ABOUT THE AUTHOR

Penelope Leach is a research psychologist specializing in child development, and a passionate advocate for children and parents. She is president of the National Childminding Association; a trustee of Home-Start; a former trustee and current research adviser to the National Society for the Prevention of Cruelty to Children; a founding committee member of the UK branch of the World Association for Infant Mental Health – and a mother and grandmother.

Penelope has a psychology Ph.D. and an honorary doctorate in education. She is a fellow of the British Psychological Society, and an honorary senior research fellow in the Leopold Muller University Department of Child & Family Mental Health at the Royal Free and University College Hospital Medical School, London, where she is currently co-director of the UK's largest-ever programme of research into the effects of various kinds of child care on children's development in the first five years.

Books by Penelope Leach include *Babyhood: infant development from birth to two years; The Parents' A–Z; The First Six Months: coming to terms with your baby;* and *Children First: what society must do – and is not doing – for children today.* This current version of the classic *Your Baby and Child* – a world bestseller for twenty years – has been written for new kinds of families in a changed and still-changing society. Parents are continually having to rethink the balance between work and home, between women and men, between mothers, fathers and other caregivers, and between the needs of different children. To be useful in today's world, a book on child care must reflect the practical implications of those new realities. The British Medical Association has awarded this version of *Your Baby and Child* First Prize in the Popular Medicine category of its book awards.

D1484668

Penelope Leach

YOUR BABY & CHILD

*New version for a
new generation*

Photography by Jenny Matthews

A Dorling Kindersley Book

LONDON, NEW YORK, MUNICH, MELBOURNE, DELHI

PROJECT EDITOR Caroline Greene
ART EDITOR Hilary Krag
PHOTOGRAPHIC DIRECTOR Sally Smallwood
EDITORIAL ASSISTANT Claudia Mitchell
DESIGNER Emy Manby
PHOTOGRAPHER Jenny Matthews
ILLUSTRATOR Aziz Khan
PICTURE RESEARCHER Sam Ruston
SENIOR EDITORS Anne Esden and Carolyn Ryden
MANAGING EDITOR Susannah Marriott
MANAGING ART EDITOR Toni Kay
PRODUCTION CONTROLLER Patricia Harrington
JACKET EDITOR Caroline Reed
JACKET DESIGNER Chris Drew

PICTURE CREDITS
The publisher would like to thank the following for their kind
permission to reproduce the photographs:

l=left, r=right, t=top, c=centre, a=above, b=below.

Collections, Anthea Sievking: 30, 47cl, 155
Sally and Richard Greenhill, Kaye Mayers: 47tl
Camilla Jessel: 13, 27, 35, 139, 400
Eddie Lawrence: 41t, 46cl
Gerald Leach: 148, 326
Oxford Scientific Films, Derek Broomhall: 22
Picture supplied courtesy of Vickers PLC: 41b
Tony Sheffield Photography: 73tl
Additional photography: Antonia Deutsch
Toys loaned by Joe Jack Foster

LOCATION PHOTOGRAPHY
Anne Sherman BDS Dental Practice, London
Clissold Park One O'Clock Club, London
Fortune Park Day Nursey, London
Pembury House Centre for Childhood, London
Royal Free Hospital, London

Published by Dorling Kindersley Limited
80 Strand, London WC2R 0RL, England
A Penguin Company

First published in Great Britain as *Baby and Child* by Michael Joseph 1977
Published in Penguin Books 1979
Second edition published by Michael Joseph 1988
Published in Penguin Books 1989
Third edition published as *Your Baby and Child* in Penguin Books 1997
This edition published by Dorling Kindersley Limited 2003
6 8 10 9 7

ISBN-13: 978-0-7513-4887-3

Reproduced by Colourscan, Singapore
Printed and bound in Hong Kong by L Rex

See our complete catalogue at
www.dk.com

To the children who were
yesterday's future and have become
today's present

A second generation of children inspired this new version of *Baby and Child*. I would like to thank all the representatives who appear in it (especially Cassie, Rory and their friends), as well as their parents, grandparents and caregivers, and all the children and adults who let us take pictures we eventually had to leave out. Every photograph is of real people rather than models, and for her sensitive photography I owe special thanks to Jenny Matthews.

I would also like to thank the design team – in particular Sally Smallwood and Hilary Krag – for their work in creating a new look for this book and ensuring that words and pictures work so well together.

Without the editor, Caroline Greene, though, the sheer size and complexity of the project might have overwhelmed us all. I thank her for her knowledgeable interest in the subject as well as her professional skill in the medium, and I thank her for being a pleasure to work with.

Penelope Leach

CONTENTS

THE NEWBORN

THE SETTLED BABY

THE OLDER BABY

THE TODDLER

THE YOUNG CHILD

INTRODUCTION

YOUR BABY AND CHILD is written from babies' and children's points of view as far as we can understand them because however the society in which they are brought up changes, and however the demands made on parents may shift and alter, those viewpoints remain relatively stable, vitally important and often neglected.

This book looks at children and their experiences from shortly before birth until the beginning of their compulsory schooling. It looks at the successive tasks of development with which they are involved, the kinds of thought of which they are capable and the extremes of emotion that carry them along. Babies and young children live minute by minute, hour by hour and day by day and it is those small units of time that most concern the people who care for them. But everything a child does during those detailed days reflects what he or she is, has been and will become. The more you, and any other adults who regularly care for your child – let's say a daughter – can understand her and recognize her present position on the developmental map that directs her towards being a person, the more interesting she will seem. The more interesting people find her the more easily she will get the attention of all the adults who are important to her, and the more willing attention she gets, the more satisfied and satisfying responses she will give.

So taking a baby's point of view does not mean neglecting the viewpoint of parents or other caring adults because they are inextricably intertwined. The happier you can make your baby, the more you will enjoy being with her and the more you enjoy her the happier she will be. And when she is unhappy – as of course she sometimes will be – you will usually find yourselves unhappy as well. Your baby affects you just as much as you affect your baby. In fact if you have spent years learning to maintain a businesslike distance between your professional and personal lives, you may be astonished to discover how difficult it is to maintain any distance at all between adult lives and baby matters. It is because you and your baby affect each other, for better or worse, that although this is a book, it does not suggest that you do things "by the book" but rather that you do them, always, "by the baby".

Raising a child "by the book" – by any set of rules, predetermined ideas or outside instructions – can work well if the rules you choose to follow fit the baby you happen to have. But even a minor misfit between the two can cause misery. You can see it in something as simple and taken-for-granted as the "proper" way to keep a newborn clean. Bathed each day according to the rules, some babies will enjoy themselves, adding pleasure for themselves and a glow of accomplishment for parents to the desired state of cleanliness. But some will loudly proclaim their intense fear of the whole business of nakedness and water. However "correctly" you bathe such a baby and however clean she becomes, her panic-stricken yells will make your hands tremble and your stomach churn. You are doing what the book says but not what your baby needs. If you listen to your baby, the central figure in what you are trying to do – and your only reason, after all, for reading the book – you will defer the bath and use a face cloth. Then both of you can stay happy.

This kind of sensitively concentrated attention to a real-life child who is a person-in-the-making, is the essence of love. Loving a baby in this way is the best investment that there is. It pays dividends from the very beginning and it goes on paying them for all the years that there are. This baby is, after all, a brand new human being and you are his or her makers and founders by virtue of your loving care, whether or not there are genetic links between you. As you watch and listen to her, think about and adjust yourselves to her, you are laying the foundations of a new member of your own race and of a friendship that can last forever. You are going to know this person better than you will ever know anybody else. Nobody else in the world including your partner, however devoted, is ever going to love you as much as your baby will in these first years if you will let her. You are into a relationship that is unique and can be uniquely rewarding.

Loving a baby or child is a circular business, a kind of feedback loop. The more you give the more you get and the more you get the more you feel like giving... It starts in the very first hours. You chat to your baby – let's say a son, this time – as you handle him, and one day you notice that he is listening. Because you can see him listening you talk to him more. Because you talk more he listens more and because he is listening he is less inclined to cry. One magical day he connects the sound he has been hearing with your face and, miraculously, he smiles at you. Less crying and more smiling from him certainly predispose you to provide more and more of the talk that so charmingly pleases him. You have created between you a beneficial circle, each giving pleasure to the other.

It goes on like that too. A crawling baby tries to follow you every time you leave the room. If his determination to come too makes you increasingly determined to leave him behind, each trivial journey to the front door or the washing machine will end in miserable tears from him and a mixture of claustrophobic irritation and guilt for you. But if you can accept his feelings and cheerfully slow your pace to his and help him go where you go, he will pay you back in contented charm and turn the chore you had to do into a game you both enjoy. Later still your toddler or young child will chatter endlessly to you. If you half-listen and half-reply the whole conversation will seem, and become, tediously meaningless for both of you. But if you really listen and really answer, your child will make more sense and because he or she says more, you will feel increasingly inclined to listen and answer. Communication will flourish between you.

So this whole book is orientated towards you – the parent, parent-figure or any caring adult – and the child as a unit of mutual pleasure-giving. Fun for that child is fun for you. Fun for you generates more for him or her and the more fun you all have together the less time and fertile growing space there will be for pain and problems.

I have written the book in this way because experience with the children of many families who let me share their relationships with each other as part of my research, as well as with my own children and grandchildren, constantly reminds me that pleasure is the *point* of having children but that pleasure is horribly vulnerable to life's other stresses. We are at last beginning to revise the traditional assumption that every stable couple will want a child. But while we acknowledge that parenthood is and should be a genuine option, we are far from acknowledging the increasing practical costs and emotional implications of exercising it. Although responsibility for the safety, health and wellbeing of a child has always meant anxiety and hard work, new strains of those, coupled with crippling guilt, threaten to counterbalance, even overbalance many people's joy in parenting. There may be anxiety about balancing the equation of time spent with children and time spent earning money to spend on them; guilt over spending too little or too much time at home or at work and giving too much or too little attention to children, partners or personal fulfilment. And there is always hard work because raising children *is* hard work whether you are at home and hands-on, at work and in remote control, or some of each.

For millions of parents, money and jobs are too scarce for these to be matters of choice. But even amongst intact and relatively privileged couples there are women who feel guilty about enjoying home-based life with a baby because they "ought" to be earning money and work-experience, if not for now then against the real possibility of marriage breakdown and lone parenting later on; women who feel guilty about enjoying working outside their homes because "my children need me"; even women who, having achieved good compromises between paid career work and unpaid caring work, feel they do neither "properly" and are guilty about both. Fathers seldom fare better. For every chauvinistic male who still behaves as if children — even his own — are women's business, there is another who wants to take an equal part in his child's life and upbringing but must fight long tradition and prejudice for the right to be there enough to learn how, let alone keep on doing it while maintaining the mortgage.

Whoever and wherever you are, having a child makes a difference; for almost everyone it means making compromises, and for many there are new kinds of family to be made, new styles of parenting to be explored. When something works out well and the organizational practicalities of life run smoothly for a while, please try not to waste a good time in guilty fretting because you are not "perfect parents". Nobody is. You probably could not even describe such parents and I certainly would not try because they are mythical. Anyway, children do not need superhuman, perfect parents. Yours only need you: the good-enough parents they happen to have and will take for granted as perfect because you are the ones they know and love.

Guilt is the most destructive of all emotions. It mourns what has been while playing no part in what may be, now or in the future. A prime purpose of this book is to help you find the courage to dismiss unnecessary guilt so that you can find positive courses of action which will truly benefit your child where your self-reproach will not. Whatever you are doing, however you are coping, if you listen to your child and to your own feelings, there will be something you can actually do to put things right or make the best of those that are wrong. If your new baby cries and cries whenever he is put in his cot, guilty soul-searching about your "mishandling" or his temperament will get none of you anywhere. Stop. Listen to him. Consider the state that his crying has got you into. There is no joy here. Where is he happy? Slung on your front? Then put him there. Carrying him may not suit you very well right this minute but it will suit you far better than that incessant hurting noise. And when, and only when, peace is restored you will have a chance of finding a more permanent solution. If your three-year-old panics when you turn out her bedroom light, stop. Listen to her; listen to your own feelings. While she is afraid, there can be no luxurious rest for her or well-earned adult peace for you. Put a light on again and let both of you be content. It does

not matter whether she "ought" to be scared of the dark; it only matters, to everyone present, that she is.

Bringing up a child in this flexible, thoughtful way takes time and effort, matching hard, committed work to long-term rewards. But what worthwhile and creative undertaking does not? Bringing up a child is the most creative, most worthwhile and most undervalued task you will ever undertake; furthermore while all your previous personal experiences and professional competencies will feed into your parenting, not even the most "relevant" will prove to have prepared you for it. Don't expect that your track record in keeping a major company running smoothly will make running a family a cinch or assume that happily caring for twenty small children in a classroom every day means that just one in your own home will be easy. Yes, fifty centimetres and three kilograms of infant can, and undoubtedly sometimes will, reduce two or more intelligent, competent, organized adults to anxious, exhausted, incompetent jellies.

Every creative person is also a craftsperson, who must learn the tools of her art just as a tradesperson learns the tools of hers. There is a craft to this project too. If you accept, and insist that everyone who cares for your child observes, the principle of striving for everyone's intertwined happiness in all your dealings with her, you will be able to see that while there are seldom right or wrong ways to do the things that need to be done, there are usually choices to be made between ways that maximize or minimize the sum of your household's happiness; ways that feel easy or difficult and ways that seem effective or ineffective. A large part of this book is devoted to helping you to find what works for you, whether the issue is changing the nappy of a two-week-old who hates being naked or a two-year-old who hates keeping still; coping with your own distress over leaving a three-month-old or a three-year-old's distress over leaving you; or finding fun play, satisfactory care and appropriate education for a child of any age. Please don't make the mistake of thinking that even the smallest of these detailed concerns are trivia that should be beneath your notice – or let adult companions imply that they are beneath theirs. Daily life with a baby or small child is made up of hundreds of minutes of minutiae. The more smoothly those minutes roll by, the more easily hair gets washed, food is eaten and transitions are made from being awake to being asleep, being alone or being in company, being on a swing or walking home, the more time and emotional energy you will have for enjoying him, and yourself with and without him. So details are important, even domestic ones. You can organize nappy-changing in many different ways, but as a five-to-ten times daily occurrence it will have to *be* organized – and the way that best suits your particular house and household, including your baby and yourself, will be the best for you. You can store playthings in many different ways, but the way that makes clearing up easy for you, or easy for you to delegate, while keeping the room tidy enough for your tastes and the toys available enough for your child, is worth thinking about.

This book does not lay down rules because there are none. It does not tell you what to do because I cannot know what you should do. But it offers you a complex and, to me, entrancing folklore of child care which, once upon a time, you might have received through your own extended family, combined with some even more complex and, to me, entrancing results of child development research. I hope that you enjoy it. I hope that it will help you to enjoy discovering the person who is your baby, and to enjoy looking after that baby person and helping along the processes that gradually turn him or her into your child. If it plays a part in helping you to make your child happy and therefore in making yourselves happy, helps you to revel in your child as your child revels in you, it will have done its job.

The baby for whom you are reading this book may not be your first. Second babies are supposed to be "easy" but you may find the first months of this second round dauntingly difficult, especially if your first child has taken up a great deal of your time and energy for the last couple of years. If she needed so much from you, how can this one possibly manage with less? And if everything you give him has to be taken from her, how can you bear it? You know that your toddler must be helped to accept the new baby but in advance of that planned and wanted birth you may find yourself bitterly resenting him on her behalf. She is a person whom you know and love; he is a stranger. After the birth, though, don't be surprised if your feelings swing just as immoderately the other way. You knew that your toddler was likely to be jealous, but on your new baby's behalf you are a tigress; so protective of him that you hurt her feelings – and then you hate yourself.

Caring for babies and small children demonstrates Parkinson's law in reverse: somehow, time and energy expand to meet the demands made upon them. All other things being equal, you will do as well by the new baby as by the first and you will not seriously deprive either in the process. It is not because second babies are easier; it is because their whole situation is quite different.

First babies have the often unenviable task of turning people into parents. That first time around you had to learn all the

practical, craft aspects of parenting. You had to learn how to change a thoroughly soiled nappy without having to change all your clothes as well; you had to learn to manage a breast or bottle with one hand so as to hold the telephone with the other, and you had to discover how wide your doorways were before you could stop being afraid of banging her head on the frames. Although the new baby may seem amazingly small and fragile in comparison with your tough little toddler, you know all that. The skills stay with you, like riding a bike.

In reality, your days are going to be fuller this time, and you'll have fewer chances of catnaps, but that doesn't necessarily mean that you'll feel even busier and more tired. First babies take up every available moment of parents' time because even when they are asleep and needing nothing, parents still can't get on with anything else because they are hanging around just in case. But you know better this time. You know that your baby will cry when he does need you and far from dithering about until he does, you will be snatching every moment to spend with your toddler.

Your first child really *needed* your undivided attention because she not only had to demand some one-to-one attention but also to expose you to the realities of child care, like teaching you not to try to write your novel when she was around and awake, and only to invite the kind of daytime visitors who would pretend they had really come to see her. Your second baby will find that if you are there at all, your attention is fully child-centred (although he may have to claim the one-to-one from his sister) and whether you are there or not, he will find much more to entertain him because she is. You wouldn't have left her sitting in her highchair for a minute after she finished her lunch, but he stays there, absorbed in watching her finger-paint with yoghurt and then watching you clear it up. You always took her for a walk after her afternoon nap but he will get taken out and about on her affairs and try out the sandpit and the big swings at a much earlier age. Staying at home for an afternoon (because she has a cold) may be a change for him rather than an unfair deprivation. As for her, your beloved first-born: being the older rather than the only child may be tough on her for a while, but she has had all your attention to compensate her for being the one you learned on, and she may enjoy having you house-bound by a new baby even before she can begin to enjoy him. And one day, with any luck, she'll do that too.

But what if you have two (or more) together? Twin babies share a womb, parents, most of each other's company and almost all the major landmarks of childhood from birthdays to starting school. Neither they nor anybody else is going to forget their twinness or miss their difference from one-at-a-time children so you don't need to emphasize it. It is their individuality that is at risk, so do make sure it does not get lost in their duality. You may find you need to make a conscious effort to treat your twins or triplets as two or three singles rather than a pair or a trio. You'll probably find that's easier to do if you remember that being fair does not mean treating the children exactly alike but taking equal trouble to meet the needs of each. You may have difficulty with other people, though. To anyone outside the intimate family, a baby is a baby is a baby. If you had had one, your family and friends would not have needed to study him closely in order to recognize the Andrew of your birth announcement; they could safely have assumed that any baby you were carrying or nursing was indeed that person. But since you have had two it is vital that everyone makes the effort to know which is Andrew and which is Angus rather than lazily referring to them as "the twins". Otherwise, when you come into the room with a single bundle they will have no idea who they are greeting.

The more you can force people to realize that the twins are not the same, the more readily they will see them as separate children and the easier it will be for you to bring them up to know themselves as unique individuals. The effort is not usually very great. Non-identical twins may or may not look alike. They are just brothers or sisters or one of each, after all. Even identical twins seldom look very alike in the early weeks because of differences in birth weight and birth experience.

Meeting the needs of twin (let alone more) babies at the same time is far more difficult to begin with than meeting the needs of two of different ages, though it will probably be easier in a few months' time. The basic problem is the sheer incompetence of human newborns – especially their inability to support their own heads or turn their bodies to reach a nipple. Picking a new baby up, carrying him so that he feels secure and holding him so that he can suck and breathe at the same time takes two hands. If you have two babies, you really need an extra pair of arms and hands to go with them. A second parent is ideal but if that is impossible do try to think of somebody else. She does not have to be deeply involved or take terrifying responsibility – it's only arms you are short of – but she does need to be with you, whenever nobody else is, for at least the first few weeks.

Meeting the needs of babies who are eventually going to have special needs isn't necessarily extra-difficult in itself. Many genetic and neurological problems are not manifest until several months have passed, and even conditions that are diagnosed

immediately – as Down's syndrome often is, for example – do not necessarily make affected newborns more demanding to care for. Extra difficulties tend to come from within adults rather than from babies. It might help a little to remind yourself that whatever diagnosis or prognosis you are given for your baby, he is a newborn baby first and foremost and, at this stage in his life anyway, far more an ordinary than an extraordinary child. It will certainly be more helpful, though, to have somebody else to remind you of that and help you begin to think about the future and face whatever you have to face. Be persistent in your quest for information from the professionals and for a support group of other parents.

ABOUT THIS BOOK

The book is organized by approximate age-stages, starting with what we know of a baby's life in the womb, and ending approximately five years and five sections later. The age-structuring is user-friendly (every parent always knows *exactly* how old her child is!) but if you use it to judge a baby or child's progress you will be misusing it. Child development is a process, not a race. Every baby in the world starts from the same place and follows a similar course, passing certain milestones in a predetermined order. But every baby follows that course at his or her own personal rate, with idiosyncratic spurts, lags and pauses, and no prizes for speed. So whether or not your child is the age indicated for the Older Baby or the Young Child, you will be ready for each new section when he or she has completed most of the developments of the one before.

This edition of YOUR BABY AND CHILD does not have a separate medical reference section – there are now whole books devoted to children's physical illnesses and to accidents and first aid. A new feature, though, is the tinted boxes you will find scattered through each section of the book containing some strongly held parents' points of view (not always the same as mine); often-asked questions, and some notes of special hazards and safety guidelines.

Of course, the baby or child for whom you are using this book may not be yours in the conventional and biological sense. She may have been adopted into your family; you may have joined his as a step-parent; she may be your professional charge as a nanny or day care provider. The "you" to whom the book is directly addressed is you whatever your relationship. I mean the word to apply to both parents when both are involved, to either one when he or she is coping alone, temporarily or permanently, and to anyone who cares for any small person. Babies don't care about genetics, they only care about caring.

"You" is an ungendered word, so carers can be people, irrespective of sex. Not so babies. Short of dehumanizing both genders as "it", English insists that an individual child is either male or female. The text drifts from one gender to the other, chapter by chapter. If gender has a particular bearing on a point being made, you will find a boy or a girl specified. Otherwise, whichever gender the text refers to, what is said applies equally to both: to your child or the child you are thinking about.

THE
NEWBORN

Getting together

It takes three to make a birthday. Most mothers and a still increasing number of fathers remember the birth of their first child as the most important experience of their lives, but the person for whom this day is most vital is neither of you two but the third person: the baby.

Recognizing that baby as a real, separate person, even though he or she started out as part of you and goes on being completely dependent on you, is an important aspect of becoming a parent and one that modern technology has made easier. Even two generations ago, babies were almost wholly mysterious until the moment they emerged from their mothers into the shared outside world. Now, thanks to new imaging techniques, more and more is known about the development of babies before birth. We know, for example, that foetuses move around in all the ways that newborn babies do; that by the end of the first trimester hands are opened and closed and there are swallowing and breathing movements; that by fifteen weeks – still before most mothers can feel even their most energetic movements – foetuses can suck their fingers, and that during the last trimester they drink, pee, cough and hiccup their way through days and nights that are already divided into organized cycles of activity and inactivity – and much of the activity looks remarkably like play.

You have probably seen your baby on an ultrasound scan and proudly shown around a first blurry picture taken months ago when he or she was still small enough for a recognizable part to fit on the screen. You may even know whether to expect him or her. Such images are astonishing proof of the existence of a Real Baby in there, especially if you are lucky enough to see some of your fluttering feelings as his or her gymnastics. But even they don't make you aware of the extraordinary fact that the foetus will be yours not only by virtue of genetics but because your unique influence impinged from early on and is still doing so. As you contemplate your growing bump, being aware of your own influence over what's inside it can forge a powerful link between unseen foetus and tangible baby, between being pregnant and being a parent. Those organized cycles of rest and activity, for example, common to all foetuses and alternating approximately 40 minutes rest with 80 minutes of activity while mothers sleep, adapt to *your* activities when you are awake. When you are physically busy and stressed, your foetus tends to be quiet; when you are resting and relaxed, he or she will get moving. By the end of your pregnancy you may be able to predict the baby's active times; differentiate between "deep sleep" (quiet and unresponsive); "light sleep" (quiet, but with bursts of rhythmic kicking and perhaps hiccups) and "active awake" (bursts of thrusting, vigorous activity); and recognize and use a fourth "alert but quiet" state, in which touch or sound readily stimulate the foetus into making gentler, smoother movements.

In the last trimester, the baby inside you does not only react to sounds, to different kinds of touch and to changing light levels but also "learns" them, reacting differently to those that are new and those that have become familiar. A strong light shone on your bulge in your foetus' line of vision is liable to startle her while a softer light stimulates her to turn towards it, but if there is a very bright light over your bath and it is therefore part of her daily experience, she will become accustomed to it. The sharp sound of a dog barking may startle your baby in the womb, too, but if the dog is yours and often barks, she will get used to that sound (just as a born child gets used to the sounds of her household) and may be relatively undisturbed by that particular sound when she has been born. She will get used to the gentler sounds that are commonplace while she is in the womb, too, especially your voices. Most newborn babies clearly "prefer" female speech because they have heard so much of it in previous months, but the preference is less marked in babies whose fathers have been around and talking to, or close to, the bulge.

None of that means that an unborn baby can be given an educational head start, of course, or that playing great music or reading great literature to babies in the womb will give them a lasting taste for it. Although we still have much to learn about prenatal development, it is unlikely that foetuses are capable of intellectual understanding; more likely that they pick up on sensory stimulation, responding to rhythms and intensities in music or dancing, and perhaps to the emotional tones of speech and touch. So don't expect to "educate" or "accelerate" your unborn baby. Just enjoy the fact that he or she has long been in two-way communication with you and will be born yours in a social as well as a physical sense.

Nobody really knows what getting born is like. Although it is tempting from our standpoint to assume that babies' birth experiences must be of claustrophobia and violence – something like being a potholer trying to wriggle through an impossibly narrow passageway during an earthquake – we cannot actually know what babies feel about what happens to them. Still, we know a lot about what happens. We know, for example, that unless babies are induced or delivered surgically, they themselves play a large part in initiating their mothers' labours. We know from babies' physiological reactions to labour – surges of adrenaline; rapid shifts in heart rate – that the experience is physically dramatic. But we cannot be sure that the baby-in-transit feels pain and panic: whether the foetal distress that means physical danger also means emotional distress.

Not knowing exactly what babies feel during birth does not excuse anyone for behaving as if they felt nothing, concentrating on safety to the exclusion of comfort or kindness. During labour and birth, combining highly developed birth technologies with highly skilled and personalized midwifery can optimize babies' likely comfort without jeopardizing their safety in any way. And once they are safely born, simply accepting them as people and treating them accordingly can do a great deal to ease their transition into independent life. Whatever a baby may experience when being extracted from her mother with forceps, it is surely reasonable to assume that resulting facial bruises are painful and to translate the possibility that newborn jitteriness is due to "cerebral irritation" into the likelihood of her having a headache. And yes, babies do feel pain when people stick needles in them.

Inexorably forced out of a warm, liquid haven, through a tight passage backed with bone, into a world of light and noise and texture, every bit of the baby's nervous system reacts with shock. It is the shock of birth that triggers his gasping efforts to breathe for himself. The placenta, which fed his circulation oxygen from your bloodstream, has finished its work. He must breathe. But if nobody hurries to sever the umbilical cord, the blood still pulsing in it buys him a little time. If we wait on him gently, he may make this vital transition for himself, replacing the old brutalities of slapped bottoms with the beauty of a first breath without crying.

Safely breathing, babies need time to rest, recoup, muster their strength and discover new kinds of comfort in a new kind of world. Your belly, soft and slack now, forms an ideal cradle but your baby cannot rest unless the surroundings are toned down. Medical personnel may have needed to talk and move around under bright lights while they ensured a safe delivery. But now that your baby *is* safely delivered the lights can be turned down lest they hurt eyes that have scarcely seen light before; the room hushed lest suddenly un-muffled noises are startling.

If all is dim and quiet, warm and peaceful, the baby, close to your familiar smell and sounds, will begin to relax: breathing steadies; the crumpled face smooths itself out and tight-closed eyes may open. The baby's head lifts a little, limbs move against your skin and, gently helped up to your bare breast, he or she may suck or at least nuzzle, discovering a new form of human togetherness to counteract new separateness. These are your baby's first direct contacts with this new world, first moments of a new lifestyle: let them be made in peace.

The baby must be weighed. But why must he be weighed now? His weight will not change in half an hour. He must be washed. But why now? The vernix that has protected his skin for months is not harming it just because he has been born. He must be dressed. But why now? Your warmth, a soft wrapping and the heat of the room are all he needs. He must have a dressing on the cord stump, a physical examination, a cot to lie in. You must be washed and changed, moved to a bed, given a drink, settled to sleep. All these things must indeed be done, but none of them need be done right now. Your baby is born. He or she is living independently. High-powered hospital time has run out. It is time for a pause of warm and peaceful intimacy among the three of you.

It is important that mothers and fathers should be helped to greet their babies the moment they can actually see and touch each other in the world they will share, and being the very first physical comfort to her newborn keeps a mother exactly where she belongs – at the centre of the baby's existence. The first minutes of independent life cannot be like that for every baby though, and are not irreplaceable. Physical safety comes first. If, for her own sake or yours, the baby must be delivered by Caesarean, hauled out with forceps, resuscitated, nursed for a while by professionals rather than parents, don't despair of giving her the very best possible start, or decide that you have missed the boat on bonding. First minutes matter; good ones optimize what is to come, but missing them will not leave a permanent gap in your relationship or weakness in the bond that links you. Two generations ago, after all, it was rare for fathers to be present, and commonplace for women to be anaesthetized for delivery, yet bonding failure was no commoner then than now.

The truth is that bonding is only sometimes the instantaneous shot of magic glue parents often expect. The greyish, bloodstreaked, wrinkly baby who eventually emerges from you, with her big heavy head, primitive-looking cord and perfect miniature ears and fingernails will certainly grab at your heart and turn your stomach over. But the sensation may be closer to incredulous panic than to

recognizable love. For many (perhaps most) parents, "bonding" is a learning and adapting process; a coming to terms that only comes to feel like real love when it seems to become reciprocal. A man who misses his baby's birth, her first hours of life, and all but formal visiting hours for a week, may seem to have missed a critical period for bonding with her, finding it subsequently all too easy to remain more or less untouched by fatherhood. But when a mother finds it difficult to establish a bond with her baby, it is never because of anything as simple as external circumstances or timing. It is feelings that erect barriers between people, and having the courage to recognize and address those feelings that can pull them down.

Newborn babies need comforting after the physical stress of labour, the physical shock of birth and those first breaths. But if none of it went as you planned – an induction, constant monitoring, lots of painkilling drugs, perhaps, when your birth plan was for minimal intervention – it may be difficult for you to see your own triumph in producing this beautiful baby through a sense of failure because you did not do it as you intended. Preparation for birth misfires if birth comes to seem an end in itself rather than merely the means to a baby's safe beginning. If your mind is on your own "performance", or what your partner or the midwives thought of it, you may be unable to focus on the baby.

Newborn babies need comforting after the physical stress of labour and the shock of being born. But if the labour and delivery have stressed and shocked you to a point where you urgently need sympathy and tender loving care yourself, you may have no sympathy to spare for the baby and nothing left to give. Unless sympathy, care and comfort are quickly forthcoming, you may even see the baby as the cause of your own distress: aggressor rather than joint victim.

Newborn babies need comforting after the shock of birth, but if there is something shocking about a baby's condition or appearance, such as a birthmark, or a harelip, you may be unable to accept that this is, indeed, the baby you knew while he was inside and have been waiting to meet on the outside. Given time, rejection usually yields to protection, but facts about your baby's condition will help to ease your pain and speed the process.

Newborn babies need comforting but when a baby also needs emergency care you may not dare to feel that you can do it. If she is whisked away to intensive care, incubated, intubated, her life linked to machines and the experts who run them, you may feel impotent; feel that the baby belongs to the hospital, not to you.

Feelings like these are normal feelings. They will not remain between you and your baby but they may hang around for longer than they need to if, horrified to find that you feel anything but love, you smother them in silent guilt. Almost every new mother has a real need to talk about her labour and delivery – perhaps to hospital staff, certainly to her partner or whoever companioned her through labour, and hopefully to friends with babies, perhaps including others from her antenatal classes – and the more problematic the whole experience, the greater that need. Don't be surprised if you need to talk through it blow by blow and over and over again; getting it straight and into proportion; getting used to what happened. Women who can find no one to talk to or who are too shaken by the birth experience to make themselves talk, tend to find themselves brooding over it until the birth becomes something they do not want to think about but cannot clear from their thoughts. Only when the experience has been sufficiently worked through will it slip comfortably away to the back of your mind, leaving you free to give yourself wholeheartedly to mothering the baby you have produced.

Sharing the experience of childbirth makes a difference to both parents – and therefore almost certainly to the baby, even if we cannot say exactly what the difference is or how it comes about. Women who have had committed birth partners who trained with them through pregnancy, tend to see that as ideal. The beauty of such a partner is that he (or maybe she) is totally involved emotionally yet unaffected physically. That does not only mean that he can help you make the best possible use of the coping techniques you have been taught, and give you physical support, but also that as you progressively abandon your normal self to the birth process, you can leave him as your alter ego watching over your interests and the baby's. As labour progresses, drawing you deeper and deeper into the vortex of birth, he may become your only link with reality. Midwives and doctors come and go, checking up, listening in, but as the world becomes a blur of strange effort they vanish into the fog, leaving his the only face you can still see clearly; his words the only ones you can still understand. What finally emerges is a truly mutual baby.

But although more and more couples are taking birth partnership for granted, and labouring women's partners are now welcomed by almost all hospitals whether they are biologically fathers or not, there will always be some people who do not want it that way. Every pair of people who are going to have to incorporate a child into their partnership must find a way of incorporating the experience of childbirth into their relationship, but it certainly does not have to be *that* way, nor indeed any way that seems supportive to outsiders, provided that it does to both participants. Neither fathers who sit out difficult births in waiting rooms, nor mothers who prefer all-female support in the delivery room are necessarily failing their partners. Feeling together matters far more than being together.

The first days of life

Going into labour can feel like the climax to long months of waiting but it is not really a climax at all. You were not waiting to give birth, you were waiting to have a baby and there is no rest-pause between the amazing business of becoming parents and the job of being them. Do try not to expect too much of yourselves during these first, peculiar days. All three of you have a tremendous amount of adapting to do and the calmer and more accepting of yourselves and each other you adults can be, the calmer and more accepting of this new lifestyle your baby is likely to be. Anyway, panic is particularly pointless right now because today's feelings and behaviour have so little to do with tomorrow. By the time your baby reaches her one-month birthday everything will be different because she will be beginning to settle into life outside the womb, and you two will be beginning to settle into parenthood.

Most couples remember this as an intensely emotional and confusing time, and no matter how often they were reminded that labour is called labour because it is hard work, most women are amazed by the depth of their dragging tiredness. For at least the first week or so after birthing your baby you are liable to feel everything too much: elation and exhaustion, stitches and pleasure, responsibility and pride, selfishness and selflessness. If reasons make it easier for you to accept your own feelings, remind yourself that your hormone balance is disturbed, your milk is not fully in, your cervix is not yet closed and your whole body is striving for postpartum equilibrium. But don't look for reasons to use as excuses because you don't need any. It is perfectly acceptable to feel extraordinary. *All* newly delivered women do and so do most of their partners because even if somebody else's body births your baby, becoming a parent is soul-stirring stuff.

As for the baby, what she has to cope with is without parallel in human experience. While she was inside you, your body took care of hers. It provided her food and her oxygen, took away her waste products, kept her warmly cushioned and protected, held the world at bay. Now that it is separated from yours, her body must take care of itself. She must suck and swallow the milk that is food and water, digest it and excrete its wastes. She must use energy from that food to keep her body functions running, to keep herself warm and to keep on growing. She must breathe to get oxygen, and keep her air passages clear with coughs and sneezes. And while she is doing all that the baby is bombarded with new sensations as the world rushes in on her. Suddenly there is air on her skin, warmth and coolness, textures, movements and restrictions. There is brighter light than she has ever known and there are things to see, coming into focus and blurring out again. There is hunger and emptiness, sucking, fullness, burping and excreting. There are smells and tastes. And there are sounds which, even if they are familiar, are heard differently in a dry world. Everything is different. All is bewilderment.

Your newborn baby has instincts and reflexes and working senses and in many ways she is amazingly competent. But she has no "knowledge" as we usually understand that word, and no experience of living in this postnatal environment. She does not know that she is herself, that the object she sees moving in front of her face is part of her (let alone that it is called a "hand") or that it goes on existing (let alone being part of her) when it drops out of her sight. She does not know that you are people either (let alone people called "parents"). She is programmed to pay attention to you, to look at your faces and listen to your voices. She is programmed to suck when you offer her a nipple and to recognize the smell of your milk and prefer it to anyone else's. She is programmed to survive and grow and learn, but it may take her a while to get going.

While she remains a newborn, rather than a baby who has settled into life outside the womb, her behaviour will be random and unpredictable. She may cry for food every half-hour for six hours and then sleep without any for another six hours. This morning's "hunger" does not predict this afternoon's because her hunger has no pattern or shape as yet. Her digestion has not settled; hunger signals have not taken on a clear and recognizable form for her. She simply reacts to momentary feelings. Her sleep is similarly formless; ten-minute snatches through the night and a five-hour stretch in the day tell you nothing about how she will sleep tonight. And she may cry for no reason that you can discover and stop as inexplicably as she began. Her crying has few definite patterns of cause and effect because, apart from physical pain and nursing, she has not yet established consistent differences between displeasure and pleasure.

Anyone who looks after a newborn baby – parent, substitute-parent, or professional – inevitably lacks the first essential for watch-ful care: baselines. The baby is brand new. However much you know about babies in general, neither you nor anyone else knows anything about this one in particular. You do not know how she looks and behaves when she is well and happy so it is difficult for you to know when she is ill or miserable. You do not know how much she "usually" cries because she has not been around for long enough for anything to be usual, so there is no easy way of knowing whether this crying suggests that anything is amiss. You do not know how much she usually eats or sleeps so you cannot judge whether today's feeding or sleeping is adequate or excessive. Yet her wellbeing is in

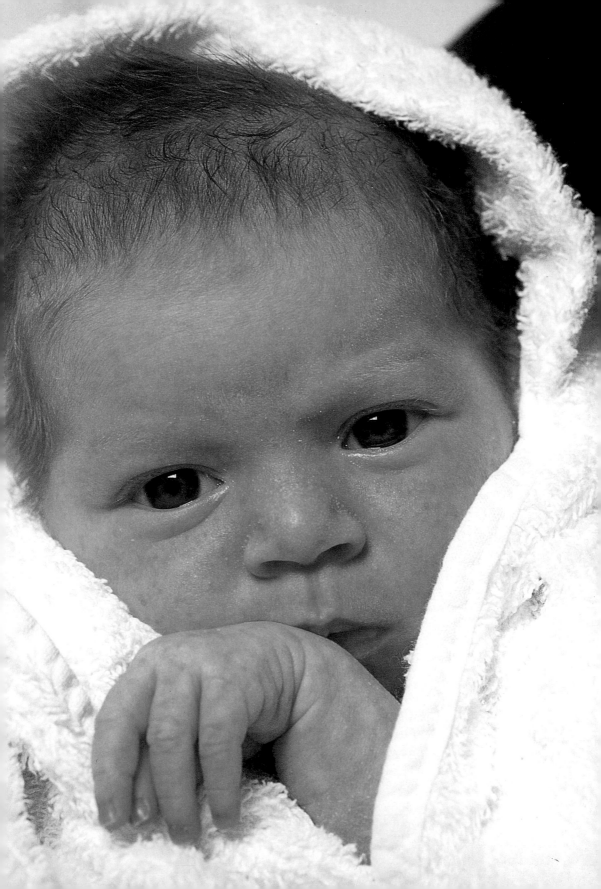

your hands. Even without baselines of usual behaviour against which to judge, you have to make continual assessments and adjustments while you learn the baby and she learns life. There is a lot of learning for all of you. It may take only a week after her birth for you to feel secure in your caring and for her to feel secure in her world. But it may take a month. Once you and she have established your baselines, got to know each other, everything will suddenly seem much easier and smoother for all of you. You will be dealing with a baby person rather than a newborn.

In the meantime, even if you are the baby's biological mother, don't torment yourself with anxiety if you do not feel anything for her that you can recognize as love. Love will come but, in contrast to the bolt-from-the-blue sensation of instant bonding, it may take time. And why not? However you define that word "love", it must have something to do with two people interacting; getting to know each other, liking what they know and wanting to know more. You and your new baby do not know each other. Furthermore, as long as she is brand new she is neither lovable nor loving. She is not truly lovable because she has not yet got herself into predictable, knowable shape nor had time to produce the characteristics which will make it clear for evermore that she is a unique person. You may love her on sight because she is your baby; the fulfilment, perhaps, of needs, dreams or plans, personal or mutual; but you cannot instantly love her as one person loves another because she is not fully a person until she is settled. She is not loving because she does not yet know that the two of you are separate; know of her own existence let alone yours. She will learn to love you with a determined and unshakeable passion unequalled in human relationships. But it will take time.

So if you have mixed feelings towards your baby, don't take them as a guide for the present or a warning for the future. Furious irritation at her crying can be swept away in a moment by a rush of overwhelming tenderness as you cradle her heavy, downy head. But your pride in being a parent can be as suddenly swamped in claustrophobia as you realize that you are committed to this child for ever and will never again be free to be an entirely separate individual person. It's true that nothing will ever be the same again, but it's also true that when the pendulum of your feelings stops swinging so wildly, that thought won't panic you. So even if the idea of an early break for the freedom of the workplace tempts you, don't succumb. Give yourself as much time as you can to adapt to your new reality before you pull yourself away from your baby into a work setting where you almost have to pretend that nothing has happened and she doesn't exist. When you do go back to work it's better to go *as* a parent than as a fugitive from parenthood.

If you are the baby's biological mother, your body will start loving her for you, if you will let it, even before she is settled enough to be a person. Whatever your mind and the deeply entrenched habits of your previous life may be telling you, your body is ready and waiting for her. Your skin thrills to hers. Her small frame fits perfectly against your belly, breast and shoulder. That surprisingly hard, hot head keeps placing itself perfectly for your cheek to rub, and once she learns to latch on and you start to produce milk, the pleasure of nursing, and the link it makes between you, is startlingly strong.

But even without the link of biological motherhood or father-hood, revelling in a baby's physical presence, the feel of her cradled in your arms, the ridiculous size of her hand in yours, ensures that she can join in this essential business of loving. New babies do not lie passively, leaving it to caring adults to make all the advances. If you will have your baby close, she will make advances to you, too. Give her the chance and she will see to it that love comes.

Your baby's physical reactions are your best guide to handling her in these very first days. Child-rearing plans and policies are no use to you yet because plans and policies can only be judged by the consistent responses they evoke and nothing you can think up will get consistency from an unsettled newborn. The baby needs to be handled so that her new life outside you is as close as possible to life in your womb. Her needs are simple, repetitive and immediate. She needs food and water in the combined form of milk; she needs warmth and comfort from lightweight clothing in cuddling arms, and soft wrappings in a small, safe bed; she needs just enough cleanliness to keep her skin from getting sore and she needs protection. That is all she needs. The powders and lotions, mobiles and furry toys, swinging seats and glorious clothes that tempt you in every baby shop will be fun for you to buy and nice for her later. But for now she is a bundle and she should be a bundle. Wrap her safely, hold her closely, handle her slowly, feed her if she might be hungry, talk to her when she looks at you, wash her when she is dirty and give her peaceful time to come to terms with life. Unless she is actually ill and under medical care, there is absolutely nothing that it is your duty to do to her if it makes her jump or cry. If handling her brings peaceful contentment, you have got it right; if it brings distress, you haven't. Let her reactions guide you.

If you can manage this, the baby will gradually come to realize what she needs and to realize that she gets what she needs when she needs it. By the time she is a settled, knowable, lovable small person, she will know the world to be a good place to be alive in. And that, after all, is the best start you can possibly give her.

What helps when bonding has been delayed?

If mother and baby don't bond instantly, what are the ideal circumstances for doing so gradually?

Don't entertain the idea that instant bonding is the ideal so that without it, there's a problem. And don't countenance the idea that this bonding business is exclusively female, either.

"Bonding" is not a neat entity and it's not just for biological mothers and babies. It is also for fathers – biological or not – and babies, and, in a sense, it is for all parenting *couples* and babies too. Whatever their relationship to the baby and each other, the people who are going to play "mother" and "father" need to come to terms with each other in these new roles, and mutually bond with the baby into a new threesome unit. All that is much more likely to happen quickly and smoothly if you can be together and undistracted. An hour in the hospital birthing room is better than nothing, but two weeks at home is much better (though not as good as longer still).

A new-baby-plan is at least as important as a birth plan and you need to start thinking about it well in advance. Paternity leave or its equivalent for the biological or adoptive mother's partner is crucial. Try for it officially and paid, but settle for using up annual leave if you must. Yes, it will be sad to be short of leave-time at Christmas or in the summer, but there will be other holidays and never another start to this baby's life in your family.

Unless you are planning on a home delivery, explore the possibilities of early discharge from hospital. Wherever you decide to have – or end up having – your baby, get home as soon as you possibly can. Even if the hospital genuinely encourages rooming-in and breast-feeding, it cannot be the ideal place to get to know yourself as mother and this baby as yours, because it is not *your* place. Furthermore, even two nights away from your partner are two nights too many. Two days as a visitor, while other people look after you and you look after the baby, are liable to

make him *feel* like a visitor: "How are you both? Can I pick him up?"

Try to make the first days at home into a babymoon, especially if there is no older child to divide you or hurry you towards "normality". Plan to centre the life of the whole household in, on and around what has just become a family bed. Surround it with adult luxuries – from bowls of fruit and magazines to CD-player and TV – and baby necessities. Consider swapping your phone for a cordless model; easier to use in bed, and invaluable later on when you need to phone and be phoned while breast-feeding or burping the baby or just cuddling.

Think carefully about the help you'll need and who should be asked (or allowed) to give it. If your partner will be there to care for you and share the care of the baby, any other help is at least as much for him as for you. If he will not be there all the time, somebody else should definitely be there for you. A lot of women have to put up with being alone in the house with a newborn, but for the first week or so most people find it scary. The ideal fourth person for a babymoon will care lovingly and luxuriously for both of you while *you* care for the baby – and won't come into the bedroom uninvited. Thinking your baby is the most beautiful ever born is an essential qualification; knowing useful things like which popper pops to which or why the baby's faeces are black, and telling you *if she's asked*, is a bonus.

And think about visitors. You'll want to see them, in fact babymoons thrive on a party atmosphere of congratulations and flowers and presents. But you won't want to see them without notice or for long at a time and you won't want to cook for them or listen while they talk about the things they talk to you about when you haven't just had a baby. Real friends will organize themselves, each other and the unreal crowd. Otherwise, tell everyone to telephone first, get an answering machine and discipline yourself not to pick up until you've heard that it's the right person for the moment.

Newborn
Characteristics

Although you may have found out a lot about your baby before birth, seen him or her on a scan, even carried a photo, seeing that baby for the first time is still overwhelming. You are going to have a thousand questions – and hundreds of concerns – but right now all you really need to know is whether the baby is okay – amid all that blood and vernix. The midwife will tell you that. She has been assessing the baby even as she helped him or her out of your body and onto your belly. She watches carefully as the baby begins to breathe; ready to help by sucking fluid out of his nose and mouth if necessary. She times the cutting of the cord (a privilege that may be offered to the father) so that the baby's circulation benefits from the blood that's pulsing from the placenta, notes the colour of the skin and feels his or her muscle tone.

Unless you already knew that you were birthing a boy rather than a girl or vice versa, this is the moment when you'll discover your baby's sex, though you may be surprised to realize, later on, how slow you both were to ask – or look. A living baby is the primary concern: daughter or son is secondary.

If the midwife notices anything about the baby that might worry or interest you – such as marks from forceps or an unusually full head of hair – she will probably point it out. Otherwise, once she is sure that the baby is breathing freely, she will concentrate on completing the third stage of labour and helping you get comfortable for your baby's introduction to the breast.

Your baby's birthweight will probably be the next thing you are told about him. Normal babies come in a large variety of shapes and sizes, so why does it matter to everybody exactly what this one weighs? Because the birthweight, whatever it may be, is your baby's own personal starting point for growth.

Average birthweight babies The average birthweight for babies is around 3.4kg (7lb 8oz). But that average conceals many variations. Boys are usually a little heavier than girls; first babies are usually rather lighter than their younger brothers and sisters; while on the whole large parents have large babies and small parents have smaller ones. So your baby can be exactly the right size for him without being average.

Heavy babies If you give birth to a 4.5kg (10lb) baby you will be rightly proud of yourself for having delivered him and he will probably look more beautiful and seem more mature than most of the other newborn babies in the ward as he will be well covered with fat. But don't be surprised if the hospital staff keep a special eye on him for a few days. Not all extra-large babies are extra-healthy. A few have become exceptionally heavy because their mothers have diabetes or pre-diabetes and extra, or widely variable, quantities of sugar have crossed the placenta. Such babies may have metabolic problems in the first days of life so it is important for medical staff to be sure that your particular one is just a well-grown baby whom nature meant to be large.

Lighter babies If your baby is below average birthweight but weighs more than about 2.5kg (5lb 8oz) he will be treated like an average birthweight baby except that he will probably be encouraged to feed more often. The chances are that you are smaller than average too and that this is a healthy baby who is meant to be small.

If the baby weighs 2.3kg–2.5kg (5lb–5lb 8oz) he will probably be taken to special care as a precaution, however healthy and lively he seems to be. Babies who are born weighing under 2.5kg (5lb 8oz) are more likely to have trouble with breathing, with keeping warm and with sucking. So to play safe, all babies who are under this weight are started off with special care. Don't jump to the conclusion that there is something wrong with him. If there are no problems he will probably be returned to your bedside within a few hours.

Small babies used to be kept in hospital until they tipped the scales at a particular weight. Nowadays decisions about taking babies home are based more on how they are managing their new way of life and, above all, on how quickly they settle to feeding.

If your baby is born weighing less than 2.3kg (5lb) then he probably is lighter than nature meant him to be. The lighter he is the more special the care he will need. The particular kind of care will depend partly on whether he is light because he is pre-term or because he is small-for-dates.

Pre-term babies Most very small babies are small for the simple reason that they have been born pre-term – before the completion of the usual 40 weeks in the womb. Missing time in the womb means that the baby has missed out on some growing time. It also means that he has missed out on some getting-ready-for-independent-life time. The more weeks inside the womb he has missed, the more difficulties he is likely to face. A baby born after 36–38 weeks gestation will probably only need to have things made very easy for him, by being kept in an incubator with extra warmth, extra oxygen and tiny feeds of breast milk at frequent intervals. A "younger" baby may need more help than that. He may need to have some of the responsibilities of independent life taken right off him for a while. He may be fed, for example, by a tube passed down his nose into his stomach because he is not yet able to suck or swallow for himself. He may even have a respirator to breathe for him.

Small-for-dates babies Small-for-dates babies have "intra-uterine growth retardation" (IUGR), meaning that they have not grown as much as they are expected to have done during their time in the womb. They may have spent the full 40 weeks in the womb but still be very small at birth. Or they may have been born pre-term but be even smaller at birth than they ought to be after that period of gestation. The immediate treatment given to a small-for-dates baby will be similar to that given to a pre-term one, but it is still important to know which is which.

A baby who really is small-for-dates has usually been short of nourishment in the womb. The placenta may have been inadequate or you may have had problems with your health that prevented the baby from getting all he needed for optimal growth. The baby's small size does not predict later developmental problems. IUGR is widely thought to be a *protective* mechanism that by reducing a foetus' demand for calories, lets him or her develop adequately despite a limited supply. But whatever its cause, a low birthweight does put a baby at risk for many neonatal complications. If medical staff can establish that this baby *is* small-for-dates rather than pre-term, you and they together may be able to work out what made your womb a difficult environment for him, and correct it for any baby you may have later on.

Although antenatal care in a modern centre should mean that you had routine foetal measurements and scans that dated the baby's conception and produced a record showing whether or not he grew at a consistently normal rate, none of these scientific data is infallible. Staff will probably check back on them but you may find they also question you closely about the dates of your last menstrual period. If you were one cycle wrong and the scans did not absolutely contradict what you told the operators, your 1.8 kg (4 lb) baby may not be small-for-dates at all, but four weeks or more pre-term.

SPECIAL CARE

Special care for newborns is now so sophisticated that even very small babies often do remarkably well. Treatment may start before birth. If labour seems to be beginning very much too early, it can sometimes be stopped, or at least deferred, with drugs. Even a short delay may allow hospital staff to assess the coming baby's condition and act to improve his chances of survival. If the lungs are still very immature, for example, it may be possible to treat the baby while he is still in the womb. Administration of a particular hormone can speed up maturation of the lungs and may prevent Respiratory Distress Syndrome after birth.

Incubators An incubator, or isolette, is our nearest (and not very near) equivalent to an artificial womb. The baby can no longer rely on your body to operate his but cannot yet rely on his own. The incubator acts as a halfway house between total physical dependence and being a completely independent physical entity. If he is managing reasonably well immediately after delivery, it may be used only to give him steady warmth, peaceful isolation, controlled humidity and perhaps a little extra oxygen. If he is having problems, it can be used to help him with the functioning of almost all his body systems. Whether it is used to give your baby a great deal of help or only a little, the incubator is a very safe place for him to be. As long as he remains in it he will be under constant supervision by specially trained nursing staff. Specialist doctors will keep a careful eye on his progress, while the highly sophisticated machinery of the incubator itself will record any changes in his condition, and set off warning signals whenever he needs attention. But, even though you know that an incubator is the best place for your new baby just now, having him in there will probably make you utterly desolate. Your whole being is keyed up for physical contact with the new baby, but the process which started with conception, ran through pregnancy and birth and should have culminated in a baby to hold, has been interrupted. Your body yearns

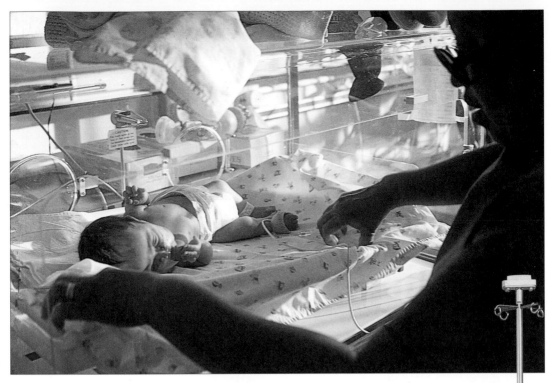

MicroLite
Ultraviolet light for babies who are jaundiced.

Vacutron
Suction for clearing the baby's airways.

Athena Monitor
Monitors the baby's vital signs such as heartbeat and breathing.

Port Doors
Allow staff, and you, to touch and handle your baby.

Controller
The "brain" of the incubator, this controls the baby's environment (humidity, warmth, oxygen and so on).

Remote Alarm Module
Connected to the monitor and nurses' call. It beeps and flashes as soon as the baby begins to have problems. The pole also holds bags of intravenous fluids.

Try to work with the incubator. It's not keeping her from you, but safe for you.

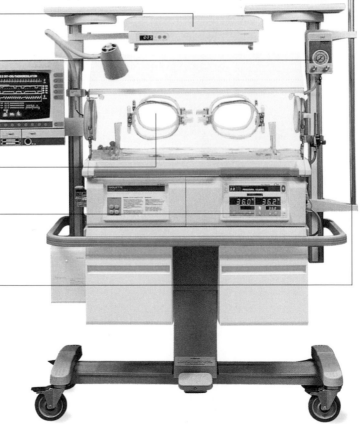

for the baby but instead of being in your arms, he is lying, looking strange and other-worldly, in a machine that would look at home in a space laboratory.

Coping while your baby is in special care

Any period while any baby is in special care is bound to be difficult for the parents, and the worse his condition the more agonizing the anxiety will be. If you have another child – a larger twin or a toddler sibling – who also needs parenting, these postnatal days may seem downright impossible. And if you have to add the physical pain of a Caesarean wound or a lot of stitches, you may truly wonder how to get through. Your physical recovery must be the priority, for everyone's sake, but you may have to sacrifice your partner's company so that while you rest, he can act for both of you in relation to the new baby and any children at home.

However, the more time your partner and you can spend with the new baby, the better. The fact that he is unready to live without special care does not mean that he is unready to use loving social contact with parents. He had that all the time he was inside you, after all. Don't abandon him now. If the incubator is in a nursery facility attached to your maternity ward, you will probably be allowed to go in whenever you like. If the baby is in a special care unit separate from your ward but in the same hospital, the sister of your own ward will arrange a wheelchair for you until you are fit to walk. If your baby has had to be transferred to another hospital, perhaps because he needs to be in a neonatal intensive care unit, it may be possible for you to go too. If not, you should still be allowed to go there as soon as you are well enough to travel.

Working with staff

Special care staff are specially trained to help shocked parents as well as to nurse premature and sick babies. They will know how important it is that you should feel fully involved as crucial members of your baby's team of caregivers rather than feeling like observers. They will be eager to explain the baby's condition and all the gadgetry because once you understand exactly what problems he is having, and how any tubes or gadgets which are attached to him are intended to help, he will stop seeming like the hospital's baby and start seeming more like yours.

Preparing to breast-feed

The baby is yours and there is one thing you can do for him that nobody else in the world can do: get your breast milk supply going. All very small babies, and those who are ill, especially need to have breast milk as soon as they are ready for any milk at all. Often the milk is given by tube or dropper until the baby is strong enough to suck for himself. Even if your baby is not ready for milk yet, you can be certain that he will need to be breast-fed when he is stronger. You can get the supply established while you are waiting for him. The hospital staff will show you how to use an electric breast pump to express your milk – much quicker and easier than expressing by hand (see p.59) or with a manual pump. Even if you eventually have to go home leaving the baby in special care, it will still be worthwhile expressing your milk not only to be fed to him now, at the hospital, but also to ensure that you have a good supply for him in the future when he joins you at home.

Kangaroo care Unless your baby is very fragile indeed, you will be encouraged to touch him through the glove-holes of the incubator from the beginning. Soon, staff may suggest that you stroke and massage him, not just for your sakes but for his, and they will probably encourage you to help with his physical care in the incubator. If he is in reasonably good shape, it will not be long before you can take him out and hold him for a minute or two.

In some hospitals, though, you will be encouraged to hold your baby from the beginning, however tiny he is and however many tubes festoon him. "Kangaroo care" is a system of nursing pre-term newborns that uses the mother's body instead of an incubator. Named after marsupials whose young emerge from inside their mothers' bodies at a very early stage in gestation, and climb into a pouch on the mother's front, it really does come as close as we can get to putting the baby back inside to finish off.

Kangaroo care evolved in South America to cope with a shortage of incubators and a high infant mortality rate. Babies, dressed only in nappies and bonnets, are placed between their mothers' breasts, face to face and skin to skin, and then covered with blankets. The South American babies who were nursed like this did as well as the few for whom there were incubators. Now increasing numbers of European hospitals are introducing this kind of care but as an extra to, rather than a substitute for, incubators. Some studies have shown that even a small amount of kangaroo care – perhaps an hour a day – leads to more rapid weight gain, an earlier readiness to suckle and often to an earlier-than-expected discharge home. Kangaroo care doesn't only help babies, of course, it also protects parents from the horrible helplessness of watching a baby fight for life and not even being the people who can do most to help.

Actual and expected birthdays Even without that, though, some parents, recovering from the shock and disappointment of not having their babies with them immediately, do manage to look on this time as if it was an extra bit of pregnancy: a sort of hiatus between having the baby invisible inside and fully part of their lives outside. From a pre-term baby's point of view that's a good way to look at it because although he grows and develops during the weeks between his actual birth and his originally expected date of delivery (EDD), they are still something of a developmental hiatus and it will be important to allow for that whenever he is compared with other children of the "same" age. Although his birthday is the day he was born (just as it is for any other child), and he is therefore six weeks old six weeks later, he will not be comparable with full-term babies who are six weeks old until six weeks after his expected, rather than actual, date of delivery. It's useful to keep your pre-term baby's gestational, or "corrected" age in mind right through the first two years, although its significance will gradually diminish. There's an enormous difference between a baby who is truly three months old and a prematurely born one whose corrected age is only three *weeks*, but that difference between the two of them will be much less noticeable by the time they reach their second birthdays.

The first full medical check

Some time in the first 24 hours after her birth, your baby will get a thorough medical check. This should be done in front of both of you so that the doctor can not only assure herself that all is well but demonstrate and explain that it is. If you are not able to go to the nursery, the examination should be done at your bedside.

If your partner has to leave the hospital, which is likely if he has to look after an older child, it is worth telling the senior nurse or midwife that he would like to be present when his baby is examined, and asking approximately when the doctor is expected. These are some of the checks that will probably be carried out.

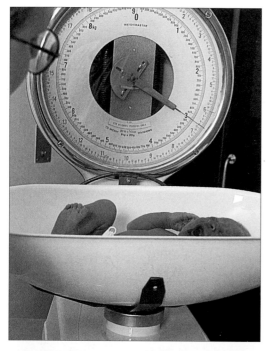

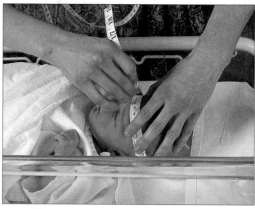

Weighing and measuring. *Your baby will probably be weighed again (left). Average weight is 3.4kg (7lb 8oz); 95% of newborns weigh between 2.5kg and 4.5kg (5lb 8oz and 10lb). Her length will be measured. Average length is 50cm (20in); 95% of newborns measure between 45cm and 55cm (18in and 22in). Her head circumference will be measured (above). Average is about 35cm (14in); normal range is 33cm to 37cm (13in to 14¾in).*

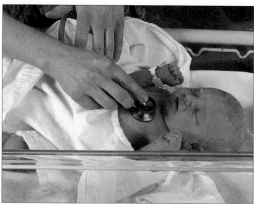

Checking the heart and lungs. *The doctor will use a stethoscope to listen to your baby's chest and make sure that her breathing is strong and steady and her heart sounds are normal. Harmless heart murmurs are not uncommon in newborns.*

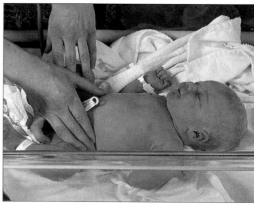

Checking internal organs. *By feeling your baby's tummy, the doctor will check that the internal organs, such as her liver, kidneys and spleen, are the right size and correctly positioned. She will also check for normal pulses in the groins.*

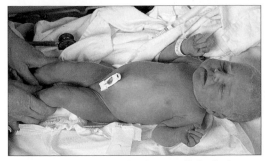

Checking the limbs. *The doctor will check that your baby's pairs of limbs match in length, that there are 10 each of fingers and toes and that legs and feet are properly aligned with no sign of club foot.*

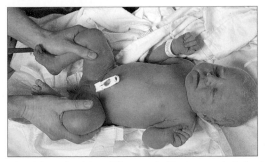

Checking the hips. *Then, probably to your baby's displeasure, she will check the hip joints for dislocation or the tell-tale clicking that suggests instability and a risk of dislocation later on.*

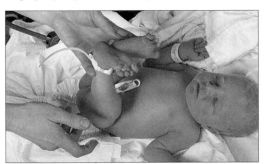

Checking the genitals. *You already know whether your baby is a boy or a girl but now the doctor makes sure that the genitals are normal and checks whether a boy's testes have descended (see p. 49).*

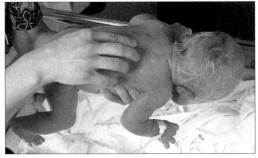

Checking the spine and anus. *Holding the baby face down along her forearm, the doctor checks that all your baby's vertebrae are in place and that her back passage is open.*

Checking the eyes and palate. *A finger to suck calms your baby during an inspection of her eyes, and then it checks that there is no cleft in her palate.*

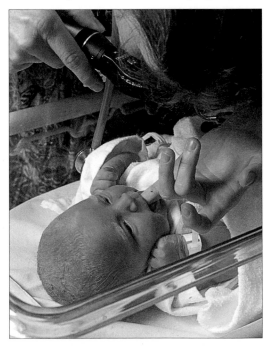

Although this first medical check-up should be an excellent opportunity to ask questions, it does not always turn out that way. Doctors are sometimes in a hurry. New babies sometimes howl throughout. And new parents are often not yet capable of constructing a coherent question, let alone taking in the answer. Questions and concerns tend to surface later. As long as you are in the hospital, there will always be someone to ask; don't hesitate. In your first week or so at home, though, even daily visits from a midwife, and a telephone number you can call in between, may not seem enough. There are still a lot of hours to get through and so many things about a new baby that can seem worrying.

NEWBORN PECULIARITIES

A newborn baby's physiology is not the same as that of an older baby, a child or an adult. It takes time for this new body to settle into life outside the womb and to become fully efficient. During this settling period some babies display all kinds of colour changes, spots, blotches, swellings and secretions, many of which look very peculiar. Most of them would indeed be peculiar if they occurred in an older person, but they are normal, or at least insignificant, when they occur in the first two weeks of life. Hospital staff take these newborn peculiarities for granted and, because they know that they are nothing to worry about, often forget to warn parents about them. The result can be unnecessary panic just when you need all the peace you can get. The following list describes some of the commonest of these phenomena and tells you why they happen and what they mean. If you need direct reassurance or if you are not sure that what you see matches what is described on the list, consult your visiting midwife, or phone your doctor. Above all, do remember that these things are normal or unimportant only in a newborn baby. If you notice one of them after your baby is two to three weeks old, you should certainly ask for advice from your health visitor or clinic.

Skin Newborn skin has an overall pinky-red hue (whatever colour it will be eventually) because it is so thin that the underlying blood vessels show through.

Uneven colour

Uneven colour. Because the circulation is not yet fully efficient, blood may sometimes pool in the lower half of a baby's body, so that when he has been still for a long time it looks half red and half pale. And sometimes a full ration of circulating blood does not reach the baby's extremities so that as he lies asleep, his hands and feet look bluish. As soon as you pick the baby up or turn him over, the skin colour will even out.

Spots. Because the skin is fragile it is easily damaged – nappy rash is not the only common kind of clothes chafing. And because the pores do not yet work efficiently, it is very liable to develop spots. Common kinds are "neonatal urticaria", consisting of a rash of red blotchy spots with tiny red centres that come and go on different parts of the baby's body, each group lasting only a few hours; tiny white spots, usually on the nose and

Milk spots (milia)

cheeks, called "milk spots" (milia) that may last for several weeks, and the grimly named but harmless "toxic erythema" – irregular red blotches with pale middles that look like a collection of insect bites. They may spoil your baby's complexion for a while but they do no harm and need no treatment.

Blue patches. Called "Mongolian blue spots", these are just temporary accumulations of pigment under the skin. They are more usual in babies of African or Mongolian descent but can also be seen in babies of Mediterranean descent or in any baby whose skin is going to be fairly dark. They are nothing to do with bruising or with any disorder of the blood.

Birthmarks. There are many kinds of birthmark; only a doctor can say whether the mark that worries you is a birthmark and if so whether it is the kind that will vanish on its own or not. But remember that red marks on the skin often arise from pressure during the birth. This kind will vanish within a few days.

Peeling. Most new babies' skin peels a little in the first few days. It is

Cradlecap

often most noticeable on the palms and soles. Post-mature babies may have extra-dry skin, and babies of Afro-Caribbean and Asian descent often have skin and hair that is much dryer than babies of European descent. On the whole, the fewer and simpler the products that are applied to new babies' skins, the better. If dry skin requires an emollient to keep it from cracking, choose a hypoallergenic

baby lotion or a pure vegetable oil. *Scurf on the scalp.* This is as normal as skin peeling elsewhere; it is nothing to do with dandruff and does not suggest lack of hygiene. A really thick cap-shaped layer of brownish scales, known as "cradlecap", can be a nuisance. It sometimes spreads to the baby's eyebrows and behind the ears. Your doctor may suggest that you try a special shampoo, ointment or oil.

Hair

Any amount of hair on the head, from almost none to a luxuriant growth, is normal. Babies born late, after extra time in the womb, may have a great deal of rather coarse hair. Whatever it is like at birth, most of the newborn hair will gradually fall out and be replaced. The colour and texture of the new

hair may be quite different.
Body hair. In the womb babies are covered with a fine fuzz of hair called lanugo. Some, especially babies born prematurely, still have traces, usually across the shoulder blades and down the spine. This hair will gradually rub off in the first week or two.

Head

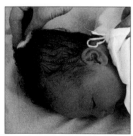

Moulded head

Oddities of shape. Babies' skulls are designed to "give" under pressure. The second stage of an unassisted labour may dramatically elongate your baby's head, while forceps sometimes leave depressions as well as bruises. The suction of a ventouse doesn't usually affect the actual skull but often raises a doughnut-shaped swelling on the top of the head. If your new baby looks like a prize-fighter, being born gave him a hard time. But that doesn't mean it damaged him.
Fontanelles. These are the areas where the bones of the skull have not yet fused together. The most noticeable lies towards the back of the top of the baby's head.

Fontanelles are covered by an extremely tough membrane and there is no danger whatsoever of damaging them with normal handling. In a baby without much hair, a pulse may be seen beating under the fontanelle. This is perfectly normal. If the fontanelle appears sunken, so that there is a visible "dip" in the head, the baby is probably dehydrated (usually due to very hot weather or a fever) and should be offered water or a feed, at once. If the fontanelle should ever appear to be tight and tense and to bulge outwards even when the baby is not crying, he should see a doctor urgently as it could be a sign of illness.

Eyes

Squinting. Many babies whose eyes are perfectly normal have a squinting appearance in the early days of life. If you look at your baby closely you will probably find that it is the marked folds of skin at the inner corners of the eyes that make you think they are squinting. These folds of skin are perfectly normal

and become less and less noticeable during the baby's first few weeks. Until the baby has strengthened and learned to control the muscles around the eyes, it is quite usual for there to be difficulty in holding both eyes in line with each other so that they can both focus steadily on the same object. As your baby looks at your face, you may suddenly notice that one eye has "wandered" out of focus. A "wandering eye" almost always rights itself by the time the baby is six months old. But point it out to the doctor at your next visit so that a check can be made on its progress. A true squint means that the baby's eyes never both focus together on the same object. Rather than moving together and then one wandering off, the eyes are permanently out of alignment with each other. If you are the first to notice that your baby has a "fixed squint" you should report it at once to the doctor. Early treatment is both essential and highly successful.

Swollen, puffy or red-streaked eyes. These are very common in the first hours after birth and result from pressure during it. The swelling may make it difficult for your baby to open his eyes at first, but it will soon subside. Any recurrence of trouble with the eyes, once newborn problems have resolved, should be promptly reported to the doctor.

Yellowish discharge/crusting on lids and lashes. This suggests a very common mild infection, resulting from contact with blood during delivery, and known as "sticky eye". It is not serious but the baby should be seen by the doctor who may recommend drops or a solution for bathing the eyes.

Watery eye. New babies don't usually shed tears when they cry, but may shed them when they are *not* crying if the tear ducts have not fully opened to allow tears to drain away via the nose. Ducts usually open by the end of the first year.

Puffy eyes

Ears

Discharge. While it is normal for a baby's ears to produce wax, which is an antiseptic protection for the ear canal, it is never normal for them to produce any other kind of discharge. If you are not sure that the substance you see coming from the ear is wax, consult your doctor. If it is wax, she will be only too pleased to reassure you. If by any chance it is pus, treatment is urgent. Never poke around inside your baby's ears; you could damage the ear drum. Like all body orifices, ears are self-cleaning. Confine yourself to washing around the outside.

Protruding ears. Some babies' ears do seem to stick out a great deal but that doesn't always mean that they are set on in a sticking out position. Newborn ears are soft and malleable and also look very different once the head takes on a more mature shape and more hair grows.

Mouth

"Tongue-tie". The tongue of a new baby is anchored along a much greater proportion of its length than is the tongue of an older person. In some babies the anchoring fold of skin is so long that the baby has almost no tongue which is free and mobile. In the past such babies were thought to be "tongue-tied". It was believed that unless the anchoring skin was cut so that the tongue was free, the baby would not be able to suck properly or learn to talk. Now we know that a true tongue-tie (one that does cause problems and will not right itself with normal growth) is exceedingly rare. Most of the growth of a baby's tongue during the first year of life is in the tip so that by the first birthday the tongue is fully mobile. In the meantime, its close anchorage has no ill effects.

Blisters on the upper lip. These are called "sucking blisters" because the baby makes them himself with his suction. They can occur at any time while the baby is purely milk-fed. They may vanish between feedings and they are unimportant.

Sucking blister

White tongue. While they are being fed only on milk, babies often have tongues that are white all over. This is absolutely normal. Infection or illness produces patches of white on an otherwise pink tongue.
Fluid-filled papules on the gum are harmless (and common) cysts.

Yellowish-white spots might suddenly become visible on the roof of your baby's mouth when he yawns widely. Although they look worrying they are equally harmless. Both will clear without treatment and will have vanished well before a first tooth is likely.

Breasts

Swollen breasts. It is perfectly normal for babies of both sexes to have swollen breasts in the first three to five days after birth. This is due to hormones flooding through the mother just before the birth. The hormones are intended for her but they sometimes get to the baby, too. The swollen breasts may even have a tiny quantity of "milk" in them. They should be left strictly alone as any attempt to squeeze liquid out might introduce infection. The swelling will die down in a few days as the baby's body rids itself of the hormones.

Abdomen

Cord stump. Your midwife or doctor will check the cord stump and make sure that your baby's navel heals cleanly (see p.100). If you should see any signs of infection — redness or discharge — report it immediately.
Umbilical hernia. A small swelling close to the navel, which sticks out more when the baby cries, cannot actually be called "normal", but is very common indeed. It is caused by a slight weakness of the muscles in the wall of the abdomen that allows the contents to bulge forward. Almost all such hernias right themselves completely by one year and most doctors believe they heal more quickly if they are not strapped up. Very few ever require surgery.

Genitals

The genitals of both boys and girls are larger, in proportion to the rest of their bodies, at birth than at any other time before puberty. During the first few days after birth they may look even larger than normal because hormones from the mother have crossed the placenta, entered the baby's bloodstream and caused temporary extra swelling. The scrotum or the vulva may look red and inflamed. All in all the baby's sexual parts may look conspicuous and peculiar. But don't worry. The doctor or midwife who delivered the baby will have checked that all is normal. The inflammation and swelling will rapidly subside during the baby's settling period and he or she will soon "grow into" those apparently over-large organs.
Undescended testes. A boy's testes develop in the abdomen. They descend into the scrotum just before a full-term birth. If the doctor cannot feel them during her examination of the newborn, it may be that they are "retractile". They have descended, but they can still go up again into the abdomen and do so in reaction to the touch of cold hands. Provided that they can be "milked" down, they will eventually descend on their own. An undescended testicle is one which cannot be persuaded into the scrotum after a full-term birth or by the time a premature baby reaches his expected date of birth. If you cannot ever see or feel both your son's testes in the scrotum, mention it to the doctor who checks him at around six weeks of age.
Tight foreskin (phimosis). The penis and the foreskin develop from a single bud in the foetus. They are

still fused at birth and they only gradually separate during the first few years of the boy's life. A tight foreskin is therefore not a problem a new baby can have. You cannot retract his foreskin because it is not made to retract at this age. You cannot wash underneath it because it is only meant to be cleaned from outside in babyhood. Circumcision (surgical removal of the foreskin) of a young baby is very rarely medically advisable and, if it becomes necessary later on, it is often because of attempts to retract the foreskin forcibly before it was ready to retract of its own accord.

Elimination and secretions

Feeding, and therefore digesting food and excreting waste, are processes that are established gradually over several days. If you are accustomed to changing the nappies of even somewhat older babies, the contents of these first ones may surprise you.

Meconium. First stools consist mostly of this greenish-black sticky substance that fills babies' intestines in the womb and has to be evacuated before ordinary digestion can take place. Almost all babies pass meconium in the first 24 hours. If a baby is born at home, the midwife must be told if none is passed by the second day. Failure to pass meconium might mean that there is an obstruction in the bowel.

Blood in stools. Very occasionally blood is noticed in the stools in the first day or two. It is usually blood from the mother, swallowed during the delivery and passed through the baby, unchanged. But to be certain, keep the nappy to show to the midwife.

Reddish urine. Very early urine often contains a harmless substance called "urates" which appears red on the nappy. As it looks like blood you may prefer to keep the nappy to show the midwife.

Frequent urine. Once the urine flow is established, your baby may pass water as often as 30 times in the 24 hours. This is entirely normal. On the other hand a baby who stays dry for four to six hours at this stage should be seen by the midwife or a doctor. It is just possible that there is some obstruction to the flow of urine.

Vaginal bleeding. A minute amount of vaginal bleeding is common and insignificant in girls at any time in the first week of life. It is due to maternal oestrogens passing into the baby just before birth.

Vaginal discharge. A clear or whitish discharge from the vagina is also quite normal. It will stop in a very few days.

Nasal discharge. Many babies accumulate enough mucus in the nose to cause sniffles or some visible "runniness". This does not mean that the baby has a cold or other infection.

Tears. Most babies cry without tears until they are four to six weeks old. A few shed tears from the beginning. It does not matter either way.

Sweating. New babies' heads are so large in relation to the rest of their bodies that newborns readily gain and lose heat from them. Keeping your baby's head covered will help keep him warm enough, but when he is too warm and begins to sweat, it may prevent the evaporation that should cool him. Many babies sweat a great deal around the head and neck even when their heads are not covered. This has no importance unless the baby shows other signs of being feverish or unwell. It is a good reason, though, for rinsing the head and hair frequently as the salty sweat may otherwise irritate the skin in the folds of the neck.

Vomiting. Spitting up a little milk after feeding is normal.

Opposition to circumcision is new-fangled nonsense; it didn't do me any harm.

We're expecting our second baby — a boy. I had naturally assumed that he would be circumcised before we brought him home from the hospital but, to my astonishment, my wife is strongly opposed to the idea. I thought it was something she had read about circumcision being painful that had put her off but although my offer to look into the question of anaesthesia was well received, it hasn't really changed her mind. She says circumcision is a cruel and archaic practice; I say it didn't do me any harm and it's important for hygienic reasons.

It is always difficult for an adult to reject his own childhood on behalf of his offspring. And it's especially difficult for a man to accept that the way his penis is may not be the best way for his son's to be. However while you feel that circumcision did you no harm, other circumcised men say that the procedure left them with a lifelong sense of having been deformed. The world has learned a lot since you were a baby, and it's that accumulating knowledge your wife wants your child to benefit from.

There is no rationale for "routine" removal of the foreskin from the glans of the penis. The idea that it was more hygienic was based on the notion of smegma gathering beneath an intact foreskin that in a baby is difficult to roll back so it can be washed off. We know now that the foreskin and the glans penis are fused at birth and meant to be. The foreskin only gradually separates. You cannot wash beneath a baby's foreskin and should not try. It may not be possible (or necessary or desirable) to wash beneath it until a little boy is four or five years old — and entirely capable of doing it himself. Furthermore attempts at rolling back fused foreskins often make tiny

splits. Those minute wounds heal leaving scar tissue which prevents natural separation. That's a common reason for an uncircumcised baby coming to need the operation when he is older. Your son doesn't need his foreskin stripped off to keep his penis clean any more than he needs his nostrils slit to keep his nose clean. And it won't reduce his eventual partners' risk of cervical cancer either; that finding was statistical lack of sophistication — or error!

But if there are no physical reasons *for* infant circumcision, there are very strong reasons against it: so strong that in most countries it is carried out only as part of religious ritual. The United States is alone in continuing to carry out the procedure as part of the routine medical care of new babies.

Circumcision is not just the quick snip many people assume but described by one leading American paediatrican as "among the most painful interventions performed in neonatal medicine". All babies react with panic-stricken crying, many with something close to hysteria, some go into shock. Local anaesthesia — though not perfect or itself painless — is certainly better than nothing, but when it wears off it does not take the pain of the raw penis with it, or help with the hurt of urination or give back the baby's pleasure in being held and cuddled. Anaesthetized or not, circumcision means a nasty few days for all of you.

When babies need operations for their own good, parents have to see them through as best they can, hoping they will forget the pain, the powerlessness, the betrayal. But why spoil your baby's first week with you, and yours with him, when there is no possible good to balance the probable harm?

GOING HOME

Going home from hospital may be more of an effort and less of a thrill than you expected. However eager you were to leave, the hospital can seem like a haven of safety once you are out on your own. And however recovered you felt compared with women who had birthed their babies only hours before, you are still exhausted; your hormones are working overtime to start producing milk, and with all that physical upheaval, you are also up against the emotional turmoil of introducing a new person into your life and your family.

However peculiar you feel now, though, try to believe that your new self, new family and new responsibilities will seem quite ordinary and manageable in a few weeks. Try to be patient and gentle with yourself. In fact why not take your baby and your partner and retire to bed? It's not too late to start a babymoon (see p.37). Lean, heavily, on your partner or anyone else who offers support. Let them look after you while you look after the baby. And don't, *please* don't, try to accomplish anything practical or professional. This is a time for people and their feelings. Talk out your own and your partner's; play out your toddler's, and keep that baby close.

The blues "Baby blues" or "fourth-day blues" are not an inevitable part of the postnatal days, but they are very common. Sometimes they are triggered by real problems with your health; real concerns about your baby or the real separation from your partner that being in hospital entails. But even if you had an easy delivery and now have a beautiful, healthy baby and loving support at home, you can suddenly find yourself in floods of tears. Don't let those tears frighten you. And don't decide that because you are crying you must be unhappy. Tears of this sort spring partly from physical and emotional anticlimax after the birth, and from hormonal chaos as your body struggles to adapt to not being pregnant any more and to making milk. If you can calmly let them flow – even weep luxuriously into your partner's neck – they will probably stop as suddenly as they began.

Postnatal depression Postnatal depression is not at all the same as the blues. It can sneak up, or overwhelm you, weeks, even months after your baby's birth and last for a long time.

Depression is a real illness. Any major upheaval in life can touch it off in an individual who happens to be vulnerable: a bereavement or divorce, a house-move or a redundancy. In the end people almost always recover on their own. But when the upheaval is a birth, there's a baby to think about.

Deep down, your postnatal depression is about being this baby's mother so it is as much about him as about you, and bound to affect your image of the baby and therefore his own developing self-image. Postnatal depression matters to your baby on a more superficial level too. Your baby needs your loving care and if you're depressed you cannot give it, desperately though you may want to. Depression drains everything of joy and colour, saps your self-confidence and energy and turns you in upon yourself in anxious spirals. Even if you can find the drive to meet your baby's physical needs or arrange for someone else to do so, depression will deny you your pleasure in him and therefore deprive him of being your joy as well as your responsibility. So, if you should suffer from postnatal depression, you will need practical and emotional, and possibly medical, help quickly and as much for your baby's sake as for your own.

The question is: will you get it? If you are feeling utterly worthless, you probably will not feel worthy of your doctor's time. If putting on your clothes takes superhuman effort, telling somebody how you are feeling will probably be beyond you. If you already feel guilty because your baby suffers from your incompetence and your mother blames you for it, you're not likely to want to expose yourself to any more criticism. At least one in ten of new mothers suffers some degree of postnatal depression – and "suffer" is no exaggeration. Partners, grandmothers and friends should all be alert to the possibility so that as their mouths open to say, "Do pull yourself together", they suggest help instead. Friends are crucial. The experience of postnatal depression and the help that is needed is very different for different women but almost every study suggests that while complete separation from the baby is valuable to no one, support and companionship from other mothers is invaluable to all.

Whether you've a few intimates or a big casual group, your female friends will be more crucial to you now than ever before.

*Give breast-feeding
a chance; it probably
won't be long before it's
bliss for both of you.*

FEEDING
AND GROWING

If there is a decision to be made about whether a baby is to be breast-fed, it has to be the mother's because she is the only person in the world who can act on it: it is her body, her lifestyle and specifically her mothering rather than interchangeable parenting that is primarily in question. But the fact that fathers cannot breast-feed does not disqualify them from taking part in the decision–making, or excuse them from responsibility for how that decision works out. Women are far more likely to decide to breast-feed if their partners assume that they will want to nurse – or at least like the idea of them nursing. And it is often a partner's informed support that enables a woman to carry on through early breast-feeding difficulties. So if there is a decision to be made about how you are going to feed your baby, it is yours, but not yours alone unless you are going to be on your own.

But is there a decision to be made at this point? Unless breast-feeding seems beyond your personal pale – something you don't even want to think about doing, despite all you have heard about it during your pregnancy – you'd be sensible to begin by nursing your baby. Starting off with breast-feeding keeps your options open for the long term while giving the baby a boost of benefits in the short term. If you find you don't enjoy it, or it doesn't suit you for very long, you can always wean your baby (gently) from the breast to a bottle, knowing that you have given him or her a really good start. But if you start with a bottle, it's too late to change. You cannot switch from formula to breast milk, because unless the baby has been nursing regularly, your breasts will not be making any milk.

Immediate advantages of breast-feeding
Don't listen to anyone who suggests that it is not worth starting breast-feeding unless you plan to go on at least for several months. It's worth starting however short a time you think you will do it for. Being nursed for any period, even for a day or two before your milk comes in, is worthwhile for your baby:

■ While the baby is establishing your milk supply, he will be getting the colostrum which breasts produce first of all. Colostrum gives the baby water and sugar (which he could get in the form of "sugar-water" from a bottle if he was not to be breast-fed) but it also gives him just the right amount of protein and minerals plus many important antibodies from you that will protect his health while he is building up his own immune system. There is no artificial equivalent of colostrum, which is why even a few days at the breast give babies a head start.

■ *Your* milk (not just anybody's breast milk) is the only milk that will be uniquely right for your baby. It will adjust itself to his age and stage so its exact composition at the beginning will depend whether he is born pre-term or full-term. It will keep on adjusting itself to conditions, too, so if the weather is hot and he needs extra water, your breasts will provide it.

■ If your baby is genetically predisposed to allergies, exclusive breast-feeding will protect him from early exposure to "foreign" milk proteins while his digestive system grows up a little.

■ Research suggests that health benefits of breast-feeding, even for a few weeks, may be dramatic and lifelong. Recent studies, for example, suggest that it helps to optimize brain development and minimize the chances of neurological problems.

Nursing for as little as two or three weeks will probably give you more of the worst breast-feeding has to offer than of the blissful best, but it will certainly give you some physical advantages:

■ Your uterus returns to its pre-pregnancy state much faster.

■ Frequent night feeds are much easier.

■ Once your milk supply is established, the hormones released in nursing help to relax you and combat stress.

But if breast-feeding briefly may work well for you both, breast-feeding half-heartedly may not work at all. Nursing is most likely to be a pleasure if you ignore anyone who suggests that it won't be; that you'll get too tired or that you won't make enough milk. Those dire warnings easily turn into self-fulfilling prophecies, especially in the first days after birth when they have kernels of truth. Trust yourself to provide, and your baby to take, everything he needs (and surround yourself with people who also trust you both). Don't even buy bottles, or formula, or dummies, unless you live more than an hour from a source.

Advantages of longer-term breast-feeding Breast milk is the milk nature intended for human babies rather than cow babies and the count of known differences in the composition of the two now stands at over 100, by no means all of which can be ironed out in manufacturing formula milks. New research findings make the list of advantages for your baby longer and more scientific every year:

■ Breast milk (yours, remember, not just anybody's) goes on being the only milk that will be uniquely right for your baby, adjusting itself to his age and stage and to conditions.

■ Breast milk adjusts itself to your baby's appetite within each feeding – which maximizes his contentment and helps prevent obesity. The first milk your baby gets (the foremilk) is low-calorie so your baby can satisfy his thirst and desire to suck without getting to feel too full or risking getting too fat; the milk he then gets as he empties the breast (the hindmilk) is richer in fat and calories and *will* make him feel full, signalling his appetite to switch off when he has had enough.

■ As long as your baby is exclusively breast-fed he is far less likely to suffer from infections – particularly gastro-enteritis, but including colds and middle-ear infections.

■ If your baby is genetically predisposed to allergies, continuing breast-feeding will help to protect him.

■ As well as the many advantages of breast milk, nursing at the breast can provide more sucking satisfaction than a bottle because a baby can go on comfort sucking – and getting tastes of something that is not air – even when the breast is effectively empty.

Longer-term breast-feeding will benefit you too – provided your other relationships and your lifestyle can accommodate it:

Nursing mothers seem enslaved.

We are mature first-time parents-to-be. Of course we understand the advantages of breast-feeding but we are amazed by the extent to which friends with babies seem to be tied to them by nursing. We recently gave a party to which five babies came because they couldn't be left at home. It must be possible to breast-feed without being enslaved.

Breast-feeding certainly *is* a tie between mother and baby, but whether that tie feels like a chain or a ribbon of honour depends on the woman (and her partner), the baby, their lifestyle and day-by-day circumstances.

If your baby is to have no food other than breast milk and is only going to take that directly from your breasts, it is probably going to be at least three months before you can confidently leave her for more than an hour at a time. Is three months per child slavery?

Some small babies adopt such regular schedules that they really can be counted on not to get hungry or thirsty within three hours of a feed – long enough to take in a movie or dinner, if not both – but most don't and can't. The trouble is that if a burp or a fire engine wakes your baby two hours after she nursed, she's likely to need suckling to settle again, and if you are not there, nothing else will do.

Nothing. Don't let anyone tell you that if she woke and cried when you weren't there it wouldn't really matter. Once a baby who knows no other way of eating or drinking has focused on wanting to nurse, nothing will distract her and she may cry inconsolably, sometimes hysterically, more or less indefinitely because as she gets more and more exhausted, she also gets hungrier and more thirsty. Agony for the baby and agony for whoever is caring for her: longing to help but helpless.

But while your baby has no other source of food than your breasts, will you have to leave her? If you take her around with you wherever you go, you can go almost anywhere you might want to go as a treat. Okay, cinemas and clubs are tricky, but parties are fine (your small visitors didn't spoil anything did they?) and so is shopping or going out to lunch if you choose from among the ever-growing number of establishments that pride themselves on being baby-friendly.

■ Breast-feeding forces you to sit or lie down and take the rest you need; perhaps the only rest you get. Night feeds are easier even though there may be more of them.

■ Breast-feeding helps you to get your figure back because the extra fat your body laid down was in preparation for lactation and it rapidly comes off you and onto your baby. It may, or may not, be an advantage to you that some of the fatty tissue in your breasts is likely to have been replaced by milk glands so that after weaning, the breasts are slightly smaller than their pre-pregnancy size.

■ Breast-feeding will probably relieve you of pre-menstrual tension in the long term as well as menstruation in the short term. It will not reliably prevent you from becoming pregnant, though.

■ Breast-feeding is thought to reduce the risk of breast cancer developing before the menopause.

■ Breast-feeding that is going smoothly saves time and trouble: nothing to buy and store and run out of; nothing to mix or sterilize; nothing to keep cool or re-warm; nothing to fetch in the middle of a TV show or the night. And nothing to wash up. It even costs slightly

less to buy the extra food your baby needs and eat and process it yourself, than to buy it ready-processed from a formula manufacturer.
■ Unless you prefer to keep it very private, breast-feeding makes it easier to take the baby out and about with you, even to public places or workplaces with no track-record as baby-friendly. Nothing but nappies to carry on a trip or run out of when the car breaks down; and nothing your baby needs from anyone but you.

Advantages of bottle-feeding Almost every mother can make, and almost every baby can take, breast milk. "Almost" is accurate but still leaves a few who cannot. If your baby cannot have your milk because medication that is vital for you would be damaging to him; or if he especially needs your milk but cannot nurse because he is immature or ill, or prevented by an anomaly such as cleft lip and palate, the advantages of bottle-feeding from the beginning will be obvious to everyone. If you and your baby cannot sort out the demand and supply of breast milk to his satisfaction and your comfort, the advantages of bottle-feeding will all too readily become obvious to both of you, even if the nursing problems were unnecessary or reversible. Be careful though; sometimes apparent advantages of bottle-feeding at the beginning of a baby's life are less because bottle-feeding is wonderful than because breast-feeding takes longer to become so:
■ Getting a baby started on the bottle is easier than getting him started on the breast because you only have to consider his comfort and competence, you can take your own for granted.
■ Bottles of formula from the beginning let you off the intense (and sometimes uncomfortable) physical and emotional involvement with your baby that establishing breast-feeding requires.
■ If you are neither pregnant nor breast-feeding, your body is no longer enmeshed with your baby's wellbeing, so it can belong to you again. Instead of soul-searching about whether your body can adequately nourish his, you know that almost anyone can feed him. The bond between father and baby may be tighter because he can feed him from the beginning, but the bond between you and your baby may be looser because you don't have to.

Getting the best from both breast and bottle Many of the physical advantages of breast-feeding are to do with the milk rather than the process of nursing. With the help of bottles, you may be able to give your baby breast milk without the breast (and you) having to be there for him. This may be particularly important if you very much want to breast-feed (or your baby especially needs to have breast milk rather than formula for some medical reason such as a familial tendency to allergy), but you have to return to work at an early (but hopefully not too early) date.

Provided you have had time to get your milk supply fully established, it may be so copious that as long as you nurse your baby freely (probably frequently!) at night and before you leave for work in the morning, you can also express enough breast milk for daytime bottles. If you're going to rely on expressed milk for part of your baby's feeding you will almost certainly want to use a breast pump. Expressing milk by hand is a useful technique in emergencies, but collecting whole bottles of milk is achingly slow work. There are manual and electric pumps available ranging widely in sophistication.

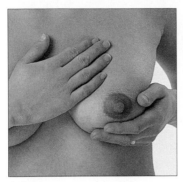

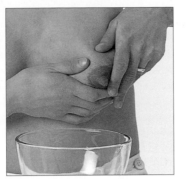

1 Support your breast in one hand. Use the other palm to stroke repeatedly down to the areola, all round the breast.

2 With fingers under the breast, run your thumbs down to the margins of the areola and the milk ducts beneath.

3 Press in and up with your thumbs so milk squirts from the untouched nipple. Repeat all around the breast.

You may not find the most expensive the most comfortable. Try to arrange to hire for a trial period before making a major investment.

Most of the emotional and social advantages of breast-feeding do depend on one-to-one nursing but it doesn't have to be all or nothing. It may be possible for you to be there and nurse the baby yourself most of the time if only someone else can feed him from a bottle some of the time.

Not all babies switch happily between breast and bottle, and rather few can do so before they are two or three months old. However, once yours will accept a bottle to enable you to go to work, there's no reason why he cannot be fed the same way at a weekend occasionally, to enable you to do something for fun. If you've nursed him during the day on a Saturday and can express in the early evening what he will need later on, his father, grandparent or trusted sitter could free you to go out or simply to sleep.

If, like many women, you have problems with expressing breast milk (or finding the time to try) and there is no particular reason to avoid giving your baby formula, ordinary bottle-feeding may seem, and prove to be, a much easier option once you go back to work. But provided you have got your baby established on the breast, formula-feeding by day need not necessarily mean the end of all nursing. Not every woman's supply of milk is dependent on expressing during the day. You may find that yours keeps up in response to the stimulation of your baby feeding in the early morning, through the evening and at night, and that your baby can nurse at night and take bottles of formula by day, without getting confused between the two kinds of nipple or rejecting either.

Although some babies never have bottles at all and others are never put to the breast, "breast" or "bottle" isn't a clear-cut, once-and-for-all choice for many women. Many breast-fed babies have some bottles; even exclusively breast-fed babies may have bottles of expressed breast milk. In fact, the chances are that you will use both, whether sequentially, interchangeably or occasionally.

BREAST, BOTTLE, OR BOTH?

Feeding plans (like birth plans) are often overtaken by events. Whatever your intentions, and however clear-cut they may be, it's quite likely that you, like each of these three women, will find yourself doing something quite different. Plans are good, but plans that don't work for you and your baby aren't good plans, so have no qualms about letting them go.

Angela's story

The feeding plan. To breast-feed for her baby's sake during her three months' maternity leave, then bottle-feed with formula.

What happened? Breast-fed exclusively for five months and partially for almost a year. Only bottles used were for expressed breast milk. Only formula given was from a cup.

What changed her plans? To her surprise, Angela enjoyed nursing and found herself miserable at the prospect of stopping, for her own sake as well as the baby's. Perhaps her little daughter, Amy, could sense that she was half-hearted about the bottles she offered; anyway, Amy made it very clear that she did not want to stop breast-feeding either. She would have nothing to do with formula from a bottle. With her maternity leave running out, Angela tried expressing milk for her baby to take from a bottle. She found expressing easy and Amy would accept it as long as someone other than her mother offered it to her, so she was fed that way until she was five months old and seemed ready to drop her lunch-time bottle feed in favour of solid foods and a cup. At that point, Angela and her childminder found that Amy drank formula from a cup just as willingly as breast milk so Angela thankfully stopped expressing and storing breast milk to cover her daytime absences. But that did not mean an end to breast-feeding: to Angela's delight, her milk remained plentiful even when she was only nursing before and after work – and in the night.

Maria's story

The feeding plan. To breast-feed for at least the first year or until her baby was entirely weaned, with the help of her five months' maternity and annual leave, and the crêche facilities at her workplace.

What happened? Used relief bottles of formula from two months; entirely weaned from breast to bottle at four months.

What changed her plans? Maria never found nursing quite as easy as she had expected. Although her baby, Jonathan, fed well, she had not realized how frequently a baby might need to suck to build or increase the milk supply. Her partner was generally supportive of her breast-feeding, but certainly did not consider it worth suffering for. If Maria had a bad night or the blues, he invariably suggested that Jonathan should have a bottle so that she could have a rest. Two months after the birth, Jonathan was still nursing very frequently, especially through the evening, and his father began to realize that there was no prospect of being able to go out and leave him "between feeds". A month later, Maria was not only very tired but also was feeling an uncomfortable mixture of guilt and anger towards her partner. She agreed to see whether an evening bottle of formula would settle Jonathan enough to give them some time together and he took the bottle so well that they were soon able to go out for the evening leaving him with a babysitter. Maria intended those evening bottles to be the only ones Jonathan had, but cutting down his evening nursing quickly reduced her milk supply and the baby began to look for the bottle at other times of day. By four months he was fully bottle-fed. Although it was a relief to Maria not to have to struggle with breast-feeding any more, she regretted letting it become a struggle. She felt that now she knew what to expect she would be able to manage better with a second baby even if her partner was not more wholeheartedly supportive.

Jessica's story

The feeding plan. To breast-feed for as long as her baby wanted. She had waited a long time to have a baby and was now nicely placed to take a long maternity leave and then join her husband in their own business, sharing work and child care flexibly between them. Nursing was part of her image of herself as a mature and serene mother.

What happened? The baby was bottle-fed from day three.

What changed her plans? Jessica had a long second stage of labour. However, the baby, Sam, sucked well within minutes of birth so, although the midwives felt she would be better off staying in the hospital overnight, they gave in to Jessica's determination to go home within a few hours, as planned. Once out of their hands, though, Jessica could not get Sam to latch on properly and her husband tried in vain to help. The baby slept a lot that night but his parents felt too anxious to relax and by the next morning both were exhausted and convinced that Sam must be getting dehydrated. By the time the midwife arrived, Jessica's nipples were sore and so were her feelings. The midwife reassured everyone and helped Jessica get Sam on, but that night the milk came in with a rush that left Jessica in pain (and crying) and Sam unable to latch on and crying. The father (who may or may not have been crying also) sent for his mother-in-law and went out to buy bottles.

FIRST FEEDS FROM BREAST OR BOTTLE

Newborn babies don't need much food in the first three or four days of life. Breast-fed babies get minute quantities of creamy colostrum. Some bottle-fed babies are given sugar-water first in hospital; others are given formula from day one. Either way, it is the water part of those drinks that they need most. They probably will not take much, anyway. Feeding is something babies have to learn.

Because they take little food to begin with, breast-fed babies in particular usually lose weight for four or five days before they start to gain. It is quite usual for a baby to lose 225 g (8 oz) over the first five days and then gain it back over the next five. A baby's weight at 10 days old is therefore expected to be roughly the same as it was at birth.

When a newborn baby is thirsty or hungry he feels uncomfortable so he cries. But at this early stage he does not cry to be fed. He does not know that the discomfort he feels comes from hunger; that sucking will bring him food or that food will make him feel better. In fact, a basic equation of babyhood that he needs to discover is: "sucking equals food equals comfort".

Some babies are so ready to suck that this vital learning takes place quickly and easily. They may have been practising sucking their fingers in the womb (we know that some babies do) and once they

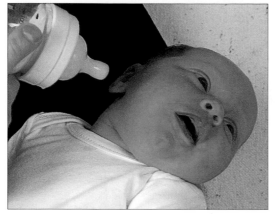

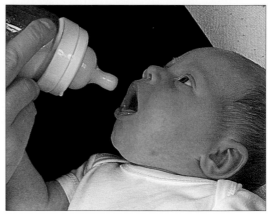

1 Bring the baby to the bottle as you'd have to do if it were a breast: instead of trying to put the teat straight into her mouth, stroke that cheek first so she turns towards you.

2 As she turns her head, your baby's lips will purse. When the teat or your finger touches them they will open. Your baby's wide open mouth tells you she is ready.

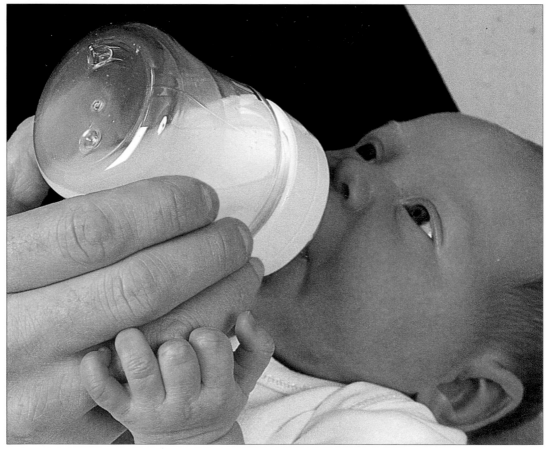

3 If you now put the teat into your baby's mouth, she will probably draw it deeply in and settle to rhythmic sucking. Keep the bottle tilted so that milk covers the teat and hold it firmly. Her suction is strong and needs something to pull against.

are born they suck anything that comes their way. Of course, when such a baby is offered the breast or a bottle he sucks that too. Sucking gives him colostrum or milk and that makes him feel good. After two or three repetitions, the feeding lesson is learned.

Other babies are quite different. They cry piteously with hunger-pain but when their mothers try to put a nipple or teat in their mouths they yell around it. Even a taste of colostrum or formula does not stop the crying because the connection between that taste and comfort has not been made yet. It will be made, though. However much of a struggle your early attempts at feeding may be, you can be quite sure that your baby has been born with a set of sucking reflexes and that if you evoke those reflexes (rather than trying to plug his yelling mouth with your nipple or a teat) he will suck. And once he has sucked a few times and discovered the food-comfort it brings him, all will be well.

Beware of nipple confusion Getting milk from a breast and getting milk from a bottle require completely different sucking techniques and very few newborns are willing or able to learn both at the same time. A large mouthful of warm, soft, nipple-plus-areola cannot feel much like a smaller but stiffer bulb of rubber, latex or silicone. And that contrast alone is enough to cause problems because if the baby tries to suck your nipple the way he does the artificial one, he'll make you sore and get no milk; but if he tries to suck the rubber the way he nurses from you, he'll take it so far into his mouth that he'll make himself gag.

Conventional wisdom has it that babies find bottle-feeding "easier" and therefore won't work at breast-feeding once they have a taste for it. But since babies who have a taste for breast-feeding are often difficult to persuade into taking bottles, the point may simply be that they like to feed the way they're used to feeding.

Nipple confusion may lead to poor nursing and breast problems. So, since your breast milk supply depends on your baby's sucking (which the supply of milk in a bottle does not) don't risk it. If you want to breast-feed at all, try not to introduce your baby to a bottle (even for water or expressed breast milk) until your milk supply and his technique is well established. Some mother-baby pairs can cope with occasional bottles at three weeks, but you'd do better to wait until six weeks if you possibly can and twice that long if breast-feeding is a real priority for you.

Introducing a bottle after that time may take considerable tact and patience. If you are going back to work, do allow a week or so for the baby to learn to accept however many daily bottle-feeds he is going to have to have, while you are still available. He may take the bottle most readily from you, because he is used to you feeding him. On the other hand, he may adamantly refuse bottles from you because he can smell the breast milk he is used to, although he will take them quite readily from his father or caregiver. You may need to experiment with types of teat and size of hole, too.

The rooting reflex A baby who is awake, alert and at least somewhat hungry will respond to any gentle, breast-like touch or stroke anywhere on the side of the face by "rooting": actively turning his head to search for the nipple while pursing his lips in readiness for it. When those pursed lips touch something nipple-like, he opens his mouth widely, ready to latch on.

If you are breast-feeding and holding your baby on your left arm, ready to feed him from your left breast, rolling him over so that he lies on his side facing you will evoke a rooting response. As you turn him, you will stroke the right side of his face with your arm and then the bottom of his right cheek and the corner of his mouth with the underside of your breast. So by the time your two bodies are aligned, his mouth will already be pursed, and provided his mouth and your nipple are at the same height they're likely to touch.

If you are using a bottle, the process is the same except that since you want the baby facing up (rather than in towards you), you may want to start her rooting by deliberately touching her cheek and the corner of her mouth with your finger.

Working with rooting and sucking reflexes What happens then is crucial (though once things go smoothly you won't experience the successive steps in slow motion the way they are described here). The baby registers the feel of the nipple or teat on his pursed lips and as a reflex response opens his mouth widely. If you then (and only then) fill that open mouth by putting the teat into it or by moving him on to the breast so that the nipple leads the way and a good mouthful of areola follows it, he will latch on and probably begin to suck.

Why only probably? Because the rooting reflex that gets your baby on to the breast or bottle doesn't actually start him sucking. Sucking reflexes develop later than rooting reflexes – pre-term babies often root as if they'd love to suck long before they are capable of doing so – and have to compete in the first day or two with babies' gag reflexes. It is far more urgent for your new baby to get mucus out of his airways than food into his stomach, so don't be surprised or feel rejected if a mouthful of breast makes him gag and spit up rather than suck and swallow.

It is all much simpler than it sounds when written out. In fact if your baby's first feeds go smoothly you don't need to know about the reflexes his learned behaviour is building on. It is when they are not going smoothly that it's worth having a clear picture of the processes in your mind so that you can at least avoid working against them:

■ Keep the cues straightforward. If you touch both cheeks instead of one, for example, your baby will not know which way to turn his head; if you hold both cheeks to try to do the turning instead of leaving it to him, he will be confused and fight you.

■ Give the cues in order. It's important to get him rooting for a feed before you actually invite him to suck, so don't start even a bottle feed by touching his lips with the teat.

■ Respect the timing. If your nipple is still in your bra, or the bottle in its warmer, when your baby's pursed mouth seeks, touches something and opens, you will miss the magic moment for putting him on and you may have to start again.

■ Above all, remember that feeding is something for your baby to do and for you to facilitate. It is easy to be too active, as getting him latched on seems the most important and difficult thing you've ever done. But you can't force your baby to suck and it's better not to try.

If a baby's sucking reflexes are respected and used in his very first feeding experiences he will quickly learn the lesson that "sucking equals milk equals comfort". But it helps him to learn and it helps him to get enthusiastic about the whole feeding business if the feeds are kept comfortable and peaceful, and the more enthusiastic he becomes, the more comfortable and peaceful *you* will feel. It is not always easy to arrange life for your baby exactly as you would like it in a busy hospital, especially if your baby is in the nursery rather than beside your bed. If they really will not allow rooming-in, what about an early discharge? For the smoothest possible start:

■ Avoid even trying to feed a baby who is very upset and screaming. He will not suck well. While he is overwhelmed by his feelings there is little chance of him discovering that he can suck himself better. At home, it will be better for both of you if he is always picked up and offered food before he reaches that point. In hospital, staff sometimes misguidedly keep your breast-fed baby away from you and waiting for his feed because they want you to rest, especially at night. And nurses may be making up feeds for the bottle-fed babies at certain hours so unscheduled feeds are not available. If, despite all your efforts, your baby has been kept waiting and is upset, he needs soothing by close wrapping, rocking or walking before you attempt to persuade him to suck.

■ Noise and movement may distract your baby from sucking. If this seems to be a problem and you are at home, try excluding everyone but your partner from the room while you are nursing, at least for a few days. If you are in hospital, you can at least position yourself so that your body is between your baby and the room and your face is directly above his. If you can get him to focus on you, other things will be less distracting. Wherever you are, keep up a gentle stream of talk. Your voice will block out the other sounds.

■ Don't try to force a sleepy baby to stay awake. In the very first days many babies are too sleepy to suck for long, especially if they were dosed with your pethidine. It really does not matter if your baby goes to sleep after a few sucks because if he is mature enough to need more food, he is mature enough to wake again and ask for it. On the other hand it *does* matter if he is upset by being bounced around and having his feet flicked in misguided attempts to make him take the "proper" amount all at once. Feeding should be gentle bliss.

■ Make sure your baby gets properly rewarded for the effort of sucking. In breast-feeding, a somewhat pendulous breast (especially one that is not yet full of milk but only has some colostrum in it) can block the baby's nose when he tries to suck so that instead of being rewarded, he gets in a panic because he cannot breathe. Either move his bottom further in to your body so that his forehead moves fractionally away, or use the fingers of your free hand to depress the breast a little just above the areola so his nose is clear.

In bottle-feeding, a teat with too small a hole may frustrate your baby. Instead of an easy reward for his sucking he has to work for every sip and in these early days he may easily give up. If you up-end the bottle, milk should drip out of the teat at a rate of several drops per *second*. If it is slower than that you need a larger-holed teat.

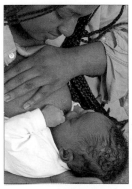

While baby and breasts are both new to feeding you may need to look for positions that suit both.

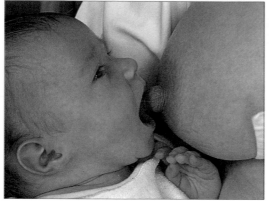

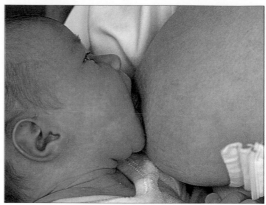

1 A good latch almost guarantees a good feed for your baby that's comfortable for you. Roll her body (not just her head) in towards you. When the open mouth says she's ready...

2 ...move her onto the breast (not the other way around), lower jaw well down the areola, mouth full of breast and the nipple drawn right back in her mouth, safe from friction.

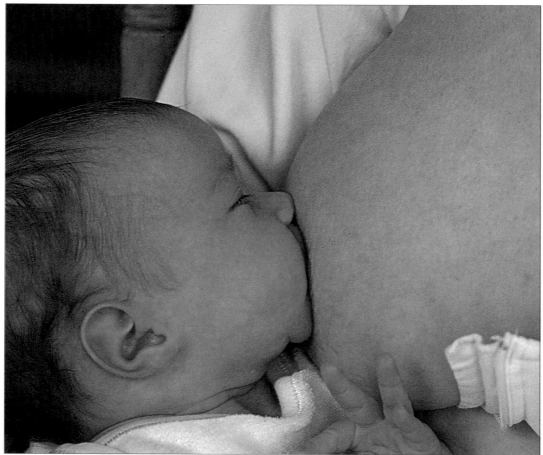

3 Chin resting firmly against the breast, lips rolled back rather than pouting, she doesn't suck milk from the nipple but presses the milk sinuses with her jaws and tongue so it squirts down her throat. Is she getting any? Listen for the sound of swallowing – and watch her ears wiggle.

Getting Started with Breast-feeding

Getting started with breast-feeding is not always easy. Just as many babies need to be tactfully shown how to use their sucking reflexes, so many breasts have to be gradually persuaded into easy performance of the function for which they are designed. Many first-time mothers find the first few days worrying, strange and uncomfortable; as a result some abandon the attempt to breast-feed within a week of the birth. Don't give up before you have given yourself a chance to experience the glorious time ahead when these early problems are over and the milk is there, like magic, whenever the baby wants it and wherever you want to be. It's because they know, from experience, that this happy state is coming, that mothers who have breast-fed one baby hardly ever give up on breast-feeding the second, however difficult the early days may be.

Don't be surprised or disheartened if the whole feeding business is a struggle as long as you remain in hospital. The availability of expert help seems comforting but may not be of very much practical use. Helping someone persuade a new baby on to the breast is rather like helping her tie a necktie. You can do it yourself or let her do it; two of you together make a muddle. You will probably work things out better when you and your partner and the baby can be together in your home surroundings with everything (including any expert help) under your own control and the privacy you need to experiment without feeling a fool.

Sometimes hospitals actually sabotage breast-feeding by giving babies bottles or dummies. Until your baby is established at the breast and dedicated to sucking your nipples for food and comfort, being given latex wannabees for either is liable to confuse him. Furthermore, getting food or water or even just comfort from a bottle or dummy will lessen the urgency of his next request for the breast and the enthusiasm with which he nurses. And it is on his urgency, enthusiasm and capacity that your breasts' milk production (and therefore his food supply) depends.

Unless your baby is pre-term or ill and under special care, he does not need to be nourished by hospital staff. You can do it. You can produce *all* the food and fluid your baby needs now he has been born, just as you did beforehand. Your colostrum is exactly what he needs today. Your milk will be exactly what he needs in a day or two. You can make enough milk and you can deliver it to him. He will like the taste. It will suit his digestion. It will nourish him perfectly.

It will probably be three to five days after the birth before colostrum is replaced by breast milk. Your baby should be put to the breast regularly, both to get that vital colostrum and to practise feeding while your breasts are still soft. Without practice in the whole business of sucking, the newborn will find your larger, harder, milk-filled breasts more difficult to cope with.

When the milk does come in, don't decide that it is no good because it looks bluish and watery compared with thick yellowy colostrum, or the creamy-looking formula given to the baby in the next cot. Breast milk is meant to look like that. It is perfect.

To sit comfortably, find a low chair that supports your spine when your feet are flat on the floor, or wedge firm cushions behind you (right). Don't bend over or lift the baby. Use a pillow to bring her mouth level with the nipple. The football hold (far right) with a pillow under the arm holding the baby, may help with latching on — especially if you find one breast difficult, or after a Caesarean. Don't miss feeding lying down (below). It is often bliss for both if the pillows are right.

Comfort during feeds Comfort and relaxation go together, and being relaxed helps the milk flow so getting comfortable really matters. Different positions may work for you at different times of day and stages in your baby's life, but to stay comfortable all through a feed you will usually need pillows or cushions for support. Your baby's mouth needs to be level with your nipple without you holding him up or bending down.

Possible early problems Along with your milk you may (or may not) acquire various minor, short-lived but uncomfortable – sometimes really painful – problems. Describing them does not mean you have to have them and having them does not mean that there is anything the matter with you or your mothering. The size of your breasts, for example, has no relevance to their ability to produce an abundant supply of milk. Milk is produced in deeply buried glands, not in the surrounding fatty tissue.

Engorgement After the birth and delivery of the placenta, production of the placental hormones, progesterone and oestrogen, is reduced in favour of prolactin, the hormone that controls your production of milk, and oxytocin, the hormone that controls the "let-down" reflex that delivers that milk to your baby. Often the milk "comes in" overnight so that your breasts suddenly become large and tightly swollen both with milk and an increased supply of blood. Sometimes the chemical messages the breasts receive are over-emphatic and they become engorged: rigidly hard, hot and painful, with even the areolae around the nipples distended.

Breasts in this state are always uncomfortable and may be extremely painful. Fortunately the hormonal imbalance will settle down within a day or two. Your breasts will never again be so large, tight or uncomfortable, even when you are producing three times as much milk for a larger and hungrier baby.

If your baby can latch on and nurse, he will relieve you of enough excess milk to reduce the painful tension in your breasts. If the areolae as well as the breasts are swollen and hard, he may not be able to latch on, though, and any efforts he makes will be frustrating for him and painful for you. You will first have to soften the breasts a little, by bathing them repeatedly with warm water, and then very gently expressing some milk by hand (see p.59). Go carefully: swollen tissues are easily bruised. In between feeds, cold compresses applied to your breasts will constrict the blood vessels and help the swelling to subside. A packet of frozen peas makes the easiest usually available compress. If you divide the contents of one packet between two larger plastic bags, so that the peas are loosely packed, you can actually fit them to the shape of your breasts so that the whole surface is covered. If you can neither stand to be without the support of your maternity bra nor fit your pea-compresses inside it, try round cabbage leaves, selected for size and shape, pre-cooled in the fridge and changed as they warm.

The let-down reflex and after-pains Babies are helped to get the milk from their mothers' breasts by the draught or let-down reflex. When the hormone oxytocin is released into the blood, the muscle fibres around the milk glands contract, forcing their milk down into the milk ducts – and sometimes all the

When a leak matters, try gently pushing the nipple in, as if it was a doorbell.

way out. All lactating women have this reflex but some are far more aware of it than others, or find that as time passes it takes less and less to evoke it. The warm buzzing sensations in your breasts – and spreading dampness in your shirt – may only start when you feel your baby sucking or hear him crying; but seeing or thinking about him may be enough, or even seeing or thinking about any baby.

Almost all breast-feeding women need breast pads to absorb drips inside a properly fitting supportive bra. But if you have a pronounced let-down and a copious milk supply you will also need a sense of humour. If your baby demands breakfast while you are cleaning your teeth, your breasts may spray milk all over the mirror.

Once breast-feeding is established you may find that your milk will not let-down if you are tense, anxious or embarrassed. The baby latches on and sucks but gets little or nothing and may come off again, howling indignantly. The milk will not flow comfortably until you can find enough privacy for relaxation.

Oxytocin also makes the muscles of your uterus contract, which is why breast-feeding tends to speed up your womb's return to its pre-pregnancy size. Some women feel those contractions as mild "colicky" pains. A few find them a very uncomfortable part of starting breast-feeding. They tend to be rather worse after later babies than after the first, but they are only noticeable for two or three days.

Sore nipples

Don't play tug of war over your nipple; release the baby's suction instead.

The mistaken idea that nipples got sore from the unaccustomed use of suckling was responsible for a lot of misery both for mothers (who had sore nipples) and babies (whose sucking time was rationed). Indirectly it was also responsible for a lot of breast-feeding "failures" because soreness affected supply and rationing affected demand.

The principal cause of nipple soreness is not unaccustomed sucking but *any*. Nipples are not for sucking on. If they are drawn in and out over the baby's gums and tongue the friction certainly will make them sore and he will not even get much milk. So the principal cause of sore nipples is poor positioning. Your baby must draw the nipple right to the back of his mouth followed by a good mouthful of areola. The two together make a "teat" that is held in place by his suction while his jaws squeeze the margins of the areola and breast tissue, squeezing milk from the milk glands. Never subject your nipple to suction by pulling your baby off it, either. Wait until he pauses for breath before easing him off your breast. Or break the suction by inserting a gentle finger in the corner of his mouth.

If you get a bruised feeling where his gums have worked on the areola, adjust your position at the next feed so that a different part takes the main stress.

Avoid washing nipples with soap in late pregnancy or while breast-feeding. They have built-in lubrication from tiny glands around the areola ("Montgomery's tubercles") which it's a pity to remove as it is more effective than any cream you might use to replace it, and more hygienic, too. Don't massage and scrub nipples to harden them. They are made for the job of breast-feeding so they don't need any special preparation. And you don't want them tough, you want them flexible and elastic.

At the end of a feed, express a drop of hindmilk from the breast your baby has just finished, and use it as a lotion to cover your nipples and areolae. Then let them air-dry if you can. Warm (not hot) air from a hair dryer will speed things up if you are in a rush.

It is important to keep your nipples as dry as you can. Plastic-backed breast pads tend to keep them damp (though they keep your clothes dry), so keep these for special occasions when the state of your clothes matters. Ordinary pads will keep your nipples drier. Dry bras are important, too. Expensive though they are, it's important to have enough maternity bras so that you can not only wash them every day but change them the moment a breast pad lets you down. You may be able to cut down the number of expensive bras you need to buy by wearing sleep bras or crop tops at night.

Warm, sore patches and hot, painful lumps Very occasionally one of the tiny tubes that carry the milk from glands to nipple gets blocked. Milk gathers above the blockage and cannot escape. You will have a red, sore, possibly swollen patch but you have not got mastitis or a breast abscess – yet.

If you can clear the blockage all will be well. Bathe the breast repeatedly with hot water and massage it gently from above the red patch towards the nipple. Then get your obliging baby well latched on and the milk flowing. If the lumpiness and pain subside, feeding the baby has helped the milk duct to clear itself. If they do not, see your doctor the same day.

Mastitis If the milk does not start flowing so that the blockage is cleared, swelling will increase and eventually substances in the milk will burst through the cell walls into the breast's connective tissue and small blood vessels, making a larger and more painful lump. Those substances have no right to be there and your body will react to them with inflammation as it would to any other foreign protein – from a mismatched blood transfusion for instance. You will feel feverish, shivery and ill. Now you *do* have mastitis, but it is not necessarily infective – yet. You need to see your doctor and you need to keep on trying to clear the blockage with your baby's help. If you can, all will still be well, but if you cannot, and especially if you cannot bear to feed the baby from that breast at all but "rest" it, the inflammatory condition is very likely to lead to infection. Then you *will* have infective mastitis and if a pocket of pus should form, you will end up with a breast abscess.

As well as advice about massaging the breast and getting your baby latched on correctly to drain all parts of the breast including the blocked and swollen part, your doctor will probably give you antibiotics. You may feel better so quickly that you find it difficult to believe that there was an infection for those antibiotics to cure. There probably wasn't. The chances are that the antibiotics helped you because they are effective against inflammation as well as against infection and they reduced the swelling and pain so that it was easier for you and your baby to get the milk flowing again.

If you can ensure that all segments of your breasts are regularly drained, you can often avoid further blockages. And if you react fast to the very first signs of a blockage beginning, you will probably never have mastitis again. It is poor feeding technique rather than repeated infection that causes recurrence; improved feeding technique rather than medication that prevents or controls it. So if you develop a *second* warm red patch on one of your breasts do check your baby's positioning, and discuss possible causes with your health visitor or a breast-feeding counsellor.

Do you and your baby find feeding from one breast easier than from the other? If you do it may be to do with your handedness (right-handed women and their babies often prefer left breasts). See if your baby gets a better mouthful of that breast if you use a football hold (see p.68).

Is your milk supply so copious that your baby does not really have to suck but just lies there gulping milk that pours into his mouth? In order to make him work his jaws and tongue so that your ducts are squeezed empty and refilled, make sure you keep him on the first breast until his desultory sucking and only occasional swallowing suggest that it is "empty". He may not even need the second.

Supply and demand How much milk have you got? How often should the baby have it? In breast-feeding these two questions go together because your breasts will make as much milk as your baby sucks from you. The more he takes the more you will make. The more often he takes it, the faster you will make more. This is why a mother can make exactly the right amount of milk for a 2.7kg (6lb) baby or exactly the right amount of milk for twins who weigh 5.9kg (13lb) between them. This is why she can make enough for the baby in his second week of life and also in his twenty-second week.

Almost every mother *can* but not every mother knows it. Breast-feeding is a natural supply and demand system and therefore depends on babies being allowed to behave naturally. The system often fails if they are kept to unnaturally rigid schedules, and sometimes does not work easily because they are interfered with in quite minor ways. It's therefore important to understand how the natural system works.

Once birth has instigated its natural sequel, lactation, the breasts make milk and the baby drinks it. As the breasts are emptied, so they at once start to make more milk. If the baby had his fill at that first feed, he will be satisfied for some time – perhaps for as much as two hours – so the breasts will only make about that same amount of milk again. But if he did not get quite enough at that first feeding, he will be hungry quite soon. He will want to suck again. If he is allowed to, he will empty the breasts yet again and they will be stimulated to make more milk.

The more often he empties the breasts, the more milk they will make. Eventually, perhaps after a day, perhaps after a week, the breasts will be making so much milk that the baby will stop being hungry so often. Instead of nursing every hour or two he will only empty the breasts every two or three hours, so they will slow their production down to that level. That level of production will not be right for the baby for long, of course, because he is growing. A day or a week later he will need more millilitres than he is getting at each feed so, hungry, he will again ask to nurse more often. The extra number of feeds serve the double purpose of keeping the baby satisfied and signalling the breasts to make more milk. When the breasts have responded by increasing the supply, the frequency of the baby's

Colostrum (left) is perfect first food and medicine. After that babies need one breast at a time: all the thirst-quenching foremilk (centre) then all that nourishing hindmilk (right).

demands will decrease again, and so it will go on. It's a simple system and it almost always works, if it's given the chance:

■ Nurse your baby as often as he is hungry. For the first week or so after your milk comes in that will probably be whenever he wakes up and may be as often as every hour, probably with a slightly longer interval once or twice in the 24 hours. Certainly 12 or 15 feeds at this stage is not even unusual, much less undesirable. As long as you get the baby well latched on each time so that your nipples do not get sore, and as long as you can use these almost non-stop feedings as periods of rest, it does not matter how often you suckle him.

■ Nurse your baby for as long as he likes. Traditional advice to limit sucking-time to "two minutes (or five minutes) each side" was bad advice that must have contributed to many "nursing failures". The composition of the milk changes as your baby sucks. Thirst-quenching, low-calorie foremilk comes first, then richer, more concentrated hindmilk. Babies who were only allowed two minutes at each breast were effectively given two helpings of soup but no main course. Feed your baby for as long as he likes at one breast. It's good for the breast to be emptied, diminishing the chances of blocked milk ducts. And emptying it is good for your baby, ensuring that he gets a complete meal including the hindmilk, an opportunity for comfort sucking after that if he wants it and a lesser chance of "colicky" pains later. Offer the second breast after the first is finished, but don't be surprised if he doesn't want any more. Next time he wants to nurse, offer the breast he didn't empty this time.

■ However often your baby nurses, don't offer a bottle instead of a breast you think is empty. Even if he sucked very recently there will always be a little milk available, and letting him take it is the best possible way to speed up the refilling process.

■ However often your baby nurses, don't offer a bottle as well as the breast because you feel he must have more food. Frequent sucking will sustain him while it cues your breasts to make more milk.

■ Unless your baby is ill and you are instructed to do so by his doctor, don't offer extra drinks of water when your baby has ad lib breast milk available, even if the weather is very hot. Breast milk meets the demands of thirst as well as hunger, adjusting its composition to do so if necessary. Your baby does not need anything else and even plain water from a bottle may cut down the time he spends nursing and possibly confuse him into expecting latex teats instead of your nipples.

Worries about your milk supply

Don't hurry to give your baby supplementary bottles. Even if the milk supply is not copious, you and your baby together can build it up provided you have confidence in yourself, you give your baby all the time he wants at the breast, and someone gives you loving care and comfort while you do it.

Consider your reasons for thinking you haven't enough milk. There are only two real signs of milk-scarcity. The first is failure to gain weight. That means that your baby is going on losing from his birthweight although he is more than a week old; or he's not gaining on it after the second week, or he has not gained more than 30 grams or so, if that, in *any* of the next few weeks. Don't expect your breast-fed baby's weight gain to fall into the same pattern as that of your niece who was bottle-fed from birth, or as the weight gain charts (which, in many books, are based on bottle-feeding). Your baby is not failing to gain weight just because he gains 85g (3oz) this week instead of the "recommended" 225g (8oz) or because his gain is widely variable from week to week. The second, and more immediate sign of milk-scarcity pinpoints shortage of fluid rather than shortage of food. New babies commonly urinate so frequently that it's rare to find one in a dry nappy. If yours stays dry for two or three hours, or doesn't thoroughly soak at least six to eight nappies in 24 hours, he probably isn't getting enough (see below).

If you are worried about your milk supply because your baby cries a lot, the reason is more likely to be to do with *how* you are feeding him than *how much*. Ask yourself:

■ Are you letting the baby suck whenever he likes? It doesn't matter to him if he has to suck very often to keep himself satisfied and while he is doing that he is correcting any temporary shortage of milk.

■ Does your worry about your milk date from an increase in your work-and-stress load? A temporary shortage when a mother first comes home from hospital or first starts coping with a household (and perhaps a toddler) is common. But if it lasts more than a day or

---

PARENTS, TAKE NOTE

Dehydration

Getting enough to drink, and retaining fluid long enough for the body to use it, is crucial to everyone's health and wellbeing, but especially to babies'. The younger your baby is, the more easily she may become dehydrated and the more serious it is likely to be if she does. It's mostly because of the risk of dehydration that many conditions are taken more seriously in small babies than in anyone else – even infants just a few months older. Any fever, for example, raises the body's fluid requirements. Any vomiting or diarrhoea deprives the body of fluids. All those three together will not only deplete a young baby's fluid resources terrifyingly fast, but will also suggest that her stomach and intestines are inflamed so that even if she drinks, her body cannot use the liquid. Seek medical advice immediately.

Your baby does not have to be ill to become somewhat dehydrated, though. In the first few months what she drinks is also what she eats. If she is not getting quite enough milk she will gradually become mildly dehydrated as well as hungry and slow to gain weight. And if what she is taking is only marginally adequate, any additional call on her body's fluid resources – such as an extra hot day – may render it inadequate. Babies who are getting and retaining enough fluid wet themselves so frequently that any dry nappy is a rarity and a nappy that stays dry for more than a couple of hours is a warning signal. If you are using high-performance disposables, though, be careful about using wet nappies as a reassurance or dry ones as a warning because it can be difficult to be sure which is which. The ultra-slim kinds are so efficient at wicking wetness away from the baby's skin and holding it in the "gel" in the middle, that the small quantity of urine passed by a newborn is almost undetectable and unless the nappy is soiled, it looks unused. If this type of nappy is your choice, try to get into the habit of weighing in your hand the nappy you have just taken off against the new one you are about to put on. On direct comparison a dry nappy is distinctly lighter than one that's concealing even the smallest amount of wetness.

two, or coincides with your partner going back to work or your mother going home, you need more help and more rest.

■ Are visitors, older children, or even the people who are supposed to be helping you, getting in the way? In the early days of breast-feeding, the let-down reflex can be inhibited by other people so that the baby cannot get the milk that is there for him.

■ Are you uncertain of the quality of your milk? Don't be. Except in exceedingly rare cases of illness or medication for illness, breast milk is always perfect. If your breast-fed baby has spots or digestive discomfort, they would certainly be as bad and would probably be worse if he was bottle-fed.

■ Have you started taking contraceptive pills? You are right to use contraception from the first time you make love after having the baby, because breast-feeding is not an adequate protection against pregnancy even if your periods have not started again. However, the hormones that prevent pregnancy tend also to reduce milk production. If oral contraception is your choice, you need to be prescribed the lowest possible dose. Even then, you may make slightly less milk for the first few days that you take it, though after that your body will adapt.

■ Are you in touch with a breast-feeding counsellor? Your own community midwife, health visitor or doctor may give you excellent advice and support but a trained counsellor is a true specialist, while an experienced breast-feeding mother from a postnatal support group, like the ones run by the National Childbirth Trust or the La Leche League, may be able to give you the kind of one-to-one, ever-available support that makes all the difference.

GETTING STARTED WITH BOTTLE-FEEDING

We have no real alternative to the breast-fed baby's colostrum, so while the bottle-fed baby may start life with one or two drinks of sugared water, formula milk will be offered by the second day. This is much sooner than a breast-fed baby would find milk, so your baby may take very little. The water content is needed much more than the food content, so don't worry.

If your baby does take all the milk offered, she may gain weight from birth instead of after a few days' weight loss. Although early weight loss often worries parents, don't be too enthusiastic about every few grams your baby gains; bottle-fed babies can get too fat.

Choosing a Cow's milk is ideal for calves but it is not the natural food for babies.
babymilk Babies under a year old should not be fed on any kind of unmodified cow's milk - liquid, dried or evaporated, from dairies, supermarkets or health food stores, or on goat's milk either. It is fine to give tastes of milk products, such as yoghurt, from four months if that is when you are starting "solid" foods, but it's better to use babymilk for mixing cereals until at least six months, and to stick with that formula for your baby to drink from a cup as well as from a bottle, until the end of the year.

Modern babymilks are more or less extensively adapted to bring made-up feeds as close as possible to breast milk. In the UK such milks must meet the recommendations of the Department of Health and must constitute complete nourishment for the first months of life, requiring no additions other than boiled water.

Recommended babymilks vary, though, in their convenience as well as their constituents. From time to time there are medical or dietary concerns about particular formulations. Make your choice in consultation with your midwife or health visitor. Don't use milks that are intended for special circumstances (such as soya milks intended for babies who are allergic to cow's milk products) on a whim, or switch from one brand to another because you think your baby is "colicky". And do read the labels on various brands so that you know exactly what you are feeding to your baby:

■ Whey-based milks are the most like breast milk, with similar levels of protein and minerals. Casein-based milks (which are sometimes advertised as suitable for especially hungry babies) may be slightly less easy for a young baby to digest.

■ All babymilks have added vitamins and iron so you should take your health visitor's advice about whether to give your baby the normally recommended multivitamin drops in addition to the particular formula you have chosen.

■ Of the various formulations available, ready-to-mix milks are the cheapest and, among those, the powders cost less than the liquid concentrates. They are more trouble to measure and mix, and require most attention to sterilizing, but they are lighter than the liquids to carry home and they don't need refrigeration after opening.

■ Ready-to-pour liquid formulas need no mixing and are available in various sizes of can and carton, including individual sizes. You pay for their convenience, though, and not only in money. If you are using ready-mixed milk, you are lugging home and finding storage space for water you would otherwise add to concentrated milk.

■ If you are more concerned to maximize convenience than to minimize cost, and neither the weight of your shopping nor storage space is a problem, some babymilks are available in ready-to-use form, sealed into disposable "bottles" that only need the addition of a sterilized teat. As well as being ultimately trouble-free, these are also untouched-by-human-hand-hygienic.

Preparing bottle feeds You cannot safely take a happy-go-lucky approach to preparing bottles, especially while your baby is very young. However relaxed you choose to be about other aspects of home-hygiene, punctilious, perfectionist attention to washing and sterilizing bottles really matters. About 12,000 babies each year are hospitalized for gastro-enteritis in the UK alone.

There are bacteria everywhere. We all carry them on our hands and our clothes. We breathe them, eat them and excrete them. Most of them are harmless. Very few types will make us ill unless we take in such a large number all at one time that our bodies' defences are overwhelmed. But a new baby, especially one who is not breast-fed, does not have strong defences against common germs. It takes time for her to build up immunity to them. In an ordinarily clean home, she will cope with the few germs that she sucks off hands or toys. But when she is feeding it is different. Milk, especially milk which is

Making bottles means taking trouble but giving them is a pleasure.

Bottle-feeding is treated as taboo.

Although statistics say most babies are bottle-fed, every baby but mine seems to be breast-fed. I felt pressured at birth-preparation classes and in hospital, and now I'm beginning to get out and about with my baby I get surprised, even shocked, looks whenever I produce a bottle. I wish people would remember that not everyone wants to breast-feed and not everyone can.

Only a minority of babies are breast-fed for more than a week or so after birth, and only a tiny minority are given nothing at all except breast milk for several months. So it is true that most babies are bottle-fed and if it doesn't seem that way to you, it's probably because breast-feeding is commonest in the very first weeks after birth. It may also be especially popular in your particular geographical area and social group.

Of course it's just as wrong that you should be made to feel uncomfortable about bottle-feeding as that another woman should be made to feel uncomfortable about breast-feeding. Once the decision is made, your comfort and the baby's is all that matters. I'm not surprised you felt some pressure before birth, though. Midwives, health visitors, doctors and birth educators do all tend to push prospective parents to think especially carefully about nursing because they know that if they take an entirely even-handed approach to both methods, breast-feeding will not actually get a fair chance.

Breast-feeding does not get nearly as much exposure as bottle-feeding. In today's small families, many young people scarcely see a nursing baby before they have their own first child so breast-feeding isn't taken for granted. On the other hand, manufacturers spend millions of pounds a year advertising baby milks and bottle-feeding equipment, and sponsoring paediatric and child care events, so young people all grow up with those names and images as a taken-for-granted part of having a baby.

If a woman is going to breast-feed, the decision needs to be made before birth, so that the baby can be put to the breast immediately. The later an attempt to nurse is left, the less likely it is to succeed. The decision to bottle-feed can be taken at any time and implemented immediately.

A woman has nothing to lose by deciding to nurse – and her baby certainly gains. If the decision proves wrong, or her mind or circumstances change, she can always switch to a bottle. But a woman who decides to bottle-feed loses out on options as surely as her baby loses out on colostrum. Once she has missed her chance of establishing lactation, she cannot switch to the breast.

The more successfully breast-feeding has been "talked up" during pregnancy, the sadder it is for women who had every intention of nursing their babies but find they cannot. Yes, of course it's true that not every woman can breast-feed. A few are too ill to get lactation going, for example. A few find themselves on medication that would do their babies no good at all. Some cannot establish and keep up their supply while their pre-term or ill babies are in special care.

But it certainly wouldn't help the situation to warn pregnant parents of these possibilities because in breast-feeding fear of failure is the very thing most likely to provoke failure. Almost all women, including many who try to nurse but succumb to painful breast problems or the tyranny of the baby scales, would have been able to breast-feed if they had had enough self-confidence, support from partners and others (especially mothers) and skilled, sensitive professional help on demand.

around room temperature, is an ideal breeding ground for germs. So while your baby might pick up a few off her own fingers and deal with them perfectly well, she will pick up an enormous, and possibly overwhelming number from a bottle which has been left standing around in a warm room. To keep your baby's milk as free from bacteria as possible:

■ Check the expiry date on babymilk containers before you buy, and again before you open one you've been storing.

■ Avoid dented or damaged cans.

■ Keep packets of powder closed, opened cans or cartons of liquid closely covered and refrigerated.

■ Wash your hands before handling the milk or equipment, especially after using the toilet or handling pets or their food. If you use liquid babymilk, keep a special can-opener for those cans and sterilize the top with boiling water before you puncture it.

■ Wash in hot water and detergent (or in a dishwasher) and then sterilize everything you use in measuring, mixing or storing babymilk. That means measuring spoons and mixing jugs as well as bottles, teats and teat covers. Provided that you put a sterile teat cover over the sterilized teat on your ready-filled bottle, that teat will still be sterile and safe when you take the cover off to feed the baby.

Bacteria which escape your precautions (by landing on the sterile teat as you put it on the bottle, for example) cannot multiply dangerously while milk is boiling hot or while it is icy cold. It is the in-between temperatures that help them to flourish. To minimize the chances of bacteria breeding:

■ Cool made-up milk quickly, preferably by putting it in the body of the refrigerator (not the door) while it is still hot.

■ Keep a made-up bottle, or opened container of ready-to-pour milk, cold until the baby wants it. Don't put a bottle to warm in advance of her waking up, or keep it warm if she drops off to sleep for more than a few minutes in mid-feed. Never put warm milk in a vacuum flask or electric bottle warmer: keep *water* hot and stand *cold* milk in it to warm.

■ Throw away any milk the baby leaves. Don't try to save that half-bottle for next time and don't pour the now unsterile remains of one feed back into your jug of sterilized babymilk in the refrigerator.

Measuring and mixing babymilk
When you combine milk powder or liquid concentrate with boiled water, you are constructing both your baby's food and her drink. If you do it in exactly the proportions the manufacturer suggests in the mixing instructions, you will end up with a feed that is as close to the composition of breast milk as it is possible to get with that particular milk formula. The baby will get the right amount of nourishment and the right amount of water.

Research workers have found that feeds made out of powdered babymilks are often measured inaccurately. In parts of the world where babymilks are beyond the means of many people who use them, the powder is often made to last longer by being mixed into double quantities of water, making big feeds of starvation food value. In the West, parents sometimes seem to treat making up their baby's milk formula as if it were creative cookery. Making a baby's bottle is not like making instant coffee or custard. You cannot make it "better" with extra powder, or less fattening (but no less nutritious) by adding extra water. If you add extra powder, the milk will be too strong. The baby will get too much protein, too much fat and too many minerals in proportion to water. She may get fat because you are giving her too many calories, and thirsty because you are giving her too much salt. If she is thirsty, she will cry, and you will give her another bottle. If that bottle is also too strong she will be even more thirsty. The end result can be a baby who cries a lot, does not seem terribly well or happy, puts on a lot of weight, and seems to need a lot of feeding. Follow the manufacturer's instructions exactly, and especially:

■ Never guess at quantities. Measure water accurately by boiling it (to sterilize it) first, and measuring it when it has cooled. If you measure the water first and then boil it, some will be lost in evaporation.

■ Measure milk powder accurately by over-filling the scoop provided and slicing off the surplus at scoop level with a knife. If you wipe the surplus off on the edge of the tin or smooth it off with a spoon, you will almost certainly end up with a somewhat packed or heaped scoop, containing more powder than it should. Shaking off the surplus may leave you with either too much or too little.

■ Measure liquid concentrate accurately by pouring it either directly into the bottle or into a marked-off measuring jug and then holding it up (or getting down) so that it is at eye level as you read off the marked millilitres. If you check the level with your eye above it, you will think there is less milk than there really is.

If you really do make up your baby's bottles exactly as the manufacturer recommends, and as long as you resist the temptation to add a spoonful of cereal in the vain hope of a better night, or a spoonful of sugar to make it "nicer" and persuade your baby to drink more than her appetite says she should, you can treat the resulting milk as if it was breast milk. The baby can have as much as she eagerly drinks (and no more), as often as she is hungry. You don't need to carry your scientific accuracy in making the milk on into feeding it.

But formula milk is *not* breast milk, of course, so it will not adjust itself to your baby's changing needs. In very hot weather, or when she is feverish, your bottle-fed baby may get caught between the rock of lost appetite and the hard place of thirst. She may need extra plain, cooled boiled water so that she can drink without eating. You certainly have nothing to lose by offering water regularly.

A bottle is not a breast, either; a baby who tries to go on sucking for comfort when she has finished feeding will get extra food that she does not want if the bottle is not empty, and mouthfuls of air and then a vacuum and flat teat if it is. If your baby would like to go on sucking, try offering a (clean, short-nailed) finger.

Supply and demand How much and how often should bottle-fed babies be fed? Bottle-fed babies do best if they are treated as much like breast-fed babies as possible, so of course milk should be offered whenever the baby seems to be hungry and removed only when eager sucking ceases. The fact that she is being bottle-fed and you can therefore see exactly how much she is taking does make a difference though. If what she wants is only half what you expected you may be tempted to push her to take more. Try not to. After all, if the bottle were a breast you would not be able to see how much she'd left. If she cries only an hour after drinking 85 ml (3 oz) of formula, you may find yourself declaring that she cannot possibly be hungry again already. Try to accept that although her stomach cannot yet be empty, she feels a need to have her food topped up. After all, if that previous feed had been breast milk, you would just assume she hadn't had very much.

A brand new baby is used to having her food supply continually replenished by transfusion feeding in the womb. Now her needs must be met by digestion of food from a stomach that starts full and gradually empties. While she gets used to this dramatic change and all the new sensations that come with it, your baby may demand food at intervals that are just as irregular and almost as frequent as they would have been if she had been breast-fed.

If you offer her a bottle whenever she seems hungry and take it away the moment she loses interest, she will only take the amount she needs. If she drinks it all, you can assume she needed it. If she takes a little, the comfort of sucking and of your care will make her feel better. If she drinks none you have gained important information: this time it is not food she wants. And what have you lost? One bottle of formula.

If you stick to these principles in your baby's first weeks, you will never have to worry about whether you ought to feed "on schedule" because the baby's own schedule will gradually evolve out of her digestive pattern. Met willingly, these irregular demands will probably level off by themselves in a few weeks. It takes rather longer for a baby to digest formula than breast milk – eventually around three hours. True hunger signals are tied into the near-completion of the digestive process. Once her digestion is working more maturely and she has got used to this new kind of hunger, she will neither feel nor express distress until she has digested the last meal so her requests for food will fall into a pattern similar to a conventional schedule.

Exactly the same process of maturing and settling into a feeding pattern will take place if you keep your baby to a strict four-hourly schedule from the beginning. Offered feeds only at 2 am, 6 am, 10 am, 2 pm, 6 pm and 10 pm, she will eventually expect, and be hungry for, food at those intervals. The difference is that these early weeks will be miserable for you all. The baby will wake and cry. If you are determined not to feed her because it "isn't time" you will probably try every other method of comforting her, which will be hard work. But because what she really wants is food, and she is getting hungrier and hungrier while you are working away at other methods of comfort, nothing you do will really soothe her. By the end of the session you'll be lucky if you can feel anything but an unhappy mixture of guilt and anger and helpless despair. To crown it all, when the clock does at last say the "right time" and you give her a feed, she will probably not suck well or take enough milk to keep her happy until the next scheduled meal. All that crying will have tired her and filled her stomach with air. She will probably fall into exhausted sleep after a few millilitres and wake up again an hour later to repeat the whole miserable performance.

So don't fall into the trap of thinking that feeding your baby whenever she seems hungry will get her into the habit of demanding food frequently. She does not wake from habit, she wakes from hunger. When she is mature enough not to feel hungry so often she will not wake up and cry.

BURPING

There is always air in your baby's stomach. He swallows some while crying or just breathing as well as when he feeds. If you feed your baby in a fairly upright position, the heavier milk will find its way to the bottom of the stomach and the lighter air will gather at the top. When the stomach is uncomfortably distended with milk and air the baby will be able to burp some of the air out without taking (much) milk with it.

Burping midway through feeds Some babies swallow so much air that their stomachs get uncomfortably distended before they have had enough milk. They need a half-time burp to make room for the rest of the feed. A baby who needs to burp will stop sucking and may drop the teat or nipple and fuss. If you hold him upright for a minute or two, he will burp and then return to his feed. If your baby is sucking happily, though, there is no need to remove the teat or nipple just in case he has too much air in his stomach. If he is still sucking, he is not uncomfortably full and should be left to feed in peace.

Burping after feeds Burps are basic to life with most babies but much more of a bane to some than others. Every baby ends feeds with his minute stomach distended with milk, but while that distension makes one baby writhe and squawk with discomfort, it leaves another blissfully asleep. Most babies relieve the pressure a little by burping, but where one only needs the opportunity of being held upright for a minute or two, another needs long minutes of parental ploys and patience. And while one baby can be counted on to burp (in the end) and be done with it, another sometimes needs several repeat performances.

If a fully fed baby is comfortably asleep, he certainly doesn't have to burp right now but he may need to later. If you put him against your shoulder and rub or pat his back gently, you can combine taking precautions with having a cuddle. But don't feel that you must not put him down until he has burped. He may not have taken in much air this time. If he hasn't burped in three minutes, he probably isn't going to. If he needs to burp later, he will, with or without your help.

If your baby is one of the few who really seems uncomfortable until he has burped, but not one of the many who do it easily, you'll probably try many different methods and positions. Do take care not to let creative experiment and the stress of the moment combine to blind you to anatomy. For instance a sitting-up position is often recommended for burping, but a small baby held sitting may easily have his stomach folded so that it is difficult for the air to escape. Lying flat in any position – even face down across an adult's lap, a position some babies find very soothing – encourages milk and air to mix so that one cannot come up without the other. It is upright positions that encourage air to rise above the milk in the stomach, and escape without bringing milk with it.

The best position for burping – and patting and walking, dancing and rocking; and seeing the world from a hug.

Bringing up milk Almost all babies sometimes bring up some milk along with the air especially when adults try to force burps from babies by energetic jouncing or over-enthusiastic patting. Usually the quantity of milk brought up is very small, although it may look a lot because it is mixed with saliva and spread all over your shoulder. If you are getting worried about the amount of food your baby is losing, try spilling five millilitres of milk on purpose to give you a standard of comparison. "Sicky" babies bring back milk at every feed and sometimes more than once. They may reduce your clothes to ruins and you to despair without doing themselves any harm at all. Check with your health visitor or doctor if you are worried, but unless the baby is failing to soak his nappy (without being given extra drinks of water) or to gain weight, you can be sure he is not losing more from his feeds than he can spare.

If there really is a lot of milk coming up, there are several possible reasons for it:

■ The baby may have sucked more than he could comfortably hold. He is sensibly bringing back the surplus.

■ Feeding while lying flat meant that the air couldn't rise above the milk. Try holding him more upright.

■ Being bounced about mixed air and milk together so they could only escape together. Handle him gently immediately after feeds.

■ Crying while waiting to be fed, or in mid-feed when he was thought to need a burp but wanted to suck, put a lot of extra air into his stomach, followed by the rest of his milk.

■ The bottle was held too flat, so that the entrance to the teat was not always covered with milk. The baby had sucks of nothing but air between sucks of milk and it all got mixed up together in his stomach. Keep the bottle tilted.

■ Too small a hole in the teat meant that the baby had to suck very hard and therefore swallowed air with each mouthful of milk. Check that milk drips out of the teat at several drops per second with the bottle upside down. (Don't check with water; because it is thinner it comes out faster than milk.)

Vomiting If a baby brings up milk some time after feeding, it will be curdled because digestive juices will already have been working on it. If an hour or more has passed since the feed, it may smell nasty. The baby may only have had some air trapped inside the stomach which has now come up bringing the partly digested milk with it, but there may be a digestive disturbance or the beginning of an illness. If the baby seems unwell, especially if he is feverish or has any sign of diarrhoea, consult your doctor or clinic. If the baby seems perfectly well let hunger guide feeds as usual and just keep an eye open for any symptoms.

Projectile vomiting This is quite different from hiccuping milk up with some air or from ordinary vomiting. The baby spurts milk out towards the end of a feed with such force that it may hit the floor or a wall as much as a metre away. A baby who does this regularly does lose more nourishment than he can spare so consult your health visitor or doctor without delay. She will probably arrange a time when she can sit with you during a feed and observe the vomiting for herself.

If the baby's vomiting is "projectile", the most likely explanation is a condition called pyloric stenosis. This is a fault in the muscles of the outlet between stomach and bowel; milk comes up because it cannot go on down. More usual in boys than in girls, it is easily and permanently corrected by a small operation.

FOOD AND GROWTH

New babies need as much breast milk or properly made formula as they willingly drink. Only under exceptional circumstances do they need anything else whatsoever before they are four months old.

Unlike most breast-fed babies, those who get formula from the beginning may lose none of their birthweight, or lose a little but regain it within a few days of birth. Once they have regained their birthweight most babies gain weight at something close to 28g (1oz) per day, whatever kind of milk they get. Day-to-day variations are the rule rather than the exception, of course, but the average weekly gain for a full-term healthy baby is around 170g–225g (6oz–8oz).

Many new parents find it difficult to leave it up to babies to decide how much milk to take. They want to know exactly how much they "ought" to have so as to be sure to provide it. But there is no general "ought" for all babies, or even for bottle-fed babies. Feeding a baby is not an exact science because babies vary just as much as older people in their food needs. A baby with a slow, efficient metabolism will grow well and have plenty of energy on fewer calories than a baby who burns her food up faster and less completely.

Most adults are bad at adjusting their food intake to suit their individual metabolisms; what we eat is not dictated only by hunger but also by habit, social customs and pure greed. But a small baby's adjustment is almost always perfect, at least until we confuse it for her by introducing sweet juices and weaning foods. As long as your baby is having nothing but milk, trust her appetite. Whatever quantities the baby takes, they are right for her provided she is offered as much as she wants whenever she wants it; she is contented most of the time and becoming more contented as she gets older and more settled; she is active whenever she is awake and becoming more so with age, and she is growing.

Expected weight gain
There is no specific quantity of food babies are expected to take, but there is a rate of growth that all healthy, full-term individuals are expected to match. Your baby's birthweight is her personal starting point for growth, but once growth has started (at around 10 days, say, after any postnatal loss and regain) she will grow roughly the same amount and at approximately the same rate as all other babies, whatever that birthweight was. Of course, we can narrow down that "approximately" by refining the ways we group babies. As we've already seen, there are perceptible differences between the growth patterns of breast-fed and formula-fed babies, but they are not usually treated as separate groups because there is so much overlap between them. On the other hand boys tend to be a little heavier than girls so the genders are separately grouped, and twins (even those born at full-term) are almost always smaller than singletons. Parents may also find it useful to bear in mind the likelihood of differences between babies of different ethnic groups. In the UK, for example, babies of Asian origin tend to be smaller than average, while babies of Afro-Caribbean origin tend to be larger.

A baby's overall growth follows a predetermined pattern rather like a rocket which, once launched, follows a pre-set trajectory. You fuel your child's growth with proper food and tender, loving care and as long as you do so, the upward growth curve will be steady over time. Unlike that rocket, though, your baby's day-to-day and week-to-week weight-trajectory will certainly not be perfectly steady and may wobble about all over the place. If you find yourself worrying because your baby gains 225g (8oz) one week but only 60g (2oz) the next, try to get into the habit of looking at her current weight on her *chart* (see p.88), rather than thinking about it in the abstract.

Centile charts Centile charts for recording babies' growth are invaluable. Although the statistics on which they are based, and the way they are presented vary from place to place, they all allow parents to check that the shape of the curve made by the joined-up dots of their own baby's successive weights is similar to the curves on the chart, and her weekly or monthly growth keeps her in a more or less consistent position relative to its centile lines (see p.89). If that is what you see when you study your baby's weight chart, she is gaining weight as she is expected to do however little she may have gained this week. If on the contrary, her weight gain does not just wobble about or dip so that a week's measurement falls the other side of a centile line, but falls and stays down so that the next recorded measurements start a new curve at a lower level, then expected growth is being interfered with by too little food, illness, or some other stress. She will need an extra boost of food-energy to put her back on course. Likewise, if her weight gain should rise so fast that it peaks upwards to start a higher curve, some external factor such as cereals concealed in bottles, or many sweetened drinks, may be interfering. She needs her food-and-drink formula unpadded with extra calories so that she can go on satisfying her hunger and her thirst while getting back on course.

Height (or length) matters too Weight gain alone is not an adequate measure of a baby's growth because children are not meant to get fatter and fatter but to get heavier because they grow bigger overall. Getting taller (or longer) matters too. Length changes much more slowly than weight and is far more difficult to measure accurately, but whatever your baby's length at birth, she will gain around two centimetres each month or just over five centimetres in three months. Just as there is an expected weight for a baby of any age, related to birthweight, so there is an expected length at any age, related to birth-length. A complete record of your baby's growth means charting both measures together and if the measurements are being carried out by a health professional you will probably find that the gradually increasing circumference of your baby's head is also recorded.

Changes and exceptions to normal growth Having said all this, children do not continue to grow at the same rate as each other forever. If they did there would be no point in growth charts, only birth measurements. We interfere with the regularity of growth by overfeeding or underfeeding, or introducing solid foods early or late. Life interferes too, making one child subject to many infections and another resistant to them; one physically very active and another much less so. Eventually children's own hormones interfere: the pre-puberty growth spurt takes place at different times and rates in different people. For most babies, the growth rates shown by the curves on the charts overleaf will be the norm for at least the first year. But there are many exceptions:

■ Pre-term babies: some of these will be twins or triplets. Their birthweights are not their biologically ideal starting points and since they may be very slow to get started with feeding and therefore with growing, they may do no more than hold their low position, relative to average babies, for a long time.

■ Small-for-dates babies: these also have artificially low starting points but may make startling growth during their early weeks, especially if they were partly starved in the womb. With excellent care such babies may change position from the very bottom of the lowest section of the chart to somewhere near the top of that "small baby" section.

■ Babies who are ill in their first weeks: these babies (and those who have problems that directly affect their feeding, such as cleft palate) may be slow to start gaining weight or may actually go on losing it. Again excellent care, perhaps including surgical repair, may lead to a spurt of "catch-up growth" so that the baby's personal growth curve shifts upwards and then settles down on a new, higher trajectory.

■ Babies who are bottle-fed from birth: these babies may lose no weight in the first days. They may even gain very fast from the beginning, especially if the formula is made too strong or they are encouraged to take a set amount. An even greater rise in such a baby's weight curve may be seen if solid foods are added early to the full quota of over-concentrated milk. Recording length as well as weight gives warning of that unfortunate combination of circumstances. A baby who is gaining weight faster than nature intended will not gain length to match it. The disparity is evidence that your child is getting obese rather than simply growing large.

Average is easier Society is geared to people of average size, and that includes babies. If your baby was not of average birthweight you need to be aware of it and allow for the difference. Baby clothes are usually sized by age and weight (or sometimes, less usefully, by length) but it is still easy to find yourself misled. A stretchsuit for "birth to three months" seems certain to be large enough for a newborn. But that age-range means 3.2kg–5.5kg (7lb–12lb) and length to match. It will not last your four-and-a-half-kilo baby for long. Toiletries and medicines that can be bought over the counter still sometimes carry advice according to age rather than weight, and that can be highly misleading. It's not only that a small baby needs less of any medicine than a larger one but also that the bath product recommended "from three months" might not suit her until she is several weeks older. When it comes to safety limits on equipment such as car seats, specification by age *and* weight may still leave you floundering if your baby doesn't fit the manufacturer's expectations. If she is bigger and heavier than average, for example, it may not be clear whether she should be moved from one seat or position in the car to another at a given weight, or wait until she reaches the suggested age; whether the issue is the strength of the seat or the maturity of the occupant's spine.

The further your baby is from that average size, the more you have to think – and ask. Above all, ignore the various rubrics about weight gain that you may still hear quoted as if they were gospel truth. They certainly will not be true of your baby. This one for instance: "a baby should double her birthweight in six months and treble it in a year". Which baby? If you look at the chart overleaf you will see that the saying is about right for a baby girl on the 50th percentile curve, but a very small baby on the 2nd percentile is likely to double her birthweight in three months (she'd be half-starved if it took her six) while a large baby on the 98th percentile will take longer than a year to treble hers – and would be grossly obese if she didn't.

Growth charts

The chart reproduced opposite is an example from a real chart recording the growth of a real baby. It shows centile curves that are similar shapes for all populations, and explains their universal derivation. These figures however, are based on British growth statistics for girls. Comparable figures for other populations are somewhat different.

The red line in the middle is the "50th centile" which is always the average for the statistical population being charted. That line is drawn in such a way that out of any randomly selected group of 100 of that population (in this case white British girls), 50 (50%) will weigh or measure more and 50 will weigh or measure less.

The two blue lines are the "98th centile" at the top and the "2nd centile" at the bottom. Those lines mark off the normal limits of very large and very small. Almost all babies' lengths and weights will fall between those lines, in fact out of that randomly selected group of 100 British baby girls, only two (2%) will be heavier and longer than the 98th centile, and two (2%) lighter and shorter than the 2nd centile. So, into each of the areas between the red line and one of the blue lines there will fall 48 (48%) of the group of 100 babies.

Although they are all within normal limits, there's a very big difference between babies' weights and lengths around the average line and babies' weights and lengths around the lines that chart the very large or small. That big space can be divided up by centile sub-divisions to show not just average, very large and very small, but as many in–between categories as anyone requires. It is useful to mark in at least two more pairs: the 91st and the 9th (9% of babies are bigger or smaller) and the 75th and the 25th (25% – a quarter – of babies are bigger or smaller).

The usefulness of centile charts like this one is illustrated by the successive (but not very frequent) measurements it shows of an exclusively breast-fed baby girl.

Her birthweight put her squarely on the 75th percentile (only 25% of newborn girls are heavier; 75% lighter) and her length was a little higher still. Nevertheless, for the first eight weeks of her life she gained weight rapidly (as many breast-fed babies do) so that she reached the 91st percentile.

Over the next two months, although she kept on gaining weight she did so much more slowly so that her measurements gradually returned to the 75th percentile where she began.

Thereafter, her weight gains were variable but never out of step with the established pattern. Looking at the chart it was always clear that overall, her weight was holding a position near to the 75th percentile; never below it and usually somewhat above. Meanwhile her length increased more steadily and relatively more rapidly. Having been born the length that would be expected for her weight, by the time she reached the age of nine months she was longer than all but two in every 100 babies.

Her parents – first-timers – were emphatic that without this method of recording and observing their little daughter's progress, there were many individual measurements that would have worried them. The mother, in particular, felt that the slowing up of weight gain around the third month would have led her to question her milk supply, even perhaps to consider supplementary bottles or the early addition of solid foods, if she had not been able to see from the chart that the lower gains were taking the baby back to her original weight curve rather than below it.

Centile charts make it easy to see whether a baby's length increases (above right) match her weight gains (below right) and if her overall growth is at the expected rate despite temporary peaks and troughs.

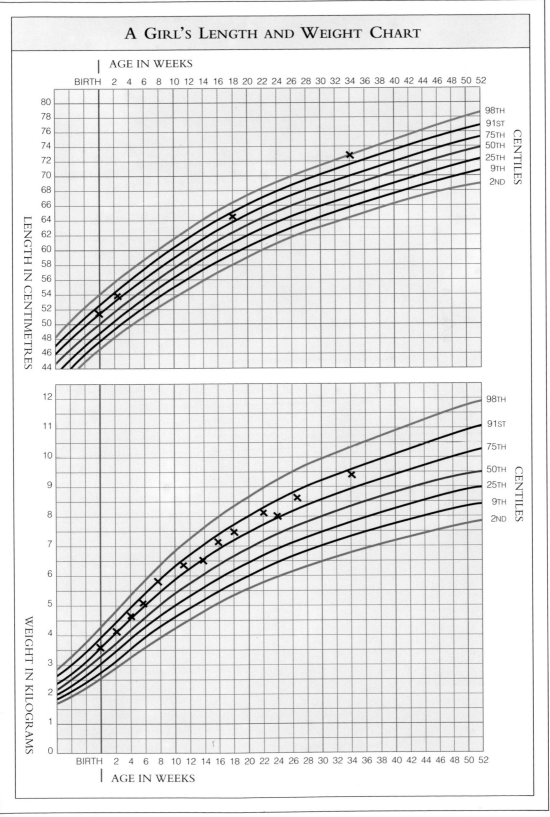

A Girl's Length and Weight Chart

Looking after your baby's body is no more difficult than looking after your own, but until you've got the knack of supporting his head, and the confidence not to drop him if he yells indignantly, it can seem daunting – and non-stop. These notes will seem simplistic in a couple of weeks – or to any experienced parent – but they are designed to give a start to each and every adult who wants to be fully involved in the baby's care. If one person – mother, nanny – becomes the acknowledged expert in the first few days, it may be difficult for father or anyone else to catch up.

LIFTING AND CARRYING YOUR BABY

New babies have an instinctive fear of being dropped which shows whenever their heavy heads are allowed to flop or their uncontrolled limbs dangle in space. They can neither support their own heads nor control their own muscles and they are only relaxed and happy when somebody does it for them. When a baby is in a cot or pram the mattress provides support; when he is in someone's arms the adult body supports his. But being picked up or put down introduces a potentially alarming moment when one kind of support is removed before the other is established.

The answer is to give new babies a moment with *both* kinds of support before either is removed. If you are picking your baby up, arrange your hands and arms under and around him while the mattress is still supporting his weight. Don't even begin to lift until the baby has felt the new security your hands are providing. When you put him down, reverse the process: keep your supporting hands in place as you put the baby down so that he has time to register the security of the mattress before you remove them.

Arranging your hands and arms takes practice before it becomes an unthinking skill. But you will not go far wrong if you think of your new baby as a badly wrapped parcel. If you pick him up around the middle, both ends will flop. If you concentrate on supporting his head, his legs will dangle. You have to gather him together so that you can move him in a compact bundle, and then move slowly, keeping to a minimum the distances he must travel through empty space. If, for example, you are picking your baby up from a carrycot on the floor, kneel down to take him in your arms. Don't stand up until he is nestled against you.

While your baby is so small it only takes one arm to hold her safely. Swing your left elbow across to brace her against you and you can have your right hand back.

Your baby isn't really a parcel, though, he's a person and deserves to be treated with respect. An important part of that is making sure that he is aware of what you are going to do before you do it – or at least is aware that you are going to do *something* before you do *anything*. Never pick him up without first alerting him to your presence by talking to him and touching him, and as you move him, always give his muscles time to adjust to each stage on the way to the new position. Babies who are plucked from their cots and deep slumber without so much as a by-your-leave must feel as though they are being swooped through the air by invisible giants.

If you are right-handed, put your left hand under her neck, your right hand under her bottom. Lean down so your left forearm follows her spine and spread the fingers to support her head.

Now lift slowly and steadily. Your arms and hands support her in the same position as the mattress and they are ideally placed to put her directly against your shoulder.

Most babies seem to like this position best of all, for being held, carried, cuddled, comforted — or burped. Most parents like it too because the baby is safely part of you and although you can't see her face, she can hear your heart.

DRESSING YOUR BABY

Some babies really hate the whole dressing and nappy-changing business and since you have to do it several times in every day, that's hateful for you. Sources of distress include:

■ Lying on a hard or cold surface, so use a changing mat or equivalent, covered with a muslin nappy or towel.

■ Having bare skin exposed to the air, especially from the waist up. It helps to have the room warm but it helps most to lay a textured fabric (another towel) over her tummy as you remove her clothes.

■ Being turned over, jolted around and having clothes put over her head. Choose front-opening garments, preferably made from stretchy material. Look for envelope necks you can open really widely, and raglan sleeves so you can put your hand up the sleeve in reverse, find your baby's hand and then pull the sleeve instead of the arm.

■ Having her legs held in the air for the length of time it can take you to clean up a copious motion with tiny wipes or cotton wool balls. Get the worst off with the tail of the nappy and then use *water*.

  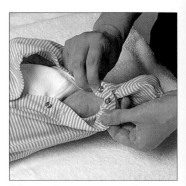

She hates being bare; hates her nose scraped. You need to be quick and neat. Stretching the neck between your thumbs leaves both palms to put it over her head.

You don't have to push and pull soft little fists. Put your hand up a sleeve in reverse; grasp hers and pull the sleeve over her arm rather than her arm through the sleeve.

More crying means more chance of getting the poppers wrong. Start the legs from the ankle, doing right and left in turn. When you reach the crutch there's no room for error.

Making sure your baby is neither too hot nor too cold

Warmth is important to new babies because while healthy full-term infants can *produce* heat efficiently from the moment of birth, they are not very good at *conserving* it. If their environment gets cool, they have to divert energy into heat-production and away from the central activities of living and growing. They tend to be fretful and restless too, and if they are allowed to get actually *cold,* there is a possibility of dangerous chilling. So keeping new babies' environments reasonably warm saves them from having to use any energy in warming themselves, and also contributes to relaxation and contentment.

Babies can get too hot though, and this will also make them restless and cross. By about four weeks after birth, getting too hot is at least as likely to be a problem for full-term babies as getting too cold because by that time they are rather better at conserving warmth than shedding it. If heavy clothes, close wrappings, highly insulating covers, warm headgear, the rainproof covers on a pram, or any combination of those, prevent air from reaching sweat-damped skin to cool by evaporation, there is a real risk of dangerous overheating.

Staying warm but not too warm

Experiments have shown that a *naked* newborn baby stops using energy to make warmth when the temperature immediately around her body reaches about 29°C (85°F). While this would be far too hot for an ordinary family room, or for a room in which your *clothed* baby was going to spend time, it is a reasonable temperature to aim at in a room where you are going to bath her while she is brand new. The rest of the time you can ensure that the air around her body stays around this ideal temperature simply by dressing her. Three light layers of clothing (such as a vest and nappy, a stretchsuit and one shawl or blanket) will keep the air inside the bundle warm enough with room temperatures around 18°C–20°C (65°F–68°F).

A baby's ability to conserve her own warmth improves with age and weight and so does her ability to spare some energy for heat-production. A baby who was pre-term and still weighs less than 2.7kg (6lb) should definitely be kept indoors when the weather is cold and should only be undressed in really warm places. On the other hand, a three-month-old baby weighing around 5.5kg (12lb) will be getting quite good at staying warm as well as being able to afford to use some energy warming herself up. Between those extremes, commonsense precautions will keep your baby warm enough but ensure that she doesn't get too warm:

■ Dress your baby according to the temperature and adjust her clothes as the temperature changes. It is just as important to take her outdoor clothes off when you come home or go into a warm shop, as to put them on when you go out. Likewise it is important to adjust her night-time coverings to the *current* temperature of her bedroom. If she needs two blankets when the central heating switches itself off late at night, she certainly cannot need more than one when she first settles to sleep during the evening. Lightweight, layered clothing and bedding make adjustments easy both by day and night. Highly insulating garments and covers – such as quilted "duvet" pram-suits and continental quilts – are dangerously hot for indoor use.

■ Your baby's head is so large in relation to her body, and probably so little protected by hair, that she can lose a lot of heat from her head unless she wears a hat. If you're concerned about her getting cold, cover her head; if she might be too warm, take her hat off or replace it with a sun hat.

Covering that big head with a hat can help your baby stay warm when it's cool and safe when it's sunny, but when he's inside and hot, leave his head bare.

■ Deep sleep renders new babies more vulnerable both to cold and to heat, so when your baby drops off, be ready to add a blanket before she has time to get cold or take one off before she begins to overheat.

■ Your baby is more likely to become chilled or overheated outdoors than indoors, because outdoor cold often comes with a cool breeze and outdoor heat often means warm sunshine. In her first few weeks, don't expose your baby more than fleetingly to either.

Signs of chilling

A baby who is managing to keep herself warm but would be happier if outside conditions relieved her of the task will be restless. Her breathing will be faster than usual and she may cry. While her hands and feet may feel cool, her chest and stomach, under her clothes, will still feel normally warm. As soon as you take her to a warmer place (especially out of a cool breeze), she will probably become calmer and more relaxed.

A baby who is losing the battle to stay warm and is in danger of becoming chilled, behaves quite differently. She is very quiet and still. She will not cry until she is beginning to get warm and can therefore spare the energy which crying takes. Her hands and feet will feel cold and even the skin of her chest under her clothes will feel cool to your hand. Do not simply add more wrappings. She is already cold and cannot make more heat for herself at the moment. Extra wrappings will insulate the coldness in. She needs to get warmer first – perhaps by being taken into a warm room and given a warm feed or by being cuddled close to adult body warmth under your coat or a blanket. After that, extra wrappings will insulate in the warmth that she needs.

If such a baby were given no help in getting warm, she could slip into the next stage of chilling which is called the "neonatal cold syndrome". This is very rare but it is dangerous. Vital bodily functions run so slowly that the baby is lethargic, floppy, difficult to awaken and unable to suck. Her hands and feet look swollen and bright pink. Her skin is very cold to touch. A baby in this condition needs urgent medical attention as she will have to be rewarmed slowly and with great care.

Beware of overheating Hot weather seldom bothers babies as long as they have plenty to drink so that they sweat freely, and loose, light clothes so that the sweat can evaporate and cool them. If your baby is born into a heatwave or your air conditioning breaks down, don't assume that she'll be less contented as a result. When it is really hot, banish clothing made of synthetics (which can prevent evaporation) in favour of cotton. If your baby is happy in no clothes at all, she could lie naked on a nappy, but most newborns seem to feel safer in at least a vest. If you take her out in her pram, use a sun-canopy instead of the pram hood, which will trap warm air around her or, better still, keep her in the cooler-feeling shade of trees.

In the car, be careful of the extra heat made by sunshine beating on the windows and also of the wide temperature differences there may be between a warm outside world and an air-conditioned car, and between an overheated static car and a moving one. You may need to keep adjusting your baby's clothing and coverings. Sun blinds on the windows will also be useful. They prevent your baby's eyes from being dazzled by sun as well as helping to reduce the solar heat gain in the car.

If the baby is irritable and her skin is damp, fan her gently to cool her by evaporation. If her skin is dry, sponge her with warm water first, and then fan her. If the room (or car or train compartment...) is unpleasantly hot and muggy, a wet towel hung across the window will produce a surprisingly speedy air-conditioning effect.

Direct radiant heat is a real hazard to small babies. Until the friction of clothes and exposure to air, wind and sun have toughened it, your baby's skin is very fragile. Guard it not only from obvious threats like sunburn and hot water bottles, but also from less expected ones like light bulbs and radiators.

Temperature control is serious business.

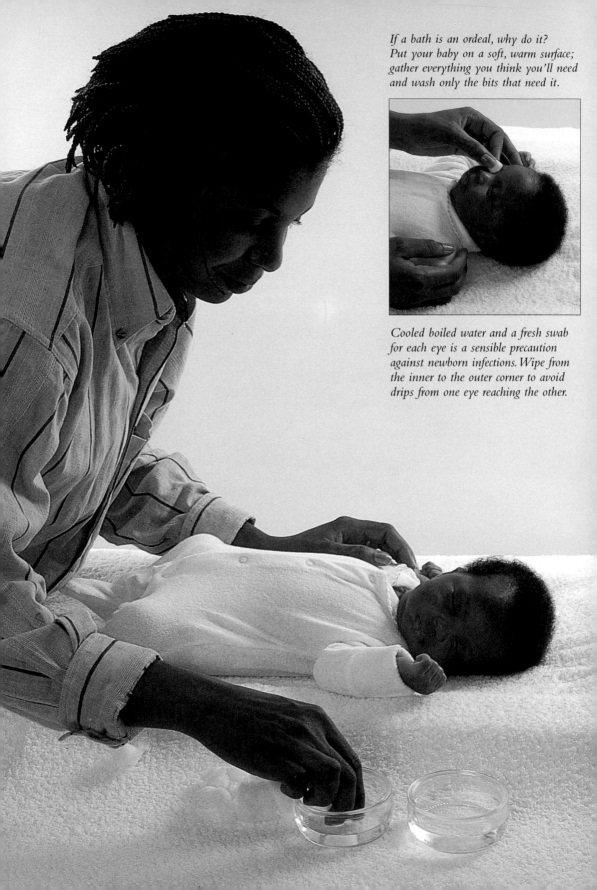

If a bath is an ordeal, why do it? Put your baby on a soft, warm surface; gather everything you think you'll need and wash only the bits that need it.

Cooled boiled water and a fresh swab for each eye is a sensible precaution against newborn infections. Wipe from the inner to the outer corner to avoid drips from one eye reaching the other.

KEEPING YOUR BABY CLEAN

Babies do not need to be kept nearly as clean as most of us keep them and newborn skin often suffers from adult enthusiasm and elaborate toiletries. Of course it is important to wash off the urine and faeces that would otherwise make his bottom sore, the dried milk that's buried deeply in the folds of his chin(s) and the sweat-salt from his head and neck. But you don't need lotions and liquids and wipes for any of that and, for the first couple of weeks at least, your baby may be better off without them. What you need is plenty of warm water and it doesn't even have to be a bath.

If, like many North American mothers, you're advised not to submerge your baby until the umbilical cord stump has fallen off, or you find that the bath is something that neither you nor your baby can enjoy just yet, you don't have to do it. You can make your baby perfectly clean by "topping and tailing" and do it without frightening him or putting yourself through the horrors of trying to hold a slippery screaming mite safely with shaking hands in a bath full of water.

This way of washing a new baby concentrates on cleaning the bits that really need it: the eyes, nose and ears, the face, hands, umbilicus and bottom. It keeps undressing (and therefore re-dressing) to a nappy-changing minimum and it can all be done without picking the baby up.

Notice that the method does not include poking bits of cotton wool up the nose, cleaning out the ears with cotton buds, or trying to pull back little boys' foreskins. All of a baby's orifices are lined with mucous membranes which are designed to bring out any dirt. So concentrate on wiping away what appears on the outside. Don't go hunting up the nostrils or into the ears with twists of cotton wool; if you do, you may actually push back the dirt. It is a good principle never to interfere with any part not visible from the outside.

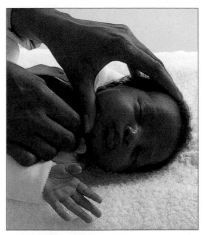

How many chins does your baby have? Getting the milk-and-dribble out of every single one is a daily challenge that a casual wipe will not meet.

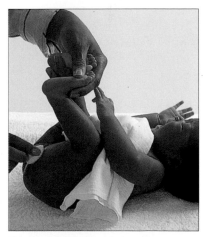

It's the rare newborn baby who can stay cheerful without any clothes, but any textured fabric laid over the tummy helps.

Which nappies?

What's the true balance of advantage between disposable and washable nappies?

Both kinds, especially the more expensive ranges, have greatly benefited from modern design and technology, and babies, as well as parents, benefit from the improvements. Some babies do still get nappy rash, but it is no longer either commonplace or linked to one kind of nappy or another.

In disposables, absorbency and bulk no longer have to go together. Slim-line "ultra" nappies with an inner layer of gelling material (sodium polyacrylate) are more absorbent (though more expensive) than most of the thicker ones that rely on the absorbency of pulp-fluff. In fact, you need to be wary of their very efficiency. Some of the top-of-the-range disposables are so absorbent, their stay-dry lining so effective and their fit so good that if they are not soiled, it is easy to forget to change them.

You are likely to use about eight or ten nappies each day to begin with, so less expensive disposables are bulky to carry home. If you have no storage problem, you can take advantage of bulk-deliveries offered by many chain stores, but don't order too many of one brand – especially in the newborn size. You may want to try several kinds before you settle for one.

"Disposable" means throwaway, not flush away and not vanishing. Disposable nappies add enormously to the growing problem of domestic waste disposal and while the use of individual plastic bags – deodorized if you like – reduces the nuisance to neighbours and garbage disposal people, it's one more load for already overloaded landfill sites. Fully recyclable disposable nappies, manufactured by environmentally friendly techniques should soon be widely available.

Washable nappies are also available in a wide range of types and prices. Terry and muslin squares are still much the cheapest but also the most primitive. Whatever kind of nappies you use, though, it's worth having some muslins in your life for general mop up.

The best washables are all-in-ones: many layers of shaped muslin, plastic-backed with Velcro fastenings. They are as convenient to use as disposables except of course for the washing and drying.

Quick-release nappies to use with waterproof pants, and shaped nappies to fit into special waterproof covers with Velcro fastenings, are both slightly less expensive.

"Pre-folds" – cotton nappies with an extra-thick central section – are less expensive still. They are the choice of most of the nappy-washing services. They provide the nappies and leave you to provide your own pins and pull-on pants, or Velcro-closing plastic wraps.

From the baby's point of view it probably doesn't matter which nappies you choose as long as she is changed often enough. No greater risk of nappy rash is intrinsic to one type or another.

From the adult point of view there's a clear-cut issue of convenience between disposables and re-usables, and within each of those classifications, more money buys you better-looking, better-performing products.

If you like everything about washable nappies except the washing, consider a service. In most cities, having clean, dry washable nappies delivered to you each week will cost about the same as using ultra disposables. If you are concerned to make an environmentally sound choice, though, it's more complicated. Problems of manufacturing and disposing of disposables make re-usable nappies seem virtuous, but to make a proper balance sheet you would need to audit all the energy used in washing and rinsing and drying them and consider the polluting effects of all those sterilants, detergents and bleaching chemicals pouring down drains and into rivers. Studies have been done but their conclusions are not consistent.

Changing a nappy   Changing your baby's nappy is going to punctuate the life of your household for a long time so it's worth making the whole thing quick and easy for yourselves. That usually means gathering together the things you need – nappies, disposal bags for disposables or bucket for washables, wipes or water bowl and cotton wool – on something that will serve as a changing table. Changing mats are fine but not essential; the cold plastic will need covering with a towel and the towel on its own will do. If you live in a house with many stairs, or have a home office, it may be sensible to have a second nappy-changing set–up in it. Not to mention supplies in the car (and maybe in both your brief-cases).

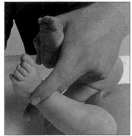

Make sure your baby's ankle bones cannot grind together by keeping a finger between them.

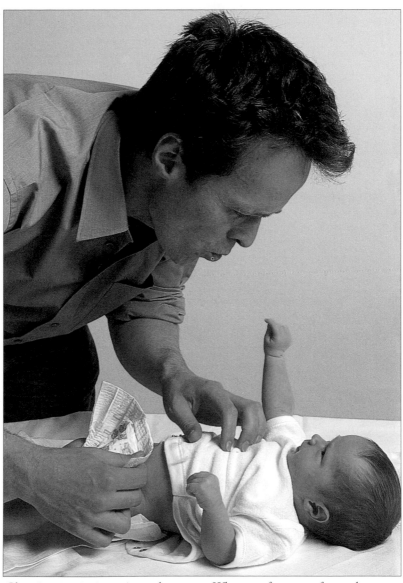

Changing nappies is routine and repetitive, but that does not mean it has to be boring for you or your baby.

What a perfect excuse for another, and another, and yet another cuddle and conversation.

CARING FOR NAVEL AND NAILS

Some parents find caring for the umbilical cord stump very daunting. The centimetre or so of thick brownish tissue looks extraordinary and they find it difficult to believe assurances that since the cord had no nerve supply the cut end is not sore. Furthermore they know that haemorrhage or infection would be a serious matter. Don't let it faze you. Within a couple of weeks there will be no cord stump: just a neat navel. Meanwhile it truly does not hurt your baby and although bleeding or infection would matter, neither is at all likely and it's especially unlikely that problems would set in so fast that you did not have ample time to notice and consult your midwife or doctor.

For the first day or so after birth the clamp or "bone" that fastens your baby's umbilical cord is left on. If you leave hospital with it still in place, your visiting midwife or your doctor will remove it. A very small amount of bleeding – a drop or two – is not unusual.

When the cord stump falls off, your baby's newly revealed navel could be sore. Go gently.

The cord stump will now shrivel and fall off of its own accord, usually in one to two weeks and should be kept as dry as possible during this time. This is not a matter of life and death; an accidental splash will do no harm. But try not to wet that area when you are washing your baby's bottom, and if you give her a proper bath before the cord has fallen off and the navel healed, don't have the water deep enough to submerge it.

Some doctors recommend dabbing the cord stump with alcohol or applying a drying, medicated powder. Others recommend leaving the stump strictly alone but cleaning around it. Your doctor or midwife will show you what to do. Either way, if a thin, yellowish discharge appears where the cord stump meets the baby's belly, you see more than a drop of blood, or the stump or general area becomes red, hot or oozy, show it to your midwife *or* your doctor that same day so that any incipient infection can be nipped in the bud.

The stump will often heal more quickly if you can reduce the friction it is subjected to. If your baby is an average kind of size, newborn nappies that are cut down in front to avoid the navel may fit well enough to serve their purpose. If not, try folding your chosen kind of nappy down.

When the cord stump finally falls off, the navel it reveals may not yet be entirely healed. This permanent part of your baby *does* have a nerve supply and *could* be sore for a day or two and it may not yet be as neat as it's going to be, so go gently and be patient. By the time your baby is two to three weeks old she'll have an ordinary-looking belly button – but whether an inny or an outy, nobody can say.

Keeping nails short A new baby may be born with long fingernails and they grow rapidly. Unless they are kept well-trimmed they can make nasty scratches on her face as she waves her hands around, rubs her eyes or tries to suck her fist. Mittens can prevent the scratches but only at the exorbitant price of concealing her hands from her.

Cutting the fingernails with scissors isn't easy because the baby's fingers are so very small that it's difficult to hold on to one at a time firmly enough to be safe, especially if she tries to pull it away. Use only special baby nail scissors. Their small size and rounded ends make them seem a little less dangerous. Try holding the finger you are working on between your forefinger and thumb, using the rest of your hand to enclose the rest of hers. That way even if she takes her finger away, there's no risk of you pinching another one. If she is impossibly wriggly (or you are very anxious) try carrying out the whole procedure when she is asleep. If cutting her nails always wakes her up, see if your partner can do the job while the baby is nursing.

If you can find no comfortable way of using scissors, two other techniques may help during the first three weeks or so while your baby's fingernails are still soft. Try peeling off the surplus nail (which looks very white and is often somewhat flaky) between your own finger and thumbnail, or try peeling it with your teeth, relying on the extraordinary sensitivity of your tongue and lips. As the nails begin to harden though, peeling becomes difficult. You might find smoothing with an emery board easier than cutting.

Don't forget her toenails. Once she begins to kick, sharp edges could scratch her legs.

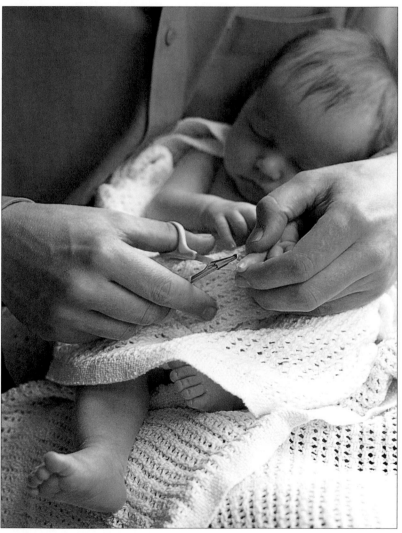

Trimming a baby's fingernails is always essential but seldom this easy. If yours wakes the moment you begin, try when she's drowsing over a feed or abandon scissors and peel off sharp surpluses with your own fingernails or teeth.

BATHING

A daily bath is still a taken-for-granted part of newborn baby care in many parts of the world. If your baby is born in a European hospital, staff will probably be anxious to give you at least one bathing demonstration even if you take him home on day one.

Although you can manage without one, a baby bath makes bathing much easier, whether you start now or in a few days' time. There are baths that fit into their own stands or clip over big baths, and special shapes to help keep your baby safe, but simple baths that can be put on any firm table, or even on the floor are probably as good as any. What matters is that you should be able to choose a warm room and a height that doesn't give you backache, and that somebody else carries and empties the bath for you. If you have no small bath, though, don't assume that the adult one is your only option. It isn't a viable option at all because the bath is too low for you and too cold for your baby. You'd be better off bathing him in a large container, such as a very well-rinsed washing-up bowl, or in a fixed basin or kitchen sink. Watch out for the taps, though. It is easy to bang the baby on them or scald him with a drip from the hot one.

Not many babies this age enjoy the business of nakedness and water so don't be surprised or downcast if yours howls throughout. In another week or two he'll probably love it. In the meantime, make the whole operation as quick and slick as you can. An assistant (aged 3, 33 or 63) to pass you things is a great help; failing that, try to have everything gathered where you can reach it so you can be *quick*. Start by washing your baby bit by bit as if you were topping and tailing him, but finish with him naked inside a big soft towel.

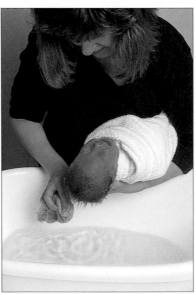

Still wrapped in her towel, hold her with her head over the edge of the bath while you first wash her face and then rinse her hair. She doesn't need shampoo yet.

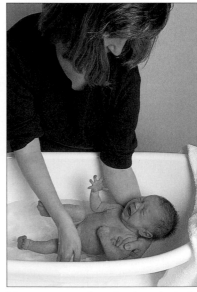

Now unwrap and put her into the bath with your right hand under her bottom, left forearm behind her, head supported on your wrist and your fingers grasping her armpit.

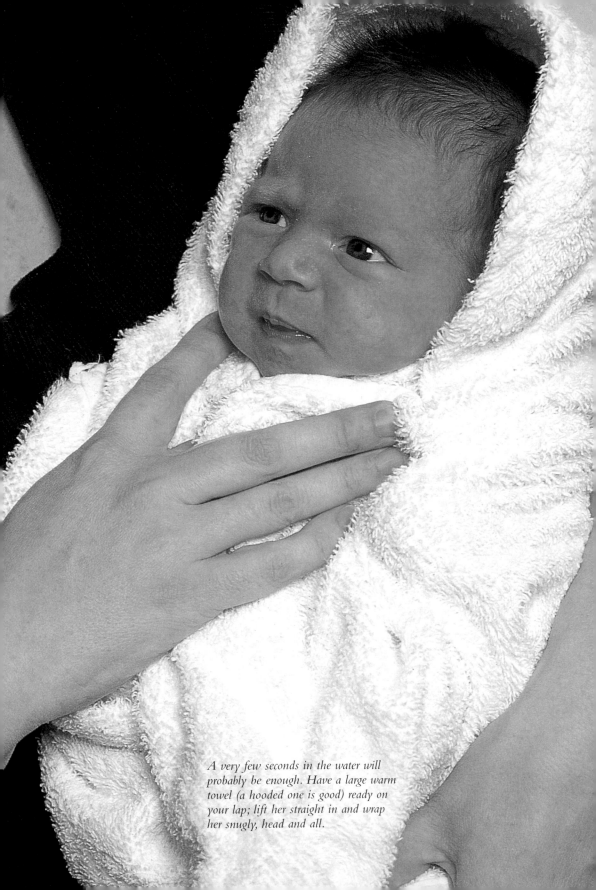

A very few seconds in the water will probably be enough. Have a large warm towel (a hooded one is good) ready on your lap; lift her straight in and wrap her snugly, head and all.

EXCRETING

The very first substance your baby passes will not be faeces but meconium: the greenish-blackish, tarry material that fills unborn babies' intestines. The passage of meconium readies your baby's intestines for the products of digestion, and demonstrates that they are in working order, with no blockage. It is important, therefore, that meconium is passed before she is fed anything other than colostrum (see p.55), and that you know that it has (or has not) been passed.

While you are in hospital, staff will be alert to meconium stools. They will note it down if one of them happens to change the relevant nappy, and ask you, if not. Once any meconium has been passed it stops being an issue (though there may be more than one blackish sticky nappy). But if you bring your baby home within a few hours of birth, make sure you know whether she has passed any or not; keep it in mind until she does and mention it to the midwife within 24 hours if by any chance she does not.

Changing stools Once your baby's bowel is cleared of meconium and she has begun to take milk from the breast or from a bottle, she will pass "changing" stools – so-called because their odd character is due to the change-over from transfusion feeding in the womb to ordinary digestion. Changing stools are usually greeny-brown, semi-fluid and frequent. But sometimes they are bright green, full of curds and mucus and violently expelled. If they look like this, don't assume that the baby has violent diarrhoea. Peculiar-looking stools are a feature of these early days.

If the stools really worry you, take the baby and one of the soiled nappies (in a sealed plastic bag) to the doctor so that he can check that there is no infective diarrhoea (gastro-enteritis). If the baby is being breast-fed, gastro-enteritis is extremely unlikely. If she is being bottle-fed, it is a possibility, but it is still a remote one if the baby seems contented and sucks well. It may be three weeks or even more before your baby settles to passing normal or "settled" stools.

Settled stools A baby who is having only breast milk will probably pass orangey-yellow stools with the consistency of mustard and only a mild sour-milk smell. But she may sometimes pass stools that are greenish, full of mucus, curdled-looking or otherwise peculiar, without being in any way unwell. Try not to take too much interest in her nappies. Concentrate on her general wellbeing.

She may have so many small motions each day that you never change a nappy that is not soiled as well as wet. On the other hand, she may have only one motion every three or four days. Both extremes and everything in between them are absolutely normal. And it is normal for breast-fed babies to swing from one to the other.

Bottle-fed babies usually pass stools which are bulkier and more frequent than those of the breast-fed baby, because formula leaves more residue than breast milk. They are a pale brown colour and smell more like ordinary stools. Whereas a breast-fed baby's food is always perfect for her, a bottle-fed baby's food may not be. If the formula you have chosen does not agree with your baby, you may get your first clues from her stools. Don't chop and change between formulas without medical advice, though.

Constipation Bottle-fed babies often pass stools several times a day as a breast-fed baby may, but they seldom go for days without passing any. If a bottle-fed baby passes no stool for a day or two and then passes a hard one which causes obvious discomfort, she is constipated. Lack of fluid is a common cause; offer extra drinks of water.

Diarrhoea If a bottle-fed baby suddenly starts to have diarrhoea she should see the doctor in case she has gastro-enteritis. If she is vomiting as well, goes off feeds and/or seems feverish or ill, then the appointment should be made as an emergency. Gastro-enteritis can be extremely dangerous to babies, especially to very young ones. The immediate danger is loss of fluid from the body due to the diarrhoea and exacerbated by any vomiting. The baby should be offered as much cooled boiled water as she will drink.

But most loose stools will be found to be due to diet not to infection. Too much sugar can cause diarrhoea. Are you adding cereal to the bottles instead of giving the formula exactly as the manufacturer recommends? Are you giving the baby lots of fruit juice? Or giving drinks of sugar water?

Too much fat can also cause loose stools. If your baby is not digesting the particular fats in her formula, the stools will smell very nasty. Take the baby and a soiled nappy to the doctor. If he feels that the fat in the milk is not agreeing with the baby, he may recommend that you change to a different formula.

Colour changes Even before you introduce any solid foods, some "extras" can cause quite alarming colour changes in the stools. Rosehip syrup, for example, will turn the stools reddish or purple. Various over-the-counter medicines will colour the stools, while if the doctor has prescribed iron for the baby, the stools may be blackish.

Urine It does not matter if your baby wets herself very often; it may matter if she does not. A new baby who is dry after a couple of hours needs watching. Her body may be using up more fluid than usual because she is starting a fever. Or she may need more than usual because it is a hot day. Give her plenty to drink and see if she is still dry after another hour. If she is (and she almost certainly will not be), ring your doctor. The baby just might have an obstruction.

Too little fluid, especially when the weather is hot or when she has fever, can make the urine extra strong and concentrated. If it is really strong, it may stain the nappy yellow and redden the baby's skin. Once again, she needs more to drink.

If the urine remains very strong, even though the baby is drinking plenty, and especially if it begins to have a nasty fishy smell, take her to the doctor. She just might have a urinary infection.

Of course if blood in your baby's urine is a possibility, you need an immediate appointment with the doctor. But pause to think for a moment. If your baby is a girl and the redness you can see is blood at all, it may be coming from the vagina rather than from the bladder. Vaginal bleeding is quite normal during the first few days of life (see p.50), and on a wet nappy can easily look as if it is part of the urine.

Your newborn sleeps wherever she finds herself and whenever she feels the need.

SLEEPING

New babies sleep exactly the amount that their personal physiology tells them to sleep. There is nothing that you can do to make your baby sleep more than this amount and nothing that the baby can do to sleep less. Unless he is ill, in pain, or extremely uncomfortable he will do his sleeping wherever he finds himself and under almost any circumstances. So your power over his actual hours of sleep is very limited. By making him comfortable you can ensure that he sleeps as much as he wants to, but you cannot put him to sleep. On the other hand if you are in a crowded bus – somewhere that's not very comfortable – you need not worry about him being kept awake. He will only stay awake if he does not need to sleep.

Separating sleep from wakefulness At the very beginning of life a baby often drifts so gradually from being awake to being asleep that it is difficult to tell which state he is in at any given moment. He may start a feed wide awake and ravenous, suck himself into a blissful trance so that only his occasional bursts of sucking tell you that he is still at least a little awake, and then drift into sleep so deep that nothing you do will wake him.

This kind of drifting does not matter at all from his point of view. But from your point of view, life will be much easier to organize later on if you know that the baby is either awake (and therefore bound to need some attention and company), or asleep (and therefore unlikely to need anything at all for a while).

So, rather than letting him drift and doze on somebody's lap, it is a good idea to start from early on to "put him to bed" when he needs to sleep and to "get him up" when he is awake. If he is always put into his basket or pram when he is really sleepy, he will soon come to associate those places with going to sleep. If he is always taken into whatever company is available when he is awake, he will make that association too.

Disturbances to sleep A sleeping baby need not mean a hushed household. Ordinary sounds and activities will not disturb him at this early age. But if everybody creeps about and talks in whispers while he is asleep, there may come a time when he cannot sleep unless they do. It is therefore important to let him sleep through whatever sound level is normal for your household. If outside stimuli disturb the baby, it will usually be because they change very suddenly. He may drop off to sleep quite happily with the television set on, but wake when it is switched off. A toddler playing around the room will not keep him awake but one coming in may wake him.

But at this stage he will be disturbed most often by internal stimuli. Hunger will disturb him; being cold may disturb him if he is not in a very deep sleep; pain will wake him and so may passing a bowel movement or burping. Sometimes the jerks and twitches of his body as it relaxes towards deep sleep will disturb him too.

Separating night from day Although human beings are mainly diurnal creatures, sleeping by night and active by day, babies do not seem to have a mechanism instructing them accordingly. They start off sleeping and waking randomly through the 24 hours and it takes time and sensible handling to persuade them to concentrate their sleeping at night and their wakefulness in the daytime. Although most adopt this pattern fairly rapidly, babies who have spent weeks in constantly lit and busy intensive care units may be very slow to adapt.

Speed up the process of separating night from day from the beginning by making a clear difference between going to bed for the night and ordinary daytime naps. Bathing or "topping and tailing" your baby and changing him into nightclothes can be part of this. Giving the supper-time feed in his room can be part of it too. Above all, try to put him down to sleep in the cot and the room that he is going to use all night, rather than putting him in his pram somewhere else in the house as you might during the day:

■ Take extra trouble over making the baby comfortable at night. If you are merely putting him to bed for a daytime nap, it may not matter very much to you if a burp wakes him a little while later. When it is night, try to ensure that he has finished with burping and that nothing that you can foresee is going to disturb him.

■ Try wrapping the baby securely (see p.116). In the daytime it does not matter if his own movements bring him fully awake as soon as his sleep lightens. At night you do not want him to wake even during the normal periods of light sleep which intersperse heavy slumber.

■ Darken the room enough to make it different from daytime, so that when he opens his eyes (as all babies do from time to time during the night) his attention is not caught by anything brightly lit or clearly

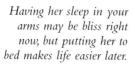

Having her sleep in your arms may be bliss right now, but putting her to bed makes life easier later.

Small babies need small beds and they need them kept close to adults.

visible. But leave a dim (15-watt) light on so that you can attend to him during the night without switching on more lights.

■ Make sure the room is reasonably warm 18°C−20°C (65°F−68°F) and stays warm. Getting chilly will wake him when he is in light sleep, and can be risky if it happens while he is in deep sleep.

■ Keep night feeds as sleepy and as brief as possible. The baby is bound to wake up because he cannot (and should not) yet get through the night without food and drink, but the less completely he awakens, the better. Make sure, before you leave him, that everything you will need during the night is gathered together. You don't want to have to carry him around while you search for a dry nappy.

■ When he cries, go to him immediately so that he has no time to get into a wakeful misery. Don't play and talk while you feed him; concentrate on soothing cuddles instead. Daytime feeds are social playtimes but night feeds are for sustenance only.

Organizing your nights

Lack of sleep, and more especially broken sleep, is the very worst part of parenting for many people. The problem is not confined to the early weeks when new babies wake because they have to be fed. All babies wake from time to time and most of them insist on adult company and comfort when they do. You can cross your fingers for the kind of baby who sleeps all night, every night, from six weeks of age, but don't hold your breath. There are a great many parents who have not managed to share a single unbroken period of seven hours sleep by the time their baby is a toddler.

There are two very different approaches to this problem area and it is worth trying to decide which will suit you, so that you start out as you mean to go on. The first approach is a basic acceptance of this small new person not just into your waking life but into your night life and your bed. Sharing a "family bed" will not stop your baby from waking up and it will not save you from night feeds in the first weeks. But if he is sharing your bed with you, your baby's awakenings and his feeding will disturb you far less than they will if you have to go to him. And, because he is where he best likes to be − close against you − he is likely to go back to sleep far more quickly and easily.

Babies who sleep in family beds from early on often wake much less than other babies as they get older. As they get older still, they may wake but find it unnecessary to wake you. After all a toddler who is with you in bed does not need to cry for a cuddle because he is already having it or can just snuggle up.

Sharing beds is not dangerous (see p.183). But family beds do have snags and it's sensible to foresee them if you can so that you can weigh up the pros and cons. The major snag is that once your baby has slept this way for a few months, you are very unlikely to be able to persuade him, without a long and miserable fight, that a separate cot in a separate room is nicer. And however much you enjoy sharing a bed with your six-week-old baby, you may find that you change your mind later on. A baby or toddler in your bed does cut down your privacy, and being with him by night as well as by day can make you feel that as an individual you are totally submerged beneath your parent-persona.

The second approach welcomes the baby into your life but

determinedly excludes him from your night life and your bed. It means doing everything you can to help him sleep happily alone. It means going to him whenever he cries for you but never taking him in with you or letting him come to you when he is older. It leaves you freer when he sleeps well but may condemn you to endless visits to his cotside when he is teething or has bad dreams and, later still, you may have to return him to his bed night after night.

Nobody can make this choice for you. You may not be able to make it either. Even if you decide on the second approach, a bad week may find you taking your baby into bed with you at 3am after all because nothing seems to matter except being allowed to get your head down. Try to be aware of the choice and think about it, though. Your worst option is an attempt to compromise, sometimes letting him sleep with you and sometimes trying to insist that he stay alone.

Helping yourselves
to get enough sleep

If you're aiming for separate beds, you can maximize your own sleeping hours even during these early weeks of night feeding:

■ Wake the baby for a late-night feed at your bedtime. If you wait for him to wake, you will be losing sleeping time. If you go to sleep for an hour and then he wakes, you've been disturbed an unnecessary time. It will not hurt him to be fed before he knows he is hungry.

■ Think of your own small-hours comfort. If you are bottle-feeding, leaving the bottle ready in the refrigerator and a vacuum flask ready-filled with hot water to warm it will cut down your work.

■ Feed the baby as soon as crying begins. If you "leave him to cry" he may indeed cry himself back to sleep, if he was not very hungry. But he will keep you awake while he is crying and then wake again, extremely hungry, just as you have got back to sleep yourself. If you "make him wait a bit" he will keep you awake with his crying and when you finally feed him he may be too tired and upset to take a full feed. He will wake you again sooner than he might have done if you had fed him promptly. If you give him water, the sucking and thirst-quenching may put him back to sleep, but the peace will not last; his stomach will soon tell him that he's been fooled.

■ Discipline yourself to sleep the moment the baby is settled. It is easy to lie awake wondering if he is going to need another burp or another few millilitres. If he does, he will let you know. Waiting for him to cry will lose you yet another piece of sleeping time.

■ Decide whether one or both parents are going to cope. Although the very early night feeds are part of the excitement of having a new baby and you may both want to be involved, there is a long stint of too little sleep ahead of you. There is not really much point in both of you waking for every feed unless doing it together makes it all much quicker. Breast-feeding mothers usually decide that a snack and a chat is not enough compensation for having a husband who is exhausted too. Most of them prefer to manage alone and perhaps get paid back with afternoon naps at the weekends. Bottle-feeding parents sometimes work out a sharing system, with one parent doing one night and the other the next. But that does not always work because some mothers find that they wake up anyway, cannot get back to sleep until they know the baby is settled again and therefore feel that they might as well give the feeds themselves.

What can we do to prevent cot death?

We're haunted by the possibility of cot death, which we do not really understand. What is it? Why can't medical professionals make up their minds and give clear instructions? What can we parents actually do to prevent it?

Very occasionally an apparently healthy baby, usually under six months old, dies in his or her sleep. Cot deaths (deaths due to Sudden Infant Death Syndrome or SIDS) are, by definition, deaths that could not have been foreseen (even by a doctor) and *are never explained* (even at post-mortem). SIDS deaths are parts of a bigger group of Sudden Unexpected Deaths in Infancy (SUDI). The rest cannot be foreseen, either, but are eventually explained.

Without knowing the exact causes of cot deaths (which wouldn't be cot deaths if they did), medical professionals cannot know – and tell parents – exactly how to prevent them. In fact exactitude may never be possible because SIDS deaths probably result from complex combinations and interactions of circumstances rather than from simple single causes. The medical profession is now mapping those complexities, though, and very successfully – SIDS rates have fallen sharply.

Detailed research comparisons are being made between the circumstances of SIDS babies and of other babies who matched them closely in every respect except that they survived. Observed differences between matched groups aren't necessarily related to SIDS of course. If a single study has more blonde than brunette babies dying, for example, it is almost certainly due to chance, but when several studies have more deaths among babies in smoking households, it almost certainly isn't. Smoke pollution is a recognized risk factor for SIDS.

Several very strong risk factors for cot deaths are so widely agreed by experts in different countries that parents everywhere are advised to take action to avoid them. These risk factors aren't the "causes" of SIDS, though, so avoiding them doesn't mean you can be *certain* of protecting your baby. Nevertheless you will enormously reduce the (already minute) chances of SIDS striking your family.

■ *Babies should be put down to sleep lying on their backs.* Sleeping on the back is safer than sleeping on the side; sleeping on the tummy should be avoided.

■ *Babies' heads must not become covered while they are asleep.* Place your baby so far down the crib or cot that the feet almost touch the end and there is nowhere to wriggle to; use light blankets tucked in so the head is exposed and uncovered. Don't give a pillow or soft toy. Don't use duvets, loose quilts or ties on bedding. Make sure the cot mattress leaves no gap in which a baby's head might get wedged.

■ *Babies must not get too hot while asleep, especially when feverish.* Keep night-time room heating (if any) no higher than would be comfortable for a sleeping adult. If a baby is feverish, use fewer covers, not more.

■ *Babies should not be exposed to smoke either before or after birth.* Failing a non-smoking household, a baby is partly protected if his or her sleeping place is kept as a smoke-free zone 24 hours a day whether the baby is in it or not.

SIDS (and SUDI) research is ongoing. While the above points will figure in almost every cot death prevention programme, additional points may also be made by various organizations in different countries. Less clear, less statistically powerful or less generally accepted risk factors include: parents' slowness to recognize signs of illness and seek medical advice; bottle-feeding as opposed to breast-feeding; and levels and details of prenatal care. Bed-sharing (see p.183) has been identified both as a risk and a protective factor and therefore remains controversial. The greatest statistical risk factor for SIDS overall may be the one which individual parents can do least to avoid: poverty.

You may never know why she's crying but by the time you've tried everything she will have stopped.

CRYING AND
COMFORTING

All babies cry, especially in their first few weeks outside the womb. Although many parents wish their babies never cried at all, they'd be even harder to care for if they didn't. Babies cry when they need something and it is because you know that yours will do so that you can assume, under all normal circumstances, that as long as she is not crying she needs nothing. It would take serious illness, severe chilling, or smothering, to make a baby suffer in silence.

Babies never cry for nothing. The statement that they cry "to exercise their lungs" is nonsense. Their lungs get all the "exercise" they need in breathing. But while crying always means that your baby is at least somewhat uncomfortable or unhappy, crying in these first weeks doesn't always mean that something is wrong. Recent research suggests that a lot of newborn crying is "developmental": that babies may cry because they haven't fully adapted to life outside the womb, or because some aspect of their extraordinarily rapid and complex neuro-physiological development is making them tense and uncomfortable.

A lot of the time, of course, your baby cries because she needs something, and then, if you are lucky, you will be able to understand what she needs and give it to her. She's hungry, you feed her, the crying stops and you both feel pleased with yourselves and each other. But if you're unlucky, it isn't at all clear what she needs. You offer everything you can think of but the crying goes on and on and nobody can feel pleased with anybody. And then there are the really grim times when you do know what she needs but you actually cannot give it to her. She's clearly desperately tired but nothing you do enables her to relax and sleep because some internal discomfort – a bellyache, perhaps, or just an impending bowel movement – is keeping her (and therefore you) awake.

A baby who cries and cannot be comforted is definitely the downside of parenting. The sound of your baby's crying is certainly meant to grab your attention (if it didn't you might ignore your crying baby) but is not meant to go on and on: it's meant to stop when it is answered, like a telephone bell. The longer the noise goes on the more intolerable it becomes and the more difficult it is not to be overwhelmed by panic or sadness. It's really difficult to go on feeling loving and sympathetic to the baby even though she seems to reject all your efforts to help her: maybe even seems to reject *you*. If the crying and the ineffectual attempts to comfort go on for too long (and at 3 am how long is that?) many parents come to feel frustrated and useless; they may begin to feel angry, too, losing sight of the fact that the baby cannot stop crying until she has what she needs and beginning to feel that she *will not* stop, that she is crying to torment them. If you feel like that you are not alone.

CAUSES AND CURES OF CRYING

The causes and the "cures" for crying that are outlined here are designed to answer those frantic questions which come into the mind of almost every parent from time to time: "What is the matter with her?"; "What can I do?" The truthful answer to both questions may well be "not very much". But somewhere in this chapter there will probably be something that will comfort (or at least explain) your baby, and even if there isn't, by the time you have given each possibility a try the episode will be over – until next time.

Hunger Hunger is the most common cause of crying in a young baby and the easiest to deal with. Research studies have shown that if the baby is hungry, only milk will stop the crying. When researchers gave babies sweetened water or dummies, they sucked but then started to cry again after a few seconds. The need is for food and can only be met by food going into your baby's stomach. Just sucking, or even sucking combined with a pleasant taste, will have no effect.

Pain Until surprisingly recently new babies were believed to be insensitive to pain. Nurses assured anxious parents that their babies didn't feel the heel-sticks that took blood for testing; doctors circumcised baby boys and surgeons carried out quite lengthy procedures without anaesthesia. These must have been considerable feats of faith because pain certainly causes crying from the first minutes of life, although it is sometimes difficult to be sure whether a crying baby is distressed by pain or by something else. For example, she may stop crying when she is picked up, and immediately pass air from one end or the other. Can we assume that the air was causing pain? It may have been giving her bellyache; it may have been making her stomach feel uncomfortably distended; or it may have had nothing to do with the crying, being passed merely by chance when she was picked up. Certain kinds of pain cause unmistakable reactions though. Your baby will probably cry heartbreakingly if her bottle or her bath is even a few degrees too warm.

Over-stimulation, shock and fear Too much of any kind of stimulation will cause crying. Loud sudden noises, unexpectedly bright lights, sharp or bitter tastes, cold hands, hot face cloths, too much laughter, tickling, bouncing or hugging can all overcome a new baby.

Sudden happenings, particularly if they involve a sense of being about to fall or be dropped, tend to cause shock and real fear. As well as crying, the baby may tremble and pale.

If there is a minor accident, such as a bang on the head while being carried through a doorway, the baby's crying is likely to be as much due to the shock of the bang as to actual pain.

Mistiming The amount of any kind of stimulation which is "too much" depends on the baby's mood and state. What she enjoys when she is awake, content and well-fed may make her cry when she is sleepy, irritable or hungry. For example, physical games which she enjoys when she is feeling sociable will reduce her to despair if they are used to "jolly her along" when she is not. Tired, sad babies need cuddles, not play. Hungry ones need food.

Mistiming feeds will obviously cause crying from hunger, but mistiming the rate at which the baby gets the milk can cause trouble too. If you offer food too slowly – by having the hole in the teat too small or by taking her off the breast or bottle to burp – the distress of her hunger breaks through the relief of feeding, so that the baby who was crying because she was hungry stays hungry because she is crying too much to suck.

Bathing or changing a baby who is very hungry will cause crying, both because it delays the arrival of food and because being handled when she needs a feed tends to irritate her. She should not be bathed immediately after a feed, either, as a great deal of jouncing around is likely to make her bring up milk, so choose a wakeful period for baths, or wake her to be bathed before she has woken herself from hunger. Nappy-changing after feeds does not matter if it is gently done, but if the baby is one who needs to burp at half-time, or drops off to sleep and needs waking up, you can change her in mid-feed.

Getting from a sleepy state to sound slumber is often difficult for small babies. Try not to make it more difficult by changing her surroundings when she is just getting drowsy. If you must take her out in the car, put her in her seat and start the expedition before she begins to drop off so that she can go to sleep to smooth motion, or wait until she is sound asleep before you start.

Being undressed Many parents assume that it is their own clumsiness and inexperience which make babies cry when their clothes are taken off. Although skill certainly helps by making the process as quick and smooth as possible, many babies cry literally for the loss of their clothes. What often happens is that the baby gets increasingly tense as her outer garments are removed and finally howls when the garment next to her skin – vest or undershirt – is taken off. This reaction has nothing to do with being cold: it can happen however high the temperature of the room or the undressing hands. The baby misses the contact between the fabric and her bare skin. She does not like the feeling of her skin exposed to the air. She is crying for her clothing and will stop as soon as she is dressed again. But she can usually be kept completely calm while she is naked if a piece of textured material (a towel, a nappy or a shawl) is laid across her chest and stomach.

Feeling cold Feeling chilly will cause crying if the baby is awake or almost awake at the time. Much of the crying that goes on when babies are first taken out in prams is due to feeling cold air, especially a cool breeze. It is not a dangerous kind of cold – the crying itself will ensure that the baby makes heat for herself – but she does not like it. The crying will stop as soon as she is brought into a warm room.

Jerks and twitches Most new babies jerk and twitch when they are in that twilight zone between consciousness and sleep. A few are startled awake over and over again by their own movements. They cry, drowse, jerk and cry again, clearly tired and ready for slumber but unable to get themselves past the twitchy state and into deep sleep. Efficient wrapping up or swaddling (see overleaf) will almost always deal with this kind of crying.

Lack of physical contact Babies who cry until they are picked up, stay cheerful while they are being held and then cry again when they are put down, are usually crying because they are uncomfortable without physical contact. This kind of crying for lack of "contact comfort" is often misunderstood. Parents are told that the baby is crying "because she wants you to pick her up". The implication is that she is making an unreasonable demand on you and that if you "give in" you will start "bad habits". In fact, the reverse is true. The baby is not making unreasonable demands; in fact if anyone is, you are. She is not crying to make you pick her up but because you put her down in the first place and deprived her of contact comfort. It is natural and instinctive for a small baby to be most easily content when she is being held by somebody. In many parts of the world, babies are held and carried almost all the time. Grandmothers and older sisters take turns when mothers must be unburdened, but women carry out most of their chores with their babies slung on their backs. Compared with Western newborns, those babies cry remarkably little.

Picking the baby up and cuddling her will almost always stop the crying. If it does not, then holding her against your shoulder, so that her stomach and chest are pressed against your chest, will. If whimpers still break through the contact comfort, walk with the baby in this position; the rocking movement will soothe her and peace will descend.

You probably cannot hold and walk your baby for hours on end, even if there are two of you to take turns and you use a sling. But you can deal with most of your baby's need for contact comfort by wrapping her up in such a way that the wrapping shawl gives her the same feeling of warmth and security that she gets when she is held closely in your arms against your body.

You can also keep crying for contact comfort to a minimum by making sure that all the surfaces the baby lies on are warm and soft. Plastic laminates and plastic sheets may make life easier for you but they are horrible for her. So cover all plastic mattresses or mats with a textured fabric such as terry-towelling.

SPECIAL COMFORTS

If you have looked for all these causes and tried any of the "cures" that seem appropriate and your baby still cries, inexplicably, maddeningly, there are a few other techniques you can try. But "try" is the operative word. There may be nothing you can do but your best, right now or for the immediate future. All babies cry, but some cry more than others and parents are not responsible for either kind. You may all have to live through a difficult few weeks.

Wrapping for comfort Wrapping your baby up is rather like old-fashioned swaddling except that it is not intended to "keep her back straight" or any nonsense of that kind. It is intended simply to give her tactile comfort, by surrounding her with a warm, soft, gentle holding layer of material which prevents her own little jerky movements from disturbing her.

Efficient wrapping is magically soothing to most babies. Wrapping which is too loose may have the opposite effect. Your aim is to encase

1 Lay the baby on a soft, light, slightly stretchy receiving blanket or shawl. Take one side up, level with the back of the baby's head.

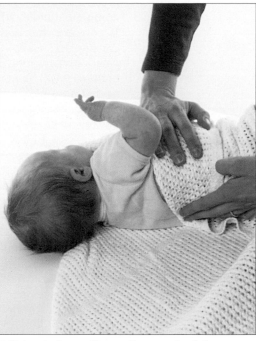

2 Bring it down diagonally over the left shoulder so that it holds her flexed elbow, leaving her hand free. Tuck the end under her.

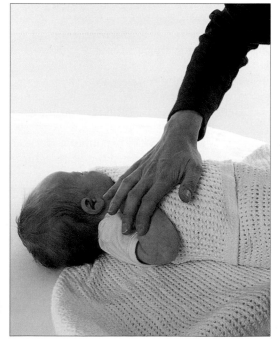

3 Take the other side straight over, right elbow held, hand free. Use as much tension as you can short of shifting the baby.

4 Lift the baby a little to secure the edge under her body – or pick up the whole securely wrapped and, for the moment, quieted bundle.

the baby completely so that her limbs are gently held in their preferred position and so that, when she moves, she moves as one complete bundle rather than feeling herself moving within the shawl. If you use the method outlined here, you need not worry about getting the wrapping too tight. It is held in position only by the baby's own weight, and this is not enough to hold it tighter than is comfortable. The ideal wrapping material is light and slightly stretchy so that it moulds itself a little to the baby and "gives" with her. A small cellular cotton blanket will do in winter. In warm weather a brushed cotton cot sheet will be comfortably warm to feel without being too hot to wear. In hot weather a baby who enjoys the comfort of being wrapped but might get too warm, will be happy if a soft muslin or gauze is used. Whatever fabric you use, a baby who is wrapped in it will be warmer than she would be if she were merely covered. Do compensate for that by reducing the layers of bedding you use.

A new baby's natural position is with her arms bent at the elbow and her legs flexed. Wrap her like this, making no attempt to straighten her out before you start. Above all, leave her hands where she can suck them if she wants and is able to do so.

Babies vary widely in the length of time they continue relaxing best when wrapped up. Let your baby be the judge: when she wants to rid herself of the wrappings she will begin to kick and struggle to get them undone.

Comforting rhythms A baby who cannot relax can be helped to do so by a variety of constant rhythmical stimuli. These seem to work by blocking out whatever internal or external discomforts were bothering her. You apply a soothing blanket of overall stimulation which wipes everything else out for the baby. It will not work if there is a simple cause for the crying which you have failed to discover. Hunger, for example, will break through everything. But it probably will work if the trouble is some kind of general and diffuse irritability or a tenseness which is preventing a tired baby relaxing into sleep.

Rhythmical rocking is almost universally effective in stopping crying and inducing sleep. Parents who find that it does not work are almost certainly rocking too slowly. Research from many years ago showed that the effective rate is at least 60 rocks per minute through a travel of about eight centimetres. Such a rate is difficult to achieve by hand, even if you have a rocking cradle. There are various automatic rocking gadgets such as clockwork swings available, and some parents find energetic use of a rocking chair effective, but you may find it easier to walk with the baby. Time yourself and you will find that a walk round the room rocks her at just about this rate. It seems likely that the soothing effect of this rate of rocking comes directly from babies' experiences of being in a walking womb. You can provide this kind of rocking and lots of contact comfort, while leaving yourself free to get on with at least a few other things, by using a sling. There are a variety of commercial slings available, but at this age, and especially when the purpose is soothing rather than transport, a front carrier that holds the baby warmly against you with her head well-supported, is probably best.

Most babies also find rhythmical sounds very soothing. You can

A different way of holding and being held can change the mood for both of you.

buy a recording of a mother's heartbeat, as heard by a baby in the womb, or rely on your own rendering of the lullaby your mother sang. Soft rhythmical music on the radio or stereo often works too, but make sure that it does not stop before the baby is properly asleep. If it does, the change in stimulation will wake her.

The burring sound of a fan heater, vacuum cleaner or washing machine often works excellently. So does the sound of a car engine. Most babies sleep peacefully in cars while they are running but tend to wake again the moment the engine is switched off, so don't be tempted to drive round the block in the small hours.

Comfort sucking Sucking will not stop a hungry baby crying unless it brings her food, but it will almost always soothe a baby who is not hungry.

There are pros and cons to the use of dummies (see p.186). Reasonably contented babies can manage perfectly well without them and it is better that they should do so. But dummies can certainly help babies who are often miserable and difficult to comfort in any other way. The furious howling mouth latches on to the dummy and all that energy goes into sucking instead of crying. Gradually the rhythm of the sucking becomes gentler. Eventually the baby goes to sleep. Even while she sleeps, having the dummy in her mouth protects her against a fresh bout of crying: whenever something begins to disturb her, she sucks instead of waking.

If you decide that your baby does need a dummy, do guard against the habit of popping it into her mouth whenever she cries – or in case she cries. Try first to find out what she needs, and provide it. Her dummy should be used only when you have tried everything else.

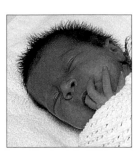

Babies who can soothe themselves by sucking their own fingers are a very fortunate few.

Some babies find and suck their thumbs and fingers before they are born and use them for comfort sucking from the first day of life. Others cannot find their own hands without help until they are several weeks old. If a lot of crying that is difficult to "cure" is worrying you and you do not like the idea of a dummy, you might compromise by helping the baby's hand to her mouth to see whether she can quiet herself by sucking it. Even if she sucks though, she may not find her small finger nearly as soothing as your much larger one.

Extra warmth As we have seen, wakeful babies tend to be fretful if they are having to warm themselves, and more contented when air temperatures around them are warm, provided they are lightly dressed and covered. If your baby is crying and you cannot persuade her to stop, a little extra warmth may calm her down and help her to relax. Although the warmth will not cure whatever discomfort is making her cry, she will probably react to the discomfort less if you can keep the temperature at around 21°C (70°F) until the episode is over. If she drops off to sleep, though, do check, before you tiptoe thankfully away, that there's no risk of her becoming overheated.

A baby who is often miserable and difficult to comfort will give you and herself more peace if you take trouble about warmth right through the newborn period. Wrap her carefully when you take her out in her pram on chilly days or take her for trips in a cold car, until she has grown up a bit. Keep her own room and any other rooms she regularly uses as near 21°C (70°F) as you can manage until she seems happier and more settled.

COLIC?

There is one quite common pattern of crying which you will not find in the previous pages. It usually begins something like this: your three- to four-week-old baby seems to cry more, and more distressingly, in the early evening than at any other time. As he becomes more settled, so that his daytime crying lessens and he becomes easier to comfort, the evening crying bouts build in regularity and intensity until they take up almost every late afternoon or evening.

Somewhere around this time you probably take your baby to the doctor. You want to know why he is having these regular and uncontrollable screaming fits and why you do not seem able to comfort him. What is the matter with him?

Your doctor will examine the baby and talk to you. He will assure himself (and you) that the baby is healthy and thriving and that while the screaming seems to you to be related to wind and abdominal pain, there is no sufficient physical reason, such as indigestion, to account for his apparent distress. By the end of the interview you will know that nothing is seriously the matter with your baby but you may still be no closer to understanding why he screams or how to live with it.

The nearest you'll get to an answer to that "why?" is probably "colic" (or "evening colic" or "three-month colic" or "paroxysmal crying"). If your doctor and your health visitor do not use these words to you it is probably because the terms are extremely unscientific. "Colic" sounds like the name for an illness needing diagnosis and treatment, potentially serious. But colic is not an illness; only a very distressing pattern of newborn behaviour with no accepted cause, no generally agreed treatment and absolutely no ill-effects except on parents' nerves. In fact, some researchers reject the notion that colic is an entity at all, seeing it as an extreme variation of ordinary newborn crying. The term is used here because your nerves matter and even an unscientific name may help you through the two or three bad months you are facing if your baby is beside himself with screaming every evening. You are the ones who are going to have to try everything you can think of to help and to accept the fact that, although every one of those things helps for a minute or two, nothing but time ends each episode.

Living with colic None of the comforting techniques that work for you and your baby at other times is fully effective when he is colicky. It is your helplessness, together with the fact that the dreadful bouts of screaming usually occur at the time of day when you are most tired and in need of peaceful time together, that makes colic so horribly difficult for new parents to cope with. Try to accept the fact that the cause is unknown. If you continually search for a cause, you will only confuse every other aspect of your baby care by changing feeds, feeding techniques and routines, all to no avail. Colic has been variously put down to overfeeding, underfeeding, too rich, strong or weak feeds, milk which was too hot or too cold, milk which flowed too fast or too slowly, allergies, hernias, appendicitis, gall bladder trouble, wind and nervous exhaustion in the mother! All these contradictory explanations share one decisive fallacy: if any one of them caused colic why should the trouble occur after one and only one feed in the 24 hours? However you feed your baby, you do not do it in a particular way at 6pm. If the baby had a physical problem, it would not reveal itself only at this time of day. If maternal fatigue was a cause, rather than a result, of colic the trouble would not occur when father or a caregiver took a turn with the bottle.

Don't be too ready to believe that your baby really does have colic though. If you jump to that conclusion when he cries in the evening for the third day in a row, you may miss some much more obvious and easily dealt with kind of distress. The chart below may help you to identify what people mean by colic. If your baby's behaviour partly fits the pattern and partly does not, you may find it easier to tolerate if you think of him as "colicky".

HE MAY BE COLICKY IF:	HE MAY NOT BE COLICKY IF:
He cannot settle after his late-afternoon or early-evening feed but starts screaming as soon as he has finished, or drops off to sleep but wakes screaming within half an hour.	He cannot settle after his late-afternoon or early-evening feed but after crying and grumbling for quite a long time, he finally goes to sleep. Grumbling without any screaming never means colic.
He does not just cry, he screams, drawing his legs up to his belly and seeming beside himself with pain.	His crying is ordinary crying even if it is hard crying and he draws his legs up to his belly.
Everything you do seems to help but only for a minute. He will suck your nipple or a dummy so you think that's the answer – but then the screaming starts again. A burp stops the screaming – but it starts again. Being rocked interrupts the screaming – but only for a few seconds. Having his tummy rubbed produces miraculous silence – but it does not last.	Anything you do brings the crying spell to an end within half an hour of its beginning. If a feed or a dummy does the trick the baby was hungry or needed to suck; either way he is not having colic. If a burp enables him to sleep, he had wind rather than colic and if cuddling or rocking or rubbing soothes him, he was lonely or too tense to go to sleep.
When you interrupt the dreadful screaming the baby remains shaky and sobbing until it starts again.	When you interrupt the crying he is calm at least until you put him back to bed.
The whole episode goes on for at least an hour and perhaps for three or four hours but is then over and done with for the night.	The episode ends inside half an hour and he then sleeps or stays happy for at least 15 minutes before he cries again. A bad day, but not colic.
A similar pattern repeats itself every day at about the same time and is never seen at any other point in the 24 hours.	Occasional screaming spells take place at any time of the day or night. They may be hard to bear but they are not colic.

I don't just hate it when my baby cries: I sometimes hate my crying baby.

Often she cries for no reason I can understand: howls when I'm washing her as if I'd put soap in her eyes and goes on as if I was just ignoring her even though I'm doing everything I can think of. I don't know why she does it when I'm only doing what has to be done. And I don't know why she won't stop when I try my very best to give her what she wants. Sometimes I think I must be a totally hopeless, unfit mother; sometimes I think she's the crossest worst-natured child in the world. It's probably both.

Your baby's in a big new world where there's plenty to upset her and when she's upset, she cries. Your baby is a big new aspect of your familiar world but do try not to let her behaviour upset you because she needs you to deal with her feelings, not share them.

Her crying is a signal that all is not well, but it's a very vague signal that tells you there's a problem but doesn't always pinpoint the problem for you and hardly ever tells you how serious it is. When your baby is crying while you're washing her, she can go just as stiff and purple over having her vest put over her head as having soap get in her eyes. It's great to buy front-opening vests as well as taking care with the soap, but it's also important to find the confidence to stay calm because *you do know how serious this is.* And it's not, very. So hang on and don't fall apart.

Just for the moment you've got to accept that your baby is going to cry a lot over little things and sometimes just as much over minute ones. That means there's no point in treading so softly-softly all the time in case she starts that you feel hemmed in. Of course you'll do your best not to let soap get in her eyes, but it's okay to say to yourself things like, "The milk can't be left in the creases under her chin. I'm being as gentle as I can be so I'll just get on and get it over even though she's bawling..." You're not ignoring the baby's crying. In fact you're taking a lot of trouble to listen and understand her. But you're accepting the fact that even when you do know what she wants, you cannot always give it to her because *you know best.* Right now she's crying because you're washing under her chin. If you stopped washing she might (or might not) stop crying for now but the chances are that she'd have a sore chin to cry about later. She does not know that but you do.

If you can stay calm while your baby cries over something that has to be done you'll not only find it easier to do what is right for her – meet her long-term needs as well as respond to her newborn distress – you'll also help her gradually to become calmer about everyday life. That face cloth doesn't hurt. Your sureness will help her towards acceptance.

It's that kind of basic confidence in your own competence as a parent – which includes your basic attachment to the baby, of course – which will stand you in good stead at the worst crying times, too: the times when you really cannot understand what she needs or wants or feels. The more she cries the more feelings of panic and guilt pollute your empathy, until the mix begins to feel like something so close to hatred that you're overwhelmed with guilt over *feeling* that way.

Your baby has no judgment; no ability to "think" the way older people do, so she certainly isn't judging you or getting at you and neither is she trying to tell you something vital that you're missing. If she's screaming as if she were in agony she probably does feel agonized, but while that means that she needs your active sympathy, it seldom means that you face a medical emergency. Her crying tells you "something's not right". You acknowledge that she's unhappy – that's for her to say – and do what you can to make her happier, but what is wrong, how wrong it is and what, if anything, can and should be done to put it right rather than just get her through it, is for *your* judgment. Trust yourself so she can trust you. You are the grown-up after all.

Rock a little, rub a little, sing a little; one at a time or all together, anything or nothing may help your baby to stop crying.

Try to keep your search for a "cure" for colic within bounds. Your doctor or health visitor might suggest trying a particular brand of colic drops before feeds; changing to a different formula if you are bottle-feeding, or experimenting with your own diet – by eliminating dairy produce, for example – if you are breast-feeding. But if nothing they suggest is helpful, don't go chasing around for other suggestions, or dosing your baby with other remedies. If there was a cure for your situation, everybody would know of it.

Instead of fretting about why, blaming yourselves or each other for doing something wrong, worrying in case the baby is ill, try for a mood of constructive resignation: you're not causing the crying and there's not much you can do to stop it. It's going to give you all a bad few weeks, so how are you going to get through them?

Although parents know they cannot cure their babies' colic attacks, most feel that they have to go on trying: that they cannot leave the babies alone for more than a few minutes at a time. Recent research suggests that they are right. Babies don't stop having colic attacks because people try to comfort them, but they scream a lot less (though they may grumble more) than babies who are left on their own. In fact some of the sessions parents remember as three hours of solid screaming turn out to have been three hours of misery and hard work for them but thanks to that hard work, only half an hour's screaming and two-and-a-half hours grizzle-moaning for their baby.

Sometimes your various ministrations obviously interrupt your baby's misery, and if they do, it's worth repeating them – perhaps in a regular cycle such as walk-and-rock; offer a suck; rub the tummy; walk-and-rock – so that a lot of interruptions reduce the sum total of screams. Sometimes nothing you do makes more than a minimal practical difference, but even then, if you listen to the note of sheer despair that develops if you put him down, it seems likely that your baby is aware when someone is (or isn't) there for him and trying to help. The more you can organize other aspects of life so you are as free as possible during the bad hours, the less stressful they will be. Ready-to-microwave meals are no extravagance at a time like this, and no real friend will hold it against you if you leave the phone to your answering machine. But these hours will be stressful all the same, so the more you can share them the better. Taking strict turns – 30 minutes on and 30 minutes off – works for some couples and is something you could ask of a rota of good friends if you're on your own. Putting the baby in his pram the moment he starts to scream and going out for a long walk helps other parents (and some of their babies) and so does putting on loud music (to compete with the sound) and dancing with the baby in a carrier so he gets rocked and the adult gets exercised... And remember: however awful the colic may be (and it may be very awful indeed) it will not harm your baby, or last for longer than 12 weeks at the most.

LEARNING FROM EACH OTHER

Some babies are much more difficult to care for than others – that's fairly obvious to anyone who's spent time with more than two. But what's less obvious is that it is more difficult for some adults to look after certain babies happily than it would be for others. Choosing your baby's temperament is even less of a possibility than choosing his or her sex: you take what you get. But what you get will make a difference to the ease or difficulty with which you settle into being this particular baby's mother or father – or grandparent or caregiver, come to that. This may be a "kind" of baby you find easy to understand, sympathize with and handle so that he or she stays on a reasonably even keel, or a "kind" of baby who needs handling in a way that does not come at all naturally to you.

All healthy newborn babies have many characteristics and behaviours in common, of course, so they are much more like each other than they are different. But even at the very beginning of neonatal life, that does not mean that a baby is a baby is a baby, and people who are "good with babies" can cope equally easily with all. A baby is an individual who is genetically unique and has already had a unique set of experiences in the womb, during birth and after it. These things all interact with each other to play a part in how he or she settles in to life and reacts to the world – and to caring adults. Those adults are also unique individuals, with years and years of experiences behind them (as babies and children as well as adults), all playing a part in complex expectations about what babies in general and this baby in particular should be like and in how they react to him or her.

If your expectations of the baby you have been waiting for are a reasonably close match to the reality of the baby you have, and the ways of handling that come "naturally" to you happen to suit him, the interaction between you will be relatively smooth and easy from the beginning. But if these things do not match – even clash – you and the baby will have to do much more adjusting to each other. Suppose, for example, that this is your second baby and that his older brother was a calm, even placid, infant who thrived on lots of stimulation and rough and tumble play. You will probably start off by handling the new baby as you handled the first – that, after all, is the kind of parenting your first child taught you – and if his reactions are similar all will be well. But if he happens to be a particularly sensitive and jumpy baby, who is terrified by anything fiercer than a gentle cuddle, your initial interaction will not be at all comfortable. Both of you will have to learn. His behaviour will affect your handling, teaching you to be more gentle; your handling will affect his behaviour, teaching him to be more relaxed.

At this very early age you have to try to care for your baby in ways which suit him now while allowing for the fact that some of his most extreme behaviours may be reactions to prenatal and birth experiences and may therefore change when he has settled down. You have

Do whatever it takes to keep him happy now, but don't assume that's what he'll need forever. New babies settle and need space to change.

to accept him for what he is today but leave it open to him to be quite different next month or next year. An energetic, busy mother and outgoing athletic father may make tremendous efforts to slow down and adjust their handling, even their lifestyle, to suit their jumpy son, but in doing so they may get so used to thinking of the baby as "nervy" or "highly strung" that they go on treating him extra carefully long after he has matured to a point where he is ready for more robust handling. If their minds are closed to the possibility of the baby changing, they may quite forget to offer him noisy toys and rough and tumble play at six months and may try too hard to protect him from bumps and falls when he learns to walk at around a year. That little boy may have real problems asserting his independence and autonomy when he is a toddler.

So whatever your baby is like now, handle him in the ways which seem to keep him happy and calm but try not to stick any labels on him. You will affect him and he will affect you; the interaction between you will play a part in forming the person he becomes, but what sort of person he will eventually be, nobody can know. That is part of the excitement of rearing a new human being.

Different "kinds" of new baby are listed here as part of useful babylore but not as part of science. Research on infant temperaments does not even attempt to group and categorize individuals before four months at the earliest and many of these typologies will have disintegrated by then as newborns become settled babies. But in the meantime, anyone experienced in infant care or observation will recognize these as common deviations from conventional expectations of tiny babies and therefore as potentially stressful for parents.

Babies who don't enjoy being held

Whatever their other characteristics most small babies revel in warm, close physical contact with adults. When a "cuddly" baby is feeling miserable, jumpy or extra-wakeful, you will often find the answer in holding and hugging, stroking and singing or jiggling and dancing. And when you cannot do any of those things you may be able to give him similar security by wrapping him up or carrying him in a sling.

"Uncuddly" babies seem to reject, even to resent, the physical constriction of enfolding arms or shawls. They do not want to drop their heavy heads confidingly onto adult shoulders or to tuck their feet snugly into adult curves. Far from relaxing them, restriction makes them furious.

Babies who don't like being held usually revel in a different kind of interaction, preferring eye contact to cuddling contact, talking to hugging. If your baby tries to escape your holding arms don't retire with wounded feelings:
■ Try putting him on a bed or rug and sitting over him so that he can study your face while you talk to him. He wants to look at you and he may start smiling and "talking back" to you rather early.
■ If you long to stroke the creases in his pudgy wrists and kiss the dimples in the small of his back, do it while he is in his bouncing cradle or on his changing mat so that he can accept your sensual pleasure in him, without feeling imprisoned. He will also be delighted if you will play with his fingers, bicycle his legs and blow raspberries against his tummy.

■ Cuddly babies don't only want body contact: they need eye and voice as well. Uncuddly babies need holding as well as looking and listening. Over a few months your baby will come to enjoy every kind of contact you offer him. But in these very first weeks, recognizing his bias towards one or the other may ease your life – and his.

Babies who never seem happy Just as there are adults who always look on the black side of everything, so there are babies who are inclined to the miseries. Babies like these usually take a long time – weeks perhaps – to settle happily into patterns of being soundly and comfortably asleep, awake and ravenous, full, awake and happy and then asleep again. They behave as if little bits of all those states stayed jumbled up together, keeping their behaviour unpredictable and preventing them from settling down to enjoy life.

A baby like this may seem tired and fretful but still not be able to relax enough to go to sleep. He whimpers and dozes his way through the afternoon and then is irritably hungry but not joyful about sucking. He is probably slow and difficult to feed. When the feeding is over he is awake but not very sociable. He soon gets tired of being held; does not seem to take much notice of being talked to but is not pleased to be returned to his cot. He probably wakes often.

Such a baby may gain weight more slowly than most and be slow to start smiling or playing with his hands. Often he even looks unhappy. He is the opposite of those "bonny babies" on the TV ads.

A baby you cannot make happy is very depressing. Like the baby who cries without apparent reason he will tend to make you feel inadequate as a parent. If his miseries go on for very long you will probably feel put-upon too because you will be lavishing love and care on a baby who seems to give nothing in return. While these feelings are very natural, helping your baby to be happier depends on keeping them at bay. Don't let yourself feel criticized by his unhappiness. It is life outside the womb that your baby does not like very much, not you. You must stay on his side or you will not be able to offer the warm, gentle, patient attention which will, eventually, help him to feel happier. Work to get him to look at you, listen to you, smile at you. Once you get him to the stage where he responds, the worst of his and your miseries will be over. As well as loving the baby whether you get any response or not, try all the suggestions for comforting crying babies (see p.114) and especially:

■ See that the baby gets plenty of milk, as much as he will willingly take whenever he seems to want it.

■ See if the baby is happier with a great deal of contact comfort. If he likes being carried around, try using a carrier so that one of you, or anyone else who cares for him, can carry him most of the time he is awake for a few weeks.

■ Limit the changes in his life until he seems much happier with what he is already experiencing. Don't, for example, try a new baby hammock or even a first drink of fruit juice until he has stopped being so miserable.

Jumpy babies All newborns can be startled by loud noises, turn away from bright lights and throw up their arms and cry if they feel they are going to be dropped. Jumpy babies take this kind of behaviour to extremes.

They may startle and cry, tremble and pale at quite low-grade stimuli. They seem to be frightened of almost everything, and perhaps they are. Perhaps it is life outside the safe, warm, dark haven of the womb which frightens them.

A jumpy baby over-reacts to every kind of stimulation, whether it comes from inside him or from outside. Hunger takes him rapidly into a frenzy of desperate crying. His own jerks and twitches stop him relaxing into sleep. Picking him up makes him tense; putting him down makes him jump. Any change in his surroundings, however slight it may be, alerts and may alarm him. With this kind of baby it isn't enough to take the telephone out of the room, even its ringing in the next room may be enough to make him jump.

The baby is not going to learn not to be frightened by being frightened. His nervous system is not going to become better able to accept minor shocks by being shocked. He is only going to become calmer by a combination of maturing and gentle handling that lets him find less and less in daily life to upset him. Caring for a jumpy baby can be a real challenge and if you see it that way, it can even be enjoyable. Set yourself to get through each day, or each bit of a day, without ever doing anything or letting anything happen which startles the baby or makes him cry. Aim to keep the stimulation which the baby receives below his tolerance level while he matures enough to be able to accept more stimulation happily:

■ Never hurry when you are handling the baby. When you pick him up, for example, he needs due warning so that his muscles can adjust to the change of position. When you carry him he needs you to move slowly and smoothly, supporting his head so that it does not wobble and never letting him feel insecurely held.

■ Keep handling to a minimum. For example, a jumpy baby will probably hate being bathed and should be simply "topped and tailed" until he is calmer. He will probably hate bumpy pram rides and wide open spaces, too, though he may actually enjoy going in the car.

■ Cut down on physical stimulation by wrapping, being careful not to make him too hot. Changes of position and being moved from one place to another will be far less worrying for him if he is properly wrapped up (see p.116). The wrappings will provide a protective cocoon between him and the outside world.

■ Make sure that everyone who handles the baby is quiet and gentle. You want him to discover that the world and the people in it are safe. A jolly uncle with good intentions and a loud laugh can frighten a jumpy baby in a way that makes him want to retreat even more from his new world. Protect him; he has plenty of time for learning to make social contacts.

Sleepy babies Babies who seem to have an almost unlimited capacity for sleep probably feel just as unready for life outside the womb as do miserable or jumpy babies. But they react to it quite differently: instead of protesting or recoiling they avoid life by staying asleep.

A sleepy baby is "no trouble". He makes almost no demands and probably has to be woken up for most of his feeds. It is often difficult to persuade him to stay awake for long enough to suck very much at a time and once he has sucked himself back to sleep he may be unwakeable. He does not seem to care very much about his surroundings or parents. He seldom cries for long but he seldom seems particularly happy either. He is playing a sleepy, neutral game.

Although the baby's lack of responsiveness may disappoint you, this is a comparatively easy "type" of baby to cope with. While he is so sleepy, you can be regaining your strength and collecting your wits in readiness for the active parenthood which will come when the baby matures a little. Meanwhile:

■ Make sure that the baby wakes up enough to eat. Occasionally an exceptionally sleepy baby who is being fed on demand fails to gain as much weight as he should because he does not demand as much food as his body needs. If you have to wake him for feeds then of course there is no harm in waking him to suit your convenience, but make sure that you do so at least every four hours and add in a couple of extra feeds if his sleepiness means that he only sucks for five minutes at a time.

■ Don't let the baby sleep through a 12-hour night from the beginning, even if he seems to want to do so. That is too many hours without water, quite apart from the food itself. And if you are nursing, it is too many hours without stimulation for your breasts. Wake him at your bedtime and first thing in the morning and bless the fact that he probably will not wake you in the small hours.

■ Don't take the baby's sleepy isolation for granted. In other words, don't let his willingness to be shut away in his cot for hours lead you to *expect* him to behave like that. Give him lots of opportunities for sociable cuddles and talk. Try to get him interested in looking at things and being talked to. If he is fast asleep on your lap after two minutes, it is fair enough to put him back to bed, but try again to play with him at the next feed. You want him to realize, gradually, that being awake is fun.

Wakeful babies   Babies vary in the amount of sleep they need, right from the beginning of their lives. Most babies will sleep for something like 16 hours in the 24 to start with. Very sleepy ones may sleep for 22 hours in every 24. A really wakeful baby may never sleep for more than 12 hours and may seldom do that sleeping in stretches of more than two hours at a time.

A wakeful baby is not usually especially miserable or especially jumpy. There is nothing "keeping him awake", he just does not sleep for the number of hours we expect of very small babies. He will take a feed and drop off to sleep immediately. But an hour or two later he is awake again, not because he is ready for more food but just because he has stopped being asleep. Because he spends so much time awake he will probably show more interest in the things around him at an earlier age than most babies. His development in every area may be rapid because he is spending extra time looking, listening and learning.

This is not the kind of baby you can care for in short concentrated bursts of time and then ignore in between. He makes himself felt almost all day and often for a good deal of the night, too. How you react to him will probably depend at least partly on how much else you have to do. A jealous older child, for example, will suffer much more from a very wakeful baby than from one who naps in a corner for much of the toddler's day. The main problem with a wakeful baby is that he is spending many more hours awake than you (or anyone else) expect, and at an age when it is difficult to find entertainment for him.

Remind yourself that he would sleep if he needed to; try to accept his wakefulness, and don't feel that he "ought" to be asleep. If you try to make him behave as other babies do, you will waste a lot of time tucking him away for naps he does not want, and you will make him miserable too because he will be bored and lonely.

There's no good reason why babies should come first.

Comforting a baby who keeps crying; trying to keep things smooth for a baby who's jumpy; entertaining one who can neither sleep nor read a book... this sounds like parenthood from hell. I don't see why I should abandon the adult lifestyle I've worked for and earned for the sake of one demanding mite, or why everyone should try to make me feel guilty if I don't. I'm not even sure it would be good for the baby to have everything her own way. Spoiling her wouldn't do her any favours because it's a rough world out there; the sooner she learns to cope with it the better.

Some of parenthood *is* hellish – but only some. The same baby who right now ruins all your evenings by crying may one day make all your mornings feel like Christmas.

Having a baby *does* make a difference to life. Few people are prepared (maybe preparation is impossible); many have patches of panic; most adapt. It's rare to meet a parent who wishes he or she hadn't had this individual child, though a few wish they'd decided not to have any.

Trying to meet your newborn baby's needs isn't just for her it's for you too, because a more contented baby almost always means less stressed-out parents. Suppose you really didn't *try* – just left your baby alone to cry between feeds – could you get on with enjoying that adult lifestyle? The truth is that it's her existence that disrupts your life and makes demands on you, not her behaviour; it's parenthood rather than your child that's bugging you.

If you really didn't try to meet newborn needs as best you can – by delegation if not in person – you'd have reason to feel guilty. This is your child, after all; you're responsible for her and she's dependent on you. But the really tough part for parents, including you by the sound of it, is trying and not succeeding. It's when you feel rejected – maybe even feel that your baby doesn't like you – that you feel like giving up and leaving her to get on with it. If she doesn't love you, why should you put yourself out for her?

But that's the tit-for-tat of a child being bullied by another child and the simple answer, of course, is that you aren't a child being bullied by another, you're an adult, a parent, caring for a tiny baby who's going to love you more than anyone ever has; but doesn't know how to do that yet and needs to learn from being loved by you.

Nothing you can do to a new baby can "spoil" her in the sense of over-indulging her. Nurturing her now is the best possible preparation for future adversity and not a matter of giving her her way. She doesn't know she's a separate person from you yet, much less a person with a will of her own and a desire to pit it against yours.

Older children are often as fascinating as they're fascinated. But black and white patterns are irresistible to newborns.

NEWBORN PLAY

Although newborn babies cannot handle toys or take part in games, even the youngest of them can certainly get bored and lonely especially if they spend more hours awake than adults want to spend caring for them.

You may need to find different ways of keeping the baby company. Park his pram or Moses basket close beside the most available adult and make sure all grown-up members of the household get into the habit of stopping for quick chats. Have him beside you while you are phoning or watching television, and find easy ways of carrying him. A sling will let you do simple jobs in the house as well as take him around shops and other interesting places.

Being carried around is perfect entertainment for a wakeful newborn. The rhythm of an adult's movements is as good as a massage or a dance and the panorama of life that he sees and hears as you stroll round the garden or up the street is as enthralling as a movie. Try some variations on the obvious ways of carrying your baby. In particular, when you are carrying him for fun and to show him things, try holding him with his back to you.

New babies inevitably spend a lot of hours lying on their backs and get less bored if they do it in various places. Later on it's a good idea to arrange different places where your baby can lie on the floor – a spare pram mattress or changing mat to carry from room to room is useful. Right now, though, you and he probably both feel that he's safer in a bed – pram, Moses basket or carrycot – that can be moved from one interesting place to another. Your baby will not see the detail of anything that is more than 25 centimetres away from him, but he will nevertheless enjoy sunbeam or lattice-blind patterns on a nearby wall; a bright curtain that is gently moving; the shapes of a big houseplant or the moving leaves of an outdoor tree or bush.

Interesting things to look at from close up are the nearest approximation to toys for this age group. Although conventional strings of pram toys and mobiles are fine, your baby will probably be far more riveted by black and white patterns on special cards or first books, tucked into the mattress on the side to which he turns his head; mobiles that are designed to be viewed from underneath (by him rather than by you!) and everyday objects of interesting shapes that you hang from a play frame or cot-gym. Change these things often so that your baby always has something new to look at.

She's studied the circle pattern, now she's focused on the checkerboard and is even beginning to touch what she is looking at.

HEAVY HEADS AND REFLEXES

There is much to learn about looking after very new babies and because they have not yet settled down, caring for them is a very demanding job. It is easy to get so involved in daily care that you find yourself treating your child like a very precious kind of object rather than a developing person, a new human being. But your baby is human and your baby is developing – every moment of every day. Don't let night feeds and wet nappies take up so much of your attention that you miss the fascinating changes that are taking place, the signs of your baby beginning to grow up.

Postures and head control

Newborns are very scrunched-up looking creatures. Whatever position you put your baby in she will curl herself inwards with her body taking up its position in relation to a head so large and heavy compared with the rest of her that it acts as an anchor and a pivot.

Until your baby's body and limbs grow a little so that her head becomes relatively lighter, and until she can get some control over the muscles of her neck, the baby's voluntary movements will be restricted. At the beginning she can lift that head a little and she will always try to turn it to avoid smothering, but movements of her limbs are restricted by her curled position while the fact that her head is always turned to one side prevents her from seeing things which are directly above her.

A baby's muscle control starts from the top and moves gradually downwards. When you hold her against your shoulder in the first hours after birth, she rests her head against you. If you hold her away from you and do not support her neck for her, that head will simply flop. Within a week she can force those neck muscles to lift her head away for a second or two. A few days later she practises controlling her head so continually that whenever you hold her it feels as if she were deliberately bumping her head against you: effort-flop-effort-flop, again and again. By the time a full-term baby is three to four weeks old she can usually balance her own head for several seconds provided the adult who is holding her keeps absolutely still. But she still needs your supporting hand whenever you carry her and especially when you lift her or put her down.

This scrunched-up creature with an over-sized head and a too big skin is not going anywhere and isn't happy trying. But as the knees push and the legs straighten it's easy to believe that false crawling is the real thing.

Newborn reflexes   During the first week of life, this baby, whose muscles are still so incompetent even in balancing her head, exhibits some remarkably mature-looking behaviours which sometimes fool parents into believing that they have produced an infant who will crawl or even walk at a few weeks of age. These are not voluntary or controlled movements, though, they are reflex behaviours which will die out over a few days and then be re-learned months later as new accomplishments at the appropriate stage of development.

False crawling   If you put her on her stomach, the baby's naturally curled-up position leads her to flex legs and arms so that she looks as if she were about to crawl off. She may even "scrabble" so that she wrinkles the rug she is lying on. The position will be unlearned when the baby becomes able to uncurl herself and lie flat.

False walking   If you hold the baby upright with the soles of her feet just touching a firm surface, she will take quite deliberate "steps", placing one foot after another while you support her weight. Once again this behaviour will quickly drop out of her repertoire. By the time she is a week old she will simply sag if you hold her upright.

False clinging   In the first days of life a baby's hand grip is incredibly strong. In theory (and in some experimenters' practice), you could hang her up by her hands and she would cling on tightly enough not to fall. But don't try it. The ability passes between one day and the next. You might choose the next for your experiment.

But although the baby's extraordinary strength of grip passes off, some degree of reflex hand grip remains. If you put your finger or a rattle into her closed fist, her hand will grip itself around it. When you try to remove it, her fist will close even more tightly in a reflex attempt to hang on. This reaction to the feel of a grippable object in her palm will remain through all the weeks that must pass before the baby is ready to learn to take hold of objects on purpose. So hanging on with her hands is not something which, like crawling or walking, she has to unlearn and then learn all over again. In this instance the reflex reaction eventually gives way to deliberate action.

The reflex response which leads a baby to hang on to whatever she finds in her hands may be left over from pre-history when our ape-like ancestors' children kept themselves safe by clinging to their mothers. Today's human babies cannot cling on to an adult's clothes with their hands, arms and legs, as baby monkeys cling to their

mothers' belly fur. Yet they seem to want to. Almost all babies are happiest and most relaxed when they are carried in a face-to-face position and older ones like to have their arms around the adult's neck. When new babies are not being carried, being closely wrapped up, or even having a piece of warm textured material laid across a bare chest and stomach as if they were pressed against a warm mother, usually calms the fretful and pleases the calm.

The Moro response If your baby, who would like to cling to you, feels that she is about to be dropped, she produces a violent and obviously distressed reflex which is called the "Moro response". You will see it if you jerk her arms while you are holding her hands: her arms will snatch up at yours and her legs curve convulsively upwards as if seeking a body around which to clasp themselves. If you put her down carelessly, so that your hands start to release her before she feels the firm security of the mattress, you'll see an even more violent version: she will throw out both her arms and legs and then flex them convulsively; her head will jerk back because the reflex movements have upset her head control; she will probably cry out in fear.

There's no fur for your baby to grab to save himself from a fall, but the Moro response is a reminder to adults that he feels insecure. Like other reflexes, the Moro response has lost its direct usefulness to the baby because, unlike her furry ancestors, she does not have the muscle power to save herself from a fall by grabbing hold of something. But the response is still indirectly useful. Every time your baby reacts in this violently startled way you will know that you have handled her too roughly, too unexpectedly or without taking enough care to support her heavy head. Moro responses are a hint to parents to take more care.

SENSES AND SENSATIONS

Each of your baby's five senses is in working order from the moment of birth if not from before. There may not be much smelling or tasting in the womb, and there is probably too little friction for much sense of touch, but babies certainly hear before birth, and see, at least to the extent of differentiating degrees of light and darkness. But while your brand new baby does not have to learn how to see, to hear, to sense touch through the skin, or even to smell or taste, he does have to learn to interpret those sensory messages. After all, although he can see differences between one object and another, he has no experience to tell him that an object that looks like this is a face, a breast, a teddy bear or his own hand. As soon as a baby comes out of the womb, all his senses are bombarded with stimuli and learning through the senses goes on from that moment.

Since new babies cannot tell us what they feel or think about things we have to make deductions from their reactions to them. Researchers have developed ingenious ways of assessing a baby's thoughts or feelings about particular stimuli without his direct co-operation, and of measuring those responses so that babies can be compared with each other, or with themselves over time. Given a choice of things to look at, for example, a baby will look first or look for longer, or turn his eyes further to see, the sight he "prefers". Given a headset and two recorded voices linked to a dummy and the different rates at which it is sucked, babies as young as 48 hours learn to choose to hear their mother's voice rather than a stranger's. Often we cannot say more than that babies respond with pleasure to certain kinds of sensory stimulation and with distress to others, but even that simple information contributes greatly to our understanding.

Touching and being touched Babies do not only enjoy touch, they need it. Skin-to-skin contact comforts and relaxes newborns and also produces deeper breathing and therefore more oxygenation. New and older babies react with calm pleasure to warm, soft, firm pressure, especially up the front surface of their bodies – a precursor, presumably, of the hugs we all enjoy. Newborn skin is acutely sensitive to texture, moisture, pressure and temperature. Your baby will certainly be aware of differences in the softness of clothing fabrics; the tightness of a nappy around his tummy or the normal variations in the temperature of his bath water. From the first day of life onwards, a baby may be distressed by the exposed feeling of nakedness – however warm the air around him – and if he is distressed he may be comforted by the feeling of any textured fabric laid over his abdomen.

Touch elicits some newborn reflexes too. Babies react to the feel of an object in their fists by gripping onto it, to a stroking touch on the cheek by rooting and to a solid surface under the soles of their feet by stepping movements.

For many years it was assumed that infants' reactions to pain – to having a heel jabbed with a lancet to get blood for testing, for example – were a matter of reflex. Indeed, as late as 1986, American surgeons thought that infants as old as 15 months were incapable of feeling pain. A comprehensive medical review proved otherwise. Its conclusion – that newborn responses to pain are "similar to but greater than those observed in adult subjects" – is generally accepted by medical authorities although it is not always acted upon. If a procedure would hurt you, it will hurt your baby.

Smelling and tasting

Newborn babies seem to share adult reactions to smells, turning away, with disgusted expressions, from the smell of rotten eggs; looking pleased at the smell of honey. In some respects, though, their ability to differentiate between one smell and another far surpasses ours. If a breast pad worn by his mother is put to one side of a baby's head with a breast pad used by another mother placed on the other side, the baby will "choose" the mother-smell, turning his head to that side in 75% of trials. In rather the same way, babies react as adults do to various taste categories, screwing up their faces, even crying, in response to bitter, acid or sour tastes. But a baby is far more sensitive to some tastes and degrees of taste than we are. He can differentiate accurately between plain, slightly sweetened and very sweet water, for example. We know this because experimenters showed that while babies will suck bottles containing any one of these, they will suck longer and harder as the sweetness increases. No wonder it is so difficult to control the sugar-intake of older children.

Hearing, listening and making sounds

Babies can sense and differentiate sound vibrations while they are still in the womb and they react with soothed pleasure after birth to recordings of sounds which they have lived with before it: not only mothers' heartbeats, but particular pieces of music or television theme tunes which they shared with her, willy-nilly, in the final weeks of pregnancy. In contrast, loud, sudden sounds will make your baby jump. The sharper the sound the more extreme will be his reaction. Thunder rolling round the house will not bother him nearly as much as a plate smashing on a hard floor. Just as clearly as he dislikes these sounds, the baby enjoys (or at least is soothed and relaxed by) repetitive rhythmical sounds. He will enjoy music, but he will enjoy the rhythmical pounding of a drum or the steady whirr of your vacuum cleaner just as much – as far as we can tell.

Voices, perhaps familiar from life in the womb, are the sounds your baby prefers: she's listening even though she's not looking at you.

But while any baby with normal hearing clearly hears all these sounds, the ones to which he listens, with obvious concentration, are the sounds of people talking. He has a built-in interest in voices and in voice-like sounds. Because they come from the adults to whom he must attach himself, the caretakers without whom he cannot survive, he is programmed to pay attention to them.

Unless you are on the look-out for it, you may not notice how much your baby enjoys your voice during these first weeks. At this stage his looking and listening systems are still separate. He listens without looking for the source of the sound he hears, so he often listens to your voice without looking at you. If you watch him carefully, though, you will see his reactions to your loving prattle. If he is crying, he will often stop as you approach the cot, talking. He does not need to see you or to feel your touch first. If he is lying still when you begin to speak to him, he will start to move excitedly. If he is kicking, he will stop and freeze to attention, concentrating on your voice. When you talk, your baby listens; when you talk directly to him, his heart rate goes up. And as we saw at the beginning of this chapter, if he is given a way of choosing whether to hear your voice or that of a stranger, he will almost always choose yours.

It will be a long time before the baby can understand your words but from the first days of his life he will react to your tones. When you talk softly and caressingly the baby reacts with pleasure, but if you speak sharply to an older child while handling him, he will probably cry, while if something should make you cry out in fear while you are holding him, he will be instantly panic-stricken.

Your baby's only deliberate sounds during these early days are crying. It may seem to you that all the crying sounds the same, but in fact there is a repertory of different cries which represent different states and intensities of feeling, and you will probably find yourself reacting differently to each. When the types of cry are analyzed by sound spectrograph you can actually see differences of tone, duration and rhythm between them. A baby's pain cry, for example, has a particular intensity and a unique rhythm. When you hear that cry you will probably find that you are thinking of nothing but getting to your baby – fast.

A hunger cry is quite different. It has particular patterns of sound and pause which are the same for all babies but quite different from any of your baby's other cries. If you are breast-feeding, that particular cry may start the let-down reflex so that your milk starts to flow even as you get up to go to the baby. If you are bottle-feeding, the cry probably directs you to the kitchen to start warming the bottle. Hearing that cry, you will have no doubt at all that the baby needs you, but you probably will not have the sense of urgency that comes with a pain cry.

Fear sounds different again. The fear cry is a sound of pure desolation and is highly infectious. By the time you reach your baby your own pulse will be racing and adrenaline will be flooding through your body, readying it to fight any danger to protect him.

Your own feelings are the best guide to reacting appropriately when your baby cries. If you find yourself at the cot side before you've had time to remember the wait-a-bit policy you'd just agreed with your partner, the chances are that something you heard in the baby's cry made that the right thing to do, even if you cannot describe that "something", even to him.

By the time he is around four weeks old your baby will begin to make other sounds besides crying. He will make small gurgly googly noises when he is relaxed after a feed and little tense whimpery sounds when he is building up towards hunger cries. He is moving towards the next stage in communication – cooing – and a new kind of crying – grumbling.

Seeing, looking and focusing Babies can see, clearly and with discrimination, from the moment of birth. If your baby seems to spend a lot of waking time gazing blankly into space or looking towards a brightly lit window or at lights or blowing curtains, this is not because babies are incapable of seeing anything more detailed, but because you do not put

Your baby will study anything interesting that's put within that short visual range, and patterns are second only to faces.

anything else within easy visual range.

A new baby can focus his eyes so as to see things clearly when they are at different distances. He can, but he seldom does because until his eye muscles strengthen, it is very difficult for him. The easy focusing distance for a new baby is about 20cm−25cm (8in−10in) from the bridge of the nose. At that precise distance he can see clearly but objects which are further away are blurred. If he lies in his cot with nothing within his focal distance to look at, he will look up at whatever he can perceive through the distance-blur. Brightness and movement (as every short-sighted person knows) are the two things that will be visible to him.

If, armed with this information, you deliberately put things close enough to your baby's eyes for him to see them clearly, he will "choose" to pay attention to much more subtle stimuli than brightness or movement. In fact he will not even choose the simple shapes and primary colours you might expect. You can test his "choices" for yourself by holding pairs of objects where he can clearly see them. He will look at a simple circular red rattle if there is nothing else close enough for him to see, but if you add a sheet of paper with a complicated black and white pattern on it, drawn in lines at least three millimetres wide, he will turn his attention to that instead. He will look at a simple cube, but add a more complex shape such as a toast rack and he will look at that. He is programmed to give his attention to complex patterns and shapes because he must learn a complex visual world.

His fixed focal distance is not a matter of random chance. On the contrary, it is exactly the distance which separates his face from yours when you hold and talk to him or when you are breast-feeding. Just as voices are the most important things for him to listen to so faces are the most important things for him to look at and he is innately programmed to study them intently whenever he can. It may even be that the blurring out of more distant objects is developmentally useful to him as it helps him to concentrate on those vital faces undistracted by other things.

New babies do not know that people are people so your baby cannot know, when he studies your face, that what he is looking at is you. He simply gives his full visual attention to any face available, or, failing a real face, to anything he sees which is face-like. His criteria of "face-like" have been studied in detail. If an object or a picture has a hairline, eyes, a mouth and a chin-line, the baby will react to it as a face. If you watch his eyes you will see that he starts at the top, scans that hairline, moves his gaze slowly down to the chin-line and then back to the eyes. Once he is looking the face (or pretend-face) in the eye, he will go on for much longer than he will look at anything else.

While it is interesting to try out this reaction by showing your baby a simple sketch of a face, or a paper plate with a face drawn on it, looking at real faces is much more valuable to him. When he has learned enough about faces you will get your reward for patiently giving him yours to study. One day soon that intent scanning will end as usual at your eyes but it will culminate in his first overwhelmingly social gesture to the outside world. It will end with his first smile.

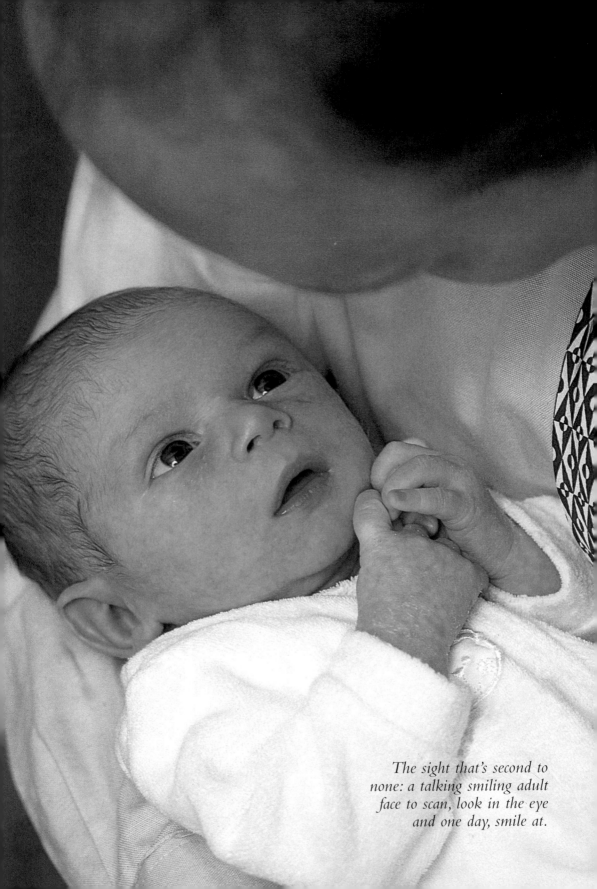

The sight that's second to none: a talking smiling adult face to scan, look in the eye and one day, smile at.

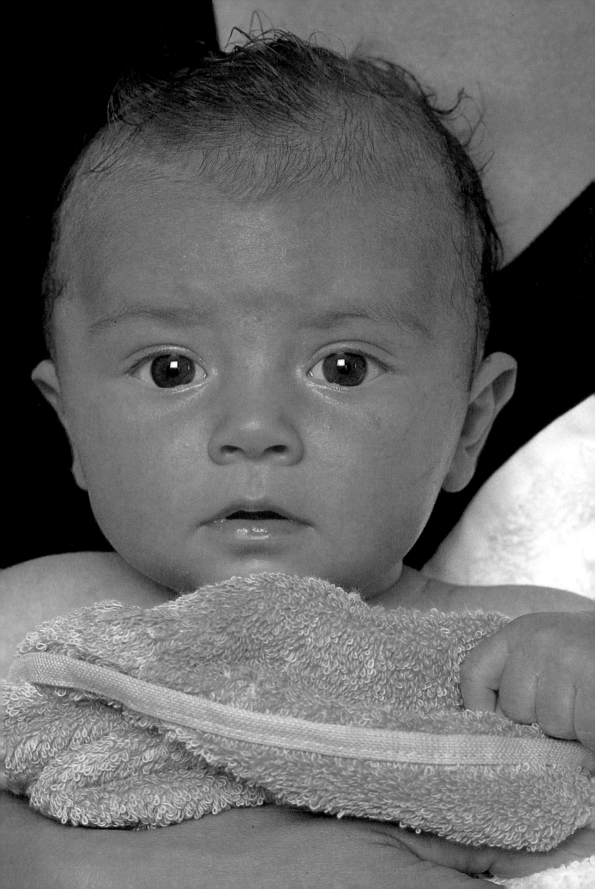

THE
SETTLED BABY

The first six months

One day you will find that you have stopped regarding your baby as an unpredictable and therefore rather alarming novelty, and have begun instead to think of him as a person with tastes, preferences and characteristics of his own. When that happens you will know that he has moved on from being a "newborn" and has got himself settled into life. Your baby may be two weeks or two months old when that moment comes and from his point of view it does not matter whether it is sooner or later. It will matter to you, though, and to everyone else who is involved in caring for him.

A settled baby is a manageable proposition. If you feel he's a little devil, at least he is a little devil you know. You can tell how he likes to be handled even if it is not the way you would choose to handle him. You know what to expect from him even if it is the worst; know what frightens him even if it is almost everything. Above all, you can tell when he is happy, however seldom that may be, and when he is miserable, even if that is almost always. So once your baby is settled you know what you are up against. Instead of trying to survive from hour to hour, get through another day, avoid thinking about another week, you can begin to work and plan for reasonable compromises between his needs and those of everyone else.

The baby will make it increasingly clear that apart from food, his prime need is for the people who are his constant caretakers. Your love for him may still be problematic, but his growing attachment to you is a matter of survival; his assurance that you will love him and therefore take care of him. As these first few weeks pass, people become increasingly interesting to him. He finds faces fascinating. Every time yours comes within his short focusing range he studies it intently from hairline to mouth, finishing by gazing into your eyes. He listens intently to your voice, kicking a little when he hears it, or freezing into immobility as he tries to locate its source. Soon he will turn his eyes and his head to see the person who is talking. If you pick him up, he stops crying. If you will cuddle and walk him, he usually remains content. Whatever else he likes or needs, he clearly likes and needs you. You can begin to have some confidence in yourselves as the parents of this new human being.

But in case these settled responses to your devoted care are not enough to keep you caring, the baby has a trump card still to play: smiling. One day he is studying your face in his intent and serious way and he scans down to your mouth and back to your eyes as usual. But as he gazes, his face slowly begins to flower into the small miracle of a wide toothless grin that totally transforms it. For most parents, grandparents and carers, that's it. He is the most beautiful baby in the world even if his head is still crooked, and the most lovable baby in the world however often he wakes in the night. Few adults can resist a baby's new smiling. Even the most reluctantly dutiful visitors have been known to sneak back to the cotside to try for one more smile, all for themselves...

When the baby smiles it looks like love, but he cannot truly love anyone yet because he does not know one person from another. His early smiles are an insurance policy against neglect and for pleasant social attention. The more he smiles and gurgles and waves his fists at people, the more they will smile and talk to him. The more attention people pay him, the more he will respond, tying them ever closer with his throat-catching grins and his heart-rendingly quivery lower lip. His responses create a self-sustaining circle, his smiles leading to your smiles and yours to more from him.

There is no harm in assuming that these enchanting early smiles are meant for you personally. They soon will be. It is through pleasing social interaction with adults who find him rewarding and therefore pay him more attention, that the baby moves on from being interested in people in general to being able to recognize and attach himself to particular ones. By the time he is around three months old it will be clear that he knows you and other adults who are special to him. It is not that he smiles at you and whimpers at strangers – he still smiles at everyone – but that he saves his best signs of favour, the smiliest smiles, for the people he knows best. Week by week he becomes increasingly sociable and increasingly fussy about whom he will socialize with. He is ready to form a passionate and personal emotional tie with somebody and if you are the most central, loving person in his minute world, you are elected. If a baby's mother is available at all, most babies select her for this first love. But the blood-tie doesn't automatically qualify you for the privilege. It has to be earned, not just by being your baby's mother but by mothering him. And mothering does not just mean taking physical care of the baby.

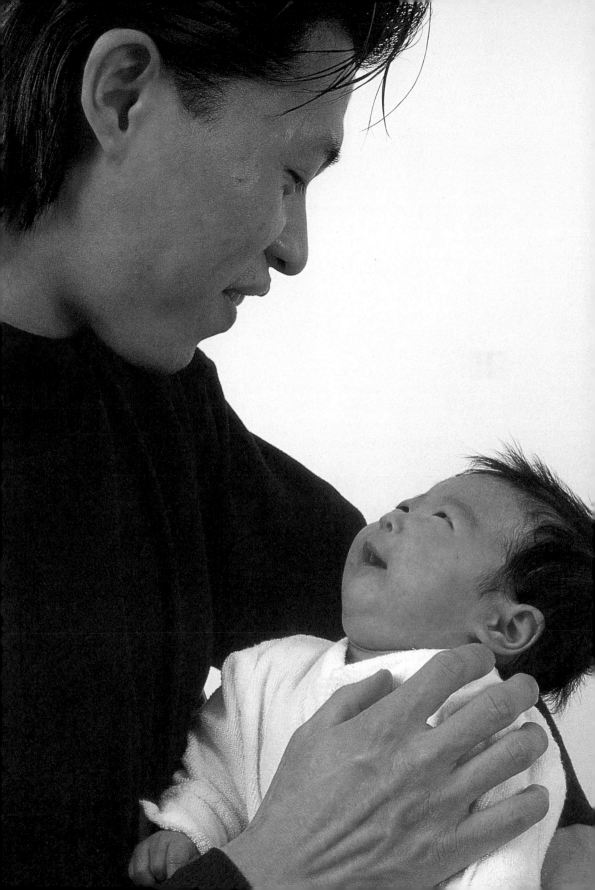

His first love is not cupboard-love, rooted in the pleasures of feeding, even breast-feeding. Babies fall in love with people who mother them emotionally, talking to them, cuddling them, smiling and playing with them. If you had to share your baby's total care with one other person and you handed over all the physical tasks, using your limited time for loving and play, you would keep your prime role in the baby's life. But if you used your time to meet his physical needs, leaving the other person to be his companion and play-mate, it would probably be that companionable adult to whom he became most closely attached. Of course your baby needs good physical care. Of course feeding is his greatest pleasure in life and therefore links physical with emotional care, but your baby doesn't just need someone who'll come and feed him when he's hungry, he needs someone to come when he needs company, someone who notices when he smiles and smiles back, who hears when he "talks", listens and replies. Somebody who plays with him and shows him things, brings little bits of the world for him to see. These are the things which really matter to three-month babies. These are the things which make for love.

Every baby needs at least one special person to attach himself to – and more are better. It is through this first love relationship that he will learn about himself, other people and the world. It is through it that he will experience emotions and learn to cope with them. And it is from the foundation of this baby-love that he will become capable of more grown-up kinds of love; capable, one far-distant day, of giving children of his own the kind of devotion he now needs for himself. Babies who never have a special person, receiving adequate physical care but little emotional response, or being looked after by a succession of caretakers, often do not develop as fast or as far as their innate drive and their potential for personality allow. And the development of babies who are suddenly separated from parenting-people is put at risk. But as long as your baby does have at least one special person, he can make other people special too. His capacity for love is not rationed any more than yours is. The reverse is true. Love creates love.

If you and your partner are fortunate enough to be able to share your baby's care from the beginning, he will probably respond equally to each of you in total (though differently since you are different people) and his emotional life will be both richer and safer for not being vested in one person alone. That does not mean though that you will get equal shares of smiles, or co-operation about stopping crying or going to sleep, on any given day. The baby who has the luxury of two available parents will often play favourites. Most babies start out most relaxed of all with their birth mothers –

perhaps due to long familiarity with their smells, heartbeats and voices, as well as to the bliss of breast-feeding. By four or five months though, fathers, rather especially the father who has not been continually involved in a baby's routine care, may suddenly find himself singled out for favour. When he does come home, or stays home because it is a weekend, his face, his talk and his play strike the baby as fresh and interesting. Because he has not spent the day trying to fit a sufficiency of chores and sanity-preserving adult activities around the baby's needs, he may be able to offer more of the social contact the baby craves.

Once that special relationship is made, sharing your time between the baby and paid outside work will not threaten it or the baby's wellbeing provided that he continues to be – and to feel that he is – your primary concern, and that the care that fills in for yours is enthusiastic and genuinely loving. Sharing your baby's care with your partner, with other relatives and/or with a caregiver whom you pay to act like family, is a modern version of the way babies used to be cared for in extended families in the West, and a Western version of the way they still are cared for in much of the developing world. Don't expect those other people to keep your baby on ice for you, though. He must get on with living and loving in your absence, however much you dread him seeing his first snowfall without you or learning to love somebody else best. The snowfall may happen but won't matter (he won't remember this year's anyway); loving any-body more than you would matter but won't happen. Once babies know their mothers and fathers from everybody else, they go on knowing. And once they love them best, they go on doing that too.

Many women don't want to share their babies with paid work this soon, though, because they passionately enjoy this stage of motherhood. The baby flatters you with his special attentions, making you feel unique, beloved, irreplaceable. He needs you for everything: for adequate physical care but for emotional and intellectual care too: play, toys, help with each successive effort and opportunity to practise each tiny new accomplishment. Whatever the baby becomes able to do, he needs and will want to do it; it is up to you to make it possible for him. Yet despite all this needing, his hour-by-hour care is comparatively easy. He is no longer irrational and incomprehensible as he was when he was newborn, yet he is not awake most of the day and into everything as he will be in the second half of the year. You still get daytime periods of peace and privacy and you can still put the baby on the floor and know that he will be safely there when you next look.

But some women hate it. Instead of taking pleasure in being so much enjoyed and needed, they feel shut in and consumed by the baby's dependence, yearning for at least a little time when he needs nothing practical and nothing emotional either. The continual effort of identifying with his feelings, noticing his needs and padding his journey through the passing days makes them feel drained, and once they begin to feel like that, practical baby care seems easy compared with coping with an infant's loneliness or boredom.

Understanding your own importance is probably the best prevention and the most likely cure. All the vital developments of these months are waiting inside your baby. He has a built-in drive to practise every aspect of being human, from making sounds, using his hands or rolling over, to eating real food or roaring with laughter. But each aspect of his growing up is also in your hands. You can help him develop and learn or you can hinder him by holding yourself aloof. You can keep him happy and busy and learning fast, or leave him to be discontented, bored and learning more slowly.

If you do help him, you and the whole family will gain because the baby will be comparatively cheerful and easy and a pleasure to have around – most of the time. If you refuse to help him, trying to ration your attention, everyone will suffer and you will suffer most of all. The baby will be difficult, fretful and little pleasure to anyone. You will be unhappy because, however much you may resent the fact, your pleasure and his are tied together. If you please him, his happiness will please you and make it easier for you to go on. If you leave him miserable, his misery will depress you and make it more difficult. You may resent his crying; resent the fact that he needs you – again. But ignoring the crying not only condemns him to cry but also condemns you to listen to his crying. So when you try to meet his needs, tune in to him, treat him as he asks to be treated, you do not only do it for him, you do it for yourself, too. Like it or not, you are a family now. You sink or swim together.

Why won't doctors tell?

I knew almost at once that something wasn't right with our second baby, but while the paediatrician at the hospital agrees that "he's having a few problems" she won't specify them and only nods when I do. She wants me to agree that "he's doing quite well really" but sounds as if that's a surprise. When my husband asked straight out, "What is the matter?" she said it's "much too soon to tell" and when I asked her to speculate about his future, she looked quite shocked and told me to "take one day at a time". Why won't they tell us what they know or at least share what they think?

Faced with the devastating discovery that "something's wrong" with their baby, parents almost always feel that breaking the news to them was badly handled. Sometimes parents are told a lot, but too soon and too fast so that, numb with shock, they can't take it in. Sometimes they are told a lot about what's wrong with their baby, but not much about what's right (parents of premature babies often suffer in this way); and sometimes when only part of a problem is obvious – such as a cleft lip – more trouble is taken to explain the unseen cleft palate than the surgery that will correct both. Usually, though, parents are not told enough, even when they are already aware that *something* is wrong.

Telling parents that the baby they have is not the entirely healthy baby they longed for is something doctors dread. Furthermore "the news" is often not clear-cut. Many genetically transmitted diseases, for example, take time to manifest themselves clearly and early signs that alert health professionals to particular possibilities may mean nothing to parents. If a baby is born with a bowel blockage, for instance, cystic fibrosis is a possible cause staff may want to test for. Cystic fibrosis is unlikely to occur to the parents, unless they already know that they are carriers. Their anxiety and attention will be focused on the baby's immediate bowel problem and it is understandable if medical staff prefer not to share the possibility of

chronic disease until or unless test results transform it into a certainty. It is often more helpful to parents, though, if doctors share their experience-based thinking, however speculative it may be.

Sharing is the hallmark of good practice here. You might get it through a full assessment of your baby. A good developmental assessment is a carefully structured opportunity to share knowledge of the baby (you have known him for 40 weeks longer than any doctor after all), observe him together (a good paediatrician can focus your attention on details of your baby's behaviour that you might otherwise not have noticed) and plan for him collaboratively. Professionals and parents are then allies on behalf of the child and at least as focused on what he can do as on what he cannot; focused on the baby as your baby, not as your problem.

A poor assessment may make you feel as if you are taking an examination with your baby as the test paper, though, and leave you still wondering what "they" think of him. If that happens you'll need to go elsewhere for information and support, but finding it will be easier if you have a diagnostic label to start from. There's probably at least a tentative diagnosis on your baby's hospital notes. You are entitled to read these but if the idea of asking for them embarrasses you, see if your own doctor will telephone the paediatrician, get an answer and pass it on to you.

That label is helpful not in itself but as the key to information and people who can be. There are parents' self-help groups, and specialist associations for people with a vast range of disabilities. With that word or phrase as a starting point you may be able to find them through your local reference library or in phone directories and help listings. And if you can get access to the Internet, you will find all that and contact with other individual parents who have been where you are coming from and can do more than any doctor to help you see where you are going.

FEEDING
AND GROWING

Once you and your baby have settled to breast-feeding, the two of you can go anywhere, anytime.

By the time your baby is around two weeks old, you will both have learned a lot about feeding either at the breast or from bottles. Those first confusing days, when neither of you knew quite how to do it, are over, but there may be new kinds of confusion ahead.

The baby wants you to feed her because she cannot feed herself. You want to feed her because you know that she must eat if she is to grow and be healthy. So you are both on the same side and worrying or fighting over feeding is a waste of both your energies and a waste of fun for you both. The fun part is important. If you watch your baby at the beginning of a feed you can see her hunger, and the feeling of the milk going down inside her lessening the hunger pain. You can see that the actual sucking is important to her too. After three or four gulping minutes she settles into a perfect rhythm; a burst of sucks and then a breath and a rest and another burst of sucking. Soon an expression of blissful satisfaction spreads across her face. The rhythm slows a little; the rest pauses get longer, the bursts of sucking shorter. Now she is drunk with milk and pleasure; almost asleep, just giving the odd suck now and again to remind herself that the milk is still there for her.

It all sounds easy. And for some parents with some babies it is easy. If your baby has begun to gain weight (and goes on doing so fairly steadily), is reasonably contented most of the time (or at least tending to become more rather than less so), and is becoming increasingly active and interested when she is awake, you can be sure that there is nothing the matter with her feeding from her point of view. And if feeding her is something you look forward to, and being fed the event she enjoys most, you can skip the next few pages. But it isn't always easy for everybody. Your baby may go on with the unsettled and unsettling behaviour which is typical of newborns for longer than you expect, especially if she was born pre-term or had particular postnatal difficulties. She may produce new and puzzling behaviours over feeding. Or you may find that although the whole feeding business does get easier, you don't find it so easy that you can relax and assume that the baby is doing well.

BREAST-FEEDING: COMMON CONCERNS

Once you and your baby have got up to speed, breast-feeding will have a momentum of its own that keeps it going even when it seems threatened by illness or absence. Right now, though, problems are common and because breast-feeding is vulnerable to your stress, even minor concerns may threaten it.

Resisting the breast   It's not unusual for babies to refuse occasional feeds or be fretful about feeding, but it is unusual for a nursing mother to be able to take that kind of behaviour calmly. A baby who rejects your breast with apparent distaste, fights away from it or will not settle to sucking

Try not to take fussy feeds personally; it's not you he's rejecting.

seems to reject *you*. The more upset she gets the more desperate you are to comfort her, but if she will not accept the basic comfort of your breast, what can you offer? To make matters worse, the crying, the rooting, the attempts to latch her on and moments of sucking, probably let down your milk so that you are dripping all over everything. Your nipples may get sore so that you begin to dread physical pain as well as emotional rejection. If it happens several times in a row do consult your doctor. An infection such as thrush may be making your baby's mouth sore.

More often, though, babies behave like this at the breast because they cannot gulp fast enough to keep up with the first flow of milk and feel they are going to drown, or because they are having trouble breathing through a stuffed up nose while sucking; because they were kept waiting so long that hunger went over the top or because their sucking efforts are not readily rewarded with milk. You may never know exactly what upset this particular feed, or precipitated the troubles that dogged most feeds for weeks.

The easiest way to cope with a one-off occasion is to accept that something has got this feed off to a bad start (even if you've no idea what) and start again. If your partner is present, he could hold the baby out of sight and smell range of your breasts and soothe and cheer her while you mop yourself up and calm down. Then shift to the easiest available setting and position for a feed. If the feed that went wrong was in public, for example, look for some privacy. If your baby always latches on more easily when you are lying down than when you are sitting up, retire to your bed or a sofa and try that. If the baby still doesn't feed really well, but eventually goes to sleep, don't keep trying to wake her. Let the whole episode go. The chances are that when she wakes, she'll feed with pleasure.

It probably will not take many one-offs or many days of recurrent problems to erode your confidence, though, so do be quick to seek help from a breast-feeding counsellor or whoever you trust most for help (even hands–on help) with nursing. Both the causes and the cures of this kind of problem are very likely to be to do with the baby's position at the breast and the way she is – or isn't – latching on (see p.66).

Milk intake For first-time parents of breast-fed babies, worries about quantities of milk usually head the list. Aware that they can neither control nor measure what's available or consumed, they wonder whether their babies can really be trusted to make and take what they need.

The answer is almost always yes, but only if parents are also prepared to trust babies to know when they want to suck and for how long. Your baby is far more likely to be able to ensure your milk supply if you are prepared to meet her feeding demands – even when she asks for the breast an hour after last time, or goes on sucking for half an hour. However frequently and lengthily she feeds, your new baby will not take more than she needs. It is impossible to overfeed a breast-fed baby unless you give something else as well as milk. A hungry baby whose mother has a copious milk supply may gain weight faster, and look fatter, than the baby next door who is also breast-fed. Don't compare them. However roly-poly she becomes, your baby is not, and will not become, "too fat" (meaning fatter than she is programmed to be at this stage in her life) unless you start adding solid foods to her diet before she needs them, or giving her syrupy drinks.

Many new mothers who are still finding breast-feeding a bit of a struggle cannot imagine anything they would like better than to worry about too much weight gain, though, because that would mean that they could stop worrying about too little. If your baby does not seem to be thriving easily and cheerfully, you will, of course, consult your health visitor or your doctor. But don't be too quick to assume that she isn't getting enough to eat, especially if you are assessing her behaviour according to traditional criteria built from observations of bottle-fed babies. They may have little relevance to babies who are exclusively breast-fed (see p.73).

Babies who demand food very frequently, for example, are often assumed to be underfed. But how frequent is frequent? Some (though by no means all) babies who are fed on modified cow's milk go three to four hours between feeds, but babies who are fed on human milk almost never do. For your baby, a two- or two-and-a-half hour interval is entirely ordinary. And that does not even mean a period of two or two-and-a-half hours asleep or away from the breast, of course. Intervals between feeds run from the start of one to the start of the next, so feeds which take longer have shorter gaps between them. Breast feeds often last longer than bottle feeds because of their accompanying comfort sucking. Your baby may start sucking at midday, finally drop off the second breast at 12.45 pm and start again soon after 2 pm...

Bottle-fed babies who produce very few dirty nappies, or very scanty, odd-looking stools, are often underfed, but breast-fed babies need not be. Even if your baby soiled three or four nappies a day in her second week, soiling only one every two days now does not suggest starvation or constipation. Some of the time some babies digest breast milk so completely that there is very little waste.

Babies have to grow and that means that however they are fed, they have to put on weight (and length). But while failure to gain enough weight does, of course, suggest that a baby is not getting enough milk, the rate and consistency of weight gain that is "enough" is questionable.

An upward trend in your baby's weight is certainly the best indication that she is being adequately fed. Since the trend may take several weeks to establish and stabilize, though, gazing at her weight chart won't do much to help you cope with immediate panic. For short-term reassurance that your baby is not starving, consider her nappies – not the soiled ones but the ones that are wet, or should be.

As long as your baby is having no food or drink other than breast milk, her food and her drink are one and the same thing and she cannot go short of one without being short of the other. Provided she wets at least six, and preferably eight, nappies every 24 hours, she is neither dehydrated nor starving. Of course making this count depends on changing your baby frequently, and if you use super-absorbent disposable nappies, you'll have to inspect them closely, too, as one pee by a small baby is almost imperceptible (see p.74).

Underfeeding in a breast-fed baby can creep up on you very gradually in a way which is unfairly difficult to spot. What often happens is this: having got breast-feeding started, your milk supply becomes plentiful during the second and third weeks while you are getting plenty of rest and not (we hope) worrying too much about the rest of your household. The baby begins to adopt some kind of feeding pattern (although it is quite likely to be two-hourly by day and only four-hourly occasionally, at night) and you rightly assume that demand and supply are dovetailing nicely.

But eventually you and your partner have to get other aspects of life going again, and so do the people who have been helping and cosseting you. A spurt of physical activity, or even just the sudden stress of finding yourself alone with your baby all day and expected to cope, can make you very tired. Whether it happens when the baby is two weeks old or four weeks old, you may find yourself wondering how you will ever integrate everything you used to do with everything you have to do now.

Getting tired and harassed tends to reduce your milk supply. And meanwhile the baby is growing. She needs more milk now than last week, so if your fatigue means that there is less available, she is bound to be hungry. Coping with her hunger so that it does her no harm is easy: you just let her suck as often as she likes, even if that is much more often. But coping with her hunger so that it does *you* no harm is more difficult because one of the reasons you are tired and harassed is that she needs such frequent feeding. And of course the more you want or need to do other things, the more difficult it becomes to let her suck when she wants and for as long as she likes.

This kind of situation is not easy to spot. The baby's behaviour may not tell you very much because discontent and crying, a tendency to wake only two hours after her last feed in the daytime and demands for two or three feeds in every night, are not new behaviours. They seem exactly like her unsettled behaviour in the newborn period, so you may not realize that she would be more settled by now if she were not hungry.

The behaviour of your own breasts may also mislead you. If you wake each morning with more milk than you know what to do with and in urgent need of a clean bra it is difficult to believe that your baby can be going short. She may be, though, especially if, as often happens, she wants most milk when you have least available.

If you think carefully back over the past few days you may recognize a pattern of your baby being content for reasonable periods between each feed you give her from, say, 4am to 4pm, but getting less and less contented from 4pm until you have had your first good sleep of the night. Her discontent may be because a just-adequate milk supply dips to its lowest in response to the demands of late afternoon. There may be a tired toddler, a messy house and a meal to get. On the other hand, this pattern may not be because you have less milk late in the day but because your baby wants more. Many breast-fed babies who feed at "reasonable intervals" during the day and during the night, like to feed almost non-stop through the evening.

What to do depends on how much you want to go on breast-feeding. If you do want to, then the baby has to be given the chance to make more milk for herself, just as she did at the very beginning when you were getting breast-feeding going. The milk is stimulated by her sucking. The more often she "empties" your breasts, the more milk you will make. When her frequent sucking has built up the supply until it meets her needs, she will suck less often. It is a beautifully simple system and it really does work. But don't expect to be sure that it is working for at least two weeks. Your baby will need the first week to stimulate you to make the extra milk she needs. It is only in the second week that you can expect to find yourself caring for a calmer and more contented baby, and then to get a nice surprise from the scales.

Helping your baby boost the milk supply

Maximizing your baby's chances of persuading your supply to match her growing demands means feeding her whenever she wants and for as long as she wants each time. That may not be easy, especially if you and the rest of your household had thought the babymoon was over and begun to think in terms of "getting back to normal", or if you are already counting the remaining weeks of your maternity leave on the fingers of one hand. No other solution is likely to work and neither will a half-hearted attempt at this one, so it's worth really pushing for the time and space you and the baby need. Some mothers find that time and space easier to come by if they declare a breast-feeding emergency and take refuge in bed for 36 hours, taking the baby with them.

If you can spend a night, a day and another night not only feeding your baby whenever she asks, but also encouraging her to suck whenever she is willing to do so, and having a luxurious rest yourself, you will get the milk-increasing project off to a flying start. Of course

Taking the time and space you and your baby need to rest and nurse needn't mean your older child is left out.

it's ideal if your partner can join you, or at least wait on you with tempting trays. But even if you have to get up to feed yourself, or take a toddler and her toys into the bed with you a lot of the time, it's still worth being there where you can be alert and responsive to every message from your baby and never in a hurry to end a feed because you don't plan to do anything but give her another.

There's nothing else you need do. Drinking extra fluids will not make extra milk unless your normal intake was keeping you dehydrated. And eating special meals won't help either, except insofar as they make you feel luxurious. Women can – and sadly many have to – produce nutritious milk for their babies when their own nutrition is on the borders of starvation. Of course it's important to eat good food so as to keep yourself feeling as energetic as possible, but bread and cheese, fruit and yoghurt interspersed with ordered-in pizza, will ensure good nutrition just as well as the "real meals" you've no time to buy, *or* cook, *or* eat.

Even before you see an increase in your baby's weight gain, there are various signs that suggest that more milk is available to her:

■ She may begin to space her feeds out a bit more, either staying asleep for longer between one feed and the next, or waking without instantly crying for the breast.

■ She may get so much from the first breast that, at least at some feeds, she takes very little from the second, or even misses it out altogether because she is deeply asleep.

■ She may be more inclined than before to posset some milk when she burps.

■ She may wet more nappies, more thoroughly than she had been doing before.

What she isn't very likely to do is give you peaceful evenings and less-interrupted nights. Don't assume that evening feeding marathons and night feeds mean that your baby is still not getting enough. They are part of the means whereby she *will* get enough. There's even some evidence that night feeding has an important hormonal effect on milk production.

Keeping up the milk supply Once you have got your milk supply up to the level that meets your baby's needs, try not to plunge back into a maelstrom of activity – especially stressful activity. Feeling peaceful – better yet, happy – helps lactation, just as the hormones released as you breast-feed help you feel peaceful... There is only one thing you definitely need to do to make sure that the milk supply remains ample, though, and that is to go on offering the breast whenever your baby seems to be hungry, and letting her suck for as long as she likes more often than not. If you (or your mother-in-law) are put off by the term "demand feeding", because it makes the baby sound so assertive, try thinking in terms of "request feeding" instead.

There are a few things it's worth trying *not* to do, though, because they definitely won't help your milk supply – worrying for example. We do not entirely understand how worry and anxiety affect physical functions such as breast-feeding, but there is no doubt that they do. Many mothers see this most clearly if they try to breast-feed in circumstances where they cannot feel relaxed: the breast is full, the baby sucks, but tension prevents the let-down reflex, so the milk does not flow in response to the stimulation of increasingly desperate sucking. Just as a farmer with a nervy cow to deal with might say, "You have to gentle her or she won't let it down", you have to try to "gentle" yourself, relax, go easy on yourself.

Being relaxed about your baby's feed-times is particularly important because trying to keep her to a schedule is certainly something to avoid, even if the schedule is one which she seemed to have settled on for herself a week or so ago. Your breasts must have the stimulation of extra sucking if you want them to produce extra milk. At this stage in her life you cannot ration her sucking without rationing her food and you certainly want to avoid compensating for scarce breast milk by giving a bottle-feed as well. If you offer your baby a bottle and she accepts it, she will be less hungry than usual so she will not instruct your breasts to make the full amount of milk she usually needs. Complementary bottles are appropriate after you have decided that you cannot or do not want to bother to produce more milk, but not before.

As long as you are struggling to keep up your supply, don't even leave a babysitter to give occasional bottles of formula. Breasts which are left full of milk for several hours receive the signal "you have made more than is needed; make less". If you don't want to take the baby out with you, it is better to leave expressed breast milk in a bottle and to pump again during any absence that lasts more than two or three hours.

You're very unlikely to get any help from patent medicines which claim to increase breast milk. Like "tonics" and medicines which claim to increase your sexual vigour, most of these are merely multivitamins and magic. They probably will not do you any harm (though while you're breast-feeding it's better not to take *any* "medicine" without your doctor's advice) but unless your diet is very deficient in vitamins they will not do you any good either.

It may be important to avoid your usual birth control pills altogether for the moment. Many combination pills actually decrease the milk supply. You need to discuss an alternative method of contraception, or at least an alternative type of oral contraceptive, with your doctor or family planning clinic. You might be advised to take a mini-pill now and return to a (marginally more effective) combination pill when your baby is four to five months old. If you have breast-fed successfully for that length of time, the whole supply-demand situation will be perfectly adjusted and well able to override the slight and temporary reduction the changeover will cause.

If things don't improve If you can dedicate two weeks to trying to increase your breast milk and your baby's contentment, you will almost certainly succeed whether you start off with two days in bed or not. But success has a price and only you can decide whether it's affordable. Almost every healthy woman can produce enough milk for even the largest and hungriest baby – or even for two – but not all of those women can do so while doing much else. And while some women are happy – or at least willing and able – to treat breast-feeding as an almost full-time activity for a few weeks; abandon all idea of "feed times" or

Making enough milk for two is seldom a problem but doing much else at the same time may be.

"sleeping through the night" and just concentrate on the baby, other women don't want to or simply cannot. If you have a toddler or older child, already a little saddened by your absence for the birth and your new distraction from him, you may feel that being available to play with him, to take him out and to care for him as you used to do, is just as important as nursing the new baby. If there is nobody who can take care of your household and you, lying about most of the day while the baby cuddles and sucks and dozes may be a lonely and uncomfortable business. And if your nipples keep getting sore and the walls are closing in on you, or you're convinced that your marriage or your job is in jeopardy, you may just feel that you've given breast-feeding your best shot and that's enough.

Just as the original decision to breast-feed was necessarily yours, so the decision to carry on with exclusive breast-feeding and pay what it costs must be yours too. Don't cut the baby's father out of it, though, unless he has put himself outside the situation by going away, actually or figuratively. There is a great deal he can do to facilitate your nursing. If he wants the baby to go on being breast-fed enough that he'll do anything he can to make that possible, you might feel like carrying on in a new spirit of joint responsibility, co-operation and breakfasts in bed.

Complementary bottles Do make a definite decision, though, or you may find that you gradually stop breast-feeding without having intended to – and regret it. You can ensure that your baby gets plenty of milk while reducing your time-commitment to breast-feeding, by giving her complementary bottles of formula. But once you start regular complementary bottles, the amount of milk she takes from the bottle will probably gradually increase and the amount she takes from the breast will decrease. Within a couple of months those bottles aren't complementary to breast-feeds any more but a replacement for them.

That may not matter of course. If you are aiming to wean your baby from breast to bottle before long anyway, complementary bottles are probably a good way to start because that gradual changeover will probably be easier on both of you than a quicker swap. And even if you aren't consciously aiming to stop breast-feeding, if you really do not much care where your baby gets her milk from provided she gets plenty and you can get on with some other things as well, the change of balance from breast with a bit of bottle to bottle with a bit of breast and then none, may not matter much to the baby (who has already had the enormous benefit of your colostrum and first milk), or to you. But if you are envisaging nursing your baby for a year or more, it may matter horribly to you.

So if you want to go on breast-feeding, don't try to cope with a scarcity of breast milk by using complementary bottles *instead* of time and effort; use them as well. Once a baby will accept a bottle at all, complementary feeds tend to reduce breast milk because the baby takes all the additional food she needs from a bottle so that she is less hungry, sucks less often and therefore gives your breasts less stimulation. It will be difficult for you to maintain, far less increase, your supply. Furthermore complementary bottle feeds tend to reduce babies' motivation to breast-feed. Even if she is reluctant to begin with, a baby who has learned that milk comes out of bottles as well as breasts is likely to get "lazy" about breast-feeding – and especially disinclined to bother about the last millilitres that need considerable sucking effort. As soon as the breast milk stops flowing freely she looks around for the bottle. And once that begins to happen, those bottle top-ups tend to reduce your motivation to breast-feed, too. Even if your baby is only taking small amounts per day from a bottle, you still have the expense of buying, and trouble of sterilizing, feeding equipment and formula. You may soon feel that you are getting the worst of both worlds.

Giving complementary bottles Choose and prepare a bottle formula just as you would for a bottle-fed baby (see p.75). Feed the baby from the breast as usual, but when she has taken all she can from both breasts, offer her a bottle of the prepared formula. The amount of formula she drinks will be roughly the amount she still needs after taking all your breast milk. It may be nothing at some feeds, quite a lot at others.

If she is only willing to drink any formula after certain feeds of the day (often the late-afternoon and evening ones when your milk supply is at its lowest), you need only offer bottles at those feeds.

It may be several days before she will accept a bottle. Babies who have settled to breast-feeding do not always take easily to a teat. If yours refuses to drink any formula at all, you may not be clear if she is refusing it because she is already getting enough from the breast or because she dislikes the new method. Persist in offering the formula for at least five days. If she is hungry, the baby will have accepted it within that time. If she still has not accepted it, she probably isn't hungry. Check on her weight gain, though.

BOTTLE-FEEDING: COMMON CONCERNS

Feeding a baby formula from a bottle instead of breast-feeding means that you have more, and he has less, control over what he eats. You may be glad to have bountiful supplies of food that are available to him whether you are or not, and enjoy being able to see exactly how much vanishes down his throat at each feed. But while you are less likely than the breast-feeding mother to feel anxious about your baby being underfed, you are rather more likely to overfeed him.

Overfeeding Bottle-fed babies do not get too fat from being allowed to drink as much properly made formula as they want, whenever they want it. If they get fat it is either because they are given extra foods or sweet drinks as well as their bottles, or because those bottles are tampered with. Unless your doctor specifically recommends it (which she might if your baby is exceptionally large) he should not have "solids" until he is at least four months old. And when he does have cereals or purées, they should always be given separately, from a spoon, never concealed in his bottle. Likewise it's important to make bottles up accurately, or use a ready-to-feed formula. A spoonful of baby rice or an extra scoop of milk powder in his bottle means that it will contain an unusually large number of calories in the usual number of millilitres. Your baby will not be able to take all his milk, if he wants it, without having to take in a lot of extra hidden calories.

When your bottle-fed baby is thirsty but not hungry, she needs water not formula.

Remember that a baby can be thirsty without being hungry and that formula milk, unlike breast milk, does not adjust itself accordingly but has always the same balance of food and water. Bottle-fed babies sometimes benefit from drinks of cooled boiled water, especially when the weather is hot or they are feverish.

If your baby does have extra drinks, encourage plain water in the hope that it becomes a pleasurable habit that largely replaces fruit drinks now and fizzy drinks later. Vitamin C-enriched fruit drinks and "baby juices" contain "no added sugar" but have a lot of fructose – natural fruit sugar – that will put his eventual teeth under threat and feeds him extra calories along with the vitamins. Modern babymilks usually contain adequate vitamin C so that your baby does not need these drinks at all, especially as he may take multivitamin drops that contain yet more vitamin C. If you want him to have fruit juices for pleasure, make sure they are a once-a-day treat, and highly diluted.

Underfeeding Underfeeding is rare in bottle-fed babies but it can happen. A baby who cries a great deal, seems generally discontented with life and is gaining weight slowly, is probably not getting enough to eat. Some of the following points may be relevant:

■ You may be trying to control the amount of milk your baby takes, or expecting him to take the same amount at each feed instead of leaving it to him. Like older people, babies are hungrier for some meals on some days than others. Make sure he gets as much as he even *might* like by putting a few millilitres more milk in each bottle than he is likely to take and letting him go on sucking until he is ready to stop rather than urging him to go on until the milk is finished. If a bottle is emptied, can you be sure that he would not have liked more?

■ You may be scheduling feeds too strictly. The baby's digestion will take around three hours to deal with a full feed, so most of the time he will not demand food much more often than this. But his appetite will vary; he will not always take a full feed. If you do not allow him to make up for a small breakfast by having a mid-morning snack, but make him wait until the next "proper" mealtime, he may not then be able to hold enough extra milk to make up. Suppose that he only drinks 85 ml (3 oz) of milk at breakfast-time instead of his usual 170 ml (6 oz). A couple of hours later he will be hungry. A small "snack" feed followed by his ordinary lunch-time feed in due course would put him back on track, but if you will not give him a bottle *until* his ordinary lunch-time he will not be able to drink his usual bottle *plus* the 85 ml (3 oz) he missed earlier. His stomach simply will not hold that much milk at one time. If this situation goes on and on it can lead to a great deal of fretfulness as well as to low weight gain.

■ You may be using a teat with too small a hole. A hungry baby will work hard and patiently to get milk however slowly it flows. But after 55 ml (2 oz) or so the acute hunger pains stop; his motivation dwindles and the baby may give up and go to sleep. He will wake again in a couple of hours and demand more food, but if the same thing happens repeatedly you may find that you have a baby who demands frequent feeds, never takes much at any of them and does not gain much weight. So make sure that the milk drips rapidly out of the teat when you turn it upside down. The baby should be able to get at least half the feed during the first five minutes of sucking.

■ He may be a very sleepy baby (see p.127). In a few weeks he will grow up enough to be more alert, but in the meantime don't rely on him telling you he needs food. Wake him for feeds at reasonable intervals and use the things that will interest him most – your face and voice – to keep him awake while he sucks. He may drop off despite your efforts and if he does, there's no point in trying to pour milk into his sleeping mouth. Instead of forcing him to take more, now, offer little and often while you wait for him to grow up a bit.

Night Feeding

Although you are almost certain to meet at least one parent whose baby regularly sleeps right through the night before he is six weeks old, most babies don't and yours probably won't. Bottle-fed babies usually need at least six feeds in the 24 hours until they are around six weeks old and many will need five feeds until they are somewhere around four months. If you are breast-feeding, your baby may nurse so often that numbers of feeds seem irrelevant. But as long as four hours is the longest your baby ever goes between feeds, you are bound to have to wake up once during your normal sleeping hours, though if you are clever, you need seldom wake twice. And once your baby is content with a basic five feeds a day – three meals plus an early-morning and late-night feed – you should be able to get a solid stretch of six or seven hours sleep almost every night.

Being woken, night after night, is a tremendous strain; more of a strain than doctors or nurses, friends or relations often realize. It is not the lost hours of sleep which matter: most of those can probably be made up by going to bed earlier or having an afternoon nap at a weekend. The exhaustion comes from the continual disturbance of your sleep patterns. Being woken, even for a few minutes, twice or three times every night for weeks on end can make you feel like sleepwalkers.

Juggling feed times so you can get more sleep

Maximum rest for you as well as contentment for the baby depend on your willingness to adapt your approach to her night-time wakings to her age and stage of development. During these first months, keeping her waiting for feeds will lose you unnecessary hours of sleep. Later on, being too quick to feed her when she wakes will doom you to unnecessary weeks of broken nights.

The secret of success in juggling these early and necessary night feeds to suit you all is to stop yourself thinking in disciplinary terms. Don't let yourself believe that doing without a feed is "good" for the baby; virtue does not come into it. Don't entertain the notion that feeding her before she is ravenous, or giving her a few extra sucks by way of a snack, is "spoiling". It is simply good sense. If – and only if – you genuinely accept that, you will usually be able to anticipate and divert a demand for food which was going to come up at a totally uncivilized hour. You do it by waking the baby up and feeding her instead of waiting for her to wake you. Why fall exhausted into bed at midnight, knowing that the baby will want food at around 2am and around 6am, when you can wake her just before you go to sleep and thus ensure that she will only disturb you at around 4am?

Abeola and Jake's story

Abeola and Jake were beginning to feel like sleepwalkers. Their little daughter, Jewel, wasn't a *bad* sleeper, in fact she slept quite a lot. But she didn't sleep any longer between feeds in the night than in the day. Most days she'd have a feed around 5.30pm and another around 9.30pm, but then she'd wake her parents at 1am or 2am and then *again* at around 5am. They decided that something had to be done. *What could be done?* Abeola knew that trying to *delay* a feed when the baby was hungry would only mean more crying for Jewel and even less sleep for her parents. But what about offering Jewel the first night feed *before* she was hungry – and before her parents fell asleep? Might that be a way of giving the baby what she clearly needed while getting a bit more of what they themselves needed – sleep? Jake was keen to try anything that might mean Jewel only woke them once rather than twice, so once the baby had had her usual 9.30pm feed, her parents didn't wait for her to wake them at 1am or 2am but instead woke her, around midnight, just before they went to sleep.

What happened? After a couple of confused nights when Jewel woke at 1am even though she had just been fed and wasn't hungry, she took to sleeping through to around 4am. Not a civilized time to be awakened, but far better than both 1am and 5am. This kind of juggling of Jewel's feed times went on working for her parents. After a few weeks it became clear that Jewel didn't need both a late-night and a very early-morning feed any more and Abeola and Jake realized that by using the same method, they could choose which of the two feeds she abandoned. They decided to try and get rid of the late-night feed so they could get to sleep earlier themselves. Instead of waiting until nearly midnight, they woke Jewel a few minutes earlier each night until eventually that late feed merged with the evening one into a single feed around 10pm. Falling thankfully into bed, Jake and Abeola could (almost) count on (almost) six unbroken hours of sleep.

For better mornings. If they'd preferred to go on with a late bedtime but to get rid of the 4am awakening, they could have juggled Jewel towards that pattern instead. By gradually pushing her 5.30pm feed forward towards 7pm they could have persuaded her to sleep through her 9.30-ish feed and on to around 11pm or midnight. In that way they could have persuaded Jewel to give them that precious six-hour sleep before waking at a comparatively civilized 6am.

Going through the night without being fed

A lot of real (as opposed to baby-book) babies hang onto sixth (and seventh and eighth) feeds way past six weeks, and not all co-operate in having late-night and early-morning feeds "juggled" for their parents' convenience by three or four months. If yours is one of the babies who seems to need more feeds by night than by day and who is still waking you constantly when she "ought" not to be waking you at all, you may well find that your patience and good sense are being eroded by sheer exhaustion. Try to hang on to them and resist the moral pressures that may be put on you to resist her. As long as you know that you are going to feed her in the end, you'd far better feed her in the beginning. She wakes (usually) because she is hungry. Because she is hungry she cries. A feed will stop her crying immediately but nothing else will stop her for any useful length of time and every recommended method of delaying that feed will delay your return to sleep, too.

Leaving the baby to cry is a common prescription, but premature and even more certainly nonsensical during this age period than later. The longer you leave a hungry baby to cry the more hungry and tired she will get. When you finally give in, the tiredness may mean that she takes only a small feed before sleep overcomes her and she will wake again all the sooner. If you refuse to "give in" and you leave the baby to scream for an hour or more, she may go back to sleep because she is exhausted. But you will still have gained nothing.

Half an hour's nap will revive her and her now ferocious hunger. You will have been kept awake through the first crying bout and now you are awake again...

Giving drinks that are not food may put your baby back to sleep for a few minutes if she was only a little bit hungry. But the water or juice and the sucking only give her a temporary feeling of fullness and a warm cuddle. It will not take her more than half an hour to discover that her tummy is still empty; she will wake you again just as you have sunk back into heavy sleep.

Giving an extra-large feed in the evening will not help unless you were actually underfeeding her before. Babyfood manufacturers sometimes try to cash in on parents' need for more sleep with advertising copy which says "for a peaceful night for your baby and you, give..." But a baby's appetite and digestion do not work like a car's engine; you cannot make her go for longer without a refill by forcing in extra fuel. If she is already taking a full feed in the evening, it will consist of as much as she wants and, by definition, she will not want any more. If you force extra calories into her, by putting cereals into her bottle, for example, she will still digest the food at a normal rate. The extra will affect her weight but it will not affect her sleep – except possibly to disturb it by giving her indigestion.

MIXED FEEDING

Breast milk or formula is a complete food and drink. Although breast milk contains very little iron so that some authorities believe that babies who have been exclusively breast-fed may need extra iron by the time they are four months old, others maintain that even that small quantity is enough because its quality and absorbability is so high. In theory your child could go on living on milk alone forever but in practice a milk-only diet would not work out very well.

Although the foodstuffs in milk are complete they are very diluted: milk contains far more water than anything else. As the baby gets heavier he needs more calories and more of all nutrients, so he drinks more milk. Eventually he reaches a point where he is drinking all the milk he can hold at every feed, yet four or five bellyfuls per day do not give him quite as many calories as his body requires. Since he literally cannot hold any more milk on each occasion, the only way he could get more food would be to have more feeds. If you had nothing but milk available for him, you would find that he began to wake again for the night feeds he had just abandoned, and to demand the bottle or breast at more and more frequent intervals through the day. Fortunately you do have something else available: "solid" foods which, although less perfect sources of all needed nutrients, are far more concentrated sources of calories than milk. Tiny quantities of a solid food give the baby the extra calories he is beginning to need without stretching his milk-distended tummy much further.

There are also social reasons for offering your baby solid foods. You are trying to bring up a human being and human beings eat as well as drink, and eat a range of foods, not just one. Your baby needs to learn that hunger-satisfying, enjoyable food can come off a plate as well as out of a breast or bottle. He needs to discover how to take it in without sucking and he needs to get used to a variety of tastes and textures. Until he has learned these things he cannot share in the pleasures of food in sociable eating: still an important part of social interaction, even if meals around a family table are no longer routine.

First "solid" foods are not really solid because mixing them to a creamy texture with the baby's accustomed milk makes them seem acceptably familiar. But once you have decided that your baby is ready for something in addition to his milk, do resist the temptation to mix it into his bottle. Instead, give it from a spoon or your finger. Feeding your baby a bottle which has a spoonful of cereal mixed into it is forced feeding – it means that he cannot get his accustomed quantity of milk (and that means water, too) without getting the added cereal as well. It deprives him of any chance of saying "no" to the cereal without saying "no" to the milk. If you are ever tempted to add *anything* to the babymilk in your baby's bottle, remind yourself that breast-feeding is nutritionally ideal and you can't spoon cereals (or medicine) into breasts...

When to start mixed feeding There are no hard and fast rules about when you can, should or must start offering your baby solid foods except that no baby should have them earlier than four months, without special medical reasons. For pre-term babies that means four months after their due dates rather than their birthdays. So if your twins were born at 30 weeks, they should wait for non-milk foods until they are around six months, unless their doctor suggests otherwise. Although generations of babies were given solid foods far earlier in their lives and appeared to thrive, modern research clearly indicates that until 18 weeks or thereabouts, baby's intestines lack some important digestive enzymes and that this renders them developmentally unready to cope with food other than breast milk (or formula). Early exposure will not necessarily do them harm, but the food will not do them any good, and may block some of the benefits of breast milk, such as easy absorption of its iron, and protection against allergy.

Once your baby has passed four months, there are two sets of cues to his readiness for non-milk food that you can use, separately or together. The first, more traditional set consists of his milk consumption, weight and number of feeds.

If a bottle-fed baby drinks an almost full bottle of formula – say 200ml (7oz) – at most feeds, you can assume that his meals are as large as the capacity of his stomach allows. To get more food he would have to have more meals rather than larger ones.

Your baby's weight gain in the last month or so tells you whether or not those quantities of milk have been enough for him up to now. If he is gaining steadily he must be getting enough to eat. But as his weight increases so will his need for food and, far from wanting to give him more meals, you are probably hoping that he will soon abandon one of the regular bottles that keep your nights so short – his late-night or small-hours feed. Unless he is offered solid foods soon that's unlikely to happen; indeed hunger may even begin to wake him an extra time.

If your baby is breast-fed, so that you have no idea of the quantities he drinks, you can use his weight, combined with his demands for food, to give you cues about when to introduce solids. If he weighs as much as 5.5kg (12 lb), he is unlikely to be able to get enough food for his needs in fewer than five feeds each day and may well need six. If he adamantly refuses to lengthen the interval between feeds, or suddenly begins to shorten it, perhaps reverting to the evening sucking binges you had thought were over forever, it is reasonable to suppose that he needs more to eat and will either have to have more breast feeds or something in addition to them.

The second set of cues to your baby's readiness to meet with non-milk foods is more impressionistic and individual. Does your baby *seem* ready to experiment with a new and more grown-up way of eating? Does he like to sit propped in a highchair or feeding seat, for instance, or does he still slump sadly unless someone holds him?

If he can be propped sitting, is he interested in what goes on at table? If he sometimes watches you eat, following each bite from plate to mouth, moving his jaws as you chew or making "ah-ah-ah" asking noises at you, it has obviously dawned on him that this process is one that you enjoy and he would like to try. It's hard to imagine a better reason for offering him a taste of something.

If your baby makes you feel positively selfish when you don't offer him your lunch, he's probably ready for more than milk. If any of the food he is begging for is suitably bland – a vegetable soup that you haven't sprinkled with salt and pepper, for instance – there's no reason why he shouldn't have his first friendly taste off your finger. If the moment the food on your finger touches his tongue, the tongue and the food are both poked out, the tongue thrust reflex is still active. This reflex protects very young babies from

choking by clearing foreign bodies, including food, out of their mouths, so if the reflex is still there, he is not ready. If he grabs your finger, though, sucks it like a lollipop and looks disappointed when it stops tasting of food and reverts to tasting of finger, he might enjoy half a teaspoonful of something of his own as well.

Enjoy is the important word. Early tastes of solid foods are intended more for education than for nutrition and the most important lesson of all is enthusiasm. Offered while your baby is still well-nourished by milk alone, minute quantities of other foods cover the possibility of his needing a bit extra from time to time but are much more a preparation for the future than a necessary part of the present. They are not meant to make a major change in his diet or to replace any part of it. Above all, the new – and not always comfortable – business of eating off a spoon does not replace or reduce the sensual delight of sucking. The beginning of mixed feeding is not the beginning of weaning.

Keep the quantity of solids down and the quantity of milk up. Don't let advertising by babyfood manufacturers convince you that your baby should match increasing quantities of solid foods to decreasing quantities of milk. Instead, feed very small quantities of solid foods and the usual amount of milk, increasing the solids only if the baby wants more as well as the milk.

Never force solid foods on the baby. Offer tastes and let him decide whether he wants them or not. At the beginning it is not always easy to distinguish between incompetence and rejection – dribbling and spitting – so err on the side of giving him less than he might want rather than more. He's got all his life to eat carrots.

Suitable and unsuitable food for early mixed feeding

Most of the baby's diet will consist of milk for weeks yet. Even when he does begin to reduce his milk intake because he positively wants more solid foods, he will still drink enough to provide almost all the protein, minerals and vitamins he needs. First solid foods are therefore needed only for their calories – their fuel – and there are calories in every kind of food. Your baby will get no more benefit from an expensive "high-protein" cereal than from an ordinary one. He does not need the extra protein in the expensive product, only the calories which are in both. So choosing first foods is more a matter of avoiding the few types that are particularly likely to cause allergic reactions than selecting those that will be particularly good for him. He can have almost any food that you ordinarily serve provided it has a taste he likes, a semi-liquid texture he can easily take, and no ill-effects on his digestion. Once he has got the idea of taking food without sucking, try to offer a wide variety of flavours so that you find out, by experiment, what your baby likes and what he does not. Even at this early stage, when taste acuity is still developing, he will have definite preferences which you should respect.

Foods to avoid in the first six months

Some foods are especially liable to provoke allergic reactions in young babies and should therefore be avoided altogether until at least six months and then introduced in tiny quantities and one at a time: wheat cereals and wheat flour (including bread); eggs (yolk as well as white); citrus fruits (including orange juice marketed for babies); nuts and peanut butter (even the smooth kind).

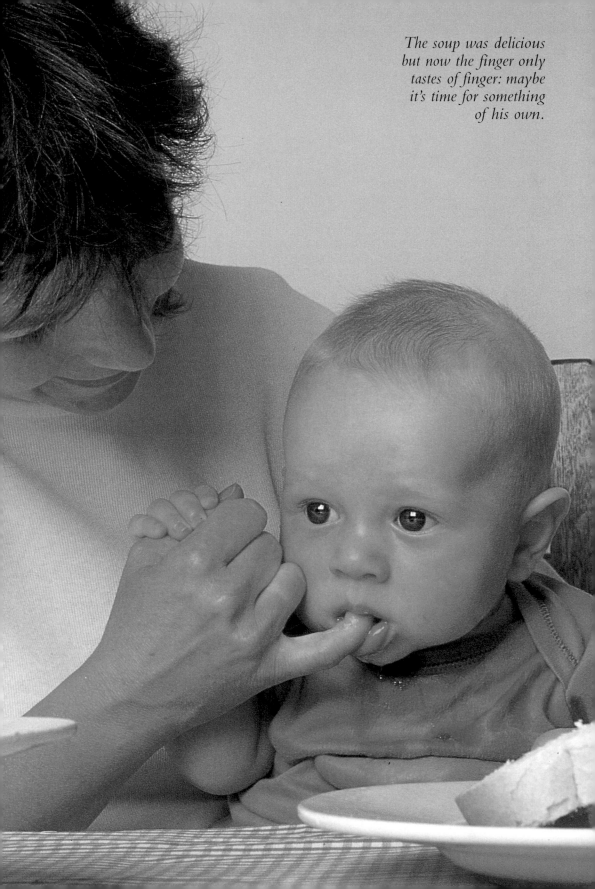

The soup was delicious but now the finger only tastes of finger: maybe it's time for something of his own.

Foods to be cautious with If anyone in your baby's family suffers from allergic disorders – including complaints like hayfever whose connection with food is not obvious – your baby may be extra-liable to them too. Let him start life on breast milk exclusively if you possibly can, and consult your health visitor or your doctor before you start giving *anything* else, whether formula milk or solid foods. Consult again before you attempt to introduce any of the high-risk items.

Avoid added salt, which can stress immature kidneys, hot spices that might burn the baby's mouth or even inflame his stomach, and coffee, tea and alcohol, which are all drugs.

Be sparing with added sugar and be sure to offer at least as many savoury foods as sweet foods. Many babies easily develop a preference for sweet foods which puts their dental health at risk. It's worth making sure that when yours joins the drink-and-a-biscuit brigade, his feelings aren't hurt by bread sticks and drinks of water rather than chocolate chip cookies and apple juice.

Don't give ordinary cow's milk (or goat's or sheep's milk) except perhaps for mixing foods. For drinking, use only breast milk or formula during the whole of the first year. If you especially want to give a more "grown-up milk", you could use a "follow-on formula" after nine months, but these babymilks for older babies eating some solid foods offer no advantages over the babymilks used from birth – and of course no advantage over breast milk. Although soya milk is often recommended for babies who are thought to be intolerant of cow's milk products, it can itself cause allergic reactions. Use soya only if it's prescribed by your doctor – and then only in the form of a soya-based infant formula.

Introduce each new food on its own and as a single teaspoonful the first couple of times. If it should disagree with your baby you will know exactly which food to avoid for a few weeks.

Remember that he cannot chew yet. If you feed him lumps he will have to swallow them as lumps. He will not like doing so and he may choke. So sieve, or liquidize his early meals. The type of foodmill often called a "mouli" is especially useful because it both liquidizes and sieves foods. If you use a liquidizer or food processor it will produce what *looks* like babyfood but still contains the pips and tough skins or fibres his digestion will find difficult to cope with. You will need to use a sieve as well.

Foods to start with Rice or cornmeal cereals are the traditional first solid foods. They are marketed specially prepared for babies and they only need mixing with formula, breast milk or boiled cow's milk.

Cereals have a lot going for them, especially the advantage of being rich in, or enriched with, iron – the one nutrient which exclusively breast-fed babies might be beginning to need. But although their bland milky taste is sufficiently like babies' accustomed food that they are seldom rejected outright, many babies prefer strained fruits or vegetables. The tastes are more surprising than the taste of unsweetened cereal, but they are also more interesting and pleasurable.

You could try sieved ripe banana or avocado, stewed apple, boiled and strained potato, yam, plantain, spinach and carrot.

Should we avoid commercially prepared babyfoods?

Is it true that commercially prepared babyfoods are poor-quality, sweet and starchy? Would it be better for babies' health if parents used only home-prepared foods?

It depends which brands of babyfood you buy, and what foods you prepare at home.

It's certainly true that some babyfoods are over-processed. Sometimes the contents of jars – a mixture of vegetables for example – are watered down and then thickened up again with a starch or gelling agent; sometimes most of the natural taste is cooked out and replaced with artificial flavourings; often a range of processing aids or "improvers" are added. Read the label. If some of the entries mean nothing to you, just remember that ingredients have to be listed in size order, so if water comes first there's more water than anything else, and the shorter the list is, the better. The best babyfoods contain nothing more or less than the stated foods.

Using home-cooked food for your baby is fine provided you are carefully storing and cooking fresh (or frozen fresh) foods that were hygienically produced, manufactured and marketed. Young babies – along with elderly people – are more vulnerable than the rest of us to all kinds of "food poisoning". The precautions you take in your own kitchen are crucial, but they won't protect your baby from carelessness in the factory or supermarket. Raw meat and poultry need to be kept well away from foods that are to be eaten without further cooking, as well as being thoroughly cooked themselves. Raw or undercooked eggs (including meringue and mayonnaise) should be avoided altogether. Most important of all, food should spend as little time as possible at the warm (rather than boiling hot or icy cold) temperatures that encourage bacteria to multiply unimaginably fast. Resist the temptation to save time by warming pre-cooked food to the right temperature for your baby; it should be brought to boiling point and then cooled and eaten. Beware of cook–chill foods (including increasingly popular baby meals) that only need heating in a microwave. There may be cool-spots and if the dish is neatly finished you may not even stir it so as to discover that it is not uniformly boiling hot.

The greater the variety of interesting foods your baby gets to try, the better, but anyone who cooks in your household will need to keep her in mind and avoid potential allergens, such as nuts, go easy on sugar and remember to wait until the baby's portion has been removed before adding salt, hot spices or wine. And you may need to plan for the days when everybody's late home and nobody feels like cooking. Chinese take-away is not good food for your baby, however carefully you strain it.

The main risk to babies' health posed by their food doesn't come from inadequate nutrition or even too many additives, though. Most experts agree that it probably comes from pesticide residues (see p.246). The only way to avoid pesticides is to buy only foods that have been organically produced: organically produced babyfoods when you want to use jars or packets; organically grown vegetables and fruits when you are cooking.

Every parent wants his or her child to have a healthy diet, but by no means every parent has the time, the money or the inclination to exclude all "non-organic" foods – or all commercially produced babyfoods. If you want to play safe but not quite as safe as that, make sure that you offer your baby a wide mixture of kinds of food, both commercially prepared and home-cooked. If the "lamb dinner" she prefers does contain a lot of thickener and not much meat, it won't harm her nutrition to eat it once a week provided she eats a different jar (with different strengths and failings) at the next meal, and something home-cooked the next day. Similarly an occasional serving of under-flavoured, over-sweetened "apple dessert" with traces of chemicals in it isn't going to damage her health, harm her sense of taste or put her off your cooking.

Home-prepared or commercial babyfoods Once your baby happily accepts one or two solid foods it is good for him to be offered a wide variety. You can buy special babyfoods for him or put tiny portions of your own cooking through a liquidizer or mouli. (Some people freeze extra portions in an ice-cube tray.) If you want him to like your cooking, make sure he has some home-cooked foods from the beginning. If he gets very used to the bland sameness of commercially prepared babyfoods, he may later reject the stronger and more definite tastes of your foods. Fresh stewed apple, for example, is nothing like "apple dessert".

There's nothing difficult about cooking for a baby although you may want to pay a little extra attention to hygiene. Drying-up cloths, beaker spouts, can openers and re-heated left-overs can all be sources of more bacteria than your baby may yet be able to cope with. At this early stage when you do not have to worry about feeding him a "balanced diet" of solid foods, he can have a tiny portion of any suitable food you cook. Some foods simply need reducing to semi-liquid texture. You can use a liquidizer and adjust the final purée with extra stock, milk or water. Most babies prefer the texture of heavy cream; a stiffer, mashed-potato texture tends to make them gag. Pippy, stringy or very rough-textured foods, like raspberries, cabbage or minced meat, need sieving too. Foods can be made less strong-tasting by being mixed with milk, yoghurt or custard. Try to avoid anything which may disgust your baby. A piece of gristle can upset eating for weeks.

Jars are an extravagant way to feed a baby at this early stage. He will only need one or two teaspoons of food at a time, yet the jars hold three tablespoons. You cannot use the remainder up over several meals because the foods will not stay fresh and safe for more than 24 hours after opening, even in a refrigerator, and you do not want to offer the same food three times running. Dehydrated foods in packets can be used as gradually as you like. If you buy several different kinds, both sweet and savoury, your baby can explore variety.

Helping your baby to eat There is no hurry; go slowly. Learning to eat solid foods is a big task for your baby. If you upset or frustrate him, by trying to force food into his mouth when he is rejecting it, you may put him off the whole business.

Doing it herself from early on will make new tastes and textures easier to accept later.

Don't assume that hunger will motivate him. When he is hungry he wants to suck milk: that's the only way of assuaging hunger he's ever known. It will take him time to discover that the stuff that comes off a spoon can have similar effects. In the meantime if your baby cries for food and then goes on crying between mouthfuls, don't assume that he doesn't want, or like, the food. If he takes it willingly, the crying may mean that he hasn't had enough: "I'm *still* hungry".

Cash in on his curiosity and interest in the way you eat and in the foods that he can see other people enjoying. Sharing in the pleasures of family eating is the very best way to introduce him to the whole idea of food-that-is-not-milk.

Make use of his ability to play with his hands. At this age a baby will not get much nourishment out of finger-foods but he will very much enjoy them. Being allowed to clutch and suck at a rusk makes up for passive spoon-feeding, and the fact that the baby puts the food

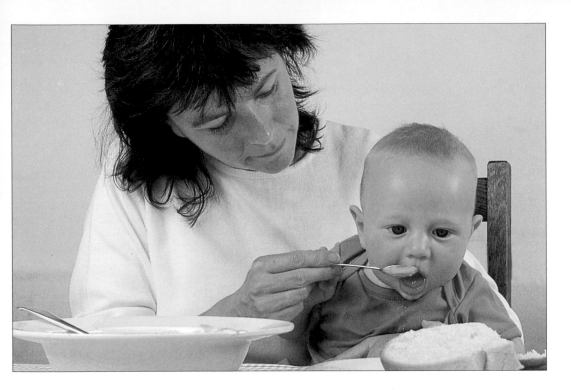

Eating from a spoon is a difficult technique to learn – even if you're concentrating.

to his own mouth makes it more likely that he will find the strange taste and texture interesting rather than infuriating. Watch him every moment though. If a crumbly piece breaks off in his mouth, he may need you to fish it out for him.

Be tactful in your timing. Don't try to teach your baby about solid foods at meals for which he is always frantic. The early-morning feed, for example, is not usually a good one to begin with. He is barely awake but he is ravenous. Let him suck in peace.

Whatever time of day you select for introducing solids, don't try to give spoon foods to your baby while he is desperate to suck. If you do, he will yell with hunger and frustration around every spoonful. On the other hand don't wait to offer them until he is full of milk. He will be too sleepy and lethargic to bother. A sandwich system can often work best: a few minutes' sucking to allay the worst of his hunger and assure him that the breast or bottle is still safely there for him; then the offer of some solid food; and then as much more milk as he wants.

Taking food without sucking is very difficult for babies until they get the hang of it. If you put the food on your baby's tongue, he does not know how to get it far enough back in his mouth to swallow. It may simply dribble out again. If you dump it at the back of his mouth, he may gag and will probably then reject spoon-feeding, sometimes for weeks. The technique that usually works best is to use a tiny flat spoon – an old-fashioned salt or mustard spoon is ideal – and to hold it just between the baby's lips so that he can suck the contents off. If he sucks at it, he will get some of it far enough back in his mouth to swallow. If he likes the taste, he may become positively enthusiastic.

It's important to know when to stop. If you use this method of spoon-feeding, your baby will be able to "tell" you when he does not want any more: he will turn his head away from the spoon or close his lips instead of sucking. But if you put food right into his mouth, you will not be able to tell when he has finished. Dribbling the food out, gagging and crying may all be signals to stop, but they may also be the result of bad feeding technique or a baby who is not very good at eating yet.

Moving towards family mealtimes By five to six months most babies are ready to begin to adapt to family mealtimes, however many "snacks" they have from the breast or bottle in between. Your baby still won't last from early supper to breakfast, though, so that stretch of time has to be interrupted either by a late-night breast-feed or bottle-feed or by an early-morning one, whichever you prefer. If you like to sleep in but always go to bed late anyway, a late-evening bottle or breast-feed may suit you better.

After a few weeks, babies who have enjoyed their first tastes of solid foods will know that food from a spoon can satisfy hunger. Although sucking milk will go on being vitally important for many months, they will have learned to look forward to solids as well. Such babies are ready to begin, very gradually, to eat more spoon and finger-foods and to rely less on the breast or bottle.

The "sandwich" system makes it easy to recognize this stage. You prepare the baby's solid food and then settle down to feed him from the breast or bottle. But now, recognizing his dish, he begins to hurry that first sucking in order to get to it sooner. If he likes what is in it, he may eat it all and then want only a token amount of milk to finish up with.

Once he begins to behave like this you can offer rather more solid foods (perhaps three teaspoons instead of one) and be prepared to abandon the "sandwich" system when he shows, by gesture, that he wants to start a meal with his solids or that, having sucked and then eaten, he does not want any more milk. He is beginning, very gradually, to shift his allegiance from milk to "real" food. But although this *is* the beginning of weaning, your baby is doing it himself because he wants to. Nothing is being forced on him and it is still important to let him set the pace. There may be days or even weeks when he reverts to wanting almost entirely milk, and there may be certain feeds in each day when he continues to need two sucking sessions. If you let him lead, you can be sure that he will take the milk/food combination that he wants and that what he takes will also be what he needs.

Eventually he will probably arrive at a pattern. First thing in the morning he will almost certainly need to suck before he can eat. This may be a milk-only feed, being given now rather than in the late evening. But if the meal is breakfast, let him suck as much as he wants and then have his solid food afterwards.

At lunch-time he will probably be eager for his solids and he may be generally less interested in sucking at this time of day. Offer him the breast or bottle after his meal, but once he shows you he is uninterested, offer a drink from a cup instead.

At supper-time he may need a suck first, to calm him down after his bath and playtime. Then he will be ready to eat his solid food before having a long peaceful suck (perhaps in his own room) to ready him for bed.

If he still has a milk feed to come in the late evening, this will obviously be a time just for simple, sleepy sucking.

During this in-between stage your baby is learning to manage with fewer but larger meals than he has been accustomed to. He will learn fast and happily if you keep the whole business of eating pleasurable for him. Often he will need a snack to keep him going. Instead of an extra milk feed, he may now sometimes enjoy something hard and edible to hold and chew. The more practice he gets in managing finger-foods the sooner he will get some actual nutrition as well as enjoyment out of them.

He will want to play with his solid foods, too, and the more you encourage him, the sooner he will learn to feed himself. Your baby still needs to be held and closely cuddled while sucking, but the rest of the time a highchair with its own tray table, or a feeding chair that brings him up to the adult table, will be more comfortable for both of you and leave you freer to help him.

Sitting right up to table with adults is fun, but all kinds of chair need a safety-harness every time.

From now on, try to think of yourself as helping the baby to eat rather than feeding him. Once he sits up to meals he will certainly want to join in with his hands as well as his mouth. Let him dabble and smear, dip his fingers in the dish and suck them and try to find out what a spoon is for. It is messy but it is vitally important. The

---

PARENTS, TAKE NOTE

Choking

Although choking on small objects, especially round ones like buttons, marbles or (poisonous) watch batteries, is more of a hazard than most people think, choking on food is generally less of a hazard. This is because pieces of the kinds of food given to babies seldom seal off a baby's airway dangerously. Don't let the horrid prospect of your baby choking prevent you from offering her finger foods.

Many babies gag if they are spoon-fed with unfamiliar foods, thick mushy textures or too large mouthfuls. Gagging is unpleasant – and babies clearly dislike it – but the gag reflex is also protective: it gets the food back to the front of the mouth where it can be spat out or renegotiated. The usual culprit among finger-foods is the too-large piece of food a baby stuffs in her mouth – or later, bites off with sharp new front teeth – that really needs chewing with teeth she has not got. She can deal with a tiny piece of toast by

squishing it between her gums while sucking and softening it, but a bigger piece defeats her. She may gag; if that fails to move the food forward she may begin to cough and splutter but it's easy to rescue her by hooking the food out again with your finger.

A smaller piece of food may be a bigger problem because it is more likely to be half-swallowed and "go the wrong way". She may need help coughing out a piece of carrot or apple she tried to swallow whole, but while the episode may be terrifying it's unlikely to be really dangerous because the food itself will not block the airway so that she cannot breathe. As long as she is able to breathe she can, possibly with assistance, cough it out. If she were alone it might be a different matter. When there is a piece of food stuck in the throat, the throat can swell, wedging the foreign body in place. That might seal off the airway. No baby should have any food or drink without adult supervision.

more he feels that what he eats is under his own control rather than simply being ladled into him, the more he will enjoy the whole eating game. The more he enjoys it now, the less trouble you are likely to have later with fads and food refusal. And lots of practice now means that he will be able to feed himself entirely independently at an early age. So try not to boss him. Skin washes, in fact it washes so much more easily than anything else that if it's warm enough, taking clothes off while he eats is a lot more efficient than covering them with a bib. Still, a bib with a pocket keeps the worst off clothes and if you are worried about what gets on the floor, a plastic tablecloth under his chair will keep the worst off that, too.

Drinking from a cup

A spout and two handles means independence for him and less mess for you.

Babies who take less milk from breast or bottle because they are taking more food from a spoon, need to make up the difference in liquid by drinking from a cup. Your baby may find drinking without sucking even more difficult than eating without sucking. By all means let him get used to sips from an ordinary beaker, but for everyday drinking it is worth getting him a "teacher-beaker" or "sippy-cup" that offers a compromise between sucking and ordinary drinking and allows him to practise holding it himself without (much) spilling. You may even find it worthwhile to buy into one of the "drinking systems" that offers a cup with a succession of tops starting with a long, soft spout from which a beginner can more or less suck, followed by a series of shorter, harder, more free-flowing spouts that gradually prepare him to manage with none.

Your baby does not need to drink large quantities from a cup because he is still getting most of the liquid he needs from milk, and "solid food" has a high liquid content too. Don't press him to take more than he wants, and don't try to tempt him by filling his cup with juice. If he needs anything to drink, he needs water.

GROWTH

Once they are settled, most babies gain something like 28g (1oz) a day, or 170g–225g (6oz–8oz) a week, until they are around three months old. Of course not every baby's weight behaves like that – or behaves like that all the time – but by looking at a centile chart (see p.89) you'll see that that's the average rate of gain not only for the average-sized babies around the middle line but also for the babies who started out big (at the top of the chart) or small (at the bottom).

After the first quarter year, the rate of growth slows down a little. In the second three months your baby will probably gain around 140g–170g (5oz–6oz) each week, and around 6cm (2in) in the quarter year. Gaining regularly still matters more than gaining a lot. A baby whose weight gain, week-by-week, has put her just below the 50th centile, so that if you join up her accumulating points her weight curve neatly follows that one, probably will not suddenly gain so little that she drops right down to the 9th. If she did, she might be short of food. However, if that baby started out just below the 50th centile but has always gained more slowly than most babies, so that her upward weight curve has always been flatter than average, she is probably a baby who is meant to gain rather more slowly than most.

TEETH
AND TEETHING

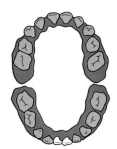

Babies usually cut first one of the two bottom teeth in the middle and then the other, starting at around six months.

Babies cut their teeth in a fairly predictable order but at widely varying ages. Your baby's first tooth will almost certainly be one of the bottom front pair but will only probably be cut shortly before his half birthday. Getting teeth earlier or later than average doesn't mean that a baby is "forward" or "backward" – in fact it means nothing of significance except that once a tooth appears that toothless grin is gone forever.

For most babies "teething" starts later than you may expect and is less dramatic. Since your baby probably won't cut a tooth until five or six months, it's unlikely that the process will trouble him before, say, four months. And it probably won't cause *much* trouble then. The first four teeth are so flat and sharp that they usually come through with nothing more notable than a slightly inflamed gum, a bit of dribbling and a lot of chewing. If you can see a red patch of gum, and your baby seems frantic to bite down on it, try rubbing it with your finger.

"Teething" is a popular, but usually inaccurate explanation for fretfulness and crying in very young babies. And it can be a dangerous explanation, too. Each year a few babies reach hospital in a serious condition because parents had ascribed what turned out to be symptoms of serious illness to teething and therefore waited too long before seeking medical help. Teething cannot cause fever, diarrhoea, vomiting, convulsions or "fits", at this age or later. If your baby seems ill when you thinks he is teething, consult your doctor: he is either ill *and* teething, or simply ill.

Teeth and chewing

When your baby is cutting her first tooth, your finger will be doubly in demand for rubbing and for chewing.

First teeth are biting-off teeth not chewing teeth. Babies start chewing with their *gums* long before they acquire teeth at the back of the mouth to help them. Don't assume that a baby with one solitary front tooth cannot chew. He will start teaching himself to chew as soon as he can get his hands and the toys that they hold into his mouth. Make sure your baby also gets foods such as peeled pieces of apple or scrubbed raw carrot to chew well before six months or he may become so used to semi-liquid foods that when he does have chewing teeth, at around a year, he won't use them because really solid food revolts him and makes him gag.

Chewing on hard foods is good for babies' developing jaws, and feeding themselves with their own hands helps them feel enthusiastic and independent about eating. Stay close, though, in case your baby pokes himself in the eye with that carrot stick. And once a coming tooth is visible, as a small, pale bump under the gum, be especially alert. When its point breaks through, it will be so sharp that your baby could grate a tiny piece off that apple and choke on it if you weren't there to help.

In the first week or two most babies lie all scrunched up as if they were still in the womb, and when they aren't being held closely in adult arms, they like to be closely wrapped. They usually feel insecure when they are lifted and frightened if their bodies, their limbs, and especially their necks are not constantly supported. Changing their clothes and bathing them and generally mucking them about is best kept to a hygienic minimum.

That changes very quickly, though. As they settle into independent life babies gradually become more comfortable and confident in their bodies and more competent at managing them. By the second month you'll probably see your baby uncurl her body, move her arms and legs for the fun of it and eventually struggle to get those wrappings off. She's ready to enjoy physical freedom as well as nestling; and to enjoy being handled and played with and carried around.

CARRYING YOUR BABY

Although babies don't mind being left in baskets or cribs when they're fast asleep, they get bored and lonely if they are isolated from the rest of the household when they're awake. You can find comfortable ways to carry your baby even when you have grown-up things to do. In a few weeks you may be comfortable using a sling on your back or on your hip as well as in front. In the first weeks, cuddle-carrying often feels best but a change is fun.

A front sling or carrier that's worn facing outwards lets your baby see where you are both going and share your view of the world.

Once he can support his own head, holding him on your hip this way round supports him from shoulder to crutch but leaves you a free hand.

A human front carrier feels grown-up and interesting to your baby and supports his spine, top to bottom.

This face-down carry often soothes crying babies. Put one hand between his legs so the hand supports him from underneath. Use your other hand to support his neck and shoulders.

KEEPING YOUR BABY CLEAN

Babies who have uncurled their bodies and begun to kick often love being bathed. Instead of lying tensely in the water, on the verge of panicked crying, she feels the water floating her body and it makes her feel light and free and powerful. It does make her powerful, too: the water supports some of her weight so she can kick harder than on dry land. For many three-month babies a bath is a favourite game and a three-minute evening splash leaves them so well-exercised and so relaxed that it's an obvious first part of a bedtime routine.

Going in the big bath

If you lie him back to kick he'll empty his little bath everywhere. It's time for the big bath.

Somewhere between three and six months, babies and their thrashing limbs get too big for any form of small bath. Be tactful about the transfer to the family bath, though. Your baby may find the vast expanse of water and the towering walls frightening at first. If the baby does seem worried, try putting the usual small bath inside the big but empty one for a few days. It will keep her splashing contained while she gets used to the look of it.

Once she does go in the big bath, holding your baby securely is more difficult because she's necessarily at floor level. Don't try to bend down to her; kneel on the floor with everything you need beside you. A small towel or special non-slip mat in the bottom of the bath will stop the baby slipping away from you and make her feel more secure too. Keep the water shallow. If it is deep she will float. Remember that the bath is wide. Unless you grasp the baby's shoulder with your fingers as well as supporting her head on your wrist, she could roll over and get her face in the water.

Some babies enjoy free kicking on dry land but still dislike being bathed. Since no baby gets over a fear by being frightened, it's best not to push it. If she's happy with that little bath you could carry on with a bath-in-a-bath or maybe a shared bath would feel sociable and safe.

Even a baby who's scared of being bathed may love it if you're in the water with him. A joint bath is for him rather than for you, though. The water needs to be warm, not hot, and it will take both your (wet) hands to hold him safely and an extra pair to lift him out.

New babies' digestions gradually settle down with the rest of them but don't expect to find that a particular type or frequency of stool is normal for your baby. Both may still be widely variable. Exclusive breast-feeding makes it very unlikely that your baby will suffer any digestive disturbance, get diarrhoea or become constipated. Try not to be concerned over several stools per day, or days without one. It does not matter either way. Even a week without a stool is not unusual, and scarlet-faced grunting when one is on the way doesn't mean constipation, only very young unaccustomed muscles.

Cow's milk formula leaves a baby with more waste to dispose of, so bottle-fed babies tend to produce larger, firmer stools and will usually pass them one to four times a day. Gastro-enteritis is a real and serious possibility in a bottle-fed baby, so a sudden attack of diarrhoea, with frequent and watery stools, means sameday medical advice. If the baby also seems ill, with fever and/or vomiting, get to a doctor quickly. Take a soiled nappy with you in a sealed plastic bag. The doctor may want to take a specimen to send to the laboratory.

Bottle-fed babies can suffer from constipation. If a baby's body requires extra water (due to hot weather or fever, for example), it will extract every possible drop from the food, leaving waste that will make a dry, hard stool that may be difficult to pass. Extra drinks of plain water are the answer but if uncomfortably hard stools are a recurrent problem after three to four months of age, very well-diluted fruit juices once or twice a day may help.

When your baby starts to eat solid foods his digestion may not break down the new substances completely so there may be colour changes and undigested particles of food in his stools. If you go on with tiny quantities, his digestive system will adapt. If stools also contain a lot of obvious mucus, though, the baby may not yet be able to digest that particular food, or it was given in a form which contained too much roughage. Withhold that food for a week or two and then offer an even smaller quantity, more finely strained.

Nappy rash Nappy rash can mean anything from slight redness to severe inflammation with sores or pustules. One can lead to the other. Soft new skin may react to toiletries even if they are labelled "hypoallergenic"; warm skin left damp is liable to chapping; acid urine stings and makes it worse and the area is a perfect breeding ground for bacteria or for yeast infections – such as thrush – from stools. The answer, then, is to use simple, or no, toiletries (warm water is wonderful stuff) and keep your baby's bottom as clean, dry and aired as you can. Wash and dry your baby immediately after every bowel movement and change him frequently in between, even if you are using super-absorbent disposables. If you need plastic nappy-covers use "breathable" types. Leave him bare-bottomed on a nappy whenever you can. If his bottom tends to get red, try coating the clean, dry skin with petroleum jelly. If that's not adequate protection consult your clinic. Some medicated ointments prevent the stay-dry layer of some disposable nappies from wicking moisture away and therefore make matters worse.

*A sleeping baby need not
keep you home or quiet!
Buggy, car seat or shoulder:
it's all the same to him.*

SLEEPING

While newborn babies often drift randomly in and out of sleep, sometimes spending long periods suspended between the two states, settled babies tend to be much more definite about the difference between the two. Once she is asleep, you can be fairly sure that your baby will not wake up again for a while; once she does wake up you can be equally certain that she will not go to sleep again until she has been fed. Not all sleep is the kind that makes you lean over to check that your baby is still breathing, though. New babies need twice as much Rapid Eye Movement (REM) sleep as adults. That kind of sleep is thought to play a crucial (though not fully understood) part in brain development. To your baby it means a relaxed body but an alert mind and lots of dreaming. To watching adults it means restless grimaces and sucking movements.

At three or four weeks of age sleeping and feeding still go hand in hand so that, left to follow their own inclinations, babies wake up because they are hungry and go to sleep because they are full. By around six weeks, though, the relationship between feeding and sleeping begins to slacken a little. Your baby will still be inclined to go to sleep while she is feeding and to be unwakeable once she is full. But she will not always sleep until she is ravenously hungry again. Instead, she will begin to wake up, sometimes, just because she has had enough sleep for the moment.

Enough sleep for your baby is still the amount of sleep she takes. Sleep laboratory studies suggest that 16 hours a day is about average for a newborn, but the range of hours that go into calculating that average is very wide indeed. Sleeping as much as 19 hours or as little as 10 doesn't make your baby abnormal – just on the sleepy or wakeful side.

Patterns of daytime wakefulness

Most babies are habitually wakeful at one particular time of day. A common one is the later part of the afternoon. The baby sleeps after breakfast through most of the morning. She has a feed at lunch-time and sleeps again, but this time she does not sleep right through until hunger wakens her. She naps for an hour or so and then wakes anyway. In many households parents or caregivers find this pattern convenient. It's a good time to pay social attention to the baby; to have her playing on the floor or riding around in a sling, or to make an expedition of taking her to the shops or fetching older children from school. If you want to, you can encourage it by waking the baby if she does not wake herself, and perhaps giving a drink of water or juice to stretch the time she waits until her next feed. An hour or two of interesting play and places and your baby will be very ready for her next feed and will probably sleep well at least through the beginning of your adult evening.

If your baby adopts a pattern of daytime sleep and wakefulness that you find wildly inconvenient, you may be able to persuade her to alter it by juggling her feeds. If she tends to nap for only an hour or so after breakfast, for example, and then stays awake most of the morning and sleeps all afternoon, an extra "snack" feed when she wakes in the middle of the morning may well put her back to sleep again. If you then let her sleep for as long as she likes, her lunch-time feed will probably come up rather late and, over a few days, she is likely to shift towards being awake in the afternoon. It doesn't always work though. Some babies will not suck if they are woken before they are hungry. Others accept the extra feed with pleasure and duly go back to sleep, but they don't sleep any longer than they would have done without it.

Adjusting night-time patterns is worth any amount of effort – but daytime ones are different because by the time your baby reaches three to four months everything will have changed anyway, and she is likely to have two or even three wakeful periods in the day. As before, a good feed makes her inclined to sleep, but as she gets older her naps get progressively shorter.

Sleeping difficulties Babies in this age group cannot have sleeping difficulties so if there are any problems they are yours, not your baby's. Unless she is ill or in pain she will sleep as much as she needs to sleep and cares very little where or when. She is still not capable of keeping herself awake, and she is no more capable than you are of waking herself up on purpose. It will be a long time yet before you need add worry about whether she can be getting enough sleep to worry about the fact that you certainly are not!

Night-time sleep Becoming a diurnal being who mostly lives by day and sleeps by night, is a biological adaptation that's commonly completed by three to four months. If your baby has reached that sort of age but does not yet sleep any more soundly or for any longer periods at night than in the day you can't teach her to make a complete difference between night behaviour and day behaviour, but you may need to help her (see p.107).

Warm enough when the covers are kicked off, cool enough when they're not, cotton baby bags solve a conundrum of comfort and safety.

Check for sources of outside disturbance too. If she shares your bedroom, your quick response to her every small sound and your anxious peeps into the cot to make sure she is still breathing, may be stimulating her to full wakefulness whenever her sleep lightens. As she gets older and more energetic, and especially once you move her from her small first bed into a big cot, she may also begin to kick off her covers so that she gets chilly and uncomfortable. Now that warm rooms and wrappings are frowned upon because of the risk of overheating and the associated increase in the risk of cot death, a lightweight cotton baby bag, shaped like a dressing gown with the bottom closed may be useful to help her feel both safe and warm. And if you start using a bag at night now, you will be sure of avoiding at least one set of later problems: climbing out of bed.

Continuing wakefulness in the evenings can be the result of "colic" (see p.120) which got your baby accustomed to spending those particular hours awake. If she did have colic but it is now over, get her up when she wakes just as you used to do, but as soon as you have given her a good cuddle, put her down again. Now that there's no discomfort to keep her awake, she'll probably drop off.

If the evening fretting has nothing to do with colic, though, and your baby is fully breast-fed, she may simply need to feed more often in the evening than you can easily believe. Believe her. It is not only that the milk supply can be somewhat scanty at the end of a busy day, but also that many babies have a growth spurt in the second month and need to build up their mothers' supply to meet it. Such babies quite often want to binge all evening and since prolactin levels are highest at night these feeding marathons are very effective.

Remember that as she gets older your baby needs to spend more and more of the 24 hours awake, so if she sleeps a great deal of the day, she is bound to be wakeful in the evening or at night. If you are taking care of her yourself, or sharing her care with your partner or a nanny, you may need to adjust the pattern of her day, reducing adults' expectations of breaks from child care, and building in more outings. If she is spending some or all of the day with a childminder or in a child care centre, make sure that she is being offered all the stimulation and play she can comfortably use. Offering too little needn't mean that your baby's caregiver is neglectful. While some young babies who are under-stimulated make it clear that they are bored and keep fussing for more attention, others are far harder to read. If your baby is getting too little stimulation in a domestic care-setting, or being overwhelmed by too much in a group setting, she may seem inactive rather than bored or alarmed, and inclined to sleep rather than fuss, until something really interesting happens, like parents coming home.

Waking at an ungodly hour of the morning usually means that your baby has had enough sleep, even if you haven't. If she still has an early-morning feed it may buy you another couple of hours' peace. Once it is clear that she doesn't need anything to eat or drink until breakfast there's nothing you can do to make her go back to sleep. Right now she will probably be happy to come into your bed so that you can at least wake up slowly. Later on she may even be content to play in her cot for a while.

Daytime sleep In the early weeks with a first baby, parents often find it almost impossible to relax or get on with anything other than baby care while the baby is awake. Only when she goes to sleep can the rest of life start up again. If she does not go to sleep, or if she keeps waking up, they feel that they have accomplished nothing all day.

That feeling is very natural while you are coping with a new and unsettled baby, but it's important to get yourself over it as quickly as you can. After all, it is only for a very few weeks that being asleep is a baby's usual state, and being awake the exception. She is a human being and very soon, like other human beings, being awake will be her usual daytime state and sleep – in the form of separate naps – the exception. You have to teach yourself to accept the baby as a wakeful member of the family and once you've stopped saving everything you need to do until she falls asleep, you will find that there are ways to do a lot of it while keeping her pleasant company. Once you take it for granted that she is a person, to whom you can chat while peeling potatoes or recount the gist of that maddening phone call, baby care and at least the domestic aspects of your life will join up.

Going in a big cot When your baby comes near to the weight limit for her first basket or crib, or begins to kick actively and try to roll over, it's time to get her used to sleeping in the big cot that she'll use until she's a big girl

Not just a place for your baby to sleep but also his special sanctuary for at least the next two years.

who sleeps in a big bed. Cots need to have high sides so that standing or climbing babies can't topple out, so most have one side that drops down to make it easier to reach the baby. Many drop-side cots also have two positions for the base and mattress so that those sides can be made effectively higher when your baby is tall enough to climb out. If you think all that barred space around her will worry your baby, let her get used to it gradually over a few nights by putting her in her first bed as usual, and then putting baby and bed into the cot.

Drop-side cots can't easily be moved from room to room, of course, but that doesn't mean your baby can no longer nap in other places. She may be able to go on using her first bed for that for a while and she'll be able to use a carrycot pram or sleep in a lie-flat pushchair for months to come, provided she wears a safety harness.

If your baby shares your bed and you mean to go on sleeping as a family, you may wonder if you'll need a cot. The difficulty of managing without one is that once a baby is mobile, her safety in a family bed depends on an adult being there to keep her from rolling or crawling out. If she has no cot of her own, you'll never be able to put her to bed earlier than one of you wants to go.

Thinking ahead about naps and nights

While your baby's eating and sleeping are still interconnected you will probably find that she usually sucks herself to sleep. She stays at the breast, or goes on with her bottle, until the nipple or teat finally falls from her mouth. Even if you hold her up in case she needs to burp, she does not surface again but is slipped into her basket or her crib already soundly off. That's a lovely, luxurious experience for your baby and it's nice for you too because, knowing she is already sleeping, you can at once turn your attention to other people or things.

But just as it is important to think ahead about the way you want to handle night waking when your baby is older, so it is important to think about this way of getting from wakefulness to sleep. A baby who drops off while she is feeding, or while you are rocking and patting her to get up wind, is not *going* to sleep, you are *putting* her to sleep. And while you may enjoy doing that now, you will not enjoy doing it for the next two or three years.

A lot of later sleeping difficulties are at least partly due to older babies who have always relied on being put to sleep not knowing how to manage for themselves. It's easy to see why. You nurse your baby until she is completely unconscious of her surroundings. Then you slip her into her bed and leave her. That's fine until she next wakes, but when she does wake (and remember everybody does wake from time to time) everything has changed. The last thing she remembers is being in your arms; now she finds herself alone in bed. Of course she is going to cry. "What's happened? Where are you?" When you come to her she wants you to pick her up again and put her back to sleep in that same way. She doesn't know how to snuggle herself down, close her eyes and go to sleep. She may only be able to drop off in your arms; she may even need to be put to the breast or be given another bottle so that she can drop off while sucking. She probably goes back to sleep easily so that you slip her into her cot without any sense of struggle. But next time she wakes the whole pattern repeats. And if you are not a bit wary, next year when she

Are family beds safe?

Is co-sleeping dangerous or not? We know there are lots of other pros and cons but all we're concerned with right now is the safety issue and we can't get a simple answer.

The reason that you can't get a simple answer is that there isn't one – or not one that different authorities and organizations in different countries can agree on. Some research findings suggest that sharing a bed with parents increases the (minute) risk of cot death because adult bedding is liable to compromise babies' breathing or make them too hot. Some studies produce no evidence that co-sleeping is a risk factor for Sudden Infant Death Syndrome (SIDS) and, to complicate matters still further, some research findings suggest that, far from being a risk factor, co-sleeping is actually *protective* against SIDS. Babies who might have given up breathing if they'd been sleeping alone are thought sometimes to be stimulated to keep going by their slumbering parents' breathing, movements and sounds.

It's unlikely that any of these findings are simply right or simply wrong. The apparent contradictions are more likely to be due to the complexity of the issue. Deaths due to SIDS are, by definition, inexplicable (see p.111). Risk factors – such as sleeping prone or being exposed to cigarette smoke – are the nearest we can get to "causes" and even those risk factors work together in complicated ways. So it may be that co-sleeping with a parent is sometimes risky (when a parent has been drinking or taking drugs, for example), sometimes neutral and sometimes protective (when a baby is starting to succumb to an infection, for example).

Cot deaths are so dreadful that health authorities understandably prefer to play safe and stay simple in the advice they give to parents. That means that any child care strategy that has *ever* been linked with any extra risk of SIDS is liable to be indicted and resulting guidelines can be confusing and potentially distressing for parents. In the UK, for instance, recent governmental reports have advised that "while it is likely to be beneficial for parents to take their baby into bed with them to feed or comfort, it is preferable to place the baby back into a cot to sleep. This is especially important if the parents smoke or have consumed alcohol". How beneficial can it really be to nurse a baby in bed if instead of luxuriating, the mother has to fight to keep herself (and the baby?) awake? And what about the harm it will do if she has to feel guilty for endangering her baby every time she loses that fight, falls asleep and only realizes that she has done so when she wakes to find that two hours have passed?

As individual parents, perhaps with the advice and support of individual health professionals, you may be able to arrive at answers concerning bed-sharing that better allow for the issue's complexities and your own circumstances and sensibilities. Of course sharing a bed with an adult *can* be a risk factor for SIDS – or for any Sudden Unexpected Deaths in Infancy (SUDI) come to that. It's all too easy to imagine what might happen if a parent was too drunk or sedated to be aware that the baby had rolled onto his tummy; the mattress was soft, the duvet was 12 togs and right over him and the pillows were not well out of the way. But that doesn't necessarily mean that bed-sharing *is* risky and that all parents should be advised not to do it, however strongly they feel that co-sleeping is right for them.

This issue of babies sleeping in family beds is not clear-cut as, for example, the issue of babies sleeping on their tummies is clear. The difference is a difference in evidence. The evidence that babies are more at risk if they are put to sleep on their fronts than on their backs is powerful and undisputed so it would be irresponsible of anybody to disregard it. But the evidence against co-sleeping is confused and conditional and there is also evidence in its favour. So, with due care, individuals are surely entitled to make up their own minds.

Full and sleepy but not quite asleep, she is all set to drop off by herself.

wakes it is still repeating. There are a great many toddlers who are still breast-fed or bottle-fed two or three times in every night because although they don't wake any more often than anybody else, there is no other way in which they can get back to sleep.

Letting your baby suck herself to sleep, and putting her into her bed already asleep, isn't something that you can, or would want to, avoid altogether. But once your baby is, say, three or four months old, it is sensible to make sure that she sometimes goes to sleep on her own so that she knows how to do it. The trick is to get her relaxed and sleepy in your arms, but make sure that she is just awake enough to be aware of being put into her crib; to experience its comfort and your departure, and to drift into sleep because sleep overcomes her.

If you much prefer putting her to sleep yourself both *for* the night and *in* the night, you could try to put her down awake for daytime naps when it does not matter so much if you have to go back to her. But eventually it is a good idea if she usually goes to sleep on her own at bedtime too. If you settle her down and she doesn't drift off but starts to cry, go straight back to her. This is skill-training not discipline. If necessary go back to her several times, until sleep does overtake her. If that seems a lot of trouble compared with just nursing her until she is asleep, think of the future. Once she is weaned and able to roll over to make herself comfortable, you want her to be able to surface in the night and drop off again, just as you do yourself. If she has never discovered how to go off to sleep without you she will have to call for help and wake you every single time she wakes up.

CRYING AND COMFORTING

Some babies cry more than others. Even once the newborn weeks are over and babies are "settled", there are some who seem more easily reduced to the miseries, more jumpy, or just less contented in general than most others. Still, even if yours is a baby who has always cried more than most and goes on doing so, the chances are that he'll cry less as he gets older. The average amount of time babies spend crying definitely peaks (at two to three hours in each 24 hours) at around six weeks.

While any drop in your baby's daily crying will no doubt be welcome, a dropping off of those long crying jags may be the most welcome of all. In the second and third month your baby may still begin to cry as often as ever – many times every day – but he will seldom go on and on despite all your efforts at comfort unless, of course, you are coping with "colic" (see p.120). Pick your crying baby up for a cuddle and a chat and the chances are that he'll stop. If he is in pain, dazzled by sunlight, teased by a cool breeze or acutely hungry, the crying may start again and go on until you do something about that specific discomfort. But most of the time settled babies will stay calm just as long as parents or carers will go on cuddling.

Many parents find that this is the change that does most to make "difficult" babies easier to live with and to love. Instead of those dreadful times in the newborn period when you felt like the most useless parents in the world, you begin, now, to know that you are magic. Maybe you wish the baby did not need your magic quite so often, but if he needs it, it's infinitely better for you to have it.

Most of the crying becomes more comprehensible, too. You still hear that now-familiar basic hunger cry. Your baby still sometimes lets out that pain cry which makes your heart thud even though your brain knows a simple burp is all he needs. But he adds a "grumbly" cry, a sort of whimpery, fretful, almost whiny sound. And he uses that one first on most occasions. He is not saying "disaster!" or "I'm starving!" just "I don't seem to be quite happy just now". Soon afterwards he adds an "anger" cry, quite unlike any of the others. It is an indignant roar: "Come back!" it seems to say, or "I want it!" or "Don't do that!"

Maybe you could not describe all your baby's different cries in words and do not recognize them in these, but you will certainly know which is which when you hear them. When your baby starts to grumble, you know that he is getting hungry or getting bored. You know it is time to do something for him and it is easier to think what to do because you are not overwhelmed by the urgency of a full-throated roar. So at least you can begin to understand his crying better, and you can usually stop it, at least for the moment. But what can you do to make him start crying less often?

All the causes and cures of crying that were suggested for the newborn baby (see p.114) may still apply to this older one. But there are some new aspects to consider now, too.

Sucky babies

It certainly works, but does she really need it?

Some babies are better soothed by sucking than by anything else and it may be difficult to distinguish the need to suck from the need to feed. A breast-fed baby can get all the extra comfort sucking he needs provided his time at the breast is not rationed and he's allowed to "empty" the first breast (and have a lovely, leisurely suck) before he's shifted over to another full one. A bottle-fed baby can't suck without feeding, so even if he is fed "on demand" he may need extra sucking. The best source of extra comfort sucking for any baby is his own hands: always available and far more hygienic than anything you can provide. Encourage him by helping his fist to his mouth a few times and by making sure you do not wrap him with his arms in, so that he cannot reach that precious thumb. Thumb-sucking usually comes later, though. Most babies cannot yet get their hands to their mouths without help or get satisfactory suction on a tiny digit.

If your baby cries a lot, cannot, or will not suck his fingers but sucks passionately on yours, you could give him a dummy. They have become increasingly common and there is no doubt that they can make a miraculous difference to a few miserable or jumpy babies. But not every baby needs one and there are cons as well as pros: don't assume that your baby ought to have a dummy. Most babies don't need them and are better off without. If your baby is miserable and you want to see whether a dummy makes a difference, try giving one just for a few months until your baby begins to put toys and finger-foods in his mouth, and at bedtime only. Peaceful evenings and nights may raise the morale of the whole family. If the baby is a happier person by around six months, you could try taking it away altogether before the baby is old enough to remember it or miss it for long. It is at the crawling and toddling stages that dummies seem most unaesthetic, unhygienic and limiting to a child's explorations.

ADVANTAGES OF DUMMIES	DISADVANTAGES OF DUMMIES
If the baby takes to it, the dummy will soothe him to sleep, soothe him when he is irritable or windy or even after a fright.	Once he is used to it he may not be able to do without it. He may want it for years and you may find it difficult to limit his use of it.
If he sleeps with a dummy in his mouth and it stays put, disturbances or the periodic lightening of his sleep level will make him start sucking again (thus soothing himself) rather than waking him right up.	Dummies often fall out during deep sleep. When your baby is disturbed or his sleep lightens, he will want it back. Since he won't be able to find it for himself he will always need help in going back to sleep.
A dummy will probably mean that he will not take to sucking his thumb.	A dummy in the daytime will limit sound-making and exploring toys by mouthing them and you may tend to plug his mouth at every protest. Unless you keep sterilizing, they're unhygienic too.

Whatever you decide about dummies, don't compromise with a "dinky feeder" (a mini-bottle filled with a sweet drink) or a propped-up bottle of juice or formula. These are the shortest road to rotted first (and future) teeth and there is also a risk of your baby sucking and choking while asleep. If you want to give your baby a drink, hold him on your lap.

Wakeful babies who are bored

A lot of your baby's crying may be due to you expecting him to sleep more often and for longer periods than he needs. He may be a baby who needs much less sleep than average (remember that some three- and four-month-old babies never sleep for more than 12 hours in the 24) or you may not yet have taught yourself to get on with life when he is around, so that you keep trying to tuck him away.

If he is a very active baby (and many wakeful ones are), the physical restrictions of wrappings and covers may frustrate him. When he must be alone in his cot or pram, try leaving him free to kick. If the weather is cold, a baby bag (see p.180) will keep him warm without restricting him too much.

Even with freedom to move around, he will get very bored if he spends a lot of time alone but awake. Interesting things to look at, swipe at and eventually touch will do a great deal to keep him happy. If you've got a garden, try putting him in his pram under a tree or where he can see patterns of light and shade or perhaps a lineful of dancing washing. If he's got to be indoors hang lots of interesting objects closely over him and change them frequently.

But there is no replacement for people. If your baby spends a lot of time awake but alone, he is probably crying because he is lonely.

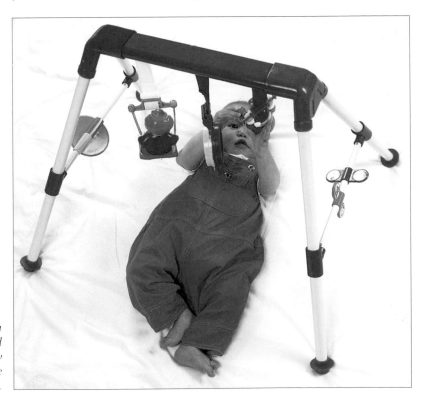

First she looks, then she swipes, reaches and grabs. Add safe-to-chew toys of her own and the fun lasts for months.

After all a baby who is asleep in the garden does not know that he is alone; a baby who is awake is alone and conscious of it. If somebody keeps him company whenever he is awake, the excess crying may stop overnight.

Keeping him company whenever he's awake doesn't have to mean sitting at home waiting for him to wake up and wishing there was someone to keep *you* company. Make the most of his portability to make your maternity leave at least something of a holiday. Breast-feeding may tie you to the baby but it does not tie the two of you to anywhere in particular. In these few months until he gets moving and begins to need a range of foods in addition to breast milk, he is easier to take along with you, to work or to play, than he will ever be again. So you can go almost anywhere and do almost anything with anybody you please and when he isn't hungry your baby will be fascinated.

All adults are fascinating to him, though, and so is everything they do. As long as he can have a cheerful carer, the baby himself doesn't need a lot of outings and entertainment. When somebody is doing simple jobs around the house or garden, he will enjoy being part of them from the vantage point of a sling. Even when nobody can carry him, there are lots of other ways to arrange for him to feel part of grown-up activities, especially now that he is old enough to be propped up. Help all members of the household get into the habit of stopping off for a chat and to tell him what they are doing. Propped in his pram with a cushion under the mattress, or in his infant seat, your baby can be taken wherever the most interesting adult activity is going on. Interesting to *him* that is. No matter how tedious you may find certain chores, they probably will not bore him. You may be fed up with peeling potatoes but he has never met a potato before; introduce him.

When he is tired of being propped, a rug on the floor is an ideal playground unless your home is full of dogs and toddlers. Your baby will not watch television but he will be happy to watch somebody else doing yoga or vacuuming and he will love to look at bright objects hanging from a self-supporting activity gym. But perhaps the best of all solutions for older wakeful babies is a baby bouncer. A soft seat harness attached by elastic cords to a door frame or ceiling hook gives him a perfect all-round view of the world and, at the touch of his toes on the floor, a delightful freedom to dance and twirl and jump... Baby bouncers make miserable babies happier and happy ones happier still. And they make babies seem like playmates to their older siblings from an early age. As soon as your baby can hold his head and upper back straight he can begin to learn his world from this entrancing new angle.

Few babies can resist a bouncer's all-round view and amazing gift of independent movement.

MUSCLE POWER

When you look at a nursery full of newborn babies, see how all their postures are dominated by the disproportionate weight of their heads, and how little control they have over their limbs or their bodies, it is difficult to believe that a single year will see most of them standing upright. Muscle control comes amazingly quickly though. Starting from the top, with babies quickly learning to balance their heads on those wobbly necks, it moves downwards in an orderly, almost unvarying, sequence. By the middle of the year babies can usually hold their back muscles steady enough to sit up more or less unsupported. By the end of the year they are finally taking charge of knees, ankles and feet so as to pull up and stand.

All babies follow the same pattern of physical development but each one goes down that path at her own particular rate. Like runners, they set off together and follow the same track, but some go fast and some do not; some spurt like hares along one stretch and creep tortoise-like along another, while others jog steadily all the way. So perfectly normal babies may be weeks ahead of, or weeks behind, equally normal babies of the same age, yet they will all be learning their new physical skills within the same developmental time-frame and in the same order. A baby may learn to sit alone early or late, but yours will certainly learn to sit before standing. A baby may omit crawling altogether in favour of walking, but if she is ever going to crawl she will do it before (though perhaps only a matter of days before) she walks.

So while milestones like learning to roll over, sit up, crawl, stand and walk are useful reminders of what every baby has to accomplish, and may be a useful guide to *what* you can expect your particular child to do next, they tell you very little about *when* the next, or any particular development will take place, and even less about when it should.

Moving past these milestones at a variable rate means that children continually shift their positions relative to each other. Comparisons between one child and another are inevitable – parents who are interested in each other's babies are bound to be interested in what each is or is not doing – but if they make parents, grand-parents and other carers feel competitive, such comparisons can lead to quite unwarranted jealousy and heartbreak. Your niece may start to sit alone weeks earlier than your daughter, but once sitting she may be content and busy and show no interest in crawling for a couple of months. Meanwhile your daughter "catches her up" by learning to sit and then "gets ahead of her" by immediately starting to crawl...

There is no "catching up" to do and no "getting ahead" because these developments are part of a process not a race. Your baby is not better or worse than your neighbour's child because she learns to manage some muscular challenge before or after her. Your baby is an individual person taking her own time along the developmental track. Compare her journey with the journeys of other individuals, by all means, but for interest not for judgment.

Head control

Self-supporting but not secure, his head will still flop if he's picked up in a hurry.

By the time they are six weeks old most babies' neck muscles will have strengthened and come sufficiently under their control that they can balance their heads upright as long as whoever is holding them keeps still. If you walk around carrying the baby, or bend down with her in your arms, her head will still flop. She needs your hand at the back of her neck as she is lifted and put down, or whenever you tip her even a little off centre.

Over the next six weeks or so those neck muscles get firmer and your baby's muscular control progresses gradually down to include her shoulders. She is growing and putting on weight, too, so her head is no longer quite so heavy in relation to the rest of her. By the time she is around three months old – or near to the equivalent if she was born prematurely – her control of her head will be complete and your supporting hand will be needed only when you pick her up, or undertake some awkward manoeuvre such as getting her out of her car seat.

As the baby's head control improves, so all her postures – the physical positions that she adopts spontaneously – change too. She gradually uncurls from that newborn position. On her back, she begins to lie flat, with the back of her head on the mattress and both arms and legs free. Turned onto her stomach on the floor, she learns to stretch her legs out from underneath her, and to turn her head to either side instead of keeping it always turned in one preferred direction. Held at your shoulder she keeps herself upright instead of curling in to rest her head in the hollow of your neck. Before long you will find that if you pull her gently to sitting position by her hands, she will bring her head with her, holding her neck in line with the rest of her spine instead of letting it drop backwards or resting her chin on her chest.

Kicking

Now she lies flat instead of curled over, she can kick her legs and wave her arms for the sheer joy of movement.

These small and gradual physical developments make important differences to what your baby can do and the use she can make of the world around her. Curled in the foetal position, her head always turned to one side, she could see nothing above her cot. Lying flat, she has a clear view above her and one that she can enlarge by turning her head. Now she can enjoy toys, mobiles and faces hung there for her delight. Now, too, her limbs are freed so that she can begin to discover the joys of physical activity.

Most babies will have "uncurled" by the time they are three months old. Once your baby has reached this stage, she will begin to look as if she is happy in her body, and having fun learning to use it. Now, if she is awake she is moving. As she lies on her back, she kicks, moving one leg after the other in a smooth bicycling action, quite different from the jerky little movements she made earlier. Her arms wave too and, as we shall see later, her hands, moving in and out of view, become her most important "toys" (see p.198). As she lies on her stomach, she practises a new kind of head control. She bobs her head up off the mattress, rather as she bobbed it off your shoulder a few weeks earlier. She is teaching herself to hold this head–up position, and once she can do so for a few seconds at a time she also discovers how to take some weight on her forearms too, so that not only her head but also her shoulders come clear off the floor.

Rolling By nine or ten weeks many babies are so physically active that if you put them on their sides, they quickly kick themselves back over to the broader base of their backs. Whether that is deliberate rolling or just wriggling aided by gravity, most babies are three months old or more before they learn the much more difficult (and potentially dangerous) technique that enables them to roll from the stability of lying on their backs to the comparative instability of lying on their sides. Beware: once your baby can roll like this, she will roll. The changing table that seemed so safe and convenient may become a real hazard between one nappy change and the next.

But think what a lot of entertainment and independence these tiny physical developments give your baby. She can exercise herself, watch her feet and her hands; roll enough to relieve skin that's tired of pressure, and change her view of the room; lift her head so that she can see something different. It takes very little to spoil all this for her though. Restrictive clothes or blankets will stop her kicking; a crumpled mat will stop her rolling; a bare white wall will take away her pleasure in being able to look around. Helping her to do what she is already trying to do, and to enjoy it, is not at all the same as pressuring her to try things she's not ready for. If she is to get the most out of her own development, she needs your help.

Beginning to move
towards sitting Once your baby can hold her head steady as you carry her gently around, and hold it clear of the floor when she lies on her tummy, her muscle control will gradually progress downwards from her neck to her upper back. If you pull her gently to sitting position, she will not curl right over, as she did earlier, so that her head almost touches the floor; she will hold up her head and shoulders, so that only the middle of her back and her hips are still saggy.

Between three and four months, trying to sit up may become one of your baby's principal preoccupations. The moment you take her hands she tries to use them as handles to pull herself up. And if there are no adult hands within reach she will try to go it alone. Lying on her back, resting after an energetic kicking bout, she will lift her head

If you won't give her your hands to help her sit up, your baby will try to go it alone.

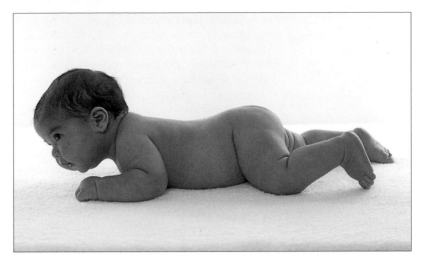

clear of the floor. A month or so later she can lift both her head and her shoulders and may get an amazing glimpse of her own feet as she does so.

All this means that the baby now needs to spend at least some of her waking time propped up. Propping her up lets her see what is going on and, crucially, makes her part of whatever social activity is available. If she is lying on her back, busy people can pass her by; propped up, people may catch her eye as they pass and pause for a smile and a chat. Propping your baby up emphasizes the fact that she is a real person.

But it needs care. It's difficult to make a baby comfortable in the corner of a sofa or armchair because as she gradually slips down, her back bends more and more, her head is pushed forward and she cannot wriggle herself back. She can be made comfortable in a pram if pillows are put under the mattress so that she leans against a firm smooth slope, and she may enjoy a fabric "bouncing chair" at the very beginning, or be happy using a portable car safety seat as a chair. But much the best solution is a baby chair, the most adjustable you can find, ideally one that goes from a nearly reclining position to a nearly upright one. A chair like this lets the baby tell you how upright she is ready to sit. If you strap her into the chair set at around its halfway mark when she is about two months old, she will relax comfortably in it. After a few days or weeks you will see her craning her head and shoulders forward from the backrest as she tries to sit more upright. If you then notch the chair up one more hole, the process will be repeated. The ideal seat is light, stable and portable so that the baby can be close to you and watch what you are doing. The best you can find may be part of a "seating system", complete with stand and tray (and maybe swing frame and rockers too) so you can turn it into a highchair (and indoor play set) and use it right through toddlerhood. If you'd rather select separate items if and when you need them, though, you'll find simple seats among low chair/rocker combinations.

By five to six months, your baby's muscle control will probably have progressed downwards to such an extent that most of her back will be self-supporting, although her hips still sag. When you pull her to sitting she may now provide all the muscle power herself, needing your hands only for balance. When you prop her, it may only be the bottom of her spine that still needs support. By the time they reach their half birthdays, many (though by no means all) babies have the muscle power they need to sit, although few have perfected the skill. If you plant your baby on the floor and take your hands away for a second, she probably will not sag, but she will tip. There is still a problem of balance left for her to solve before she sits alone.

Moving towards crawling Although quite a lot of babies look as if they are going to crawl before their half birthdays, it's rare for them to do so. Crawling almost always comes after sitting – often several months after – and despite those early appearances, it sometimes does not happen at all.

Beginning to consider crawling early depends upon babies being accustomed, and content, to spend time lying on their tummies. There have always been some babies who objected strenuously from the earliest weeks and that proportion may be increasing now that babies are routinely put to sleep on their backs and therefore have little experience of lying face-down.

Babies who do spend some of their floor-play time on their tummies quickly learn to hold their heads up, take their weight on their forearms and then to pull their knees up under them and get their bottoms in the air. By four or five months, many have discovered that they can get more purchase on the floor if they pull their legs right up and push with their feet rather than their knees. At about the same time they may learn to lift their shoulders by pushing up with their hands rather than their elbows. Now the baby has both ends organized for crawling but she still cannot put the two together so as to be on hands and knees.

Some babies try so hard to put these two positions together that they look as if they are see-sawing: head-down-bottom-up and then bottom-down-head-up. A real crawl, moving along deliberately with her tummy right off the floor, is very unusual before six months. But a see-sawing baby often covers quite a lot of ground; enough ground to go off the edge of the bed or over the top of that flight of stairs... Your baby is not fully mobile yet, but it is nevertheless high time for commonsense safety precautions.

Some babies who did not object to lying on their tummies in their first three months or so nevertheless come to dislike it and therefore abandon these preliminaries to crawling. They are often babies who are currently especially interested in looking at things and in interacting with people. Being on their tummies restricts their view of the world, so the minute they are put in that position they fight to roll over on to their backs again. Some even succeed before they are six months old.

A baby who reacts like this will probably stop objecting to lying on her tummy as soon as she can get there of her own free will by rolling over from her back. She will probably manage this soon after she has perfected rolling in the other direction.

There is no reason to suppose that babies who refuse to practise any preliminaries to crawling before their half birthdays will be later than others in actually doing it. If a baby defers first attempts at crawling until long after she is physically capable of doing it, she may experience immediate success and be roaming freely all over the place after two days, rather than two months. Some babies don't just defer trying to crawl, though. They never do it, and that doesn't matter either. Unlike the other "motor milestones" crawling is usual but not universal. Your baby may skip being a crawler in favour of being a biped.

Progress towards standing Standing is a later accomplishment than sitting or crawling because muscle control moves downwards. Babies cannot take charge of their legs and knee and ankle joints until they have acquired control over their backs and hips.

But practice starts early. Held in "standing" position on your lap, your three-month baby sags pathetically, but a month later she takes at least a little of her own weight by pushing down with her toes while she practises straightening her knees, and by four to five months the knee-straightening has become rhythmical so that it feels as if she were "jumping". Once your baby reaches this stage she may refuse to "sit" on your lap at all. The moment she is picked up she will turn herself inward, fasten her fists in the adult's clothes and fight to get herself upright. Standing gives her warm contact with your body, a chance to gaze into your face and a delightful view of the world over your shoulder, that moves as she "jumps". By the time she is six months old, you may have decided that your baby is not only a gymnast in the making but one who is convinced that all adults are trampolines...Your baby is not ready for a trampoline but she is ready for a baby bouncer (see p.188). Don't confuse bouncers with *walkers*, in which babies scoot themselves all over the floor. It's safer, and better for her development, to learn to walk without artificial aid.

PARENTS, TAKE NOTE

Keeping occasional caregivers in the picture

Babies' development proceeds by fits and starts. Some overnight accomplishments can catch parents out; that's how so many babies who can *almost* roll over on a Monday come to roll right off their changing tables on Tuesday morning.

But if keeping safe track is tricky for parents who are around all the time, it's far more tricky for people who are not. A nanny or childminder who cares for your child three days a week, the grandmother who has him on Saturdays, or even the child care centre staff who *don't* have him at the weekends, need careful briefing. As well as sudden increases in mobility, watch out for:

■ Babies who have been swiping at swinging toys suddenly learning to grab and pull. A pretty toy for looking at may not be safe to chew; a string might strangle.
■ Babies beginning to reach out and grab things. It may only be the whole dish of his own lunch but it could be the adult's hot cup of tea or a toddler's hair.
■ Babies getting hold of things and putting them in their mouths. Keeping the everyday clutter of life – pens and scissors, newspapers and knitting – out of reach is not difficult when you know you have got to, but nobody wants to find out the hard way that the time has come.

Seeing and Understanding

Newborn babies have a built-in interest in looking at people's faces and at complicated, sharply defined shapes and patterns. Both have obvious evolutionary advantages. A baby who is fascinated by people pays attention to the only source of his survival. And attention to complicated patterns and images is adaptive because he has to learn to manage a complex world.

Finding you

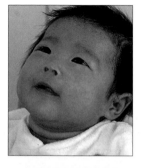

During this first half-year your baby will move a long way from merely looking, though. He will begin to understand many of the things he sees. He will learn to know one thing from another, and he will gradually begin to be able to do something about what he sees, adding action to looking by co-ordinating his hands with his eyes.

In his first days your baby will study any face, or any object or picture with the hairline-eyes-mouth pattern which makes it seem like a face. It does not take him long to learn to distinguish real faces from phoney ones, though. When he begins to smile – usually after three weeks and before six – he smiles at you, your neighbour or a face-sketch. But by eight weeks, you or your neighbour will get faster, wider smiles.

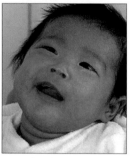

One day her steady study of your face is lit like sunrise by her first smile.

By three months, babies don't only know real faces from fake ones, they also begin to know one face from another, especially the familiar from the strange. Your baby still smiles and "talks" to that smiling, talking neighbour but he smiles more readily at you, at his father and his childminder: the people he knows and loves the most. A month or so later he knows you and he infinitely prefers you. He is not alarmed by strangers – that stage may come later – but he is restrained with them, whereas he is free, confident and joyous with you. Before he reaches six months the signs of his emotional attachment to you as individual people are flatteringly clear. On your lap he behaves as if your body belonged to him; he explores your face, sucks your nose, puts his fingers in your mouth... Handed to the stranger he is polite but decorous. When you hold out your arms to take him back, he comes to you with grins and crows of delight. He has understood that those people he keeps on seeing are his special people and he forces acceptance of that role on even the most reluctant member of the household – lodger, or teenage half-brother – by singling each out for charming attention.

Finding other interesting sights

In the first weeks of life a baby's curled-up position and limited range of vision prevent him finding much to look at for himself. However if objects are deliberately shown to him from a distance of about 20cm (8in) from his nose he will focus his eyes and indicate his interest with his body. If he was lying still, he will start to wriggle; if he was kicking, he will "freeze to attention". If the toy is moved slowly, still within his limited focus range, he will follow it with his eyes. If it is moved too fast or taken too far away for him to see it clearly, he will lose interest; indeed the minute he loses sight of the toy he has forgotten it ever existed.

Learning to reach out and touch and take the things he sees makes your baby an active participant in life.

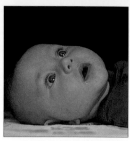

Your baby will learn by looking long before he can learn by doing. Make sure there are interesting things to see within his focusing distance.

While your baby's hands are still usually fisted he is not ready for manipulative play so he has no use for toys to play with. He can use any number of things to look at, though, and it's probably useful for him to practise focusing his eyes on different things at different angles and distances. Remember that the focusing distance that is easiest for him to start off with is 20cm−25cm (8in−10in), so any mobile or toy hung up for him to see needs to be close. If you tuck a black and white cloth "first book", a vinyl pattern card, or clear photographs of faces into his pram or crib on the side to which he naturally turns his head, he may suprise you by the concentration with which he studies them. He'll study your face even more fixedly, though. Animated adult faces − smiling, talking, singing, questioning − will certainly be the most interesting objects in the world to him, so he'll probably enjoy as much face-to-face "conversation" as there is adult time available.

Finding the best first plaything: hands

It takes a baby longer to find his own hands than to find other people's faces. Your face is deliberately put within his focal range many times each day, but his hands are usually out of sight and out of mind until he himself can do something positive to discover them. As long as his hands are continually fisted you can assume that the baby is not ready to use them. Only when they are open during most of his waking time is he ready to have things put in them; to start doing things with them.

At around six weeks your baby will probably find his still-fisted hands by touch. He grasps one with the other; pulls them; opens and shuts the fingers. But he does not know that those hands are a part of him, and, even at eight weeks, when they are sometimes open rather than fisted, he does not bring his hands up to look at them. Your baby uses one hand to play with the other as if it were an object, and if you put a rattle into that "other" hand he will grasp it and finger it in just the same way.

First adventures with a rattle can be a bridge to the discovery that hands are part of himself. Because a baby who is eight or more weeks old usually lies flat on his back, he can wave both arms freely. That means that if someone has put a rattle into his hand, he is likely to make it sound. When it sounds, he follows the noise with his eyes and that's how he comes to see, for the first time, his own hand and the rattle in it. For the next two or three weeks, toys that are easy to grasp, light enough not to hurt if they land in his eye, and make some sound when they are waved around, are really valuable. They direct the baby's eyes and attention to what his hands are doing. They help him to establish the relationship between himself and his hands; the relationship between what those hands do (wave around) and what happens (the noise).

By 10 to 12 weeks most babies don't need the sound any more, though they may still enjoy it. They have truly found their hands by now, by eye as well as by touch, and play with them constantly, watching them all the time. Your baby may lie for minutes on end, bringing his hands together; spreading them apart so that they go out of sight; bringing them back again; pulling the fingers... as concentrated as a five-year-old watching television.

Their hands are babies' best first toys. Your baby concentrates on them like a school child watching television.

Once the baby's hands are under this much control, at around three months, he will explore them with his mouth as well as his eyes and the other hand. One finger goes into his mouth; it is taken out again, inspected, put back in the mouth with a thumb for company, looked at again and so on.

Once your baby's hands go in and out of his mouth, so will everything else. His mouth has become part of his exploring equipment and he will not be satisfied that he has properly come to terms with an object unless he does put it in his mouth. Trying to stop him mouthing things is wasted effort for you and unhelpful to him. If you are worried about hygiene, make sure all the baby's playthings are suitable for sucking as well as for holding and looking at; wash them from time to time, and begin to train everyone in the household to keep potentially dangerous objects out of reach. Your baby cannot stretch out and pick things up yet, but he soon will.

Because babies' mouths are part of their exploring equipment, it is obviously a pity if they are continually occupied by dummies. Very sad and fretful babies who really cannot be contented unless they have their dummies almost all the time, probably are not ready for much play with their hands yet. But most babies can now have their comfort sucking saved for bedtime, or especially stressful times, so that their mouths as well as their hands can take part in playtime.

Starting to use hands

Babies start out by using their hands and their eyes separately, fingering things without looking at them and looking at things without touching. As long as looking and touching stay separated, though, a baby is passive: an observer of the world who looks, but cannot do anything about what is seen. To become an active participant in life, your baby has to put these two things together and learn to reach out and touch and take the things that he sees.

Getting hold of things is a very complicated business. You have to see something, work out what it is – or at least decide that you want it – estimate how far away it is, and then use careful arm movements to get your hand to it. Even then, you have to make fine adjustments of that hand in order to grasp the object. Only when you have done all that are you in a position to manipulate whatever you have got hold of: to *do* something with it. Learning this feat that we all accomplish thousands of times each day without giving it a thought, is called learning "hand-eye co-ordination": learning to put what the hands do together with what the eyes see. The development of hand-eye co-ordination in the first half of this vital year is as important as the development of crawling and walking is in the second half. What

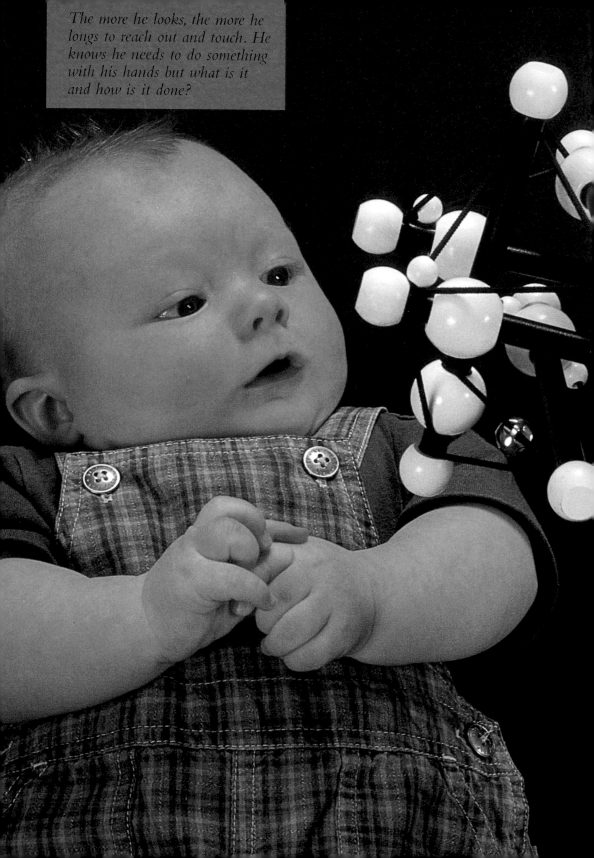

The more he looks, the more he longs to reach out and touch. He knows he needs to do something with his hands but what is it and how is it done?

is more, this co-ordination of hand and eye is of lifelong importance. The child who is good with a ball or a hammer is one whose hand-eye co-ordination is well developed. The competent driver will be well co-ordinated too.

Nothing you can do will teach a baby to co-ordinate hands and eyes until he is ready, but offering appropriate kinds of play as soon as he is ready will start him learning with all possible pleasure and speed. Babies who spend hours confined in cots or playpens, with few toys and minimal adult attention, are very slow in learning to reach out and get hold of things and that means they are also slow in discovering what can be done with things – in developing manipulative skills. As soon as those babies are given interesting things to look at and plenty of attention from adults who help them reach out for things and ensure – and cheer – their successes, their hand-eye co-ordination develops much faster.

Bored babies are deprived babies and they are usually boring to care for, too. Don't assume that because your baby is too young to *do* much in the way of playing he can't use enrichment beyond the obvious toys like teddy bears and stuffed animals, and those old friends the mobile, the rattle and the pram string.

Seeing and doing Once your baby regularly watches his hands while he plays with them, he is certainly connecting seeing with doing. Although he still focuses most easily on things that are close to him, he becomes quicker to achieve focus and better at following a moving object with his eyes, turning his head, if necessary, to keep it in sight. It will not be long before just *looking* at something that interests him ceases to be enough; he will also try to *do something about it* – taking a vague swipe at the object with whichever hand is nearest to it and sometimes looking consideringly from this hand to the object and back again.

Successfully reaching out and touching things gives your baby a sense of his own growing power and control over his own body and the outside world. He can use all the opportunities you can arrange for him. Don't expect too much, though. Although it is useful for him to practise controlling his hands and estimating, by eye, the

Swinging toys are fun to watch, and swiping gives a baby a new sense of power: "I do that and something happens!"

distance between them and the object he wants, he won't be very efficient at it yet and constant failure won't motivate him to learn any more than it motivates an older child or an adult. Try to arrange success experiences. If you are holding a toy for him, wait until he has definitely reached towards it and then put it in his hand. Things to swipe at, hung on short strings from a cot gym or playframe so that they are about 25 centimetres from his nose and well within reach of an upstretched hand, provide ideal play at this stage. Your baby will wave towards a suspended woolly ball and sometimes his hand will connect so that it swings. A light rattle, hung up in the same way, makes a change: the baby discovers that his swiping makes a satisfying noise as well as producing movement. Hang up a variety of objects that will behave in different ways when he swings them (and would not harm him if they happened to work loose) and watch him glory in the discovery, "I see that, I do this, and *something happens.*"

Touching and taking Once your baby can reach out and connect with things without having to think about it, you'll see him start to make increasing efforts not just to touch but to *get hold* of things. Swiping at toys hung over his pram or from his playframe is no longer a game in its own right. He wants to get and hold them. Most typically he looks at the toy, looks at his own nearest hand, lifts the hand towards it, "measures" the distance by eye again and then goes on repeating this until he actually manages to touch... He probably still fails to get hold of the object though, because he almost always closes his hand just before it gets there.

Swinging objects will be more frustrating than entertaining now. A cot-gym with its own intended playthings is probably the ideal replacement when he is playing on his own. Take care to select a type that has some objects down the sides; the row along the top probably will not be within the reach of a three-month baby. When he is propped up, an activity board may be popular, but remember that he won't yet manage any complicated manoeuvres like poking with one finger. He'll have most fun, and best advance his experience and skill at using his eyes and hands together, when an adult plays with him.

The kind of careful, slow reaching out that is typical of this age-stage is easiest for a baby who is held or propped in sitting position, so that his body is supported and his hands and arms are free to move. If you hold things for him to touch, don't be too quick to help him because he's struggling to make his hands obey him. If you let him make the effort right up to the moment when he manages to touch the object he wants, you can then reward him by putting it in his hand so he has actually *got* it. He will also like touching things as he sits on your lap – especially if you are not actually attending to what he is doing so he can take all the time his concentration will allow. Wearing a hard-to-break chain or a medallion around your neck is a good way to keep him happy on a bus or at an adult gathering. Your reactions to what he does soon become part of the fun, though. If any of his special adults happen to wear spectacles, removing them may be the baby's first deliberate joke.

As his half birthday approaches your baby will become so adept at focusing on things at almost any distance, and following them with

Now when he wants something he reaches straight for it, his hands opened and angled just right for its size.

He can see it and touch it, but he cannot take it. He doesn't know "two-dimensional" but he's finding out what it means.

his eyes in any direction, that he'll watch as adults go about their affairs, and even catch sight of interesting events through the window. By now he'll be relatively adept with those hands, too. He knows where they are without looking at them so when he reaches out he only needs to keep his eyes on the object and lift his arm and hand straight to it. He will learn to keep his hand open until it makes contact, and then close it around the toy. And he will discover that the best way to get hold of large objects is to go for them with both arms open, and clutch them to himself.

Show your baby anything and everything, and help him to discover what is touchable and what is not. He can see the big bus but he cannot touch it because it is too far away; he can see the sunbeams on the wall but he can't catch them. He can see flowers on the carpet but however hard he tries he cannot pick them like the flowers in the garden. Picture books will help him explore and come to terms with these conundrums and so will the small experiments his own improving manipulative skills make possible. By six months some babies (though by no means all) don't only enjoy having toys to hold and bang on the tray of their chairs but will also watch while you demonstrate what each will do and copy you in (sort of) throwing or pushing something. Your baby will probably like to have finger-foods to pick up and pop in his mouth and will try to hold his own bottle or (your) breast. And whenever he sees anything interesting, he'll reach out for it and become so quick at doing so that reaching out becomes grabbing. Be careful what objects you allow within his range: once he can get hold of things he will, and everything he gets hold of will go into his mouth - credit cards and scissors as well as rattles and rusks.

Hearing and Making Sounds

One of the excitements of reaching the four- to six-week stage, when your baby is settled into your home instead of your womb, is that she begins to link up her listening with her looking. One day she lies on her changing mat gazing absently at the ceiling while listening intently to your pleasant chat. The next day she listens just as intently, but instead of gazing at the ceiling, she searches with her eyes for the source of the voice, looking for what she is hearing.

If you haven't yet seen your baby smile in a convincingly social way, you may be due for that unrepeatable experience about now, too. Although parents don't always notice this, first smiles are usually a reaction to voice alone, not to smiling faces or even to smiling talking faces. Your baby smiles first to the sound, then, when she has visually discovered your talking face, she smiles to the sound and the sight. Only two or three weeks later still will she smile to your smiling face without the talking sound.

During the second month, babies begin to react to an increasingly wide variety of sounds. Crashes will still make them jump, music will still soothe many, but sounds in the neutral middle range become important too. Your baby's reaction to any particular sound will usually depend on the mood and state she is in when it begins. If you switch on the vacuum cleaner while she is feeling grumbly, the noise will probably act as the last straw and make her cry. But if you switch that same cleaner on when she is feeling happy and playful, it will probably just add fuel to her smiling and kicking. It is as if these medium range sounds act as a general stimulus, making babies feel more strongly whatever they were feeling before the sound began. People's friendly voices are the important exception. They, and only they, seem consistently interesting and pleasing to babies, whatever the circumstances and whatever their mood.

First social sounds Since babies have a built-in interest in listening to people's voices, it is not surprising that they usually make their own first social sounds when they are being held, played with and talked to by an adult. Babies make a few sounds that are not crying from soon after birth, but those contented gurgles after feeds and little whimpers before crying are more the result of physical states than any desire to communicate. A full stomach, a totally relaxed throat and a half-open mouth lead to "contented" gurgles. A tense throat and faster breathing lead to whimpering.

It is two or three weeks after they have begun to respond to being smiled at and talked to with pleased smiling and wriggling, that most babies begin to add some sounds of their own. Your baby may grin and kick, watching your face and producing small explosions of liquid sound. A couple of weeks later, perhaps round about three months, she will have sorted smiling out from talking. Now, if you smile, she smiles back. If you talk, she talks back.

Babies who are talked to a great deal tend to be talkative. Babies

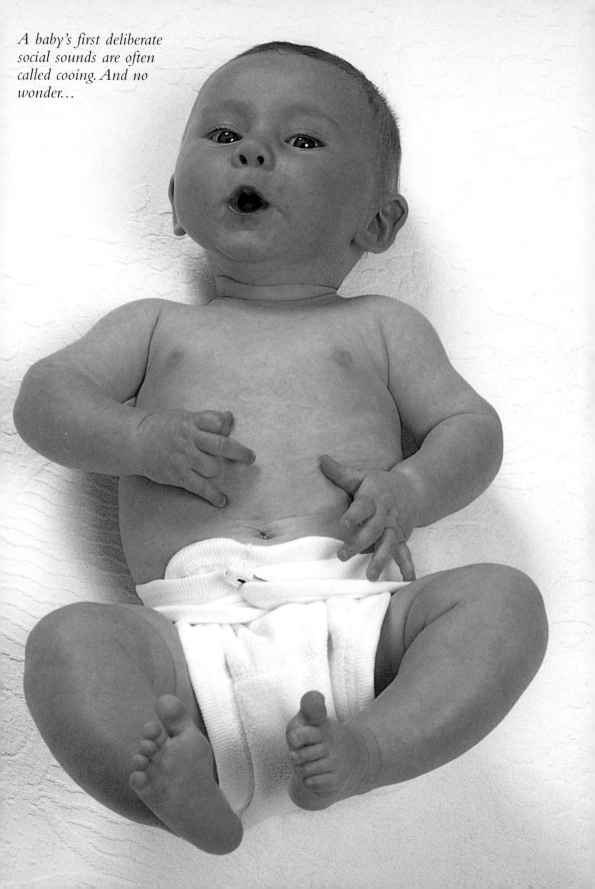

A baby's first deliberate social sounds are often called cooing. And no wonder…

who are usually cared for quietly, are not handled much at all or are attended to by someone who often simultaneously talks to an older child, talk much less. Of course babies do not only talk when they are talked to; they also talk when they are on their own in their cots. But plenty of social conversations when she is with other people usually means plenty of "practice talking" when she is alone, too.

"Talking to herself", combined with playing with her hands, is often a baby's best solitary entertainment at this age. In fact the more babies "talk" (both to adults and to themselves) the more likely they are to be content to spend some of their waking time alone. Far from getting "spoiled", babies who are given plenty of attention by adults tend to be more contented and less demanding than babies whose parents ration the attention they give.

First conversations These early vocalizations are not "talk" in the sense that your baby is trying to say something specific, of course, but they are "talk" in the sense that she is deliberately using her voice as a means of interacting with you. You say something to the baby, she makes a sound back and then pauses, as if waiting for your reply. When you say something more, she waits until you stop as if giving you your turn, and then makes some more noises as if taking her own. This is social sound-making and no sound other than a human voice can stimulate it. Research workers have tried following each sound made by babies with the tinkling of a little bell; but that sound did not make any of the babies "answer", nor affect how much they talked overall. Your baby "answers" somebody who is talking to her: she doesn't just make a sound because she hears one.

Babbling The second three months of a baby's life typically produce a positive spate of what is technically called "babble". By that time most babies have reached a stage of overall development that makes life very stimulating and exciting for them. As they kick and roll, play with their hands, swipe at objects and triumphantly touch them, they celebrate and comment with streams of talk. Your baby will still talk most of all when you talk to her, but she will seldom stay silent for long even if she is alone.

At three to four months most of the baby's sounds are open vowels. She says "aaah" and "oooh". This stage is often called "cooing" and with good reason: she sounds very like a dove.

The first consonants which most babies add to their cooing – dictated by the immature configuration of their vocal tracts rather than any intention – are K, P, B and M. They turn cooing sounds into noises which sound much more like words. The one Western parents usually notice most is "maaaa". It cannot be coincidence that names for mothers, in a majority of European languages, start with that sound. Along with a few unwary mothers assuming that their babies are trying to name them, there are always a few unwary English-speaking fathers downcast because the baby says "maaa" but does not say "daaa". In the first half-year of their lives, it's reasonable to assume that the baby is neither naming nor not naming anybody. Babies say "maaa" because the M sound comes easily to them early in their speech development. They do not say "daaa" because the D sound is difficult until later.

Going through these stages in sound-making, learning to make more and more complicated babble-sounds is built in to babies' development. Although your baby will babble more fluently if she is talked to a great deal, she will babble to some extent if she is scarcely talked to at all, or even if she never hears a single word or sound from outside because she is deaf. You cannot assume that the hearing of a baby under six months is normal just because she babbles and makes sounds. Deafness will not show itself in her voice until the second half of her first year. You can only spot hearing-loss early by watching the baby's reaction (or lack of reaction) to sounds from outside herself. If she never turns her head to look for the source of your voice and does not jump when you drop a saucepan just behind her, consult your doctor however much she talks.

Listening   By the time your baby is four or five months old she will listen intently when you speak to her, and watch your face even if you are moving around nearby rather than talking to her face to face. When you leave a space in the flow of words she will answer you with increasingly varied sounds and emphasis. When she is alone she will practise running through an increasingly rich repertoire of sounds.

Many parents assume that their children learn to talk by copying

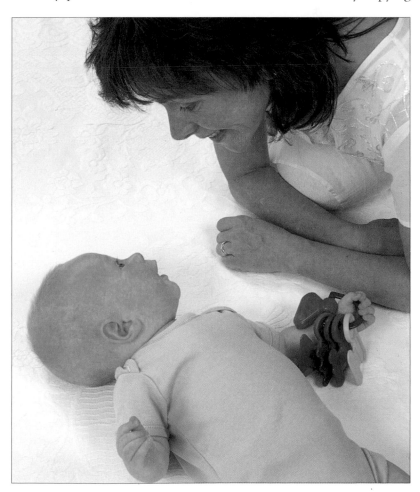

While you talk, he listens; when you pause, he talks in his turn. The art of conversation is learned long before words.

so, from this stage onwards, they simplify what they say and emphasize particular words, thinking that they are making the job of imitation easier. Babies do not learn to speak by imitation, though, and what they need from adults is not easy speech but lots of two-way conversation. Talking to your baby, now and later, as if she understands you, is the very best way to help her towards doing so. Your talk gives your baby something much more important than a model to copy: it gives her the intensely enjoyable experiences of communication that stimulate her to join in with every sound that she already can make and every sound that she can learn to make.

A wide range of babble-sounds is available to all human babies. How many – and which – sounds a baby makes depend partly on where the physiological development of her sound-making apparatus – mouth, tongue, larynx and so forth – has got to, and partly on individual talkativeness. Nationality, or the particular language or accent used in talking to a baby, probably makes no difference yet. Because the sounds babies make are universal, they naturally include noises which sound like attempts at words in any language. Individual babies learn the language of their families and communities less because they imitate what they hear than because of the selective reactions of parents, relatives and carers to particular sounds. If listening adults are English-speaking, they select the English-sounding noises, greet them ecstatically as attempts at words and dismiss the rest as "mere babble". Italian parents pick the Italian-sounding noises, Japanese parents select the Japanese sounds... In truth, though, your baby is not trying out words in any particular language; she is not trying for words at all. She is just babbling because babbling is a sociable thing to do: playing with making sounds. The sounds she makes will not become different from those of her friends from other linguistic backgrounds until she starts to make meaningful words in the second half of the year.

Although your listening baby is not trying to imitate what people say to her, she is learning their voices, learning to distinguish familiar people from strangers by listening just as she already distinguishes them by looking. Mothers' voices are usually familiar to babies from before birth – and therefore distinguishable from everyone else's – but by the time she is six months old your baby's excitement may clearly show that she has heard a friend talking in the hall. Later, when she wakes from a nap and you go into her room talking, she will begin to smile even before she has disentangled herself from the bedding enough to look at you. But if the voice she heard had not belonged to you but to a little-known babysitter, the face she lifted from her cot would have been a watchful and suspicious one.

Helping your baby to talk The age at which children say their first words, put two words together in a phrase or build their first sentences, is probably dictated more by genes than parental behaviour. Still, the ease, fluency and complexity with which your baby babbles now is related to the ease and speed with which she will learn to use real speech later on. And since her talkativeness now is at least partly dependent on stimulation from the adults around her, and her talkativeness later will dictate her readiness for many kinds of learning, making sure she gets all she can use is clearly important. Your baby is trying to join a language community. It will not help her to be committed to long daily hours with a bored young au pair who speaks no English and not much at all; to all day, every day, in a centre with too few adults to the numbers of babies and therefore little time for talk, or to a childminder or relation who keeps the TV on all day as a matter of course.

Not every parent at home finds this kind of stimulation easy to provide though. Talking to babies (even their own) is easier for some people than for others. Natural talkers chat to anyone who is around and if that happens to be the baby (or the dog), she gets the benefit. Some adults who wouldn't necessarily chat to a pet have a real sense that babies are people from day one and would no more ignore a baby than a visiting friend. Other people are naturally quiet, do not talk very much even to each other and find talking to a baby makes them feel silly – as if they were talking to themselves.

You cannot just decide to become a talkative person. If you try to force yourself to behave in a way that feels unnatural it will not strike your baby as real communication.

A few set-up situations will help you though, because your baby's responsiveness will get you going:

■ Show her a picture book, point to and name the things in it and

---

PARENTS, TAKE NOTE

Deafness

Problems with hearing cause problems with language. Early recognition maximizes the chances of effective help, so if you find yourself wondering if your baby is hearing well, don't wait and see: seek advice.

Impaired hearing is often missed in the first three or four months because even once babies have separated out their listening and looking so you think you can tell which is making them smile, seriously affected babies "coo" just like babies with normal hearing. These early sounds are not dependent on auditory input.

By the time a term-baby is four or five months old, though, there will be cues. As well as jumping when somebody makes a sharp crash (which even a baby with less-than-perfect hearing may do) most babies now often look for the source of a sound, turning their heads to find your talking face or even the TV. If nobody has ever seen your baby do that, set up some ideal opportunities, such as putting him in his chair, waiting until his attention is on another adult in front of him then speaking in an ordinary voice from

close behind him. If he doesn't react, don't panic (he may have heard you but been too busy to bother) but do mention it to your health visitor or doctor.

Before the middle of the year, your baby's cooing will have acquired consonants and been transformed into babbling and now there will be differences between the sounds he makes if he is, or if he is not, hearing-impaired. Unless there are other babies in your lives, or you can clearly remember the babbling of an older child, the difference may be difficult for you to hear yourselves, but it should be fairly clear to an experienced child health professional.

If nothing suggests that your baby's hearing is impaired except that he doesn't "say" much, it probably isn't. There are many reasons for relative quietness in infancy, such as:
■ Being a relatively quiet baby.
■ Being born prematurely and/or having health problems postnatally.
■ Being a twin.
■ Coming from a quiet/late-talking family on one side or the other.

Sharing a book is one of the most satisfactory ways of sharing an adult.

tell her what they are doing. She will enjoy it even without understanding the details, and she's entitled to library tickets, right now.

■ Tell the baby what you are doing whenever you are handling her. As you bath her, tell her which part you are soaping or what you are reaching out for. As you give her a meal, tell her what it is and what is coming next.

■ Ask questions. Of course your baby will not answer in words but she'll do so surprisingly clearly in expressions, intonations and gestures: "Is that nice?" "Where's it gone?" "Is it too cold?"

■ Talk naturally, without deliberately over-simplifying what you say. If you try to keep your words simple, the pace slow and the subject matter comprehensible, you will sound stilted and unnatural. Your baby will respond just as gleefully to your comments on the latest political developments or the price of cheese as she will to a carefully chosen sentence about the family dog. If baby talk comes naturally to you (and it probably will) by all means use it. If it doesn't, don't. At this stage it does not matter either way.

■ Try to have some play-talk time alone with your baby, even if she is one of triplets or has a sadly jealous toddler sister. This is especially important if chatting to her in front of other people makes you feel silly, or if you have an older child around who also needs lots of conversation and is infinitely better at making sure he gets it!

■ Most important of all, listen to your baby and try to answer her, in words, every time she smiles and makes noises at you. She does not need a running commentary or monologue from you every moment of the days, she wants conversation. If you are not a person who finds it easy to start many conversations yourself, you can at least discipline yourself to reply whenever she tries to start one.

A bath is a time for fun and talking, and for feeling every inch a responsive person.

Playing
and Learning

Play is much more than "just fun" to babies. Play is discovering what they can do and practising doing it; finding out about things and exploring what they find. At this age-stage play can be anything which stimulates babies to use their bodies, their senses and their emotions; to develop their thinking, their understanding and their intelligence. So while play must be fun (or the baby will not do it), not all play has to be deliberate fun. Provided the adult who is taking care of him has enough time, patience and good cheer, your baby can get some play value out of every single ordinarily pleasant happening in his day, from having his nappy changed to being fed lunch.

Being deliberately played with is very important to babies, though. Older children may long for you to play with them and love it when you do, but they can play without an adult in a way that your baby cannot. In fact for the next year or so the distinction between "playing" and "learning" that will be so important when he is older, will scarcely exist, and neither will the matching distinction between an adult playing with him and teaching him. When you or another adult carer set out to play with your baby, you can't help but be teaching him because he can do so little for, or by, himself and has everything to learn. He'd probably like an adult to play with him whenever he's awake but the time any of you can spend one-to-one with him, and without anything else you have to (try to) get done simultaneously, is probably limited. So it is worth making sure that it is used for the most appropriate, and therefore interesting and enjoyable, kinds of play you can possibly think up.

Making the most of playtime
Adjust kinds of play to your baby's moods. Like everybody else he enjoys different things when he is in different moods, but unlike most older people his moods can change in a moment.

When he is feeling tough and good, he enjoys rough and tumble play. It makes him triumph in his body and, gradually, in his own control and power over it. But when he is feeling tired or unwell, the same games frighten and upset him. He does not feel in control and powerful now; he feels manhandled.

When he is feeling quiet and affectionate, he revels in being rocked and crooned to. But when he is feeling restless and energetic, the same games make him feel imprisoned.

When he is tired or hungry or miserable, no game is any good. He does not want your play, he wants bed or food or comfort.

Being a playmate means adjusting your timing to the baby's. His reactions are much slower than yours, especially when the play that you are offering stretches new abilities up to and beyond their limits. If he is to take his full share in the "game", you must train yourself to play at his pace. If you speak to him, for example, wait five seconds for him to "answer" and then get impatient and say something else, you have done him out of his turn. Wait. It may take him fifteen seconds to find his answering sound.

The world through a baby's eyes is dauntingly difficult to understand.

If you hold out a toy for him to take, wait while he starts the painstaking process of reaching out for it, but then get sorry for him and put it into his hand after all, you have done him out of his part. Wait. Give him time to get his hand there; time to succeed in the play-task you have set him.

If you smile down at him for a few seconds, blow him a kiss and then turn away, you have left him yet again with no part in the game. He was probably going to smile back at you but you did not give him time. Now his smile fades as he gazes, puzzled, at your back.

Adjust your games to your baby's temperament. There is a "right" intensity of stimulation for each baby at any moment – enough to interest him and make him notice, but not enough to overwhelm him and make him withdraw. The swinging-in-the-air game that makes one five-month baby crow with delight will really frighten another. The gentle lullaby that makes one smile and try to sing will pass unnoticed by another. You know your own baby best; the more alert you can be to his reactions, the more easily you will be able to get your play just right for him.

Does he hate loud noises? Then don't give him a metal spoon to bang on that saucepan, give him a plastic spatula instead. Don't give him a rubber duck with a loud squeak either, put sticky tape over the squeaker hole until he has got acquainted with it and don't let your toddler pick it off to "make it work".

Is he physically timid? Then don't play "This is the way the farmer rides", bouncing him on your knee. Play "This little piggy went to market" instead, playing with his toes.

Is he physically very active? Then don't count time spent travelling in his car seat or confined in his chair as "playtime" even if he does have a toy to "play with". Put him on the floor instead and help him to "bicycle" his legs and practise rolling over.

Provide the "right" amount of novelty. Between about three and six months babies tend to be most alert to, and interested in things which are familiar enough to be manageable to them but yet slightly novel. An object which bears no resemblance to anything your baby has ever seen before may leave him cold or frighten him into retreat, but entirely familiar objects may bore him. He's found out all he can about that old rattle or familiar string of ducks across his pram; there are no more discoveries to be made and therefore no more than passing, for-old-time's-sake interest. What your baby will like best is another rattle, rather like the last one but a bit bigger, perhaps, and a different colour. A piece of paper like the one he had yesterday, but tissue this time so that it feels different and makes a new kind of rustle. A music box like the first one but with a new tune; a mobile as before but with different shapes; or a plastic bottle with bubbly water in it instead of that plastic jar...

Give your baby the chance to play with no clothes on and discover that skin is "me" and can never be shed but clothes are "outside me". By two to three months most babies take a tremendous pleasure in being naked, in striking contrast to their fear of nakedness earlier on. Naked playtimes have everything to recommend them. The baby has the chance to discover and practise new physical skills, unhampered by clothes and coverings, and he has the chance to "find" all the parts of himself that are usually hidden from view and from touch under nappies and vests. Taking off his clothes changes the texture of his world, as air or sunlight fingers his skin while he rolls and chortles. Physical play and cuddles with you take on a new dimension, too. You will probably find his bare dimpled back irresistible, and if you should happen to find blowing raspberries in his tummy irresistible as well, you may provoke his first real belly laugh.

But of course your baby needs to be warm and he needs to be safe. The centre of a double bed with a towel spread over it is an ideal naked playground as long as he cannot yet roll right over. And if it is warm enough, a rug on the grass under a tree is an idyllic place for him to play.

Help him to explore bits of his world that he cannot reach on his own. Carry him around the living room looking at all the pictures on the wall; all the ornaments; all the pot plants. Take him into the garden or the park and lift him close enough to touch a branch of a shrub if he wants to, and·can manage it.

And when you are doing chores you have done a million times before, remember that they are new to him and let that renew your interest and slow your pace. Introduce him to the tomatoes you are slicing; hold him up to dabble in your washing-up water if it's not too hot, or let him touch that bag of frozen peas for a second and find that it is too cold.

Everything you take for granted is new to your baby: he needs you to introduce him.

TOYS AND PLAYTHINGS

Throughout this age-period beloved adults are your baby's best playthings. Your body is his gymnastic equipment; your muscles supplement his so that with you he can do a thousand things he cannot yet do alone. Your face and voice together are entrancing to him; the things that you do and the things that you use all fascinate him. When you give him your attention, your affection and your help, you give him the best kind of play there is. Gradually, though, babies come to need and want to find out about the world and the things as well as the people that are in it. They need objects; playthings, toys...

Toys for an age group that will not see the TV advertisements or clamour in a toy shop have to be designed to appeal to the people who will choose and pay for them – adults. Of course they are designed to be safe and colourful, but who said babies like brilliant primary colours best? Try your baby with a black and white book or a purple rattle (if you can find one). They are also meant to be easy for babies to hold, but in an attempt to convince adults that they are getting value for money, many are made more elaborate than is necessary and therefore heavier than is desirable. Your baby will do nothing with his first toys except wave them (so extra bits to spin or pull are redundant) and he will almost certainly hit himself in the eye in the process. Real value-for-money toys for this age-stage are simple and lightweight and the better-designed also have enough variety of shape, texture and sound built in that a baby with very few skills can get a lot of experiences.

Whatever plaything you give your baby he'll look, feel and mouth it, then drop it and move on.

However carefully you choose rattles and rings, cuddly toys and mobiles, squeaky toys and balls though, bought toys alone will not be enough for your baby at this stage. Whatever you give him to play with, he will do very little with it. His main interest in objects is in getting hold of them; looking at them, feeling them and exploring them with his mouth. Once he has thoroughly examined an object in this way he is ready for a different one. Only a millionaire with unlimited storage space could buy enough toys to satisfy his insatiable curiosity about things. The answer is to lend him a carefully chosen selection of ordinary household objects – your toys – to supplement his own.

Everyday objects for play

All objects are new to new babies so they will enjoy anything you are prepared to lend. It does not matter what the object is for as your baby will not be able to make it work. Colour, size, shape, weight, sound and feel are what matter.

Sharing household things with babies does add to adult responsibilities though, because their knowledge, vigilance and commonsense are the only guarantee that those things are safe for play. You don't only need to be alert to possible hazards yourselves, you also need to alert anyone else who cares for your baby. A mother's helper – even a grandmother – who arrives and finds the baby playing with something of yours might assume that you'd passed it as safe and not realize that she should keep a special eye on it.

Remember that the baby will suck and bite at everything. Anything he plays with must be safe for him to put in his mouth.

He needs many things to examine: safe household objects are fun.

Check apparently harmless objects like tea strainers to be sure there are no edges that could hurt his mouth. Things that are safe when whole can become dangerous when broken so keep checking and be quick to throw things away at the first sign of disintegration. Yoghurt pots, for example, are very sharp once they have cracked, and can even trap small fingers or bottom lips. By accident or effort, the baby will learn to take things apart; if you want to make plastic pots or bottles into home-made "rattles", don't put dried peas in them, or anything small enough to cause choking; using two really big buttons is better. Sucking sometimes means swallowing; watch out for unexpected poisons, such as batteries, and some newsprint (assume it's all newsprint) as well as for obvious ones like remaining drops of cleaning fluid in a plastic bottle you thought was empty. It's a good principle never to use for play any empty container whose original contents would have been dangerous to your baby: if you want plastic bottles, stick to well washed-out empties that held fruit juice or baby lotion. And remember that whatever the baby holds, he is certain to drop. Avoid anything heavy enough to hurt if he happens to drop it on his face when he is playing lying down, or even his fingers if he's sitting in his highchair.

Safety precautions are more difficult to enforce when your baby shares playspace with older children. A four-year-old can learn what's dangerous to the baby but it's not fair to rely on her remembering. A toddler may actually offer the baby her felt-tip pens or sweets. It will be even more difficult when the baby crawls, so work out now how you, and any carer who looks after a range of ages, can best manage.

During these months your baby will become very efficient at reaching out to touch objects but will still have trouble in picking them up. It is only in the second half of the year that he will learn to use his fingers and thumbs separately and develop a fine pincer grasp. In the meantime he will probably approach things two-handed, trapping his target-object between his wrists and then scooping it up with his palms. That's easiest for him if he is firmly supported in a sitting position with both arms free and the object on a table or tray in front of him. Your lap as you sit up to table is an ideal support. Failing that he needs to spend some of his playtimes in his infant seat or highchair with its own table.

At this stage babies can only attend to one object at a time, and certainly cannot choose between several, let alone use two or more together. Faced with a trayful of toys, many become confused and play with none of them. Your baby will probably enjoy this kind of play most when you put one or two objects on his table, and take them away and replace them with others every few minutes when he begins to get bored.

If the baby is playing with one of your kitchen "toys" and you need to use it, offer another object as a swap. When babies in this age group are grasping things, they are actually incapable of letting go on purpose. The more you try to take away the wooden spoon you need, the more tightly his fingers will curl around it, and he will bitterly resent having it removed by force. So make use of his inability to do two things at the same time: offer him that soup spoon and he will drop the one you are waiting for.

LOVING
AND SPOILING

Playing with your baby when there are grown-up things to be done; trying to look at things from her point of view; adapting to changing needs and moods; responding to every gesture and sound; it all adds up to a lot of attention. Should your baby have so much? Is it loving or is it spoiling?

That's an argument most parents have with someone, even if it's only with each other or themselves. You need to work out what you think and find the confidence to behave accordingly yourself, and convey clear expectations to anyone else who cares for your child. If you don't, you will always be vulnerable to the charge that you are "spoiling" her; in fact as she grows older, uncertainty about "discipline" may become your Achilles' heel as a parent.

The spectre of a "spoiled child" hangs over many parents almost from the moment their first baby is born. The baby is fine and healthy, but if they are not careful they will "spoil" her. What does that mean? "Spoiled rotten" makes children sound like pieces of beef, made disgusting by being carelessly left out of the fridge past their "use by date", but children are not meat. Neither the definition of "spoiling" nor the avoiding action to be taken are agreed, yet the concept causes endless misery – and not only to the children. For fear of spoiling, mothers who only want that hurting noise to stop, deny themselves relief and leave babies to cry alone; fathers who pant home from work but fail to arrive before "bedtime" deny themselves, or are denied, hugs; grandparents are denied the pleasure of giving "too many" presents, and whole families ration their attention and therefore children's joy.

Your charming baby will not become a selfish, demanding, bratty four-year-old because she gets "too much" of any of that. There isn't even any risk that your miserable, colicky baby will get spoiled by all the extra carrying and rocking she's getting. In fact there's no such thing as too much attention and comforting, play, talk and laughter; too many smiles and hugs; even too many presents and treats, as long as parents, or whoever is in charge, give them because they want to rather than because they feel they have to; willingly rather than in response to blackmail. That bratty four-(or forty) year-old may have been indulged earlier on, but such individuals sometimes turn out to have been notably under-privileged as children. Indulged or deprived, though, what is certain is that people who become spoiled get most of whatever they do receive as young children by bullying it out of parents and others against their better adult judgment.

Getting "spoiled" does matter. Young children who will "not take no for an answer"; older children and adults who remain self-centred and insensitive to the feelings of others, think only of their own gratification and give no thought to anyone else's needs, are spoilers of everyone's pleasure. Each child does have to learn that "she isn't the only pebble on the beach"; every adult does have to be aware that she or he is not an island.

There's no such thing
as too much attention
provided you give it
because you want to,
not because you feel
you have to.

What's important to young babies in day care centres?

My maternity leave is nearly over and I'll need full-time care in a day nursery or child care centre. What should I be looking for?

No printed list can replace real-life looking and talking, but the following are all widely accepted indications of good practice for babies and young toddlers.

Day care can only be as good for your child as the people who do the caring, so look first at staff training and/or experience, support and supervision:

■ Your baby needs intimate, consistent individual care.
He should be allocated to a "key worker" who, ideally, will be primarily responsible for his hands-on care as well as for logging his progress in the nursery and any problems. Some centres encourage close relationships between key workers and children (even having them "move up" with their children at least to pre-school age).

The higher the number of staff relative to the numbers of children they care for (the adult:child ratio) the better. Recommendations for excellence are that one adult care for no more than three of these youngest children.

Babies should be in rooms containing groups of no more than six children (and two adults). Young toddlers may be in groups of nine children (still with three adults). From around 18–36 months the usual recommendation is an adult:child ratio of 1:4 and a group size of up to 12 children (and three adults).

Where a centre (or a childminder or family day care provider) cares for children of different ages in "family" groupings, there should not be more than two children under two years in any one group.

Once a child has become attached to a care provider, his security depends on her staying in the job. Everything possible should be done to reduce turnover of staff. You might ask what that turnover has been in the past year.

■ Your baby also needs high quality care.
Quality is likely to be related to pay and therefore to training and turnover, but a planned "educational" programme must be an integral part of quality care, even for the youngest babies. Don't be dazzled by an elaborate-sounding curriculum. The aim is not that babies should be taught "subjects" or even directly taught skills. What matters is that each should be encouraged in a wide range of play activities tailored to his particular needs and changing with them.

The physical conditions in which children are cared for are obviously important but subject to widely varying regulations. Consider how clean and warm and bright it is, how much daylight and sunshine comes in, and the amount of space available to each group (can two one-year-olds push toddle-trucks without terrorizing the rest?).

One room, however spacious, is a limited all-day environment for babies with a whole new world to find out about. Look for outside playspace in daily use and enquire about the availability and frequency of trips outside the nursery.

■ Your baby needs respectful care.
If babies and toddlers are to spend their days as a group yet feel themselves to be valued individuals, the nursery must support every child's self-esteem. It's a good sign if staff are not only willing but eager to work closely with you and with anyone you designate as important in your baby's life.

As far as possible physical care arrangements should allow for individual differences. Ask if every child is expected to eat the same food and take the same length nap at set group times. You could also enquire whether toddlers are helped towards toilet mastery on an individual or group basis.

Books, toys and ceremonies should reflect the cultural diversity of the nursery and be positively non-sexist and anti-violent. Staff should avoid stereotyping language, model sensitivity to disabilities or problems and be able to describe to you how they would handle a range of interpersonal issues, such as name-calling, biting, bullying and hitting back.

But those phrases, echoing down the years from our own childhoods and applied without much thought to our children, have no sense or meaning in the life of a baby, and very little in the life of a toddler. It's not that these new children are too good to get spoiled, it is that they are not nearly grown-up or clever enough to get spoiled. In order to become spoiled (or indeed to become the opposite, a paragon of unselfishness and thought for others), a child has to see herself as an individual person, completely separate from everyone else. She has to appreciate other people's rights as well as her own and she has to be able to plan to assert her own over theirs. That's far too sophisticated for babies and toddlers. Right now your baby scarcely knows that there's a difference between her hand and yours. If she wants a finger to suck, the nearest one will do. If she feels a need, she expresses it; it will be months before she knows that you have feelings and needs as well. Your toddler learns all that, of course, and it's important that she should, but she will be nearer two than one year old when she becomes intellectually capable of working out involved plans for power struggles like, "If I cry and just keep on crying she'll let me in the end."

Meeting a baby's needs is a tough job, and tougher at some times than others. Every baby has some smooth phases when her development and lifestyle mesh, and some phases when they get out of step and new needs arise so fast that for a while she has to keep demanding. If spurts in development are noticed so that the new needs are quickly met or even anticipated, she will soon stop needing to tell everybody about them so loudly or so often. But if you worry about the "demandingness" being a symptom of spoiling, or other people worry you by suggesting it, you may set yourself to resist those needs rather than to understand and meet them, and then she will have to keep on telling you about them in the only ways she can. Friends and relations who tell you that your baby is "canny", that "she's twisting you round her finger" are not so much wrong in fact as in tone. Babies near to the middle of their first year have learned a lot about their small world and the people in it. Provided they are cared for consistently by the same selection of people – parents, relations, caregivers – they will have learned what to expect of different people, and *will* now be learning how to manage them, and that's good. If your baby is ever to be a communicative, competent, confident person, it's important that she discovers now, for example, that although there's nothing she can do to stop you leaving her while she's asleep, so that she wakes up all alone, there is something she can do to make you come back as soon as she wakes and becomes conscious of needing you. She learns that you come when she cries, so she learns to summon you *by* crying and later on she'll call. That's "management" of her life and her environment and it's important she should succeed, but you may have relatives or acquaintances who call it "manipulation" and see it as important that she should fail. "Don't give her her own way" they insist; "life is tough and she'd better get used to it". You may not be able to change those attitudes but do try to insulate yourself so they cannot penetrate and hurt you. Above all, don't let yourself in for sharing your baby's care with a childminder or a nanny who wants her to believe that "those who ask don't get".

If babies nap for half an hour when adults had expected two hours' peace, only paragons are pleased to see them awake. Once your baby is awake, though, there's nothing either you or she can do to put her back to sleep so the obvious and easy answer to her cries is to get her up and help her play. The fear-of-spoiling answer is the direct opposite: "I'd meant to pick you up at 1.30pm but now you're crying for me at midday I'll jolly well see that you wait until 2pm because you've got to learn." What could a baby learn from this? What message could that supposedly "disciplinary" behaviour convey to her? "Don't bother to call me because I will not come until I am ready"? "Don't tell me when you are unhappy because I am not interested"? "The more you tell me what you need the less likely I am to give it to you"? "I will only do things for you if you do not ask"? "Face it, kid, you're helpless"?

In this situation everybody loses. The baby loses because her needs are not met, or are met only after so much delay that she loses her vital confidence that they will be met. On this occasion she may be no more than uncomfortable in the full nappy that woke her, or bored with being alone. But after a few more experiences of this policy, she will anticipate being left and become anxious; quicker to cry and fuss and slower to accept eventual comfort. Where earlier she might sometimes have been content to play alone in her cot when she woke, she has now learned to associate the cot with being alone and helpless. Soon she starts to cry the moment she opens her eyes, and then to cry before she has ever closed them, resisting altogether the cot that is sometimes a prison.

Her parents or other carers lose because the less they meet the baby's needs the more demanding she becomes. The more their determination to resist her hardens, the more anxiously exaggerated her demands become. The adults get caught in a vicious spiral which actually creates the very phenomenon they sought to avoid: an unreasonably demanding and whiny baby.

The rest of the family loses because resentful parents and an anxious baby are not much fun to live with.

If you are already feeling "put upon" and over-burdened by caring for your baby, or you are on the point of going back to work and having even more to do in fewer hours at home, it is difficult to believe that offering her even more of yourself will make things easier for both of you. If the baby runs you off your feet while your attention is rationed, wouldn't making that attention freely available mean that her demands simply exceeded your time and energy? It sounds as if the answer must be yes, but it is no. If your needs and your baby's are out of balance the answer is not that your baby's should be met *less* but that yours should be met *more*; more help so that you have more time; more support so that your energy goes further. Bringing up a baby is undeniably hard work; nothing can make it easy. But parents and carers who always meet baby's demands as fully as they can and without unnecessary delay have less work, less drudgery and less stress.

Why? An actual example from a universally stressful part of parenting may explain most clearly. The chart opposite depicts a single night in the lives of two mothers of three-month babies. Alison

	ALISON'S NIGHT	BEULAH'S NIGHT
Both babies wake and cry at 3am	Alison wakes, listens, checks time; finds baby has only slept three hours since last feeding. Puts head under pillow and tries to go back to sleep. Cannot sleep through noise of crying. Gets up after 20 minutes, feeling cross and disgruntled.	Beulah wakes. Listens to make sure crying persists, gets up sleepy but resigned.
Time awake before reaching baby	**22 minutes**	**2 minutes**
	Baby is in lather of misery. Too upset to smile at mother. Sobs shakily as she prepares to feed her. Cannot settle easily to feeding. Needs frequent burping as has swallowed so much air in crying. Takes 30 minutes to get through 85ml (3oz) of milk.	Baby stops crying as mother enters room. Smiles at her as she is lifted. Settles at once to lusty sucking. Needs burping in the middle of feed. Takes 20 minutes over full feed.
Feeding time	**30 minutes**	**20 minutes**
	Baby still needs more burping and has to be re-settled twice before she finally drops off.	Baby sucks herself to sleep at end of feed. Burps as she is lifted back into her cot, then goes instantly to sleep.
Time to resettle baby	**15 minutes**	**2 minutes**
	Alison is free to get back into bed and go to sleep herself.	Beulah is free to get back into bed and go to sleep herself.
Time from first being woken	**1 hour 7 minutes**	**24 minutes**

(who worried about spoiling) believed that she could and should save time and energy by rationing her attention to her baby. She and her partner were both determined that the baby should learn to fit into their lives rather than dominating them but found her crying far more difficult to ignore, or bear, than they had expected, so they were already concerned that they might spoil her. Beulah was on her own and enjoying her baby more than she'd ever imagined possible. She was not haunted by the spoiling spectre; she found it easiest just to do for her baby whatever the baby seemed to want.

Whichever mother you are inclined to agree with, you will see that in this real situation Alison was clearly the loser. She spent more of her night awake and she spent the time less pleasantly than Beulah too. By keeping her baby waiting for her feed Alison caused a long period of frustrated and miserable crying so that when she finally did go to her, the baby was much too upset to greet her with a rewarding smile. Even when Alison offered her the feed, the baby was too distressed to settle to it with pleasure, so Alison did not get the satisfaction of watching her luxuriate under her ministrations. On the contrary, giving the feed was tiresome and frustrating and took much longer than it would have taken if the baby had been calm. And even after all that time, the baby only took about half her usual amount before exhaustion and wind from all that crying overtook her. Because she had not managed a full feed, Alison was probably going to get woken up again in a couple of hours...

Nobody *likes* giving night feeds, but Beulah could at least go back to sleep feeling that she had done a satisfactory job pleasantly. Poor Alison was bound to feel that Babies are Hell and Night feeds a Torment, and when the 5 am summons racketed through the house she was all set to start another day feeling resentfully at odds with her baby.

New babies need what they want

Meeting a baby's needs as fully as you can means more fun and less stress today, and more sleep one day.

This powerfully proves the point where meeting babies' physical needs is concerned. However, if you feel that physical needs are the only kind that are valid you may still feel that as long as you know your baby is recently fed, thoroughly burped and wearing a nappy that is clean if not dry, you should resist her demands because "she doesn't really need anything, she just wants attention". For all your sakes do keep reminding each other that your baby is not yet old enough to want anything that is not also a need. If she wants

something, she needs it; if she needs something she can only get it from a caregiving adult. Company, comfort or a cuddle are all real needs; just as real as physical needs. Without food or warmth she will die; without social attention from adults she will not learn to live as a full human being.

Your baby needs loving adults – and love from adults – to do for her, know for her, manage for her, all the things she cannot yet do and know and manage for herself. But passive help, care without education, isn't enough. She also needs one of you, or someone who stands in for you, to demonstrate and help her practise a million different vital skills, to tell her things and to lend extra brain and muscle power to her efforts at managing herself in her world. Above all (because everything else follows from it) she needs at least one of you to be her special person; to talk to her and to love her so that she too learns to be a special individual person who can talk and who can love.

Try to feel honoured, rather than burdened, by your baby needing you so much and needing so much of you. She is probably the only person in the world who will ever love you one hundred per cent without criticism or reservation. Arrange to enjoy her company whenever you can and don't let even the first murmurs of jealousy set up stresses between you and whoever cares for her when you can't. She is probably the only person in the world who always wants to be with you. She would never prefer anyone else although she'll accept loving care wherever she finds it. Make her feel good and let her make you feel good, too. You have everything to gain and nothing to lose.

THE
OLDER BABY

From six months to one year

This half-year will see the culmination of your child's babyhood and, as she perfects the skills she worked on during her first six months, it will often feel like a celebration of it and her. By the time she reaches her birthday she will sit alone (certainly), crawl about (probably), stand up (possibly) and even say a word or two. Each of those milestones is important in itself, of course, but passing each individually is as nothing compared to the cumulative difference that passing them all will make to the person your baby becomes, and the lifestyle you share. Once your baby is mobile – whether on all fours or two legs – she will no longer have to be content with the places you put her and the things you choose to bring her. She will go anywhere that is open to her (including out through the street door...) and grab and chew anything that has been left within her reach. With ever-increasing manual dexterity, and eventually a fine pincer grip between finger and thumb, even a tiny pin, a lost paper clip or an errant pea from last Sunday's dinner will not escape her. She will discover fascinating things to do with non-chewable objects, too. She will find a wastepaper basket and empty it, find a book and scrumple it, find the TV and push its buttons, find the cat's litter tray and dabble in it... Keeping things safe from her will need endless forethought and orderliness. Keeping her safe from things will demand constant vigilance.

Constant adult vigilance will not bother your baby, in fact her increasingly close attachment to the people who care for her means that she will welcome it as extra attention and often find incomprehensible rules and reproaches funny. There is nothing more devoted than a six-month baby – except that same baby, three months later. It is a feature of these months that babies' primary attachments deepen while, if more than one adult is available to them, their range of attachments widens. A baby's first, most basic attachment is usually to the person who has been most constantly and actively engaged with her, as companion and playmate as well as nurturant carer, and for most babies under six months that is the birth mother. For a few babies, though, it is the father, while for some it may be an adoptive, substitute, or foster mother, whether related to her or not.

A primary attachment to one person doesn't mean that a baby doesn't care about anyone else, though. And since babies do not have a fixed quota of love to give, the fact that your baby has more than one person who is "special" to her does not deprive you of anything. If you have always been, or shared in being, her most basic person, you will not lose that relationship by leaving her to someone else's care while you work away from home, however much she loves and thrives with her other caretaker. The same applies, of course, to families where both parents are present and involved. If the mother is the constant companion and playmate, she will probably be the baby's primary person but, provided the father is a loving and regular part of her life, he will be "special" too, and if the mother should become boring by comparison, the allegiance of the one-year-old may change. If the father undertakes most of the baby's care while the mother comes and goes, these first relationships will probably be the other way around – and equally liable to reversal. And if two involved but busy parents share with a loving caregiver as well, the baby's emotional life will only be enriched. Believe it. If Mary Poppins should arrive in your household, make the most of it.

However many devoted, fun people your baby becomes attached to, though, she will almost certainly be true to the person she selected – let's assume it is you and that you are her mother – for her first (and arguably her most important) love affair. The baby spent her first months learning to know you apart from everyone else and to love you better. Now she loves you so much that if she could have her way, she'd have you close by all the time and all to herself. She does not want to share you, or to have you give your time and attention to anyone or anything else; she wants your attention and she feels passionately for you physically, too. Even if she was not at all a cuddly baby earlier on, she now likes to be held and carried, rocked and bounced. And when she is on your lap, she will play with your hair and your hands, stroke your face, inspect your teeth, pop food (and worse) in your mouth, as if your body belonged to her.

The possessive demands of a lover are delightful if you love him or her but irritating if you do not. In the same way, the physical and emotional relationship which most babies in this age group demand of their mothers tends to please and flatter those who have enjoyed motherhood so far, but can be too much for those who were already finding it over-demanding. Some such mothers find babies' physical demonstrativeness positively embarrassing. Expected, as an adult, to keep your own feelings under control, neither displaying them in public nor giving way to them, you may find yourself faced with a baby who is simply demanding to be cuddled and kissed, patted and stroked. She holds out her arms for more, giggling with glee if you tickle her under the arms as you lift her; sucking your nose or stroking your breast if it comes within range, and purring like a sensuous kitten when it is time for a bath or a new nappy.

If you can accept and be proud of your own prime importance to your baby, you may find that you can revel with her in the relationship. One way is to try looking at yourself through your baby's eyes. If you do you will see yourself as good and warm and loving; as interesting, exciting and funny; worthy of all this devotion, in fact as the perfect mother. If you can, you should. Your baby is practising loving for life. The more she can love, now, and feel herself loved back, the more generous with, and accepting of, all kinds of love she will be, right through her life. In fact the more comfortably you can respond to her now, the more easily she will respond to the emotional needs of your grandchildren when her turn comes for parenthood. You will help yourself, too. Finding your baby irresistibly delicious will help you, more than anything else, to ride comfortably through the hardworking and sometimes stressful months ahead.

At six or seven months all the signs of your baby's devotion are positive ones. She is nice to everybody but she is nicest of all to you. Her swiftest, widest grins, her longest "conversations" and most infectious laughs are all directed at you. For most parents and babies, though, there is a negative side to all this joy. If your baby so much likes to have you with her, it is natural that she should come to dislike having you leave her. She will probably reach a point, at around eight months, when she tries to keep you in sight every moment of her waking day; when she cannot, she will be uneasy, tearful or even panic-stricken.

Psychologists call this reaction "separation anxiety", but whether or not you see anything worthy of such a name in your baby depends on her physical as well as emotional development, and on her home circumstances. If she can crawl, and you happen to live in an open-plan space, she will keep you in sight simply by crawling after you wherever you go. But if she gets anxious about you before she gets mobile, she will be in quite a different situation. She cannot follow you so she will keep an eagle eye on you instead, starting to whimper whenever you move from her immediate vicinity.

On a good day at home you probably will not find it difficult to help your baby keep you in sight. You arrange life so that you can do your things while she does hers close by. You get into the habit of chatting to her while you work, commenting on her activities without interrupting your own. When you must leave the room, you either wait for her to follow or you scoop her up and take her with you to the front door or to the kitchen... But on another day and in another mood you may find yourself resenting her minute-by-minute dependence. You are being loved more than you can stand. Once irritation begins to grow inside you, her behaviour feeds it with each successive half-hour. You leave the room and she howls. You come back, comfort her and start to iron. She rolls and crawls beneath your feet, almost pulling the iron on to herself by its flex. A friend comes for coffee and, determined not to lose your attention completely, the baby insists on sitting on your lap, using all her new sounds to join, or interrupt, the conversation. To crown it all, when your friend leaves, you go to the lavatory, only to find your little burden thundering piteously on the door... Every mother has days like that sometimes (and fathers find first experiences of them astonishing). But knowing that they are commonplace doesn't make them fun. Looking at the baby's feelings from her, rather than your, point of view will help you keep them to a minimum.

To you, it seems totally unnecessary for the baby to cry just because you have gone to the bathroom. But when the baby loses sight of you, she minds. You are the centre of her world; the mirror in which she sees herself and everything else; her manager, who copes with her and helps her cope with other things. When you go away from her *you* know where you are going and how soon you will return, but she does not. As far as she is concerned, you might be gone forever. Out of sight is still out of mind. She registers your absence but cannot yet hold an image of you in her mind so as to wait calmly, and look forward confidently to your return. Over the next few months your baby will discover "object constancy": learn that things (and people) do not cease to exist just because they go out of sight and hearing. And, from continual experience, she will learn that wherever you have gone you will always return. But right now she only knows that you have vanished and that she feels bereft.

If you try to override her feelings, ignoring her cries, prising off her clinging arms or shutting her in a playpen to stop her following, she will get more and more anxious. The more anxious she feels the more determinedly she will cling to you. If you try stealth, often sneaking out of the room or house when she is busily occupied, she will occupy herself less and less because she will keep an ever-closer eye on your movements. Separation anxiety becomes much easier to live with if you accept that your baby's feelings are real and, in terms of her stage of thought-development, reasonable. Take her around the house with you whenever you can and let her follow when she is

able. When you must leave her, find a phrase that you always use to signal your departure ("bye-bye for now") and give her fair warning so that she does not feel deserted or betrayed. Another phrase – a "here I am again" – can mark a definite ending to the separation, something that she will gradually come to recognize and expect after any parting. You can even help her understand and practise in the safety of play. Peek-a-boo games, in which she covers (cursorily) her own face and you pretend to have no idea where she is ("Where's she gone? Oh *there* she is.") reverse the usual roles and give her the power to vanish, and control over coming back.

Learning to understand these things is a necessary condition for calm separation but may not be sufficient. Even once your baby knows that when you go you still exist and will come back, she may not want you to leave. But even if you cannot prevent her minding, or prevent her from tearing you apart by crying and holding up her arms to you as you leave for work, you can ensure that separations from you don't actually harm her by making sure that you leave her with someone else to whom she is also attached. When you go, she needs another "special" person whom she can use as her "completing half" until you come back. She cannot manage alone. She cannot manage with a stranger or even with a casual acquaintance. But she can and will manage without you if she has someone else with whom she has a real, loving relationship. Leave your baby with such a person and even if you leave her apparently drowning in a sea of despair, she will be safely aboard the life-raft of that relationship within minutes of your departure. So when you ask yourself, "Is it all right for me to leave her?" (for the evening, or four mornings or 40 hours each week), ask yourself how well she knows your substitute and how they feel about each other. Your absence is a negative but it can be balanced by a presence which is positive.

Towards the end of this first year your baby may seem to add anxiety about contact with people she does not know to her anxiety about being separated from you. Usually the two kinds of fear are mixed together because the occasions when you notice that she is extremely shy with strangers are also occasions when you want to detach her from yourself – because the children's shoe fitter needs to measure her feet, for instance, or admirers that matter to *you* want cuddles. The chances are that your baby is not distressed by strangers themselves but by what they do. She is probably happy to smile and talk to people she does not know provided they behave discreetly and keep their distance. Unfortunately many adults do not think of babies as real human beings and therefore do not extend to them the same respect and courtesy they automatically accord to older people. Some adults are shyer than others but even the least shy would be disconcerted if a stranger rushed up in the street and kissed and hugged him or her. We like to know people before we accept close approaches and physical affection from them. Babies feel the same, and deserve protection from those who try to treat them like pets.

If your baby is never handed over to anyone or forced into contact, but is allowed to peep over your shoulder at the people in shops and buses, to play peek-a-boo with visitors around your legs and to go voluntarily towards them when curiosity overcomes shyness, she will probably become more and more willing to make friends with people who are at present strangers. Letting her make the social running now will help to produce a confident toddler who is interested in new people.

Fears of being away from you and being with people who are neither you nor known friends are real fears. Like other fears they will die down most quickly in babies who are given least cause to feel them. At present your baby is too newly in love with you to take you for granted. But if you can carry her through this period of intense and potentially anxious attachment on a wave of securely returned and protective adoration, she will come to take your love and your safety for granted in the end and, grounded in confidence in her home relationships, be free and ready to turn her attention outwards as she gets older.

The more she's allowed to use her hands, the sooner she'll use a spoon. And skin does wash...

FEEDING
AND GROWING

At six months some babies are so enthusiastic about eating a range of solid foods that they are already beginning to reduce their intake of breast milk or formula. Don't feel your baby ought to be beginning to wean himself, though. Most babies this age are still having solid foods as extras, and a few are still exclusively milk-fed.

Official guidelines to infant nutrition have long recommended delaying the introduction of solid foods until at least four months: the earliest age at which most babies' digestions can begin to cope with foods other than breast milk or formula. That advice hasn't changed but concern that the introduction of solid foods should not usually be delayed much beyond this half-year point has been added. By six to eight months, some babies begin to need some non-milk foods to ensure their supply of iron. By this age most babies are very ready to try some of the foods they see adults eating, and to pick up and suck finger-foods as they do toys. Even if your baby is not very enthusiastic, it is probably worth persisting in offering tastes for him to try. He is likely to find it easier to accept new eating techniques, food tastes and textures at six or seven months than he would later in the year.

Milk matters Despite these concerns, it is widely acknowledged that some babies, such as those who are at high risk of allergies, may do best if given nothing but breast milk (and perhaps an iron supplement) through most of the year. And even if your baby has no special need to prolong *exclusive* milk-feeding he still needs to take a lot of his food that way. However enthusiastic he may be about new kinds of food and ways of eating, your baby is probably still passionately attached to the breast, bottle or both. Don't be in any hurry to wean him right away from sucking. As he takes more solid food he is bound to take less milk, but for a long time to come some pleasurable sucking will be an important support to his emotional health, just as some milk is an important support to his nutrition.

What kind Breast milk or formula will continue to be a vital source of nutrients, *of milk?* including iron, for your baby all through this year: convenient, inexpensive, and high quality health insurance during phases when the solid foods he will eat are – well, *limited*.

Don't switch to unmodified cow's milk (or goat's milk either) as a main drink before your baby is at least a year old. Quite apart from its other differences from human milk, using unfortified cow's milk as a main drink for your baby dramatically increases the possibility of him suffering from iron-deficiency anaemia.

Full- or near-term babies are born with enough iron stored in their livers to last them for four to six months, but after that their supply may run low and need regularly topping up. That isn't as easy as it sounds because babies' bodies will only absorb certain kinds of iron under certain nutritional circumstances. Breast milk does not contain a great deal of iron but it is of a type that is so readily

A complete, iron-enriched formula is the best alternative to breast milk; from a cup as well as a bottle.

absorbed that its small quantity is usually enough. Cow's milk, on the other hand, is not only very low in iron itself – a pint a day providing only about five per cent of the amount a six-month baby might need – but also makes it more difficult for babies to absorb iron from other foods. And that is important because however aware you are of the importance of offering your baby foods that will give him iron, and the vitamin C that is necessary for its absorption, he's unlikely to get more than he needs since the foods that are naturally iron-rich, like red meat and dark green vegetables, are seldom a baby's first favourites.

If you're not nursing, or you don't want to go on giving more than just one evening feed each day – give your baby formula, and make sure the one you choose is iron-enriched, as most are. If you are nursing, though, you don't have to start buying formula to use in cooking for your baby even once you're fed up with expressing milk into tiny servings of cereal. After your baby has passed six months, it's fine to use whole cow's milk for cooking and preparing his food. After all cow's milk isn't *bad* for your baby – and many cow's milk products, like cheese and yoghurt, are very good indeed – it's just that it isn't adequate as his main milk for drinking.

If your baby is bottle-fed, it's fine to use the formula he's established on right through the year as his only type of milk. He can drink it from a cup as well as from his bottle, and since you'll have it available, you might as well use it for mixing cereals and so forth as well. Don't be tempted to introduce unmodified cow's milk as a main drink as weaning progresses. If you want him to change to a different milk, it would be better to try a "follow-on" milk or older babies' formula. These milks are usually even more highly fortified with iron and vitamins but are not otherwise much different.

Hygiene Do remember that as long as your baby drinks any kind of milk from a bottle his bottle-feeding equipment must be sterilized. By six months there's no need to sterilize feeding dishes and so forth, but bottles of milk are different. The teats can easily trap traces of milk and warm milk is the ideal breeding ground for bacteria.

WEANING

Introducing babies to "solid" foods and moving them on to mixed feeding adds new foods and new ways of eating to their milk-by-sucking diet. That's important preparation for weaning but it isn't the same thing. When you start to wean your baby you're starting the process that will eventually *replace* milk as her basic food with a range of other foods, and replace sucking from breast or bottle with eating from a spoon and her fingers, and drinking from a cup.

As long as your baby has at least four bottles or breast feeds every day, she will still be getting most of the nutrients she needs from milk alone. You can assume that she is getting most of the calories and all of the protein she requires so that her solid foods are still only making up a small difference between the calories her appetite and growth demand and her milk provides, while helping to ensure her mineral and vitamin intake.

If four breast or bottle feeds are the pillars of your baby's diet, it's obviously liable to collapse as soon as she abandons even one of them, whether she does it spontaneously or because you are starting to wean her. Soon after six months some babies – usually bottle-fed babies – start sleeping through without an early-morning or late-night feed, settling down to a regular pattern of three meals (and bottles) per day with some snacks in between. Breast-fed babies of around the same age are less likely to give up late or early feeds, especially if their mothers are out at work in the day, but they often take little or no milk at midday, preferring water or juice from a cup to either formula or expressed breast milk from a bottle.

A gradual start to deliberate weaning usually reduces babies' milk intake in much the same way. Even when your baby is entirely content to abandon sucking at lunch-time and have a drink of milk from a cup instead, she will not get through as many millilitres by this new drinking method. And as the weaning process continues you will probably find that the more you persuade her to reduce her sucking, the more she reduces her milk consumption. If so, go very gently. If your baby feels compelled rather than persuaded, feels that she is no longer *allowed* to have her milk by sucking breast or bottle, she may well refuse to have it at all.

New drinks and drinking methods

A lid and a spout makes it easier for your baby to manage the change from sucking to drinking.

"Solid foods" can replace the nutrients in milk but they cannot replace all its liquid. Once your baby eats "real" food instead of some milk, she needs drinks to go with it. Don't worry if all her drinks added together don't add up to the total volume of milk she has given up, though. Those "solid foods" have a lot of liquid in them.

Cups with spouted lids are a great help from the very beginning of weaning to the very end. Drinking from a spout is a compromise between sucking and ordinary drinking and you can graduate the compromise. Using a long, flexible spout is almost like sucking and makes the change much less abrupt for a young baby. In fact using a sucky spout during the first weeks of gradual weaning maximizes the chance that your baby will consent to drink at least some of the milk she used to get by sucking.

By eight or nine months, though, you may find that your baby is less interested in a drinking method that feels like sucking than in one she can manage alone. Few babies can manage an ordinary beaker without any help before they are a year old because even if they cope well with the actual drinking they tend to spill as they put the beaker down. With a short, rigid spout, though, your baby can drink almost as she would without one, but you do not have to insist on holding the cup for her because if it lands on its side it will do no more than drip.

Whether or not your baby accepts milk from a cup as a drink at breakfast and supper, she will need thirst-quenching drinks at other meals and in between times and far the best is plain water. Although a baby who is accustomed to diluted fruit juice or "fruit drinks" ad lib may reject a drink of water with every sign of disappointment and distaste, babies who are brought up to drink water when they are thirsty treat it as the life-giving stuff it really is.

If your tap water is not safe or palatable to drink, a domestic water purifier will probably be the least expensive solution. If you prefer to use bottled water for your baby, choose carefully. Some types contain high levels of salt and other minerals.

If you want your baby to have fruit juice, buy (or make) unsweetened pure juice, dilute it well and try to offer it no more than once in a day, and as an integral part of a planned snack. Treated in that way, fruit juice can be a treat "food" with useful vitamin C in it. But kept constantly on tap, as it is in many households, fruit juice, especially in sweetened, coloured, commercial juice-drinks, is a very expensive way to put your child's teeth at risk. Furthermore, if your baby learns to regard plain water as insulting this year, she's likely to be demanding novelty flavours of "juice-box" off the TV ads next year, and cans of fizz the year after.

Weaning breast-fed babies

Only you and your baby can decide on the right time to start and complete weaning, though powerful people such as employers may have an input to *your* view. A few babies get bored with breast-feeding and take to a cup even before their mothers feel ready to start stopping. There's no way you can argue with a baby who feels this way because if she reduces the amount she sucks, she will also reduce the amount of milk you make. A few mothers see no reason to wean their babies at all but go on breast-feeding as long as the baby (then toddler, then child) asks to nurse. As long as it feels right to you and your baby either extreme, or anything in between, is fine.

A breast-fed baby whose mother can be around most of the time can go on having all her milk from the breast until she is ready to have all of it from cups, but when is she ready? If you've breast-fed your baby and never used bottles for expressed breast milk, maybe not even for water or juice, that can be an emotionally laden question. Your baby is around six months old and now you need to leave her with her father or a caregiver while you go to work. The baby eats solid food (but not a lot) and drinks water or juice from a cup (but not a lot). Does she need to have a bottle? The answer partly depends on her age. Most 20-week babies don't use cups well enough to count as anything but fun and education; a lot of 28-week babies do. In between, well, you know your baby. But the answer depends at least as much on your hours away and whether you can start slowly and build them up over a few weeks while your baby grows up a bit more. Provided she can eat solid foods and drink from a cup well enough not to feel hungry or thirsty, she can certainly cope with one feed without sucking. But two feeds, plus the potential snacks either side of them, is different. If you've got to be away from 8 am to 5 pm and your baby isn't seven months yet, doesn't eat a lot of solid foods and refuses outright to drink milk from a cup, formula in a bottle may be the easy way for her, for whoever takes care of her and for you. Don't be surprised, though, if once you've made that decision and bought the bottles, your baby rejects them out of hand and goes for more of the grown-up stuff by day and lots and *lots* of nursing by night...

If you can choose when to start weaning your baby from the breast and how long to take, do wait until her single-minded dedication to nursing has slackened, at least at some feeds, and allow time to do it gradually. Ideally you shouldn't ever have to deny the breast to a baby who is directly asking for it. She is quite incapable of understanding why you are suddenly refusing her, and may feel that you are refusing not just the breast but closeness. You shouldn't have to suffer the physical discomfort of overfull breasts, either. Take it slowly and both your baby and your breasts will usually adapt without problems. If, for example, she now enjoys real food at lunch-time and only sucks cursorily after it, you might decide to offer milk from a cup instead of from the breast, and to whizz her straight from her highchair to

---

PARENTS ASK

Should I wean my breast-fed baby in case he bites me?

My son is seven months old and has just cut a top tooth to go with his two bottom ones. The tooth is amazingly sharp and I'm suddenly terrified that he might bite my nipple. It happened to a friend of mine and she bled. My husband thinks I should wean him; he says that teeth mean solid food anyway. But I had intended to nurse him all year and was enjoying it until I got scared of this. Anyway it seems unfair to punish him for something he hasn't even done yet, but the threat's there isn't it?

However many teeth they have, most nursing babies don't bite the breast. If biting was commonly a serious problem the human race probably wouldn't have survived this long because in much of the world babies would starve to death if they were not breast-fed at least into the second year. Your husband may be right to think you should start weaning, but his reasoning, as given here, is wrong. Babies' first teeth are nothing to do with their ability to eat solid food. They don't chew with their front teeth like rabbits: they chew with their gums until they cut molars at the end of the year.

Babies biting can be a big issue for a few nursing women, but if you'd really like to go on breast-feeding why not give yourself a chance to find out if you are one of them?

Quite a lot of babies bite once. Yes, it hurts, but not so much that one episode is something to be afraid of. Mothers yell and jerk away; their babies are amazed and alarmed, burst into tears and have to be persuaded back on. Often that's the only time it happens.

If it *does* happen again you probably will be uptight waiting for a repeat. But it's still likely that you can ride through the problem in a few days if you want to go on.

Try not to repeat that violent reaction (easier said than done). Babies don't begin to understand that they hurt (so punishment's irrelevant) and may be amused or appalled. It is the (few) babies who are amused who may keep on biting: learning to do it *to get that reaction* (just as they are beginning to throw toilet rolls out of supermarket trolleys and snatch off grandparents' spectacles). Babies who are appalled may be so afraid of it happening again that they are too nervous to nurse (just like their mothers).

Try to say, "No", very firmly and calmly; slip your finger into his mouth to take him off the nipple, and end the feeding for now. Next time, make sure:
■ He's had something cool to chew on in case those slowly emerging teeth are bothering *him*.
■ Nobody has laughed at him for biting fingers or noses, or ever will again. ("No. No biting.")
■ You aren't due to talk on the phone or read to his sister while he feeds. If he felt he had to reclaim your attention, a bite might be part of that. Keep eye contact while he sucks and talk to him.
■ You don't try to persuade him to go on sucking if he's not interested, and you take him off (by breaking the suction) the moment he begins to play.
■ You slip your little finger between his gums before you wake him if he drops off at the breast – he might bite as he wakes.

her buggy for an after–lunch walk by way of distraction. By the time you get back, it will no longer be a time of day when she is used to nursing and she will probably have forgotten that she didn't nurse when it was. On this new regime your breasts will get less stimulation and although you might feel uncomfortably full on the first few occasions, your breasts will adjust and make less milk within two or three days. If you also offer your baby milk from a cup as well as solid food at her other meals, and then let her suck as much as she wants at the end of the meal, she will gradually take less and less from the breast so that you will make less. Over a few weeks she will probably reach a point where she is taking only a token few sucks in the morning and a comfort feed at her bedtime. That night–time session will probably be the last your baby will willingly give up, remaining part of your cuddly bedtime ritual for months to come. As long as she doesn't rely on breast-feeding to get herself to sleep, though, your baby may surprise you by abandoning it of her own accord somewhere nearer to a year than 18 months old.

Of course you don't have to leave it to your baby to decide when to give up that last feed and complete the process of weaning. But if you do not want to go on being even that much committed to breast-feeding until your baby is at least eight or nine months old, you might want to consider offering a bottle after all. Even if she is perfectly capable of managing without sucking during the day, your baby may not be comfortably ready to do without any at all and may especially miss sucking for comfort at bedtime.

Weaning bottle-fed babies Some parents take a very easy-going attitude to bottles and are happy to see them used as comfort objects and useful non–spill cups right through toddlerhood. Other parents regard bottles as a necessary evil to be got rid of the moment their babies are capable of eating from spoons and drinking from cups. There are advantages and disadvantages to both approaches but failing to decide which you're going to adopt is your worst option. If you let your baby do as she likes with her bottle all through this half-year and then suddenly decide that she must give it up altogether, you're all likely to have an unhappy time of it.

Babies who have constant access to bottles full of milk tend to get more and more attached to them, not only as a source of food and drink but also as a source of sucking comfort. The comfort is good for them, of course, just as the comfort of nursing is good for breast–fed babies, but constant access may not be. You might find some of the following problems:

■ A bottle-fed baby's source of comfort isn't in her mother's control as a breast-fed baby's is. So as she gets older, and more and more able to think of a bottle, and demand *another* bottle at any time of day or night, it is far more difficult to refuse her.

■ Babies who are really hooked on their bottles sometimes drink so much milk that their appetite for solid foods, and therefore their chances of an optimal diet, is ruined.

■ Toddling around with a bottle of milk in her hand or her mouth limits manual play and efforts to talk and is bad for teeth, too.

■ Sucking herself to sleep with a bottle of milk that pools in her mouth as she drowses is worse for a baby's teeth than anything else (except a bottle of sweet-acid fruit juice) and might also choke her. Right now you may think you would never allow *your* baby to do such a thing, and maybe you wouldn't. But if you reach a time when you know that a bottle means she'll go happily to sleep all by herself, and go straight off again when she wakes in the night, and that no bottle means she will not, maybe you will. Certainly a lot of tired parents do.

Weaning your baby as soon as she drinks from a cup can raise the reverse of almost all those problems. Refusing to give any milk from a bottle can lead to the baby refusing to take any milk at all – and that's as bad for her diet as taking too much for too long. Your baby may miss the sucking comfort so much that she takes to sucking her thumb and has *that* in her mouth all day. And of course cutting out the bedtime bottle can usher in problems over settling for the night.

You don't have to wean your baby very early in order to avoid long-continued dependence on a bottle. All you have to do is to treat the bottle as if it were a breast, and wean her from bottle-feeding exactly as you would wean her from nursing:

■ Introduce a cup at four to five months and gradually get your baby accustomed to the idea that milk and water can come out of this as well as out of a bottle. By six months she will probably be willing to take all drinks that are extra to her feeds from a cup. That means that only milk will now come from a bottle, not water or juice.

■ Abandon the lunch-time bottle in favour of solid foods, with milk from a cup, soon after six months or as soon as she eats enthusiastic spoonfuls rather than tentative tastes.

■ Abandon the late-night bottle (or early-morning one) as soon as the baby shows you, by sleeping right through the night, that three main meals a day, supported by snacks, are now enough. A cup of milk makes an excellent snack if your baby likes it; otherwise offer water from a cup together with hard finger-foods.

■ If all goes smoothly, the baby will now be having only two bottles per day: one after the solid part of breakfast and the other after the solid part of supper, before bedtime.

A cup of milk is a snack, a cup of juice is a treat, but when your baby's just thirsty a cup of water is best of all.

Now comes the important piece of adult-upmanship that will keep the bottle in its pleasurable place. Let the baby go on with the two bottles as long, but *only* as long, as they are drunk sitting on somebody's lap. Somewhere around her first birthday, your baby's drive to be independent and to move around the room will become so strong that she will hate sitting still. If you never, even once, let her discover that a bottle can be taken around the room on crawling adventures, there will come a day when she wants to move about more than she wants to suck.

Don't be trapped into letting the baby carry the bottle off "just this once". She couldn't carry a breast off after all. Even if you are visiting friends and you want them to see your relationship with the baby at its smoothest, don't let temptation get the better of you. Your baby is not stupid: if she does it tonight and it blissfully combines the two things she enjoys most – sucking and moving around – she is very likely to demand to carry it off again the next night and the one after.

While she is learning that she's faced with a choice, let her change her mind and crawl back for another suck if she wants to (after all she could have done that if she'd been nursing). Make her get properly onto your lap and cuddle in for it though (breasts can't be held out to babies on the floor). You may eventually have to set a limit – say one action-break per feed – or she may behave like a foal, sucking for five seconds at a time between 10-second canters.

Remember to keep the bottle entirely for milk. If you suddenly decide to give juice or water from the bottle again – perhaps because it is the easiest way to carry fluid on a journey, or get it down your baby when she is feverish – you are abandoning the idea of the bottle as a pretend breast and your baby is almost certain to fuss next time her drink appears in a cup.

SOLID FOODS

Babies in their first year are growing rapidly and have very high energy needs in relation to their body size. Most year-old babies need half as many calories as their (non breast-feeding) mothers, yet their stomachs are much smaller and cannot cope with large quantities of food at one time. That means that babies and toddlers need to eat much more often than adults and that they need energy-rich foods. Sugar calories are empty of nutrients, as well as damaging to teeth, but parents should take care not to apply any of the other healthy eating messages intended for adults to their children. A high-fibre diet, for example, is singularly inappropriate for a baby or small child. He cannot afford much space in his stomach for minimally nourishing "roughage", and far from needing it to keep him "regular" really rough stuff may give him diarrhoea. He should not have a low-fat diet either because fats are the most concentrated source of calories and he needs some. When you buy cow's milk to cook for him, or dairy produce for his use, choose full-fat versions.

As weaning progresses, your baby will drink less milk and therefore need more solid food. Do make sure that the foods you give him are a generous replacement for that milk – in terms of calories for energy and growth as well as in terms of more specific nutritional needs. A lunch of puréed spinach followed by stewed apple is rich in certain vitamins and minerals but will have nowhere near the calories of the bottle he used to have. If you serve him vegetables without meat, fish or pulses, and minimally sweetened stewed fruits, lift their food value with full-fat grated cheese or fromage frais.

As long as your baby drinks as much as a pint of formula milk – or takes two full breast feeds – every day he will not go short of "first-class" protein, calcium or vitamins, whatever else he eats. Even if his food choices are very limited and idiosyncratic – nothing but cereal and toast today – that milk will provide a nutritional safety-net. If he refuses milk altogether for a while – perhaps because he continues to resent being offered it from a cup – he will need to get all his nutrients from his meals, but it's worth remembering that a small helping of fortified baby cereal will provide that vital iron and other minerals and a daily dose of multivitamin drops will ensure that he doesn't go short of A, D or C. And even though he never *drinks*

Help your baby eat for herself because she wants the food, not for you because you want her to have it.

milk you will probably find that it plays a large enough part in your baby's meals to ensure his intake of calcium and the B vitamins. A lot gets "lost" in cooking for a baby. At least 57 ml (2 oz) to mix that helping of baby cereal to the texture most prefer, for example; 28 ml (1 oz) to cream a small potato, soften a well-cooked scrambled egg or make custard to go with his fruit – not to mention the yoghurt he likes for supper and the cheese sticks he eats in his fingers...

Home-cooked or commercial babyfoods? Ideas of which particular foods are suitable or unsuitable for babies vary dramatically from country to country and are far more to do with convention than diet. There are very few kinds of food that you eat but which your baby should not have. As long as you avoid much salt, extra sugar, hot spices, alcohol, coffee and tea, he can try anything you are cooking. You will soon find out whether he likes it and whether his digestion copes with it or not.

A lot of parents feed babies between six and 18 months on almost nothing but commercially prepared babyfoods. A few take pride in avoiding them altogether. As in most dietary matters, the chances are that you'll find your baby does best with a mixture. Provided somebody is shopping and cooking anyway, it is just as easy – and much cheaper – to adapt family food for your baby as to feed him on commercially prepared babyfoods. And good quality fresh foods will usually beat jars and packets for nutrition and taste, too, as well as educating him for later. That "lamb dinner" is the same today as it was last week; the meal you cook yourself will never be exactly the same twice over because even if you use the same recipe, your ingredients will vary. Your baby is not too young to enjoy the taste of tomatoes that have just come into season or of a gravy that is especially good. And he will soon welcome a crispy cheese topping or crunchy grated carrot instead of that inevitable purée or consistently lumpy "junior" meal. But if nobody else in the household eats much home-cooked food – relying mostly on meals out and ordered in, and on ready-prepared cook-chill dishes and convenience foods – you and he may often both be better off if he has jars of babyfood.

Creating a balance A mixture of home-prepared and commercially prepared foods will probably suit most households best. Your baby could share family meals whenever you are cooking something which he likes and which it is easy to make suitable for him by withholding seasonings until his portion has been served, and by sieving or liquidizing, mashing or chopping. When the main dish of a family meal is something he dislikes, or something you consider unsuitable, such as salt beef, a bought pie or a casserole containing wine, it could be replaced with a can or jar of commercially prepared babyfood, perhaps with some of the grown-ups' vegetables. When only the baby is to have a cooked meal, good babyfood may be better for him than whatever leftovers are in the fridge. And while fresh fruits are ideal for his sweet courses, using jars of baby fruit will save you stewing tiny portions, while other "sweet varieties" can be used to make a second course for him when other members of the family are not having one. Above all, don't scorn prepared powdered baby cereals. Rich in vitamins, fortified with iron and using valuable milk in the mixing, they are far more nourishing than the dry breakfast cereals older people eat. Served with fruit or with cheese they make an excellent breakfast or supper dish for a baby or toddler who enjoys them.

Knowing your labels Read the labels when choosing commercially prepared babyfoods: nutritional quality – and therefore value for money – varies widely. You will often find a mismatch between the name on the jar and the actual food it contains. A leading manufacturer's "apple" for example contains – in descending order of course – apple juice, natural yoghurt, modified cornflour, rice flour, vegetable oil and vitamin C. Not apple at all, but thickened enriched apple juice.

You will also sometimes find a vast list of additives to a simple recipe. Another manufacturer's "apple crumble" for example lists: rice, oat, wheat, soya, maize flours, malt, sugar, skimmed milk powder, apples, maltodextrin, vegetable fat, apple, pear, apricot and plum juices, caseinate, calcium carbonate, malt and vanilla extracts, dextrose, citric acid, demineralized whey, yeast, vitamin C, cinnamon, niacin, zinc sulphate, iron, vitamin mix. Fewer is better, but it's worth knowing which additives are which and what they imply:

■ Thickeners: if a liquid – water, juice – is the first ingredient listed, further down you'll probably find one or more "thickeners": cheap, non-nutritive substances put in to give an over-processed runny "food" a spoonable texture. Thickeners include modified cornflour, rice starch, wheat starch, gelatin, carob gum, xantham gum.

■ Improvers: although manufacturers may not put as many additives in babyfood as in adult food, they can and do add "improvers". If several of these are included, the food you are buying is very highly processed: emulsifiers, maltodextrin, hydrogenated vegetable fat, citric acid, caseinate, calcium carbonate, demineralized whey.

■ Flavourings: if babyfoods taste of natural food they don't need added flavourings. Watch out for sugar in different forms – sucrose, glucose, dextrose, lactose, fructose, maltose. In savoury combinations look out also for meat extract, hydrolyzed vegetable protein, yeast or vegetable extracts.

Playing safe Don't stop sterilizing bottles and teats just because your baby drinks follow-on milk instead of formula. Add his teacher-beaker to the sterilizer; that spout can trap bacteria-breeding drops.

Don't let your baby have dairy produce, savoury or sweet, bought from a shop with no chiller, or ice cream that is not bought ready-wrapped from a freezer. Ice cream that stays frozen is cold enough to be safe, but scoops and melted spillage may be contaminated.

Don't serve soft-cooked eggs, or anything with raw egg as an ingredient, to your baby, and be careful to keep raw chicken (and all meat) completely separate from foods he will eat without further cooking. Contamination with salmonella is generally acknowledged to be widespread. This, and all warnings concerning risks of bacterial contamination of particular foods need to be taken even more seriously for your baby than for adult members of the household. If there should be a problem with listeria in soft cheeses or cook-chill dishes, or BSE or *E.coli* in hamburger, he is the one who is most likely to be affected and much more likely to be affected badly.

SELF-FEEDING

Problems over an older baby's or toddler's eating often dominate the lives of whole families for months on end (see p.334). You can do a great deal to avoid them by cultivating relaxed and accepting attitudes now. Try to help your baby feel that eating is something pleasurable which she herself does because she wants and enjoys the food, rather than something she is made to do by adults who want her to have it. She eats, actively, rather than being fed, passively. And she eats for herself, not for you.

At six to eight months, your baby is bound to be fairly passive during eating, because she has to be fed: she cannot yet manage to feed herself. But being fed is an uncomfortable business. Try it: exchange spoonfuls with your partner and you will find that the food never comes at exactly the rate you want and the whole business makes you feel extraordinarily helpless. So keep the months when your baby must put up with this to a minimum by encouraging her to take part in the process herself from the beginning and to take it over completely as soon as she can get the food into her mouth by any means she chooses and no matter how much mess results:

■ Give your baby a spoon as soon as she will take one from you, even if she merely bites and waves it. If you let her do what she likes with the spoon she will sometimes manage to dip and lick it, and by nine months or so she will actually eat off it sometimes – though it will still have a sneaky habit of turning upside down on its way from dish to mouth. In the meantime use a second spoon yourself, swapping your loaded one for her empty one so that she can fill her mouth while you refill the spoon.

■ Positively encourage your baby to eat with her fingers. If you let her dabble in her food and then suck her fists at six months, she will soon learn to do it on purpose. When you can see that she is dipping and sucking because she likes the taste, slow down your spoon-work and let her get as much food for herself as she can.

■ Give your baby some easy finger-foods. While dipping and sucking fists is fun, picking up fingers of bread and butter, or grabs of grated cheese is even better. At six months finger-foods keep her actively involved in her meal while you feed her the mushy food. By a year she will hardly need any mushy food at all. She will eat with her fingers and sometimes with a spoon, and you will only need to help her get the last of her custard or gravy.

■ Don't try to enforce conventional notions of what goes with what. If she wants to dip cheese in her jelly, why should you care? She will adopt your ideas about food combinations in the end.

■ Don't try to *make* your baby eat anything. Many foods are good for her but none is irreplaceable. When she has had enough food it is actually better for her to stop eating, so don't keep her sitting there hoping she will eat a bit more.

■ Don't make the baby eat her main dish before she has the sweet course. At this age the thought of dessert will not encourage her to finish meat that she does not want. Later, when she understands what you are doing, it will only make her want the forbidden course more.

■ Expect a mess and arrange to cope with it. If it is warm enough

Easy finger-foods help your baby to take charge of his own eating at an early stage.

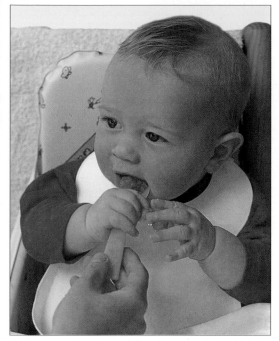

1 He can put a spoonful in his mouth but filling the spoon is difficult and anyway an empty one is good to chew...

2 He won't like you taking his spoon to refill it, or using another to dump food in his mouth so fill a second spoon and do a swap.

3 Now he can start all over again, filling his own mouth from the blue spoon while you refill the yellow ready for another exchange.

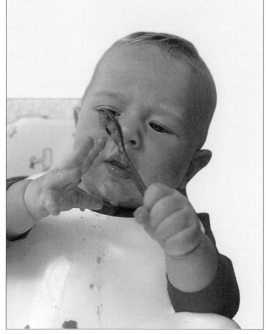

4 He'll still play with the spoons and spread food all over himself, but he'll stay enthusiastic about eating and that's what matters.

Are babies at risk from pesticides in fresh foods?

Determined to avoid the overload of chemicals in manufactured foods, we were all set to start weaning our baby son onto fresh foods cooked at home. But we've just been told that there are pesticides and other chemical residues on almost all fresh vegetables and fruits and that they are even more dangerous to babies and young children than to adults. Is that so? If it is, what on earth should concerned parents feed to their babies?

Vegetables, and to an even greater extent fruits, do commonly contain pesticide residues: up to 50% of all fruit samples in recent large-scale American studies.

Balancing the risks and benefits of pesticides and other chemicals in food is a highly technical business which often leaves commercial and environmental interests in opposition. Until recently "safe" levels for residues of various dangerous substances were based on data concerning all consumers without regard to children under five as a particular, and particularly vulnerable, group. Small children are more likely than adults to be exposed to high levels of pesticide residues on fruit because they eat far more fruit for their weight. Large samples of American pre-school children have been shown to eat six times as much fruit in total; six times more grapes; seven times more apples and apple sauce and as much as 30 times more apple juice as adults. (Most adults don't drink *any* apple juice, of course.) Some experts consider it likely that young children are also more susceptible than adults to the toxic effects of pesticides because their bodies may be less capable of detoxifying them. Target organs may be vulnerable to particular chemicals because of their immaturity: young brains to neurotoxins, for example.

The purpose of publicizing the undoubtedly greater risks to babies and small children is not to panic parents but to persuade the food industry to reconsider some "acceptable" practices and residue levels. When public protest about a particular contaminant becomes vociferous enough it can actually change government policy and commercial practice. This is how Alar (Daminozide) came to be banned from apple growing in the U.S. in the late 1980s.

Day-to-day parenting becomes impossible, though, if you succumb to helpless despair. These are real risks and often unnecessary (or greedy) risks, but they are still small compared with other environmental dangers. And there is a little (not a great deal) that you can do to minimize the risks to your own children:

■ Buy organic babyfoods: more brands are becoming more widely available. If your supermarket doesn't stock any, exercise consumer influence by asking.

■ Buy organic fruit and vegetables when you can. Standards are very strict in European countries, less so in the U.S. but you should be able to find State certification that the produce was grown without herbicides, pesticides or chemical fertilizers. Prices will tend to be higher everywhere and you cannot, of course, buy a full range of out-of-season produce because long-term storage demands chemical preservatives.

■ When you cannot buy organically grown fruit and vegetables, try and buy mostly locally grown produce that's in season.

■ When you're not sure of their source, foods with inedible heavy skins or husks (bananas, corn cobs), and foods you can peel or scrub (apples, carrots) are safer from pesticide sprays and other surface chemicals, though not from systemic chemicals picked up from soil and fertilizer, of course.

■ Serve as varied a diet as your child will happily accept to maximize safety as well as good nutrition. The wider the range of juices, or "dinners" or fruit or vegetable finger-foods he has, the lesser the chance of him taking in a worryingly large amount of any one contaminant. It was the parents of children who had drunk nothing but apple juice for months, and maybe as much as half a litre a day of it, who had most cause for concern about Alar residues.

you can strip her top half altogether: skin is much easier to wash than clothes. If she must have clothes on, though, a really efficient bib (perhaps the kind with an ever-open pocket at the bottom to catch her dribbles and misses) will keep them moderately clean, especially if you push up her sleeves and tuck extra tissues in round the neck. A thick layer of newspaper under her chair will catch the rest and can still be recycled. Or you could use a plastic sheet. If you find it impossible to feed her in public without holding her hands out of the way while you pop neat spoonfuls into her mouth, try to feed her in private. Forcing your baby to eat tidily is second only to forcing her to eat at all as the best way of putting her off the whole business.

If you think your baby isn't eating enough Beware! You may well be wrong and worrying about the amount your child eats may create problems for all of you later on. Reasonably well and happy babies who are offered milk and manageable solid foods don't starve themselves (see p.336) so try to trust yours to know how much is enough. If you cannot:

■ Look at the baby's growth. If the upward curve on her weight and length charts is reasonably steady, she is getting enough to eat.
■ Look at the baby's energy and vitality. If she is lively and active, she is not going short of food.
■ Consider the baby's milk intake and remind yourself that milk is food. She may be drinking almost everything she needs.

If you are still tempted to push food at your baby, have her health and charted growth checked by your doctor or clinic. Even if your baby is obviously well-nourished, health professionals won't grudge the time it takes to reassure you. They know how important it is for you to relax about your baby's eating before she enters toddlerhood.

GROWTH

In this second half of the first year babies' rate of growth slows even further. Between now and his first birthday your baby will probably gain at no more than half the rate of his first six months. If you weighed him every week – which would be pointless if he is in good health – you would probably find that his weight rose by only around 60g (2oz) a week with an overall height increase for the half-year of around 8cm–10cm (3in–4in).

Although the general shape of your baby's growth curves will still follow the general shape of the centile curves on the chart – and he is likely to be in or close to the segment he started out in – you may now get more "wiggles" in his weight gain. If he is severely ill for a couple of weeks, or off-colour with repeated minor infections over several weeks, he may gain no weight at all for a while and even begin to look thin. When he is better, though, he will probably catch up by gaining extra fast for a few weeks. Solid feeding may make weight gain more variable, too. Weeks when he has an exclusive passion for baked beans or cheese are likely to put more weight on him than weeks when he only wants vegetable soup and apples. Over several weeks or months these wiggles even out. Since it is only the shape of his *overall* weight gain that matters, don't set yourself up for worry by weighing him too often.

Teeth
and Teething

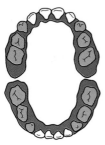

By the end of their first year many babies have matching rows of four top and four bottom incisor teeth.

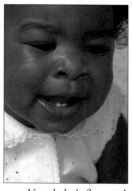

Your baby's first teeth transform that toothless smile into a toothy grin.

Teeth usually appear fast and furiously during this half-year, but not always. Don't be surprised, let alone concerned, if your baby is one of the large minority who produce teeth to a different timetable from the one suggested here:

■ The first tooth, cut at around six months, is usually one of the two middle incisors in the bottom jaw.

■ The second tooth follows close behind and is next door neighbour to the first.

■ At around seven months (or sooner or later) most babies produce one of the matching pair of top incisors and then its neighbour.

■ By eight to nine months all four of these top front teeth are often through and by nine to ten months the remaining two lower incisors appear so that babies have achieved a row of four top and four bottom teeth. There is then usually a pause.

■ Sometime around the first birthday the next tooth will appear: one of the four first molars that fill the furthest back position so far at each side of each jaw.

The sharp, flat shape of the front teeth – the incisors – helps them to come through easily, far more easily than the larger, broader molars which are to come. But although most babies don't suffer more than fleeting and trivial discomfort while cutting any individual front tooth, having two or three on the move at the same time may make your baby inclined to the miseries. Make sure that she has plenty of things to bite. Ordinary "teething rings" have no advantage over other smooth toys but your baby may appreciate the slightly chewy gel-filled kind you can pre-cool in the refrigerator.

If you want to use teething gel on your baby's gums, choose carefully. Even today, some contain quite powerful drugs, or sugar. You may find that it helps to rub the sore patch of gum with your finger, even if there is no medicine on it. Once the baby has two or three teeth, chewing on a variety of objects (*not* fingers) will also help to "file down" their exceedingly sharp points.

Teeth and weaning When babies' first teeth – those flat incisors – appear, they are so sharp that mothers sometimes wonder if their arrival signals an end to breast-feeding. It doesn't, of course. The first two teeth at least are almost invariably bottom teeth. Your baby has no matching top tooth against which to pincer anything. Although you may feel the difference when your baby plays with the nipple towards the end of a feed – and may have to stop her doing so – it will be weeks, yet, before the kind of biting which is occasionally problematically painful becomes a possibility (see p.237).

Looking after your baby's first teeth Looking after your baby's first teeth isn't always easy but it's well worth the trouble. Even though the whole set of baby teeth will eventually be shed and replaced, their health is no less important than the health of the permanent teeth. Your child has to use them for several crucial years, after all, and even when they begin to be

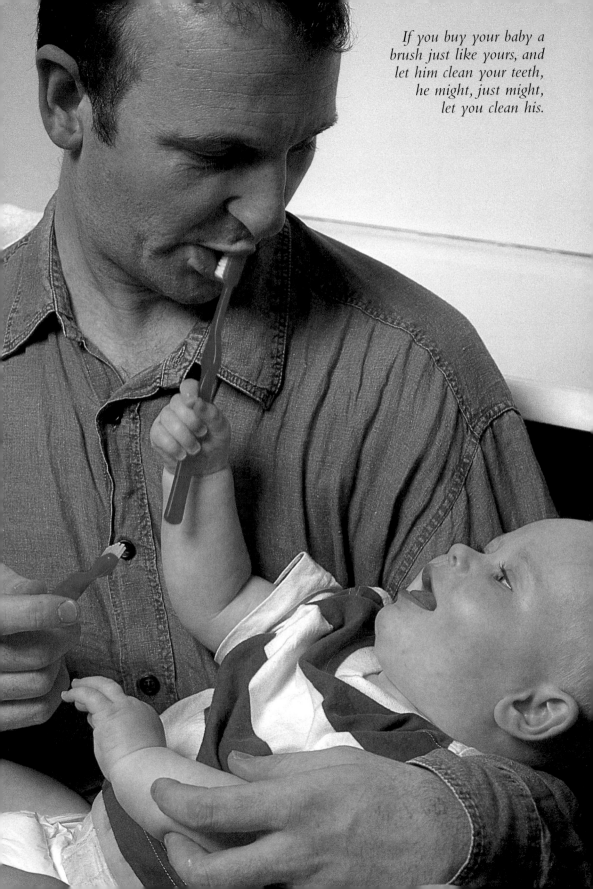

If you buy your baby a brush just like yours, and let him clean your teeth, he might, just might, let you clean his.

What's the reality of cleaning babies' teeth?

We've been told we should clean our seven-month baby's teeth (tooth!) from the beginning, but the very idea of putting a toothbrush into his mouth seems absurd and horrible. Is this really a parental duty? If so, how's it done?

Your baby's single tooth certainly doesn't need *brushing*, but unless you are giving fluoride drops on medical advice, it will benefit from the protective effect of a children's fluoride toothpaste. The easiest way to apply it is probably on your finger so you can work by feel if your baby doesn't want to let you see what you are doing. Use a peppercorn-sized helping of paste and try to cover the whole surface of the tooth.

Brushing, as well as fluoride paste, becomes more important when a baby has two or more teeth that butt up against each other, and much more important still in the second year when he eats more textured foods – even some sweet sticky foods – that might get between them and stay there. Introducing toothbrushes and rituals in the first year is really more useful as preparation and education for dental health in the future than it is for the present.

Wait until your baby is sitting up and becoming interested in trying to copy the things he sees you doing regularly, then make sure that one of those is brushing teeth.

It helps if you get identically coloured brushes for him and each of you, and if whoever is taking care of the baby today sits with him on the bathroom floor to brush, using a bowl (or maybe the bath) for rinsing and spitting so he can really see what is going on and try to do it too. Even when he learns to put his brush in his mouth he won't be able to copy that last spitting-bit yet, but it's much the most interesting part of the process

and will help to hold his attention.

When he's used to watching you brush your teeth and pretending to brush his own, try offering the baby a turn at brushing your teeth in exchange for letting you have a go at brushing his. If this ploy works you may have to elaborate it into brushing his teeth *while* he "brushes" yours. If it doesn't work, though, don't try to insist (you actually couldn't *make* him admit the toothbrush without risking hurting him); the toothpaste-on-a-finger technique is still more important. Take every opportunity to persuade him to open his mouth for you. He may enjoy showing off a newly cut tooth, or pointing out a sore place on the gum that needs rubbing.

By the time your baby's birthday is coming up and he has teeth butting up to each other top and bottom, he will probably be able to sit on your lap up to the sink, or even stand on a stool with you behind him for safety, and watch in the mirror while you brush, and perhaps count, your teeth and his. Make a point of telling him the correct name of each tooth you're attending to so that he is easily persuaded that no single tooth must be left out. Touching each tooth with the brush "to give it its share of toothpaste" often appeals to a young toddler's sense of justice and keeps his mouth open for five seconds after boredom looms.

Don't expect it to be an easy task that you carry out thoroughly, though. Few toddlers are consistently co-operative about having their teeth cleaned and however keen he becomes, your child will not be able to clean his own teeth adequately until he is at least six years old. Even if they are supervised, reminded of the technique and kept brushing for reasonable periods, younger children do not have the necessary manual dexterity.

replaced, the health and proper positioning of his second teeth largely depend on the first.

Cleaning your baby's teeth is important from the beginning and becomes more so as she cuts teeth that butt up against other teeth. But while the ideal, now as later, is to ensure that no sugary film remains in her mouth and no shreds of food stay caught between two teeth, effective up and down brushing may be impossible at this stage and the fluoride in the toothpaste is probably what matters most. Make brushing with a small soft toothbrush and a tiny dot of children's toothpaste a twice-daily routine, but if your baby resists, don't try to force her. You can't brush teeth efficiently while a baby struggles and cries and trying is likely to put her off the whole teeth-cleaning business.

Fluoride in the diet, as well as applied directly to the teeth, dramatically reduces their vulnerability to decay. Just as it was important for you to get enough during pregnancy, so it is important for your baby to get enough now. Enough, but not more than enough. Too much fluoride can discolour teeth and may have other ill effects. In some areas fluoride occurs naturally in the water; in others fluoride is added to the public supply of drinking water. If your child is not going to get enough from water you can buy fluoride drops specially for her. If you do give your baby drops, though, it may be important *not* to use a fluoride toothpaste. Check the local recommendations with your health visitor or doctor.

First teeth are just as vulnerable to sugars as later ones. Although it is important to encourage your baby to like unsweetened and savoury foods, the very best thing you can do to protect her teeth at this stage is to make plain water her routine non-milk drink. Unsweetened, diluted fruit juice is a good source of vitamin C, but although it has no sugar added to it by the manufacturer (or you, of course) it still contains natural fruit sugar. One small cupful a day might be good for your baby, but one easily becomes several so that she gets much more vitamin C than she needs and more sugar than is good for her teeth. And if she is having juice at intervals all through the day, it's horribly likely that she might sometimes have it in a bottle, too. Slowly sucking sweet drinks ensures a long leisurely sugar-bath for the whole of a baby's mouth and is the worst possible insult to her teeth. In fact if you were only going to take one step to care for your baby's teeth now, refusing to give her bottles of any sweetened drink, and making sure that nobody else who takes care of her ever does so, would be the best step you could choose.

Try to get everyone in your baby's circle to take it for granted that milk is for nutrition, water is for thirst and fruit juice from a cup is a once-daily event or an occasional treat. If you do, your child may avoid the slide from real juice to bottled "vitamin C concentrate" for babies, "fruit drinks" for toddlers and fizzy drinks for older children. Sidestepping the sweet drink habit in this first year may be a strike for dental health throughout childhood.

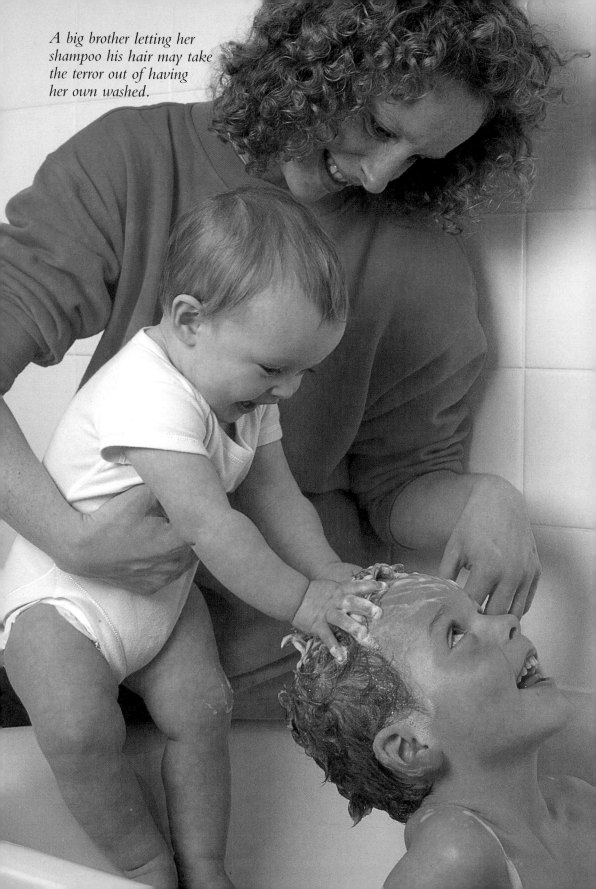

A big brother letting her shampoo his hair may take the terror out of having her own washed.

EVERYDAY CARE

As babies get older they spend more and more time on the floor and once they can crawl they get exceedingly grubby. Washing them is not as easy as a few weeks ago when they kept (more or less) still, either. Can you wash the face of someone who sucks the face cloth whenever it comes near and change a nappy while toes are being chewed? It's not easy but as long as your sense of humour stays intact, it can be fun.

HAIRWASHING

Being able to sit up in the big bath makes bath time a favourite part of the day for many babies, but may also make hairwashing a horror. Babies who can sit often don't want to be laid down, and many are nervous about lying in such an expanse of water. But having their hair shampooed sitting up is tricky. They need to tip their heads back which most find difficult; if they don't, they get water down their faces which most loathe.

If a struggle has already begun, start by giving up for a bit. The more you frighten your baby the more frightened he will become, but his short memory is still on your side. If you don't try to shampoo his hair for at least a month, he will probably forget to dread it. In the meantime you can sponge bits of food out of his hair as if it was a shaggy rug, and brush it with a soft damp brush to stop it looking lank and greasy. When you start again, set yourself to keep water (not just soap) out of his eyes. If soap trickles, don't try to rinse it off: wipe it away with a face cloth. If your baby is still afraid of having water poured on his head, don't insist on showing him that there's nothing to fear. If you try to rinse his hair while he screams and struggles, water is bound to run down his face which *is* what he fears.

As long as she lets you pull it right on, this gadget stops the dreaded drips.

You need a new approach. If hairwashing trouble has spilled over into dislike of the bath, try separating the two things by washing his hair backwards over the edge of the bath or wash basin as you did when he was tiny (see p.102). If he isn't scared of the big bath when he shares it with an adult, try washing his hair while he's safely and happily held in a lying down position (see p.176). If you rinse the front of his hair that's out of the water by the dipped face cloth method, there's no reason why he should get even a drip down his face.

STAYING SAFELY CLEAN

Cleanliness is anathema to a crawling baby but good hygiene is vital to his health. Getting the balance right means being very fussy about cleanliness around food and excreta (human or animal) but not about grubby knees or toys that go from floor to hand to mouth. "Dirty dirt" and "clean dirt" may both contain bacteria – even the potentially harmful kinds we call "germs" – but only the dirty kind – old food, mouse-droppings, the cat's litter tray, soiled nappies – provide a breeding ground for the teeming thousands it usually takes to overwhelm the defences of a child's body and make him ill.

Germs are a real hazard in the home, but chemical poisons are more common and usually more serious. Once your baby can crawl at all, he'll soon stand and try to climb. It's time to move poisonous cleaning materials from that undersink cupboard and alcohol from the dresser, and to install child-proof locks on garage or garden shed doors and medicine cupboards.

PARENTS, TAKE NOTE

Drowning

Babies can drown in the smallest amount of water it takes to cover their noses and mouths – less than five centimetres. They drown because when they fall face down they don't always put their arms out to save themselves so they may end up flat. If they happen to find themselves flat and face down in water, they don't usually hold their breath while they struggle to roll over or sit up: they draw in a deep breath ready to yell, and fill their lungs with water instead of air.

Hold on to your newly sitting baby in the bath and don't turn your back even when she sits steadily. As a crawler she may try to pull herself to standing by the edge of the bath. As a toddler she'll try to walk about in it. Don't leave her alone in the bath, even for one minute, for the next couple of years.

Garden water-hazards need attention too.

Once your child even might get into the garden alone, water butts need lids, paddling pools have to be emptied after each supervised play session and ornamental pools need to be drained, fenced or covered with safety mesh. Submerged a bare one centimetre under the surface, mesh will not show but will not let a child drown, either.

Teaching your baby to swim makes it more likely that she'll hold her breath if water covers her face, instead of "breathing" it in. Don't let early swimming proficiency lull you into a false sense of security, though. Swimming in a warm calm pool won't prevent your three-year-old drowning if she climbs onto a water butt and falls head downwards, goes through the ice on a gravel pit, slips off the bank into deep river water or gets knocked down by waves at the beach.

EXCRETING

As babies come to eat food that is more and more like older people's so the waste that is the end product of digesting that food becomes more like everyone else's. Solid foods – and eventually unmodified cow's milk – move more slowly through the intestines yet still leave a comparatively large amount of undigestible residue. The resulting stools, compared with a younger baby's, are less frequent, bulkier and smell more strongly of faeces.

Constipation   Babies still vary in the frequency with which their bodies need to evacuate waste: children and adults vary too. So a daily motion is not now, and never will be, a prescription for, or sign of, good health. Your baby is only constipated if, when a motion finally arrives, it is dry and hard enough to make its passage difficult or painful.

If your baby does have hard motions, the most likely explanation is that she is not drinking quite as much as her body could use. Very mild degrees of dehydration are quite common during the months when babies are substituting more solid foods for milk, and perhaps also being encouraged to substitute cups for breast or bottle. Offer lots of extra drinks of water and, if hard stools continue, some diluted fruit juice or vegetable juice as well.

Don't give any form of laxative unless your doctor gives you direct instructions to do so. She almost certainly will not because most doctors agree that it is a great mistake to try to override the body's natural rhythms. Never interfere with your baby's bowel habits by using suppositories or enemas either. A healthy baby's bowels open when they need to. It is not your job to control them.

Diarrhoea   New foods may still prove difficult for your baby to digest and if they do, undigested particles may appear in her stools. If there is also visible mucus, it usually means that the food was too fibrous or pippy for her. Instead of just liquidizing or mashing, try putting the next serving of that food through a mouli or sieve.

Intolerance of spicy food, a course of antibiotics, even a sudden increase in your baby's intake of sugar or fat can cause very loose and frequent stools, which may have an unusually nasty smell. On its own, this kind of non-infective diarrhoea will not make your baby ill and needs no treatment other than perhaps serving simpler food for a day or two. But if, in addition to loose stools, your baby seems unwell, goes off her food, runs a fever and/or vomits, she should be seen by a doctor on the same day. She may have gastro-enteritis. While this is not quite such a serious threat to this age group as to younger babies, the loss of fluid can still rapidly make them exceedingly ill. So get medical help quickly and, while you are waiting for it, offer your baby as much cool boiled water – or rehydration fluid if your doctor recommends it, you prefer it and your baby likes it – as she will drink.

Sensible precautions will help you avoid gastro-enteritis – and all forms of food poisoning. All the suggestions for good hygiene during the weaning period are relevant (see p.243).

SLEEPING

This second half of your baby's first year will usher in marked changes in your household's night life. Some of them will certainly be changes for the better from your point of view; others may be for the worse. The overall number of hours per day which your baby spends sleeping will probably be dropping slightly but likely changes in the patterning of his sleep will probably be more significant to you than its duration. He used to share his total sleeping fairly evenly around the clock, spending similar hours in night-sleep and napping (if you could decide which was which). Now, sleep increasingly shifts away from the daytime hours and concentrates at night. A likely pattern is a 10 to 12 hour night, and two separate daytime naps of anything from 20 minutes to three hours each. Don't expect unbroken nights, though, because if you do you will almost certainly be disappointed as well as woken up. Recent statistics from a big survey of parents in Britain's West Country suggest that fewer than one in six babies regularly sleep through the night at six months and more than one in six wake more than once a night – some of them as often as eight times.

Although some connection between your baby's eating and sleeping remains, so that a large meal or luxurious sucking still make him inclined to feel sleepy, the connection is not nearly as strong as it was. He will no longer fall asleep after each meal, and even when a meal immediately precedes a regular nap time, intriguing activities may be enough to keep him interested and awake for a while.

As we saw earlier, babies who need much less daytime sleep than the average require more care and attention from the adults who look after them, but may get considerable developmental advantages from their extra hours awake. If your baby is in a day care centre, or with a childminder or a nanny, do be sure that those aren't going to be boring, lonely hours when nobody will play because he "ought" to be asleep. A wakeful baby lives a much fuller life than one who sleeps for several hours each day and needs adults help in doing so. That means that you, and any other carers have to find ways of getting on with adult life while sharing it with the baby, rather than dividing the days into periods of baby care and periods of adult activity. All concerned will eventually get their reward: plenty of waking time spent with interested adults doing interesting things will probably turn your baby into an extremely sociable and competent toddler.

Don't be too quick to abandon naps altogether, though. Even if your baby only sleeps for 20 minutes on each of the two occasions when he's put down each day, he may well be happy to spend twice that long comfortably settled in his cot with toys to play with and interesting things to look at.

Stick to the routine of a morning and an afternoon rest even once you know that your baby won't actually sleep. Ignore a brief protest on being left – any busy and well-attached baby is bound to announce that he would prefer to stay up or have you stay with him. You may well find that after a couple of minutes he is happily playing or talking and looking at things. If he is, leave him. He may be enjoying a rest from his demanding life just as much as you are enjoying a rest from his demanding company.

Don't ignore the first grumbles of boredom, though. Go to the baby quickly even if he's only been on his own for 15 minutes. If he's left, he is bound to begin to feel that his cot is a prison. He will not go happily into it next time.

DIFFICULTY OVER GOING TO SLEEP

Taken together, the separation of sleeping from feeding and its concentration at night set the scene for less disturbed nights for you. But other developments follow a different script. Until around six months your baby will fall asleep when he needs to. Nothing except acute hunger, illness or pain will keep him awake. So if you put him comfortably to bed at night and settle him for naps during the day, you can assume that he will sleep if he needs to and that if he does not sleep, he does not need to. But between six and nine months this changes. Your baby becomes able to keep himself awake, or to be kept awake, not only by noise and excitement around him but also by internal tension or a reluctance to close out the world, or relinquish you, by falling asleep.

As soon as babies *can* keep themselves awake, many do. Trouble when trying to put babies to bed at night is one of the most common and most disruptive problems parents face. You will be lucky if you do not suffer from it at some time and to some extent with at least one of your children, so when it first strikes, don't add to your misery by assuming that everybody else's child goes to bed like an angel, or that your child's behaviour is your (or his) fault. Persistent trouble is even more likely when your baby stops having a bedtime breast or bottle feed, whether that is when he is eight months or eighteen months old. Whenever it happens, once your baby can – and at least sometimes does – keep himself awake on purpose, you can no longer assume that he will sleep if he is tired and that if he does not sleep he is not tired. The reverse can be true. He can now get over-tired and too strung up and tense to relax into sleep he badly needs.

The first signs of going-to-bed-trouble sometimes follow an obvious upset. Many babies who have been admitted to hospital, even for a few days, have trouble settling to sleep once they return home. But the disturbance that starts night-time trouble need not be a traumatic one. A holiday away from home can break the baby's routines so that problems begin when the family returns home. A new room can disturb him in the same way; even a turn around of the furniture in his old room can leave him feeling disorientated and unable to drop easily into sleep. So since bedtime trouble is a great deal easier to prevent than it is to cure, it is worth thinking carefully before introducing any optional major changes into your baby's surroundings during this age period.

Trouble over going to sleep at night doesn't need an external cause, though. Often the difficulty comes from inside your baby: from his passionate attachment to you and his determination to keep you with him or to keep himself with you. He cannot bear to see you leave, and even if you stay nearby he cannot allow himself to go to sleep because sleeping takes him away from you. So he screams and cries when you leave him; greets your return with delight and screams again as soon as you leave. If you sit with him, he will lie quietly; but as soon as you move towards the door, he will snap fully awake again. His ability to keep himself awake will certainly outlast your patience. He has nothing else to do all evening; you have plenty.

Having your baby sleep with you There may not be an "answer" in the sense of one trick that completely prevents or finally removes all stress from the nightly separation. Even sidestepping the separation itself by having your baby sleep with you in a family bed may not prove stress-free. Take a careful look at what that will mean in the near future when your baby crawls and climbs and walks, before you decide on it as a long-term solution.

If your baby isn't going to go to bed on his own, but with you, where is he going to spend the evenings until you are ready for bed? Right now it may be easy to have him around downstairs; let him drop off to sleep and then put him on the couch. It will not be so easy when he is mobile, though. He may find it difficult to go to sleep without being put to bed in some definite way, and once he falls asleep he won't be safe on the couch or anywhere but on the floor, in a cot or maybe in a playpen.

If he is not accustomed to being left to go to sleep in the evening, being left when you have an evening out may be very difficult for him – and for your babysitter.

Once you have taken him upstairs to bed with you, one of you will have to stay with him every minute he's awake, and supervise him very closely when he's asleep. Left alone he might roll or crawl out. Even if he got off the bed without hurting himself, would he be safe on the loose in your bedroom? And even if he stayed asleep, would he be safe? The studies confirming that sleeping in family beds is fine for babies do not suggest that family-sized beds with adult pillows and bedding and *no adults* are safe.

If you are breast-feeding your baby, it may be difficult to wean him completely while he can more or less help himself. Are you happy to let him nurse at night until he weans himself?

Helping your baby go to sleep alone If you prefer your baby to sleep in his own cot – whether in your room or another – there is a great deal you can do to help him release you at night. Your aim is to narrow the gap for him, between the state of being awake and with you, and the state of being asleep and without you. If he is suddenly carried away from the warm, bright living room, full of the pleasant and familiar sounds of people and TV, to a cool, dim, quiet room where he is put into a cot he knows he cannot get out of and left to listen to your footsteps receding, he is likely to panic. We cannot know what he thinks but his sobs seem to say, "You are going, you are gone, I am alone forever..."

Re-organizing his bedtime routine and his sleeping arrangements may enable you to soften this separation for him. It usually helps if bedtime starts long before the parting, and is, in itself, something to look forward to as an especially enjoyable part of his day. It may begin when you pick him up from day care or when you return from work and, after greeting each other, see his carer off. Or perhaps it begins alone with you, having supper in the kitchen, but continues with a rumbustious bath time, heralded by his father's return home. Your baby will need some winding down time, though, and ritualized time which tells him that bedtime is coming up and gives him the countdown to it. Many babies – and children, because rituals last – have a regular sequence of stories in the living room, counting games up the stairs, poems and songs in the rooms they sleep in, kisses for particular pictures or toy people and then kisses for themselves in bed. Your baby is more likely to accept being in bed if he does not feel himself completely cut off because he still has a light on, the door open and family sounds audible. And he's far more likely to let you go away a *bit* if you don't try to go away *entirely*. Try spending the next 10 minutes or so tidying away dirty clothes, readying things for the next morning and generally pottering around near his open door so he can settle himself and begin to drift towards sleep in the comfortable knowledge of your presence. Or try adding his father into the emotional mix so the baby has you *and* him for a few minutes before you withdraw leaving him to sing the last song. Eventually your baby is going to be on his own, of course, but even if he'd rather one of you stayed, that's not at all the same as being left feeling panic-stricken and bereft by your departure. If you can keep the whole nightly business peacefully low-key, these are months during which he will develop ways of giving himself security and comfort. He will use these to help himself cope with being without you.

COMFORT HABITS

A baby's comfort habits are under his own control in a way which the comfort he gets from other people is not. He cannot force you to stay with him or to go on cuddling him; the amount of comfort you will give him is up to you. But he can rely on as much comfort as he wants if it comes from himself.

This is both the strength and the weakness of all comfort habits. They are good for babies because they give them independent and autonomous sources of security; make them more able to rely on

Thumb-sucking is comfort that's within her own control and always available.

themselves and leave them less at the mercy of the adult world. But they can be bad for a baby if he relies on them so much that he cuts himself off from the kinds of comfort which do come from other people. In general, then, a baby who uses a comfort habit to keep himself calm and relaxed while his mother leaves him to fall asleep at night is doing himself nothing but good. But a baby who often uses that comfort habit during the day, when a parent or beloved caretaker is present and the world of toys, play and exploration is open to him, is showing signs that all is not well. Of course an occasional incident need not worry you. Your baby's desire to rock in a corner instead of playing, today, probably means nothing more than that he is particularly tired or is feeling unwell. But if he often behaved in that way it could mean that he needed to give himself a lot of comforting because he was not getting enough from anyone else. At the furthest extreme, a child who is almost completely withdrawn into a world of rhythmic rocking is usually showing us that he cannot manage or get satisfaction from the world of people and activity.

Sucking for comfort Sucking is the most basic of all comfort habits. Your baby may have been sucking his fingers, thumb or a dummy for months. But now the sucking takes on a new significance for him. He may be able to let you leave him calmly provided he is sucking, but not otherwise. As you leave, he sucks harder. He sucks instead of crying; uses the energy that would have gone into crying, in sucking; uses the comfort of the sucking instead of the comfort of you. Sucking is so basic that your baby may combine it, now, with other forms of comfort.

Cuddlies Dignified by psychologists with the name of "transitional comfort objects", cuddlies are soft things that babies adopt and which come to stand in for people in their minds. Cuddlies range from gauze nappies through old cot blankets to more conventional soft toys. A cuddly stays with your baby, like a piece of parental love, through the sad moment of parting. It is still there for him when he wakes in the small hours and you are not. Not all children adopt a cuddly, but those who are going to will probably do so sometime in this half-year, using it passionately either with, or instead of, sucking. A baby's cuddly takes on a very real emotional importance for him. It is his familiar; the thing that spells safety and security, wards off evil and promises your return. He may simply hold and finger it or he may use it in all kinds of elaborate ways. A scarf, for example, may be wound round his head with one end looped across his face so that he can suck his thumb through it. A teddy bear may always be held crossways so that his ear is under the baby's nose.

If your baby has adopted something in this way it will be his most important possession; the thing that his carer must never leave in the park or throw out as rubbish; the one item that really must not be forgotten when you go on holiday or left behind if he has to go to hospital. You probably will not even be able to wash it as often as you would like because you ruin its precious familiar smell. Cuddlies can never be completely duplicated because daily use contributes to their uniqueness. But with years of use ahead, it's worth doing what you can to ensure against disaster. If your child's cuddly is something simple like a gauze nappy, put two or three away for emergencies. If

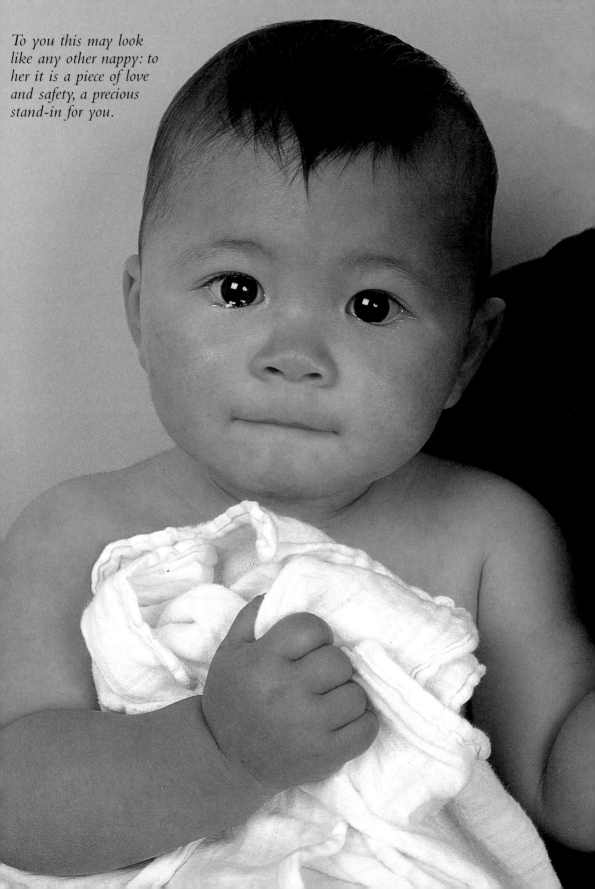

To you this may look like any other nappy: to her it is a piece of love and safety, a precious stand-in for you.

it is a soft toy, it would be wise to buy a second and put that somewhere safe. If it is a piece of blanket or a sweater of yours, you may be able to cut it in half without the baby noticing and keep the second half against the dreadful day when the first falls to pieces or gets thrown away. Such a "second" will not entirely prevent misery, because it will not look or feel or smell quite the same as the one that has shared your baby's cot for months or years. But it will be very much better than nothing.

Rituals   Some babies take the bedtime rituals adults offer and build on them. There's no harm in that but you may want to be aware that once the two of you have begun to formalize your baby's going-to-bed routine in this way, he may embroider it until a routine that took 13 minutes each night when he was nine months old takes 33 minutes when he is three. Do make sure that anyone who is ever going to put your baby to bed knows the details of his chosen ritual. His grandmother cannot be expected to cope successfully while you have an evening out if she is not equipped with the same tools for peace that you use yourself.

Rhythmical movements   When your baby was very small you probably walked with him, rocked him and patted him whenever he needed comforting. Whatever was causing him distress he found rhythmical physical activity soothing. Most older babies still find physical rhythm soothing and many find more-or-less desirable ways to provide it for themselves.

Obviously harmless rhythmical comfort habits your baby may discover include stroking his face or pulling on his cuddly. Twisting a lock of hair is harmless within limits, but can tie fine, baby hair in knots or even pull it out. A noisy nuisance, but nothing worse, is rocking on hands and knees so that the cot whizzes all over the floor. Slightly more worrying is the kind of rocking in which the baby bangs his head on the end of the cot with each rock.

Head banging   If you notice that your baby is head banging every evening you need to know whether it is the rhythmical sound and the rhythmical jar that he finds satisfying, or whether he is actually causing himself pain on purpose. The easiest way to find out is to fix several sheets of cardboard to the head of the cot. Don't use a cot-bumper or other soft padding because that will deprive him of the noise. He can still thud against cardboard but he cannot actually hurt himself. The point is that if your cardboard-padding is acceptable, pain is no part of your baby's head banging so it is nothing to worry about. But if the baby cannot settle as he usually does, or transfers his head banging to the unpadded side-bars, pain clearly is part of the point and you need to ask yourselves, and anyone who cares for him during the day, why he wants or needs to hurt himself.

Is he angry with somebody and turning that anger in on himself? Is somebody or something frustrating him beyond easy bearing? If the head banging only built up when his father went away on a trip or when he changed caregivers, his father's return, or being given the chance to get used to the new person more slowly, may deal with the whole matter. Failing any obvious extra stress in his life, offering lots of extra individual attention, and chances to play noisy, physically active games with you may relieve his inside tension.

If, instead of lessening, the head banging spreads from evenings in the cot to daytime in any old place and your baby or toddler begins to bruise himself deliberately against the walls or furniture, consult your child health clinic or your doctor. Don't let anyone put you off by telling you, "Don't worry, lots of children do it." Not many do and they need to be helped to be happier.

Masturbation If nappies and sleeping suits don't foil them some baby boys make a rhythmical comfort habit out of pulling their penises, while some baby girls adopt a version of rocking which rhythmically rubs their vulvae against the cot mattress or bars. Even if you easily accept that it is natural and right for all babies to explore the parts that are usually covered with nappies whenever those nappies are taken off, finding your baby rocking away, red-faced, panting and obviously excited, may shock you.

Try not to be shocked and if you are, try not to express it. Masturbation will do your child no harm, now or later, and discovering its pleasures early does not suggest that a baby is "over-sexed". All babies have sexual feelings (even though most adults prefer to believe otherwise) and sooner or later they all discover that rubbing their genitals feels good. The only possible harm in the situation is the harm you, or another loved adult, could do by over-reacting. If your baby is happily playing by, and with, himself alone in his cot, leave him be.

If bedtime still Sometimes, despite all your attempts to make it easy for your child to
upsets your baby let you go, with plenty of encouragement of comfort habits and lots of co-operation in making gentle rituals, a baby still gets really upset about going to bed. Pulled between a crying child and a burning meal it is easy to lose sight of your long-term goals and react to the immediate stress in ways that may lead to months of trouble. It is worth thinking the whole matter through during a calm daytime moment.

What you want is to have your baby settle happily into bed and drift contentedly off to sleep on his own leaving you free to concentrate on other things. That means that tearing yourself away leaving him to howl cannot be the right answer, even if you are capable of doing it. If you do that, he is not settling happily, and being abandoned will certainly increase his feeling that it is not safe to let you go out of the room in case you never come back. But staying with him, or bringing him back downstairs, is not a long-term answer either. You are not getting your adult evening peace and far from beginning to discover that it is safe to be on his own and that he can manage his own sleeping, the baby is getting the message that you agree with him that solitude is intolerable.

The long-term answer may involve a lot of short-term effort while you convince your baby that it is safe to let you go because you always will come back, but that it isn't any use demanding to get up again because you will not let him. You give him what he needs – reassurance – but you will not necessarily give him what he wants – more daytime:

■ Try to keep the pre-bedtime hour affectionate and enjoyable. A squabble over supper or a jealous tussle for father's attention will be enough to increase his uncertainty about how much he loves and is loved, and therefore how safe it is to let you leave him. This is not the time of day for sudden discipline.

■ Always make sure that the baby knows bedtime is coming up, by following the same evening routine of, for example, bath, play, supper, bed. Keep to going-to-bed rituals, or even invent some for your baby. Getting a teddy settled into bed, for example, can be a good lead-in to getting him settled too.

■ If, after all this, your baby cries when you leave, go back. Reassure him that you are still close by; kiss him again and leave. You may have to repeat this over and over again, but it is the only sure way eventually to convince him that you really will come but that you really will not get him up or stay with him and put him to sleep.

■ If you've been back again and again, try using your voice alone. It may be enough reassurance for the baby if you simply call pleasantly to him. If so, you can keep him calm while saving your own legs and at least *half* talking with his father. It's not exactly peace, but it may be the nearest you'll get for the next week or two.

WAKING IN THE NIGHT

Although babies can, and often do, sleep solidly for a 12-hour period, some wake frequently, even if only briefly. This kind of waking used to be called a "bad habit": babies were ignored when they woke or even scolded or smacked to "break the habit". But babies cannot wake themselves on purpose. If something disturbs yours before he has had enough sleep, or he comes awake during one of the "light sleep" periods everybody has every night, leaving him to cry or punishing him for crying is not going to prevent the same thing (or something different) from awakening him the next night. "He will soon learn not to do it," people say. But how can your baby learn not to do something which is outside his conscious control?

Outside disturbances Some of the night waking of this age group is due to the baby being woken up by external events. He no longer sleeps as deeply as he did when he was younger. You cannot necessarily assume that once he is asleep, almost nothing will wake him. Don't let visitors go into your baby's bedroom and don't go in yourselves unless you have reason to believe he needs you. Leave his door ajar so you can take a reassuring peep from a distance.

Noises which blur into the general level of background noise during the day can become disturbingly sharp in the comparative silence of the night. Heavy traffic on the road outside his room, low-flying aircraft or trains on a nearby line may all disturb him. He may also sense comings and goings around him even if they are not very noisy. It's not only visitors peeping into his room who may wake him. If he shares your room, your movements, whispered conversations and sleeping noises may all tend to disturb him, too.

Do what you can to re-organize the baby's sleeping arrangements to minimize disturbance. If you are short of space you may need to take a hard look at who shares which room with whom. If he shares a bedroom with an older child he may be woken by her nightmares and take longer to settle afterwards than she does. Would you rather have him in with you? If the room he is in is right on the lorry-route, secondary double-glazing on its windows would make a big difference; heavy curtains will help a bit and both would be best of all.

Getting cold will make him more likely to wake up. A very cool room is much less dangerous to him than it was when he was younger because he will not pass straight from deep sleep into a chilled state, but he will wake in the small hours if the heating goes off and the temperature dives. Although you certainly don't want his room to be warmer than about 18°C–20°C (65°F–68°F), you do want the baby to stay snugly warm even if he kicks off the blankets. A baby bag or blanket sleeper will keep his own warmth insulated in.

A very sore bottom, due to nappy rash, sometimes means a lot of night waking because the urine stings his skin whenever he wets himself. It's worth protecting a bottom that looks as if it even *might* be getting sore, with a thick coating of a silicone-based protective cream at night. Towards the end of the year he may have some bad nights because of teething pain with his first molars. And unless you are exceedingly lucky, there will be colds and their associated discomforts as well. You can't prevent a first awakening of this kind, but an appropriate dose of a children's paracetamol liquid may help for the rest of the night.

Internal disturbances Unfortunately most of the night crying in this age group is due to disturbances that come from within the baby and are more difficult to deal with. Whenever his sleep lightens he may come to consciousness. If a baby finds himself awake but perfectly happy, he will drop off again without telling you about it, provided he does not depend on action from you to put him to sleep. Video cameras left in babies' rooms overnight have shown babies waking and going off to sleep again without anyone knowing, far more frequently than parents imagine. But if your baby expects to be put to sleep with feeding or rocking or patting, he will have to call for you (see p.182), and if he finds himself not only awake but also anxious or afraid, he will cry for you.

Nightmares – or at least night frights of some kind – are commonplace in this age group. Of course there is no way that adults can know what form a nightmare takes because babies cannot tell, but they wake, usually, with a sudden terrified scream, appear afraid, are completely reassured by the arrival of a parent and often go back to sleep while they are being comforted.

Some babies repeat this behaviour several times each night and every night for months. Research suggests that a high proportion of them may be babies whose parents or caregivers do not pick them up readily when they cry by day either because they are afraid of spoiling them or because there are too many babies for the available adults to give much one-to-one attention. It is almost as if these babies are subconsciously making up at night for too little attention by day; making sure, during sleeping hours, of love they feel uncertain of when they are awake.

If your baby seems to be falling into this pattern, start by trying to imagine yourself into his place and see whether he might feel ignored rather than nurtured. If the answer is even a tentative "yes", you need a new policy, a new care-arrangement or both. In addition:

■ Slow up on anything that seems to be putting a strain on the baby. If you are trying to wean him from his bottle, for example, you may be going faster than he can easily bear. A return to some sucking could bring you all more peace.

■ Make sure that bedtime is relaxed and enjoyable. Going to sleep feeling warmly loved and protected may help him to stay comfortably asleep all night.

If a pattern of waking is set

If your baby starts waking in fear several times each night so that you begin to feel like zombies, taking him into bed with you the first time he wakes may bring peace for the rest of the night. Almost half of recently surveyed British parents always, or usually, deal with night waking in this way, and it may work for you as it does for many of them. Do *try* not to do it out of sheer desperation and against your own intentions, though (see p.109). If he shares a family bed during a few weeks or months of nightmares, it isn't likely that he will happily sleep apart from you just because they end. Although it may be difficult to imagine worse nights than you are having now, future nights of weaning him back to his own bed could be just as bad:

The most blissful short-term solution to night waking; but will it suit you in the longer term?

■ If your baby wakes frequently but is not afraid, simply no longer asleep and unable to get back to sleep without your help, taking him

into your bed will certainly defer the time when he can manage this feat. It may also make difficulties over going to sleep more likely and more intractable. If he can count on you to cuddle him back to sleep when he finds himself awake at 2am, he is bound to expect the same at 8pm. He can't tell the time, after all.

■ If you are trying not to take the baby into your bed, do go to him as soon as you are sure that he is really crying, not just muttering to himself. If a nightmare woke him, the disturbance will cease as soon as he sees you, hears your voice or feels your stroking hand. With practice you can give this kind of instant comfort half asleep and roll straight back into bed.

■ If he woke for no particular reason and now wants to play or, failing that, to suck or rock until he is fast asleep again, you may find that similar techniques to those suggested for going-to-sleep problems (see p.263) are equally effective with the staying-asleep variety. As before it is a compromise between leaving your baby to cry for as long as it takes him to exhaust himself and give up all hope of reaching you, and picking him up and taking him to sleep with you. You leave him firmly and confidently ("It's okay. Nothing to be upset about; off to sleep now."); when he cries you go back and reassure him ("There's nothing to cry for; we're right here.") but you don't pick him up, even if he breaks your heart by trying to climb up your arm ("Not now, darling. It's night; time to be in bed now.") instead you leave again. It can take a long time and it's not painless, but if you don't like either extreme, it's a happier medium.

That approach can be dressed up in all kinds of ways so as to dignify it as a "method". But unless you really feel it would help you to have someone else decide how many minutes you should stay away for the first night and whether or not you should pat your baby's back on night three, your best guide is probably your baby. If he's crying hysterically you'll probably stay with him until he calms down even if that's longer than your intended reassurance visit. But if his crying sounds cross and fretful rather than frightened or sad, maybe you won't go in after 10 minutes of it but will wait a bit longer in the hope that he'll drop off.

Your partner may have a large part to play in the whole process. If your baby is breast-fed or has been until recently, weaning may be getting mixed up with separating. Your baby is less likely to think about nursing if he doesn't smell breast milk. And even if nursing is long forgotten, he may find separating from mother even more difficult than separating from father when both of you are there. It's worth a try, anyway.

Early-morning waking Your baby does not know what time it is. He wakes because he has had enough sleep for the moment. Once you have finally abandoned the idea of an early-morning bottle or breast feed, it is not very likely that you will be able to persuade him to go back to sleep again. If he cries or shouts for you there is no point in trying to ignore him. You will have to go in the end so you might as well go at once. But you need not let him get up and start his day:

■ Make sure your baby has light to see by and toys to play with. If his room is dark in the early morning, leave a low-wattage night-light

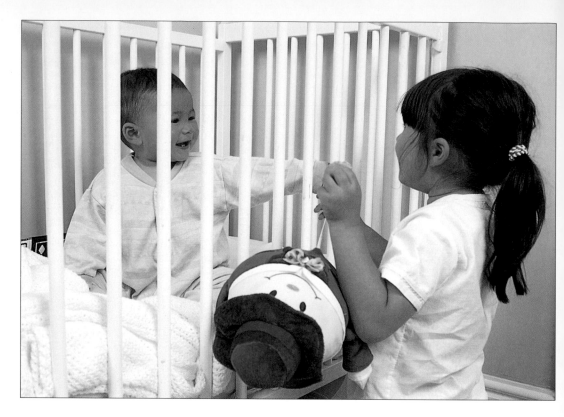

In an early-morning world with no grown-ups, children may entertain each other with astonishing sweetness.

on. Put a selection of toys in or beside his cot and he may occupy himself, at least for a while.

■ Be prepared to make him comfortable by changing his nappy, removing his sleeping bag and offering him a drink. Five minutes spent in this way may earn you another hour in bed.

■ Consider offering a baby the company of an older brother or sister if he has one who is willing. If the two of them share a room, or the older child is allowed to go to the baby when he wakes in the morning, they may entertain each other beautifully. There are no grown-ups around to create jealousy; the baby is safely imprisoned in his cot so he cannot pull hair or steal toys; he has no adults to appeal to so he offers the older child all the charm he normally reserves for them. These early-morning play sessions sometimes create, and often cement, a close and affectionate relationship between siblings. In fact accustomed to their squabbling in the public daytime, you may be amazed by their private sweetness.

You can't share those moments but you can have some morning magic of your own. You don't have to resist morning cuddles even if your bed is strictly out of bounds as a place to sleep at night. Taking him into bed with you for a family huggle when you are all (sort of) awake will not confuse the issue for your baby and will remind you of the point of being parents!

CRYING AND COMFORTING

Crying features much less in the lives of most babies in this age group than it did when they were younger. If you counted up your baby's daily minutes of crying, you would probably find there are many fewer now than at three months, let alone at the six-week peak. And even if the total hasn't dropped a great deal the impact of her crying on you and other people has probably changed. Three months ago crying sometimes seemed like a behaviour in its own right and one that might go on and on whatever you did. Now, crying is very clearly a reaction rather than a behaviour. If your baby cries, it's because of specific happenings and feelings, and if she cries a lot today compared with yesterday, it is because especially upsetting things happen, or she's feeling especially sensitive so ordinary happenings are hard to cope with.

Most of the time ordinary happenings don't cause crying, now. The more babies grow up, the more robustly they are likely to react to the hurly burly of daily life. In fact a lot of the things that used to make them startle and cry, such as sudden loud noises and quick movements, may now make them laugh. And when things do worry them, they will often express unease or alarm with anxious facial expressions and whimpery sounds, only embarking on full-fledged crying if nobody offers reassurance. But although babies in the second half of their first year tend to cry less overall, and certainly less readily and less often than before, there are particular aspects of their development that will introduce new causes of crying if they are not understood. Recognizing them in your baby, and learning to cope with them from now on, is important because they are all developments which will continue into toddlerhood. Sensitive handling, which is well-tuned to your son's or daughter's needs and emotions now, will certainly make life easier for all of you later on.

Separation and solitude Although not every older baby or toddler displays behaviour that obviously merits the term "separation anxiety", most dislike being separated from adults they are attached to. Being left by parents or other caregivers accounts for a high proportion of crying episodes. Being left by parents who do not respond to the resulting crying by coming back – as in the "cry it out" approach to sleeping difficulties – probably accounts for the longest non-stop crying sessions.

It's not only at night that babies object to being left, though. Even in the daytime, when they are up and playing, some babies are sometimes so sensitive to being left by the caregiver and to being alone in a room, that even two minutes causes crying. Don't be tempted to slip out without your baby noticing though, even if she is busy and you do only want to fetch something from the next room. If she looks up and finds you gone this time, how can she settle confidently to concentrated playing next time? A series of what are (in her terms) "betrayals" will make her far more anxious than a series of open departures and affectionate returns.

A combination of separation and solitude is what is most likely to upset your baby; being left with someone else — especially one to whom she is also attached — is far easier. So while some crying when a parent leaves home to go to work, or leaves a baby at day care, is common, it usually is and certainly should be, very brief.

Fears When your baby was younger she may have given the impression of being a little fearful of a great many things. Now, along with much greater confidence in coping with life in general, she is likely to develop intense fears about one or two particular things. She may, for example, be quite unworried now by most loud noises, but suddenly terrified by the sound of the vacuum cleaner. She may enjoy every kind of rough and tumble play but intensely dislike having clothes pulled on or off over her head. She may love her bath and everything to do with water, but then panic if she sees the water running away down the plug hole.

Fears of this kind often seem completely, even irritatingly, irrational: why should the vacuum cleaner's sound worry her when the noise of the washing machine does not? But fears are not rational. The baby's fears have to be accepted and respected because they are real, not because they are sensible. If you keep finding yourself tempted to demonstrate the harmlessness of hoovers, consider some of your own irrational fears. We all have them. Why, for example, do you mind beetles when you are not afraid of ants? And how much does it help you to know that beetles don't bite and ants might?

The best way to handle these quirky fears is to recognize and accept them, and help your baby avoid what she's frightened of as far as possible. Perhaps the vacuum cleaner could be banished except for weekends or other times when there's a second adult available to take the baby to another room. A carpet sweeper does a good, quiet, inexpensive job in between. Don't empty her bath water until she is well out of the way and don't buy clothes with close-fitting necks and no fastenings, however pretty they look. Don't *assume* that these, or any other particular things, will frighten your individual baby, though: she may be fearless, or frightened by quite other experiences. And whatever your baby's fears, do be careful not to be so obvious about helping her avoid them that she gets the impression that you share them. When she must be reminded of the existence of something scary you are helping her avoid, make it as clear as you can that you are helping her stay away from something because it frightens *her*, not because it *is* frightening or because it frightens *you*.

If you feel impatient with all this, or embarrassed in front of other people who think it's silly to pander to baby fears, remember that the more your baby has to face her fear the more intense it will become, and the less she has to experience it the faster it will die down. You cannot ever make a child fearless by frightening her.

Unexpected During these months your baby is beginning to build up a lot of
happenings expectations about people and how they behave. She is also making patterns of daily life in her mind; learning routines, rhythms and rituals. These powerful, new expectations are still being built and are in the forefront of her mind. When something happens that seems to contradict them, she loses confidence in her own understanding and

Your baby must be able to rely on you to protect her from her fears but not to share them.

feels afraid. As an example, imagine a baby who has learned that when she wakes up in the morning, either her mother or her father comes to greet her and get her up. Now imagine that a stranger walks in instead of the familiar parent. It's obvious that the baby would cry in fear, but it's not quite so obvious that it's because her expectations are shattered. Mightn't her reaction be simply due to the fact that the person who comes in is a stranger? Or to the surprise of a stranger coming without warning? At this age that's unlikely because that same stranger walking into the house to join the family for tea might well get brilliant smiles. What upsets the baby is not that she appears, but that she appears when and where she was expecting a parent. Something similar sometimes happens when a baby has built up expectations about feeding from a bottle. If she is accustomed to sucking warm milk and you feed her with cold, she will probably cry from the shock. It is not that she dislikes cold milk (she may readily drink it from a cup), it is just that it is not what she was expecting.

Totally new experiences may also be more than your baby can cope with. Her very first ride on a swing, her first taste of ice cream, or her first meeting with a horse may each make her cry. They are all potentially enjoyable but she needs time to get used to them.

Supporting your baby through unexpected or novel experiences is an important skill because as she gets older and her horizons broaden, it is novel experiences that will gradually thicken and enrich the fabric of her life. Of course it will be easier when she is older and you can use specific words, but even at six months you will probably find that you can warn her, by intonation, touch and gesture, when something unexpected or new is coming up. Foreseeing the things that may be going to alarm her, turn her attention to your own calm presence so that she receives the experience with and through you. If she has that first swing sitting on your lap, with your interested reassuring voice telling her about this new sensation and your familiar arms holding her steady, she will probably enjoy it from the beginning. And all the best first tastes of ice cream come from a cone that belongs to someone else.

Helplessness Babies have strong emotions but very little power. As far as we know, their loves and hates, their wishes and wants are as strong as ours, but because they are still physically incompetent and unable to use language, there is much less that they can do about them. Often your baby will cry because it is the only thing she *can* do. A situation has arisen in which she can do nothing to help herself. Her crying is a signal to you to take action for her.

You go out of the room. The baby wants to go with you. She cannot follow because she is not yet mobile; cannot stop you going; cannot go with you, cannot even ask you to take her along. So she cries. Another time she is playing happily in her cot when the toy which she was enjoying drops through the bars. She cannot get it for herself. She cannot call to you to pick it up for her. So she cries. Out on a walk, a friend of yours whom the baby does not know stops to chat. She holds out her arms to the baby saying, "You'll come to me for a cuddle won't you, darling?" The baby feels your arms starting to hold her out. She cannot tell you not to, or answer the stranger's rhetorical question with words; she can only cry her "no!"

The more sensitive adults are to cues from a baby that are more subtle than crying, the less often she will need to cry. If, for example, you make a point of indicating to your baby that you intend to leave the room, she can hold up her arms to ask to go too. If you are half-listening to her contented play in her cot, her dismayed silence will alert you to the dropped toy. It's not all up to adult caregivers, though. The ultimate resolution of your baby's helplessness will come from her own growing competence. Learning to crawl, for example, may be a liberation as well as a pleasure. At last she can go where she wishes and get what she needs, at least within the limits of the freedom that you are prepared to arrange and allow for her.

Trapped and helpless she can only cry, beg to be rescued, and hang on tight.

Anger and frustration Once babies can go places and do things at will, they find it intensely frustrating when adults stop them. By your baby's first birthday this kind of frustration may be the commonest cause of crying. Even her crying when you leave her in the evening has at least an element of angry frustration at being kept in her cot when she wants out.

A crawling, exploring baby has to be constantly checked for her own safety and that of other things. Removing her from the refrigerator door eight times in 10 minutes may drive you crazy but it drives her to despair. She wants to open that door and she is months away from understanding why she may not, or even from remembering that you will not let her. The more she grows up and discovers things she wants to explore and do, the angrier it will make her when she is prevented from doing them, either by you or by her own incompetence.

You have to stop a baby doing unsafe or destructive things. And she must attempt maddeningly difficult tasks if she is to learn. So some angry, frustrated crying is inevitable. But a baby who feels hemmed in by restricting adults or continually defeated by her own immaturity will not forge ahead in her development. There is a balance to be struck between too much frustration and too little.

When you or her caregiver must frustrate the baby, because her intentions are dangerous or damaging, you can use her distractibility. There is no need to have a long tussle about that refrigerator. Take the baby right out of the room and, after a brief burst of anger, she will forget about it – for the moment. Put a child-proof fastening on the door that evening and when she thinks of opening it next day she will only be momentarily furious to find she cannot. Once she knows she can't, she'll stop trying and turn to something else.

When the baby frustrates herself, adults have to judge whether she can learn by the situation she has got herself into or whether she can only fight herself into a fury of frustrated crying. If she is struggling to get the lid off the toy box and there is a good chance that she will succeed, leave her to it. The success will be worth the effort. But if you can see that she is not going to be able to manage alone, help her sooner rather than later. You will not offend her dignity by interfering. Managing alone is not yet important to her for its own sake. She just wants that lid off, no matter how.

Some babies seem to have a far greater tolerance of frustration than others; a setback that makes one howl leaves the next still smiling. You cannot do very much about these differences so there is no point in worrying about them. On the other hand, don't decide that because they are at least partly inbuilt, you'd better resign yourself to them forever. It's as much a mistake to regard your baby's temperament as set for life in this half-year as it was in the first. She may develop exceptional patience and staying power later on even if she is easily frustrated now. On the other hand, being placid now doesn't guarantee that she'll never take life hard. If you stay tuned-in to your baby week-by-week, and handle her day-by-day in the way her cues to you suggest, you are doing the best you can.

But even though some babies do cry more readily than others and some of these kinds of crying are bound to occur, the overall amount that your baby cries is some kind of index of her contentment. If nothing ever seems to go right for her for more than five minutes at a time (and as a result it's hard for the people who care for her to stay cheerful) it is worth trying to work out what it is that most often upsets her. Apart from physiological states − pain, illness, tiredness, hunger, thirst − her crying is most probably a reaction to lonely separation or fear, a signal to you to take action on her behalf, or an explosion of frustration and rage. If you can work out which emotion in what kinds of circumstance is causing most of your baby's crying, you may be able to offer whatever it is − extra security, a quicker response, greater freedom − that will transform her into a happier (and therefore easier) baby.

PARENTS HAVE THEIR SAY

My beloved baby's clinging is giving me cabin fever.

I've stayed home with my son for nine months. I hoped not to go back to work until it wouldn't matter to him. But he cries every time I leave the room and I can see myself peeling him off me to send him into school when he's five. I love him more than I thought possible and can't bear to go, but I've got cabin fever and can't bear to stay. And, yes, there's money. We can manage on one salary, just, but I worry about how I'd care for him if something happened to his father, or our marriage. Nobody ever says it, but I think it would have been better if I'd gone back when he was six weeks old so we never got used to being together.

This is the real, complex dilemma that is shared by millions of women. It's usually over-simplified because only a woman who is being torn apart by it has the right to say what her problems and priorities are.

It's not just your baby who wants you to stay while you want to go: *you* want to stay, for yourself as well as your baby, *and* you want to go. It's not that you *have* to earn right now, nor is going back to work primarily to do with self-image, self-fulfilment or even career prospects. Money is tight, now; more would ease things, but it's money in the future that really worries you, and being entirely dependent on your baby's father. You're not just scared by the pain of separation that looms over you both, but by the possibility that what you've done so far hasn't been worthwhile.

It's true that if you'd gone back to full-time work when your baby was six weeks old, you'd have sidestepped some of this. But while you were free of being clung to, you'd have missed a million hugs. It doesn't sound as if you really doubt that you made the right choice. And at least you did *have* a choice.

Your underlying worry − that maybe your baby is *too* attached to you (and you to him) − is groundless. The end of the first year is usually a very clingy age and stage; that's probably what's brought on your cabin fever right now. But he wouldn't be any *less* clingy if you'd always worked full-time; you'd just be there for less of it.

Similarly the fact that he'll probably take it harder when you start leaving him than he would have done when he was a few weeks old doesn't mean that it would have been better to leave him sooner, *or* that it would be better not to leave him ever, at all. The time you have had being together ad lib has given your relationship solid foundations that will support a different lifestyle, especially if the change is not sudden and total. He will cry when you go, celebrate when you come home, learn that other adults can care for him and that it's safe to let people you love leave, because they always come back.

Of course you won't like seeing his face fall when he sees you pack your brief-case; crumple when you put on your coat. But your job is to help him manage strong emotions, live with and through them, not to keep him in a lukewarm world where nobody is ever very sad but nobody is ever very happy either.

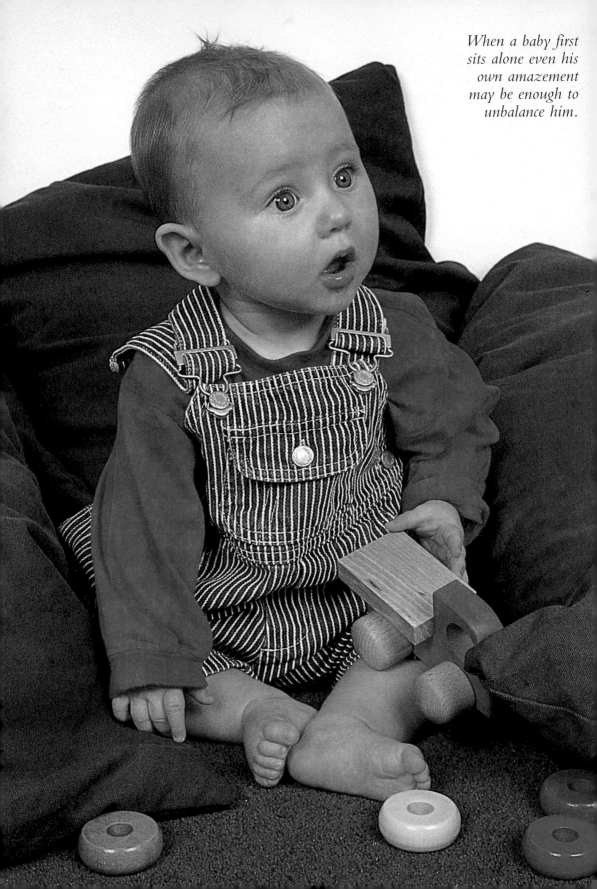

When a baby first sits alone even his own amazement may be enough to unbalance him.

MORE
MUSCLE POWER

Six-month babies often seem happy in their bodies. They use all four limbs smoothly and rhythmically. They enjoy physical movement for its own sake and keep testing the limits of their own strength as they struggle to roll right over or to lift their shoulders even further from the floor. They seem to understand, now, that all their different bits make up bodies that are all of a piece.

As we have seen, muscular control starts at the top and moves downwards. So at this stage the baby's use of his upper half, his head, shoulders, arms and hands, is well ahead of his use of his lower half. He can use his arms and hands for accurate reaching out, and he can use his head to track moving objects with his eyes. He does not yet have similar control over his hips, knees and feet. It is mastery of these muscle groups for which the baby will now struggle. The fight to stop lying around and become a sitter, a crawling quadruped and a walking biped is on.

SITTING

If you put your six-month-old baby squarely on his bottom on the floor, spread his legs apart, get him balanced and then slowly remove your hands, he will probably stay "sitting" for three or four seconds. His muscular control has already progressed downwards to a point where he can hold himself straight from the top of his head to his bent hips. But it has not yet reached a point where he can balance himself in this position.

By seven to eight months some babies will have solved this balance problem for themselves by leaning forward and supporting themselves with both hands flat on the floor in front of them. If your baby takes up this position he will be comparatively stable and he will certainly be sitting, but it will not be a very useful kind of "sitting alone". With both hands occupied in providing balance, he cannot play or even suck his thumb. And because he has to lean forward to get his hands securely on the floor, he cannot see anything very interesting either.

Most babies will be eight to nine months old by the time they achieve independent balance, without support from an adult or their own hands. But even now, sitting may be more for practice than for use. Even when your baby can balance in sitting position for a minute or more, he still topples over as soon as he turns his head or reaches out a hand. It will take him another month of constant practice before sitting replaces lying down or being propped, as the position in which he carries on most of his waking life.

Helping your baby to sit The drive to sit is built-in to your baby's development. You do not have to do anything to make him want to sit or even to teach him how. But while he will be ready to practise balancing in sitting position at six or seven months, he will not be able to get himself into sitting position without help until he is around nine months. Giving him the opportunity to practise, by getting him into position, is therefore up to you.

He will make it clear he wants you to sit him up. While he lies on his back on the floor he will sometimes crane his head and shoulders up in a desperate but unavailing effort. If you kneel beside him, he will grab for your hands and use them as levers to pull up by. After a while he may become so enthusiastic about sitting up that every time you go to him as he lies in his cot or on the floor, he will offer you his hands, hoping for another session of the pull-me-up-to-sitting game.

You cannot play the sitting game all the time so you have to find ways to help him practise balancing alone, too. Where and how you do this is important. Sitting, as he is accustomed to do, strapped in a chair or buggy is no longer enough for the baby. It is still a good position for play but he cannot really practise balancing alone with that amount of back support available. On the other hand, sitting completely unsupported is not yet possible for him. He needs a compromise between the two.

The best compromise is to put your baby on the floor surrounded with cushions or with rolled blankets or quilts or in a purpose-made "play ring" such as you might find at a nursery. When he is six or seven months you can wedge the protective padding under his buttocks so that he has just enough support at the base of his spine to sit for a minute or two. When he goes over backwards or tips himself forward into crawling position the padding gives him a soft landing. Experience of this sort of protection may mean that your baby never bothers to balance himself with his hands on the floor. Even if he does go through this stage it will be over quickly because he will be confident that he will not hurt himself. When you can see that his balance is improving, you can arrange the padding so that it surrounds but does not actually support him. It will still mean that when he waves both hands in triumph at finding himself sitting alone he falls comfortably.

A month or so later your baby will be sitting steadily as long as he keeps perfectly still and concentrates on his balance. But sitting still is not his idea of fun. That padding will still be invaluable whenever he stretches forward just too far or falls over backwards because he makes a wild gesture with his arms.

Staying safe on the way to steady sitting Once your baby has really started to practise sitting alone he will try to get himself into sitting position by any "handle" he can get hold of, and he will try to balance himself wherever you put him to sit. This means that some of the equipment which was safe for him in the early months may now be dangerous.

Beware of buggies and lightweight prams. If your baby goes to sleep in a lie-back buggy or carrycot pram, he may wake to find himself wedged against the side of it, get hold of the edge, manage to get himself almost to sitting position and tip the whole thing over. If he is left propped sitting in such a vehicle while you are busy, he may work his way forward and try to balance without support. When his balance fails and he flops forward with a thump, both the brakes and the chassis will be put under considerable strain.

Once he reaches this stage lightweight transporters are best used only for transport. Of course your baby will still be able to fall asleep in his buggy while you're walking or shopping, but for safety's sake he should not be left to sleep in it without immediate adult supervision. If you want your baby to be able to nap in friends' houses, or start his night in a portable bed while you are having a sociable evening, a travel cot may be a worthwhile buy, especially if you also plan to camp or go away for weekends or holidays. Such a cot folds up for easy transport, safely replaces a drop-side cot all through toddlerhood and will even double as a playpen.

Watch out for lightweight chairs. A younger baby keeps up a steady pressure on the back of his chair. When he cranes forward he moves his head and shoulders but leaves his bottom and most of his weight squarely in the base of the seat. Now, he struggles to get right forward; he balances for a few seconds and then relaxes his muscles and hits the back of the chair with a thud that can make it tip. If the chair is on the floor, a fall will be frightening and painful. If the chair was on a table or work surface, it would be a serious matter.

Even if your baby has not yet reached the stated maximum safe weight, it's probably time to give up bouncing cradles and adjustable rockers, except those that have their own stands and can be turned into safe, steady highchairs for use into toddlerhood. The seat alone should no longer be used for anything except perhaps picnic meals where you are constantly present. If you do not want to buy the stand, the baby now needs either a separate highchair or a low chair-table combination. Whatever he sits in:

■ Use a separate safety-harness always. The chances of your baby trying to stand up in a pram or chair and falling right out, are almost as great as the chances of him tipping it over. He should wear a safety-harness, as a matter of course, whenever you put him into anything that is meant to restrain him, such as a chair, pram, buggy or car seat. The exceptions, of course, are his cot and playpen. It will be a long time before he can climb out of those and their design is intended to provide safely limited freedom. Using a safety-harness is much less irksome if you have a separate one for each regularly used item of equipment. If you have to go into the kitchen and get the harness off the highchair in order to put it on the baby and his buggy, the day will almost certainly come when you will not bother. That will be the day your baby discovers how to tip himself out.

■ Stop putting your baby to sit in armchairs or on beds. Constant sitting practice means constant tumbles, but the best kind of tumble is from the floor to the floor. If your baby tumbles from a chair or sofa he is unlikely to do himself real physical damage, but damage to his nerves, morale and confidence can easily delay both his progress and his pleasure in sitting up.

■ Don't leave your baby alone on the floor, especially if he is surrounded by cushions, while he practises sitting. If he fell face down into them, he would almost certainly lift his head and roll free, but he could fall with his arms awkwardly trapped; he could smother. Padded or not, your almost-sitting baby is also almost crawling. He should never be left free and alone in a room, not even for the few moments it takes you to answer the door.

When she can roll right over she'll slither, get her knees right up and then crawl – but often backwards.

CRAWLING

Many (but not all) babies learn to crawl at the same time that they learn to sit alone. The two developments may parallel each other closely except that your baby will be slower to perfect his crawling than his sitting. At six months he can sit alone for a second but cannot balance, and can get into crawling position but cannot progress. At seven or eight months the baby can sit steadily and play at the same time, and a month or two later he can also crawl anywhere.

Babies who do not master these techniques simultaneously will almost certainly learn to sit alone before they learn to crawl. It is not unusual for a baby still to be an immobile sitter on his first birthday.

Although "crawling" is usually taken to mean progress across a room on hands and knees, quite a lot of babies adopt other manoeuvres, either before, or instead of, a conventional crawl. Early mobility may come from skilful rolling over and over, with a slither to take the baby the last half-metre to his objective. A slippery floor may help your baby learn to get about by pulling himself along on his elbows, with his legs straight out behind him. If he finds this satisfactory, he may be late in learning to pull his legs up and push with his knees.

Babies who learn to sit steadily comparatively early sometimes adopt a "bottom shuffle" instead of a crawl. The baby pushes himself around on his bottom using one hand to propel himself. From his point of view this method has a lot to recommend it. He saves himself the effort of going from sitting position to crawling position and back again, and he keeps one hand free even while he moves. He can see what is going on better than a conventionally crawling baby, too. Bottom-shuffling babies often leave out conventional crawling altogether and go straight on to pulling themselves into standing position and cruising around furniture.

Some babies learn to crawl in the ordinary way but then discover that they can move faster on hands and feet than they can on hands and knees. A few leave hands-and-knees out altogether and "walk like bears" right away.

So while the following paragraphs describe average progress towards ordinary crawling, different rates of development or idiosyncratic methods of getting around do not suggest that there is anything amiss with your baby. He must learn to sit alone and he must eventually learn to stand and walk alone. How or whether he

gets around the room in between is far less important.

If something he wants is just out of reach, a six-month-old baby who is lying on the floor on his tummy may pull his knees up under him, push up with his hands, and often manage to get his tummy right off the floor. For a moment he is in true crawling position but he will not get anywhere. Just as he still has a problem with balance when he is trying to sit, so he has a problem with actually moving forward when he is trying to crawl.

During the seventh and eighth months, babies who choose, or are willing, to spend some of their floor-time lying on their tummies often make it very clear that they *want* to crawl. If you watch carefully you can see the effort that is being made; see that the baby is "thinking forwards". Thinking isn't doing, though. Very few will manage to cover any ground at this age.

Towards the end of the eighth month the baby will probably give up lying on his tummy altogether. As soon as he is placed face down, turns over or collapses from one of his sitting adventures, he gets himself on to hands and knees. He learns to do everything but move along. He rocks backwards and forwards and he swivels himself around and around, following your progress around the room or the cat's escape from his attentions. It is at this stage that he may be so desperate to get moving that he develops all kinds of peculiar ways of getting around, none of which is a true crawl. He may rock, swivel, roll over and squirm on his tummy, so that one way or another he does actually get from one side of the room to the other. However,

Going forward from sitting, she finds herself on hands and feet, walking like a bear.

this is not useful progress any more than sitting while using his hands for balance is useful sitting. He still cannot choose to go in a particular direction, and if he sets off because he has caught sight of something he wants, he will have lost track of it by the time he has finished playing acrobats and come to rest again.

It is during the ninth month that most keen crawlers actually begin to make progress. To their fury it is sometimes backwards. The baby fixes his eyes on something he wants and makes a mighty effort. His control of his upper body is more developed than his control of his legs, though, so he tends to push harder with his hands and arms than with his knees. Instead of finding himself closer to the thing he wants, he finds himself moving backwards away from it. This is a short-lived phase, however infuriating for your baby. Once he can crawl at all he will soon get his direction right and adjust the power of his pushing.

Helping your baby to crawl Your baby does not need your help with the preliminaries to crawling as he needs it for the preliminaries to practising sitting. All he needs from you is opportunity and he will get plenty of that provided he spends a good part of his waking day on the floor. He can get into crawling position from lying on his tummy or rolling there from his back, as well as by going forward from propped or independent sitting. There are, however, a few things which you can do to make early crawling enjoyable and safe for him:

■ Protect your baby's knees. Their skin is still soft and easily chafed. Even in summer he will be more comfortable if he wears cotton dungarees or light trousers when he is trying to crawl on grass or rough textured carpet.

■ Foresee possible dangers. He will learn to crawl without learning any extra good sense. Steps between rooms, staircases, splintery floors, and unsuitable objects left lying around can all cause accidents.

■ Watch out for unexpected spurts in ability. Even before he can actually crawl across a room the baby may roll and squirm himself out of the safe corner where you left him and into danger. Take action to child-proof the rooms he will use before he is fully mobile.

■ Remember that part of the desire to crawl is a desire to get hold of things. Something that looks really entrancing may give him just the extra surge of motivation he needs to get moving. Make very sure that when this happens it is not a pencil or a pin cushion that has caught his eye.

■ Don't leave your baby free, alone, in a room, but don't keep him imprisoned in a playpen either. Being alone may mean that he gets into danger. Being enclosed will take away all the fun of crawling and much of the point of the tremendous efforts he is making. He needs a safe floor, safe interesting objects and constant supervision.

■ Don't try to keep your baby clean. Fussiness about hygiene is essential in the kitchen and the lavatory but out of place when your baby is playing on the floor. Ordinary household dust will not harm him and skin is the most washable of all materials. Don't dress him nicely if you are going to mind when his clothes get grubby. Dress him in work-clothes designed for warmth, protection and comfort, and change him into party gear only on special occasions.

STANDING

While learning to sit up and to crawl often go approximately together, standing and walking are definitely later accomplishments.

At six months most babies love to be held standing on a lap, and behave as if they were on a trampoline, "jumping" by bending and straightening both knees together.

During the seventh month they begin to use alternate feet instead of both together. They "dance" rather than "jump", and they often put one foot down on top of the other, pulling out the underneath one and then doing it all over again.

First he bounced and then he danced, but nowadays he walks, solemnly, the full length of his grandfather's knee.

At this stage, the baby cannot bear anything like his full weight. Nor is he yet "thinking forward" as he does at this age when he tries to crawl. It is not usually until around nine months that he begins to get the idea of using his feet to go forwards, placing one foot in front of the other. Now your baby "walks" two steps to the end of your knee and then collapses, giggling. If he is held securely, with his feet on the floor and with you taking most of his weight, he may now enjoy making a few wobbling steps.

By 10 months the baby's control of his muscles has usually moved downwards to his knees and feet. At last he can take his whole weight, standing squarely on his flat feet, keeping his knees braced, though still sagging forward a little at hip level. He has reached the same point in standing that he reached at six months in sitting. He can stand, but he cannot balance.

Once the baby can take his full weight and stand square on the floor provided somebody balances him, he will soon learn to pull himself up to a holding-on standing position. Most babies will do this before they are one year old, starting by pulling themselves, hand over hand, up the bars of a cot, playpen or stairgate. If you give him the opportunity, your baby may use you in the same way, crawling up to you as you sit on the floor, and then hauling himself up by your clothes to stand triumphantly, balancing by your ear or hair.

When the great moment comes for your baby to stand, make sure tipping furniture doesn't let her down.

Just as newly crawling babies are often flummoxed by their inability to crawl forwards rather than backwards, so newly standing ones often find it impossible to sit down again. For two or three weeks on end your baby may find something to pull himself up by as soon as he is set free on the floor, but shout piteously for help as soon as he reaches standing position because he cannot let go and sit

down again. As soon as you come to the rescue and sit him down, he repeats the performance. It can be a tiresome phase because you have to go to his assistance every couple of minutes and both of you get tired and frustrated. It will not last for long, though, especially if you refrain from plucking him free and dumping him in sitting position, but lower him gradually to the floor. Every time you do that you help him acquire the confidence either to let go with his hands and sit down with a plop or to lower himself by sliding his hands down his support, not releasing it until his bottom reaches the floor. In the meantime, if you are both getting fed up, extra rides to the shops or the park in his pram or buggy may help. He has not yet got to the stage where he will even think about walking when he is out on an expedition. He will happily sit and watch the world going by, resting both his muscles and your nerves.

Within a few weeks of first pulling himself up to standing position, your baby will learn the assisted walking we call "cruising". He pulls himself up as usual so that he is standing facing the back of the sofa or the bars of his cot. Gradually he inches both hands together along the support and then follows them by stepping sideways with one foot. Left straddle-legged, he will usually sit down, looking dumbfounded by his own achievement. It is a major one. That shuffle was his first step. Never again will he be a baby who cannot walk.

As long as the baby feels that he needs to take some of his weight on the hands that cling to his support, he will have to move those hands together. But practice brings confidence; within a few days or weeks of that first shuffling sideways movement he will have become convinced that his legs will bear his whole weight. He will then be able to stand further back from his support and pass himself hand over hand along it. Every time he moves a hand he moves his leading foot one step sideways and then brings the other foot up to join it. If you watch him carefully you can see that it is the moment when one foot is actually moving, leaving all his weight on the other one, which still worries him. Gradually his balance improves. By the end of the year you will probably see him standing right back, holding on to his support at arms length, using it only for balance. Very soon now he will be ready to let go altogether and stand quite alone.

Her first cruise takes her around a chair and into life on two legs.

Staying safe on two feet You cannot help your baby learn to stand by putting him in standing position as you sat him up to practise sitting. Given the opportunity and some careful attention to his safety, he will pull himself upright as soon as he feels ready to do so.

Giving him the opportunity is not difficult. If he is free in a room with furniture, he will hold on to that; if he is in his cot, he will pull himself up by the bars; if nothing better presents itself, he will grasp your hair or the family dog's neck. The problem is that many of these adventures will lead to falls and while some are inevitable at this stage of a baby's development, too many, especially when they take place from standing up, can hurt his confidence as well as his head. Later on, when he is walking freely, he will learn to put his hands out as soon as he feels himself falling. Toddler tumbles are usually no worse than grazed knees and palms. But at this early stage it is particularly difficult for him to protect himself because his head is still large and heavy relative to the rest of him; his balance is precarious and his hands are taken up with trying to hold on. When he falls he is likely to fall awkwardly. It is worth planning protection for him:

■ Consider the furnishings in the room. Flimsy pieces are dangerous because they will support him as he first grasps them and begins the leverage part of his getting up, but they will topple over as his hands and his weight move upwards and he pulls. He will then fall from his most unbalanced position neither sitting down nor standing up, but halfway between the two. Tall flimsy objects, such as a hat stand or wicker plant stand, are the worst of all. They will not only topple over but, because of their height, will also fall on the baby. Some obviously hazardous pieces can be wedged in place; others can be positioned so that they are inaccessible to the baby. A few would be better removed to another room for a few months, until your baby can get to his feet unaided.

■ Watch out for dangers above the baby as he pulls himself up. He will not be able to reach out for things while standing until he can spare a hand from holding on, but he may try to pull himself up by a hanging tablecloth or dangling electric cable. Neither a coffee pot nor a table lamp will do his skull any good.

■ Don't start using a sleeping bag at this stage if your baby has not been accustomed to one. He may try to stand up while he is in it;

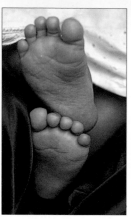

Bare feet help newly standing babies to feel the floor and balance. Don't hurry them into shoes.

Going at your baby's pace

will certainly fall and may bang his head on the bars of his cot. But if he is accustomed to a sleeping bag don't hurry to give it up. He's unlikely to try to climb in it if he has always worn one and this simple fact may keep him safely and happily in his cot later on when your friends' babies are driving them mad by trying to clamber out.

■ Don't put shoes on your newly standing baby. He does not need them to *support* his feet, now or ever. He only needs shoes to protect his feet once he is walking freely enough to do so outdoors and on all surfaces. Shoes at this stage will make it far more difficult for him to balance because they will cut down the sensations his feet receive from the floor and the sensitive adjustments of his toes. They can be slippery too and may cause an accident.

■ Don't put socks without non-slip bottoms on your baby unless all your floors are carpeted. Ordinary socks turn hard floors into skating rinks; your baby may fall and even if he does not, the difficulty of standing under these conditions will badly shake his confidence. He is safest in bare feet. When cold is a problem, use non-slip socks or play boots.

Don't try to make the baby walk holding your hands. At this stage he may not like walking with all that empty space around him and only wobbly hands to hold on to. He will probably feel safer doing his cruising around something solid. If you want to give him the chance to practise pulling himself up when you are out in the park where there is no furniture, kneel or sit on the ground and let him use your body as if it were inanimate.

Don't try to hurry your baby on towards independent standing and/or walking. Standing, cruising and eventually walking alone are all dependent on the baby's confidence and his motivation as well as on his muscles and co-ordination. If you try to hurry him you may slow up his development by causing falls that make him afraid. If he seems to have managed one stage, such as learning to pull himself upright, but does not seem to be moving on towards cruising or standing alone, it may be because he does not actually want to go further with the walking game at present. Pleasure in crawling all over the place at will may mean that he has no motive for learning to walk just yet. Although many babies will pull themselves up and cruise before their first birthday and some will walk independently, a large minority will not get onto two feet at all in their first year.

LIVING WITH YOUR MOBILE BABY

Newly mobile babies are not always easy to live with. Being able to get around a room enormously increases their ability to get themselves into danger or to break and destroy things; yet the mobility does not bring even the smallest amount of extra commonsense with it. You have to watch your baby, every waking minute, or make sure that somebody is doing so. You have to prevent what you cannot allow as well as help with the activities you approve of, and somehow you have to make sure there is space for the baby to do his baby things that does not take over the space that rightly belongs to other members of the family. Many parents find this the most difficult of all

Is it a good idea to use a playpen?

Now that our daughter is crawling and starting to walk, my husband and I keep arguing about whether it's more important to keep her safe or give her freedom to explore; specifically, are playpens good or bad?

The difference between safety and imprisonment is often in the eye of the beholder – and most of us are not very logical about it. For example, we all recognize that playpens are an issue (whether we are in favour of them or not) but we all take cots for granted. We all use those cots to stop our babies falling or crawling out of bed, but most of us aren't comfortable with the idea of using nets over the top to stop them *climbing* out. Everyone has to work out their own position on these gadgets. Perhaps the best starting point is to consider their effect on the baby.

A playpen confines a baby to a small area that can be completely controlled and therefore kept almost completely safe. Until she is mobile, she can only use a small area at a time and what comes into it is bound to be controlled by adults, so at this stage the playpen is no disadvantage to the baby and there's no reason why adults shouldn't use one if they find it worth its space. They may not, though. A baby who stays where you put her isn't very difficult to keep safe.

Once the baby is crawling, though, everything changes. Now the playpen actually prevents her from doing the two things she most wants to do: get around and explore. Those are things parents want babies to do, too. The challenge is to keep her safe while she explores (which is difficult and disrupting to adults who must live with safety gadgets and keep a constant eye on the baby), not to keep her safe at the expense of exploration. Some families find it possible to compromise, giving crawling babies the freedom of the floor most of the time but themselves the relief of the pen sometimes. Most babies quickly learn to protest loudly at any gesture towards confinement, though, and that makes a difference. If your baby doesn't mind five minutes in the pen with her toys from time to time, and those five minutes ensure your sanity, why not? But if she *does* mind, and loudly tells you so, then putting her in there is imprisonment.

So why does a drop-side cot seem different, even when a baby cries and holds up her arms and begs you to lift her out? Perhaps because it is making sure the baby doesn't do something she *shouldn't* (get out of bed without anyone knowing and crawl around the house all alone when everybody else is asleep). So why not a net to keep a climber safely in her cot? Because the minute she tries to get out, finds that the net is stopping her and fights its confinement, that cot has turned from a safe haven into a prison cell.

Keeping a baby safe and giving her freedom to explore are both so important that it's better to think in terms of a balance between the two rather than an absolute choice between them. You've achieved the best balance when your baby *is* kept safe but doesn't *feel* restricted so a baby-proofed play area is better than a playpen; a sleeping bag that prevents her trying to climb out of her cot is better than a net that foils her.

stages in child-rearing so anything you can do to make daily life easier for yourselves will be worthwhile. After all you are aiming to enjoy these months, not merely to survive them.

Arranging the physical circumstances of your home so that it is easily shared by all age groups can make a big difference. Even if it takes a whole weekend of hard work to reorganize the living room so that breakables and books are out of reach, it will be worth it. If you don't, caring for your baby will be largely a matter of taking things away from him and taking him away from things, day after day.

Where one particular issue becomes a focus of trouble, take action to make it totally impossible for the baby. If he is always escaping from the living room and trying to climb the stairs, put up a stair gate and leave it there. The danger and the trouble are both removed together. If he insists on messing around with the magazine rack, remove it out of reach. Once it has gone it cannot cause trouble. Sometimes this kind of preventive action takes a bit of ingenuity and has ongoing nuisance-value for adults. If your baby will *not* stop opening the refrigerator door to see the light go on, for instance, you may have to find, buy and install a child-proof catch and then live with it. It is a bore for everyone (including the baby!) but better than endless rows.

Arrange basic safety precautions. Don't forget to discuss what they should be and how they should be used with any and all adults who ever care for your baby and any and all older people who use the affected parts of the house. Your nerves will stay in better shape if you know your baby cannot fall downstairs, electrocute or burn himself.

Be positive with your baby. Try to provide a permitted equivalent to every action you have to forbid. If he may not empty out that drawer, which may he empty? The answer "none" is bound to lead to trouble once he has got the drawer-emptying idea; the answer "this one" will satisfy you both.

Use his distractibility to defuse arguments. If he insists on playing with the wastepaper basket, remove it out of sight and give him something else. He will have forgotten in two minutes. If you can't move the object, move the baby. Five minutes in another room and he will have forgotten any but the most entrancing games.

Put fun for everybody before tidiness. If you try to sweep every crumb and tidy each muddle as it occurs you will go mad. And if you expect your child's carer to keep the place spick and span she will not be able to put her commitment to your baby first. Decide when you really want the place cleaned up (whether that is twice a day or once a week), do it all in one almighty blitz and then try not to worry until the next blitz is due.

SEEING AND DOING

It takes babies much of their first six months to discover that their hands are part of themselves, and that by conscious effort they can make them reach out and get hold of things. It's a triumph, then, that by the middle of the year, your baby has "found" her hands once and for all and can wave them, reach out and grab with them as directly and immediately as you or I. Before your baby can begin to make her hands perform more and more complicated manoeuvres, though, she has to learn to use different bits of them separately. It will take her most of the next half-year to acquire the key aspect of human dexterity: the pincer grip of forefinger and thumb.

Day-to-day changes in the way your baby uses her hands are minute, even though the overall change between six months and one year is enormous. Furthermore, exactly how she learns her increasingly fine hand control will depend on the objects and opportunities she is given for practice. But although it is difficult to catalogue, your baby's growing ability to make her hands do as she pleases is as crucial as being able to control her legs and feet, and walk.

Touching as well as taking hold

At around six to seven months babies begin to understand that they can use their hands to explore things by other means than grabbing hold and mouthing them. While your baby's most usual reaction to a toy will still be to reach out and grasp it, put it in her mouth and then take it out and look at it, she will sometimes use her hands simply to touch, stroke or pat. This small development is more important than it seems because it enables the baby to find out something about objects which are not graspable. As she lies on the carpet, for example, she will stroke it, exploring its texture. Even three or four weeks earlier she couldn't have done that because she would have concentrated her energy on trying to pick up the bafflingly flat flowers in its pattern. The flowers would have defeated her by being ungraspable and the rest of the carpet would have gone unexplored.

Feeling with her hands lets a baby learn about things she can't grab and suck.

Once your baby has discovered that feeling things with her hands can give her some information about them, you will probably notice her becoming increasingly interested in different textures and sensations through her fingers. She will stroke the tray of her highchair; feel the window pane and pat her blankets. You may even get your hair stroked rather than having it grabbed by the handful! As well as buying (or making) "texture toys" with surfaces of velvet, sandpaper and silk, let her play on grass, carpet, matting, wooden floors, so that she can discover with her hands the fascinating differences. Now that she need not grab and mouth everything she touches you can even bring her the pet rabbit to stroke.

Differentiating arms and hands

At six months your baby probably still usually behaves as if she thinks her arms and hands are single units. When she holds onto someone, she wraps her arms around the nearest bit rather than holding on with a hand. If she wants to call attention to something, she gestures in its direction with a broad sweep from the shoulder. Expansive gestures are characteristic of babies' very physical reactions to things that interest them, but your baby will gradually learn also to use her

In a mirror she meets an image that looks warm and graspable but feels cold and flat.

lower arm, from the elbow, and her hand from the wrist. By eight or nine months she will have a repertory of gestures, probably including a royal goodbye wave of the hand only.

While your baby is learning to use different parts of her arms separately she is also learning to differentiate the various sections of her hands. At six months she grasps objects with her whole hand, picks things up by using her cupped hand as a scoop and tackles large objects by using both hands together as if they were a pair of tongs. During the seventh and eighth months she begins to make use of her fingers and thumbs for grasping and for holding on to objects. A month or so later she will probably have such fine control over her separate fingers that she can use an index finger to point or to poke.

Opposing fingers and thumbs

During the last three months of the first year your baby will use her new manual ability and control to develop a more mature grasp and grip. Instead of trying to pick up small objects by using her whole hand adjusted to a small cup or scoop, the baby learns to approach them with her forefinger and thumb using a pincer grip. This change may not seem to make much immediate difference to her daily life and play, but it is crucial to her future as a human being rather than any other kind of mammal. Right now, though, that pincer grip may be a mixed blessing, enabling your baby to retrieve the smallest and most ancient crumb from the floor under the kitchen table, or pick up the one stray pin left on the sewing machine.

The fine pincer grip that captured the apple and delighted the baby is a crucial development that's unique to humans.

While your baby is acquiring these new and delicate ways of getting hold of things with her fingers, she must also tackle the unexpectedly difficult problem of letting go of things she is grasping. At nine months most babies understand the idea of letting go. If you hold out your hand and say "give it to me", she will hold the toy out to you, clearly realizing that you want her to release it. But the actual process of uncurling her fingers in order to release what she is grasping is still very difficult for her. If she sits there holding out the toy but with her fingers still curled around it, don't assume she is teasing you. She probably cannot think how to proceed. You can help by putting your own hand flat under hers, mimicking what she feels when she plays with objects on a table. When she feels her hand and the object on a flat surface, she can relax her fingers easily.

Most babies will have discovered how to uncurl their fingers voluntarily and in mid-air by the tenth or eleventh month. Once your baby has discovered how to let go of things she will probably practise at every opportunity and with enormous pleasure. You may face weeks of toys being dropped from her cot; food being dropped from the highchair, face cloths and soap flopping over the edge of the bath, socks left behind her buggy and trails of shopping cast out of the supermarket trolley. This phase can be made even more fun and more educational for her (as well as marginally less tiresome for you) if some of her small toys are fastened on to her cot or buggy. She will throw them out and then joyfully discover that she can fish them up again. Fastening them on requires some care, though. Don't use string or tape in case the baby gets it wound around her neck or even gets herself generally entangled. Use short lengths – 15 centimetres or less – of something with a breaking strain the safe side of strangulation.

Some knitting wools are ideal because they break easily but watch out for acrylics and other synthetics which might not.

Towards the end of the year just dropping things will give way to a deliberate throwing and to an equally deliberate placing of objects. Your baby needs a light ball to roll and throw – a foam rubber "indoor ball" is ideal – and she needs "placing toys" such as bricks and threading rings. She will also practise filling and emptying almost any kind of container with almost any collection of objects. Purpose-made small toys are fine, but potatoes or oranges with a carrier bag to pack and unpack will probably keep her happy for as long as it takes you to put away the week's shopping.

Helping your baby to handle objects

Until a baby can explore the world for herself it's up to adults to bring bits of it to her.

Until she becomes mobile your baby has to rely on you to bring the world to her. She cannot go and get things for herself so she has to wait for people to bring things to her. Do make sure that everybody brings her plenty. Even before she can do anything much with objects, she is ready to learn about them by looking, sucking and feeling. If she is only given rattles, rings and woolly balls, and all those interesting household objects are kept out of range, she will be deprived of endless fun and learning. If someone else cares for your baby in her home or in yours, do make it clear to her that you would like your baby to share her "toys" and "games". Your baby can use all the objects you can possibly offer her but she'll enjoy them more if she is given one or two at a time and allowed to get everything she can out of them before they are swapped for fresh ones.

At six months a single plaything probably takes up her whole attention. She literally cannot think about two things at the same time, even if they are two identical things like two little red bricks. Watch what happens if she is holding one of these in her left hand and you offer her another. Right now, she will not take the second with her free right hand and hold them both. Instead, her attention will turn to the new brick and the one she was holding will drop out of her hand and mind.

Around the seventh month you will see that change. Now if you give her two rattles or two bricks, she probably will hold one in each hand. Although just holding them is good practice for her, she will probably still treat the two toys separately rather than making each more interesting by combining the two. It will be a few weeks yet before she bangs those two rattles together to increase their noise.

Most babies become able to hold two objects, one in each hand, at just about the same time that they begin to use fingers and thumbs separately. Those two developments together will probably suggest that your baby is ready to enjoy exploring more complicated objects and shapes. She will practise threading her separate fingers through any rings that come her way, whether they are her own threading rings or the handles of your tea strainers. She will poke her index finger into the indentations on an egg poacher, and use it to trace out the features of a doll's face or the swirly patterns on a table mat.

Becoming able to hold one thing in each hand and both at the same time opens up a world of delightful combinations.

Your baby learns the properties of many different objects by handling them and she learns how to use some of them by fortunate chance. After all she originally made her rattles sound by randomly waving her arms around and that's how she learned to wave and

A miracle of understanding: it's not the first time this baby has pulled a string but it's only now that she follows the cause and effect.

sound them on purpose. But increasingly, as this half-year passes, she learns how to use objects by watching other people. By late in the eighth month she may even be ready to copy actual demonstrations. If you now give her a thick stumpy crayon and a piece of paper, for example, and then take a similar crayon yourself and scribble on the paper with it she will try to do the same. She may not manage to make a mark, but her actions will imitate yours and next time she gets a crayon she will try again. Toys on strings also often produce a miracle of understanding for the baby. At seven months, if you hand her the end of a string you have attached to a toy car, she will probably pull it more or less by mistake. Even when the car moves towards her she will show no understanding of what she has done. But within six weeks or less, understanding of that cause and effect dawns. As the string moves the car, her face lights up with amazement, and she will pull that car towards her as often as you are prepared to move it away from her again.

Your baby's willingness to copy what adults and other children do will increase steadily from now on. If adults take her where older children are playing, and also show her how to do what they themselves are doing, like unscrewing lids, threading the holder-rod through the toilet roll, putting the key in the lock and pouring out drinks of water, your baby will try to copy. She will be getting good ideas for things to try to do and she will be motivated to try to do them; those two things together mean that her manual development will proceed as fast as it can.

As your baby gets more and more competent with her hands, do encourage her to use her skills all the time. Even if you have to do a lot of the feeding and washing, she should have a spoon at mealtimes and a face cloth at bath time. You can show her how to pull off her socks and turn the pages of her board books. She can put the potatoes in the vegetable rack as well as bricks in a box; bang the piano as well as her tambourine and throw a ball for the dog when you do. All these things, and thousands more, are new experiences for a baby. They are fun and learning and what is more they mean that she will feel properly involved with adults and the things that they do. She does not really want to be kept separate from the rest of the household, with special toys and special games that are only for her. She wants to join in. The more all the adults who take part in her care will slow their pace down to hers and put up with her messes, the faster and more happily she will learn.

LISTENING
AND TALKING

Although many babies will not produce a single recognizable word before their birthday, this half-year is crucial to their language development. Babies learn language long before they can speak. First they must listen to other people's words and learn to understand what they mean. Only then will they be able to produce meaningful words of their own.

The importance of a baby's listening and understanding is often underestimated because the importance of babies' own word production is over-estimated. If you find yourself spending a lot of time and energy trying to persuade your baby to produce word-sounds by imitation, do remind yourself that you are trying to bring up a person, not a parrot. An imitated sound isn't a useful word unless it has agreed meaning. If you persuade your baby to imitate the sound "da-da" (or to utter it when you do, instead of as a random part of his babbling) and then you throw your arms around his father and leap up and down saying, "Daddy! He said Daddy. Did you hear him?" that imitated sound may actually acquire agreed meaning and become a useful word. But he will not learn to talk by means of that kind of concentrated teaching of one word at a time, but by gradually decoding the mass of speech sounds with which he is surrounded. Concentrate on giving him lots of talk to listen to; plenty of opportunities for grasping the meaning of the words he hears; an immediate and pleasant social response to the sounds he makes and lots of verbal games and rhymes and jokes.

The how and why of language learning Just as many people assume that babies learn words by imitation, so they often assume that babies learn to speak in order to say what they want or feel. Neither everyday observation nor research supports these simple ideas. Imitation clearly accounts for only a very limited part of language learning since, as we shall see, many of children's early words and phrases are not, *cannot* be imitations. When did you take your baby to the gate of a meadow and tell him to "see sheeps"? As to expressing needs, babies manage to communicate with their caretakers for the whole of their first year without using words, so why should they suddenly feel a need for them? Anyway, when first words are produced they seldom have anything to do with a baby's needs. Your baby will be unusual if he first learns to say "biscuit" or "come" or "up". He may start with words that express need by protest: "mine!" or even "no", but the chances are that he will start with the name-labels of people or things which are emotionally important or pleasurably exciting to him.

Two main bodies of research have been influential in explaining how – and why – children acquire language. The older, pioneered by Chomsky and Lenneburg, postulated an inbuilt human language capacity or "Language Acquisition Device" which underlies children's ability to learn the particular language of their community, and to do so at incredible speed and under a vast range of conditions.

The more recent, better known through the work of psychologists such as Jerome Bruner than through its Russian pioneer Vygotsky, sees language as social rather than biological, and its development as dependent on "social scaffolding" provided for children by parents and other adults. Neither theoretical position alone accounts for the full range of observations. As with most nature-nurture controversies, it seems clear that both play a part and that takes some pressure off parents. Your baby will learn to talk even if his language learning does not get a great deal of social scaffolding. But the scaffolding is certainly worth providing when you can because it clearly makes a difference.

Every aspect of your baby's development will proceed more smoothly and happily if you don't feel pressured or pressuring about it, but that's especially true of his language development. Early sound-making is a playful activity. Making "conversation" is a game. Throughout this half-year your baby will do almost all his talking, whether it is to an adult or to himself, when he is pleased and excited or at least happy and content. When he is cross and unhappy he will not talk; he will cry. Whenever you hear him carrying on a "conversation" with himself, making a sound, pausing as if for an answer and then speaking again, you will find that his noises sound like pleasant, friendly or joyful speech, but never like cross or irritable speech. When the time finally comes for your baby to produce real words they too will be in a pleasant context. If "ball" is to be his first word it will not be spoken in angry demand but in pleased comment. If your name is his first word, he will not use it first as a reproving whine but as a delighted greeting.

Developing
speech sounds In the middle of this first year most babies will carry on long babble conversations with an adult, making a sound, pausing while the other person replies and then answering back again. The baby will continue for as long as you will go on, looking and speaking directly to him. He cannot yet talk to you if he cannot see you, or even respond vocally if you call to him across the room.

Most of the sounds are still single syllable cooing noises. He says "paaa" and "maaaa" and "boooo". He intersperses them with laughter and gurgles and hiccups of delight.

During the seventh month the baby becomes increasingly on the alert for speech sounds. He begins to search the room with his eyes if you call him when you are out of sight. He will look for the source of the voice on the radio, too, ready to respond with conversation as soon as he can discover who is talking.

At about this time your baby becomes able to control his vocal apparatus sufficiently to repeat sounds and you may hear him turn his cooing noises into two-syllable "words". He says, "baba" and "mumum" and "booboo". Gradually these "words" become more separate from each other, with less musical cooing between them. Once this happens, usually by the end of the seventh month, there are new sounds on the way. This batch is more exclamatory and less dovelike: he says, "imi!", "aja!", "ippi!". These new two-syllable "words" seem to make the baby increasingly excited by his own sound-making. Once they are in his repertoire, he may wake you each morning with a dawn chorus of delighted talk in which he behaves exactly as if you were in the room and talking to him. He will exclaim, pause, speak again, pause and then say some more, and he will go on for minutes at a time, entertaining himself until you choose to go and join in the conversation with him.

During the eighth month most babies begin to take an interest in adult conversation, even when it is not directly aimed at them. If your baby happens to be sitting between you as you talk over his head, that head will turn from one of you to the other as each speaks. He behaves as if your conversation were a tennis match he was closely following. But the talking game is too good for the baby to let himself be left out for long. Soon he learns to shout for attention. It is not a yell that he produces or a squeal or a cry: it is a definite and intentional shout. This is often the very first time that a baby uses a speech sound with a specific communicative purpose in mind.

Soon after the shout, many babies learn to sing. Of course the song is not elaborate: four notes up or down a scale is about average. But it is quite definitely musical and usually set off by your singing, by music on the radio, or theme tunes on television.

Communicating without words Language and speech are not the same thing. You and your baby have been communicating without words since the day he was born (or maybe earlier still) and as this first year passes you will find yourselves communicating in more and more speech-like ways. In fact before his first birthday your baby may be using language in every sense

Communication can take many forms and works through all the senses.

except that he cannot yet control his vocal apparatus enough to produce spoken words. He may be using a range of gestures whose exact meanings are clear to all sensitive observers, such as nodding and shaking his head for yes and no; pointing at things in answer to questions about where and what things are; hugging for hello or love; waving goodbye and sometimes "go away". If someone says to your 10-month son, "Will you come to me for a cuddle?" and he vigorously shakes his head, what is that if not language?

Clear evidence that the demands of forming spoken words hold up the development of language comes from households that sign instead of talking. Babies who use British Sign Language, or American Sign Language, typically produce their first recognizable signs between seven and nine months, about three months earlier than most babies in hearing households produce their first spoken words. The explanation is probably part biological and part social. Gaining control over the hands and fingers is easier for babies than gaining control over the vocal apparatus. Additionally it's easier for parents to model, decipher and manipulate babies' signs than their sounds. No wonder this is the peak age for all babies, normally hearing or not, to enjoy learning those word-and-gesture songs and games that involve their own bodies – "This little piggy went to market" and "Round and round the garden".

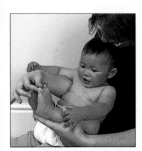

Action rhymes combine bodily and verbal play, gestures and jokes in a way babies find irresistible.

Getting close to words

As well as exciting developments in communication, the last quarter of the year usually produces notable speech developments too. Instead of making any and all sounds that his vocal apparatus will produce – like an older child blowing a clarinet every which way – your baby will begin to confine himself to the range of sounds he hears around him – to real tunes. At the same time his *forms* of speech suddenly become much more elaborate, with long drawn out series of syllables being produced. He begins to inflect and change the emphasis of his sounds, too, so that listening parents hear varied sounds suggesting questions, exclamations and even jokes among the babble. Then the forms of speech change yet again. This time the baby does not just add more and more of the same syllables to what he says; instead he combines all the syllables that he knows into long complicated "sentences", such as "Ah-dee-dah-boo-maa." Some babies can actually make themselves understood with this meaningful-sounding nonsense language; others sound as if they are talking, but in a definitely foreign tongue. Whether you can understand it or not, though, the jargon sounds so realistic that sometimes, if your mind is on something else when he starts to talk, you may find yourself saying, "What did you say, darling?" forgetting for the moment that he cannot really have "said" anything. He soon will, though.

Many babies produce their first "real" word during the tenth or eleventh month. We cannot be exact, because first words are surprisingly difficult to identify. "Mummy" is a good example. When a seven-month-old baby says "mum", few parents will be fooled into thinking it is a real word because they do not expect a seven-month-old baby to talk. But when that same baby makes the same sound at 10 months, it is different. You are expecting words now so you tend to find them among all that babble, reinforce them, and forget that the actual sounds your scaffolding has elevated to word-status have been in his repertoire for months.

There is no particular point in trying hard to identify your baby's first words. It does not matter whether he uses any or not at this stage. His expressive, fluent, varied jargon, especially if it is backed with gestures like pointing, is absolute assurance that he is going to speak when he is ready.

But the stages the baby goes through in getting to words are interesting and finding them interesting will make it easy for you to help his language development along. Interest will make you listen carefully to what he says. Listening carefully will probably make you answer him with more adult talk. Being listened to and answered is what he most needs for his speech development.

It will probably be shortly before his first birthday that your baby will get the idea of using a particular sound to refer to a particular event or object. It may still take him a while to sort out exactly which sounds belong with which, though. One baby used a word that sounded like "buddha" to denote everything desirable or interesting: his drink, book, favourite game and playmate were all "buddha" for a few days. Then it took time for him to "decide" what sound to use as a name for a particular object. He used the word "bon-bon" when asking for his ball. Later he used the word "dan" about the same ball. On each occasion it was clear that he meant that ball and did not mean anything else, but he behaved as if all that mattered was to use a word – any old word would do.

There may be weeks of confusions such as these before your baby moves on a stage and starts to use one sound, and only one sound, to refer to one and only one object. Even then the sound he uses may still not be a "word" in the adult sense. It may be an "own-word" (like "dan" for ball); a sound that the baby has invented, and attached to a particular thing or a particular person. But even if the own-word has not the slightest similarity to the "proper" one, it should be counted as a word if you know what he means by it. After all, the whole point of speech is communication between people. If you know that your child means "bus" when he says "gig", then "gig" is a word and he is talking to you.

How babies learn first real words Your baby grabs hold of individual words from the mass that echo around every waking hour of his life. The words he picks on are usually related to something that interests, excites or amuses him (so he is listening when they crop up) and occurs frequently so he gets lots of clues to their meaning.

A baby hears a word like "shoes", for example, over and over again in daily life as the one constant sound in a large variety of statements. In one day you may say to him, "Where are your shoes?"; "Oh, what dirty shoes!"; "Let's take your shoes off"; "I'll put your shoes on"; "Look what nice new shoes." That word "shoes" is the one sound which occurs in all those sentences and it is always associated with those things that go on his feet. Eventually he will associate the spoken sound with the objects and when he has made that association, he will have learned what the word "shoes" means.

Your baby will probably learn the meanings of dozens of words before he actually says more than one or two. He will first use words which mean something joyful or exciting to him. Perhaps he has in fact understood that word "shoe" for several weeks but has never said it. When you take him to a shoe shop and buy him a pair of bright red slippers, his pride in them as they glow on his feet may be what stimulates him at last to say "SHOES!". Similarly, a little boy had clearly known for months that the recurring word "Toby" referred to the family dog; but it took the sadness of missing him when he spent the night at the vet hospital, and a sudden rush of affection on his return, to stimulate the first use of his name.

First words often come slowly but understanding of words goes on apace. If your baby has only used a word or two by his first birthday, don't assume that he is not learning language. He is listening and learning to understand.

Learning to talk in two languages Children learn to speak the languages that are spoken to them. If your baby lives in a bilingual family, or in a community where one language is spoken at home and another at nursery, he will learn both. His early overall language development may be a little slower, but he will soon catch up. And even if he does not maintain and remember his "second" language, there is evidence to suggest that learning it will have given him some intellectual enrichment.

Helping your baby to listen, understand and talk Lots of loving, interesting, two-way talk is the best overall help that you can give to your baby's language development, but there is talk which is positively useful and talk which is less useful. Consider the following suggestions:

■ Talk directly to your baby. He cannot pay attention and listen carefully to general conversation. If he is in a room with his whole family and everybody is talking, he will be lost in a sea of sound. You say something and he looks at you, only to find that your face is turned away to his sister. Sister replies, brother interrupts with a half-finished sentence that ends in an expressive shrug, and meanwhile somebody else has started a side conversation – and the television has been switched on. Third or fourth children, especially in families where the children are born close together, are often actually delayed in their language learning because they get so little opportunity for uninterrupted one-to-one conversation with adults. Even if you are coping with a baby, a toddler, and a four-year-old who never stops asking "why?", try to find at least some times when you can talk to the baby alone.

■ Don't expect him to learn much language from strangers, or as much from a succession of caregivers, as he will from you and other people who are special to him. Babies learn the meanings of words by hearing them over and over again in different sentences and with varying tones of voice, facial expressions and body language from the speaker. The more familiar he is with the person who is talking, the more likely he is to understand. Even at the toddler stage he may be quite unable to understand a stranger's words because the accompanying expressions and tones of voice are strange to him.

■ Think carefully before you employ a caregiver who is not fluent in your language. A nanny or housekeeper cannot model good speech for your baby unless she is fluent herself. If everything else about her seems exactly right, you might consider employing her on the understanding that she uses her own language with your baby – who will therefore be brought up bilingually.

■ Make sure that you use the key labelling words when you talk. The baby is going to single out label-words which continually recur in different sentences, like that label-word "shoes". So when the two of you are hunting under the bed, make sure that you say, "Oh, where are your shoes?" rather than, "Oh, where are they?". The child's own name is a vital label for him to learn. He will not think of himself as "me" or "I"; indeed, English grammar makes pronouns extremely difficult for a child to learn because the correct word depends on who is speaking. I am "me" to myself, but I am "you" to you. So at this stage, you use his name-label, too. Don't feel embarrassed because it is "baby talk". "Where's a biscuit for John?" you can say as you rummage in the biscuit tin. It will mean much more to him than, "Where's one for you?"

■ Talk to the baby about things which are physically present so that he can see what you are talking about and make an immediate connection between the object and the recurring key word. "Wasn't it funny when that cat we saw ran up the tree?" will not mean nearly as much to him as, "Look at that cat. Do you see her? The cat is going to run up that tree. There! A cat in a tree..."

■ Use picture books in the same way. Big clear illustrations of babies and older people doing familiar things will entrance him: "Look, the Daddy's doing the washing up... can you see the mugs?"

■ Talk about things which interest your baby. Not all your conversation can be about immediately visible things, but if you tell his father the story of the squirrel he saw in the park that evening, he will pick up the subject matter and, perhaps, the labels for the things he learned while they were visible, like "squirrel" or "nut".

■ Overact, using lots of gestures and expressions. You can make your meaning much clearer to the baby if you point to the things you are talking about, indicate the thing you want him to crawl over and get, and generally "ham" your message a bit. Babies with vocal, outgoing parents often learn to understand and use exclamations first of all because they hear them used over and over again and with exaggerated inflections and infectious excitement: "Oh dear!" you may say when he falls down and, "Up you come!" as you lift him from his cot.

■ Try to understand your baby's words or invented words. You will motivate him towards ever-increasing efforts at speech if you show that you care what he says; that it matters to your understanding whether he uses the right word or not; and that you will always try to understand any attempt at communication that he does make. Of course this is a subtle message to try to convey to a 10- or 11-month baby, but the general idea will get across to him if he sees you taking trouble. For example, if he makes a sound and gestures towards something when he is sitting in his highchair, you might look to where he is pointing, and list for him all the things that you can see which he might have meant. If you hit the right one his pleasure as he repeats his own-word will be immense and so will his interest in

Good books and useful talk go together.

the correct version you then offer him. If you see him crawling around looking for something, using a nonsense-word questioningly, join the hunt for the nameless object. Once again, when it is found, the baby will be thrilled to have found it; thrilled with your understanding and thrilled with the name-label you provide.

■ Help your baby to use his few words in obviously useful situations. If you are playing together and you can both see where the ball has rolled to, ask him to get it for you. When he crawls back with it you can confirm that he understood you correctly by thanking him, using the word again: "Good boy, you've brought your ball." If you then carry on playing ball with him, the whole transaction of words and actions will have an obvious and pleasurable point, and the word will probably stay in his memory.

■ Don't correct or pretend not to understand own-words. It's important to give your baby the correct version of a word he has mispronounced, but trying to make him say that word again "properly" will only bore him. He does not want to say the same thing again better, he wants to say something else now. Your corrections are unlikely to have any effect anyway because, as we have seen, he is not imitating language but developing it. His own-word will evolve into something more correct in its own good time but not at your command.

If you pretend not to understand the baby unless he says something "properly", you are doing worse than boring your baby: you are cheating him. He has communicated with you; said something and made you understand his meaning. He has therefore used a piece of language. If you refuse to acknowledge it, you spoil the flow of his *language* in favour of mere *words*. Furthermore he may not be able to produce the "correct" word, because that word has not evolved for him yet. If his own-word is the best that he has to offer, rejecting it will hinder rather than help him. After all, it is pleasure, affection and excitement that motivate early speech. Refusing him his bottle until he says "milk" instead of "bah-boo" will make him frustrated and cross. You are more likely to get tears than words.

PLAYING
AND LEARNING

Safe, suitable floorspace is now a priority for your baby's play and learning.

This is a very physical half-year for most babies; a span of time during which they will often be so preoccupied with struggling to sit up alone, to get across the room on their own or to stand up on two legs, that play with toys takes second place. Reaching these physical milestones takes enormous physical effort, endless practice and considerable courage. It's lucky for their continuing development that babies have a powerful in-built drive for mastery that keeps them trying even when physical or neurological problems pile seemingly insuperable difficulties in their way. A baby who can crawl will crawl. Nothing but actual confinement or heavy plaster will prevent it. A baby who can pull up to standing position keeps doing so despite frights and bumps when fragile furniture topples. And the persistence with which he or she will go on trying to stand alone – wobbling, falling, getting up again – is remarkable. Most adults would send for a wheelchair after two days of it but the drive in your baby ensures that she will press on just as far as she can. Don't torment the near-crawler by suddenly refusing to pass her the toy she gestures for because "you can get it yourself if you really try". She would if she could and when she can, she will.

Babies do not begin to crawl or walk *because* they want to go places under their own steam. Nevertheless, these new physical achievements do gradually earn them large new measures of autonomy. All their short lives they have had to rely on adults to bring them bits of the world to handle and explore; now they become able to go and find things for themselves. Instead of having to accept passively whatever playthings and ideas are offered to them, they can begin to act on their own ideas about what they want to do, and decide for themselves what they will play with. This new measure of autonomy of action doesn't usually come with new emotional independence, though. The fact that your baby becomes more able to manage some bits of her time and play without adults does not necessarily mean that she will be more willing. Most babies want and need constant emotional support and encouragement as they learn the difficult lessons of growing up, through play. Indeed your baby may, as we have seen, become more rather than less clingy as her first birthday approaches.

Safe physical freedom

Sitting, crawling, standing and eventually walking, are occupations in themselves for your baby. At this stage she is just as keen to practise crawling or standing for its own sake as to get to somewhere or reach something. So the main thing she needs for her play is a floor and freedom to use it. If the household has not yet set up a playspace for her, it will need to now. She must have some area of floor which is suitable and acceptable for her constant use. The ideal floor is large, uncluttered (especially by any delicate, breakable or tippable furniture), reasonably soft and warm, easily cleaned and near to the hub of activities of any adult who is at home. Only a fortunate few will have such a floor; others will have to compromise and invent.

Unless you and your family are very short of space overall, it is not difficult to make over a piece of floor for a baby. A hard, cold, stone or tiled floor can be partly covered with carpet tiles or even with cheap matting, which can be hard on knees but is not bad for heads. An extra layer of underlay or old carpeting pads your baby's falls and your nerves. If you want your baby to play on the living room floor but not to ruin its fitted carpet, consider putting down a dhurrie in her special area or you could put down playmats for her – the kind that will later be playthings in themselves because they are marked out with road systems or farm layouts.

A dining room opening out of the kitchen can often be made suitable for a baby, without losing its basic use, if the door between the two rooms is left open and a stair gate fixed across. This gives the baby a view of an adult centre of operations, without giving her access to a kitchen that may be small and dangerous. With thought, though, a larger kitchen can itself be made safe enough for supervised play. As well as confining obvious dangers, like knives and cleaning fluids, to wall racks, locked cupboards or high shelves, use safe appliances such as cordless kettles, and safety gadgets such as cooker guards. Don't forget to watch out for less obviously lethal dangers as well, such as household rubbish bins (complete with sharp tin cans and poisonous used batteries) and seriously unhygienic dog food or cat litter trays.

It is worth putting thought and effort into this playspace for your baby because it will be basic to the household's life for many months and some obvious-seeming solutions will not work well for any of you. A special playroom in some out-of-the-way part of the house, for example, will not work, however beautiful it is. If you make your baby stay there, she will be extremely lonely and bored, as well as at risk, without your constant presence. You will probably find that adults either abandon it and let her play in the (unprepared) kitchen or take their jobs from their natural places in order to do them companionably in the playroom.

Some families have so little living space that the idea of setting up somewhere special for a baby seems ludicrous. It isn't though. The less space there is, the more crucial sharing it out becomes. If a baby or toddler must play in an already crowded family living room, she is bound to endanger her own safety, other people's possessions and the sanity of any older children, unless it has been carefully adapted for her. A playpen is only a very partial (and short-term) answer. Although a small area of space where she is safe both from wrongdoers and from wrongdoing may be better than nothing, even a baby who willingly goes into a playpen cannot do and learn all that she should if she is constantly confined. She will feel less shut in if a play corner is marked off less formally, perhaps with a piece of furniture, such as a couch or bed, that she can eventually use to pull up or climb on. A corridor or hall often makes extra space that a baby or toddler can use as long as any stairs can be gated. And even the most unpromising outdoor space – garden, porch, yard or balcony – is worth the trouble it may take to make it safe because even if it is too small for crawling around, it enlarges the baby's horizons – and adults' tolerance for messy play with sand and playdough and water.

Keeping your baby close to the functioning centre of the household, and finding imaginative ways to give her safe freedom that does not impinge unacceptably on anybody else, is not only good for her but also for everyone else in the household. If your baby has suitable playspace that is close to the adults who care for and companion her, there will be days when she will occupy herself on it and around them for a great deal of her waking time.

Of course your baby needs other kinds of play too, especially sociable play and talk. But it is easier to enjoy paying her your full attention, to be alert to the need to protect her from dangers and to be patient about keeping other people's possessions from her clutches, if you don't have to do it every single moment.

Changes of scene and associated changes of activity are important. They broaden the play possibilities which are available to a baby, and stop her getting bored. At this age-stage, so little is familiar to your baby that a simple move to another room can be as interesting to her as an outing is to a toddler. A romp on your double bed, for example, is a glorious game for a baby of this age and may be a relief from trying to crawl or stand. Play with toys on the hard floor of the kitchen makes an interesting change from the carpeted floor of the sitting room, especially if someone takes the time to show her how differently her wheeled toys behave. And trips outdoors combining buggy riding with, perhaps, a crawl on the nearest available grass, are vital. The more she can be taken out and about with adults, the better. A 20-minute trip to the shop or the library that you might once have found boring is full of new sights and sounds and sensations for your baby. By the time you have shared her amazed delight at the cat sitting on the wall; helped her name the truck that stopped at the traffic lights and seen her notice those lights changing, you may even see the community with fresh eyes yourself.

Different kinds of play, with different people in different places, keep a baby learning and stop her getting bored.

Toys and Playthings

Freedom to get moving and eventually to start exploring is more important to babies during this age period than actual toys. Many of the playthings suggested for younger babies will please this age group in new ways once they can sit up alone to manipulate them and crawl across the floor to find them. However a few new things will give your baby particular pleasure because they are especially appropriate to this particular stage of development.

Once she can crawl, your baby will much enjoy things that roll along. Whether they are actual balls, wheeled toys or household objects such as napkin rings, she will crawl to get hold of them and soon learn to push them and then give chase. Choose large objects (no marbles, however much she would like them) and check all wheeled toys for sharp or protruding bits, especially around the axles.

Learning to let go of objects at will is an unexpectedly important passport to new kinds of play. Your baby will enjoy dropping things out of her highchair or buggy. She will learn to *throw* things, and that can include permitted and shared games with beanbags or foam balls, to balance the forbidden jokes like throwing things out of your

Discovering that she can be the cause of that tuneful effect makes her feel unusually powerful.

Concepts like "full" and "empty" need careful study. Can he be sure there's nothing in there?

shopping trolley as fast as you put them in. Above all, she will begin to enjoy putting things into containers and emptying them out again. You can buy pots of safe, interesting objects for this purpose, but small blocks and a shoe-box or oranges and a basket are just as good.

As she learns about cause and effect and discovers her own power over objects, your baby may also begin to enjoy simple musical instruments such as a drum, tambourine, maraca and xylophone. Some babies are still alarmed by sudden sounds, but many enjoy the noise such an instrument makes (even if adults do not) and revel in the realization that it was their own actions that produced the sound and that they can produce it again whenever they please. Even if your baby is not an enthusiastic early musician, she need not miss out on this joyous sense of power. Offer her some toys which do something when a button is pushed or a lever is pulled, or start her on this particular journey of discovery by finding her a jointed "dancing doll" whose limbs move if she pulls the string, or a duck that quacks when she pushes it. And whenever she does something with a toy, *tell her* what she's done and what is happening.

As her linked understanding of speech and of concepts such as "up" and "down" and "full" and "empty" increases, books, and the kinds of talk that go with "reading to" a baby this age, become more and more important. Show her (ask her) where the dog or the daddy is in the picture: pop-up and lift-the-flap books will probably become her favourite. Tell her (and ask her) what the cat or the cow says. Read her some rhymes for their rhythms and jokes. Do some action games that end with a surprise tickle; games that name fingers and toes and noses and ears will help her both to be aware of different bits of her own body and to learn the names of them.

Personal care helps understanding, too. The routines and rhythms of everyday care help your baby to feel loved and cared for and,

gradually, to begin to care for herself. She has her toothbrush, you have yours, and she may surprise you by handing you the right one when you weren't aware that she knew either the words or the differentiating sizes. A bath can be "too hot"; the hot tap is a "no!"; ducks float but face cloths don't and one day she will lift her arms for her T-shirt. Is all this play? Yes, at least it ought to be.

Organizing toys Your baby will not remember what toys she owns during these months except that she will notice if special things (like her "cuddly") are missing. You cannot assume that she will know what she wants and go searching for it if it is not immediately available. If toys are put away in cupboards out of sight, they will be out of mind too. That does not mean that it's ideal for her to have everything she owns permanently strewn on "her" floor, though. She will get bored with all her toys just because she has seen them so often. Some toys actually age without ever being used because the baby comes to regard them as totally familiar. At this stage a toy hold-all – such as an old-fashioned baker's basket or a large smooth plastic storage tray – kept in a corner of her floor, is a good compromise. If everything in current use ("real" toys and loaned household playthings) lives in there, clearing up between play sessions will be easy and quick; your baby will be able to see some of her toys and will quickly learn where to go when she wants something.

A baby who cannot yet crawl needs to be given a few toys at a time as she sits in her chair or on the floor. Even once she is mobile and can help herself, she will probably play more concentratedly if you get out a small selection and just put them on the floor for her. Either way, as soon as she loses interest in what she's got, pick those playthings up and get her out a new batch. Towards the end of the year her mobility and speech may both have reached a stage at which you can ask her what she wants to play with and encourage her to help herself from the hold-all. Don't be surprised if there are days when she empties it out and plays with nothing in particular. Emptying out is the game; with a bit of encouragement filling up again can be part of it!

If your baby usually has more toys than you feel she needs, perhaps because she has grandparents who lavish gifts on her, or older siblings whose toys she has inherited, you may like to keep some on a high shelf or in a cupboard, to be produced occasionally. As well as toys she is not quite ready for, they might be toys that need extra-close supervision, toys that need specific play environments, like water toys for the paddling pool, or toys that make so much noise you cannot stand them all the time. Because your baby is still most easily absorbed by playthings that are somewhat novel but not incomprehensibly so, toys that are produced only on special occasions tend to keep their play value for longer than most others.

Even a lavish supply of real toys cannot entirely meet your baby's desire for novelty, or keep up with her insatiable desire to explore and learn about things. Keep a box or basket into which you put things the baby might like as you come across them. Each shopping trip will produce some. You might save a cardboard box or cereal packet she will enjoy filling with small toys, or a tube she can post things

Your baby need never be short of playthings if you'll share your "toys".

through. Around special holidays, like Christmas, there will be gift boxes and shiny ribbons. Clearing out a cupboard at home or at work might produce a lidded plastic pot that can be filled with water and a squeeze of bath liquid so it bubbles when she shakes, or a plastic scoop you don't want any more or an empty squeeze bottle you can wash out and give her to play with in the bath. And can't that computer print-out be recycled next week with scribble on it rather than today? If you are clever about this, and maybe enjoy it as a way of thinking about fun with your baby even when the two of you are apart, you will always have a "new toy" for her, ready to be produced on a grumbly day or when the weather keeps her in or a visitor comes and takes your attention from her. No plaything will do instead of you, but a new one might allow you a few minutes' conversation!

Including your baby in adult play

Almost mobile, imitative and devoted, eight- to nine-month babies often prefer adults' "toys" and games to anything intended for them. Watching and sharing adult activities helps babies learn about the world, its objects and people, so the more you can take yours around with you the better. But unless you happen to farm, cook or raise rabbits for a living, most of your important activities will probably be ones she cannot share. She cannot come with you to most office-based jobs and if you do take her with you most office activities will be incomprehensible and therefore boring to her. And even if she is lucky enough to have a parent who works at home, word processors and fax machines will not interest her for long, and telephones usually mean adult talk that is not for her.

The activities which really will interest and involve your baby, now and through early childhood, are domestic ones and it is because these are so peculiarly suited to companioning and teaching small children that people sometimes lump child care and housekeeping together as if they were the same activity. They are not the same at all, of course. Efficient housekeeping means getting routine chores done as quickly as possible: companioning a child means slowing the pace and structuring the activity so that there is space and time for her to do it too.

If a caregiver comes to your home to take care of your baby while you are at work, don't feel that it is wrong to expect her to do anything around the house because the baby ought to have her full-time attention. Likewise if your baby goes to a childminder, don't expect her not to do anything but play all day. After all, your baby wouldn't have *your* full attention all the time if you were at home. Some concentrated play with an adult is important, of course, and you will want to be sure that the caring adult would always give the baby's needs priority over anything else, not only if she especially needed a whole afternoon's cuddling but also if the two of them fancied the sunshine in the park. But babies often find adults who do *nothing* but watch them play, and try to join in, both boring and intrusive. Your baby will enjoy her days more if she spends them in ordinarily busy company, as long as that busyness includes her, safely, cheerfully and verbally, and never leaves her trapped in a playpen while the adult "gets on".

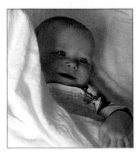

Cooking delights most babies, who will see it as "messy" or "water" play even before the connection with nice things to eat dawns. It is easiest for the adult to work safely if the baby sits in her highchair and is handed odds and ends to mix, pummel and taste.

Housework can seem like a good game played all over the house if the baby is bounced on the bed that is being made, plays peek-a-boo around the furniture and has a clean duster to wave. It's not a good game for babies with any tendency to asthma, though, as dust (and especially house-mites) is a common allergen. The "toys" involved need some thought, too, as almost all cleaning chemicals are dangerous. You may want to banish the most lethal liquids – such as bleach – from your household, and replace pressurized sprays with products that are kinder to eyes as well as the environment. Laundry and ironing are neither much fun nor safe "games" for a baby. Although they are the chores working parents most often want to delegate, they are probably best saved for nap times.

Gardening can be as good a game as cooking, provided the weather is fine and there is earth for the baby to scrabble in and grass to crawl on. Although there are real safety issues to think about, don't let a list of them convince you that being outside is more dangerous than idyllic. Just as kitchen implements can be dangerous, so you need to be careful not to use power tools – mowers, trimmers, hedgecutters – while children are in, or liable to arrive in, the garden, and to keep sharp implements and poisonous chemicals locked away. Of course your baby should not be exposed to too much sun, or to disease-carrying ticks, but these are only hazards in particular parts of the world at certain times of year. Of course she shouldn't come in contact with poisonous plants, but if you don't grow (or tolerate) any, she won't. More difficult to avoid is the risk of toxocariasis infection from earth that is fouled by cats or dogs. Although this can happen anywhere, the risk is much more concentrated in cities than in rural areas. It's wise for adults who are gardening with children to wear gloves and remove them before wiping noses. Small children themselves should do their "gardening" in fresh compost in their own seed trays that are stored under cover.

Shopping, whether it involves a saunter to a shop nearby for two items or a major supermarket expedition, can be a treat. Your baby will enjoy the sociability of meeting local people she knows well; but she will also enjoy riding in a trolley, helping herself to things off the shelves, opening the packets and sampling the contents... Accept the inevitable and let her help herself to something innocuous, like a French bread stick, right at the beginning. Struggling with something she knows is nice to eat but cannot easily manage, and something that is also interesting to hold and play with, will (probably) distract her from trying to destroy every shelf display and open every purchase. Unpacking shopping is almost the best game of all. If somebody deftly removes any eggs, tomatoes, or other squashy or dangerous purchases, she will unpack the cans and the oranges and roll them all over the floor.

ENJOYING THE
BRIDGE FROM
BABY TO TODDLER

Being a loving parent is a demanding practical job that is also tough emotional work, especially during periods when your child seems to be changing particularly fast so that you have to keep changing the way you interact with him. The months around a baby's first birthday are often one such period. Learning to move around under his own steam and to stand, and becoming able to understand a lot of adult words and say a few, may seem to transform your baby into a different person. They don't, though. The small person who cries for you in the middle of the night standing up in his cot is the same person who cried for you lying down. He hasn't really changed and he isn't really developing faster than before, it's just that these particular developments have a dramatic impact. He isn't a little baby any more but he is still a baby. Don't let yourselves expect too much of him.

Staying on your baby's side The more calmly you can all cross these bridging months out of babyhood the readier you'll be to find your toddler terrific rather than terrible. Somehow you have to find ways of staying on your baby's side whatever he does; making the most of the good bits of each day, seeing the funny side of the other bits, and never letting yourself, or any adult who is involved with him, see him as the enemy. An absolute determination to enjoy yourselves as parents can help you take positive pleasure in being clever enough to guide your baby without him noticing, distract him before there is a clash and save him before there is an accident.

Like many parents you may find that life gets bumpier as your baby gets older. He does a lot now and not all of it is what you'd choose. He doesn't say much yet, so it's not clear how much he understands. He's keener on being with you than on co-operating. You may have days when everything he does seems irritating. You will certainly have moments when you get angry. Don't be too upset if you find you have yelled at your baby. Although he will certainly be frightened, it may be easier for him to cope with adults who occasionally vent their feelings in a brief loss of temper than with adults who bottle everything up and become silent and withdrawn. Your baby needs to be able to rely on cheerful companionship from any adult who cares for him; without it he is bewildered and lonely; he cannot flourish in an emotional vacuum.

Don't let yourself and your anger right off the hook, though. Yelling may be easier for your baby to cope with than adult withdrawal, but that doesn't mean that it's good for him to be yelled at, however righteous the reason.

First thoughts about discipline It's at this stage in babies' lives, and in the context of these quarrels, that many parents begin to think and talk about discipline. The timing is fine but the context is not. Your nearly mobile, nearly talking baby is certainly capable of understanding what "no" means,

As your baby becomes a toddler, try to stay on her side, enjoy what you can and see the funny side of the rest.

and of beginning to co-operate with adults, even (sometimes) when he doesn't actually want to. But he isn't ready to cope with adult anger when he *doesn't* co-operate because the reasons for the anger are beyond his understanding, so that it seems to him to gather out of nothing: a vengeful act of God; a thunderbolt.

Your baby has no way of knowing that the thing he did or that just happened – milk down your clean shirt, a brief-case emptied out – was one more minor disaster and your "last straw". Even if he had sensed your previous tension he will not have understood what caused it: the failed alarm call that left you late in getting up, late in getting *him* up, late getting off to day care and work. He doesn't understand much about your feelings or your affairs, nor should he. They are not yet his concern. If you scold, he may enrage you further by laughing; if you shout he will jump and cry. If you lose your cool to a point where you actually punish him physically, shaking him, smacking him or dumping him in his cot, he will be as amazed and horrified as you would be if the family dog suddenly turned on you and took a chunk out of your leg. Until the reasons for adult anger become comprehensible, no punishment can teach him anything useful. When they do, he will be able to learn without it.

Suppose he pulls a mug off the coffee table and breaks it.

A waste and a lot of work for you but she doesn't know that. She meant no harm, however great the harm she's done.

Momentarily terrified that the coffee was hot you justify your angry scolding on the grounds that he should not have touched it because you have told him not to many times, and anyway he should have been more careful. But think a minute. He touched the mug because it was there: his vital curiosity told him to examine it and his memory and understanding are not yet good enough to tell him which things are forbidden. He broke it because his manual dexterity is not yet adequate for handling breakable things gently. So was the accident really his fault? What was the mug doing left within his reach? He is being punished for being what he is: a baby.

Now suppose that he tips all the food out of his dish on to the freshly washed floor. In fury you say that "he ought to know better". But ought he? A few minutes earlier you helped him to tip all the bricks out of their bag onto the floor. Is he supposed to share your ideas about the difference between food and toys? As to the clean floor, he probably watched you sloshing bubbly water over it earlier on. Is he supposed to understand that soapy water cleans things, but gravy dirties them? Once again you are being cross with him for being the age he is and for behaving as people in his age bracket are meant to behave.

Whatever other people may sometimes suggest, going gently with a baby this age cannot "spoil" him or create behaviour problems for later. In fact the more consciously you love him, and enjoy the way he loves you, the better. If you let yourselves realize and reciprocate his inexhaustible desire for smiles and hugs it will be obvious that the last thing he wants is to displease you. It will be a long time yet before he can understand what pleases you, though. Your pleasures are not the same as his. You don't like gravy on the floor...

PARENTS, TAKE NOTE

Shaking

However irritated you get with your baby, *don't shake her*. If you have to pick her up and remove her from the video player six times in a minute, *don't shake her*. Even if she bites your nipple or your sister's newborn baby, *don't shake her*.

Your baby is gradually growing into her head but it's still large and heavy compared with the rest of her and although her neck can support it perfectly through all ordinary activities – including the kind of rough-housing she enjoys – she's still extra-vulnerable to whiplash injuries. These may occur in a car accident, or if somebody hits her on the head. They are horribly probable if anyone shakes her.

Shaking can make your baby's head move backwards and forwards so violently that her brain is jarred against the inside of her hard skull. Sometimes tiny blood vessels tear and bleed into the brain. Sometimes a blood clot forms and presses. Just shaking your baby could cause blindness or deafness or fits – or death.

Being a parent and a person balances best if your baby joins in with the things you like to do.

COPING CONFIDENTLY

Since your child isn't a little baby any more, you are not new parents. But sometimes this transition out of babyhood threatens your sense of being experienced, good-enough parents. This is often a stage in a baby's life when he is very aware of his attachment to parents and very reluctant to be separated from them – for minutes or hours. But it is often a stage in *parents'* lives when they are expected to re-orientate themselves away from the nursery and towards the adult world. The baby clings, the outside world beckons and parents are caught in the middle.

Balancing these demands isn't easy, especially as the downside of the deepening closeness that develops during your baby's first and most completely dependent year is that you come to mind more and more about *his* feelings, as well as your own. You cannot be happy if he is not; furthermore if he is unhappy, you'll probably feel responsible. Whenever things aren't perfect for him, you are liable to decide that it's because of something you have done or left undone, and feel guilty about it.

Guarding against guilt

Guilt is probably the least useful of the common emotions aroused by being a parent. In fact guilt can keep you so busy regretting what you did and didn't do in the past that you've no time to think creatively about the present or plan for the future. If you can keep guilt under control, all of you will be happier.

It may help to remind yourselves that being parents does not make you all-powerful. Try as you may, sacrifice yourselves as you will, you cannot always make the outside world behave as your child would wish and you would prefer. You long for the bigger children next door to let him hug them, for invading viruses to clear before his ear starts to hurt, or for the accident-snarled traffic to loosen up so you get to the nursery before he notices that you are late. But since you cannot make those things happen, you cannot be to blame when they do not. Things *will* sometimes go wrong for your baby. Trust him to cope in an age-appropriate way, and instead of wasting your energies castigating yourselves or each other for what has happened already, use those energies to support him through what will happen next.

Helping your baby to cope with separations

Young children feel secure when they are cared for by parents or loved carers, in predictable ways and usual places. At this particular age and stage, any separation from you and from home is potentially upsetting, even if the reason for it is something that is meant to be a treat, such as a weekend at the seaside with grandparents. Equally, any potentially upsetting event will be easier for your baby if one of you can stay with him.

People matter more to your baby than places. If he could choose, he would certainly rather come with you on the most boring business trip (or trip to the corner shop or the bathroom come to that) than be left behind. He cannot choose, of course, but when you are making those grown-up choices for him, try to do it at least partly from his point of view. Will that weekend away be a treat or will it turn into misery for everyone when the first bedtime comes up? Only you can know the answer but it will probably depend on

Before a grandparent stands in for you, the baby needs to know him as a trusted carer as well as a beloved treat.

whether or not your baby knows the grandparents not just as treat-type people but as reliable carers. That's the question that has to be considered whenever somebody takes on the role of a baby's primary caregiver for the first time, even a beloved father or experienced child care provider. Of course they can cope with teething pains and temperatures and really well-used nappies, but does the baby know it; trust them to do so?

If the honest answer to that question is "no", the few hours in a conference crèche that would have suited you so well, or the weekend that's meant to be a treat for him, are not a good idea. Your baby needs some, or more, getting-to-know-you-time first. But if there is no time because the separation from you isn't a minor convenience or a treat but a necessity – perhaps because you have to go into hospital – the importance of being at home and following his usual routine as much as possible, will probably be thrown into high relief. When fathers cannot be around, the most helpful relations or close friends are the ones who will move into your home to care for your baby, rather than offering to care for him in theirs.

Taking your child to hospital

Coping with a young child who is badly hurt or seriously ill is definitely the downside of parenting. If it is an accident that brings a baby to hospital, parents often feel desperately guilty themselves, even (or perhaps especially) if they were not there when it happened, and furiously angry with whoever was in charge, whether or not the incident was actually caused by anybody's negligence. Even if your baby is in hospital because of illness or planned surgery, you may find yourself feeling guilty over your own inability to save him from pain and fear. And of course if his life or future health is at stake, there will be your own fear to deal with as well. Parents who have to cope with this again and again because their babies require a series of interventions, say that it gets a little easier but not much, and that a support group of parents whose children have similar conditions is tremendously helpful. The first time, though, don't be surprised if your partner suddenly announces that it would be best to "leave him to the experts" or if you find yourself backing off to "keep out of everybody's way".

What you'd both really like to do is run away and hide until the whole thing is over and you can take your baby home again. It's understandable, heaven knows, but it's what your *baby* would like least. There are only a few circumstances in which parents owe small children absolute priority. This is one of them. Your child needs hospital care for his scalded skin, his dehydration or his heart surgery, but for his whole self and sanity, he needs the personal kinds of care which cannot come from nurses; cannot come from anyone but you. With you to support him, he will cope with the strange place and the scary happenings; separated from anyone he loves and trusts, the whole experience may add up to an emotional disaster.

If you wonder whether other children at home, his twin, perhaps, or a toddler brother, can manage without you, remember that they are not ill and are not in a strange place. Of course someone must look after them while you are away, but if the choice is between leaving a well child with a less-than-favourite person and leaving an ill one with strangers, the decision should be obvious. In a two-parent family, though, that choice should not be necessary. Employers should recognize fathers' need for compassionate leave under these circumstances (or at least resign themselves to it) as they would mothers', and children's hospitals should welcome either parent to room-in with a baby or small child. So even without extra help from relatives and friends, two parents can cope with children both at home and in hospital, swapping over as suits everyone best.

Coping with illness at home Most of your child's illnesses will be run-of-the-mill colds and middle-ear infections; in no way dramatic but still likely to pose questions about his care. If a child is usually looked after with others – in a nursery, with a childminder or even by a shared nanny – he will have to be kept away while he is obviously infectious. So who is going to take care of him? The question highlights the precarious position of employed parents who have no back-up network from family or close friends. Taking a couple of days off work every few weeks is so difficult for many parents, and inconvenient for their employers, that the corporate world is beginning to produce adult solutions. Special "sick-child day care" is being set up in some cities, and a few firms are even experimenting with schemes to keep qualified child care people on call ready to be sent to the homes of key workers kept home by children's illnesses.

Those solutions are not child-friendly, and they are especially unfriendly to babies and toddlers who can't happily be cared for by strangers when they're well, let alone when they're ill. If you would not leave your baby in a totally strange nursery, or at home with a complete stranger, when he is perfectly well, it's clearly not appropriate to do so when he is feverish and plastered to your front like a baby monkey. Sick babies need, and are surely entitled to, care by people they know and trust. And parents of sick babies are surely entitled to give that care. Try for an accommodation with your employer; if unpaid leave is out of the question, you should at least be able to take annual leave at short notice. And if you want to keep those days off to an absolute minimum, look for a child-friendly arrangement for odd days of convalescence. Having a grandparent come to the house and indulge him for a day really might be a treat.

Introducing child care Babies and toddlers flourish when they are cared for by people with whom they have close, mutually loving relationships – and they can have several of those. If you are the only people in the world your baby trusts and feels close to, it would certainly upset him to be left with anyone else, *tomorrow*. But that does not mean that you're committed to ensuring that one of you stays with him 24 hours a day indefinitely. On the contrary: it may mean that it is time to help your baby form an attachment to at least one other person he can comfortably accept when you are not there. After all, even if you don't need day care right now, because one of you plans to go on staying at home with him, or you mean to cope with his care between the two of you and home-based work, plans could change or disasters could strike. Your baby loves you best and it's very unlikely that anything will change that, but loving a few other people a *bit* makes life safer.

I want shared care not shared love.

I resent the idea that working full-time means sharing our small daughters' upbringing with their carer. Even more I resent the suggestion that the baby will – and should – get "attached" to her. She's our child. The fact that we're out of the house from 8am–6pm five days a week doesn't change that. I employ someone to take care of my children and I expect her to do as I tell her. I don't want her input to their values and personalities any more than I want advice on interior decorating from the person who cleans my house. I don't want the children diverting love that belongs to us to anyone else either so I use au pairs on six-month contracts. The language difference makes sure that the girls are thrilled to see us each evening and if an over-close relationship should form all the same, it ends before it can threaten the family.

A house and a child are not the same. A house is an object so you can metaphorically put it on ice and it will just sit and wait until you're ready to use it again. A child is a person so she goes on being and growing and changing when you're not there. Furthermore very *young* people need to involve adults in those processes and will form relationships with whoever is around. Lack of a common language may hamper the adult but the children will probably deal with it by beginning to learn whatever language their carer speaks to them. As for affecting their attitudes and behaviour, she will not be able to help herself, even if she actually tries to obey your orders and serve your children rather than caring for them. Babies and toddlers use adult faces as mirrors, seeing their own behaviour reflected in facial expressions. Even if she does not, or cannot, say a word, they will soon learn what she thinks of their eating or weeping, their games and their squabbles. And they will care what she thinks, even if you don't.

I wish you could believe that your little girls would be thrilled to see you each evening even if they'd spent the day with somebody who spoke fluent English and had loved them both ever since they could remember.

They are indeed your children and spending the working days without you will not change their awareness of that or their feelings about you. Children's love for adults is not rationed, or channelled. It cannot be used up or diverted. Indeed the more people children have to love and feel loved by, the more lovable and loving they are likely to be. Don't project the threat that might be implicit in, say, a close relationship between your husband and another sexual partner, onto a close relationship between your children and another caregiver. You do not have to try to keep your children loveless through the working days in order to ensure your due measure at weekends.

Going back to work, or more work It does not matter whether the person who makes it possible for you to go to work without guilt is a grandparent, nanny, au pair, childminder or nursery worker. What matters is that your baby has time to get to know the caring adult and comes to love her; that the adult reciprocates by loving *him*; and that you accept and encourage their relationship with pleasure rather than envy.

Your own acceptance is always important when you want your child to accept arrangements he did not choose and might prefer otherwise. If parents are relaxedly sure that what they are doing is right, or certainly *all* right, children can come to take almost any lifestyle for granted, even far from ideal arrangements, like having one parent work away all week and only come home at weekends.

When you're at work your baby needs to be with another adult who she knows and trusts as a loving caregiver.

Whether he's been used to having you home all the time, or to spending just a couple of afternoons a week with another mother and baby, you can be quite sure that even the most clingy one-year-old will eventually take sympathetic day care in his stride if you can give him enough time to adapt.

Don't expect your baby to accept a new carer in a week. He needs time to get to know her with you before he faces life without you, and he needs brief times alone with her before he is committed to periods that seem to him endless. If the new carer is in a new care-place – a child care centre instead of home, perhaps – the adaptation will be greater and take longer.

Do remember that once your baby has settled with a carer he will have come to love her. Changing carers does not just mean going through the getting-to-know-her process all over again, it also means losing somebody who has become important. Of course you cannot leave your baby with someone who proves unsuitable, but do choose as carefully as you possibly can in the first place. It's astonishing how many parents settle for a nursery without having seen every other child care facility; it's even more amazing how many nannies are hired without their references being checked first. Although you cannot ask any carer to guarantee a long-term arrangement, do avoid those that are obviously temporary (like a nanny who plans to marry on another continent next year). And once you have entered into an arrangement, do think very hard before changing it if the baby is happy and doing well. It may be very irritating to come home from work to a messy house but if it is occupied by a cheerfully chortling child who has obviously had a good day, you may need new plans for the housework rather than a new nanny. You may find a carer who is perfect in all respects, but it's far more likely that you will have to settle for someone who is right for your child and tolerable for you.

The kind of person and arrangement you need depends primarily on who is already available, or could make themselves available, to care for the baby. If two of you are sharing his parenting, your absence at work leaves only half a gap. Even if you are not sharing day to day, it makes a difference if there are two of you, each with enough flexibility at work that you can cover for each other and the carer when plans go awry. And some fortunate families also have a wider network of caring people: family members nearby, or close friends with babies, who can be counted on in emergencies and get paid back within a complex network of friendship and obligation.

The kind of job you mean to take is also crucial, especially its hours. If you are only going to work for half-days, at least to begin with, your child's basic care and upbringing will remain squarely in your hands. Provided he is safe and contented with his carer, it will not greatly matter if he is under-stretched or over-indulged during those periods. On the other hand, if you are going to take on a full-time job, especially one that has no flexibility and may even involve extra hours or travel, your baby will spend more than half his waking hours with the carer and you will have to accept that you are sharing not just your baby's daily care but his upbringing. His self-esteem, discipline and learning will be influenced almost (though not quite) as much by her as by you. You need to choose accordingly.

What's the range of available choices in day care?

I realize that the quality of any actual day care depends on the people who give it, but can you outline the range and pros and cons of possible kinds of care?

Three main categories of child care cater for parents working or studying outside their homes.

Carers who live in may seem to offer the ultimate security for children and freedom for parents, especially as most will babysit while you go out in the evening. Remember that your home will be her home, though. She will have every right to be there when you don't want her as well as when you do.

A qualified nanny is employed only for child care so you may end your working day cooking her evening meal, and spend your weekends doing housework. A mother's help will reckon to do anything you would do if you were at home, but may find the job just as lonely, boring and underpaid as you did (and after all it's your child!). Au pairs *can* be marvellous, but most are no more domesticated or child-centred than you were at 19; don't speak the fluent English you want your child to hear and learn and seldom stay longer than nine months. That's a lot of losses for your child.

Daily carers, in your home or theirs, may be easier to get on with because you do not have to share private lives or draw awkward lines between time "on duty" and time "as family". Going out to work may be just as difficult for them as for you, though, especially if they also have children. And you will have to arrange (and pay for) evening babysitting.

You may be able to share a daily nanny with another family: make sure the adults are compatible and the children manageable together. A daily mother's help may be happy with part-time work to match your hours away, especially if she is working her way through college, but make sure she has enough interest and energy left over for your child.

Carers in their own homes (childminders; family day care providers) exist in every country but their quality varies widely.

In America some such care is unregistered and uninspected. In the UK and most other EU countries, there are registration and inspection procedures, strict controls on the permitted numbers and ages of children, and increasingly widespread provisions for training (including training for work with children with various special needs) and for support and back-up.

If a relative or friend offers to care for your child as an informal, unpaid childminder, think before you cheer. If she doesn't need to be registered you have only your personal relationship on which to base the assumption that your baby will be safe with her and anyone else she chooses to have in her home. And favours this big are sometimes offered with more enthusiasm than forethought and quickly go sour.

As for group care in nurseries or child care centres (see p.218), national and local policies concerning the provision of day care places vary widely. In some countries, public or charitable bodies provide places for almost all who want them and set national standards of excellence; in others, scarce places are over-subscribed or confined to groups with special needs for day care.

Forward-looking employers increasingly offer workplace day care as a perk to staff. There are big advantages: you need only be away from your child during your actual working hours; you can visit during breaks and you are on the spot in case of illness or crisis. But possible snags include rush-hour travel; your child's isolation from your home community and the fact that if you're off sick she can't go to day care and if you change jobs, she loses her place.

Chain, and privately owned day care centres are expanding to meet booming demand, though many don't accept under-twos whose care demands extra resources. Quality varies, as do costs, but standards of good practice (including education rather than just babysitting) are being agreed, which is a necessary, if not sufficient, step towards meeting them.

THE
TODDLER

From one year to two-and-a-half

Your toddler is no longer a baby, feeling himself as part of you, using you as his controller and facilitator, the mirror in which he sees himself and the world. But he is not yet a child either; ready to see you as a person in your own right and to take responsibility for himself and his own actions in relation to you. He has begun to be aware that you and he are separate people but he does not take it comfortably for granted. Some of the time he asserts this new-found individuality, yelling "No!" and "Let me!", fighting your control and his own need for your help each time an issue presents itself. But some of the time he clings to you, crying when you leave the room, holding up his arms to be carried, demanding with open mouth that you should feed him.

His in-between behaviour is confusing for you but it is painful for him. He has to become a person in his own right but it feels safer to remain your possession. He has to begin to reject your total control over him yet it is easier to accept it. He has to develop likes and dislikes of his own and to pursue his own ends even when they conflict with yours, yet conflict feels desperately dangerous to him. He still loves you with an unrivalled passion; depending on you totally for emotional support. The developmental imperative of independence conflicts with the emotional imperative of love.

If you expect your toddler to remain the comparatively biddable baby he was, he will have to clash with you directly. He needs your love and approval but his drive to grow up will not allow him to accept them at the price of too much dependence. But if you expect him to change overnight into what he will be – a sensible child – he will feel himself inadequate. He needs your help and comfort and if they are withheld from him, he cannot manage. Babied, he is bolshy. Pushed on, he is whiny.

There is a middle road which allows him to adventure but ensures him against disaster; helps him to try but cushions his failures; gives him a firm framework for acceptable behaviour yet pads it so that it can contain him without bruising his dawning sense of being his own boss. Finding that middle road depends on understanding some aspects of toddlers' development that are not always obvious, and on refusing to be fooled by appearances. In many ways your two-year-old seems much more grown-up than he feels. His walking, his talking and his play develop to a point where outwardly he seems little different from a three-year-old, but his inward understanding and his experience do not match up to them. If you treat him as a baby, you will hold him back. He must come to understand. He must learn by experience. But if you treat him as you would treat a pre-school child, you put him under intolerable pressure. He must be helped to understand. He must have experience made manageable.

The key to understanding your toddler lies in understanding the development of his thought processes. It is only as these mature that those conflicting emotions and misleading abilities can come together to form the reasonable and manageable whole we call a child.

Your toddler's memory, for example, does not yet operate as it will when he is older. He may remember people and places and songs and smells as well as you do yourself but his memory for some kinds of details is still very short. When he was a baby, doing baby things, this was neither very important nor very obvious. But now he is trying to do more grown-up things it is both vital and conspicuous. Day after day he trips and tumbles over the step between kitchen and living room. Wild with irritation and plagued by worry over the bumps on his head, you wonder whether he will ever learn. He will, but it will take time. He cannot "bear that step in mind" until repeated experience has etched it into his memory. When he was a baby it would have been your job to prevent him crawling over the edge. When he is a child it will be your job to point the step out to him. But right now your job is to modify the painful potential of that series of experiences and to jog that memory. You may need to pad the step and issue endless reminders.

Just as his memory of events in the past is selective, so is his capacity for forethought. Although he can anticipate your work-day departure from the brief-case in your hand, he cannot anticipate the results of his own behaviour. If he can climb that step-ladder, he will do so without thinking ahead to the problem of how to get down again. Often difficulties with memory and with forethought combine to get him into trouble. He has been scolded again and again for playing with the buttons on the television set, but as he approaches it again today neither the memory of past scoldings nor anticipation of the new one that is coming is strong enough to give him pause.

Those buttons demand to be pressed. They draw him like a magnet.

It is because your toddler cannot think ahead that he cannot wait a second for anything. If he wants it at all, he wants it now and the clamouring begins even as he watches you remove the wrapper from the longed-for ice-pop. If neutral waiting for things he likes is difficult for him, putting up with even minor discomfort now, in order to be more comfortable later is impossible. Wailing with misery because the ice-pop has made him so sticky, he will still fight off the face cloth that brings relief. Most of the time he is still a creature of this moment only.

Similar immaturities in toddler thinking may get him into trouble in his relationships with people, too. He loves you. Everyone tells you that he loves you. He tells you that he loves you, and when you get that big hug, wicked grin or contented chuckle, you know he loves you. Yet it may be quite rare for him to behave in the ways we adults think of as "loving". He cannot put himself in your place or see things through your eyes. He will hate it if you cry but it will be the feelings your tears arouse in *him* which he dislikes, rather than the feelings the tears suggest in you. It is not his job yet to consider other people's feelings, he has to come to terms with his own first. If he bites you and you bite him back to "show him what it feels like", he will howl his hurt and outrage as if biting was a totally new idea to him. He makes no connection between what he did to you and what you then did to him; between your feelings and his own.

Even his own feelings are often still a mystery to him. It is the combination of being unsure what he feels now, and unable to remember what he felt last time or predict what he will feel later, that makes decisions so difficult for him. "Do you want to stay here with me or go to the shop with Daddy?" seems a simple and insignificant choice. But it is neither straightforward nor unimportant to the toddler. Which will he enjoy more? Which did he enjoy last time? Which does he feel like doing now? He does not and cannot know. He dithers and, whichever is finally chosen for him, he is miserable.

He will have to learn to make his own decisions, of course, that's part of growing up. But he will learn faster and more happily if he practises on decisions where he has nothing to lose. If he has two biscuits, "Which are you going to eat first?" is a question he can consider without stress. He has them both. Nobody is going to take away the one he decides against. He can change his mind six sticky times if he pleases.

Toddlers acquire language at widely varying ages, but early words often get them into trouble by suggesting that their understanding is greater than it is. Your child learns new words and uses them correctly, but he often misses the subtler meanings those words convey to adults. He may well use the word "promise", for example, yet he cannot possibly understand the concept it usually conveys. If you offer him five minutes more play if he promises to come straight to bed afterwards, he will happily say "promise". But the word is nothing but an agreement label. After that five minutes he wants a further five. He cannot understand the reproach in your voice as you say, "But you promised..."

Words often make trouble over truth too. Your toddler may talk fluently enough to issue accusations and denials long before their accuracy means anything to him. He talks as he feels. It might have been the dog that made that puddle on the kitchen floor: he wishes it had been and says that it was. During a quarrel with his sister, he falls and hurts his knee. He says that she pushed him – which she did not. But although she did not hurt his knee, she did hurt his feelings. He is telling a kind of feeling-truth which just happens to be different from adult truth.

Later on you will be able to demonstrate the value of promises thoughtfully made and reliably kept; of truth (usually) told, and lies (mostly) avoided. But it is too soon yet. Don't corner him with concepts he cannot understand. Your toddler is doing his best to please, but he *is* only a toddler. If nothing less than child standards can please you, he is certain to fail.

Your toddler's developmental clock has told him that it is time to stop being a baby and move towards being a separate person. If you treat him as a baby, he will fight you every step of the way and, in the end, he will win his independence because he must. But he will win it at a terrible price paid in lost love.

That clock does not yet read "childhood", though, so attempts to manage and discipline him as you would a child will not work either. You will be faced with a lack of comprehension that looks like defiance, and every battle you join will end with love lost. So don't try for absolute control and don't join moral battles. Your toddler will be "good" if he happens to feel like doing what you want him to do and does not happen to feel like doing anything you would dislike. With a little cleverness you can organize life as a whole, and issues in particular, so that you both want the same thing most of the time. Your toddler has his bricks all over the floor and you want the room tidy. If you tell him to pick them up, he will probably refuse. If you insist, a fight will be on and you cannot win it. You can yell at him, punish him, reduce him to a jelly of misery but none of that will get those bricks off the floor. But if you say, "I bet you can't put those bricks in their bag before I've picked up all these books," you turn a chore into a game; an order into a challenge. Now he wants to do

what you want him to do, so he does. He did not pick up (most of) the bricks "for Mummy"; he did not do it because he is a "good boy". He did it because you made him want to. And that is the best possible way to go. Conduct your toddler through his daily life by foreseeing the rocks and steering around them, avoiding absolute orders that will be absolutely refused, leading and guiding him into behaving as you want him to behave because nothing has made him want to behave otherwise.

The payoff now is more fun and less strife for you all but that does not mean that the moral imperative demands a different line. The later payoff is seriously important. This toddler, who does not know right from wrong and therefore cannot choose to behave well or badly, is growing up. Soon the time will come when he does remember your instructions and foresee the results of his actions; does understand the subtleties of everyday language; does recognize your feelings and your rights. When that time comes your child *will* be able to be "good" or "naughty" on purpose. Which he chooses will depend largely on how he feels about the adults who are special to him and have power over him. If he reaches that next stage of growing up feeling that you are basically loving, approving and on his side, he will want (most of the time) to please you, so (with many lapses) he will behave as you wish. But if he reaches that stage feeling that you are overpowering, incomprehensible and against him, he may already have decided not to bother trying to please you because you are never pleased; not to let himself mind when you are cross because you are cross so often; not to expose the depth of his loving feelings for you because you have not always seemed to reciprocate.

If you ever wonder whether you are being too gentle and accepting with your toddler, or anyone ever suggests that it is time to toughen up, look ahead. If your child reaches three or four no longer seeking your approval, not feeling co-operative, not confident of loving and being loved, you will have lost the basis for easy, effective "discipline" all through childhood. At this in-between toddler stage, a happy child is an easy child. A child kept easy now will be easy to handle later.

A healthy diet doesn't have to be dull…

Eating
and Growing

By the beginning of the second year your baby will be ready to share most family foods and to have meals at the times which suit the rest of you, provided she can also have some snacks in between.

If you are cooking fresh foods, you can make most of them suitable for a baby. Fried foods might be too fatty for her, but her portion can be grilled or dry-fried in a non-stick pan. If the sauce has wine in it, or hot spices or more garlic than she likes, it can be replaced with plain stock or yoghurt. Otherwise you will rarely need to do more than cut foods up or mince or mash them while you are serving.

If you are not doing much cooking for the rest of the family, or you use a lot of prepared cook-chill or frozen dishes whose additives and flavourings you cannot control, you may find that some commercially prepared babyfoods are still useful. For example, if you do not provide a cooked breakfast for anyone else, a helping of baby cereal will give your toddler much more nourishment than a similar-sized helping of adult breakfast cereal. If you do not usually provide a sweet course, "toddler desserts" or "fruit varieties" will save you stewing half an apple or cooking a minute custard.

Adult convenience foods need to be used with some care. Although most frozen foods have the same nutritional quality as fresh food, canned and dehydrated foods are often nutritionally poor. A bowl of canned tomato soup, for example, may fill your child's belly but it will not provide enough calories or useful nutrients to count as the main dish of a main meal. Dehydrated foods usually contain a great deal of salt. Although the baby's ability to cope with salt does improve with age, too much will still place a strain on her kidneys. Furthermore these foods often contain a variety of preservatives, colourings and artificial flavouring agents such as the ubiquitous monosodium glutamate. Although most countries have stringent regulations to control the use of chemicals in food, many people believe that we should all be better off if we ate fewer of them. So while there is no need to go to extremes – the occasional gravy made with a stock cube will not hurt your baby now – it is not a good idea to feed her a steady diet of these manufactured foods.

The same caution applies to adult soft drinks. If you read the small print on a bottle of fruit squash, you will probably find that it contains a variety of sweeteners, flavourings and colouring agents and very little real fruit. An occasional drink of one of these products will not do a toddler any harm but for regular consumption and plenty of vitamin C, stick to diluted fresh fruit juice. Of course if a toddler needs a snack, there is much to be said for a drink of milk while if she is simply thirsty, there is no drink better than plain water.

Worries about toddlers' eating After being bombarded with detailed advice about feeding a baby, parents who seek advice on feeding a toddler usually find themselves fobbed off with the all-embracing and mysterious prescription "a good mixed diet". When they enquire what such a diet consists of, they are told to "give plenty of complex carbohydrates, like whole-meal bread and pasta; give meat and fish every day; give well-cooked eggs; cheese; milk and plenty of fresh vegetables..." Realizing that their toddler dislikes and refuses almost every one of those items, they decide that she cannot be eating properly. The seeds of anxiety (and therefore of eating problems) are sown.

What is a mixed diet and what's so good about it?

A "mixed diet" is one in which some of each of a wide variety of foods are eaten in different combinations, every day. Its virtue lies in the fact that an individual who eats that diet over a long time will get everything her body requires under all circumstances. If what is needed is not in one food, it will be in another. If not enough of one nutrient is eaten at breakfast, the deficiency will be made good at lunch. So if your child does eat a good mixed diet, you need not even try to work out what she needs or is getting of any specific nutrient because day-by-day and week-by-week the two will match up.

This is a major advantage because working these things out is complicated. Total food needs and requirements for specific nutrients vary both from person to person and in the same person from one day to the next. Your own entirely adequate diet, for example, may suddenly fall short of the exceptional need for iron brought on by a series of heavy menstrual periods. Working out what you are getting from specific portions of food is even more complex. We know, for example, how much protein is in 170g (6oz) of lean lamb. But how lean is lean? We know how much vitamin C is in 115g (4oz) of freshly picked raw spring cabbage, but how much is available and absorbed after the cabbage has been picked, transported, stored, cooked and kept warm? On a mixed diet these vexed questions need not concern you. The individual who has some meat or fish and/or some beans, nuts and pulses; some cheese, eggs, milk or yoghurt, will be getting more than adequate protein whatever the quality of each item. And if she also eats a range of vegetables and fruit, boiling the vitamin C out of that cabbage will do no harm to her diet (though it may offend her taste buds) because there will be plenty in the baked potato or the fruit salad.

Wide variety, that "good mixed diet", is the safe and easy way to feed anyone, child or adult, well. Aim at it, by all means, but don't feel that without it your child must be poorly nourished. Her diet can be both good and mixed enough without having to include all the foods that are conventionally considered "good for her". The value of any one food lies in the use which the body can make of its constituents, so no food is magically good-in-itself, only as good as the sum total of what is in it. Furthermore, anything that is in one food will also be in some others so no single food is absolutely necessary. A generation ago milk, for example, was thought essential for children and there were endless rows over undrunk mugfuls. Now milk is recognized as a food that some children do better without, and that even for the rest is only an easy-to-take package of useful nutrients. The valuable proteins, minerals and vitamins milk contains are in other foods too, especially the many foods made from it. There's no virtue in a cup of milk that isn't in a cup of yoghurt, any more than there's special virtue in an egg gazing one-eyed off a plate. The milk

The wider the range of foods a toddler is offered the better, for snacks and treats as well as meals.

and egg in the pancake your child enjoys is just as good (or bad) as the traditional English nursery breakfast she deplores.

So if your child does indeed eat a conventionally good mixed diet, she will certainly be getting everything she needs and you need not think any further about her food. Don't even bother with the rest of this chapter. But if she doesn't eat that kind of diet, don't worry. If you read on, you will almost certainly find that provided you offer a wide range of foods, she gets enough of everything important from the combinations she likes, whatever individual foods she rejects. Be a little wary, though, of *new* Western conventions about healthy eating which may lead you to limit the range of foods you serve and therefore the range from which she can choose. Of questionable value to adults, many of these notions of healthy eating are un-questionably wrong for small children.

Calories In societies where calorie-counting means the fewer the better, and "low-cal" is an advertising point, it's important to remember that calories (technically "kilocalories" or "kilojoules") are not nutrients, like fats or proteins, but a measure of the total energy our bodies get from foods. Good health absolutely depends on sufficient calories to keep bodily functions ticking over and to fuel activity, while children's bodies need a surplus over today's needs to fuel tomorrow's growth. Those amounts are not the same for different people, though, nor even for children of the same ages and sizes and stages of growth. It is essential to offer your child plenty, but it is also important to understand that however little she chooses to eat, it is enough if she is well, energetic and growing.

All foods contain calories – when industry eventually succeeds in producing calories-free edibles, they will be food substitutes rather than foods – but in widely varying concentrations. Fats (including oils) are the most concentrated source of calories, so foods that are rich in these contain most of all. One slice of bread thickly spread with butter gives a child more energy than two slices eaten plain; one potato served as French fries yields as many calories as three potatoes served boiled. A child who seems to flourish on remarkably little food may be eating it in a high-calorie form.

Carbohydrates Sugar is pure carbohydrate, the kind many people eat too much of, and not to be confused with the complex carbohydrates of which they may eat too little. Most carbohydrate-rich foods are bulky ones made from grains such as wheat, maize and rice, and from roots such as potatoes, yams and cassava. These are staple foods all over the world. People get most of their energy from these foods because, although their calories are less concentrated than in fats, they are eaten in relatively large quantities.

The low concentration of calories and the high bulk in these foods are important in themselves because they mean that people can fill their stomachs, and give their digestive systems plenty of fibre to work on, without risking obesity. If your child is eating at all, her appetite will ensure that she gets enough of these bulky foods for energy, especially if you serve most of them simply. If she doesn't learn to expect sweetened breakfast cereals and salty potato chips, she'll probably enjoy corn flakes and baked potatoes.

Don't be in a hurry to get her eating less processed carbohydrates, though. Since eating patterns do become habitual, a gradual introduction to wholemeal bread and brown rice as well as the "white" varieties may help your toddler to choose a sensible diet later on. But a "high-fibre" diet is not appropriate for children in this age group. Your child's stomach is still very small so that she needs to eat little and often and needs food that is relatively high in calories for its bulk. Whole grains, and especially fashionable additions of bran, may actually give her diarrhoea.

Fats Many families rightly try to keep down their consumption of fats as a whole – because of their high calories – and animal or saturated fats in particular, because of their association with cholesterol and heart disease. A relatively low-fat diet is fine for a toddler. Even if she eats no visible fats, such as butter or margarine, and has very few fried foods, she will get the minute traces of "fatty acids" her body requires from invisible fats in commercially produced foods. Unlike older members of the family, though, your toddler should have whole, rather than skimmed milk, and full-fat dairy products such as cheese and yoghurt. She needs the fat-soluble vitamins they contain. And even if those are made good in a daily dose of multivitamin drops – as they must be for children who, having been weaned from the breast, are being fed an entirely vegan diet – the extra calories and extra palatability of the full-fat products are appropriate for her. If she is eating well she can, if you wish, have semi-skimmed milk (but not skimmed) towards the end of the year, and join the rest of the family in its choice of other dairy products.

Protein Protein is vital in children's diets as their bodies use its constituents as the building materials for growth. In the rich countries of the West, however, food manufacturers have overplayed the concentration and total amounts of protein children need, and the difficulty and expense of providing it. Although "high protein" is an advertising point, a child who is offered as much as she wants to eat of a variety of foods is most unlikely to need extra protein.

Protein is made up of a number of amino acids. Your child has to eat some of these in ready-made form because her body cannot manufacture them out of the others. These vital amino acids are already present in the correct balance in animal foods like meat, fish, eggs, milk, cheese and other dairy produce, which used therefore to be referred to as "first-class" protein foods. But there are amino acids in other foods too. The vegetable proteins in bread, potatoes, beans, nuts and grains can complement each other so that a careful mixture results in a complete protein intake for an adult. For growing children, though, there remains a small imbalance in the amino acid composition of these proteins that is best corrected by the addition of very small quantities of animal protein. That does not have to be meat or fish, of course, it can be milk or anything made from it. Bread and cheese, for example, or porridge and milk, provide a child with protein that is just as "first-class" as that highly recommended, widely rejected, expensive slice of meat.

On this basis most toddlers get an ample supply of protein. They may refuse eggs, but they eat puddings and cakes with egg in them.

Don't feel you must always hold back favourite foods. They may be good for him.

They may refuse meat and fish but they eat hamburger and chicken, sausages and fish fingers. They may live in vegetarian families where no meat products are served, but they eat a range of bean, pulse and nut dishes and some eggs, cheese and other dairy produce. The protein they are getting is not as concentrated as it would be in butcher's meat, but balancing the sum total of other vegetable proteins, it is ample.

If your child does not eat enough foods to make a good mixture of vegetable proteins, or like any of the less concentrated forms of animal protein, don't forget milk. As long as she gets as much as one pint of milk per day, either as a drink or in cooking, she will not go short of protein whatever else she does or does not eat.

But while vegetarian diets that allow dairy products, and perhaps eggs, are no problem for growing children, vegan diets that exclude all animal products, including milk, are dramatically different. Soy milk formulas are an imperfect substitute for breast milk; vitamin B12 is found only in animal products; providing enough calcium without dairy products is difficult, and an adequate intake of protein will probably depend on using tofu and other soy-based products. Unless you yourselves are very knowledgeable about the implications of strict vegetarianism for growing children, you will need ongoing dietary advice from an interested health professional.

Calcium and other minerals

Your child needs an adequate calcium intake both for the proper development of growing bones and teeth and for the correct functioning of muscles and blood clotting. There is a useful amount in bread, flour and other cereals, but a more concentrated source than this is needed and the easy and obvious one is milk. A pint a day will ensure your toddler's calcium intake. Even if she does not appear to drink that much milk, you can (and probably do) "lose" it in ordinary cooking. It takes at least 30 ml (1oz) of milk to scramble an egg, make her a pancake or cream her potatoes, and twice that to mix baby cereal, or make custard or a creamed soup. And there's the equivalent of twice that amount again in a pot of yoghurt, a serving of ice cream or a mug of cocoa.

He needn't drink milk to get its goodness. Foods made from milk are just as good.

Try cheese too, remembering that this is also a concentrated source of protein. Given the chance, many small children develop a passion for cheese: in cubes to eat in their fingers, grated over vegetables, in sauces, or spread on bread.

The other minerals your child needs are either so widely distributed (like phosphorus) that she is bound to get plenty or, like iron, they are used and re-used by the body so that, provided her stores are adequate after weaning, daily supplies are unnecessary.

Vitamins

Most vitamins are widely distributed so that the child who is getting plenty of food automatically gets plenty of vitamins too. However, giving the three vital ones as (carefully rationed) daily drops ensures that your toddler will get enough even when she's having an unhungry phase or eating very oddly. These are:

■ Vitamin A: the main sources in the diet are liver, then milk, butter or fortified margarine. Carrots yield "carotene" from which our bodies can make their own vitamin A. Your child will probably get enough from these sources but a supplement is a safety measure.

■ Vitamin D: the only concentrated food sources are egg yolk and fatty fishes. Pale skins make their own in sunlight, but a supplement is essential, especially in winter and for black children.

■ Vitamin C: widely available in fruits and green vegetables, this vital vitamin is nevertheless quite difficult to provide in adequate daily quantities because it is destroyed by both light and heat. Green vegetables displayed in daylight, cut up ahead and then boiled in water will have lost most of their vitamin C by the time they are eaten. Quick cooking, instant serving and use of the cooking water, with its dissolved vitamin content, in soups or gravies help, but it is still difficult to know how much has reached the child. Potatoes have plenty of vitamin C just under the skin, but when they are served in their jackets some is lost because of heat; if they are peeled and then boiled, even more vanishes.

Fruit is a better source of vitamin C because it is either eaten raw or with its cooking water served as juice. Citrus fruits, which are naturally packaged against light as well as usually served raw, are an ideal source. A whole orange or its juice every day should give your child all the vitamin C she needs. A daily serving of one of the commercially prepared vitamin C-enriched baby juices serves the same purpose. There is no harm in giving this as well as the dosage of vitamin C which is in the multivitamins. Try not to let your toddler get into the habit of drinking those baby juices ad lib, though. It may be more difficult to control her intake when she can ask for what she wants in words than it was when she was a baby, but if you are going to control her consumption of sweets, it is silly to let her have endless cups of sweet drinks. Even the brands labelled "no added sugar" contain enough fruit-sugar to put teeth and dietary balance at risk.

Don't quarrel over green vegetables for the sake of their vitamins. Fruits are a richer source.

Mealtime Behaviour

If you have done everything you can to relax about your toddler's diet but you still find yourselves worrying, you may be more anxious about eating behaviour than about actual food intake. Food costs money and preparing it takes time and care and love. It's easy to feel hurt when your toddler refuses it. The mess he makes as he plays with food he is not going to eat goes against everything adults have been taught about "good manners" and seems wantonly wasteful. And his eagerness to get down and get on with life after a few mouthfuls prevents the meal – perhaps a rare family supper – from being a peaceful social occasion. Understandable though these feelings are, it is a mistake to let them get mixed with worries about the child's actual diet. You are trying to feed him so that he can grow healthily and you are trying to teach him to behave in socially acceptable ways. These are separate tasks: both important, but totally different.

When you try to insist that your child eat some peas or broccoli, is it for vitamin C or discipline? There are many better sources of vitamin C. There are better issues for discipline too.

When you say that he "ought" to eat everything on his plate, are you thinking of him having enough to eat or of "not wasting good food"? He is the only one who knows whether he has had enough to eat or not and isn't it more of a waste of food to force it down a reluctant child than to feed it to a keen cat? When you say that he cannot have any pudding until or unless he eats the main course, is it because you truly believe that the first course consists of more important foods, or is it because you know he likes sweet foods better and you think he ought to pay for them by ploughing through his meat and vegetables?

Of course it is up to parents to choose when to discipline their children, but those who choose mealtimes may pay a high price. Some parents become so embroiled in eating battles with toddlers that the whole family's life is ruined by them, often for months at a time. There are households where all mealtime conversation is banned except stories and nursery rhymes designed to distract the toddler while parents ladle in some food. There are parents who refuse all invitations to visit friends for meals because toddlers will only eat at home. A lone mother fired the best nanny she'd ever had for refusing to keep the toddler for two hours at the lunch table to try to get him to eat, and her friend chose a childminder largely because she spent the children's nap time cutting tiny tea-time sandwiches into animal shapes.

It is curious that we get so uptight about toddlers' eating because they get hungry just like everybody else and when they feel hungry their bodies tell them to eat, and eat they do. Very few toddlers with serious "eating problems" are thin; most are actually rather fat. But trouble begins because the child does not eat what you offer, when you say or in the way that you approve. The more you try to impose rules and regulations on eating and table manners, the clearer it becomes to the toddler that his highchair is a marvellous place for a fight. Soon he knows that a meal is the one situation in which he can

Family meals help toddlers to enjoy eating what you eat and behaving as you behave.

always get your attention (even divert it from his father or his sister) and evoke your concern. That situation is irresistible to the child's growing sense of his own power and independence.

A long time ago a research study carried out at a nursery in London showed that year-old babies who were offered trays containing a wide range of suitably cooked and cut up foods three times each day, selected for themselves, with no adult assistance, persuasion or instruction, diets which, while they were wildly unbalanced day-by-day, were perfectly balanced in the longer term. Like them, your child may have a bread jag and then a meat passion and then eat almost nothing but fruit for a day or two without doing himself any harm at all. If you can accept that and trust him to know best what he wants and needs to eat of the foods you offer at any particular meal, major eating problems are unlikely.

Avoiding eating problems You are much cleverer than your toddler. If you foresee the possibility of mealtimes becoming a battleground, you can stay one jump ahead by resolutely refusing to become involved. It takes two to make a quarrel. The first steps are to do with your own feelings:

■ Believe that your child will never starve if he is offered adequate food. This is not a careless generalization but true of all children except those for whom by reason of youth or disability, the mechanics of eating are an impossible challenge. Is yours one of these? Those mechanics are only beyond him if he does not eat for himself even when it's his favourite food and he's hungry.

■ Check your child's weight and its consistent upward curve on his growth chart. If you are not convinced that it *is* increasing as it should, have him checked over at the clinic or by your doctor.

■ Go on seeking reassurance until you honestly believe that your job is only to offer good food, not to force it down your child.

■ Share this process with any adult who shares the care of your toddler. If his father, nanny or childminder continues to pressure him to eat, your campaign will not work.

The next steps are to do with encouraging your toddler's independence in all areas where you conflict, especially at meals:

■ Present his food in a form that is reasonably easy to manage and don't help him unless he asks or gestures for help.

■ If he asks for help, don't scoop food straight from the plate into his mouth so that you are feeding him. Load the spoon for him and let him take it in his hand and put it in his mouth so you are helping him eat.

■ Make him feel that eating is something active which he does because he wants the food, not that being fed is something passive which he accepts because you want him to have it.

■ Let him eat by any method or combination of methods: fingers and fists as well as spoon. He needs to feel that getting the food he wants is what matters, not getting it in any particular way.

■ Allow him to eat in any order or combination. If you can keep his pudding or the fruit bowl out of sight until he loses interest in his cauliflower cheese, fine. But once he thinks of that pudding and asks for it, refusing it until he has eaten his first course will quickly make him realize that you care more about the main course than the dessert and by the laws of toddler contra-suggestiveness that will instantly make the pudding seem even more desirable. Likewise if you will not let him dip bacon in his cereal, he may well decide that he will not eat either of them. Just don't watch if the combination makes you queasy.

■ Don't take too much trouble over your child's food. You're bound to resent it when something that's taken you half the morning goes straight on the floor. Keeping a toddler's meals simple helps to keep the emotional temperature down. Think what he is likely to eat. If the answer is "bread and butter, cucumber and ham – again", give him that. If he eats it, fine; it's an excellent lunch. If not, you will not have wasted much.

■ Don't ever use food as a reward, punishment, bribe or threat. Remember that you're aiming to keep the child's eating separate from discipline. If he is hungry, he should eat as much as he wants of whatever is available. If he is not hungry, he should not eat. If he has ice cream, it should be because that is the dessert you're offering today, not because he has been a good boy. If he cannot have ice cream, it should be because it is not available today rather than because he has been naughty.

■ Let the meal end when the child has had enough. If you have accepted that what he eats and how he eats it is up to him, it follows that not eating any more or not eating anything at all is up to him too. Try not to weaken at the last moment and try to coax just a few mouthfuls down him.

■ Try to keep mealtimes enjoyable. Sitting still is his least favourite occupation and he still finds it difficult to join in general conversation so trying to make him sit up to table through a whole family meal is likely to lead to trouble. If you want him to feel part of a family group at table, let him sit up with you, eat what he wants and then get down to play. If you do not feel able to allow him to leave a family table before others have finished, feed him on his own for another year or so.

Meals and snacks Toddlers cannot manage on three meals a day. They have to eat between those meals because they need a high intake of calories relative to their size yet their stomachs are too small to hold much food at a time. Snacks are not an indulgence but a necessity. Your child may need something when he wakes up, to keep him going until breakfast. He will certainly need a mid-morning and a mid-afternoon snack, and if he has his last meal of the day an hour or more before he goes to bed, he may need a bedtime snack as well.

If your child has to wait too long for food, his blood sugar may dip so low that he runs out of energy, patience and good cheer. When a toddler wakes from an afternoon nap crying and cross, the effect of a small drink of milk can be close to miraculous. So try to make sure that nobody in your household takes a moralistic attitude to snacks. Food is food and there is no dietary law which says that it is better to eat three times a day than twice or six times. It is all a matter of commonsense and convenience mixed with social convention.

Make sure that your toddler's snacks *are* food, though: planned and nutritious mini-meals. The main argument against eating between

To stay in control of snacks serve treats at meals and simpler fare in between.

meals is that snacks fill children up so that they "cannot eat their dinners". If a child eats a snack that isn't very nutritious – a packet of chocolate biscuits, for instance – when he is not really very hungry, he may well refuse that "good dinner" and indeed he ought to refuse it or he risks obesity. But the child who eats a nutritious snack when he is really hungry is unlikely to refuse his meal an hour later. And even if he did eat less of it, he might not be losing anything because the snack – cheese cubes and apple, say – was at least as good for him as those fish fingers.

As your toddler gets older, then, be a little wary of snack *foods*: the vast array of attractively packaged, heavily advertised fun foods that he will see in every shop and in the hands of many of his peers in strollers. He needs something to eat between breakfast and lunch, but if what he gets in between is more delicious, easier and more fun to eat than anything he gets at mealtimes, you may find yourselves in a situation where snacks work against his nutrition instead of being an integral part of it (see p.439).

Fat toddlers If you think your toddler is obese, check his current position on his growth chart (or ask the clinic to do so). A child's ideal weight goes up in strict relation to his height. If he is gaining weight much faster than he is gaining height, he is certainly getting fatter. But if his weight remains inside the 98th centile line, he is not medically overweight. And remember, many babies who are rather fat in the last weeks before they get moving slim down very quickly once they get onto their feet.

Many young toddlers are plump without being fat. Some of them are children who are meant to be big; they were big babies, they are big toddlers, they'll be big children and eventually big adults. But a lot of them aren't particularly large or heavy. They just *look* plump because their faces are very round, with baby cheeks; they don't have much in the way of necks or waists yet, and their tummies stick out.

A toddler who is getting fatter is probably eating a diet which is high in carbohydrates. But he needs carbohydrate foods to satisfy his appetite and give him energy. And he needs the useful range of proteins, vitamins and minerals they contain. So don't try to limit his carbohydrate-rich foods – or indeed any of his real *foods*. Look instead at his consumption of sugar, and particularly sugar in drinks.

If your toddler is a thirsty child who gets through a large bottle of concentrated vitamin C fruit syrup in a week, he will be getting far more vitamin C than he needs, which does not' matter, and an amazing amount of sugar, which does. Quite apart from the potential damage to his teeth, those drinks alone will be giving him a lot of extra calories without the satisfied full-feeling that comes from eating, or even drinking milk. If he is just thirsty, plain water is the best of all drinks. If he is also hungry, he would be better off with a proper snack – with yoghurt and fresh fruit, for example, or with milk and a plain biscuit.

Your toddler is growing fast. If you reduce his intake of "empty calories" even a little – and get rid of the habit of sipping sweet drinks all day – you will probably nip any tendency to obesity in the bud. Do be sure, though, that he gets the opportunity for all the exercise he wants. Is he free on the floor when he is at home and awake, or does he spend a lot of time in his pram or playpen? Is he taken to places where he can safely play actively? When he's taken out, is it in the car or the buggy? And if it's the buggy, does he get to push it some of the time or does he just sit in it?

As your child graduates from crawling to walking and then learns to climb and run, he'll want to be constantly on the go. The more exercise he takes, the better for his health, his enjoyment, his learning – and his physique.

GROWTH

Once past the first birthday your baby's weight gain will probably slow down to around 30g–60g (1oz–2oz) a week, although a faster or slower rate of gain may, of course, be perfectly right for your toddler. As we have said, there is a wide variation around the "average" at all ages.

Unless she has been ill or has had major feeding troubles during the first year, there is not much point in going on with regular weighing now. To weigh every week would be absurd as the scales may not be accurate enough to weigh to the nearest gram and simple things like passing a motion before or after the weighing will be enough to produce a false gain or loss. It is probably best to weigh and measure every three months, so that you can see your toddler getting heavier and taller both at the same time.

The proportions of a newborn baby's body are quite different from those of an older baby, but the changes that take place during this year are even more dramatic. When a baby of around a year first gets up on her own two feet parents are often very worried by her appearance. Her head is still large in relation to the rest of her and her neck seems non-existent. Her shoulders and chest are thin, her belly sticks out, her legs seem bowed and her feet have no arches. But in the course of a year, all that will change. The year-old baby is still the right shape for life on all fours. By the time she is two her proportions will have changed so that she is much better suited for life on her hind legs. A year later still she will probably have slimmed down and elongated, so that she develops the lithe and leggy elegance typical of an active pre-school child.

A year on his feet will turn your round-bellied, bow-legged, flat-footed baby into a slimmed-down toddler.

TEETH AND TEETHING

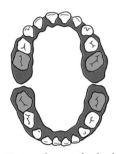

First molars at the back, and pointed canines in the gaps, leave only second molars to come.

Your toddler is likely to be "teething" throughout almost the whole of the second year, and may suffer a great deal more from it than he did in the first. The teeth which are most likely to cause discomfort are the first molars, which will probably come through between 12 and 15 months, and the second molars which will appear towards the end of the second year. The sharp, pointed canines are usually cut in between and with relatively little trouble.

Molars are big and blunt and therefore slow to push through. While teething will still not make your child ill, this second year teething probably will sometimes hurt enough to make him miserable and irritable. When a tooth is imminent, the cheek on the affected side may be hot and red and everything he does for comfort (such as sucking or biting) may also cause pain. A toddler who relies on sucking his thumb or a dummy may have a particularly difficult time settling to sleep because the sucking does not only hurt while he does it but sets up a hurting that goes on after he has stopped. Sucking milk from the breast or a bottle may also make the gums hurt, of course, and that's liable to hurt his feelings. Let him suck for as long as he feels it is worthwhile, but offer drinks from a cup as well so that if sucking stops after a couple of painful minutes he will still get enough to drink.

This level of trouble will only last a few days with any one tooth, and there is not a great deal you can do specifically to help, but doing *something* often seems better for both of you than doing nothing:

■ Something cold to bite on may be comforting. Gel-filled teething rings may not withstand toddler teeth, but a raw carrot that has been cooled in iced water in the fridge can be very effective, especially as its shape allows the child to place it exactly where it is needed.

■ Rubbing the affected gum with your finger sometimes helps, but if you are ever going to use a teething gel, this is the time.

■ Cold winds often seem to make teething "toothache" worse. If it is winter, do try to find a design of hat, balaclava or hood that your child will actually keep on, or keep him indoors (or in a car or weather-protected buggy) until the acute teething episode is over.

Find a hat your teething toddler will really wear. Her jaw and ears need protection from cold winds.

Teething and illness

If your child seems to be in real pain that does not seem to relate directly to sucking or chewing, do be alert to the possibility that teeth are not the cause or the whole cause. At this age, earache is very common and sometimes gets confused with teething pain. If your child has a temperature, he may or may not be teething but if he is, he is certainly unwell as well. If he has no temperature but keeps putting a hand to the side of his face or pulling at an ear, only a doctor can tell whether it's the ear, a tooth or both that are bothering him. Do have him checked over. Your doctor probably cannot do much for your teething toddler, but she should be able to make you feel all right about giving children's paracetamol to relieve the inflammation and pain.

Building strong teeth

The formation of strong teeth which will resist decay depends on diet. The baby's first teeth formed during your pregnancy, so they depended on your diet then. But you can still do a great deal to ensure the strength of later teeth, as well as to look after the ones the child already has. Make sure that your child continues to get plenty of calcium and of the vitamin D which enables the body to use it for laying down bones and teeth (see p.333). If weaning from the breast or bottle has dramatically reduced his milk intake, make sure he gets dairy products such as yoghurt and cheese, instead.

Keep an eye on his intake of fluoride. This mineral does more than anything else to strengthen tooth enamel and help it to resist decay, but it is a good thing that your child can have too much of. If there is an inadequate amount in the local water and he therefore had fluoride drops as a baby, it may be time to stop them and rely on fluoride toothpaste instead, but give him only pea-sized helpings and teach him to spit, not swallow. If he goes on with the supplement it may be better to use a non-fluoridated toothpaste. Ask your doctor or your dentist.

Caring for teeth

Don't let yourself drift into dentally challenging habits like giving bottles of milk to take to bed, or drinks (other than water) after his teeth have been cleaned for the night. Even plain milk contains enough sugar to cause dental trouble if it washes around the teeth over a long period. If you really feel you must give something to suck, make it a plain dummy or a bottle of water.

Brush the teeth regularly especially once the molars, which have irregular surfaces to which food can easily stick, have been cut.

Your aim is to clear all food debris from on or between the teeth. Use a small, soft toothbrush with a pea-sized helping of children's fluoride toothpaste and an up and down motion. Don't let your toddler get into the habit of sawing from side to side; it doesn't clean teeth and may damage gums. Clean the teeth at least twice every day and make sure that the last time is after supper so that food remnants do not stay in the mouth all night.

Cleaning teeth thoroughly is a great deal easier said than done. If your toddler would allow you to look carefully in his mouth under a good light, you'd probably be appalled at the number of bits of cereal that had withstood your best after-breakfast efforts. If you can see them, though, you can brush them off, so do everything you can to persuade your child to co-operate so you don't have to brush blind. Once copying you, or having a turn brushing your teeth, no longer interests him, try a mirror. If he will look at his own teeth, so can you. If he will point at them with a finger – to count, or perhaps name, them – he might let you point with that brush.

Seeing her own teeth (with your torch and mirror) will help her see the point of cleaning them.

Sweets

Take control of sweets before your child meets them. If you do not eat sweets yourselves and your child has few older friends, you may be able to prevent him from meeting a sweet until around the second birthday. It is probably worth trying. If the rest of the child's diet is sensible, even this period without sweets will help those first teeth to get a good start. But however careful you are, you are bound to meet the sweet problem eventually. Children see the pretty packets in shops, see the advertisements so cleverly aimed at them on television, see other children munching and sharing. Your child will want to know what they have got and once he does know, he will want some too.

Sweets are certainly bad for your child's teeth. But carefully selected, they do not have to be worse than many other foods; sensibly handled, sweets do not have to become a major issue. Highly refined sugar makes enamel-attacking acid in the child's mouth. Every time sugar is eaten, teeth are at risk; the more times per day they are put under attack and the longer the sugar remains in the mouth, the more likely it is that there will eventually be holes for a dentist's attention. But this applies to all sources of refined sugar, not only to sweets. Endless sipping (let alone sucking) of fruit syrups will do just as much harm as the worst kind of sweet, while a slice of cake will produce as much acid as the least deplorable kind of sweet. So it is much more sensible to take reasonable care over all sweet foods than ban all sweets while feeding the child the rest of a normal Western diet.

Sweet food which is eaten quickly will do little harm because the acid which is produced is gone from the mouth before it has time to eat into the tooth enamel. A slice of cake or a piece of chocolate is therefore much less harmful than a lollipop which the child sucks all afternoon. Chewy cakes and sweets are usually worst of all since fragments tend to stick between the teeth and stay there until the next thorough brushing – or even past it. This indictment sadly applies to many of the "healthy" foods which are often suggested as alternatives to sweets. Raisins, dates and other dried fruits – whether loose or in "bars" – can cling so tenaciously that even though their sugar is unrefined, it can do considerable harm. Some dentists even regret advocating apples after meals as small pieces of sweet apple skin wedged between the teeth can do as much harm as the sugary film the apple was intended to remove.

So, when your child reaches the stage when he must have sweets or feel conspicuously different from other children, select the particular sweets carefully and control the manner in which he eats them. Choose types which dissolve quickly, such as chocolate or fondant sweets. Encourage him to eat all that you are going to give him in one short session, so that he eats a portion of four sweets in 10 minutes rather than one every half-hour for two hours. Make sure he has a drink of water as soon as possible after he has finished them, and make sure that his next teeth cleaning session is thorough.

Visiting a dentist Modern dentistry is increasingly preventive rather than curative, so don't wait (hopefully for years) until your child has toothache. Take him to see a dentist at least once before his second birthday and then try to make regular dental care part of his taken-for-granted routine. Dentists who undertake sessions in child health clinics are usually especially good with toddlers and will make early visits fun so that later treatment is more easily accepted. They will also lend you their expertise and authority in teaching your child to look after his teeth.

Taking small children to dentists can cost a lot in stress, even where treatment does not cost money, so it's easy to decide that such visits are a waste of time because first teeth are going to fall out anyway. Don't. Most first teeth have nearly a decade of hard work in front of them and their health and spacing is vital to the second teeth.

EVERYDAY CARE

You're the one who knows his face needs washing, but he's the one who owns the face.

The job of taking care of your toddler's body belongs to you but that body belongs to her and her increasing awareness of the fact is an important sign of growing up. It does mean, though, that everyday care takes a lot of patience and a lot of tact. Toddlers often don't realize when they need their noses wiped or their wet socks changed, and can't do most of those things for themselves anyway, yet they bitterly resent being handled like objects or possessions. Caring adults need time and imagination. It's when you are in a hurry that shortcuts like giving that nose a quick swipe without so much as a by-your-leave seem tempting. If you imagine yourself into your toddler's (damp) socks, you'll be aware of how offensive it is to do things to her by force and without explanation, and you'll be able to find ways of turning almost everything you have to do for your child into something the two of you can do together right now and that she'll soon begin to do for herself.

It is worth taking all the trouble you can. The process of making your care into self-care is an important part of toddler development. Furthermore, this can be a very contra-suggestive and bolshy stage. Tactlessly handled, everyday care issues easily become triggers for tantrums that cost you stress and time and teach your toddler nothing.

Toddlers get incredibly dirty and they should. Clean clothes, hands, face and knees at the end of the day either mean a swimming expedition or boredom. If you want the enormous pleasure of a clean, neat child with shining hair and pretty clothes, make sure you don't miss the two minutes after she is dressed in the morning and put into her pyjamas in the evening. Being a toddler is hard physical labour. Like any other labourer your child can start and end the day clean, but in between needs sensible, comfortable, washable clothes and freedom to get on with the job.

UNDRESSING AND DRESSING

If you engage your toddler in the business of getting clothes off and on you'll save yourself a great deal of trouble because even if she can't *do* much of it yet, at least she won't make it impossible for you.

Undressing is comparatively easy, of course; in fact you may wish it was more difficult when shoes and socks are cast out of the buggy, and your toddler entertains herself at nap time by taking off her nappy. If you have to keep telling her off for mistimed and misplaced undressing, though, do make sure you encourage and congratulate her for doing it at bedtime. She can even begin to learn how to undo fastenings like buttons and zippers.

When it comes to easy dressing, co-operation really is the key and is usually most efficient and enjoyable if the child manages her own body and the adult manages the clothes. You hold the sleeve or trouser leg open and at the right angle: the child puts in her hand or foot and pushes. Later on she can learn to pop up poppers too. Putting things over her head may be a mobile business though. Unable to do it herself (and probably not keen on having it done

Co-operation is the key to easy dressing and undressing...

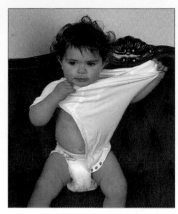

...the more she's encouraged to do as much as she can for herself...

...the more willingly she'll let you do the difficult bits.

anyway) she is likely to toddle off, laughing, leaving you to pursue her, T-shirt at the ready, and pop it on when you catch up. Do choose stretchy, loose-necked, or front-fastening tops. Having tight ones pulled over her nose, or getting stuck halfway, blind and smothered, is seriously upsetting to some children.

Nappies The days of the changing mat are numbered, if not over. Captured and laid on her back, the toddler will probably roll away and suck her toes. Distraction may work: lay her on the nappy and then hand her a really interesting toy, kept specially for the occasion. She may become still at least for the few moments it takes her to examine the toy and you to wipe and tape... If she's soiled, though, she probably won't give you long enough to clean her up or let you hold her feet out of the way. You will probably find the whole nappy business easier with her standing down and (if necessary) momentarily captive between your knees.

Clothes Don't let choice of clothes make trouble between you and your toddler. She will feel very strongly about it. The main concern will (and should) be comfort, but, boy or girl, your child may surprise you with strong feelings about what he or she looks like, too.

Clothes should protect the skin and keep the child warm and dry. They should never be stiff, heavy or physically restricting. They should not have to be "looked after", by the child or by you.

Buying inexpensive clothes is a better way to save money than buying clothes too big. Garments that are oversized will not look or feel nice while new and by the time they fit they will be shabby. Cheap clothes will not last, but with any luck the child will grow faster than they disintegrate. The biggest extravagance of all (though one you may sometimes want to indulge for your own pleasure) is buying different clothes for different, and special, occasions. Many will be outgrown after a couple of wearings.

Both sexes will be least restricted and best protected in long trousers or leggings while they spend their time crawling and falling. Dungarees or overalls avoid tight waistbands and chilly gaps when tops separate from bottoms but you will need elastic-waisted trews once your child uses a pot independently; all-in-one garments or zip flies are too difficult. Avoid thick sweaters, especially tickly polo necks. Add extra, light layers when it is cold.

Shoes and socks Don't make your child wear shoes at all until she is walking out of doors. Bare feet are safer as children use their toes to help balance. They are more comfortable too unless floors are cold. If cold is a problem, find some play boots or "slipper socks", which are heavy woollen socks with a non-slip sole attached. Or buy socks with special non-slip patterns on their soles. Don't let the child wear ordinary socks without shoes, especially if you have hard floors. The combination can be dangerously slippery.

Once your child needs real shoes she needs to have them properly fitted and then checked every couple of months. She cannot tell you if shoes are too short or narrow: the bones of the feet are still so pliable that they can be squashed up enough to cause damage without causing pain. Use a proper shoe shop or specialist children's department and make sure the feet are measured for width as well as length. Remember that if her feet have grown so that she needs a bigger size now than you bought last time, any extras, like rubber boots, will be too small as well.

Your child doesn't need expensive shoes but he must have shoes and socks that really fit.

Provided shoes fit properly they need not be grand leather ones with "good support". It is muscles that support feet. Sneakers or canvas play shoes are fine provided they do not squash or chafe the feet and provided their fastening – lace or T-bar – keeps them correctly positioned so that the child's toes do not slide forward and crumple themselves.

Once she wears hard shoes, your child will need socks to prevent rubbing and absorb sweat. The fit matters; socks which are too tight will soon distort toes. Watch out for shrinkage in cotton socks. When the child is standing, there should be at least three millimetres spare material over the longest toe. If it is a stretch sock designed to fit a range of three sizes, don't buy it if your child already needs the largest size: buy the next size-grouping up.

When you buy new socks which are bigger than the last ones, be sure to clear all the old ones out of drawers. It is no good having two pairs the right size and four more which are too small.

BATHING

An evening bath is much the easiest way to remove the day's embedded grime. You need not hold the child in the water any longer, but don't move out of arms' reach or leave the room. A one-year-old may fall if he pulls up to stand holding the slippery bath edge (try to teach him *not* to stand up in the bath). A two-year-old may turn on the hot water (try to teach him not to *touch* the taps). Either could drown in five centimetres of water. If the bath bottom is very slippery, use a rubber mat or small towel. If the hot tap stays burning, wrap a face cloth around it or cover it with an oven glove kept for the purpose. Above all, *stay close*.

With all safe, provide lots of floating toys and plastic beakers and let your child have fun while getting clean.

Although most toddlers love baths, treating them as warm water play, a few find the whole thing frightening. If yours is one of them, don't try to force him. Some of the methods suggested earlier (see p.176) may still serve to re-introduce him to enjoyable bathing, or sharing a bath with a parent, sibling or friend may help. In the meantime you have to get the dirt off somehow and he certainly will not lie still for a blanket bath.

Try to work out what it is that frightens him. If it is the big bath itself, he may be entirely happy to have a bath in the kitchen sink (mind the tap). If it is the amount of water, he may be happy to sit in the almost empty bath and use a hand shower if you have one with trustworthy temperature control.

Hairwashing Many small (and not so small) children loathe having their hair washed. You may not find the answer here because there may not be a complete solution. Any of the tricks suggested for younger babies (see p.253) may still work, but there are a few extra ones to consider now that your child is older. If hairwashing (and indeed brushing and combing too) makes real misery, would less hair make less misery? A short style can be sponged clean, is easily cared for and encourages thick, healthy hair growth too.

Provided he enjoys it, taking your child swimming may help him get used to water in his eyes. Furthermore, the hot showers provided for bathers can make an ideal setting for a quick rub with non-sting shampoo. The child is wet already; wants to get warm and has you in there as well.

If the child likes going with you to the hairdresser, you may be able to use the new passion for "let's pretend" games to set up hairdressing at home. With a little ingenuity, you can set up a "backwash". Provide "sir" or "madam" with a plastic bib, a choice of shampoos and much chat about hairstyles and water temperature and he will probably let you do the whole job with a hand shower. If the game goes well, this is the moment to snip any straggly ends too. If the child happens to have seen people in the hair salon having manicures, coping with fingernails will follow naturally; the whole thing can turn into a pleasant weekly spring-clean. Don't push your luck by insisting on blow-drying the hair if, like many toddlers, yours is scared of the dryer. Once rubbed, the hair will dry quite fast enough if you just settle him in a warm corner for a story.

Hands and nails Short fingernails are important to hygiene, and hands really do need washing before meals and after the child has used the pot or "helped" you change his nappy. Handwashing will help prevent his colds from spreading to other people, too.

Although your child cannot actually cut his own nails you may be able to keep his interest and co-operation if you let him choose the order in which they are cut and specify how long each should be. Don't cut them uncomfortably short: enough nail should be left that it stands just proud of the fingertip, following its natural curve. If scissors are difficult, try nail clippers. If your toddler hates having his nails cut he may prefer a nail file or an emery board. If you give him one of his own to use while you use yours, he can soon learn to help.

Your toddler will probably like the feeling of handwashing if you get your own hands soapy first and then take the child's hands between them. Soon he will get the idea of making bubbles by soaping hands. Right now you will have to give a bit of help and watch that soapy fingers don't go near eyes, but by the third year your child will make a good job of doing it alone, especially if he has a box or stool to stand on to reach the basin. Do guard that hot tap though. If there's a chance that your toddler might turn it on alone, you may need to reduce the temperature of the whole domestic hot water supply. 50°C–55°C (120°F–130°F) will not actually scald him, 65°C–70°C (150°F–160°F) may.

Wherever his hands have been, they'll soon be in his mouth. Make handwashing a habit – and fun.

Immunizing toddlers against those mild diseases of childhood is pointless.

Our baby had the polio, Hib and DPT triple vaccine when she was tiny and I must admit that she didn't have any reaction more serious than a coin-sized swelling from the Hib vaccine. She's a year old now, though, and due for another triple vaccine against measles, mumps and rubella (MMR). We've been warned that she might get a mild version of measles about a week after the shot, or a mild version of mumps about three weeks after it. We've also been told that there's a slim but terrifying chance of serious side effects like fever, convulsions or even brain damage. Since the illnesses themselves are usually mild anyway, we can't see the point in having her immunized. If she catches the illnesses she'll be protected for the rest of her life (rather than needing another injection before she starts school) but since they are all quite rare now, the chances are she won't.

It's true that these illnesses are usually milder than the ones she was immunized against as a small baby. In fact German measles (rubella) and even mumps are often so mild that they would not, in themselves merit the protection of immunization. Those injections don't just protect children against the illnesses, though, they also protect them against the complications which can render these infections serious, even fatal. Where children are not immunized against mumps, for example, complications such as deafness are frequent and the mumps virus is the commonest cause of viral meningitis. As for measles, of unimmunized children who catch it, about one in fifteen suffers from complications that may include chest infections, febrile convulsions ("fits") and brain damage. In parts of the world without effective immunization programmes, thousands of children die each year as a result of measles. In the UK there were about 90 such deaths annually before the vaccine was introduced: now a death from measles is a rarity.

The "mild version" of measles or mumps that occasionally results from immunization carries no risk of complications and is therefore more trivial than even the mildest naturally occurring infection. Serious side effects of the MMR vaccine are as bad as the worst complications of the naturally occurring diseases but much, much rarer. About one child in a thousand will have a febrile convulsion after the first injection, but as many as one in a hundred children who have measles will have a febrile convulsion because of it. As to encephalitis: while about one child in a million will have inflammation of the brain after MMR immunization, about one in five thousand will suffer it after measles. About a third of those children will be left with some permanent brain damage.

Many diseases are now rare in countries where most children are routinely protected by immunization. But that does not mean that a child in such a country doesn't need immunizing because she's unlikely to come into contact with specific illnesses. Now that so many people travel abroad, a child may be taken on holiday to countries where infectious diseases are still commonplace, or diseases may be brought in. By immunizing as many people as possible, fewer and fewer people catch these diseases so the diseases become rarer and rarer, and some eventually disappear. But as long as there is even a small reservoir of a particular infection, a dropping off in immunization rates will always increase the risk of the disease making a comeback. In this sense immunization protects the whole community (especially children who cannot be immunized for special health reasons) while it protects your child.

TOILET MASTERY

Sitting her bear on the potty is often a first step towards sitting herself there.

By the time of their first birthdays some babies have adopted quite regular times of day for passing bowel movements – often immediately after (or during!) meals – and since they can also sit steadily by themselves and understand quite a lot of what is said to them, their parents sometimes decide to sit them on potties at these times. People call this "toilet training" but there is no training in it at all. The baby is simply being put in the right place at the right time for the movement to be caught in a pot instead of a nappy.

Catching a baby's motions may seem harmless even if it is not doing anything towards her eventual toilet mastery. But it is a mistake. If you start doing it when she is 12 months old she may not object: the potty will seem no odder to her than some of the other places that you sit her down. But two months later she will probably hate it. She does not want to sit still anywhere for a minute longer than she need, and sitting on a potty seems to her the most pointless kind of sitting of all. When you sit her in her chair she gets something to eat; when you sit her in her buggy she gets to go somewhere; when you sit her on her potty she gets nothing – except the movement which she was going to have anyway. So if you are open to her feelings about the matter, the potty that you introduce early will be abandoned again within a very few weeks. If you try to insist that she sit on that potty, you run a real risk of starting a battle that will actually *delay* your child's readiness to manage her own toileting needs when she is physically able to do so.

If you begin before your toddler is physically ready you will be asking something impossible of her. There is bound to be stress. If you try to insist on co-operation before she is emotionally ready, you will be trying to impose your will on her in an area where you cannot win. There is no way you can force your child to use that potty, so attempting to toilet train her against her will invites her to experience successful defiance.

There are other reasons for avoiding early "training" too. A little frivolous arithmetic will show that however successful you might be at catching your baby's motions, you will not save yourself any time and effort by doing so. Research has shown that no matter when you begin to introduce a baby to a potty, she will, on average, become reliably clean and dry in the daytime by the middle of her third year. Suppose that you start putting her on a potty at 12 months, six times per day: you will have done so 3285 times before you reach your objective – a child who is out of nappies. You will have had to undress and redress her on each occasion (3285 times in *addition* to all those ordinary dressing times) and you will have failed to catch the motion a good many times too so that there will still have been soiled nappies to deal with. If you wait until your child is ready to move towards true toilet mastery – at 24 months, say – you have only to go through this process about 1000 times for the same effect. Since changing used nappies is far quicker than taking (hopefully) unused ones off, offering a potty and putting them on again, you have everything to gain by waiting from your own point of view as well as hers.

Helping your child towards toilet mastery

Although the phrase "toilet training" is deeply embedded in the Western child care tradition, it is a misnomer. The process is not really a matter of training; of making the child do something for you, or to obey you, but a matter of helping her do something for herself. The end result is that she will take autonomous charge of her own toileting: recognizing her own full bladder or bowel and doing something socially acceptable about it, such as telling an adult or going to the toilet or to find her potty.

However early you start, your child is unlikely to be entirely reliable, even in the daytime, before the third year. However late she seems to be in acquiring control, she will not set off for big school in nappies unless some neuro-physiological or emotional problem puts that control beyond ordinary reach.

Until around 15 months old most toddlers move their bowels or pass water without realizing that they are going to or even being aware that they have done so. You can get an idea of where your child has got to in this by watching her if she happens to pee when you take her nappy off or when she is naked. If she does not even look at the puddle she produces it is because she does not realize that it is anything to do with her. She is not yet ready for a potty. But if she regards that puddle with interest, and especially if she clutches herself, she is making the vital connection between the feeling of urination or passing a motion, and the sight of what is produced. A child who knows when he or she *has* performed even without yet knowing what is going to happen in advance, is not ready to *use* a potty but may be ready to meet one.

What kind of potty?

When they decide to give up nappies and take charge of putting their faeces and eventually their urine somewhere else, some children choose to put it where you do: in the toilet. They don't want anything to do with special potties on the floor; they want to get up on the toilet (with the help of a stool) and sit there like a grown-up (on a special seat that won't let them slip through). Right now, though, the toilet isn't a good option for your toddler because she'd have to be taken to the bathroom and lifted on by an adult. She needs a potty to start off with so that she can feel in charge and in control of the whole toileting business.

The child's potty needs to be comfortable to sit down on and feel perfectly secure even if she wriggles while she is sitting. It must be difficult to tip and, of course, easy to clean. A boy needs a shape that shields the front.

A "potty-chair" is a good buy. Sitting down and getting up are easy and there is good back support. The actual pot lifts out for cleaning and taking on trips but with any luck your young toddler won't easily get it out, so spills are minimized. If you can find the kind of potty-chair that is made in the shape of a miniature toilet, it may be worth its extra cost because it's easier for your child to think of herself as being just like you when she's using it. Most other gimmicky potties, such as those that play a tune when used, are of dubious value. If your child likes the tune she will soon learn that a toy that's dropped in produces it just as readily as a bowel movement. And supposing she *hates* music with her motions?

If you want him to sit on that potty, make sure it feels stable and that he can easily get off.

Introducing a potty At this stage you only want to make sure that the child knows what the potty is for and realizes that one day she will use it. Both points are perfectly obvious to you and if she has older brothers or sisters or spends time in a group, they may be obvious to her too. But an only child may be mystified. After all adults use a toilet, not a potty. The two items do not look at all alike.

Show her the potty, tell her that it is for putting whatever she calls urine and faeces in when she is big enough to want to stop wearing nappies. Then put it in a corner of her usual play place (unless she objects) or beside the toilet she most often sees you use. Don't actually encourage her to use the potty as a hat, but if that's what it takes to help her make friends with it, so be it. If she is ready to be interested at all she may sit her teddy bear on (or in) it. Eventually (maybe tomorrow but maybe in six months' time) she will want to sit on it herself. When she does, don't insist on taking her nappies off. She only wants to see what sitting on that potty feels like. She is not ready to use it yet.

Judging when your toddler is ready The right moment to encourage your child to use her pot is soon after she becomes aware when she is *about* to produce urine or a motion, rather than only being aware after the event. A coming bowel motion usually impinges on her first. The child may stand stock still, red in the face and watery-eyed, just as she has done every time she opened her bowels for months. But this time she also clutches herself, looks at you and makes sounds of anticipation. Until today, everyone in the household knew when she was passing a bowel movement *except* her. Now she knows too and if she chooses, she can put that movement in the potty instead of in her nappy. But remember that we are talking only about bowel training and that the choice is, and will remain, the child's.

Helping your toddler take charge of bowel movements Becoming "clean" is far easier for a child than becoming "dry". Most children only move their bowels once or twice a day (if that) and many are naturally regular in their timing, so the whole matter is quickly turned into a once-a-day routine and dealt with for the day. Furthermore, if a toddler *wants* to use that potty, it's easy to help her. The signs of an imminent motion are quite clear to a watching adult, and the interval between the child becoming aware that a motion is imminent and actually passing it gives ample time for her to tell and get to the potty.

Nappies that are still needed for urination can be tiresome to a child who is trying to use the potty for everything else. If you know that your toddler is likely to move her bowels immediately after breakfast or on waking from a nap, it may be helpful to let her stay bare-bottomed at least for a while. Make sure that the pot is in its usual place; wait until she tells or signals that a motion is on the way and then casually suggest that she might like to sit on the potty so that it goes in there.

If the child says "no" (now or in the coming months) don't try to insist, or even go overboard in trying to persuade her. You are trying to help her take charge of herself and she cannot be forced to do that. If she seems to like the idea or even if she does not seem to care either way, produce the potty or remind her where it is, help with her clothes if she asks you, stay with her for as long as she chooses to sit there and be calmly congratulatory if anything happens.

Many toddlers who are introduced to the idea in this casual way and at just the right moment, will stop having bowel movements in their nappies altogether within a couple of weeks. But if your child does not take so readily to the idea, you need to be cautious yourself and to make sure that your partner or carer is cautious too:

■ Don't try to force the child to sit on the potty even if you can see that she is about to have a bowel movement. Toddlers are extremely contra-suggestive. The clearer you make it that you really want her to sit there, the less likely she is to want to. And the more interested you seem to be in what comes out of her, the more likely she is to feel possessive about her faeces and threatened by your desire to flush them down the toilet.

■ Try not to seem especially bothered. It would be better still not to *feel* especially bothered. If you are thrilled when your toddler "succeeds" and disappointed when she "fails", keep your feelings off your face and out of your voice. Above all don't imply that use of the potty is a moral issue by calling her "good" for using it or "naughty" for not doing so. Using a potty instead of nappies is just a new skill which she is learning. Faeces in the potty deserve a quiet word of pleasure about how grown-up she is getting. Faeces in her nappy or on the floor need an equally quiet word of sympathy and the possibility that she might put them in the pot tomorrow.

■ Don't try to make a toddler share your adult disgust at faeces. She has just discovered that they come out of her. She sees them as an interesting product belonging to her. If you wipe her with fastidious fingertips and wrinkled nose; rush to empty the potty and are shocked and angry if she examines or smears the contents, you will hurt her feelings. You don't have to pretend to share her pleasurable interest – discovering that adults don't play with faeces is part of growing up – but don't try to make her feel they are dirty and disgusting. If your child knows her faeces are disgusting to you, she may feel that her whole body disgusts you – and therefore that it (and she) is disgusting.

■ Don't ever try to tamper with the natural bowel pattern unless you are following medical instructions you believe to be necessary. Laxatives to make it "easier" or suppositories to induce a motion at a convenient moment are completely inappropriate. It is her body. If you forcibly tamper with it, she really will feel that you are trying to overwhelm her.

■ Help your toddler to manage for herself but don't leave her to manage alone. If you have not reached this early stage until late in her second year, she will be able to go to the potty herself, manage her clothes with minimal help and get on and off as she thinks fit. Go with her when she asks; sit admiringly by and then get her permission to wipe her bottom for her (remember to go from front to back for a girl so that faeces don't come into contact with her urethra which risks urinary infections) and to empty the potty and clean it. She may prefer you not to flush while she is in the room, but if she likes to flush herself, let her. The more she feels that the whole business is up to her, the better.

Be tactful about flushing. Those are his products. Unless the flush scares him, let him do it for himself.

Your toddler will probably recognize a full bladder at about the same age that she recognizes a coming bowel movement, but doing something about it is far more difficult for her and will probably come considerably later.

When toddlers first start to notice the sensations of a coming pee there's no useful interval before they produce a flood. The exclamation that means "I'm going to" is simultaneous with the puddle. If the first you know of it is "Oh dear!" be sympathetic. It was the first she knew of it too.

But even before your toddler is ready to pee in a potty on purpose, she'll know that urine *can* go in there as well as in a nappy because she'll often pee while she's doing a poo. If she's mastering bowel control easily your toddler may spontaneously add urine control as soon as she is physically capable of it.

She will not be physically able to keep herself dry until there's time for action between knowing she's going to pee and doing it. The first sign of readiness is acquiring the momentary control over coming urine which some older children call "clenching your bottom". The child realizes, just in time, that urine is coming. She clenches the muscles around the urethra and the anus and stops it. Although "clenching your bottom" is a breakthrough, it's not very useful in itself. These muscles are too low down for efficient control; the pressure in the child's abdomen is already high; the urgency is extreme; she can hold on only for a few seconds and only while standing stock still with legs crossed. If she moves towards the potty she will urinate. It may be another three months before your toddler learns to take charge at an earlier stage, by recognizing a full bladder and tightening the muscles of the abdomen. Now she can delay the flow for several minutes and can walk without losing control. Now she can make for the potty – if she wants to.

Even once your child becomes aware that she needs to pee while there is still time to get to the potty, becoming "dry" will probably be a long, slow process and easily becomes boring for all concerned. Children urinate many times a day and on each occasion being absorbed in play can mean a lapse of attention and soaked clothing. And even when a child manages not to wet herself for a whole day, she still can't count herself dry because since she can't wake herself to pee in the night she's got to go on waking up in wet nappies every morning. Unless all the adults who share in her care are extremely tactful and gentle with her about it, your toddler may easily get discouraged and withdraw her co-operation.

Aim for as many "successes" as possible, from the very beginning. Once it is clear that there is time for action between knowing she needs to pee and peeing, pick a day at home when she wakes up from a nap dry, and delay dressing her. Suggest that she sits on her potty but if she does not want to, or sits for a moment and gets up without doing anything, make no comment. Just leave her bare-bottomed, potty to hand, and encourage her to sit there when she feels the need. If she pees in the potty (or during an emergency dash to it), be gently congratulatory. If she gets absorbed in play and makes a puddle, mop it up without comment. Either way, the episode is

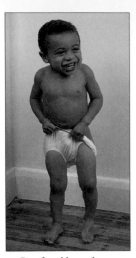

Comfortable and easy to manage, terry trainer pants keep floods off carpets but potties on the agenda.

closed and it's time to get dressed as usual. If the weather is warm, though, and you can leave her naked in the garden, so much the better. In fact it's worth waiting for summer or holiday time if you can. Each experience of feeling and seeing herself urinate will help to clinch the connection between the feeling and what happens next.

After a few days of occasional casual successes and no objections, suggest to the toddler that she can manage without nappies when she is at home and awake, and that you will help her. Don't make a big thing of it or she may feel demeaned by having the nappies back on for outings, naps and the night. Just point out that she will be more comfortable without nappies while she plays, and that if she needs to pee, her potty is close by. Do realize that this is a puddly stage. And do be actually sympathetic about her frequent accidents: "Bad luck, you left it a bit late, didn't you? Let's mop it up..."

Once she uses her potty most of the time at home, consider getting her trainer pants so that she need not wear nappies when she goes out, and so that flood-damage in the home is reduced. Think carefully, though, before you opt for disposable trainer pants. Some of these absorb urine so efficiently, and keep the toddler feeling so dry while they do so, that instead of helping "training", they set it aside. Plastic-backed terry-towelling trainer pants don't take potties and toilets off the agenda because they will not absorb a complete pee, but they are comfortable for the child to wear; easy for her to pull down and up and just absorbent enough to avert embarrassment in public places.

During this stage it is a good idea to introduce the child to the toilet as well as the potty. She, or he, will probably like the idea of doing as you do. If a little boy wants to use the toilet the way Daddy does and stand to pee, but still finds it awkwardly high, he may be happy to sit for a while longer if you remind him that everyone sits on the toilet to do poos. If he's determined to stand, he may prefer to go on using the potty for peeing and use the toilet only for bowel movements. Both boys and girls will need a box or firm step to help them on and off the toilet, and a small seat clipped over the large one so that they do not feel that they are going to fall in. Once children sit on the toilet though, it's even more important to be tactful about flushing. Many children hate the noise and are frightened of the idea of things being sucked away. They have so little idea of the relative sizes of things that they may actually think that they might be flushed away too. So let your child pull the handle herself if she enjoys doing so. If not, leave it until she is out of the bathroom.

Once she is more or less reliable at home in the daytime, abandon nappies as part of her day clothes and make them part of her night wear only. Although you will still get a fair number of pools, giving up nappies, or disposable trainer pants that do the same job, is important. While she still wears them sometimes, your child cannot take it for granted that every feeling of bladder fullness means a trip to her potty or the toilet. You cannot expect her to think, "I'm going to pee in a minute; am I wearing nappies or not?"

With many children, urine training will go smoothly from this point on. You will get fewer and fewer accidents until you suddenly realize that you have stopped taking mopping up for granted as one of your daily tasks. But there are some pitfalls:

■ Don't continually nag and remind your child to sit on the potty. You want her to feel that pants are more comfortable than nappies and that using a potty is quicker and easier than being changed. If you keep nagging, you will make her feel that life was easier when she had those safe old nappies on and that being put into pants has spoiled it all. A lot of reminders don't help anyway. You are trying to help her recognize her own need to go and do something about it for herself. If you keep reminding her, you are doing her thinking for her. You may actually delay the moment when she is fully and independently reliable.

■ Don't expect a toddler to be able to urinate without feeling the need. She will not discover how to urinate when her need is not urgent and therefore recognizable until she is at least three years old, so it is useless to send her to the lavatory before an outing "so that you won't need to go later", and it is bitterly unfair to be cross with her for an accident in the supermarket "because you ought to have gone before we came out..."

■ Cultivate your skill as a lavatory-finder. Once your child wants to stay dry she must be able to rely on you to find her somewhere to pee, quickly, wherever you find yourselves when the need strikes. Note the whereabouts of the facilities in shops and streets where you regularly go. Be patient if you have to get off a bus, leave the motorway, lose your place in the post office queue or come home in a hurry. Get into the habit of carrying a potty when you go out for long periods. And always, *always*, have dry pants available. You are the one who wanted the child to stop wetting herself. Once she has stopped she will be really upset if circumstances keep her waiting so long that she loses control after all.

Lavatory talk   Our language is full of euphemisms for toilets and the functions we perform in them. Adults find it easy to adapt their language to the company they are in, but small children do not. Yours will accept whatever words you use when you first invite them to perform on a potty, and they will go on using the same words for years no matter where they are. So do give those words a bit of thought. An invented baby-name for a bowel movement may seem entirely appropriate for a two-year-old but make you squirm when your child uses it at four and be incomprehensible to her teacher a year later. Correct medical terminology from the beginning may seem the answer, but unfortunately classmates will be mystified and teachers and other parents are likely to giggle if your child announces, "I need to urinate."

There is no general answer to this very minor problem because acceptable terminology will vary from time to time and place to place. Wherever you live there will be a fine line between the over-medical and the vernacular, the acceptable and the rude. It may help to ask parents of older children what words are being used.

Now that your child is no longer a baby, you cannot count on him to drop off to sleep when he needs to, wherever he is and whatever is going on, or to stay asleep while you carry him around. From now on, his sleep needs are going to have to figure in all your plans and will inevitably impose some restrictions on your freedom. To keep those restrictions to a minimum, you need to make some lifestyle decisions now.

Is it more important to you to be free to come and go as you please *with* your baby or to be able to count on being free to come and go *without* him? Within limits either is possible but both are unlikely. If you want to take the baby with you wherever and whenever you go, you can. Your child will be happy to accompany you out to supper with friends, to be taken away for weekends, even to go with you on working trips at home or abroad. If you live and work in a child-friendly world, or have the confidence to insist that any world that wants *you* must be friendly to your child, everyone (and particularly your toddler) stands to gain a great deal. You will have a price to pay, though. A baby who is kept up and taken out and about on occasion to suit your convenience is not very likely to go happily off to bed alone at a conventional hour, just because that is what would suit you tonight. You may find that he hangs around with you until all hours most nights of the week and that his daytime sleep is unpredictable because it depends on how tired he is from those nocturnal junketings. Such lack of routine will not hurt *him* (at least until he has to conform to the outside routines of school) but when you hear all your friends confidently planning to get their children to bed early and meet for an eight o'clock movie, it may hurt *you*.

If you want to be fairly sure of adult peace and privacy in the evenings and of a nap-time break from your child's demanding company during the day, you can set up a regular routine of naps and bedtimes and your baby will come to expect and accept them. But there's a price-tag on that approach too. Routines only work if they are kept to almost all the time. That means fitting days out around his naps and evenings out around his bedtime. It means leaving him at home with a babysitter even on occasions when he'd be welcome where you are going. And it means keeping as close to your workaday patterns as you can even at weekends or when you are on holiday.

Sleeping patterns Most toddlers sleep between 10 and 12 hours at night (though seldom in an unbroken block, unfortunately). The difference between those hours and the child's total sleep requirement is then made up in daytime naps of anything from 20 minutes to three or more hours.

At the beginning of this age period almost every baby will need two daytime naps and most do best if those sleeps are arranged to break up the waking day fairly evenly. If your baby wakes before 6am (which many babies do) he may droop by 9.30am and then need a second rest in the early afternoon.

Around the middle of this second year you may meet an awkward phase when two naps are too many and one is not enough. Your child

Even twins who adopt identical comfort habits may have different sleep needs.

 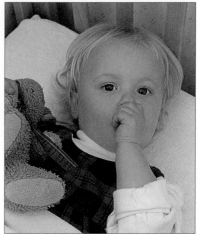

really needs one-and-a-half naps. You may meet a similar difficulty in a further year's time when he may need half a nap.

The toddler makes it clear that he is not ready to go back to bed at the beginning of the morning but that does not mean that he can last all through it. If it's left up to him he'll probably stagger on until midday, getting more and more exhausted and whiny, and finally fall asleep in his highchair over his lunch. If he is put to bed at 11.30 am, because it's obvious that even if he's kept up he's far too tired to eat any lunch, he will go to sleep at once, but exactly the same thing happens in the afternoon. He has his late lunch, does not want to go back to bed during the afternoon, but cannot stay comfortably awake until a reasonable bedtime. You may find yourself serving your child lunch at 11.15 am or putting him to bed for the night at 5.30 pm.

By the end of the second year this awkwardness can usually be resolved into a single nap taken either at the end of the morning before a late lunch, or at the very beginning of the afternoon after an early lunch. You may need to think carefully about which pattern will fit in with your child care arrangements or with your other children. You may not even be in a position to choose because if your child is in a nursery, or with a childminder who cares for another child of similar age, group play and group outings will depend on group naps.

Some two-year-olds are so sensitive to daytime sleep that the timing of their naps is crucial to the lifestyle of the whole household. If yours naps early in the nursery day and then stays awake all afternoon he may need putting to bed the moment you get him home, leaving you no wakeful time to spend with him. On the other hand, some toddlers are so refreshed by even a 10-minute sleep, that if they are allowed to close their eyes after 3pm, bedtime recedes far past a time that is tolerable for parents. You may find yourself *refusing* your child a nap; begging his caregiver to keep him awake – and then being foiled by the ride home because a tired toddler will drop off in a car or a buggy and there's very little you can do to prevent him.

Waking from naps Whether they are at home with a parent or nanny, or being cared for elsewhere, toddlers often have to be woken from naps so that everyone's day can have some pattern. If your child goes to sleep at

If you are going to have to wake your toddler, do it while there's plenty of cuddling time in hand.

11.30am, he might stay asleep until 3pm if it was left to him. Sometimes, perhaps, it can be. If you plan to take him to a party that evening, a long sleep may be just what you would choose for him. But usually group plans prevail and even a one-to-one carer will not find it easy to manage a day with no lunch, cancelled plans for the afternoon, and an older child who needs meeting from school.

Waking your toddler from a nap takes tact and time. He will probably bitterly resent being disturbed, and need at least half an hour of peaceful cuddling and conversation before he feels ready to face the world. If you try to wash or dress him, he will howl. If you hurry him to a meal, he will not eat it. If you rush him off to meet another child from school, he will whine and moan and make it impossible for you to pay proper attention to the school child. So, wake him gently while you still have plenty of time in hand and let him make a gradual transition from being asleep to being awake, from being cocooned in his cot to being loose on the floor.

Getting over-tired

This is a common but underrated problem in this age group. Your toddler is working extremely hard physically, emotionally and intellectually. People who imply otherwise, saying that small children have "nothing to do but play", can never have spent time really watching what that play involves. As your toddler learns to walk and to climb he pushes himself to the limits of his physical strength. Because he is learning he falls down, bumps himself, surprises and hurts himself many times each day. His daily life at this stage must be something like an afternoon spent by an adult learning to water-ski or to skate.

Like the rest of us, the toddler manages his body less and less well as he tires. His physical co-ordination becomes less efficient so that he has to put more and more effort into everything he does, and the more effort he has to make the more tiring it becomes. If you watch a toddler in a public playground, you can see this happening before your eyes. When he arrives, keen and fresh from a rest, the child rushes around managing everything beautifully. Most of the sand that he digs goes into his bucket and he can get three rungs up the climbing frame and laugh when he's pushed on the swing. An hour later it takes him 10 minutes to fill that bucket; all his sandpies break; his hands slip every time he tries to climb and the swing makes him cry. There's an emotional price to pay for "having fun".

Along with the physical efforts he is making to co-ordinate his own body, the child is also striving to understand and manage the world. Why does the swing, swing? What happens to the sand that doesn't stay in his sieve? And why do other children sometimes claim the see-saw when he wants it? That playground is noisy; there are lots of strange adults as well as children; it may frighten him or it may excite him, but it certainly will not relax him.

Physical tiredness, excitement and tension, often intermixed with some frustration and anxiety, can build up to a point where the toddler no longer knows that he is tired, does not see how to stop and rest, and cannot relax anyway. This is a phenomenon every child care worker recognizes – and dreads. Toddlers need rescuing before they reach this point and that's not always easy to manage for several at the same time. Don't assume that a child who is still rushing around is not tired: look at what he is doing and see whether he is finding it more difficult than he was finding it half an hour ago. If he is, then he needs a rest. Don't assume that a child who has difficulty in getting to sleep at night is not getting tired during the day: he may be getting over-tired, and it may be the resulting tension which is keeping him awake. The answer is not necessarily more sleep, but it is probably more rest.

Resting without sleeping

Try to find some ways of giving your toddler both physical rest and relaxation from stress without actually putting him to bed. Quiet occupations that he enjoys now, between bouts of energetic and effortful play, will be useful for years to come. TV – or soon-to-be-favourite videos – are not the obvious prescription they may seem, at least at the beginning of this age period. If TV holds your child's attention at all at 15 or 18 months, he certainly will not find it easy and relaxing.

When two naps are too many and one isn't enough, your child needs to rest without sleeping.

Different families will select their own "resting occupations". Try for some you enjoy yourself because since no self-respecting toddler will sit down alone to anything for more than five minutes, they will almost certainly depend on you doing something with the child. Whether you choose drawing together, doing puzzles or reading aloud, activities that get your exhausted toddler off his feet for 10 minutes today can be the basis for keeping him occupied whenever circumstances make it desirable that he should keep still in the future. And after all, even when he's old enough to relax with a video, he cannot watch TV while you are travelling or sitting in the doctor's waiting room, can he?

SLEEPING PROBLEMS

Many parents believe that every toddler except their own goes peacefully to bed at the right time every night, falls asleep on his own and stays asleep until morning. There is a general belief that if you are kind but firm no night-time fusses should ever happen. It is a myth. When research workers give parents a chance to describe what actually happens in their houses, it becomes clear that at least 50% of all children between the ages of one and two make a major fuss about being put to bed.

Trouble over going to bed at night

The reality is that night after night toddlers are rocked and sat with, cuddled, taken back downstairs, nursed to sleep on parents' beds, fed, scolded and fed again. In the real world many parents will do almost anything to avoid a fuss at bedtime. It wrecks the evening for the whole family and is especially likely to be the last straw for parents who have been at work all day and desperately need not only peace for themselves, but also assurance that their child has not missed them too much. With a meal to be prepared and eaten, news (or at least evidence of togetherness) to be exchanged and possibly older children needing attention, most parents will do whatever it takes to get that toddler to settle down quietly. They know that bringing the child downstairs again is not really a solution but if it works for tonight, that is good enough – until tomorrow.

Teaching your toddler how to go to sleep without you

If you have always nursed or rocked your baby to sleep, you may not be having nightly commotions but you are probably finding that getting him to sleep takes longer and longer. He can keep himself awake in your arms for more and more songs and he can snap from apparent slumber into furious wakefulness the moment you try to put him into his cot. With the whole performance to be repeated every time he wakes in the night, you would probably be sensible to try and teach him to drop off by himself even if it seems to make your evenings worse for a while (see p.257). The longer you go on nursing him to sleep, the more difficult it will be to teach him to do it for himself. In a few months' time he will not just cry if you try to leave him while he is awake: he'll beg for what he is used to with pathetic cries of, "Up-up Mum" and commands to, "Walk about." Leave it another year or more and he'll climb out of his cot and follow you.

If your toddler has a bottle, giving him one in his cot and letting him suck himself to sleep is a temptingly easy way to teach him to drop off on his own. If the appalling effects on teeth and the (faint) possibility of choking aren't enough to put you off, think about what will happen when he wakes up later in the night. Having gone to sleep with one bottle of milk he is almost bound to demand another whenever he awakens. Some babies get through three bottles a night in that way – bottles an adult has to fetch and maybe warm. If only sucking seems to bridge the gap for your toddler between your departure and his falling asleep, and he isn't interested in sucking his own thumb, a dummy might be a better solution (see p.186).

Making your toddler let you go

Leaving your child sad means a gloomy evening for everyone. Help her feel it's all right to let you go.

Teaching your baby *how* to calm himself and drop off to sleep without adult help is one thing; persuading him to do it is often quite another. Even if he doesn't need you to rock him or rub his back, he may prefer you to stay with him – and say so, loudly. Parents used to be told that a little firmness would quickly resolve this conflict of interest. If they would settle the child down, leave and stay out of the room however much he cried, he might cry for two hours the first night but it would be one hour the next, then half an hour and then peace every evening. Although this cold-turkey method seemed to work perfectly for some families, nobody knows how many parents really went all the way with it so the success rate remains a matter for speculation. Some of those who thought it had worked found that the peace bought by a week of misery only lasted until the next tooth or stuffed up nose; others went as far as they were prepared to and never got from misery to peace. If you look at it from the toddler's point of view it is difficult to see why it *should* work. Your toddler cries because, for the moment, he cannot bear you to go away. So what messages do you send to him by going away and staying away despite his howls? "It's no good you crying because I *have* gone away forever/nobody's listening/I'm not going to come back no matter how sad you are..." None of those is likely to make him feel safer about bedtime tomorrow; in fact they are surely likely to increase his unease about letting you go at all.

Most of the sleep experts who advocated this plan have softened their recommendations and it's just as well. A determined toddler can keep himself awake and crying for much longer than most parents (or their neighbours) can stand. And if you are going to have to go to him in two or three hours' time, when he is convinced that you have abandoned him forever, you had much better go now.

Letting your toddler make you stay The opposite approach is to give the toddler what he wants, by staying with him or taking him back downstairs. Although it is kinder than leaving him to cry, it is not really any more sensible if you think again about the message your behaviour will convey to him. "You're scared of being left and you're right, it is worrying to be left all alone so I'll stay with you/take you with me..." Once again this is not a message likely to make for easier bedtimes later on. How can the child come to believe that it is perfectly all right to be left to go to sleep if you suggest otherwise? And how can he accept that bedtime is the end of his day if he has nightly proof that crying will get him an extension?

The middle path The approach recommended for older babies (see p.258) can serve as a compromise that will solve the conflict of interests between you and your toddler rather than requiring a power struggle. After all, you don't really want to win a battle that leaves your child desperately alone, and you certainly don't want him to win some more daytime. What you want is for him to settle *happily*. The message you're sending is something like this: "There is no need to cry; nothing to be sad about. We are right here and will always come if you need us. But it is the end of today and time for you to go to sleep."

Settle the child down cheerfully, going through your usual "goodnight" rituals. Leave confidently, and if he cries wait a few seconds to see if it is just a protest statement. If it's not, and the crying starts to build up, go back into the room, reassure him: "It's all right, off to sleep now." Repeat just that last "goodnight" and leave again.

Repeat this performance (allowing for the burning vegetables) for as long as it takes the toddler to settle down. As long as he is unhappy enough alone to cry, one of you visits every few minutes. But however angrily or pathetically he cries, each visit consists only of that brief reassurance and reiterated "goodnight". "I am still here," you are saying, "but there's no more of today."

Don't stay away for more than three minutes at a time (which is longer than it sounds!) or stay in the room for more than 30 seconds, or get cross, or, above all, get the toddler out of his cot.

Do try to get the toddler to realize that you are always around, but that at this time of day you are completely boring.

It sometimes takes as much as a week for this approach to work. If it takes longer than that it will probably be because you weakened. If you get so fed up one night that you decide to leave your toddler crying alone after all, you will have to do all over again the whole job of convincing him that it's safe to let you go. Equally, if you cannot stand going backwards and forwards to him any longer and decide to take the toddler back to the living room, you'll have to start again on convincing him that once he's in bed for the night he stays there.

An even easier alternative Since he is likely to be harder to convince the second (or seventh) time, it's sensible not to embark on this plan unless you are both really determined to go through with it whatever happens. If you are doubtful whether you can, why not try a plan that's easier for your toddler (and not too time-consuming for you) for the moment, and hope it works so well that you never have to try anything else?

If your toddler will lie peacefully as long as you stay with him, you could try sitting by the cot until he is asleep for a few nights, then making a strategic withdrawal to sit by the window, and then gradually increasing your separateness by tidying first his room and then the nearby bathroom. Once he can stay relaxed and let himself get sleepy with you a *little* distance away, you're on the way to calm separation as long as you increase that distance gradually. Don't hurry, though. If you can leave the room as soon as you have settled him down in a week, and get straight on with your adult life after two weeks, you're doing well.

Waking in the night Although your child is now old enough to keep himself awake on purpose he still cannot (and never will be able to) wake himself on purpose. Waking up in the night is not a "habit". You cannot teach your child not to do it, either by ignoring him when he wakes or by scolding him for it. In fact, night waking has nothing to do with discipline, and parents who tell you, smugly, that their children know better, are fooling themselves. Don't let them fool you.

Waking without fear All children surface several times each night and usually turn over. If nothing interests or disturbs them, they drop straight down into sleep again without anyone ever knowing that they have woken. If your child insists that you know about all his awakenings in the night, even though he can put himself to sleep without your help at nap times and bedtimes, check some of the following:

■ Do you wake and go into the room whenever he murmurs or moves? You may be disturbing him. If a toddler appears to sleep much better when father rather than mother is in charge, it's almost always because *father* sleeps better. Your child is not a fragile little baby any more: if he wants you, he will let you know.

■ Does your toddler go to sleep on top of the bedclothes and then get cold in the small hours? If so, either put him in a sleeping bag or blanket sleeper or keep a separate cot blanket to drape over him and his toys at your own bedtime.

■ Does your toddler's room get pitch dark on moonless nights? If so, give him a 15-watt night light. It will not stop him waking, but it may stop him needing to call you when he does wake.

■ Does he use – and lose – a dummy? If he does, put two or three dummies close beside him when you go to bed. If you are exceptionally lucky he will be able to find one without crying for you or it.

■ Is he being disturbed by outside sounds? As with a younger child some room re-allocation and sound-proofing may help.

■ Does your toddler get hungry in the night? Some toddlers are so tired by bedtime that they cannot eat as much supper as they need. Breakfast then seems a long way off. An earlier meal with a drink of milk and a snack at bedtime may be a better pattern in these months.

■ Does your toddler get thirsty? A few parents, even at this early age, believe that restricting evening drinks will help nappies do their job. It won't. If the brand you are using leaks, change brands. Your child must drink as much as he wants right up until bedtime.

Waking up afraid This is the more usual kind of night waking. Nearly half of every group of toddlers studied by research workers suffers from it. The waking is due to some form of nightmare, but of course we don't know what the child dreams, thinks of or sees while asleep.

Some children wake up terrified several times each night for a while and then not at all for months. Others wake three or four times a week for months on end.

The waking may take the form of instant panic, so that you find the child sitting bolt upright in the cot, clearly terrified. On other occasions it is as if he is grief-stricken, so that you find him lying down, crying as if something dreadful had happened.

Either way, if you arrive quickly the drama is usually over in 30 seconds. One glimpse of your familiar figure, one soothing pat and the child is asleep again. He remembers nothing about it in the morning. If you don't arrive quickly, though, things tend to go from bad to worse. The toddler becomes more and more afraid as he listens to his own frightened voice crying in the night-quiet. When you do come to him he is shaky, tense and sobbing. Instead of being reassured by a glimpse and a pat, he may need 15 or even 30 minutes' cuddling and talk before he can settle into sleep again.

Dealing with nightmares Coping with the nightmares is simple: you just get to the child as fast as you can the moment you hear him crying. But preventing them is much more difficult; and it is prevention you will long for when you have had to haul yourself out of bed in the small hours eight nights in a row.

Beware of suggestions such as tiring the child out during the day or giving him more to eat at supper-time. An over-tired child, or one who has been encouraged to eat more than he actually wanted, is more, rather than less likely to have bad dreams. Sometimes a more general approach to the child-as-a-whole does seem effective, though. We do not know exactly what causes nightmares either in toddlers or in older people, but we do know that they are often associated with anxiety and stress. If your toddler is finding some aspect of his life particularly stressful and you can relieve that stress a little, the nightmares may become less frequent. And even if they don't, he'll still be better off.

Is there a new baby present or imminent? Have your work and child care arrangements recently changed? Is his father away from home a great deal at present? Has his special teacher at nursery just left? Any radical change in a toddler's small world is liable to have made him anxious whether he shows it during the day or not. You may not be able to remove the cause of his distress but you can probably help him cope with it, by being extra-loving and tolerant and, perhaps, by talking to him about what is happening. Even a child who does not yet use many words often understands enough of that complex mix of words and voice-tones we call language to be reassured by a simple acknowledgment from his parents that they know he is upset and understand why.

Have your toddler's desire for independence and autonomy, and your determination to socialize him, landed you. in the thick of battles about food or potties or "disobedience"? However hard he fights you while he is awake, a baby-bit of any child in this age group is liable to be worried by battles with parents or people who stand in for parents. The more displeasure he evokes the more he feels he's risking. If you can possibly relax the peak demands you are making on him for a while, and assure him that he can cope and is coping with everything you want of him, he may feel safer.

Have you just returned from a holiday? Has he been in hospital or ill for a long time at home? Happenings which temporarily take him away from home or break up his accustomed routine can have a disturbing effect. Sticking carefully to a more than usually rigid nursery-type routine for a few weeks may give him back a feeling of structured security.

All these suggestions really add up to the same idea: that a toddler who is having a lot of nightmares may benefit from being treated, for a while, as if he were a little younger than he really is. Something is making him feel worried and unable to cope with the demands made by his life. Baby him a little so that he can meet all demands with ease, and the nightmares will probably diminish.

Night wandering Late in the second year a new reason for not leaving your toddler to cry alone at night often emerges: if you will not go to him, he will learn to come to you. Climbing out of his cot at night is a development to be avoided at all costs. It is dangerous in itself because the cot sides are high for a toddler. And it can land him in danger because if he gets out safely without you hearing, he is loose and unsupervised around the house. But physical danger is not the only consideration. If your child discovers that he can get out of bed and come to find you while he is still too young to understand that he should not, he will probably do so night after night. It is disturbing enough if he keeps appearing in the living room; worse if you never know when he is going to appear in your bedroom. If your toddler is going to share your bed it is both safer and less stressful for everyone if you decide that it is so and arrange things accordingly.

Preventing night wandering The best way to prevent a child climbing out of his cot is to prevent him ever considering the possibility. Once it occurs to him to try, the combination of persistence and rapid growth that is typical of toddlers will probably keep him trying until he succeeds. Make sure that he has no strong motive, and sees no easy possibility.

If he knows that someone will come if he cries, whether it is before he has fallen asleep or during the night, he will not have an urgent and desperate reason for trying to get out. The times when he is most likely to try to come to you are the times when you have refused to come to him.

If he is never taken back into the living room during the evening, or into your bed during the night, he will not have an alluring picture in his mind of the companionable pleasures he is missing by being in his cot. It is the toddlers who can envisage a cosy family group, or an even cosier sleeping couple, from which they are excluded, who try hardest to get out of bed.

Two simple pieces of parent-upmanship are also worth considering. If your toddler wears a sleeping bag, and has worn one for as long as he can remember, he will know that he cannot walk about until someone has taken it off, so he will call rather than trying to set off. And if a cot with an adjustable height base is set to its lower position as soon as he can pull himself to standing, and there are no big toys he might stand on in it, the sides will always seem to him unscalable.

Dealing with night wandering

If the night wandering habit does start, it is extremely difficult to break. Only physical restraints will certainly keep toddlers in bed if they are bent on escape, and physical restraints are unacceptable. Locking the bedroom door, stretching netting (or even something prettied up and called a "sleeping tent") over the top of the cot, or putting a child to sleep in a safety-harness, are all potentially dangerous, emotionally as well as physically. They are short-sighted responses to the problem, too. Keeping your toddler in his cot by force guarantees that he will come to regard going to bed as imprisonment. Once that happens there is little hope of contented bedtimes and peaceful nights.

Unfortunately *teaching* your child not to get out is a notoriously uncertain undertaking with someone in this age group. You are most likely to succeed if you make absolutely sure that your toddler gains nothing by his exploits that he cannot get by calling. Try to make sure that you hear the moment he starts to climb (you will probably need a baby monitor, turned up rather high) so that you can meet him before he so much as reaches his bedroom door. If he is always put instantly back to bed again, he will probably give up.

Even without quite such a quick response you can make sure that night wandering does not get him anywhere desirable. If he appears in the living room, hustle him straight back to bed; do not give him even two seconds to be charming. If he appears in your bedroom, take him straight back to his own. Letting him cuddle in beside you is asking for nightly repeat performances.

If a cot with sides he can't climb over and parents who come when he calls are the basic equipment for keeping a toddler in bed, it follows that this is not yet the ideal time to promote him to a "big bed" (see p.462). If there is a new baby on the way, plan to buy or to borrow a second cot.

Early waking

Early-morning waking is even more common amongst toddlers than amongst younger babies, but it is often easier to live with. Most toddlers are at their best and most cheerful first thing in the morning. If yours wakes you up at 6am, it is more likely to be with loud conversation or song than with crying or grumbling. Some toddlers will simply occupy themselves with talk: bouncing their cots around and bossing their teddy bears about. Others welcome visits from any available older children, swapping charm for service until the grown-up world appears. If your toddler insists on you coming to him, try one of the following:

■ Leave some toys and books beside his cot when you go to bed. Simply getting them through the bars will occupy him for a long time.
■ Make sure there is enough light. It's hard to keep it out in summer but in winter leave on a low-wattage night-light.
■ Teach the toddler to recognize a signal which means it is a time that your household counts as morning. If he knows he can expect one of you as soon as he hears your alarm clock going off or the radio going on, he may actually be willing to wait until it does.

Occupation for your toddler in the morning may mean an extra half-hour's sleep for you.

CRYING AND
COMFORTING

Toddlers tend to live on an emotional see-saw with anxiety and tears on one end and frustration and tantrums on the other. Their feelings, positive and negative, are as powerful at this age as they will ever be and they often seem even stronger because they are so very new. If your toddler sometimes seems so easily upset or offended that it is really difficult *not* to be upsetting or offensive, it may help to think of her as someone who hasn't yet had time to get used to what she feels. She is painfully sensitive because she has not yet had time to grow a protective skin over her feelings; she has not had enough experience to know how to cope with them; she cannot control herself.

If you think coping with your tantruming toddler is stressful, try two setting each other off in turns.

Adults who talk disparagingly of "the terrible twos" are usually reacting to the violent expressions of negative emotion that are typical of this age period, and ignoring the glorious expressions of positive feeling that are equally typical. Your toddler is probably as quick to laughter as to tears; as dramatic in displays of love as hate; as thrilled by her own unexpected triumphs as she is downcast by disasters. And if she is self-centred and liable to embarrass you with public tantrums, she is also enormously affectionate and funny.

Most of a toddler's troubles, tears and tantrums arise from a basic contradiction in what she wants from the adult world. The desire to be independent, to shake off parents' absolute control and become a person in her own right, weighs down one end of the emotional see-saw. The contradictory desire to go on being a baby, who can absolutely depend on continual protection from the adult world, weighs down the other end. Day-by-day, hour-by-hour, even minute-by-minute that see-saw goes up and down. One moment the toddler demands autonomy with shouts of "me do" and "go 'way!" The next moment she turns back into a baby again, weeping bitterly because you have left the room.

That see-saw can only be kept in balance by somebody standing in the middle, adjusting to these rapidly changing emotional needs and damping them down so that neither end hits bottom. If you surround your toddler with too much close care and protection, her need for increasing independence to go with her increasing maturity will break out in anger and frustration. If you give her too much space, so that she doesn't just feel independent but lonely and uncared for, the need to be close and protected will break out in separation anxiety. Keeping an approximate balance between the two is the essence of your job as a parent and of what you should be asking of anyone else who takes care of your toddler.

ANXIETY AND FEARS

Anxiety and fear are normal human emotions but they are not comfortable ones. As we grow up we learn to cope with most situations that make us anxious and to avoid most of the things we are frightened of. But your toddler has scarcely begun that process. Right now she lacks the experience to employ protective strategies for herself and the power to force adults to do it for her.

A toddler who is anxious when she is left alone at night will probably have developed comfort habits that help her manage those uncomfortable feelings, like sucking her teddy bear's arm or twiddling her cuddly around her ear. But even those simple defences are not truly in her own power. If a jealous older sister hides that teddy bear or the cuddly gets lost at the supermarket, there is nothing she can do about it – except cry.

If she feels worried when you leave the room without her during the day, she can usually keep her anxiety level down by following you. But if you go into the bathroom and lock the door, she is powerless. She can never be quite sure of being allowed to feel safe.

It doesn't always take clear-cut outside events to make your toddler feel anxious, though; her own feelings, sliding out of control, are often more scary than their original cause. She is annoyed with you for taking away that screwdriver, but the anger, which she intended to frighten you, frightens her as it builds up. If you will change the mood, the anger and the anxiety will die down, but she cannot make you. There is nothing she can do to stop you answering her anger with your own until she is driven into a frenzy of furious fear. She needs adult help in managing her feelings.

Helping your toddler cope The very first step in giving a toddler this kind of emotional support is to get into the habit of tuning in to her, watching and listening closely to her, so that you pick up all the clues that she can give out as to what her feelings *are*. It will be a long time yet before she can take you by the hand and say, "Daddy, I'm scared those dogs might come rushing over" or, "I don't usually mind thunder but this lot is just *too* close." In the meantime you have to notice without being told. Not all adults (even parents) always take notice of even the most obvious clues to toddlers' feelings. Next time you are at the beach or in a public playground, turn yourself into an observer and count up the number of instances you see and hear of children crying, screaming or shouting fears that adults blandly ignore. You may be shocked to find how many adults you hear saying things like: "You aren't scared of that"; "You like it really, you know you do...", sometimes while forcing a passionately resisting child into the water or higher on a swing. Of course these phrases are only a "manner of speaking". Of course adults don't really mean to suggest that they know what children feel better than the children know themselves. But toddlers are not acquainted with "manners of speaking"; to them it must often seem that the adult world not only refuses to empathize with their feelings but is also incapable of understanding the word "no" however loudly it is shouted.

If ignoring a toddler's feelings is unhelpful, provoking them is unkind. Unfortunately it is always the individuals who "rise" most easily who get teased the most, and nobody but an adolescent rises more readily than a toddler. It's one thing to be (privately) amused by the little dance of fury that precedes your toddler's tantrums, quite another to provoke it for your own amusement. It's fine to play chase games while she screams in mock-fear but cruel to carry on for one second once that fear is real. And of course it's great to rough-house and tickle and laugh, but never past protest or into hysteria.

Clues to anxiety and stress If your toddler is feeling rather anxious about life, a little pressured, perhaps, to grow up faster than she feels she easily can, you may see some of the following signs:
■ She will probably be more clingy than usual, choosing to go with you rather than to stay in the room alone; choosing to hold your hand rather than to run ahead; choosing to sit on your lap or your hip rather than on a chair or the floor.
■ She may seem extra "good" – or less "naughty" than usual. She is feeling extra-dependent on you so whenever she can remember what it is that you like her to do, she tries to do it. She does not feel very adventurous either so she isn't tempted to get up to much mischief.
■ Anxiety will probably show clearly when she is in strange places

and with people she does not know very well. If her own teacher is on holiday she may not want to stay at day care. If you take her out to tea, she may turn shy and spend all afternoon with her head in your lap. Even a new park doesn't make her want to explore because she's too busy keeping close to you so as not to get lost.

If you pick up this kind of cue from your toddler, try to arrange for all the adults who are important to her to offer large extra rations of affection, attention and protection for a few days or weeks. If you caught it in time, the see-saw may swing back to the level again. If it carries on tipping further into anxiety, you will probably begin to see more definite signs:

■ The toddler may have new or extra difficulty in going to sleep. She may build up her bedtime rituals; add new members to the family of comfort creatures in her cot; cry piteously to have the light left on and call you, endlessly, after you have left her.

■ She may enter a phase of nightmares (see p.363).

■ She may seem to lose enthusiasm for food, preferring the more "babyish" items in her diet and refusing to feed herself as independently as before.

Once a toddler's general anxiety is at a high enough level for it to affect sleeping and eating, she is very likely to produce sudden fears of specific things. It is as if all that general anxiety bottled up inside is looking for a means of expressing itself.

Handling specific fears

When your child meets a new creature, introduce him, but don't insist he makes friends.

When toddlers have fears that parents feel are "reasonable" they are usually handled gently. Nightmares, for example, frighten us all, so the child who wakes screaming, sweating and shaky will usually receive instant sympathy and comfort. But many toddler fears do not seem "reasonable" to adults. Instead of sympathy, frightened toddlers may get only exhortations not to be "silly".

If your child shows fear, accept that fear. It may not seem reasonable to you, but what has reason got to do with fear? You may not share it, but you are not the one who is feeling it. If you find yourself tempted to scoff, think over your own private fears and ask yourself whether they are all "reasonable" and how you would feel if you were not allowed to avoid their causes. Do you, for example, like large, harmless spiders?

It is helpful to tell your toddler when there is (truthfully) nothing to fear, but it is not helpful to tell her not to be afraid. If you say, "It will not hurt you, but I can see it frightens you so we won't go any closer," your child will feel that you are on her side. If you say, "There's nothing to be frightened of, you silly girl," you offer neither reassurance nor support.

Most toddler fears are based on a natural and self-protective fear of things that are strange. Small children tend to be wary of new things until those things have proved themselves harmless. Since most things in the environment either provide this proof or go away, fears often pass as suddenly as they appeared. But some fears do not vanish so easily especially if they are not handled tactfully. Instead of coming to terms with the strange thing, making it part of the familiar world and accepting it, the toddler focuses more and more fear on it until it turns into the kind of fear which is technically called a phobia.

Phobias Phobias in small children are very common and do not necessarily suggest that there is anything unusually amiss. The world is a frightening place to a toddler. There are a great many things which she cannot yet understand or cope with. It is not surprising that general fears sometimes become focused in this way. More than half of all children develop at least one phobia during their second and third years and a large number of them share fears of the same things. In Western countries dogs head the list. Darkness and the wide variety of monsters that flourish there come a close second. Insects and reptiles, especially snakes, come next, and loud noises like fire-alarm bells and ambulance sirens come after those.

Phobias are different from ordinary fears. A child who is simply afraid of dogs, for example, will show her fear when, and only when, she meets a dog. The rest of the time out of sight is out of mind. Fears like this usually vanish when (and if) the child discovers that dogs are not hurtful. If she does not make this discovery spontaneously, you may be able to help by showing her the tiny puppies in the pet shop window or your neighbour's furry poodle safely on a lead.

A phobia of dogs works on the child through her new imagination. She is not only afraid when she meets a dog, she is afraid when she sees one in the distance, looks at a picture of a dog or even thinks about one. She not only tries to avoid going where she knows there are dogs, she tries to avoid going where dogs might be. If the phobia becomes very acute she may have to ride in her buggy in the street in case a dog should come by; keep out of the park because dogs may be playing there; abandon a beloved picture book because there is a dog on page four and throw her toy monkey out of her cot because at night it reminds her of a dog.

Handling phobias Phobias are not open to rational explanations because it is not the dog-in-reality that is causing the trouble, it is the dog-in-her-mind. You cannot help your child to get over this particular kind of fear by showing her that the thing she fears is harmless. Taking her to visit that charming puppy or poodle is counter-productive because such a visit will make your toddler feel so overwhelmingly afraid that her phobia is likely to be strengthened. For her, dogs *are* to be feared because dogs make her feel those horrible fear-feelings.

Since provoking more fear can only make matters worse it's best to tackle phobias only indirectly; by trying to lower her general level of anxiety to a point where she no longer has so much fear inside her that she needs to focus it on something:

■ Help your toddler to avoid the fearful thing but be careful not to let your behaviour suggest to her that you are also frightened of it. If she wants to climb into her buggy in case there should be a dog in the street, let her do so, but make it clear that you are only giving her a ride because you understand that she is frightened, not because you feel there is any genuine danger. Fear is very infectious.

■ Look for specific causes of stress in her life (see p.363) and see what can be done to lessen the strain. You obviously cannot get rid of that new baby but you may be able to help the toddler with her feelings about her (see p.427).

■ If you can find no specific cause, baby the toddler for a while. It may well be that she has forged ahead in growing up and becoming independent faster than is really comfortable for her. The see-saw has hit the ground on the anxiety/fear side and you will have to work at making her feel safe again.

■ If the phobia is taking over family life, limiting the toddler's play and making it impossible for her to go to places she used to like or to do things that she used to enjoy, seek help through your local clinic or through your doctor.

Bravery and fearlessness

Sometimes parents find it difficult to handle their children's anxiety, fears and phobias with sympathy and sensitivity because they cannot accept that it is normal for a toddler to have any at all. Some parents are actually ashamed of the child whom they see as a "coward", a "wimp" or a "cry-baby", especially, even today, if that child is a boy.

It may be helpful to sort out in your minds the very real difference between being brave and being fearless. Being brave means doing or facing something that frightens you so a brave child is, by definition, afraid... It may be perfectly appropriate to ask your child to be brave about an injection or a thunderstorm, but if you do it's surely only fair to acknowledge that she is afraid, and make it clear that you recognize and appreciate the effort she is making. Refusing to allow her to express her fear will not help your child to behave bravely this time. Refusing to admit that there was anything to fear and be brave about in the first place will not help her to behave bravely next time.

When your toddler wants to go adventuring alone, give her as much freedom as you safely can.

A child who is fearless is, by definition, *not* afraid, so if a fearless child is what you want, don't frighten her. Trying to make a child adventurous and fearless by forcing her to do things that frighten her is a contradiction. If you carry your child, screaming, into the swimming pool or into the sea because you want her to be fearless in the water, you are really asking her to be brave – very brave. The more you demand brave behaviour from a toddler, especially if you also demand that she conceal her fears, the more frightened she will become and the more effort it will cost her to behave as you wish.

If many demands of this kind are made on her, your toddler may suffer from so much fear and anxiety that she becomes less and less the fearless child you yearn for. Continual stress may tip her emotional see-saw further and further away from the independence you are trying to encourage, dropping her down towards clingy dependence. Things can reach such a pitch that it is impossible for her to be the adventurous, autonomous small person you'd like her to be because your demands keep her so busy trying to get your protection and support.

INDEPENDENCE AND FRUSTRATION

Your toddler is rapidly developing a sense of being a separate independent person with personal rights, preferences and ploys. She no longer sees herself as part of you, so she no longer easily accepts your total control over her life. She wants to assert herself and it is right that she should do so. Her "wilfulness" is a sign that she is growing up and that she feels secure enough at present to try to manage things for herself.

Toddlers like to be together but need adults to help them avoid hurtful tit-for-tat.

But life is very difficult for a toddler to manage. She does not understand things very well yet; she often wants to do things which the adult world cannot allow and she is still very small and physically incompetent. Her efforts at independence inevitably lead to frustration. While some frustration is inevitable, too much can damage the toddler's self-esteem and make her waste time and energy in fury which she could better spend in learning.

Frustration by adults

Adults can easily frustrate a toddler's new sense of independence, her feelings about herself as a separate person and her sense of dignity. As soon as she feels harried, bullied, pressured, she digs her heels in. Any issue will do for a row. It can be her pot or her clothes, her food or her bed. If she feels you insisting, she will resist. But if she feels she is being allowed a measure of choice and control over her own life she will use that pot (maybe), eat the food (probably), stay in bed (usually), come when she is called, leave when she is told and love it.

However respectful adults are of her feelings, there will be innumerable occasions when your toddler has to be prevented from doing what she wants or made to do what she would not choose. The more comfortably she can go along with necessary compulsion the more she will learn from it, so cultivate not only obvious virtues like tact, humour and patience, but also talent as an actor too. Are you in a hurry to get home? Swoop the toddler into her buggy when she wanted to walk and all hell will be let loose. However, act as if you had all the time in the world but offer, just for fun, to be a horse and pull her, and you will get home as fast as she can persuade you to run.

Frustration by other children

Toddlers – even babies – are often deeply interested in other children in their own age group. Given the opportunity, many make real and lasting friendships. But even the best of toddler friends are often frustrating and hurtful to each other, because they cannot yet put themselves in each other's shoes so as to understand each other's feelings. If they both want the same toy, the chances are that the dominant member of the pair will take it, the other will cry and adults will feel vaguely displeased with both of them. If one longs to hug and the other doesn't want to *be* hugged, you may be hard put

to it to decide which you are more sorry for. Social skills will develop with practice. In the meantime, don't expect toddlers to sort things out for themselves. They need adults to keep the peace and to explain them to each other. There's nothing useful to be learned from pulling hair and being bitten.

Frustration by objects
The objects your toddler tries to use often refuse to behave as she wishes because she is not yet very strong and her fine co-ordination is still not always accurate. Battles with objects or with frustrating toys are often educational. The toddler is finding out what things will and will not do and this is essential information for her. She may be frustrated because she cannot force her rectangular bricks into the round holes of a hammer-peg toy. But the fact that square pegs will not fit into the round holes is something she must learn; there is no point in concealing such facts from her.

They can't yet put themselves in each other's shoes but if you explain them to each other they can start again.

A little frustration of this kind will keep your toddler trying and keep her learning. But too much works the opposite way. If she often faces impossible tasks all alone and therefore often meets total failure, she will give up. Be ready to step in and help when (and only when) you can see and hear that your toddler is becoming more and more frustrated and therefore less and less efficient. Even at that point, try to see what her problem is and to offer the minimum help that will enable her to succeed; just doing it for her is not helpful.

The frustration of being so small

When a toddler understands what objects are supposed to do, understands how to make them do it, but cannot manage because she is not big or strong enough, she needs help. There is no pleasure or learning in such a situation, only grief and giving up. Children do not need rooms full of expensive toys, either for their pleasure or for their development. But they do need the equipment they do have to be physically appropriate for them. The toddler may long to push her sister's doll's pram but be too small to reach the handle. She may long to throw her brother's football but be too light to manage its weight. If she cannot have a toddle-truck or a pram of her own, and an inflatable beach ball or plastic "football", she is better off with none at all until she is bigger. If she is to feel as big and strong and competent as possible to manage her world, when most of that world is unmanageably large, it's important that her own possessions, at least, should be in scale with her.

One day she'll be as big as them, but today their game just doesn't fit her.

Any toddler who bites or hits should be bitten or hit back.

The woman whose toddler bit my one-year-old was obviously concerned, but although she apologised she didn't punish him, and when I suggested it she only carried on about him being upset by his new baby brother. Trying to understand children's feelings and why they behave the way they do is fine if it helps to prevent them doing wrong (I'd have had some sympathy if she'd given her little bruiser something to bite and vent his anger on) but, while I admit I wanted to see that child punished because he hurt mine, I think parents like her have lost sight of the basis of discipline: punishing a child who does wrong in an appropriate way. My little boy has already had a dirty mouth washed out with soap and if he ever bites anyone I shall bite him back to show him what it's like.

Biting is the aggressive toddler behaviour most parents dread the most. Throwing heavy objects, even kicking, may be more dangerous, but biting hurts feelings as well as flesh, terrorizing victims and enraging their parents. Biters are sometimes excluded from day care, playgroup or nursery school and their parents made to feel like pariahs. Punitive reactions to biting are therefore much commoner than to other kinds of misbehaviour. Your response to infantile bad language is unusual but the "bite him back" argument is familiar and understandable although it's still wrong-headed.

When a baby or small child bites he must immediately be given to understand that biting is not acceptable. Teeth (and "claws") are natural weapons for all young mammals so children don't know "by instinct" that biting (and pinching and pulling hair) is forbidden. You convey that by removing your baby from the breast with a firm "no biting", or putting your toddler down from your lap or away from another child with the same message. He doesn't have to understand *why*

he is not to bite as long as he understands that he's not to. Even if you don't find the idea of an adult biting a small child barbaric, doing it to "show him what it's like" is as pointless as it's painful because he won't get the point. Three is the earliest a child is likely to be able to put himself into another child's shoes sufficiently to see any connection between what they do and what is done to them, what they make others feel and what they feel themselves.

In fact, because children do most of their social learning by example, biting back (or similar painful punishments) make it much more difficult for them to learn not to be violent. How can a child learn that biting is beyond the pale if his parents do it? To become assertive but non-aggressive, children need to know that it's *never* acceptable for anyone (in the family, day care, or the classroom) to hurt another person on purpose. Hitting back in retaliation isn't acceptable between children, and neither is the kind of retaliation we call punishment between adult and child.

If being violently punished makes children more likely to be violent, so does being encouraged to "take it out" on a special cushion or punch-bag. Harmless violence is still violence. Although the activity may divert an aggressive child from his intended victim this time, it confirms his tendency to react physically next time he is angry or frustrated. He needs adults to show clear disapproval of *all* violence.

Biting must be stopped, but can't be stopped by adults coming down to children's level. Aggressive acts stop when adults stop them, always and instantly; show concern for the child who's been hurt and acknowledge the feelings of both parties. As children begin to talk, help them learn to negotiate with each other as equals rather than as aggressor and victim: "We don't bite (or hit or grab); we *talk* to each other..."

TANTRUMS

Although it is toddlers who are notorious for tantrums, they are not unusual in babies as young as nine months and a lot more four-year-olds than their parents admit are still capable of lying in the middle of the supermarket, drumming their heels.

Don't classify every show of anger or defiance as a tantrum. Toddlers can pull away, yell, even stamp their feet or go so stiff that you can't fold them into their buggies, without having tantrums. A full-blown tantrum is something special: the emotional equivalent of a blown fuse. Once a tantrum is underway it is not something that an adult can interrupt or a child can stop to order. A tantrum is most likely when a load of frustration – often spiked with fear or anxiety – builds up inside the toddler until she is so full of tension that only an explosion can release it. Sometimes the build-up is slow. There may be afternoons when you know at lunch-time that a tantrum is brewing and you'll be lucky to make it through to bedtime without one. Sometimes, though, a tantrum strikes so fast and unexpectedly that it really is as if the child's fuse blew because somebody pushed the wrong button. While the tantrum lasts, the toddler is overwhelmed by her own internal rage; lost to the world, and terrified by the violent feelings which she cannot control. However unpleasant your toddler's tantrums are for you, they are much worse for her.

A real tantrum is like an emotional blown fuse; horrible for you but worse for your child.

Children's behaviour during a full-blown tantrum varies, but your particular child will probably behave similarly each time: she may rush around the room, wild and screaming. Remember that she is out of control so anything movable that happens to be in her path will be knocked flying. If you do not protect her she may even crash into solid walls and heavy furniture. She may fling herself on the floor, writhing, kicking and screaming as if she were fighting with demons. Anyone who gets within range is likely to get kicked so be careful if you try to pick her up. She may scream and scream until she makes herself hoarse; makes herself retch; even makes herself throw up. She may scream and turn blue in the face because she has breathed out so far that, for the moment, she cannot breathe in again. Breath-holding tantrums are the most alarming of all for parents to watch. The child may go without breathing for so long that her face looks greyish and she almost loses consciousness. It is quite impossible for her actually to damage herself in this way. Her body's reflexes will reassert themselves and force air back into her lungs long before she is in any danger.

Coping with tantrums

Although tantrums are part of daily life with some toddlers, they may be much less frequent or rare with others. However liable your child is to tantrums, though, you can prevent many by organizing your toddler's life so that frustration stays within the limits of her tolerance most of the time. It's always worth avoiding tantrums if you can do so without compromising your own limits, because they do no positive good to either of you. When you must force your child to do something unpleasant or forbid something she enjoys, do it as tactfully as you can. When you can see that she is getting angry or upset about something, try to make it easier for her to accept. Of course she must have her coat on if that's what you have said, but

When the screams subside into sobs, the furious monster becomes a pathetic baby who needs a cuddle.

perhaps she needn't have the zipper done up yet? There is no virtue in challenging children with absolute "dos" and "don'ts" or in backing them into corners from which they can only explode in rage. Leave a dignified escape route.

If your toddler does go into a full-blown tantrum, remember that her overwhelming rage terrifies her; make sure she does not hurt herself, or anyone or anything else. If she comes out of a tantrum to discover that she has banged her head, scratched your face or broken a vase, she will see the damage as proof of her own horrible power, and evidence that when she cannot control herself you do not have the power to control her and keep her safe either.

It may be easiest to keep the toddler safe if you hold her, gently, on the floor. As she calms down she finds herself close to you and she finds, to her amazement, that everything is quite unchanged by the storm. Slowly she relaxes and cuddles into your arms. Her screams subside into sobs; the furious monster becomes a pathetic baby who has screamed herself sick and frightened herself silly. Comfort time.

A few toddlers cannot bear to be held while they are having tantrums. The physical restriction drives them to fresh heights of anger and makes the whole affair worse. If your child reacts like this, don't insist on overpowering her. Remove anything she is obviously going to break and try to fend her off anything she might run into.

■ Don't try to argue or remonstrate with the child. While the tantrum lasts, she is beyond reason.

■ Don't scream back if you can possibly help it. Anger is very infectious and you may well find yourself becoming angrier with every yell she utters. But try not to join in. If you do, you are likely to prolong the outburst because just as the toddler was about to calm down she will become aware of your angry voice and it will start her off again.

■ Don't let the child feel rewarded or punished for a tantrum. You want her to see that tantrums, which are horrible for her, change nothing either for or against her. If she threw the tantrum because you would not let her go out into the garden, don't change your mind and let her out now. Equally, if you had been going to take her for a walk before she had the tantrum, you should take her all the same as soon as she is calm again.

■ Don't let tantrums embarrass you into kid-glove handling. Many parents dread tantrums in public places but you must not let your toddler sense your concern. If you are reluctant to take her into the corner shop in case she throws a tantrum for sweets, or if you treat her with saccharin sweetness whenever visitors are present in case ordinary handling should provoke an outburst, she will soon realize what is going on.

Once your toddler realizes that her genuinely uncontrollable tantrums are having an effect on your behaviour towards her, she is bound to learn to use them and to work herself up into the semi-deliberate tantrums which are typical of inappropriately handled four-year-olds. Assume that your child will not have a tantrum; behave as if you had never heard of the things and then treat them, when they occur, as unpleasant but completely irrelevant interludes in the day's ordinary events. It sounds easy, but it is not. A mother whose

Time-out really works, even for babies.

I don't agree with smacking children and I don't think punishments like "no TV" do much good, but "time-out" really does work. When my son was two years old we had a time-out chair in the hall with a kitchen timer. Now he's four and he understands the whole system. If he sees me looking cross he'll ask, "Is it time-out?" and because he finds four minutes quite long (one minute per year of age), he really tries to avoid it. It's worked so well that I don't want to wait so long with my second child. She's nearly a year and can't sit on a chair yet, but someone suggested using a "naughty cot" instead of a chair and lent me the travel cot she'd used that way. I've put it in the spare room where there aren't any toys or anything and when she's naughty I'll put her in there to cool off.

The basic idea of a time-out is the sensible one of taking a child out of a stressful, no-win social situation, and giving him or her (and maybe the parent or caregiver) a chance to calm down so they can come back and start again with the slate wiped clean. Adults often take a similar kind of break when they feel themselves losing their cool, perhaps excusing themselves to go to the bathroom when political discussion at a party threatens to overstep polite bounds.

Time-out is especially popular amongst families who are consciously looking for alternatives to physical punishments like smacking or spanking, and it is often effective. After due warning, a child who won't stop being a pain is put by herself without toys or distractions, on a special chair or in a particular place. She has to stay there for a certain number of minutes, timed from when she stops "playing up". The child knows what she's done wrong, what she should have done instead, and what she now has to do to put it right (and earn her release). And as long as she co-operates there is no violence or humiliation. Unfortunately many children won't co-operate, though, and the moment they begin to resist, time-out

begins to deteriorate. If you tell a child, "Go into time-out" and she says, "Shan't", what are you going to do? Carry her – by force, and maybe kicking and screaming? If you put her in the room and she comes straight out again what are you going to do? Hold the door? *Lock* the door? Suddenly you're into a kind of punishment that although it's not painful is as physical and humiliating as a spanking.

If time-out is not a good idea for children who won't co-operate, it's obviously a bad idea for a child who *can't* co-operate because she isn't old enough or has particularly limited understanding. A baby who's put in a "naughty cot", as you suggest, is effectively imprisoned. Even if she understands that she's there because she kept throwing her food she won't understand that her banishment is for a finite time or that her sentence only begins when she stops screaming – which she probably can't do on demand, anyway. So are you going to leave her there until she's screamed herself into exhausted sleep or only until you calm down enough to turn back into a grown-up? And can the experience teach her anything other than that being left alone in a cot is something to be feared?

Time-out is only useful if children can co-operate, but if children do co-operate, time-out needn't necessarily be a punishment. Running around the garden to let off steam is surely more effective than sitting in a corner. For all children, though, *time-in* contained and cuddled by an adult is more likely to be effective than any kind of time-out. The toddler whose behaviour has gone beyond the pale doesn't need pushing further out but bringing back in. He doesn't need to be isolated from you but to be with you. If he can't stop hitting and head-butting the other children in the wildly playing group because his tenuous self-control has gone for the moment, he needs you to take him out of the situation and lend him your control until he's taken a breather and can take charge of himself again.

20-month-old boy asked her to take the cover off his sandpit said, "Not now, nearly time for your bath," and went on talking to a friend. The child tugged her arm to ask again but got no response. He then went to the sandpit and tried in vain to open it himself. He was tired and the frustration was too much for him. He exploded. When the tantrum was over and his mother had comforted him, she said, "I feel really mean. That was all my fault; I just didn't realize he wanted to play in the sand that badly." And she took the cover off for him after all.

That mother's behaviour is easy to understand but also an excellent example of how not to handle tantrums! She said "no" to the child when he first asked for help without giving any real thought to his request. The child's own efforts to uncover the sand did not show her how passionately he wanted to play there because she was not paying attention to him. Only when he threw a tantrum did she realize that he really did want that sand and that there really wasn't any good reason for forbidding it. Of course she meant to make it up to the toddler by giving in after all, but it was too late for second thoughts. Hasty though it was, she should have stuck to her original "no" because by changing it to "yes" after the tantrum she must have made her child feel that his explosion had had a most desirable effect. It would have been better for both of them if she had taken a moment to listen and think when the toddler asked for help rather than giving in when he screamed.

It is not easy being a toddler rocking wildly between those anxious and angry feelings. It is not easy being a toddler's parent or caregiver either, striving to stay on the centre of that emotional see-saw and to hold it in equilibrium. But time is on everybody's side. A lot of the emotional turbulence will have settled down by the time she has completed her metamorphosis into a young child.

She will get bigger, stronger and more competent and learn to manage things better; that means that she will meet less extreme frustration in her everyday life. She will get to know and understand more, too, so that her life contains fewer frightening novelties. As she becomes more fearless she will stop needing quite so much reassurance from you. And gradually she will learn to talk freely not only about the things that she can see in front of her but about things she is thinking and imagining. Once she can talk in this way she will sometimes be able to accept reassuring words in place of continual physical comfort. With the help of language she will also learn to distinguish between fantasy and reality. Once she reaches this point she will at last be able to see both the unreality of most of her worst fears and the reasonableness of most of the demands and restrictions which you place on her. She will turn into a reasonable and communicative human being. Just give her time.

Even More
Muscle Power

The outstanding physical achievement of this age period is learning to walk alone, and it is a real developmental landmark. Those first staggery steps across open space mean that a new person is demonstrating the evolution that most obviously marks human animals off from the rest: being a biped who uses only his back legs to walk on and therefore has his front "legs" free to do other things. But mobility doesn't only enable a child to cover distances and move through spaces. Moving around also enables him to understand them; to co-ordinate what his eyes see with what his body does and to refine skills he's been working on since he began to co-ordinate his eyes and hands (see p.199), such as judging distances or recognizing two-dimensional representations of three-dimensional objects.

Exciting though it is to see a crawler pull himself up, stand and then walk, skilful hands are just as essential a part of human inheritance as upright posture. So if yours should be a child who is unlikely to walk unsupported, remember that he is still developing as a toddler in all but name. He can fulfil his potential from a wheelchair later on provided specialized help from the beginning ensures that other aspects of his development are not distorted.

Faced with a gap too big to reach across, she edges as far into the centre as she can…

Between the day when they first haul themselves into standing position and the day when they set off across open space, babies progress through several distinct phases. Your baby may have reached any one of these phases on his or her first birthday – there's wide variation in the ages at which different children learn to stand and walk – and nobody should try to hurry him into bypassing the next.

Stages in learning to walk

Each of the following phases has to be gone through in sequence though one child may pass through them all in a matter of days while another child will take several months.

In the first phase the baby, who has already learned to pull himself up to standing position by cot bars or heavy furniture, learns to "cruise" along the support by sliding both hands to one side so that he is off-balance and then sliding his feet along one at a time until he is standing straight again. He does not trust all his weight to his feet alone or even to his feet supported by one hand (see p.284).

The second phase ushers in a much more efficient and confident kind of "cruising". The baby stands back a little from his support so that all his weight is on his feet and he is using his hands only for balance. Instead of sliding both hands along together when he wants to move he moves hand-over-hand. By the end of this phase he is moving hands and feet in rhythm so that at critical moments he is relying only on one foot and one hand for support, the other member of each pair being in motion.

The third phase gives the baby an increased range of mobility because he learns to cross small gaps between one support and the next. If the furniture is conveniently arranged, he will now be able to get around the room, moving along the sofa back, crossing to the window-sill and then to a chair... He will cross any gap that can be spanned by his two arms, but he will still not release one hand until the other hand has first caught hold of something else.

The fourth phase brings the child's first unsupported step. Now he will face a gap between supports that is just too great for his arm span. He will hold on to the first support, move his feet out into the centre of the gap, release his hand and then lurch a single step to grab his new support with the other hand. Once the child can cross a small gap in this way he will also be able to stand alone. Often he will

...then risks everything on a single step to the new handhold and safety waiting on the other side.

He's got no brakes and his steering's off but he's a biped now and forever.

discover this by mistake. Perhaps he is standing up holding on to the back of a chair when you cross the room towards him carrying his mug. Without thinking about gravity, he lets go of the chair to hold up his arms for the drink; he probably does not even notice that he has let go of his support.

Once your toddler can take even a single unsupported step to get from one handhold to another he will soon be ready for the fifth stage. He will still do most of his walking with support, but if there is no convenient supporting furniture between him and his objective he won't stop, stymied, but will toddle two or three steps to get where he is going.

The sixth phase brings him to fully independent walking. He may not yet walk very far without a supported rest or a brief sit down on the floor, but when he sets off to cross a room he moves in a straight line irrespective of whether or not there is anything to hold on to along his way.

Helping your child towards walking

Don't hurry and don't worry. Once he has got onto his own two feet (phase one), you can be quite sure that he will eventually walk, however slowly he seems to progress. He may be content with the mobility crawling gives him. He may be using his efforts and energies primarily on other aspects of development such as manual play or beginning to talk. Let him take his time.

Offer opportunities to practise the phase already reached rather than pressure to try the next. When he gets to phase three, for example, you can give him enormous pleasure by sometimes arranging the furniture so that he finds he can get himself all the way around the room or even from one room into an adjoining one. At phases four and five he will probably love it if you kneel down a couple of paces away and invite him to toddle into your arms.

Protect your child from falls. He is accustomed to the kind of bump he gets when he topples over from sitting position, but falling down from standing may frighten him, especially if he bangs his head, and several frights in a row may put him off the whole walking business for weeks.

Slippery floors make independent walking seem as difficult to babies as walking on ice seems to us. Your child is safest with bare feet because he can feel the floor and use his toes for balance. Ordinary socks are dangerous on a hard floor and he will not be ready for real shoes until he is walking freely outside (see p.345).

Rowdy older children playing around your baby make the middle of the floor feel very dangerous to him. Make sure that he gets the chance to practise walking when there are no human trains around to knock him down.

Don't worry about brief setbacks. As well as weeks or months when your child seems to make no progress towards walking because he is concentrating on something else or getting over temporary nervousness, there may also be short periods when his ability to walk seems to have gone backwards.

A brief but acute illness, such as a middle-ear infection, can mean several days of high fever and minimal food or exercise. At this stage of his life the combination can reduce his muscle tone, energy and

Standing up merits a fresh look at safety

The baby-proofing of your home that you undertook when your child first started to get moving may not be adequate once she's on two feet. Think again about any safety gadgets that seemed unnecessary then; they may be badly needed now. Think about safety catches or bars on low windows, for example, and new fastenings, placed out of reach of a suddenly much taller, standing child, on any external or garage doors and garden gates.

Gadgetry apart, it's also time to take a fresh look at any rooms your almost-toddler *ever* uses, scanning especially for hazards she can reach from her full height that she can't reach from sitting, and for things she can't do while holding onto something but may do when she stands with both hands free. Is she now going to pull the phone or the iron or the kettle down on her head? Might she fall out of her cot unless you lower the base? Can she reach up to the front plates of the hob or reach across to hot drinks on the very middle of the coffee table?

Learning to walk also brings its own very particular hazards in the form of furniture that will tip over on top of her if your child tries to use it to pull herself up to standing. Lightweight, spindly pieces such as cane coat racks or umbrella stands, standard lamps and high stools are the most obvious dangers, but many ordinary upright kitchen or dining chairs will tip over on her if a child grabs the back rather than the seat, especially if there's already a heavy jacket or bag hanging from it. The heavier the piece and the sharper its edges, the greater the likelihood that the baby will be injured as well as frightened.

Children cannot learn to cruise and walk without pulling themselves up to standing position so trying to ban the pulling up isn't the answer: you have to make it safe. Banish as many unstable pieces of furniture as you can, at least until your child can get up and down freely without holding on to anything, in favour of things like couches and heavy coffee tables that have a low centre of gravity. If you don't want to banish a standard light, you may be able to wedge its base under a heavy armchair; if you're uneasy about the stability of a tall bookcase, bracket it to the wall.

Consider supplementing the pull-up potential of your furniture with a toddle-truck. Your child can use it anywhere in the house, not only for getting up but also as a substitute for cruising, in rooms where the furniture is not conveniently arranged. She can also use it in parks where there's no furniture at all. Obviously toddle-truck design is vital. A push-cart or doll's pram meant for older children will not do because it will tip when your child pulls up (so she lands flat on her back) and rush away from her when she tries to walk (so that she lands flat on her face). Even something that is advertised as a toddle-truck may be unsatisfactory if it is a cheap version whose pull-up stability depends on an added load of blocks rather than its own intrinsic centre of gravity and balance. A quality toddle-truck, with or without its blocks or your child's teddy bear, will not tip when your child grabs the handle and pulls up and will not go forward faster than she does when she walks with it. It will help to keep her safe; help her to find her first walking adventures fun and increase her mobility. With years of use ahead as a brick cart, first doll's pram or wheelbarrow, it would be hard to find a better first birthday present.

Nothing beats a toddle-truck for getting up and getting about.

courage to such an extent that he regresses a phase or two for a few days. If he was cruising confidently before the illness, he may go back to crawling and pulling himself to standing. If he was walking two steps between supports, he may go back to cruising. There is still no cause to worry or hurry. He will repeat all the learning phases again but in hours or days instead of weeks or months.

Even an emotional shock or high level of stress can cause your baby to abandon his newly acquired walking. A separation from you, a stay in hospital or the arrival of a new baby are as likely to send him back to crawling as back to a bottle. As soon as he feels safe he will move forward again.

When he reaches phases five and six and can toddle at least a few steps, do remember that he still cannot get from sitting to standing position without help. Although progress towards fully independent walking is almost invariably rapid from this stage on, your child cannot abandon crawling as his usual means of getting around because he has to crawl to something he can pull up on before he can stand up.

First walking   A newly walking child has no brakes and no steering. Once he has got up speed he cannot stop quickly enough to avoid falling down the steps or steer accurately enough to avoid the lamp-post. In restricted indoor space he may be reasonably safe because he cannot get up much acceleration. But while big open outdoor spaces, such as parks, will delight him, practising his walking in busy streets or crowded shops is liable to be dangerous. It's probably better if he sits in his buggy while you are in the street and saves his walking practice for a shopping centre or mall's open spaces or a visit to the park on the way home.

But if most of his outdoor life has to be passed in streets, or if he will not stay in that buggy, he will have to be held. Holding hands can be very uncomfortable for both of you. Your arm is not long enough to allow your hand to hold his at a comfortable angle so his shoulder will be continually wrenched upwards. And locked together that way, he will not be able to follow his natural inclination to stop and look at things and then to dash ahead. For the next few months you may both be far more comfortable if you use reins. Although often maligned on the grounds that they restrict children's freedom, reins can in fact increase the freedom that can safely be made available to toddlers at this stage (see p.388).

By his second birthday your child's brakes, steering and general control over his legs will probably have improved to a point where he can walk steadily over quite long distances, although children vary, of course, at all ages in the distances they are willing to walk. He will also be able to get to his feet, start, stop and sit down, all without needing support.

Doing other things while walking

Once he's steady on his feet it's fun to play while walking instead of playing at walking.

When a child first learns to walk a few steps alone, the business of moving along on his own two feet takes up all his energy and concentration so that he cannot do anything else at the same time. If he wants a toy he will have to stop, sit down, get the toy and then go through the whole business of finding something to pull himself up by, again. If he wants to listen to something you are saying, or look at something a little way away, he will stop, and probably sit down, to do that too.

But once a child is walking freely, constant practice soon makes it easier for him. By 18 months or thereabouts he will have learned to get up without pulling himself to his feet and he will have become so steady that he can pay attention to other things at the same time as walking. He will learn to stoop down, pick up a toy and walk along while he carries it. He will learn to turn his head so that he can look at things while he walks and listen to you when you talk to him. He will learn to glance back over his shoulder too, and once he can do that, a pull-toy to take along with him will be very popular.

How toddlers use this new kind of mobility

Most adults think of walking as a means of getting from one place to another. Most toddlers do not. Don't expect yours to walk in the same way as an older child. He will not because he cannot. Understanding the limitations and the peculiarities of his walking can save you a lot of irritation and friction.

For a toddler, walking is not a going-along activity but a coming-and-going around a central adult. Your child will do most walking when you keep still; least when you are moving around. Anyone who regularly takes care of a small child will sympathize with the mother who said, "He makes me wild; this morning I was busy doing the chores and he kept whining and clinging around me until I thought I'd go mad. Now I'm sitting down with nothing to do but play with him and he's rushing around all over the place as busy as a bee." That is life with a toddler. In the morning the child had to keep a close eye on his mother because he never quite knew where she was going to be next. But once she had fixed herself in one position he could go adventuring, come back and go again safely. Your toddler will likewise do his best walking when he knows exactly where you are and knows he can get back to you in a hurry.

Adults as home base If you do fix yourself, perhaps on a park bench, your toddler will usually leave you at once, toddling off in a straight line in any direction. Unless there are hazards close by there is no need for you to get up and follow him. Research has shown that newly walking children seldom go further away than about 60 metres. He knows exactly where you are. When his outward journey has taken him to his own personal distance limit, he will start back again, often making several stops along the way but always getting closer. The homeward journey may end before your child actually comes into contact with you, though. He may stop several feet away, closely examine a twig or a leaf and then set off again without ever looking directly at you. He will go on like that all afternoon.

Problems with early walking This coming-and-going pattern is built into your toddler. It has a logic of its own but that's likely to be very different from your logic and quite difficult to understand. Your logic tells you that if you move to a different bench or a new patch of sun, there's nothing to prevent your toddler coming to you there and using this new base just as he used the old one. But your move – all four metres of it – disrupts the toddler's pattern. Although he can see where you have moved to, and although he wants to come and join you, his built-in rails lead back to where you were, not to where you are. So he freezes where he finds himself; he may even cry. You can call, you can wave, but whatever you do he will not come. You will have to go and get him, bring him to your new base and let him start out all over again on a new set of rails.

A toddler does not learn to follow or to stay with a moving adult until he is around three years old. Until that time he will ask for transport as soon as you signal your intention of moving off. Unfortunately adults don't always understand that the toddlers, who plant themselves squarely in the way and hold up their arms to be carried, are not being lazy or tiresome but following an instinct for self-preservation. If you watch the apes at the zoo, you will see that the moment an ape-mother moves purposefully away, her baby will become motionless and cry. Sometimes the mother will call angrily to the baby, just as you sometimes call to yours, but her baby will not move until she fetches it and will not accompany her without being carried and neither will yours.

Many a pleasant afternoon in the park has its ending ruined by a toddler's apparently wilful refusal to walk home. You know that he is not too tired to walk; he has been rushing to and fro for the past hour and could clearly go on rushing towards home. But attempts to make him do so will cause sad trouble.

When he holds up his arms to be carried, it isn't that he won't come along but that he can't.

If you have no buggy with you and you do not want to carry the toddler, you will probably take his hand. Being physically joined on to you helps him to stay close, so for a few yards he will manage. But holding hands is not enough. Progress will be slow and jerky. The child will keep stopping; you will yank him on again. He will steer off in the wrong direction, you will pull him back. A few minutes of this will probably be enough for both of you. The toddler will keep getting in front of you, almost tripping you up; holding up his arms, begging for a lift. You may lose patience and drag him along by the

Until he learns how to follow, only the lifeline of a lift can keep him where he needs to be – close to you.

hand or you may decide to let go and leave him to follow at his own pace. He will not, because he cannot.

Left to his own devices while you move slowly on, the toddler will lag, stop, go off on side tracks and probably sit down. His behaviour looks like teasing and most people would describe it that way and tell you to keep walking because "he'll follow soon enough when he sees that you mean it". But your toddler does not know how to follow you. If you really do move off purposefully, you will lose him. If you go slowly, you will have to keep going back, retrieving him and setting him on the right course again. It would save time if you

---

PARENTS ASK

Which restraint will keep a not-yet-streetwise toddler safe?

My 18-month girl is just starting to walk. We live in an inner-city area so most of her outings, with me or with her nanny, are in busy streets and shops. Since it's not always easy to make her hold hands and it's obviously not safe to let her walk on her own, we need to use some kind of restraint. Which is better, reins or a wrist strap? Or would you recommend something like one of these radio-beepers that go off when a child gets a certain number of metres away?

It's important to decide what kind of danger you are trying to avert before you try to decide which – if any – gadget might help.

The kind of outing you describe can be dangerous in two very different ways. Firstly there's the danger of a child toddling or tumbling into the road or under a vehicle in a car park or shop's forecourt. Secondly there's the danger of her getting separated from you or from her nanny and lost, or even abducted. Radio-beepers are not intended to protect children from road accidents and probably wouldn't do much to protect such a young child against getting separated in a crowd. If these electronic gadgets are potentially useful to any parent, it is probably to those whose older children – say five years old or more – are liable to wander off while playing outdoors or in public spaces.

Tying a toddler to her accompanying adult helps avert both kinds of danger. Although somewhat older children may well feel that a wrist strap is more dignified, toddlers are certainly safer and more comfortable with a harness and walking reins. If a tiny child gets

even one step away from you in a busy area, a wrist strap that joins the two of you is hard to see. If somebody tries to walk between you, he will trip over the strap himself and certainly bring the toddler down. It's even possible that a toddler who slipped her father's hand, but was supposedly still safely held by her wrist strap, could try to pass the other side of a bollard and be jerked off her feet. Wearing a harness and reins, the toddler moves just ahead of the adult rather than out to the side. The adult can see the child and there is no apparent space between them for anyone else to try and move into.

Furthermore if the harness is properly adjusted, those reins will save, rather than cause, falls. If your toddler trips, you can save her by tightening the reins. If she suddenly goes on strike about walking and sits down somewhere dangerous, you can actually lift her to her feet and to safety; the harness will keep her upright.

Even if she is kept safe, though, it would be sad if walking on reins over litter, through a forest of adult knees and with her nose on a level with a thousand exhaust pipes, really made up *most* of your toddler's outings. She needs to be able to explore (a reasonably clean and sometimes "natural" environment) at her own pace and to come and go freely rather than being forced, however kindly, to keep moving at yours. In fact, even if she begs to be allowed to walk from the beginning, it may be better to keep her in her buggy or a back carrier while you transport her as rapidly as possible to the freedom of more child–centred places.

carried him from the beginning. It would save time, effort and irritation if you always brought a sling or back carrier or buggy with you on these expeditions and took it for granted that he would ride whenever you wanted to move on. He does not want to get separated from you; he dreads losing you and will instantly panic if he thinks he has. He is only asking you to help him stay where you both want him to be: close.

Climbing and other muscular adventures

Teach him to stop at the top, turn round on all fours and come down feet first on his front. The same technique works for getting off sofas as well.

Around the middle of his second year your child may be so dexterous and sure on his feet that you will almost have forgotten those staggery steps he took only six to nine months earlier. Soon he will begin to walk in different ways for fun, walking round and round getting giddy and giggly, walking backwards as well as forwards and eventually running rather than simply toddling fast. Once he can run, he will soon be able to jump so that both his feet leave the ground at the same time. He will even be able to kick a ball after a fashion but because balancing on one leg for more than an instant is still beyond him, it will be a shuffling kind of kick.

Your baby may have begun to scramble onto chairs or up momentarily unguarded stairs even before he could walk, but now he can walk he will certainly also climb. At 15 months he will crawl up stairs and, left to himself, probably try to crawl down them too. By 18 months he may be ready to try climbing stairs on hands and feet instead of hands and knees, putting one foot up a step and then bringing the other foot up to join it. If there are more than three or four steps, though, he is horribly likely to sit down for a rest halfway – backwards, into space – so make sure there is always an adult right behind him. It's important to let him practise, though, and by this time you may be able to begin to teach him to come down stairs or steps safely by a method that will also work for getting off beds and sofas. Just before he gets to the edge of whatever drop he is tackling, stop him and get him to sit down and turn around so that he comes down feet first and backwards, on his tummy. If you make a game of turning him over and gently pulling him over the top the first few times, he will probably get the idea. He will go on needing help as well as supervision, though, because he will often do his stopping and turning around while he is still far from the brink and then what is he to do? Not many toddlers can crawl backwards.

Toddlers vary widely in their respect for stairs and their competence in climbing. Some can walk up reasonably shallow stairs, one foot at a time but without needing to hold on, before their second birthdays, and a few can walk down the same way provided there is a bannister or a person to hold. But many will be almost three years old before they are competent, and certainly before they can be trusted to keep on concentrating and therefore go safely up and down on their own.

Unlike older children, intrepid toddlers who insist on climbing not only stairs but furniture, builders' ladders and the big children's play equipment, can't be assumed to know their own limits. If a four-year-old heads for the top of the climbing frame when nobody is taunting or teasing her, the chances are that she'll do fine; when a one-year-old does it the chances are too high for comfort that he didn't have a clue what he was starting and won't remember, or be able, to keep holding on. If he wants to climb he needs to learn to choose his mountains and develop his technique – so don't forbid him to climb a single rung or step; teach him to climb selected ones safely. However careful you are about child-proofing places where he plays, and supervising him elsewhere, though, you'll be lucky to keep him right out of trouble for the next couple of years. You may have to be content with keeping him out of the accident and emergency department.

Finding the confidence to run and dance By the time your toddler reaches his second birthday just *walking* will probably not be much of a challenge, but *running* will still pose problems with braking and steering. He will probably love to play running-away games, but he'll need a sympathetic adult rather than a competitive older brother to play them with because it will be months before he can dash off, glance back at a pursuer and dodge to avoid a catching hand. He will soon be able to play games that mean sudden starting and stopping, like "grandmother's footsteps" and "statues", and may enormously enjoy them, and he may be so pleased with his new agility at getting up and down off the floor that if he is introduced to games like "musical bumps" and "ring-a-roses", they are an instant hit.

Some children respond to music and rhythm from earliest baby-hood but by their second birthdays most of those who get a chance to see older children and adults dancing will dance themselves at every opportunity. Even if yours is not a culture or community in which everyone dances, it is worth making sure that small children do, both alone and with parents and carers. Once your toddler begins to move his feet and knees in rhythm, he'll feel his hips and shoulders and arms and hands all moving with them; it's fun but it's also control and co-ordination.

As your toddler moves past his second birthday you will notice that whatever he tries to do with his body, his movements are gradually becoming much neater and more precise and predictable. If he is paying attention to what he is doing, he can carry something breakable with little risk that it will fall out of his hand or he will fall on his face. He will begin to be able to put complicated sets of movements together, too, so that he can jump in the air with both feet (momentarily and a couple of centimetres) off the ground and walk on tiptoe. Soon he will even be able to ride a wheeled toy that he has to propel by pushing with his feet. Not bad for somebody who could scarcely stand on those feet not much more than a year ago.

LEARNING SPEECH

Learning to understand and to use speech is a crucial element of toddlers' graduation from babyhood into childhood. Until she can talk, many people will see your child as more baby than person, needing to be "talked to" with special gestures, little words, lots of physical contact, and needing to be listened to with interpretative personal skill. She is whining: what does she want? Is she tired? Hungry? Bored?

The sheer usefulness of speech was vividly brought home when a 17-month-old girl, sitting in her car seat, began to fuss. "What is it, darling?" her mother said to make conversation, assuming she was getting bored and expecting no real answer. "Bee!" she shouted. There was indeed a bee on her sleeve and since nobody was in a position to look at her and see it for themselves, talking was her only route to rescue.

Speech is not only need-fulfilling, though. Once a child can really understand and use speech, you can discuss things with her. Things that are there to be seen like that naughty dog chasing the cat up a tree; things that are not there but will be, like Mummy who will soon be home from work; things that will never be "there" in the sense of being visible, like thunder or electricity or joy.

Language is for communication between people – speech is not just one person saying words. A few separate words on their own are not even very useful, as you will know if you have ever tried to use a phrasebook in a country whose language was totally foreign to you. It's easy to look up and spell out a vital question such as, "Where is the toilet, please?" but what use is that if you cannot understand the answer? Understanding language is still far more important to your toddler than actually speaking it. Once she really understands, she will communicate with you. If you try to teach her to imitate word-sounds before she understands their meaning, you are treating her like a parrot, not a person.

Talking timetables Speech is important, though, and since every parent knows that, few are immune to anxiety about the possibility of a child being a "late talker", especially as there's so little agreement as to how late is late. Depending on who gives you the information you may expect your child's first word at 7, 10, or 15 months; expect 50 words at 18, 24, or 30 months and listen for word combinations at 16, 24, or 30 months. If you look in the most widely used of all developmental tests, the Bayley scales of infant development, to see when the average child says two words you will find the answer "14 months", but you will also find that it derives from a range of ages from 10 to 23 months. That wide range is partly due to nature, partly to nurture and partly to the real individuality of children. Being a twin exemplifies all three.

Twins talking Premature birth usually means a slower start to speech which may not equal out before three years. Twins are often premature. Early competence in talking largely depends on the amount of time a baby spends in one-to-one communication with a loved adult. Being a twin tends to halve that time. The style of a parent's talk, especially whether it is mostly open-ended or mostly controlling, is also important. Coping with twins (or very close siblings) generates some complicated conversational patterns, including parents talking to both children simultaneously; talking to one with the other listening and both children talking at once. Above all it generates an acute need for some kind of control over a pretty uncontrollable situation. And young twins often function as a linguistic team, answering half an adult's question each; competing to get their comments in first and talking faster (if less) than most singletons.

Late talkers Provided that your child listens to people talking, hears speech and clearly understands more and more language, try not to worry if her own words come slowly. Putting her under pressure to imitate your speech, or to name the object she wants before you will give it to her, will drain the pleasure out of the communication game, make her feel inadequate and possibly slow her up. Remember that boys often start talking a little later than girls, that children in bilingual households may produce fewer words in each language to start off with, and that toddlers with older siblings very close to their own ages need more one-to-one talking time than it's easy to give. The prescription is the same for all: lots and lots of fun talk with adults.

If your toddler isn't talking at all by two-and-a-half, though, it would be sensible to get advice from whichever health professional carries out developmental checks in your community. It's important to have her hearing evaluated because even if it was normal earlier on, repeated ear trouble can reduce hearing enough to delay speech. And it's important to assure yourself that there's no developmental reason for speech delay, such as a (very rare) condition known as Specific Language Impairment (see p.504), which requires treatment by a skilled speech therapist. The chances are still high, though, that your toddler who doesn't talk much yet, soon will. Einstein was three years old when he started and yes, his parents did worry about it.

Helping your child towards language Like babies, toddlers have an in-built interest in human voices and a natural tendency to listen. You can build on this as you did earlier:
■ Talk as much and as often as you can directly to your toddler and try to make some of these private conversations between you and her. If you are talking, or reading, to her and an older sibling, she will not get as much repetition and explanation as she can use and as she will get if she is alone with you. Look at her while you talk. Let her see your face and your gestures.
■ Let the toddler see what you mean, by matching what you do to what you say. "Off with your shirt" you say, taking it off over her head; "Now your shoes," removing them.
■ Let the toddler see what you feel by matching what you say with your facial expressions. This is no age for teasing (what age is?). If you give her a big hug while saying, "Who's Mummy's great horrible grubby monster then?" you will confuse her. Your face is saying, "Who's Mummy's gorgeous girl?"
■ Help your child to realize that all talk is communication. If you chat away to yourself without waiting for a response or looking as if you want one; or if you don't bother to answer when she or another

Twins work together and play together but don't always do much talking together.

*Listening and talking
and being understood
are the keys that
unlock language.*

member of the family speaks to you, she is bound to feel that words
are just meaningless sounds.

■ Don't have talk as background noise. If you like to have the radio
on all day, try to keep it to music unless you are actually listening. If
you are listening, let her see that you are receiving meaningful
communication from the voice she cannot see.

■ Act as your toddler's interpreter. You will find it much easier to
understand her language than strangers do and she will find it much
easier to understand you and other "special" people than to understand strangers.

■ Help the child to understand your overall communication; it does
not matter whether she understands your exact words or not. If you
cook something, put plates on the table and then hold out your hand
to her saying, "It's lunch-time now," she will understand that her
lunch is ready and will come to her highchair. She might not have
understood the words "lunch-time now" without those other cues to

go with them. She will learn the meanings of the words themselves through understanding them, again and again, in helpful contexts.

■ Share enthusiasm, emotion and emphasis; whether you are expressing a flood of love for the toddler herself or exclaiming over a flock of rare birds in the sky, those are the speech qualities that will catch and hold her attention and motivate her to try and understand what you are saying.

Labelling things that matter First words are almost always labels; names for people, animals or other things that are important to them. After name-labels for a person or two and perhaps a pet animal, they are likely to add a label for a favourite food or toy. It will not be a general food-word like "supper", produced out of hunger. Hunger will lead to whining, not talk. It will be a name for a specific food, often one with special emotional connotations. Pronunciation is difficult, though, and toddlers often shorten and simplify words they understand and want to use, so that even parents and caregivers can only be sure which is which by context or trial and error. A small boy used "buh" for "bottle", "biscuit", "banana" and "book". At his supper-time the word acted as a collective noun because he got all four together, but at other times of day one "buh" was not at all the same as another. His childminder was especially thankful when "bopple", "biccit" and "ba-ya" left "buh" for book, and book alone.

Many children do not get further than this before the middle of their second year. New words often come slowly at first, being added, perhaps, at a rate of only one or two each month. But the child is storing up understanding of language and eventually, often shortly before her second birthday, will produce a burst of speech. It is not unusual for a child who says only 10 words that are clear enough to be counted at 18 months, to be saying, and *using* 100 words six months later.

The new spate of words will almost all be for things that are part of, or concern, the child herself. If adults help her, she will learn the names for parts of her own body; find her hairbrush and name it, avoid her face cloth while naming it and escape from her cot, by name. When she begins to extend her words to things that belong outside her own home they will still be things that are important to her. She may learn to name the birds she enjoys feeding with crumbs but she will only speak of the school that is important to her sister if taking and fetching her is also an important part of her routine.

Although these single words are all simple name-labels for familiar objects that the child can see, she uses them in an increasingly varied way as she readies herself for the next stage of speech. You can help her along by paying attention not only to the word she says but to the way she says it. She may label the family pet "dog" and you acknowledge that he is indeed a dog. But next time she uses the word she puts a question mark after it. "Dog?" she says, watching him trot across the garden. Answer the question mark: tell her where the dog is going. She may even make moral judgments with her single words. Watching the dog scratching in your flower bed she may say, "Dog!" in tones of deep disapproval. Make it clear that you have understood her by agreeing that the dog is being very naughty.

Everything in the world has a name, and so does what it does.

Using more than one word at a time Once she has acquired a good collection of single words and has learned to use them with varying intonations and meanings, your toddler will move on to the two-word stage without any prompting. Don't confuse phrases she treats as multi-syllable single words with this new and more advanced stage of speech: "Up-you-get" and "give-me" don't count as two word phrases if they are always strung together in the same way. Some toddlers do learn phrases as phrases, though, picking up and trying out (complete with intonations) the ones that frequently recur in the speech of adults who are important to them. One two-year-old solemnly congratulated his mother on a delicious pancake in exactly the tone her father, his grandfather, always used: "Jus'as it shou' be, my dear."

Don't expect your toddler's first creative phrases to be grammatically correct. She has to decide how to add a second word in order to communicate a fuller or more exact meaning, not in order to speak more "properly". She will not go from "ball" to "the ball" because "the" adds nothing to what she wants to say about the ball. Instead she will say "John ball" or "more ball". Don't try to correct her. If you do, you will limit her pleasure in communicating with you. It's important to help her feel that each new effort she makes in this difficult business of talking is worthwhile. When she says, "ball?" she may mean one of a number of things, but when she says, "John ball?" it is much easier to guess that she means, "Is this John's ball?" or perhaps, "Will John play ball?"

Two-word phrases make it much easier to understand your toddler's thought processes. You will be able to see, for example, that she is beginning to be able to think about things which are not actually visible. If she wanders around the room saying, "Ted?", "Ted?" you may guess that she is thinking about her teddy bear, but once she wanders around saying, "Where Ted?" you will know that she is searching for it. You will be able to hear her early concepts forming too (see p.402). After weeks of calling all animals "pussy"; she may now meet an Alsatian dog and say, in tones of doubtful amazement, "BIG pussy?" You will know that while she still does not have a separate word for dogs or for any animals-that-are-not-cats, she does have a sufficiently clear concept of cats themselves to be quite aware that this large dog does not fit into it.

Sentences and grammar Once she has begun to make and use two-word phrases your toddler will soon add another word or two so as to make sentences. Some of what she says may surprise you because she will not be copying the things she hears you say but following strictly communicative and logical rules of grammar which will usually be quite different from the "correct" grammar of whatever language you happen to speak.

Don't try to correct your child's grammar. It will do no good because she will not alter what she says to suit your instructions. On the contrary, it may do harm because your disapproval will put her off. She needs to feel that any message she communicates is welcomed for itself, so just listen to her instead.

Listen to the order of the child's words. She rarely gets this wrong. If she wants to tell her sister she is naughty she will say, "Naughty Jane." But if she wants to tell you that her sister is naughty, she will say, "Jane naughty." If she wants to tell you that she has seen a bus she will say, "See bus", but if she wants you to come quickly to the window and see the bus for yourself, she will say, "Bus, see."

Listen to the way your child makes past tenses. Most English verbs are made into the past tense by adding a "d" sound. It is because she over-extends this rule that the toddler says, "He goed" and "I comed." Sometimes for good measure she adds the "d" sound to an irregular verb that is already in the past tense so that she says that she "wented" or that she "beened".

Listen to the way she makes plurals. Most English words are pluralized by adding, an "s" or a "z" sound. Your toddler applies this

---

PARENTS ASK

How do the pros and cons of baby talk balance out?

Our daughter is 18 months old and very chatty. Her 13-year-old half-sister has recently pointed out that her father and I both use a lot of "yucky baby talk". She herself talks to Lucy as if they were both grown-up. In fact she seems to use the longest words she can think of, and I must admit that Lucy hangs on every one. She's succeeded in making us self-conscious (which I'm sure was her intention) but is she also right? Would it be better for Lucy if we stopped using anything but standard speech?

Lucy is lucky to have such varied conversationalists in her home, and especially lucky to have a teenage sister who engages with her and whose surprising polysyllables keep her talk interesting.

Baby talk is almost universal amongst parents, whatever language they speak. Babies are usually addressed in a higher-than-usual pitch, with lots of question marks, repetitions and emphases. Generally speaking, babies like it. Their attention is more readily attracted and held by "parentese" than by ordinary speech. Later on, parents' tendency to talk to toddlers rather slowly and in short sentences with simple grammatical constructions seems sensible; after all that's the kind of talk we find easiest to understand when we're struggling with a new language. And most linguists agree that repeating key words and expanding children's telegraphese into whole sentences really helps language skills. Child: "Cat up it." Father: "The cat went up? Did the cat go up? What did the cat go up?

Did the cat go up the tree?" Child: "Cat up it tree."

"Yucky baby talk" probably refers to the one common kind that may not be very useful, though: using "simplified" or incorrect words instead of correct ones. It isn't actually any easier for a child to learn "doggie" than "dog", and "duck" and "train" are surely simpler than "quack-quack" and "choo-choo" (and who hears trains saying "choo-choo" these days, anyway?). Using a toddler's "own-words" (or mispronunciations) in family conversation can be a friendly, flattering thing to do (and they aren't usually yucky, either) but if everyone eats "yoggit" and talks about sending for a "politeman", Lucy may be four years old and embarrassed in public before she corrects herself – and you.

Finally, do try not to mis-educate her because you're trying to keep things simple. A whale is not a fish so don't call it one just because it appears in a sea picture with a lot of what she has just learned to call fish. She can cope with the fact that there are mammals who live in water. And don't mis-label chimpanzees or orangutans as monkeys: if you want a broad classification she will have to learn "apes", but why shy away from those proper names? Toddlers lap up new words, the more interesting the better. So teach her orangutan yourself, and get your older daughter to stop criticizing your conversations with Lucy and get on with teaching her the names of all known dinosaurs instead. Diplodocus and Apatosaurus should keep them both happy.

rule logically to all words so that she talks about "sheeps" and "mans" and "mouses".

Listen to your toddler using phrases which she has understood for many months as single words. When she comes to use them with another word, she cannot separate the first two to get the grammar right. She has heard "pick up", "put on" and "give me" over and over again. Now she says, "Pick up it", "Put on them" and "Give me it."

And listen out for the beauty of words your child creates to convey her own meanings: "Bellvan" for ice cream van; "Mummygo" for brief-case.

A toddler's early sentences are her very own original telegraphese, developed out of her desire to communicate interesting and exciting things rather than imitated from teaching adults. A small boy, taken to his first football match and thrilled by the scene, grabbed his grand-father's hand exclaiming, "See lots mans!" He could not possibly have copied that, the longest sentence of his short life, because there are almost no sounds in common between his version and the adult, "See what a lot of men." In his excitement, Charlie had thought up his sentence all for himself.

Your child will speak her language and she will listen to you speaking yours. Your quick and understanding response to the things she says will keep her interested in communicating with you, while your correct speech keeps a model in front of her to which she will gradually adapt her own. When she rushes into the kitchen saying, "Baba cry, quick!" you know that she means her baby sister is crying and you should go to her at once. You show that you understand her language but you answer in your own: "Is Jane crying? I'd better come and see what's the matter." If you insist on correcting your toddler's telegraphese and making her say things "properly", you will bore her and hold up her language development. She is not interested in saying that same thing more correctly; she wants to say something new. Let her speak in her own way and don't pretend that you do not understand her when you do.

If you reply to your toddler only in her own "baby talk", you will also hold up her language development because you will not be providing her with new things to say. So along with letting her speak her way, make sure that you speak your way, too. Let her ask you for a "biccit" if that is her word for it; let her tell you that she has "eated it". But you offer her a "biscuit" and ask her whether she has "eaten it" yet. As long as you both understand each other and as long as you both say plenty to each other, all will be well.

PLAYING AND THINKING

Today's play is tomorrow's serious business.

For small children there is no distinction between playing and learning; between the things that they do "just for fun" and things that are "educational". Toys and other playthings are fun – if they were not, children would not use them and so they would learn nothing from them – but they are also tools for finding out about the world and acquiring grown-up skills. All children, in all societies, enjoy and learn from playthings, but commercially produced toys have taken on a particular importance in Western societies. Although there's certainly an element of competitive consumerism in the toys we buy for our children and they want us to buy, it's not all mere (let alone over-) indulgence. Our children have a particular need for toys to help them master in play aspects of the real world and the way it works which life in modern Western urban environments conceals from them.

In other places (and times) toddlers and young children understand the point and begin to acquire the skills of the family activities that go on all around them. Cows and goats are milked so that everyone can have milk to drink; musical instruments are played so that everyone can dance. Children can see, and soon understand, adult concerns – crops flattened by unseasonal weather, or water coming through the roof – and "use" most of the adults' tools, from spades to washtubs. In contrast, modern urban toddlers are cut off from most of the meaningful basics of life. Productive work goes on away from home in a mysterious place called "the office", or even more mysteriously "down town". Instead of producing obviously useful stuff like milk, it produces something called money that is either incomprehensible paper or invisible electronics. A lot of adult play is equally mysterious – meetings or the drinking of special drinks – and adult worries are completely inexplicable: possibilities of redundancy or promotion; changes in taxation or mortgage rates. Even home-based activities which toddlers would like to share often involve gadgets that are too dangerous or delicate for them to handle. To your toddler, hand-washing and line-drying would be fun, but to you, most laundry is better done by those machines he may not touch. And even if he has already been introduced to your computer, he's almost certainly forbidden to play with the TV's remote control or the buttons on the video recorder.

Nothing you can do will make an urban high-rise the ideal environment for a new human being, but a wide range of playthings will certainly help you to ensure that your toddler understands something of the natural world which is concealed under concrete, and some of the principles of how things work which are hidden in all those gadgets. There are thousands of toys on the market and many more playthings available at the cost of a little imagination. Making good choices for your child depends on understanding how his thinking is developing and where it has got to, and on taking account of what is already available to him.

The world of the one-year-old

The one-year-old's world is here-and-now reality. He is not yet concerned with imaginary matters; he is too busy making sense of what is, to be ready for what might be. He cannot cope with the past or future either, even to remember yesterday or plan for tomorrow. His job is to come to terms with real people and real things as they come before his eyes.

He has already learned an enormous amount about the real world as it is revealed to him by his five senses. He can recognize familiar objects even when he sees them at peculiar angles, like his bottle, presented endways on so that all he sees is a white disc. He can recognize familiar sounds, knowing his father's voice even while he is still out of sight. He can recognize the feeling of many things, finding his cuddly by touch alone, and if you bake cupcakes the smell will alert him to something nice to eat and his sense of taste will discriminate between his favourite chocolate ones and the rest.

But your toddler's interpretations of the world are not always accurate. He can still be fooled by people and things which do not appear as he has learned to expect. He has clear expectations of your appearance, for example. If you come home from the hairdresser with a new style, or emerge from the swimming pool changing rooms in a swimming cap, you will contradict those expectations. He may not know you. He may even be alarmed by your combination of strangeness and familiarity. Similarly, if he expects his father's daily homecoming around that corner and on foot and he emerges from a friend's car right outside the house, the child may go on gazing up the road for him. Even as his father greets him, he may glance puzzledly from his face to the point where he expected him to appear. The world is an unpredictable place and only now is he ready to begin to cope with inconstants.

Being an explorer

When your toddler can have freedom to explore, he'll seldom get bored.

Sometime during the first half of his second year all your toddler's new abilities come together in ways that make it easy for him to learn. He is mobile. He can go and find things and angles on things which you could not bring to him as he sat. He has seen that table many times but now he can view it from underneath. His reaching out, grasping and letting go are competent. He can get hold of the things he wants to find out about. His vocalizations are highly expressive. He can question and exclaim, even without words, and people will answer him; tell him things, show and help him. Soon he will use real words himself and they will both help him to understand and help him to remember what he finds out. His need for sleep is diminishing a little and, when something really interests him, he can keep himself awake. So he has more hours for finding out, for learning. He learns by exploring. When you set him free in an interesting room he moves around from object to object, looking, touching, tasting, smelling and listening. He has no particular purpose in view. He examines an object as a mountaineer climbs a mountain: because it is there. But he may examine a hundred things in an hour.

Because almost everything is new to him, he does not easily get bored unless he is confined in a highchair or playpen. If that room was interesting yesterday and this morning, tiny changes in it will start him exploring it all over again this afternoon. The dining table was laid for a meal but now it is bare. The coffee table has acquired a lot of papers, but the wastepaper basket he emptied on the floor has been (wisely) hidden. As for his own things, the bricks that were spread out higgledy-piggledy have been piled up, and it takes him quite a while to recognize his lorry because it has been left upside down with the wheels showing.

The explorer turns research scientist
A toddler cannot have too much exploring time or too much variety to explore. As he picks things up for the sake of picking them up, drops them because dropping things is fun, puts them in his mouth to understand them better, he is playing and learning.

When he's done enough basic exploring, the toddler begins to experiment as well. He still picks things up and puts things in his mouth, but now he does it purposefully; he is trying to find out what he can do with them and what they taste like. He fingers, drops and squeezes things *to see what will happen*. He is carrying out an endless series of basic experiments.

Those experiments gradually teach your toddler the rules which govern the behaviour of objects in our world. It is not fanciful to call him a "scientist" because most of these rules are ones which real

So what does happen to her playdough in your garlic press?

scientists observed, examined and explained generations ago. The toddler does not understand them but he discovers them for himself.

He discovers that when he drops something, it falls down. Always down, never up. He does not understand the concept of gravity, but he observes its constant effects. He discovers that when he pushes a ball or an apple, it rolls – always; but when he pushes a brick it does not roll – ever. The ideas of solid geometry mean nothing to him either but he is learning to live by its rules.

When he tips a beaker of water, he gets wet; when he tips a beaker of sand, he does not. The water soaks into his clothes but the sand cascades off when he stands up. He could not describe to you the different properties of liquids and solids but he is finding them out all the same.

Discovering group identities As he learns how different objects behave, the toddler begins to realize that there are similarities and differences in what he can do with them as well as in how they look. He has bricks in different colours and shapes, but although they *look* different he discovers that he can build with any or all of them; that those various bricks are more like each other than any of them is like anything else. Gradually he will learn to make more and more groupings of that kind: foods, animals, flowers. When he was newly crawling, he tried to treat the family dog and cat as if they were toys and was sadly surprised when they rushed away. Now he knows those pets are not toys. He treats them differently.

Moving towards mental concepts Once your toddler recognizes similarities and differences and uses them to form groups in his mind, he is on the way to making a vital intellectual stride: forming concepts.

Adults organize their perceptions of a complex world by using a more sophisticated version of the same grouping technique. We sort, compare, contrast and group innumerable objects, facts, people, feelings and ideas, "sort through" what we know of the world and form the information into complex concepts. It is those concepts which allow us to join new information up with what we already know and to communicate freely with each other on the basis of shared knowledge. If I talk about an "insect", for example, you will instantly know the broad parameters of what I am talking about. I shall not have to spend the first minutes of the conversation explaining to you that an insect is a living creature rather than a man-made one or that it is smaller than an elephant. Likewise, if you say something about "jealousy" I shall know that our discussion is in the area of uncomfortable feelings of envy and loss. You need not explain the concept of jealousy to me because we already share it.

We label our concepts with words so it is difficult to see toddlers' progress towards concept-formation until or unless they use language, and not easy until they have more than single words. If your toddler is making groupings and learning name-labels both at the same time, you may hear him call the family pet "dog", and wonder if he has a concept of dogs. Not necessarily. His use of the word "dog" starts as a simple label for one particular thing – that individual animal. To make a concept of dogs he has to put *all* dogs – your own, the ones he sees in the park, picture book dogs and toy dogs, into one

She knows the sheep from the pigs and the cows, and she's beginning to see them as families.

single category in his mind and use that label "dog" for the whole group. He will only do that when he recognizes that although each member of that mental group is different, they are all more like each other than they are like anything else. You may suspect that he has reached this stage when he turns from the family dog to his picture book and points out all the dogs on a page of mixed animals. If he eventually says something like: "Dog, bow-wow! Horse go neieieigh!" you can be sure he has got there because he will have picked out one of the characteristics that differentiate dogs and horses (the sounds that they make), generalized them to all members of each group (all dogs bark, all horses neigh), and contrasted the two groups (dogs don't neigh, horses don't bark).

Once his thinking has reached this stage your toddler will spend a great deal of time sorting and classifying in play, but his concept-formation still has a long way to go. Toddler-type concepts are still firmly attached to the visible world. If you show your child a page of mixed pictures or a box of mixed toys, he will (or at least he *could* if he happened to feel like it) find you all the dogs or all the cars. But he cannot find you all the "nice" or "heavy" or "round" things. These are abstract ideas and they come slowly.

Moving towards abstract ideas in the third year

Abstract concepts enable us to refer to and discuss people and objects that are absent or imaginary, and play with and debate ideas without physical reference. That is still impossible for a very large majority of two-year-olds. Your child may vaguely understand abstractions like "soon", but he probably still needs concrete signposts like "when you've had your lunch and your nap" to comprehend "this after-noon", and nothing you can say will really help him with more distant time concepts like "next week".

He is feeling his way towards abstract concepts, though, and beginning to be able to think and play in ways that are further and further removed from real objects in his hand or in front of his eyes. He begins to be able to think about familiar objects when they are not there; to remember them and to make future plans for them. Out of sight is no longer always out of mind. Called in for lunch from playing outside, he can leave the garden, eat the meal, and return afterwards to exactly the same point in his game. Although that may not sound very clever, it demonstrates remarkable advances in his thinking. He had a picture of his game in his mind. He remembered it through the meal, planned to go on with it in the future and carried out the plan without adult prompting.

Becoming an inventor in the third year

Once your child can think like this he is on the verge of imaginative play. First original ideas expressed in play are crucial developmental landmarks, but unless you are alert for them they may pass un-recognized. A saucepan worn as a hat, for example, does not look brilliantly original to you because you have often seen children wearing saucepans on their heads. But your child has *never* seen such a thing. He invented that hat out of and for his own head.

Early imaginative play doesn't always seem very different from the imitative play which has been going on for months, but if you watch carefully you will see that it is. When he was 18 months or there-abouts, your toddler loved to be given a cloth so that he could help you clean your car. Now, a year later, you see him take a T-shirt off the clothes-airer, dip it in the dog's water bowl and clean his pedal-car with it. He is not imitating a present parent; he is being an absent one. He is inventing a cloth and water bucket, pretending a toy car is real, and imagining himself as a grown-up.

HELPING YOUR CHILD TO PLAY AND THINK

If adults provide space, equipment, time and companionship for play, young children see to the development of their thinking for them-selves. Your child is a scientist and inventor; too much teaching robs him of that role. Your job is only to make sure he has laboratories, research facilities and an assistant when he needs one. Within the limits of safety and acceptable behaviour, what he actually does with play materials is his business, too. Of course he cannot be allowed to scribble on the walls or throw blocks at his friend, but that does not mean that he should be told what to draw on paper, or helped to use the blocks "properly, for building". He needs the true scientist's independence to follow his own chains of thought and not share them until he's ready.

Although you are responsible for ensuring that your toddler has good play facilities, you don't necessarily have to provide everything he needs at home or be the principal adult companion in his play life. If he is at a nursery all day in the working week he may want to spend his daily time at home in close interactive activities with you, and the weekends may be primarily times for getting out and about. If he is based at home, but mostly with a nanny who has few other responsibilities, he may be able to enjoy a playroom rather than needing to do all his playing in space he shares with you.

Whoever takes daily care of him, and whatever your exact arrangements, try to see to it that there's an overall balance in his possibilities for play. If he spends his days without outside playspace, for example, after-work trips to parks and playgrounds and weekend visits to countryside will be important, but if he spends much of his

Don't pack your toddler's time so tightly that there's no peace for amazing discoveries.

time in a garden full of toddler equipment, books and conversation may be what he needs from you. If he is cared for in a group he may benefit from peaceful time without competition, but if he is home-based and without siblings, the companionship of other children will be crucial.

Make sure the toddler has basic playspace which is close to you or whoever cares for him. He is still better off with a suitable and sociable corner in the living room than with a special room where he is expected to be solitary.

If you, or other children, share that space, you must make sure that he can play freely without getting into danger or making himself unpopular. Many of his five-year-old sister's playthings are as hazardous to him as he is to them: that party balloon, for example, that he may not only burst but choke on. And their relationship will be loudly ruined if he snatches her pencils whenever she tries to draw. If you have space for a playpen, it can protect the older child (inside) from the roving toddler (outside). You and your laptop or sewing machine would be sociably safe in there too. If space is short or you have no playpen, you may be able to shift a sofa or open out a clothes-rack to toddler-proof a corner.

Organizing play materials Your toddler cannot play well if someone has to hunt for what he wants and then, when it's found, half of it is missing. His things need organizing just as efficiently as a kitchen or a real laboratory. Toy cupboards hide a mess from your visitors, but they also hide his possessions from the child and encourage you to let them get in a muddle. Many parents grumble that their children have hundreds of toys that they never play with. Usually it is because the toys are incomplete, broken or simply forgotten. Try to arrange to have toy shelves in his main playspace and take pride in their organization. Big toys stand at the bottom so that he can get them without breaking his toes; other toys can stand directly on the shelves where they will look very attractive. Vital collections of small objects – cars, stones, counters, farm animals – can be kept sorted into cardboard boxes, plastic ice cream cartons or plant trays, and stored where you have some control over what gets emptied out two minutes before supper or gets into the hands of even younger visitors. If you stick one of each item on the outside of the box, the toddler will be able to see for himself what lives where.

Toys stay interesting for longer if children cannot see all of them all of the time. Your toddler may feel that he has more variety if some of his things are kept in the particular places where they are used. A special drawer in the kitchen for his "cooking" things will keep him from turning yours out. A basket of bath-toys could live by the bath, while outdoor toys could have their own place on the balcony or in a shed. Especially nice books, difficult puzzles and music cassettes will probably be better appreciated if they are kept in the living room, to be used when he has an adult's attention, while things he likes to play with in bed can live in his room.

At this stage toddlers are only just beginning to have their own new ideas about what to do with playthings or how to combine them to make them more interesting. You can help by showing him

Well-organized toys help concentrated creative play, alone and together.

that his farm animals can ride in his lorry and his blocks make stables. It's also worth setting up an "odds and ends" box in which all the household's adults squirrel away interesting packaging materials, scraps of cloth, cardboard tubes, plastic jars and so forth. With any luck the box will always contain the potential for a new cereal-packet garage for cars that have become boring or a new costume for a doll who has lost her novelty-value.

Out and about Toddlers who are home-based need changes of scene, especially if weather or illness keeps them indoors all day. Make use of the kitchen or bathroom for messy play and break up stretches of time with sessions away from his basic play place, perhaps listening to music in the sitting room or romping on your big bed.

Outdoors is so important that life with small children who have access to a garden or yard is completely different from life with those who have none. If there's no garden, make use of any outside space

Five minutes outside can take ten minutes getting ready, but the change is still worthwhile.

there is. Making a balcony safe isn't easy but it can usually be done by stretching strong nylon mesh from the railing to hooks set into the masonry. If the resulting cage will take your weight, you can be certain it will take his, even if he tries to monkey-climb it.

Outings are an important part of toddler life. If your toddler is cared for in a nursery he may seldom be taken off its premises so he'll need to get out and about when he's with you. If he's with a nanny at home, or a childminder at her home, do all you can to encourage outings. Even the most mundane trips can be fun. He's at the age and stage where the combination of familiar routes with the novelty of the small changes that take place day-by-day is ideal. He will not get bored of taking and fetching older children from school or with local shopping expeditions, even if you do. Yesterday he saw a bus, a dog, Mrs Jones and a tramp. Today he sees a motor bike, two cats, Mr Smith and a milkman. Let him join in with this ever-changing world: greet Mr Smith, load the clothes at the launderette and feed the end of his biscuit to a pigeon. If you do, he will enjoy and learn from that ordinary little walk as much as from an elaborately arranged trip to the zoo.

Parks and meadows give him a completely different range of experiences from those he can get indoors or in the streets. He needs to know about wind and rain and sunshine, about grass and mud and twigs, about puddles to splash in, banks he can climb and the half-frightening freedom of wide open spaces. In many parts of the world, wintry weather is an ordinary part of his environment and he needs to discover it. A waterproof suit and boots for him and enough clothes and courage for his adult escort can make howling winds, rain and snow into adventures.

A toddlers' club or playground set aside for children under five will probably be a favourite place for your child, but think carefully before you take him to ordinary playgrounds intended for older children. It's not only that the equipment will be too big and fierce, but also that outside school hours the crowds and the noise may be too much for him, and he will find no peace for his small experiments. He is only just discovering how to make a sandpie; he will learn nothing useful from having his early efforts trampled on.

Local facilities and imagination can provide a range of winter outings, though not all of them are free. Many facilities, such as swimming pools, are quiet enough for toddlers during the school day, and there are all kinds of improbable public places which can give them new and exciting experiences that are less boring for their caregivers than yet another wet walk. Riding on buses and trains is always popular and watching them at their terminals is free. Shopping malls or large department stores can seem like fairyland to a toddler, especially when nobody is even trying to accomplish useful shopping but only to have fun. They are warm, bright, full of people and fascinating objects and the expedition can finish with a ride up the escalators and down in the lifts. Museums and art galleries are often empty on weekdays and, outside major cities, some of them are still free. They can give your child a quarter of a mile of warm carpeted space and his escort some chance to look at the exhibits. He may even surprise you by wanting to look too.

Who's treading in
whose footsteps?

Your toddler wants to be near a trusted adult as he plays and will often welcome help and participation in what he does, but he does not need or want to be told what to do. His play is exploration, discovery and experiment. If adults insist on showing him what particular toys are "for", demonstrating the "right" way to do things and telling him the answers to questions he has barely formulated, they will spoil the whole process. Make sure that all the adults who regularly care for your child understand that the art of joining in a toddler's play is to let him be playleader. Provided adult dignity will permit a subordinate role, grown-up companionship can greatly enrich his play:

■ Give your toddler physical help. He is still very small and incompetent. Often he has a plan in his mind but is frustrated by his physical inability to carry it out. Lend him your co-ordinated muscles, your height and your weight, but make sure that you stop when his immediate problem is solved. He wanted you to carry the watering can to the sandpit, but did he ask you to wet the sand?

■ Offer partnership. Some games require a partner – and usually not another toddler. He cannot play "chase" if nobody will run (slowly) after him. He cannot practise rolling and receiving a ball if nobody more skilful will play. Try, sometimes, to arrange unlimited time for these games. Many toddlers have to nag ceaselessly in order to get a grudging game from an adult and then they spend most of the 10 minutes allotted to them waiting for the dread words "that's enough". You cannot play with him all day but even if it is somebody else's job to play with him a lot, do try, sometimes, to seem willing, or even eager, to play yourself, and let him have the luxury of going on until he is ready to stop. He learns by continuous repetition. If ball-rolling is on today's agenda, he may need to roll a ball for 20 minutes at a time.

■ Offer casual demonstrations and suggestions. He can use any number of these provided they are not made bossily or at tactless moments. If he is playing with ping-pong balls and you happen to have the cardboard tube from a paper roll to hand, pick up a ball and show him the interesting thing that happens if you roll it through the tube. He is free to take up the suggestion or not, just as he pleases. If he is playing with crayons and paper, show him how you can make dots instead of scribble. He may or may not want to have a try himself. But don't bustle up with the ping-pong ball or the chalks

Toddler drawing is
about discovering what
crayons do and how to
make them do it.

Don't expect toddlers to "play fair". They need adults to help manage their friendships.

when he is busily engaged with his teddy. If you do, you rudely imply that what he is doing has no importance. You are interrupting him.

■ Help the toddler to concentrate. He will probably find it hard to work for more than a few minutes at a time on anything that he finds at all difficult – especially if it involves sitting still. That means that he will not be able to get much satisfaction out of his most advanced new activities like puzzles or fitting toys. If you will sit with him, talk, support and encourage him, he will be able to go on for longer, perhaps for long enough to get the tremendous satisfaction of completing his self-imposed task.

■ Help your child to manage with children he doesn't know well. Given plenty of opportunity, older babies and young toddlers can build real and lasting friendships with each other, but acquaintances can be difficult playmates. Your child will get great pleasure (and many new ideas) out of playing alongside other children, but unless they know each other well, be prepared to conduct the party for them both. They are not old enough to be left to "fight their own battles" or to "play fair", "take turns" or "be nice to visitors". They need protecting from each other so that neither gets hurt physically or has to watch a "friend" destroy a mysterious arrangement of counters or break down a careful sandcastle. Give them similar materials and let each do what he wishes, guarded from interference. Both will play, pausing now and then to watch the other; enjoying each other's presence. If they eventually begin to talk directly to each other, rather than communicating through you, a real friendship may be in prospect.

Older children can be wonderful company for a toddler and pro-vided they are not expected to do it all the time, playing at the younger level can be fun for the older ones. Rigid separation of age groups – even year-by-year groups – is peculiar to Western societies and of questionable value, especially now that the mixed-age experience of a big family of siblings and cousins is rare.

All children can benefit from opportunities to experience being leader as well as follower; or baby as well as big one. When a mixed age group finds itself together and away from the peer-pressure of anyone's classmates, do encourage joint play but supervise it while everyone learns how it's done. An eight-year-old who has never played with a toddler before may let himself be "caught" three times in a game of tag, but the fourth time his natural desire to win will overcome his new awareness of this staggery small person and the game will end in tears. You can help with tactful (and congratulatory) reminders; by holding hands with the youngest children so they can keep up with the bigger ones; by taking the little ones to be spec-tators of alternate "rounds" so that the others can play unhindered, and eventually by helping the whole group to find a game which has natural roles for everyone so that each can play at her own level. On the beach, wave-jumping suits everyone from the ripple-splashing baby (with his hand in yours) to the breaker-jumper. At home, any variety of "mothers and fathers" or "hospitals" provides a range of roles. Don't assume that the toddler will be the baby or patient, though; he may end up giving a bottle to a seven-year-old who is making the most of his first opportunity in years to be the baby.

TOYS AND PLAYTHINGS

Toddlers will play with whatever is available to them. They need raw material to explore and experiment with but they do not (yet) care whether it comes from a toyshop, is passed on by a friend or is assembled from junk materials. It is impossible to generalize about which of the thousands of available toys your child should have because it depends what she already has, and chooses to spend time on. But there are various types of plaything that every child will enjoy and learn from in one form or another during this age period.

Natural materials

The messiness of clay is part of its point.

The world is full of small hidden creatures.

If your child is to understand the world and how it works, she needs to know which materials are natural and where they come from. If you live in a city apartment and don't have a garden, your child won't acquire that knowledge automatically. It's up to you to make sure she realizes that concrete is artificial and that not all water or milk comes out of taps, bottles or cartons. And it's important to give her different materials to explore, and to tolerate messy play, so she can discover how they behave.

Water. Play with plain, bubbly, coloured, warm or cold water will teach her that it pours, splashes, runs, soaks and feels cold in the end even if it's warm to start with. If she blows, it bubbles. Some things she puts in it float, some sink and some dissolve. It can be carried in things with no holes but it leaks through a sieve or cupped hands and seeps through fabrics. The child will play in scale with the quantity you provide, so while a paddling pool is glorious and a bath is obvious, a washing-up bowl on lots of newspaper, with small containers to fill and empty and extras such as ice cubes, food colouring or a whisk, are good too.

Earth and clay. Natural versions of these materials are so messy that children are usually given playdoughs instead. However, part of the unique value of clay lies *in* its brown messiness. Your child needs to discover – and be able to enjoy without shuddering – the

way it squidges gloriously in the hands yet can be rolled and pounded, shaped and moulded. Soon she'll realize that more water makes it sticky, less makes it too hard to handle and drying out changes it into a solid.

Playdough. Shop-bought or home-made playdough is a superb play material but children really need to have it as well as, rather than instead of, clay.

Sand. "Washed" or "silver" (not builders' sand which might contain cement) links water and clay or dough play because wet sand behaves rather like dough but with interesting differences, while dry sand behaves like water but is different again. A solid that is not solid and a liquid-like substance that is not liquid. Again scale matters more than quantity. A beach is heaven and a sandpit (with a cat-proof lid) is an excellent buy for the garden, but a couple of kilos of sand on a tray in the garage or even in the kitchen can light up a winter day. Failing sand, a kilo of rice is sometimes a worthwhile gift. Provide spoons and containers in scale and encourage "play cooking" – the first steps towards interest in the real thing.

Stones and leaves. Playing with these won't teach geology or botany; your toddler is not ready for that. But she is ready to observe that shiny stones dull as they dry, green twigs bend but later snap, and the world is full of fascinating shapes, textures and creatures.

Basic science and engineering

Blocks are for sorting now, building soon.

Posting boxes prove that shapes and angles matter.

So that's why un-building is tricky.

It's not enough to get it in, it has to go through.

Your child has to learn how things work and how to make them work; discover principles that seem obvious to us, and perfect fine manipulations that we don't even have to think about.

Filling and emptying. Filling cups with water or sand, paper bags with oranges or your handbag with small toys, and then emptying them out again, is an early step towards more sophisticated manipulative play. Along with useful manual skills your child learns how much water fills or overflows which cup; how many blocks fit into that box, and what happens when the containers are overturned. She needs lots of interesting objects, varied containers and patience from caring adults.

Sorting and classifying. Noticing the similarities and differences between things and learning to group them in her head, is one of your toddler's most important thinking-tasks. Grouping things with her hands helps her do it with her brain. Watch carefully and you will see your child beginning to identify all her cars as distinct from any other toys; later you will see oranges separated from potatoes. Later still you may see her considering universal dilemmas, such as whether the apple goes with the ball because they are both round, or with the biscuit because they are both edible. Your child will sort and group whatever comes to hand but it's fun to have large collections of natural objects with less definite differences, such as stones or shells.

Manipulating objects. When your child builds on all those skills and learns to manipulate things, toys really come into their own. They must be well-made, though, so that once she discovers how two objects fit together, they do actually fit.

Blocks. Building blocks will be part of her play for several years and she needs at least 60. Different colours are fun but different shapes are more important. They must all be in scale so that tiny ones are quarters and small ones are halves. Tip them and they are higgledy-piggledy; put them end to end and make a line that may be a train or a fence or a pattern; pile them with the smallest underneath and they fall, build on the largest and they stand.

Fitting toys and stacking toys. Different versions of these help her discover – and prove to herself – that round balls will not go into square holes; big things will not fit smaller ones; complex shapes only fit together if the angle is right. There is scope here for making as well as buying. Your child will use a first "post box" made by cutting block-and-ball-sized holes in a cardboard carton, weeks before she can manage the simplest one from a toy shop. Plastic beakers that will build up or fit inside each other as well as being used in the bath are a cheap and easy version of many stacking toys. Many kinds of "play people" that fit into holes on vehicles and playground equipment have a long and varied play life.

Formboards and jigsaw puzzles. You can create first "formboards" by cutting out dough shapes and helping your child put them back in the holes. She will probably also like a first jigsaw where whole figures lift out by a knob. Soon she'll be ready to tackle standard jigsaws with a few large pieces.

Hook-on and threading toys. Any hook and ring will join together; two hooks will too but two rings will not. Why? The toddler will hook a plastic quoit with your umbrella or experiment with a train with simple couplings. Closed rings are fun to thread on anything long and thinner. Threading rings on a rod is fun; so is discovering the threading order that makes them a pyramid. Eventually she will enjoy threading curtain rings or cotton reels onto a piece of wool or a shoelace.

A special place to bounce is good for all of you.

Going over the top is a tense moment.

Foot-power comes before pedal-power.

Toddlers must run, climb, jump, swing, roll, push and pull. It's using their bodies to the full that teaches young children to control and co-ordinate them. Although every day should be full of physical activity, special facilities and equipment do help to protect both your furniture and your child!

Rough-housing. Toddlers fall down a lot and it often hurts. Most love being thrown about by an adult who's got the knack of rough-housing safely. And throwing herself about painlessly – on inflatable play equipment or on your big bed if that's allowed, or on a gym mat or giant floor cushions – is the kind of fun that encourages physical confidence and adventures like turning head over heels.

Climbing. Climbing frames give most children a lot of pleasure and valuable, varied play over many years. A foldaway wooden cube, 1.2m (4ft) square can be used indoors (if you have room) as well as out, doubles as a playhouse and is ideal right now. For permanent garden use and for the future, buy the biggest frame (wood or metal) you can afford, site it on grass for safety and keep it interesting for years with extras such as a sheet-cover to make a tent, scrambling nets and climbing ropes.

Swinging. Swinging gives children a glorious sense of power and freedom, appeals to their innate sense of rhythm and teaches them a lot about weight, balance and gravity. Your toddler needs a small swing with a safety seat. Later on, though, an ordinary garden swing isn't the only, or always the best choice. Its fun is limited; it depends on someone else pushing, and it can be unexpectedly hazardous, too, when several children are in the garden together and feet are flying. A convenient tree branch, or the central walkway of a big climbing frame will take alternatives such as an old car

tyre on a rope or a more elegant, bought, monkey swing.

Running for fun. For an urban child (even one with good access to gardens or parks) enough safe space to run freely, as far as she wants, without anyone calling cautions after her, is intoxicating. An older child or adult to run with will make her braver; she'll even begin to get the point of games like "tag".

Throwing, catching and kicking. Few toddlers can catch a ball, but all enjoy and need big, light balls to chuck around, kick and capture. An inflatable beach ball almost as big as herself is a glorious variation: your toddler will lie across it and roll over on and with it. Bean bags, easily made at home and filled with rice or lentils, make an interesting change because they neither roll nor float.

Push-pull toys. Large scale toys to push or pull are a "must". That toddle-truck is still a good buy – usable indoors or out, for dolls, sand or a friend. Doll's prams, lawn mowers and sit-on-or-push animals may all be fun once your child walks steadily enough to cope with toys that might tip or run away.

Ride-on toys. Your toddler may enjoy being pushed along on a wheeled animal but the best buy at this stage is usually a low stable toy with swivel wheels – a first car, for example – which she can sit on and push along with her feet. This is preparation for the first tricycle, pedal-car or tractor which many children will begin to be able to manage by the time they are two-and-a-half and which will lead, in due course to a real bicycle.

Imaginative play

A miniature world puts your child in control.

A real job with real tools feeds imagination.

A hat and a scarf and she's someone else.

While your toddler is learning to sort and group objects, to understand their behaviour and to manipulate them by hand, she is also becoming able to imagine objects and pretend their behaviour. Although much imaginative play will take place with the child as the main actor – the doctor or the mother – a world in which she can play God is also valuable.

Miniature worlds. If your toddler has little cars or zoo or farm animals, with some bought or home-made garages or barns, or dolls' house-sized people and an environment for them, she will start by sorting them, but then move on to creating and acting out their stories and disasters.

Domestic play. Domestic chores may bore you, but they are among the few adult activities which toddlers can easily understand and share or imitate. At first your child will simply want to be given a cloth like yours so as to wipe things too. Later she (or equally he) will pretend to be a grown-up with domestic responsibilities for cooking, cleaning and child care. The "home corner" is usually the most popular facility in any playgroup or child care centre. Although your toddler will like to be lent some of your domestic tools, most of them will be so much too big for her that she will need toy versions of manageable size. Look for replicas of real equipment rather than irons that play tunes or cookers in the shape of Disney characters.

Dolls and soft toys. Don't reject soft toys as too babyish or dolls as inappropriate for any age or either sex. Apart from the familiars who guard the cot at night, a large family will be well-used for a long time and so will a selection of dolls' clothes and equipment. The toys will people imaginary games from tea-parties to rides on chair-trains and receive and relieve a lot of

uncomfortable feelings as your child inflicts on them some of the bites and pinches she is learning not to give to real people. Don't be surprised if your child subjects them to harsh discipline, shouting more crossly than you ever shout and even hitting them when you never smack. Children try out the exasperated as well as the loving aspects of parenthood, and play out events from fantasy as well as from reality, as they think about themselves in relation to adults.

Dressing up. One of the most important kinds of imaginative play is pretending to be somebody else: role play. Your child will experiment with the roles of everyone she observes just as she tries out your domestic roles. Dressing up helps this kind of play along but your toddler neither wants nor needs "dressing up clothes" in the sense of a ready-made fireman's or nurse's uniform. Instead she needs "props" which, to her at least, identify the character. Hats are often key items and a collection of plastic helmets, hats, caps and headdresses, as supplied to nursery schools, can be a good buy. Otherwise the toddler needs the use of your (current or abandoned) handbag, brief-case, shopping basket or sports bag; your tie, sunglasses or running shoes, together with a collection of adaptable cast-offs. A jacket that is no longer even good for gardening magically transforms its wearer into a grown-up man. A handbag signifies a grown-up lady and it only takes an old nightdress to transform her into a bride or a queen.

Looking and listening

Adult attention helps your child sit and concentrate.

Lots of books enrich your child's development.

Help your child feel and make a rhythm.

Although your toddler seems to be on the go all day, it's important to her future education that she begin to learn to enjoy play that demands more thought than muscle and to enjoy looking and listening without much doing. It's adult participation that helps toddlers understand and concentrate.

Books. These are crucial to education, so helping your child to make friends with them and learn to value them is really important.

Picture books. She needs books with clear, detailed pictures of recognizable people and objects she can learn to name and point out.

Tough cloth or board books. There's special value in books she can be allowed to look at alone, especially at nap time or in the early morning when she is in her cot.

Story books. Every child needs stories with large, detailed illustrations, and adults to read them to her. Teach yourself to adapt difficult words, edit out boring bits and put in explanations as you go. Share every picture in detail and encourage your child to find characters and events in them. "Reading" pictures is a necessary start towards reading text. Emphasize interesting-sounding words and play up rhymes and verbal jokes: your child doesn't have to understand every word to find them hilariously funny – hence the success of the inimitable Dr Seuss.

Reference books. As soon as she begins to ask questions about the world she needs to know that books have answers.

Books you read to yourself. Seeing you enjoying books tells her that reading is not mere child's play.

"Books" on cassettes. The more she is read to the better. She can get extra reading time from nursery rhymes, in the car perhaps, and later "turn the page" combinations.

Music. A sense of rhythm seems inborn in almost every child but musical sense can also be taught. Listen with your toddler to whatever music you prefer as well as to children's songs and nursery rhymes. Encourage dancing or marching or clapping. Help the child to hear how the melody rises and falls and to feel its meaning through her body. When she begins to sing recognizable songs, she's ready for other instruments. Two saucepan lids or a tambourine can serve as an instrument, but your child will need something accurately tuneful, too. Banging a piano is fun, if you have one, but a good xylophone (from a music shop) is easier for her to play and an electronic keyboard is easier still.

Television and video. Most television leaves toddlers cold because it leaves them behind. Instead of waiting while she takes it in (as you do when you read to your child), it moves on regardless and she gets lost. Toddlers who seem glued to the TV screen are often not *watching* at all, but almost hypnotized by the noise, colour and movement. But there are a few TV programmes for three- to five-year-olds that your child may already get new ideas and words and songs from, especially if you, or whoever is taking care of her, will watch too. And some children's videos come to serve toddlers like favourite story books: revealing more and more of themselves with repeated viewing.

Live theatre. If your local park or library offers children's shows, with puppets or the simplest comic magic, your toddler may enjoy them, especially if she goes with siblings or friends, and shouted participation gives her a glimpse of the magic of being part of an audience. If you have a chance to take her to a real play staged for her age group, grab it. Theatre for under-fives is so rare that if it is put on at all it is usually by dedicated, and excellent, companies.

Painting, drawing and collage

When it comes to brushes, the more the better.

After fingers and sponges try cork or potato prints.

It's not what she makes but how she makes it.

The second year is not too early for these grown-up sounding kinds of play provided you don't expect your toddler to use a brush, pencil and scissors right away.

Painting. Putting paint on paper is the point at this stage. Do not expect your child to produce a picture *of* anything. It's "just a picture".

Finger painting. Unless getting her hands covered in paint makes your child anxious, first painting is best done with fingers. It releases her from the effort of trying to control a brush, and means that there's no barrier between those thick, rich colours and swirling textures and herself. Dress (or undress!) her and the surrounding floor or table as you would for play with water or clay. Put a small quantity of each of several colours (black is often a favourite) in a palette or on a plate, stand that on a big sheet of paper and encourage her to smear and blob, mix the colours and see how they change.

Sponge painting. When she wants a change from fingers, painting with a sponge is easy and fun and so is making prints with variously shaped and textured objects. Handprints are often the most fun of all and handprint patterns make excellent "cards" for relations and friends.

Using a paintbrush. If your child is going to use a brush, painting at an easel is easier than at a table. Toddlers are hopeless at rinsing brushes between colours so you'll need a brush for each pot. Even then the colours in the pots and on the paper are likely to end up non-descript brown.

Drawing. When your child starts to draw, she takes the first step towards writing, but even that first step is frustratingly difficult for most toddlers. Get yours interested by drawing for her, "magicking" a cat or whatever she asks for. You don't have to be any good at drawing! Provide chunky wax crayons as

soon as she can hold them in her fist, and big (at least A3 or broadsheet newspaper sized) sheets of paper. Rolls of lining paper are cheap. The clean side of used computer print-out paper is ideal. Help her discover that she can make marks, and eventually scribbles.

Felt-tip pens. If your toddler is into painting but still finding a brush tiresomely difficult to handle, if she longs to draw but is still unable to press hard enough to put much colour on the page, then big, non-toxic felt-tip markers, made for children, act as a compromise between painting and drawing; almost as richly coloured as paints; almost as graphic as pencils. Unfortunately they dry up if the tops are left off and they're not *totally* washable.

Non-paper surfaces. Drawing on a blackboard with coloured chalk, or on a plastic laminate "whiteboard" with felt-tips makes an interesting change. It's better not to put boards on walls, or allow chalking on outdoor concrete, though. How is your toddler to resist other walls or floors?

Collage (or cutting and sticking). Your toddler won't yet be able to cut out with scissors or stick bits and pieces on paper to make actual pictures. Still, it's not too soon for her to enjoy what she *can* do with paper and a washable glue-pen, and to get exciting experience of different textures. If you give her ready-cut coloured paper, bits of foil and ribbon and string, she will stick them on with much glue and glee. If you show her how to tear and scrumple tissues, she will add drifts of them. And if you give her a ration of lentils or pasta and show her how to sprinkle them *onto* glue, art will be indistinguishable from creative cookery.

Moving Into Early Childhood

Your toddler isn't a baby any more but she is still *your* baby. Feeling able – and allowed – to stand still, or go backwards sometimes, helps older toddlers to deal with their remaining ambivalence about getting older, and go forward most of the time. So even if your child is more clingy and less independent than you'd like, try not to push. "Independent toddler" is a contradiction in terms, anyway.

A lot more is expected of many two-year-olds and three-year-olds than was expected of you at that age. It's fine for most, but some are subjected to more pressure than they can easily withstand. Modern working patterns and hours, coupled with awareness of the importance of education in the earliest years, mean that by the time they reach their second birthdays some toddlers are spending longer days in child care centres or nurseries than ten-year-olds spend in school, meeting curriculum and social demands that are close to what used to be thought appropriate for half-days for three-year-olds. Many others are at home, of course, at least part of the day, but even for them, scarcity of space, siblings and safe neighbourhoods may mean that a lot of input is needed from outside and much of what is available is "educational". However much your toddler enjoys swimming lessons or music or gymnastic classes, don't lose sight of the fact that she is not only expected to acquire specific skills but also to form a learning relationship with a teacher. She may manage, but she may not. It's a lot to ask at this stage in her life. If you're at home with two children under three, or your childminder is, and that weekly class is one of the social highlights of the week, it can be difficult to accept that the child who won't participate or let anyone else concentrate has not under-performed but been over-faced. Maybe there is a carer-and-child group available that will be less demanding of her and an equally welcome break for you.

Many two-year-olds spend longer in nurseries than ten-year-olds spend in school.

It's fine to have high expectations of your individual child that she is eager, and usually able, to meet. In fact one of the most effective ways to smooth the path into childhood is to assume that your child is intelligent and sensible, co-operative and kind, and react with surprise and sympathy when events suggest otherwise. Expectations of your child in competition with others are a different matter, though. Watch out for the deeply entrenched assumption that children who go fastest today go farthest in the long run, because that's the winners and losers route into childhood. The manufacturer says that "educational toy" is "suitable for ages 12–24 months" but that doesn't mean that a two-year-old who ignores it is failing. She may be busy with other things. She may be uninterested because it's a boring, ill-designed toy. "We expect all our three-year-olds to know their colours and the days of the week," says the owner of the best nursery school in town. Is it *really* the best? Don't let your child's pleasure and pride in learning nursery rhymes or getting to the potty in time (*almost* always) be dimmed by her inability to name the difference between her red T-shirt and the yellow one.

Child development is a process, not a race. There are no prizes for going fastest or getting there first and the more you can believe that, the smoother the path into childhood will be, for your toddler and for you. You have enormous influence over your child but you are not responsible for bustling her along from helpless baby to competent person: the developmental process will move her along at the rate that is appropriate for her. So don't use up all your parenting time and energy in acting and reacting. Save some for being the warm, congratulatory bystanders of your toddler's efforts to do for herself more and more of the things you used to do for her: the caring companions of her play; the unfailing supporters and facilitators of her own growing up.

EARLY LEARNING

Your child has been learning with and from you since the moment she was born and she will go on doing that, whether or not you are conscious of teaching her. But as she emerges from the personality crises of toddlerhood, and as her language burgeons, giving you a window into her increasingly sophisticated thinking, you will probably find yourself considering her education in a more formal sense. A "good education" is certainly important to later happiness, but despite the increasing emphasis that is placed on formal performance tests and assessments, try not to let yourselves equate education with school, at this stage in your child's life, or the value of education with examination success at any stage.

Once school becomes an educational goal instead of an eventual educational tool, it is easy to put too much emphasis on the formal aspects of the learning that will go on there – on reading, writing and numbers, for example – and to feel that you can and should give your child a head start: "When my child starts school she will learn to read and write. If she's already learned to read and write at nursery school she will be a school success from the beginning, but if she's going to learn to read and write at nursery school she'd better go to a playgroup first so that she gets a flying start at nursery. Maybe I can persuade the playgroup to take her as soon as she's two if they can see that she's ready. But will she be ready? We'd better find a toddler group now and start practising playgroup skills..." Your child, and any adults who share her care with you, will have a more relaxed time and feel more confident if you let each stage in her education do its own job. Toddler groups are not meant to teach children "playgroup skills", or indeed anything specific. They are intended to provide caring adults and their charges with shared fun, with social learning as a useful extra. Playgroups are not meant to prepare children for nursery schools, either. Although the differences between groups with different titles are sometimes scarcely detectable, playgroups and nursery schools take philosophically different approaches to meeting the educational needs of three- to five-year-olds. As for getting a head start into school itself through early academics: the legally compulsory ages for starting school are set where they are because educationists believe that those are the most generally appropriate times for the very beginning of formal academic learning.

Learning at home If you let your child lead, you cannot teach her too much, too young. But if you go ahead, dragging her along behind, you risk putting her off the whole business of being taught. The simple answer to "how much should I teach my child at home?" is "as much as the child herself invites".

Your two-year-old is not likely to invite you to sit down with flash cards and teach her to read, but she may well become fascinated by what the postman brings, irritated when everybody vanishes behind the Sunday papers and amazed by your absorption in a book with no pictures. Let her into the secret of reading and let her decide whether to accept it as information about adult behaviour or to experiment with the idea for herself. If the reading-game takes off with advertising hoardings, television slogans and road signs, by all means play it with her. Many children can recognize "exit", "stop" and "toilet" long before it occurs to anyone to teach them to read. Once your child understands that those squiggles mean something, that they constitute a useful and enjoyable code-system in older people's lives, she may try to follow with her finger the words you read aloud to her and want her name written on everything from her door to her T-shirt. She may, but she may not. It doesn't matter either way. It is her interest in, and understanding of, the point and process of reading which is important, not the level of her skill.

If your child does lead you into teaching her academic skills, do try to do it by putting her in the way of discovering interesting things for herself rather than exercising her slowly improving memory in rote-learning. Saying, "One, two, three, four, five..." isn't counting; unless she knows that those words are the names for numbers of things, and can comprehend the differences between the groups they are names for. Until then it's a useless, boring chant. If your child is going to count, let her start with named objects rather than named numbers. If she can seek and deal out a spoon for you, a spoon for me and a spoon for Daddy, there'll come a time when she'll find the word "three" useful and eventually she'll discover that four comes after three because it is the one more spoon she needs to get out, just today, because Granny is coming. And once your child is interested in numbers at all she will not just be counting but adding, taking away and dividing (or sharing out).

Widening horizons The bigger children get, the more input they can use from a wider world, but they cannot get interested in things they have never seen, or lead the way towards activities they have never thought of, so it's up to you to introduce your child to what is available. Whether you do it yourself or by proxy, through a nanny or childminder, offering your toddler new opportunities, large and small, is a crucial, and highly enjoyable, part of easing her forward into childhood. Do bear in mind, though, that while it's up to adults to offer, to explain, maybe to demonstrate, it's then up to children to accept or reject. If you buy her a toy that she has not asked for because she did not know of its existence, you may have to help her understand its instructions; you may have to demonstrate its potential, but after that it's up to the child to use it as she sees fit – or not at all. It's the same when you introduce your child to the library and the idea that she can have any

Everyday expeditions can enlarge your child's resources without straining yours.

number of new books to look at and to listen to. You hope that she will enjoy books and you probably try to build them in to pleasant routines like bedtime, but you don't try to make her listen to stories when she would rather be doing something else, or sit still for the end of a book that's lost her attention. It's equally important to introduce her to many different skills, but even more crucial to let her decide for herself whether to go for them. She could not invent the idea of a huge pool of cold water to immerse herself in, but if you take her and show her, swimming may become her favourite game and an early skill – or something that scares her out of her new swimming pants. The more ideas, activities and skills you can offer your child the richer will be her choices, as long as you keep those choices genuinely open. The apocryphal story of the father yelling at his toddler on the beach, "I've brought you here to paddle now b..... *paddle*" vividly illustrates the inadvertent pressure you can put on your child by spending so much (money or effort or time) that she must repay you with her pleasure. Whether your practical circum-stances, personality and mood direct you to offer your child a lot or a little, beware of sacrificing so much that you obligate her. If an afternoon at the zoo will strain your resources so that you will be really upset if she looks at pigeons and people rather than peacocks and penguins, take her to the local park instead.

Play with other children   Babies enjoy, and toddlers increasingly need, the companionship of other children, but arranging for your child to have a comfortable amount can be difficult. If she is in all-day child care she may spend more time than you would choose in shared group activities. If she is a third child following twins she may seem perpetually left out. If she is a first child, and cared for at home, she may see no other children regularly and still be unaware of the joys of friendship and the possibilities of group play. Small families, working parents with a range of child care arrangements, and un-child-friendly environments mean that if children who are not yet old enough for school are to have the peer companionship they increasingly need, adults usually have to organize it. Many kitchen calendars have more entries for the two-year-old than for both her parents put together.

Carer and
toddler groups
Carer and toddler groups go by different names in different places but are all designed as much for adults' as for children's benefit. They aim to provide parents and other carers with a pleasant place to meet and talk with others, and to provide children with play activities that will, hopefully, occupy them fully so that some adult relaxation is possible. In some towns and most cities there are also at least a few other meeting places for adult-small child pairs, such as one o'clock clubs, under-fives drop-in centres and young family centres. A few will provide facilities (as well as acceptance) for children with special needs. Describing the variety makes the provision sound far better than it is, though. One small area may have a choice of groups while another has only one, and vast rural areas have nothing at all.

If you can find – or perhaps start – an informal group which meets even once or twice a week, it will certainly introduce your child to social life while it improves your own. But however good the play arrangements (and some toddler groups, especially those run in pre-school playgroups' premises, have excellent facilities) such a group will not serve similar educational purposes to a pre-school group and is not meant to do so.

One important difference is that your child remains entirely in the care of whoever takes her there. However friendly the other adults, or however skilled the early years worker which a well-established group may employ, your child does not have to depend on any but her own adult, in emotional matters like sorting out fights or kissing banged knees or for personal service in the lavatory or at drinks time. The group compels no expansion of her input from the adult world or of her communication with it.

Although such groups usually refer to themselves as groups they seldom function that way. There is no membership or subscription payment so parents tend to bring children when it suits them to do so and not otherwise. If a group is the one-and-only in the district and open only once a week, its membership may in fact be fairly consistent, but a drop-in group that is available all the week may contain different combinations of children at each session. Your child will probably always find playmates for the afternoon but unless individual families make private agreements about when to go, she may get no chance to find out about real, individual friendships; about being part of a little gang within a bigger group or about ways of coping with children whom she finds difficult.

But the most important difference between carer and toddler groups and pre-school groups, such as playgroups, "play schools" or nursery schools, is the basic difference between the kinds of play-learning experience they can offer. The toddler group may have many of the same toys and activities as a playgroup and your child may much enjoy the chance to use equipment she does not have at home, but the toddler group does not have the trained teacher who makes a good pre-school group into something much more than "just play" (see p.542).

A carer and toddler group can provide the company your child is beginning to need and you are beginning to miss.

HAVING A NEW BABY

Although your toddler is not a baby any more, being *your* baby is still important to her. Being ousted from that position by a new baby brother or sister is a very common but always considerable bump on the road into early childhood. That doesn't mean it's unfair to do it to her though. You have an absolute right to have another baby if you want to and to have it when you want (or when it happens). There isn't an ideal age gap from children's point of view. Whether yours is one or four when the new baby comes (eight or twelve are a bit different) she *won't* like it, but she *will* cope and it's perfectly reasonable to expect that she will even be glad you did it – one day.

Parents who love one child and look forward to the next often find the idea of the older child being resentful and jealous almost unbearable. But although it's natural to want your toddler to share the family's pleasurable anticipation, pretending that she's looking forward to and will love the coming baby does not make her more likely to do so. Things will probably go more smoothly if you can face the truth: you are asking your child to put up with feeling supplanted and however you dress the facts up, she is going to mind.

Just for fun, imagine a husband breaking the news to his wife that he is going to bring a second woman to live with them in the marital home. If he used the various phrases that are used to tell small children about new babies, how would the wife feel?

PARENT TO CHILD	HUSBAND TO WIFE
"We're going to have a new baby, darling, because we thought it would be so nice for you to have a little brother or sister to play with."	"I'm going to take a second wife, darling, because I thought it would be so nice for you to have some company and help with the work."
"We love you so much we just can't wait to have another gorgeous boy or girl."	"I love you so much I just can't wait to have another gorgeous wife."
"It'll be our baby, it'll belong to all three of us and we'll all look after it together."	"It'll be our wife. She'll belong to both of us and we'll both look after her together."
"I shall really need my big boy/girl now, to help me look after the tiny new baby."	"I shall really need my reliable old wife now to help me look after this young new one."
"Of course I shan't love you any less, we'll all love each other."	"Of course I shan't love you any less, we'll all love each other."

It wouldn't go down well, would it?

When we love people we want to be enough for them. The fact that they want another person makes us feel jealous and pushed out. So assume that your child is going to feel jealous and instead of trying to induce pleasurable anticipation of an event which she can barely understand and would not look forward to anyway, concentrate on building up her ability to cope with it. That means making sure that all the relationships between existing family members are as secure and happy as they can be; building up any aspects of her life that are at least somewhat independent of you and doing all you can to pace the demands you make on her – from using a potty to accepting a new childminder – so that well before the baby is actually born, she's feeling competent and in control of everything that's expected of her.

Telling your toddler about the coming baby If your older child will still be under about 18 months when the baby is born, pre-verbal and really still a baby herself, there isn't a great deal you can do to prepare her. She will undoubtedly be amazed, and probably furious, when you leave her and then come home with somebody else to whom you pay attention. On the other hand because she is so young, she will very quickly forget that she ever was the only one. And at least the fact that she isn't old enough for you to talk to her about the baby means that she will not be able to suggest that he go home now! If she immediately turns into a truly terrible tantruming toddler, you – and most psychologists – may wonder whether it was the new baby which transformed her. But since nobody will ever know what she would have been like at that stage in her life if the baby had been born much later, there's no point worrying about it.

If the gap between the two children will be two years or more, assume that your toddler understands at least the general sense of most of what you say to her now and that her language will increase dramatically over the next few months. Talk to her about the baby even if she only understands half of what you say; that half is far better than nothing and infinitely better than not trying.

Don't start too soon though. Your toddler's time sense probably cannot encompass months. And even if it can, why add the burden of having to try to explain the inexplicable, to your despair if something should go wrong with the pregnancy? Use the early months of pregnancy for talking to her about families; point out her friends' brothers and sisters and try to find some very young ones for her to watch, especially at the breast. If you can help her accept that most families have more than one child in them, having a second child in her own may feel less like a punishment (or betrayal) for which she has been singled out.

Tell the child yourself before someone else lets it out though. Around six months is probably ideal, but tell her sooner if you cannot trust friends not to drop hints or comment on your shape in front of her. Left to herself she will probably notice nothing until you are so huge that she keeps sliding off your non-existent lap.

Making new space for the newcomer Try to foresee the things that will make your toddler feel most pushed out and arrange in advance for the new baby to have his own places, not hers. If she often sleeps in your bed, for example, either resign yourselves to sleeping with both children (do you need a bigger bed for a larger family?) or persuade the older child into her own cot well before the baby comes. If she sleeps in her cot, think carefully before "promoting" her to a bed so as to free the cot for the baby. If you are determined not to buy or borrow a second cot, it's certainly better to move the toddler out early enough for the cot to stand empty for a few months and, hopefully, stop feeling to her like hers. But if she wouldn't have been ready for a big bed if there hadn't been a sibling coming along, she'll probably be even less ready because there is. If you are going to have two children under two, why *not* two cots?

If you are breast-feeding, tail off and stop as soon as you can, even if your milk supply seems unaffected by your pregnancy and nobody's yet pushing you to wean her for your own sake. If your toddler not only remembers the breast (which she certainly will) but also still yearns for it, watching you nurse the new baby will make her both sad and angry.

Make any lifestyle changes well in advance, especially if they directly affect her. If having two children is going to mean that you have help in the house for the first time, or that you give up your childminder and care for both children at home during a long maternity leave, do it well in advance, even if it means you pay for, or use up, several weeks you don't really need. If your child has to get used to having a stranger around at the same time as she's getting used to the baby, it will add enormously to her stress, and you certainly don't want her to feel that you are staying at home because of the baby when you did not stay at home just for her.

Do everything you can to get the child's separate life going well. If you plan pre-school for her and she will be three by the time the baby arrives, consider starting her a bit early. If she is not going to pre-school or is too young to start yet, work at establishing a network of friends she likes to play with and other houses she likes to go to. She is going to need things to think about other than you and that baby; places to escape to and ways of showing herself how different she is from the newcomer.

Foresee the weeks around the birth. She has time now to get used to whatever arrangements she will have to accept then, when she is under stress. If you are having the baby in hospital and she will spend a night or two with Granny, arrange a couple of preliminary visits and make them treats. If her father will care for her and does not usually take much part in her routine care, make sure he understands exactly how to get the bacon "just right" and which soft toy is which. Small details will loom large when the child is missing you.

Wherever you deliver the new baby, someone else will have to undertake a large part of the older child's care for a week or two. Two parents and two children can be ideal, but if full-time parenting will be new to your partner help him to integrate himself in advance. Nothing is more demoralizing than a child who wails, "Mummy do it" whenever her father offers help – and it will not do much for your milk supply either.

Coming up to the EDD   Tell the child where the baby is (again) and help her feel it move. Once she has accepted (or had forced upon her) the fact that there is going to be a new baby, physical evidence of its existence will help her to face the reality and to get interested in the whole affair.

Try to make the baby real for her by discussing names and speculating about sex, but don't describe it as, "a brother or sister for

Being able to feel the baby makes him real and interesting to the toddler.

you to play with". It will not be that for many months. It is *your* baby and she needs to know that. Talk ruefully about how helpless it will be and how it will cry and wet its nappies. Tell her that she was just the same when she was tiny; show her some photographs of herself as a baby and think up some funny stories about her infant misdeeds like the time she peed on Granny's dress, sicked up in the bus or bit the doctor. Aim to inculcate an attitude of tolerant and amused superiority.

Keep birth arrangements to yourself until you are sure of them a couple of weeks before your due date. Even then, be careful not to make promises you may not be able to keep. If you have promised to have the baby at home, your departure to hospital will seem a betrayal. If you have guaranteed only to be gone for 24 hours, the days that follow a Caesarean will seem a lifetime. Play safe, be vague.

If you plan to have the baby at home, think carefully about how closely your older child should be involved. Of course you want her to feel part of this family occasion, but it may be better for both of you if she isn't actually present for the birth – or for the second stage of labour; or transition; or those last, whopping first-stage con-tractions... The reality is that unless you are phenomenally lucky, you will need to concentrate (and have your partner concentrate) on your labour once it is fully established, undistracted by the need to try to protect your child's feelings, and that labour and birth aren't a spectator sport anyway. It's difficult enough for most adults to come to terms with all that blood, sweat and tears (remember how you, or your partner, felt about that first video?); imagine how the scene is likely to strike a three-year-old, especially when it's *Mummy*. She needs a tactful companion in the house whose priority is *her* and who will tempt her away to pre-planned and promised activities at the right moments.

If you are having the baby in hospital, do say "goodbye" before you leave, even if you have to wake the child to do so. Of course that's hard on whoever is going to care for her for the rest of the night, but it is much better for her to face your departure at 2am than to wake at 7am and face what will feel like desertion.

Don't promise that she can visit you in hospital, even if children are allowed. If you have to be away from her for more than 24 hours, coming to see you will help, but only if you seem like yourself. If you should have a drip set up or so many stitches that you cannot move without wanting to screech, it may be better for her to wait.

Coming home When you come home, remember that it is you the child wants, not the baby. She is going to have to accept that baby's presence and the care you give him, but give her a chance to register your return first. Come into the house to greet her on your own, leaving the new person to somebody else for a few minutes.

Unless your older child is so accustomed to babies nursing that she's likely to take it for granted, try to show her how the new baby breast-feeds before your milk comes in. If your breasts are engorged, your discomfort and the new baby's difficulty in latching on will not leave you with much attention to spare. If your older child was also breast-fed, remind her. She'd probably like to see photographs of herself nursing. Later on, when she can actually see milk dripping and leaking, your child may ask to try some. She's probably not asking to suck, and you certainly don't have to let her if you're not comfortable with the idea, but do give her a taste of breast milk off your finger so that she can see she is not missing nectar.

Although of course you'll do with the child as many as possible of the things you did before, there are bound to be many times when you cannot, and at least some when the reason is obviously a conflicting claim by the baby. On those occasions, it's usually best to come right out into the open and say what you know the child must be feeling: "I know you're waiting and I'm sorry it makes you feel cross, but I've got to feed the baby first. I know that must seem unfair, but little babies simply can't wait for their food so I must do it now. He will go to sleep when he's full, though, and then we'll play."

It's important to make it clear to your child that you are responsible for the baby and that you will never neglect him – even for her. However much she may seem to want you to put her first, it would be truly terrifying for her if you did. After all, if you ignored the baby's crying to play a game with her, how could she be certain that nothing could ever make you ignore *her* distress?

Accept any offers of help from the older child, but don't make too much of the "you're my big girl" line. She may not be feeling at all big. Indeed she is probably feeling that being big is her whole trouble; if she were tiny, you wouldn't have wanted that beastly baby or at least she'd be getting as much attention as him. To have to help in order to get your approval may be the last straw.

Offer the child chances to behave in a babyish way for a bit, and make it clear that far from having to be "grown-up" to keep your approval, you love her devotedly even if she decides to be more babyish than the newcomer. You could offer her a turn in the baby

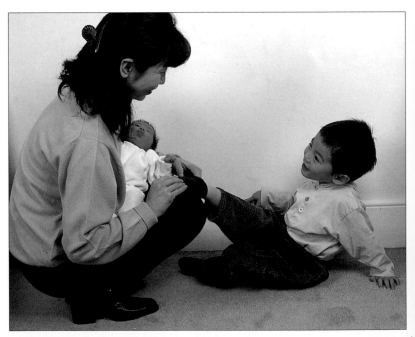

When there's a baby around, a bit of babying will help your older child.

bath and a babywipe for her face. You can cuddle her, pat her back and sing to her. It may sound absurd but from the child's point of view it is not. You want her to feel that while the baby gets a lot of things she does not normally get, he is not getting anything she cannot have, but only things she has grown out of and replaced. Not, "I'm not allowed his milk" but, "I'm old enough to have apple juice."

Try to minimize not only your child's jealous feelings but also her guilt about them. Don't ask her to love the baby, for instance. She cannot. If you ask her to she may pretend that she does but inside she'll be worried that you would hate her if you knew what she really felt. It's better to accept, even suggest, that the baby is a considerable nuisance to her just now, while assuring her that having a brother or sister is ordinary and okay and that one day the two of them will be friends and companions. Protect her, as well as the baby, from any chance that she might hurt him. If she does, she will feel horribly guilty however nice you are to her about it or however much you pretend to think it was an accident. Watch carefully when she makes approaches to the baby; make clear and consistent rules about when (and if) she may hold him, and use a cat net (which she will think is against cats) to catch the balls and blocks that get thrown into the Moses basket or pram by-accident-on-purpose.

Try to find some real advantages to being "the oldest" to balance the inevitable disadvantages. This may be the moment for a few new privileges, carefully tailored to her age, stage and particular yearnings. A later bedtime, perhaps, or a regular Saturday expedition with Dad and without the baby. If their father is willing and able to take a full part in the care and companioning of both of them, he can make all the difference to the older child's reactions to the new baby. When there are two parents for two children, the pull between their differing needs is much less obvious and painful because he can cope with the baby while you do something with the older child, and be there for her when, inevitably, the baby wants to nurse at all the wrong moments. Even fathers who have always been close to their first children often find that this period of family transition cements their relationship. The child is under stress, but because she feels let down by her mother's involvement with the newcomer, she turns to her father.

Restoring your child's equilibrium, and your own However upset your toddler may be by the new baby's arrival, she will eventually accept him and even (improbable though it may seem right now) get something out of the new family constellation. To hurry that time along, work to make the child feel that *the baby likes her.* We all find it easier to like people who like us and the toddler is far more likely to feel some affection for her new brother if early advances seem to come from her. Fortunately this is easy parental sleight of hand because you know (and the child does not) that the baby will smile at anyone (especially a child) who puts a smiling face close to his and makes noises. So as long as you can get your toddler to smile, the baby will; and once he smiles you can play it up a little. "Mary is the one he really likes" you can say to admiring visitors. When your older child acknowledges a special relationship – "He'll stop crying for me" – you'll know you are over the worst.

Must only children be lonely children?

We have one child aged 26 months and, dearly though we love him, neither my partner nor I want another. Our reasons are basically selfish – we enjoy our present lifestyle and know that we couldn't afford the child care that makes it possible twice over – but we don't want to be selfish at our son's expense. Will he suffer for being an only child, as most of our friends and relations suggest? Are only children necessarily lonely children?

The "only child" is an unhappy concept, but the unhappiness, and even the concept, is mythical. There is no evidence to show that children suffer for lack of siblings. Indeed, the sparse research that has been done tends to suggest that first-born children are in many ways more "successful" than the later-born. Every first child is an only child, at least for a while, and most only children could become first children.

Research into birth order effects is beset by this kind of definition difficulty. Your son will only be counted as an only child if he *never* has a sibling, but if you had another baby when he was 10 or 12 years old that wouldn't undo his experience of growing up without siblings. And it does not make psychological (as opposed to statistical) sense to count the teenage sister of a newborn as the older of two children, in the same sense that your son would be the elder of two if you had a new baby next year.

If there is an unhappy mythology surrounding only children, an equally mythical warm glow surrounds the concepts of brother or sisterhood, and especially the fun of being part of a large (three children? four? more?) family. That view of family life is certainly strengthened by children's literature, much of which was written when large families were ordinary, older siblings expected to nurture and share with younger ones, and the world outside home considered safe for exploration by unsupervised children

with bikes or dogs. The fact that some siblings bully and burden each other and that five children sharing a computer in a modern city flat might not have as much fun as five sharing two ponies on a farm between the world wars, is forgotten. In fact, it's so difficult for people with a sibling (or more) to imagine life without, that they tend to see every only child almost as the bereaved child they would be without their siblings.

In reality, of course, an only child is not deprived of beloved siblings but only of the opportunity of having them. And he has considerable balancing advantages, such as never having to grow through the pain of being supplanted, and never having to share his or her parents.

The decision to have one child rather than two or five is yours. It's not selfish to make it for your own reasons because being wholeheartedly wanted by parents gives babies the best possible start. Furthermore it would be pointless to try to make that decision for your son's benefit because there's no way of knowing how that one circumstance among many would impact on him. Instead of worrying about whether your decision is right, try to make sure it's not wrong by being conscious of stereotypes like the "spoiled only child" when you are thinking about his upbringing, and insure him against the most likely kind of loneliness by cultivating cousins, or honorary cousins, the children of close friends and perhaps only children themselves. Regular visits by other families, built into your family's celebrations and holiday rituals, will give a "familial" foundation to your son's childhood. Like any other child, he will rely on friends from day care, school and the neighbourhood for everyday companionship. On holiday weekends and religious festivals, though, all families tend to turn inward and that's when the only child is most likely to feel not only lonely for peers, but also uncomfortably spotlit by the undiluted attention of adults.

With any luck, two or three months of tactful handling and lots of affectionate attention from you both will carry the child through to a point where she can be amusedly patronizing about the baby. Try very hard to get her there before he gets mobile. While he lies where he's put, he is only in her way in the emotional sense, but once he can crawl into games and snatch crayons, biscuits and hair he will be a practical nuisance too. If your child can say, "Oh isn't he silly!" or, "He's trying to copy me!", their relationship will survive. If she simply dislikes him, you will all be in for a difficult couple of years.

Twins are tough competition, but even their brother will like them if they like him.

Even when first jealousy has blown itself out and your older child has almost forgotten life as the only one, you'll still need to give some thought to balancing their needs. If she starts school at the same time he starts playgroup, both will need all your emotional support and you will have to share it out or overdraw on your resources. There will be problems in suiting treats, expeditions and holidays to their differing age-stages; problems in nursing one who's ill without neglecting the other, and in coping fairly with one who gets his own way by charm while the other fails to get it by bullying. And as long as they both depend on you emotionally there will be jealousy on both sides. A younger child's jealousy (or even a twin's) can be just as painful, so don't go overboard in guarding your older child from the green-eyed monster.

Try not to assume, even as they grow older, that your children love each other. Parents often take this love so much for granted that they insist that children are "very close really" even when constant quarrelling and bitter complaints suggest otherwise. Even twins, who almost always are very close, may be so as much by necessity as by choice. Both need to be offered opportunities for separateness, and if one wants it and the other does not, both need help in coping with hurting and being hurt.

As toddlers move into early childhood they find it easier to treat each other decently.

Two or more children in a family, including a step-family, have to tolerate each other and behave decently. Adults can and should insist on that. But those children do not have to love each other; given the inevitable jealousies that arise from sharing you, they may not and you certainly can't make them. Don't make them pretend; don't force them into each other's company. If you let them work it out, they may eventually surprise you (and each other) with their mutual affection and loyalty.

THE YOUNG CHILD

From two-and-a-half to five years

A young child does not emerge from your toddler on a given date or birthday. She becomes a child when she ceases to be a wayward, confusing, unpredictable and often balky person-in-the-making, and becomes someone who is comparatively co-operative, eager-and-easy-to-please at least 60 per cent of the time.

Children change and grow up gradually. They do not transform themselves overnight, turning from caterpillars to butterflies under our eyes, but this particular change from toddler to child, whether it takes place at two-and-a-half or four, does have something of that sudden and magical quality. Looked at factually, the developments that take place in your child's third year will probably not be as great as the changes of the second, but they seem tremendous because they make her so much easier to live with and to love. It is as if by making it safely through infancy and toddlerhood, your child has, in some almost mystical way, "got there".

So where has she got to? People often call this the "pre-school period", but that's not only a mundane name for a magic time, it's also a misnomer. These three-ish to five-ish years are not a waiting time before school or even a time of preparation for school but an age-stage properly called "early childhood" that has a developmental agenda of its own. That agenda has nothing to do with school. It is exactly the same in societies where formal schooling starts much later or not at all.

A lot of the magic lies in her language. Adults characteristically do very little and say a great deal. We use words instead of actions, berating ourselves and others with guilty introspection and scolding rather than with hair-tearing and blows. We talk about what our troubles are, rather than howl about what they make us feel. We call on the phone rather than on foot and we make lists rather than buy 10 items one at a time. Everything we do and feel and think is somehow mediated through words. In complete contrast, toddlers say very little and do a great deal. They express themselves in action and demand action from us. With a toddler you cannot only explain, you also have to show. You cannot send, you have to take. You cannot keep her safe with words, you have to use your body. That is the crucial gap between you that begins to close as toddlerhood gives way to early childhood. Although pre-school children are still very physical in their reactions to their feelings and to the world, still readily capable of tears and tantrums, they have learned enough language and enough of the thinking that goes with it to be able to join us in using words as well. At last you can talk to your child, have what you say listened to, understood and accepted, get reasonable answers back, even make a joke without pulling funny faces and still get a laugh. Alongside the unique feeling-links between you, the lines of communication we use in friendship and in other kinds of love are opening up. It is this, more than anything else, that makes the child seem like a "real person".

This small person has built up a lot of experience and a lot of accomplishment in the past year or so and it begins to tip the balance of what she needs from adults further from care and closer to companionship. She can wash her face (if you tell her); put on her boots (if you leave them the right way round); get her own drinks (if she can reach the tap) and climb in and out of chairs, cars and trouble. As she feels more able to manage her world and herself in it, so you can devote increasing time and energy to the exciting business of introducing her to a wider world and its ideas.

As she uses the kaleidoscopic pieces of what she has learned, shaking them together in her mind to form and re-form different patterns of thought, she begins to remember from day to day. She applies what she learned yesterday to what she does today and she looks forward to tomorrow. Because she can look forward she can wait a bit, too. The offer of a game when you have finished what you are doing does not always drive her into a frenzy because she wants to play now. She can enjoy simple choices, asking herself what she enjoyed last time, wondering what she feels like now. She can begin to understand (though not necessarily to keep) promises; to recognize (though not reliably to tell) the truth, and to acknowledge (though not always to respect) the rights of other people.

She can begin to acknowledge your rights because her feelings of individuality are secure enough that she can see you as a separate person in yourself. She no longer sees you as a semi-detached part of her or takes you for granted as a slave whose desire to do other things than look after her is at best incomprehensible, at worst illegitimate. She may not understand why you should want to talk to adult friends, but she sees that you do; sees that you enjoy talking together the way she and her friends enjoy playing; sees the reasonableness of your case. So this is the age of bargains: the beginning of the practical and emotional trade-offs on which adults' relationships subtly depend. "If I do this, will you do that?" appeals directly to her finely balanced sense of justice and makes it easy to find ways around almost every potential clash.

Seeing you as a real whole person brings her love for you, and for her other special adults, much closer to adult concepts of love. She becomes able to experience genuine sympathy and unselfish concern; capable of offering something because she thinks you might want it rather than because she feels like giving it. If she should see you crying, she will not simply be frightened and angry at the feelings your tears call up in her, she will be sorry for you because of the feelings the tears suggest you are experiencing. She would like to help you, like to have some part in making you feel better. If she comes and hugs you, it may not always be an attempt to reclaim your attention from whatever is bothering you, but rather an attempt to soothe you with her own attention. Toddlers, even babies, also give as well as take, but it's far easier to see which is which once they grow into childhood.

As she watches you and the other adults who are close to her or who catch her imagination, the young child strives to understand your various roles and your behaviour towards each other. Most of her social learning takes place through identification and she will "be" all kinds of people from her own baby sister to the bus driver. Above all, though, she will try to "be" you, singling out and imitating characteristics that may surprise you. Despite all your efforts to keep roles and play gender-free, for instance, both girls and boys often adopt a surprisingly sexist view of family life, seeming always to be involved in domestic play when they are "Mummy" or with mechanical matters when they are "Daddy". The accuracy of your child's observations may sometimes be uncomfortable. As she looks at her father, you will sometimes see a reflection of your own, supposedly private, coaxing expression on her face. As she cares for her doll-family you will hear familiar turns of phrase and the expressions you are least proud to recognize as your own.

It is through identification with adults in general and with you, her special people, in particular, that the young child begins to take in and make part of herself, instructions and demands which previously came from people outside her. Now she begins to scold herself (and anyone else below her in status, such as the baby or the cat) for carelessness you had not even noticed. She warns herself against actions you had not known she was contemplating and she tries to

Unconditional love is a nonsensical notion.

Who came up with the absurd idea that it's wrong for parents to love children more when they are nice and less when they are horrible, or to love the ones who behave themselves more than the ones who don't? I have a four-year-old boy and two girls who are three and one. The boy has always been difficult (I didn't realize quite how difficult until I had first one and then another easy little girl) and now he is having problems at nursery school. The head teacher says his refusal to do anything but play is within normal limits for four and had the cheek to suggest that I should stop "pressuring" him and comparing him with his sister because that's making him feel that I'd love him more if he'd learn something. Well of course in a sense I would. Every parent would rather have a successful child than a loser. I pressure my son because he doesn't try hard enough and I think that's right. How are children to learn to work and do better if everyone just says, "That's okay, we love you whatever you do."?

There's a big, important difference between what children do and who they are. And there should be an equally large and even more important difference between approval of an action and love for a person. Nobody with any sense would say that parents should approve of their children's throwing macaroni cheese on the floor, tantrums in the playground or wobblies over going to bed. Children need to know that behaviours of that sort are unacceptable, almost as much as they need to know that chores and kindnesses and effortful self-control are appreciated. Disapproval (as well as approval) of things they do helps teach children to behave as they should, which is part of a parent's role. On the other hand, disapproval of how they *are* does nothing to help them be the people parents think they should be.

Children's development – physical, intellectual, emotional – is unique to each and not a race between them. Parents do not need to hustle them from one stage or accomplishment to the next because provided children are offered appropriate experiences, the developmental process can be relied upon to move them along at the rate that is appropriate for them. And there is no point in pressuring a child to learn letter sounds or songs or pencil control because he will not, cannot and should not devote his energies to such activities until he is ready, however unhappy you make him.

Parents who are over-controlling and interventionist do make children unhappy. Furthermore they often cause the very kinds of "failure" they are trying to avoid, by failing to be some of the things their children most need them to be: models, caring companions, unfailing supporters and facilitators of their overall development as individual people. It is that kind of global supportiveness that defines unconditional love and is the foundation of children's ego development. From earliest infancy, when babies learn who they are by seeing themselves reflected in their parents' faces, the self-esteem and self-respect that will maximize children's fulfilment of their potential, their resilience in adversity and their ability to esteem and respect other people, depends on feeling loved, respected, even celebrated, for who they are now, not for what they do or might become in the future.

Loving a child unconditionally means loving him whatever he does (however much his actions this morning were disapproved of) and making sure he knows it. More than that, it means making sure that he can compare himself with his sister (and, later, with classmates at school) safe in the knowledge that extra achievement, though good in itself, *wouldn't* bring him more love, and that failure, though a pity, carries no danger of losing him the love he's got. "Nobody loves a loser" you say, but nothing creates a loser faster than fearing loss of love.

run everything just the way she thinks you want it. Because she is very young and inexperienced, she will sometimes go too far so that she sounds bossy and smug. From time to time you may find yourself looking forward to her more babyish and less virtuous moods, or even tempted to squash her when she asks yet again: "That's right isn't it, Daddy?" or "Aren't I good?"

Goody-goody behaviour may sometimes be irritating (especially to siblings) but it is a triumph for your child's development – girl or boy – and a gold star for the relationship between you. It means that your child who is no longer a toddler consciously wants adult approval, wants you to be pleased with her and is prepared to put some effort into seeing that you are. You have always known that she needed love and approval, but a year or so ago she often seemed not to care whether she got it or not and never seemed to know how to earn it. Now your child is actually asking you to tell her what behaviour does and does not earn approval, so she is ready to learn any social refinement of being human which you will teach her. Since that was what you were aiming at all along, her obvious desire to please should make it easy to be patient and gentle with her. She knows now that she wants your love and she has learned how to ask for it. Give it to her in full measure.

EATING
AND GROWING

By three or four, children who do not have food and eating mixed up in their minds with love and discipline (see p.334) are often enthusiastic about food. They use up an enormous amount of energy in their daily lives and eat to replace it. Provided there is enough food available, a child like this will certainly take in enough calories; hunger will see to that. And if the food is adequate in proteins, vitamins and minerals and offered sensibly, he will also select a diet that is well-balanced for his needs. Your child may still refuse particular, valuable foods like meat or green vegetables, but that will not matter provided he can obtain equivalent nutrients from foods that he enjoys, such as cheese and fruit.

Helping your child to eat sociably

If your child is enthusiastic about eating it is because nobody has spoiled for him the natural relationship between feeling hungry and enjoying food. If that's the case he will be ready, now, to start to fit in with the social aspects of mealtimes. Go easy, though, even if he's about to start staying all day at nursery. You don't need to clamp down at home to ensure that he fits in elsewhere. Children who eat enthusiastically at home and enjoy other aspects of day care or nursery school life often adapt very happily to group lunches. As long as your child finds food that he likes available, and isn't pressured to eat what he dislikes, you are likely to find that he imitates the other children and eats more foods more neatly when he's with them than when he's with you. Knowing that he *can* do it, you can certainly raise your expectations of his social eating at home, but do it gradually. If you suddenly insist that he eat spaghetti bolognese because he eats it at nursery, or demand a vast improvement in table manners overnight, you could still put your child off eating and make problems for yourself:

Your child may enjoy the greater independence of group mealtimes...

■ Teach table manners by example rather than by exhortation. On the whole your child will come to behave as the rest of the family does, so if you are suddenly irritated by his eating with his fingers and leaning his elbows on the table, make sure he is not watching the rest of you doing the same thing.

...and eat what the other children eat.

■ Promote the child to eating arrangements like your own. He will imitate adults more readily if he sits on an ordinary chair (or a small but extra-tall version specially made for young children) rather than in a highchair, and if he has a place setting like everybody else. He cannot learn to take care of china and glass and to manage a fork, spoon and eventually a table-knife, if he is only given plastic.

■ Help him to acquire new tastes. If your pre-school child knows, from bitter experience, that he will be made to eat anything that is put on his plate, he will probably refuse even to try new foods, in case he does not like them. He will feel much more adventurous if you allow him to taste before the meal or to have a tiny bit of the new food on a teaspoon, and then decide whether he wants to be served with it or not.

It's good for growing children to make food part of fun.

■ Get the child used to foods which will make life easier for you – and make him more a member of the family and less the baby of it. A child who is generally enthusiastic about food will usually accept new foods if he sees you eating them with pleasure. Accustom him to whatever will be available on camping trips, picnics or in your local restaurants. Above all, try to get him used to eating cheese. Bread or biscuits with cheese and a tomato or an apple, is a perfectly balanced meal which takes 30 seconds to prepare and another 30 seconds to clear up. It is easily portable, available in any roadside café in any Western country and conventionally appropriate at any time of day. If your child will happily eat that combination you need never interrupt a day's activities in order to think of a meal for him.

Family meals   Few of today's families can have every meal together because busy people come and go at different times. But it's a pity if every meal is a kitchen-scramble, with mashed potatoes dolloped from saucepan to plate and food eaten by one, kept hot for another and cooled for a third to microwave three hours later. And it's even more of a pity if there aren't any meals with mashed potatoes because home cooking has entirely given way to cook-chill and take out. Preparing and cooking food is basic to human survival and caring, and sharing it is basic to kinship and friendship. If your pre-school child grows up without any home-cooked family meals he'll miss out on an important traditional aspect of family communication and togetherness. Furthermore, if he never experiences food as something more than fuel, he will have no chance to acquire a sense of occasion around relatively formal meals so he's almost certain to "let you down" when there's a really important party.

However busy your household, it may be a good idea to commit yourselves to one weekend meal that is formal enough to be fun. Your pre-school child could be involved in the cooking, at least to the extent of seeing that potatoes start out muddy and have to be boiled and skinned before they are mashed. He could make the table look pretty – perhaps picking flowers for the middle or folding paper napkins – and he could change into clean, tidy clothes for the meal. If the grown-ups have a drink beforehand, a special drink for him adds to the fun. During the meal, food is served on dishes and everyone, including the child, helps themselves and each other. It is obviously an occasion for something specially nice to eat and for at least some conversation which will particularly interest him.

In this kind of atmosphere your child will not feel nagged at if you show him a more conventional way to manage a fork or get peas to his mouth. He will feel honoured that you are letting him in on the grown-up world. It is realistic too. Why shouldn't he eat with his fingers when he is having supper alone in front of the television? What matters is that he should be able to behave inoffensively at table when the occasion demands it.

Faddy eaters   Not every young child eats well, of course, but real eating problems now are almost certainly a hangover from the toddler period and need handling similarly (see p.336).

However, a lot of pre-school children get labelled "faddy" or "difficult eaters" when they are only trying to exercise the same rights to personal taste and appetite that adults take for granted. In well-fed, Western societies most people would rather stay hungry than eat food they really dislike. Yet outside institutions, adults seldom face the choice. They buy and/or prepare what they do like. Only young children are faced with food chosen and prepared by someone else and are then expected to "eat what is put in front of them". So do be sensitive to your child's dawning tastes in food. After all, where those tastes are similar to yours, you accept them without question; it is when a child's tastes differ from everyone else's that he tends to be called "faddy".

While every family will work out its own attitudes to individual food tastes, there is a reasonable middle-road which will go a long way to avoiding mealtime trouble for all concerned:

A CHILD'S POINT OF VIEW	YOUR POINT OF VIEW
It is unreasonable to serve a meal or dish you know the child dislikes and then be irritated when he leaves it. Serve him something he normally eats even if it means substituting an egg or some cheese for the family main dish.	It is not reasonable to pander to momentary whims. If the menu is liver and bacon which he normally enjoys, he does not have the right to demand egg and bacon instead. If he does not want liver today he must make do with the bacon.
It is unreasonable to try to force him to eat a particular food. You won't succeed but you may put him off that food for life.	It is not reasonable to give him more than his share of what he *does* like. He needn't have salad greens but he can't have everybody's tomato.
It is unreasonable to insist that the child eat all the food on his plate if you put it there. Let him say how much he wants or help himself. He may then come back for more.	It is not reasonable to let him spoil food. He's entitled to leave the muffin and only eat the cherry off the top – but not to take more muffins just for their cherries.
It is unreasonable to try to insist that he eat at all if he says he is not hungry.	It is not reasonable to refuse him anything to eat when he says he is hungry.

Snacks Although young children can manage with larger and more widely spaced meals than toddlers, most still need to eat much more often than adults. If you are using up that much energy, it is a long time from breakfast to lunch and from lunch to supper. Children who are hungry at other times need food-fuel. A formal mid-morning and mid-afternoon snack is a necessity and will almost certainly be part of his routine whether he is at home, at school or in day care.

Problems arise because hunger gets confused with greed. Often it begins at home and at the whim of the adult in charge. The child says he is hungry and the adult gives him a chocolate biscuit. Next time, he does not say he is hungry, he says he wants a chocolate biscuit. Hunger or greed?

Problems are exacerbated because arguments about whether young children should eat between meals get confused with arguments about *what* they should eat. A vast market in fun foods has grown up during the last 10 years. Like sweets, fun foods are heavily advertised and attractively packaged. Vast fortunes ride on making children want this one rather than that and the result is that children do want them and many families over-react against them.

Snack foods are said to be "all rubbish; no goodness in them". But which foods? Dairy ice cream from a reputable manufacturer, for example, is nourishing, if sweet, food, at least as good for your child as a home-made custard. Even the lowly plain potato crisp is only potato, with the water removed, fried in vegetable oil. As such it is a surprisingly good source of vegetable protein and only the added salt makes it worse for a child than a helping of French fries.

Snack foods are said to be "fattening". Since all food contains calories, all food is fattening if it is food in excess of the amount the child needs. A child who eats adequate meals and a lot of snacks will certainly get fat but a child who eats snacks instead of part of his meals will not. There is nothing devilish about snack foods which makes them more fattening, calorie for calorie, than the same kind of food which is served on a plate.

Snack foods are said to prevent children eating their meals, but if they do it is because we make food in the hand more attractive than food on a plate. Snacks foods are almost always bought because the child is hungry, chosen by him, and eaten because he wants to eat them rather than because anyone else cares one way or the other and in circumstances that are enjoyably different from sitting up to table. No wonder many children would rather have that packet of "sesame crunchies" than their lunch, even if both are available simultaneously. The answer is to treat snack foods as food (which is what they really

Regular snack-times can be important social interludes in your child's day.

are) rather than as treats (which is what will make trouble). A child should not get potato crisps because he has been good any more than you would offer him cabbage for this reason. His ice cream should not be withheld because he has been tiresome any more than you would refuse to serve him meat. As with sweets, if you keep the emotional temperature down in this way, remaining problems over snacks should be easy to handle.

The trick is to make sure that if you are prepared to serve them at all, you offer the child the kinds of food he likes best as occasional parts of his regular meals, while keeping simpler foods freely available for eating between meals when he is genuinely hungry. Instead of waiting for him to nag you for chocolate biscuits while you are out shopping, serve one, with an apple, as a sweet course at lunch. Instead of taking a moralistic attitude to pleas for potato crisps, serve them occasionally in place of that boring mashed potato.

Your child will still need snacks, but once they have ceased to be his only chance to eat his favourite foods, he will not want them more than his main meals. A mid-afternoon snack might be a drink and bread and butter. If he is hungry enough to welcome bread and butter he is hungry enough for a snack to be sensible. He will not eat bread and butter from greed, and the iced, cartoon character biscuits he might have eaten from gluttony are coming up on the supper table to be eaten or left as he thinks fit. The whole situation is emotionally defused.

Defuse arguments about snacks by letting your child help himself to a prepared selection.

By four or five, or whenever you think your child is old enough to understand, you may like to give him some control over his snacks by establishing a supply of certain foods which the whole family knows are available at any time they want them. There might, for example, be a tin which is kept filled with plain biscuits and crackers, and a fruit bowl with apples and bananas. Equally there might always be a dish of cheese cubes, raw vegetables and raisins ready in the fridge. Different families with different tastes and budgets will find their own basics, but for all families the point is the same. These are "I'm hungry" foods. Anyone who cannot wait for the next meal can have some.

Sweets Just as snacks become problematical because we allow hunger to get confused with greed, so sweets are hard to handle because we let them symbolize love. A sensible approach to all sweet foods goes on being important (see p.341) but it will not keep sweet-problems at bay for long unless you also monitor your emotional approach to sweets and the subtle messages your child receives about them.

Almost every human being likes sweet things. Research has shown that from birth babies can distinguish between plain and sweetened water and that if they are offered a choice as part of an experimental procedure, most of them suck longer on sugared bottles. Unfortunately, instead of calmly accepting that sweet foods are pleasant, Western societies, with their copious supplies of cheap refined sugar, have made the buying and eating of actual sweets part of their pleasure rituals. In many families boxes of chocolates are an accepted part of any outing and an expected purchase on any feast day. Sweets are bought as presents, sent as "thank yous", hidden as surprises, given

If sweets don't stand for love your child may like fruits just as much.

When your child wants to spend his own money, sweets aren't the only good things available.

to make bruised knees better or disappointments bearable. Sweets are used to convey or to stand in for love, and it is in this light that children yearn, whine and badger for them.

If you use sweets as rewards and treats, your child is bound to place an emotional value on them as well as liking the taste. If a grazed elbow gets him a chocolate drop along with your hug, that chocolate drop will come to seem comforting to him. He will want sweets whenever he is miserable or hurt. If you buy him sweets when you are especially pleased with him, he is bound to see those sweets as being part of your loving feelings; want you to buy sweets to show that you love him; even feel unloved when you do not. If you pay with a sweet for anything unpleasant, like an injection, he is bound to see sweets as something he is owed whenever anything nasty happens. He will want payment in sweets every time you make him do something he dislikes. But if you can keep sweets out of the emotional arena and treat them as coolly and calmly as you treat other particularly nice-tasting foods such as fruits, none of this trouble need arise. Many children passionately enjoy strawberries and will eat as many as they can get during the short season when they are locally available. But how many of those children whine and cry and throw tantrums for strawberries, or even beg for the tasteless imports that are available year-round in many supermarkets?

If you can manage a cool approach, sweets will probably never be a major issue in your household. But sometimes, as children get older and spend more time with other children's families, they begin to compare what they get with what others get and to feel deprived. That's when your whole attitude to especially-nice-things-to-eat will be important. You want your child to regard sweets as just one more nice thing in a life full of nice things, some of which are foods, so encourage him, sometimes, to buy himself a different kind of food-treat. The actual shopping is half the point. Many small children only get the chance to shop for themselves from the sweet shop, but being allowed to choose and buy a beautiful red apple from the greengrocer or a shiny brown bagel from the baker can be just as much fun.

If you still need to formulate a sweet "policy", perhaps because your child is cared for by several adults who need to agree a stance, remember that parents who try for the strongest and most righteous line tend to have the most trouble. Strict rationing, for example, tends to focus children's attention on what is not allowed.

The policy which most often seems helpful is the simple one of not keeping sweets in the house. If there are no sweets, the child who asks can be told so, calmly and honestly. Nobody needs to get into the more potentially painful questions such as "would you give me some if there were any?"

Willingly buying the child a small packet of the least damaging type of sweets at some regular times (such as on the way home from Saturday shopping) may also prevent a lot of difficulties. If the child knows (and is reminded by his current carer) that he will get some sweets then, he is more likely to accept a refusal to buy any right now. You can reduce the damage those sweets do to your child's teeth by banning the most damaging types (such as toffees and lollipops) altogether and encouraging him to finish what he wants of the sweets he's got in one go. After all, he wouldn't expect to carry a half-eaten cake away to his room and put it away for later.

Although you are not going to have sweets around the house or let your child nibble on them for hours at a time, you don't want to make them seem as scarce, and therefore desirable, as diamonds. Make him feel that sweets are nice-but-ordinary by occasionally using them as part of meals – serving grated chocolate with a dessert, perhaps, or decorating a cake with jelly beans.

Obesity The natural growth pattern tends to slim older toddlers down so plump roundness is less usual in the year or so before school and fat children are more conspicuous. Really obese five- or six-year-olds are often made a butt by others and may also get into a vicious circle of being less active than most children because they are fat, and fatter than most children because they are inactive. So if your child really is overweight it would probably be right to do something about it before he starts school.

If you think your child may be too fat, look at his upper arms and thighs. If there are rolls of fat in those areas, straining the sleeves and legs of clothes that otherwise fit him, he probably is too fat.

A campaign to slim your child down is not something to under-take lightly, though, because it is not only his present happiness but also his future attitudes to eating and to his own body-shape that may be at stake. Before you take action it may be a good idea to take your child and his growth chart to the doctor. She will be able to help you work out whether, and by how much, your child's weight gain is outstripping his gains in height, and whether his current obesity is recent or part of a long-term pattern.

If you and the doctor do decide that your child is too fat, your aim should not be to make him lose weight but to slow his weight gain down so that as he grows upwards, less and less of him bulges out. Over the next 18 months or so your child will grow about 13cm (5in) taller. If you can hold his weight gain over that period down to only 1kg–1.5kg (2lb–3lb), he will end up a much slimmer-looking child.

Look first at your child's consumption of fats. You can cut his calories very substantially without him noticing the difference or going without anything useful, if you just reduce his table fats and fried foods. A 28g (1oz) slice of bread contains about 70 calories. If you add a normal spreading of butter you add another 70 calories with no extra value except some vitamin A which he is having in his multivitamins anyway. Use a low-calorie spread and experiment to find new spreads he will regard as a treat, such as cottage cheese.

Remember that almost all foods you normally fry in butter or oil can be dry-fried with no extra fat at all if you use a non-stick pan. Frying by this method is better for everybody. Remember, too, that many foods which your child likes crisp can be made that way by being dry-baked in an oven. Roast potatoes have about twice the calorie value of boiled ones, but not if you cook them on a non-stick pan in a very hot oven. Crisp bacon cooked by this method actually loses most of its fat.

Although the child may not be drinking a great deal of milk by now, it would certainly be sensible to give him semi-skimmed.

Miniatures, like these mini-muffins in sweet cases, make a little go a long way.

Consider what else he is drinking: fizzy drinks are high-calorie as well as bad for teeth. Serve plain water at meals and as a thirst quencher. If fizz is the point of treat drinks, mix low-calorie squash or fresh juice with plain soda water. Ice cubes often make simple drinks seem fun.

Obviously you will try not to let a child who is already fat eat a great many sweets and high-calorie snack foods. But while it sounds simple to substitute fresh fruit (but not bananas) for dried fruit and sweets, jelly for ice cream, plain rusks or water biscuits for sweet ones, bread for cake or buns, cutting down on these sweet and enjoyable foods takes tact if the child is not to be made miserable. A very useful trick is to buy, make or serve miniatures. Ten tiny sweets seem more to a child than three big ones. Three finger biscuits seem plenty yet will not contain the calories of one full-sized one. You can even make home-made cakes in paper sweet cases or split a 113g (4oz) packet of sweets into eight 14g (½oz) cellophane bags. A whole bag of sweets seems to him a generous portion; he will readily accept that he's had enough when they are "all gone".

As well as taking in rather fewer calories, using more up in energetic activity will help your child's weight to stabilize now, and may reduce his risk of obesity later on. While toddlers are usually very active provided they are allowed physical freedom, young children may have grown out of running about for its own sake – and become addicted to television. So if you are seriously concerned about your child's weight, look to his way of life – and to the energy levels of the adults who look after him. Every child, but especially any child who is overweight, needs both other children and adults to run with, after and away from. He needs people to help him learn to kick and throw a ball and perhaps to acquire traditional playground skills like rolling a hoop or skipping rope. Above all, though, he needs the adult carers on whom he'll model himself to be imaginative, energetic people, not couch potatoes.

GROWTH

It's fun to record a child's increasing height, but difficult to be accurate.

The pre-school period sees a further slowing in growth rate. Your child will probably gain around 2.3kg (5lb) and 9cm (3½in) in the third year, dropping to 2kg (4lb) and 6.5cm (2in) during the fifth. Don't worry if the gradual change from being a stocky, curvy two-year-old to a slimmer, straighter five-year-old makes the child look comparatively thin for a while. The toddler plumpness will eventually be replaced by muscle but this takes time. In the meanwhile legs and arms may look positively fragile.

There is no point in frequent weighing and measuring now. But twice-yearly checks are sensible. If weight and height rise together you will know that growth is proceeding normally. If weight rises much faster than height, you will know that the child is getting fatter. If the height does not rise perceptibly during six months, you should measure your child again three months later. If there is still no increase, take chart and child to the doctor. A very few children do lack a particular hormone which is vital for growth. It can be given to them at a growth clinic and will re-start normal growth, but it may

Help your child to trust her body and take pleasure in using it.

not be able to make up for the height the child has already failed to gain. So get advice before much growing time has been lost.

Measuring a child's height accurately is difficult. Don't try to use a tape measure directly. Instead, stand the child up against a wall or door, heels flat on the floor and touching the wall, head straight so that he or she is looking directly in front. Now put something flat and rigid (such as a book) on the top of the head so that it flattens any sticking-up hair. Make a mark on the wall, and then use a tape to measure from the floor to your mark. If you always use the same wall or door for measuring your children, you can name and date your marks so that over the years you accumulate a permanent record of who measured what at which age.

PARENTS ASK

Can it be wrong to help a child stay slim?

My four-year-old daughter looks just like me. She is already very fashion-conscious. We both enjoy dressing in mother-daughter outfits and she does a bit of modelling, which she loves. Unfortunately, though, she also takes after me in a tendency to put on weight. I've fought this all my life and I'm determined that she shouldn't face the same battles. At home we just don't have fattening foods in the house. She already knows the danger foods and when she asks for something like chocolate or ice cream at the supermarket I show her the "light" versions and we get those. When she goes out, though, other people try to sabotage our efforts, and not only people who mean to be kind and give her "treats", either. A teacher at her nursery school insists she has the ordinary snack. She says it's wrong for a young child to be diet-conscious and that I'm setting her up for eating disorders like anorexia. All I'm trying to do is help a pretty little girl avoid the misery of being a fatty. Can that be wrong?

Even more than the rest of us, babies and young children are all of a piece, physically, mentally and emotionally. To your daughter, her body is herself so her self-image depends on being able to take its good looks and appropriate behaviour for granted. Although you don't intend it that way, your constant concern over what she eats, and your active control of her diet, must tend to suggest to your daughter that she cannot trust her body; that if she let it alone it might betray her.

Furthermore, if she feels that you don't approve of her body, or only love it on condition that she "controls it" or even "makes it better" (ie. thinner and less "greedy") she may feel that you do not approve of *her* or that you only love her on condition that she co-operates with your slimming programme. It is never right to predict the effects of early childhood experiences on individuals, but your daughter clearly is receiving some potentially damaging messages about hunger turning into greed unless it is controlled; food needing to be rationed from outside rather than by appetite, and about fat being ugly and bad while thin is pretty and pretty is good.

It sounds as if those were lessons you learned yourself as a sad child who felt her weight was her problem. Your anxiety to protect your daughter from similar experiences is understandable, but the form it is taking is unfortunate. You are tending to treat her as if she were a miniature version of yourself; your foil, now, in the matching outfits, and your second chance in the future, via the modelling and so on. I'm sure you realize, when you think about it, that it's not your daughter's job to be you, to be like you or to become what you might have been. Her job is to be herself, an entirely separate, growing individual, and your job is to love that person whatever she looks like and support her whatever she becomes. You may find it easier to do that job if you have some outside help in learning to love yourself.

TEETH AND TEETHING

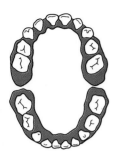

Sometime in the third year, your child will have a complete set of 20 first teeth.

Somewhere around two-and-a-half years old your child will have a complete set of first (milk) teeth consisting of 10 teeth in each jaw: two molars (double teeth) on each side, one canine (eye tooth) each side and four incisors across the front.

Last to come through are the second molars, the double teeth right at the back. Like the first molars that came through a year or more ago (see p.340) cutting them can make your child's jaw ache and her gums inflamed and sore.

The completion of the set of teeth makes teeth cleaning even more important than before. Each tooth now has another one butting up to it on one side or on both so food debris can easily become trapped in between. A small-headed toothbrush, used with an up and down motion from the gum margin to the top of the teeth, will clear most of it but it takes a careful, well co-ordinated adult and a co-operative child to make sure the back teeth and back surfaces of teeth, are cleaned as well as the front ones! Anything that makes your child more enthusiastic about the teeth-cleaning business will help you do a more thorough job.

Looking after teeth In an ideal world we would all clean our teeth after eating. In the real world twice a day is the best most of us can manage – or make our children manage. Make sure that your child's teeth are cleaned after her last food in the evening so that she does not spend all night with food debris between her teeth. Make cleaning them after breakfast a regular habit too. Then try to see that she has a drink of water, which will at least rinse her mouth, after meals. Remember that sweet foods which stay in her mouth for a long time are the worst for her teeth, so try to keep sticky sweets like toffee and long-lasting ones like lollipops away from her and, when she does have sweets, encourage her to eat what she wants and get the whole thing over rather than nibbling over a long period.

Fluoride has a strengthening effect on tooth enamel even when the teeth are fully formed and through, making it far more resistant to the acids that otherwise eat into it and let in bacteria. If you live in an area where there is little naturally occurring fluoride in the drinking water and routine fluoridization of supplies is not generally approved, do consult your doctor, health clinic or dentist. Most health professionals believe, based on accumulating experience, that routine use of a fluoride-containing toothpaste provides enough. These pastes have already reduced the decay rate among children both by their direct effect on teeth and because some fluoride is inevitably swallowed during brushing. Indeed, research findings suggest that the amount of paste some children swallow can, in itself, lead to a gradually accumulating overdose of fluoride. So ration toothpaste carefully. If your child's tooth enamel seems especially vulnerable, your dentist can apply one of a variety of fluoride products directly to her teeth.

Going to Having made a familiarization visit to the dentist during her second
the dentist year (see p.342) your child should start regular check-ups at least
every six months by the time she is two-and-a-half.

First teeth are vitally important. The second set does not even start
to come through until she is around six, so these first ones have to
last for years. Furthermore they keep the proper spaces open for the
later teeth, and help her jaws to grow to their intended shape. So
don't take a happy-go-lucky approach to early dentistry. Above all,
don't wait to make an appointment until the child has toothache.
Pain means that you have missed the stage where only superficial
enamel was affected and a repair would have been easy and painless.
The pulp is damaged and the cavity is much larger than it need have
been. Try to find a dentist who enjoys working with very young
children. If your young child can build a relationship with her dentist
before she first needs treatment, she is likely to accept any later
treatment trustingly.

Dental treatment Dental techniques have become far less traumatic in recent years. Of
particular importance to very young children is the fact that
superficial cavities that once had to be drilled and filled to prevent
them progressing can now be treated and controlled with fluoride. If
your child does have to have a cavity drilled, though, she will not
enjoy it, however much she likes her dentist. Don't make a drama out
of it but don't pretend that it is nothing either. A superficial cavity in
the enamel probably will not hurt even when it is drilled, but a cavity
as deep as the pulp may. Modern injections, with prior numbing of
the gum, are relatively painless but your child has nothing to compare

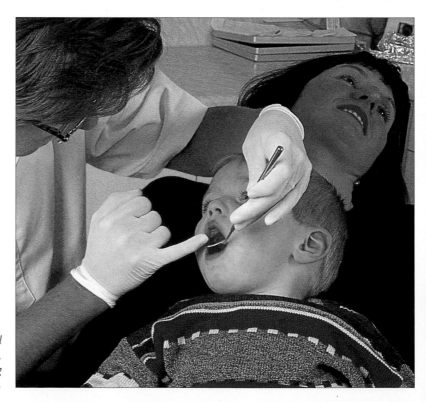

*The right dentist will
make a child's visits fun,
even if that means putting
you in the chair too.*

them favourably with. And even if there is no pain, the wet whine of the drill is hard for a child to bear, especially if a top tooth is affected. Explain what the drill is for and, with your dentist's co-operation, show the child her cavity in the mirror. It feels huge while it is being drilled; seeing how tiny it really is can be comforting. Help her to feel that she has some control over the situation by arranging with the dentist to stop drilling at once if the child signals (perhaps by raising her hand) that she needs a rest. This is really important. If she feels helpless and tortured she may panic, now, or the next time she sits in that chair.

With tactful, expert handling most young children will tolerate any dental treatment that is needed, but a few – especially the unfortunates who develop multiple cavities in their first four years of life – will find it impossible to co-operate. Discuss any problems and proposed solutions privately with the dentist. It is possible that an empathic parent, especially one who is phobic of dentistry, is not the best person to help the child. She might manage better with the other parent. Sometimes two children together – even literally together in the chair, worked on in turns – can support each other. Just occasionally a dentist who specializes in work with young children can help your child to accept needed treatment if she has her one-to-one, with nobody to intervene in the relationship.

A dentist cannot work on your child by force, though, so if all else fails the two of you have to decide whether to leave the cavity for a few months, hoping that the child's nerve will improve, or whether the treatment is urgent and should therefore be carried out with the help of a mild sedative, or even a light general anaesthetic given by an anaesthetist. If your dentist insists on giving general anaesthesia herself while carrying out the dental treatment, find another dentist.

Accidents and teeth Teeth are not rooted directly into the child's jawbone but into a strong pad of highly elastic tissue which acts as a shock absorber. It takes quite a hard bang to knock a tooth out.

Occasionally a direct blow will drive a milk tooth back into the gum from which it emerged. You will probably be able to see or feel its top, just as you could when she was first cutting it. In most cases the tooth will emerge again of its own accord. If the nerve has been damaged, the tooth may "die" and this will mean that it turns a dull yellowish colour. Show it to your dentist, but don't be too worried about it. Even a "dead" tooth can usually safely be left to do its job until the second teeth begin to come through.

A tooth which gets broken or chipped is more serious. The sharp edge may cut the child's tongue as she eats or even cut through her lip next time she falls. Take her to the dentist. She will file the sharp edge down or she may decide to "cap" it.

If a tooth is knocked out, or if it is left still attached but out of place, take child and tooth and go straight to your dentist or to the nearest dental hospital. Second teeth can often be re-implanted so that they re-attach themselves. First teeth usually cannot be replaced. Your dentist must decide whether to leave your child with a gap until her second teeth arrive to fill it, or whether to make a single false tooth for her.

EVERYDAY CARE

Learning to care for herself is an important part of growing up.

During these years children's increasing awareness of their own individuality shows clearly in their sense of physical dignity and dawning desire for physical privacy. Your three- or four-year-old may feel very strongly indeed about all aspects of his, or her, physical appearance, but if he cares what he looks like it will be for him, not for you. Both boys and girls will resent being brushed and prettied up like poodles for you to show off.

Of course your child's general cleanliness, health and wellbeing are still the overall responsibility of adults, but the more you can help him to manage the details of his daily routines, the less you will offend that precious sense of self. Practically, it will be good for you, too. Every task your child performs for himself is one less for you to do or arrange to have done. Every piece of self-care is preparation for school, where none of the adults has special responsibility for his physical care. And habits set up now may last for many years.

MOVING TOWARDS INDEPENDENCE

Don't expect fast learning; many of the chores of self-care are boring and repetitive. But there will be progress. If your child will dab his face with a face cloth at two and wash it with one of you standing over him at three, he will (usually) wash it when he is told to at four and (sometimes) go and wash just because he is dirty at five.

Making self-care easy If your child is to try to do things independently, you need to make it physically possible. If your house is dark your child will probably refuse to run his own errands. Reliably lit halls or corridors or stairs make it possible. If a child is to cope in the lavatory, the door handle and flush must be in reach and the lock manageable or out of reach. Walk around your home considering your child's size and safety. Is the water hot enough to scald? Are his drawers too heavy to open or liable to pull right out onto his toes? Can he reach his toothbrush without encountering razors or pills; reach a mug without chipping your best wine glasses? Children cannot do the impossible and will not even try if their efforts are accompanied by frantic exhortations to "be careful" so arranging their independence is up to adults. If there are no coat hooks they can reach, how can you expect them to hang their coats up?

Learning to choose Making decisions is part of growing up. Your child must learn to consider what he should do, rather than simply doing (or not doing!) what you say. You cannot leave many choices entirely to your child, though, because in these early days he will often make decisions that are bad for health (like "deciding" only to clean his teeth once a week) or intolerable to you (like "choosing" to wear her party dress to school). The best way to provide decision-making practice within safe limits is usually to organize life so that your child is completely free to decide between carefully limited choices. He can clean his teeth now or after his story, and choose between the two dishes you are offering for supper.

Clothing that is easy to manage means more independence for him and less work for you.

Choosing clothes

Who says two blues don't go with purple and bright red?

Parents are often surprised at how strongly children as young as three or four feel about what they wear. It isn't only a question of comfort, or even developing clothes-sense but also of developing me-sense. Clothes are part of self-image; and of the image of self that is projected to the world. Who does your child feel like being, or want to be thought to be today? And if there is a group of children that is important in his life, how does he want to appear in that?

Your child is not old enough to choose new clothes to buy or even to select which clothes to wear, but he is certainly old enough to be entitled to some say. It is his body, after all. Why should he present it dressed to someone else's taste? Try to offer him two or three outfits or garments that are suitable to the occasion and acceptable to you, and let him choose freely from amongst those. Try to play fair on the freedom front. If they are both okay in themselves, must you veto the scarlet top because he proposes to wear it with the orange trousers?

A fuss over clothes is a wearing way to start the day. Your child may respond better to being given a choice of clothes for the morning before he goes to bed the night before. If he seems to resent a very limited choice, you could try clearing all special occasion and out-of-season clothes away so that he can choose from amongst the remainder. Sometimes, though, it is *less* choice that is needed, and your child may happily settle for a sort of private "uniform" for weekdays, alternating two pairs of trousers (or skirts and tights) and two sweatshirts. However you manage choice of clothes, do make sure they are as easy as possible for the child to manage. Go for buttons or toggles he can cope with alone rather than slot-in zips which are difficult. Unless he or she pleads for zip flies, stick to elastic-waisted trousers, shorts and skirts and buy shoes with Velcro fastenings when you can. Keep tiresome extras like gloves and hats to a minimum and sew on those that are essential (such as mitts) so they do not get lost.

Coping with the chores of everyday care

Most young children still hate having their hair washed or even thoroughly combed through, while fingernail and toenail cutting is boring and teeth are often brushed in a hurry. A weekly "spring cleaning", undertaken on a regular, agreed evening, chosen not to clash with a favourite TV programme, and conducted with pleasant ceremony, is often the easiest way for both of you. Maybe you could do some personal care chores for yourself at the same time. Set aside plenty of time; rushing will make the child bolshy. You must have time to let him try everything and the child must feel that he gets lots of relaxed attention in return for co-operation.

Your child still cannot cut his own nails but he can use an emery board to smooth the results of your cutting. Make sure his toenails are cut straight across. Cutting them in a curve (as you do his fingernails) makes them more likely to grow inwards.

Teaching your child to brush his teeth effectively himself is liable to be a struggle, but so is doing it for him. To finish off the cleaning process on spring-cleaning night, make a game of, "How well have we cleaned your teeth this week?" helping him to use a disclosing agent which stains areas of remaining plaque bright pink. Getting every bit of that pink off is a real challenge and when it is done you will know that the teeth really are clean, for now.

Hair has got to be washed but if washing it causes problems let the child decide the easiest way. He may choose any of the methods suggested for younger children, but just being allowed to choose, and therefore exercise some control, is what matters most. Using your shampoo or conditioner may help too. Once the shampoo is on, let your child do most of the rubbing himself, design soap hairstyles and have a mirror to look at them in. When the dread business of rinsing is over, teach him to check that his hair is free of soap by making it squeak between his fingers. Don't forget a final no-tangles cream rinse, and the sooner you can teach him to comb it through himself, the better, because then you won't have to do it.

There's a fun way to do almost everything that has to be done.

TOILET MASTERY AND AFTER

There is wide variation in the ages at which different children succeed in mastering the toilet business. A few (more girls than boys) are able to give up nappies altogether by the time they are three; many more are completely reliable about using the toilet or a potty by day, but still need nappies at night. Quite a lot who can manage their bowel movements are still in nappies or pull-ups because they cannot hold on long enough to get to the potty to pee.

Problems with becoming dry If your child seems totally oblivious to pots, toilets or indeed to urine itself, make sure that he does in fact understand what you want:

■ Make it clear to the child that you are confident that he will soon be able to take charge of his own urination and that you look forward to him using the pot or toilet just as you (and a personalized list of people he likes and admires) do. It sounds obvious, but it is possible that this message has been overlaid by the care you have taken to avoid toilet training pressure.

■ Make sure that the child actually sees some of those people, adults and peers, using the toilet. Imitation can be a great help.

■ Help him to be aware of wetting. Modern disposables absorb urine so efficiently, and keep the child feeling so dry and comfortable, that they may be concealing the whole business from his attention. Once he has begun to urinate in a potty or toilet, take him out of nappies as much as you can when he is at home and awake. Plastic-backed towelling trainer pants will do something to protect your carpets.

■ If you use disposable pull-ups at all, do keep them for very special occasions. If these amazingly neat and efficient garments enable your three- or four-year-old to "pass" as dry, they may reduce his motivation for mastery, or at least put the whole business out of his mind.

The child who still shows little sign of taking charge of urination may simply be a late developer in this respect. If you look back to the toddler section you will probably be able to see that he (or less commonly she) is following the ordinary sequence for gaining control, even though success is coming later, or more slowly, than it often does.

There is some evidence that being late in acquiring bladder control runs in families. If you can check your own achievements, by asking your respective mothers to search their memories, the answers may comfort you. But if both mothers insist that you were "trained" before you were two (or one!) don't be cast down. At least one of them, if not both, is probably looking back through a glow of nostalgia. There is also evidence that toilet mastery is more difficult for boys and takes most of them longer than most girls. If you are comparing a girl who was dry early with a boy who seems as if he might stay sopping wet forever, stop. They are not comparable and he will not. All children, except those with severe mental or physical difficulties, or very specific neurological disorders, learn to keep themselves dry in the end, and not such a distant end, either. How many children have you seen start school in nappies?

Temporary physical problems can make toilet mastery more difficult though. A child's sphincter should function in such a way that it is either firmly closed or entirely open. If your child is constantly damp rather than occasionally soaking, urine may be dribbling uncontrollably. Much more commonly, infection in the urinary tract, most often cystitis in girls, makes urination unusually frequent, overwhelmingly urgent and painful. Staying dry sometimes taxes adults under those circumstances; young children don't stand a chance. If your child is one of the considerable number who has a succession of these infections, don't worry, or let him worry, about toilet mastery until hospital investigations and definitive treatment are successfully completed.

Building on early mastery When, and only when, your child is reliable enough about daytime soiling and wetting to be out of nappies, you can begin to help him to generalize his accomplishment. Becoming able to manage the whole business of excretion independently, under almost any circumstances, will give his self-confidence and sense of himself as a competent individual an important boost.

Getting used to full-sized toilets Your child may have been using the toilet for months, but if he has always preferred a potty, now is the time to start a gentle switch-over. Once he can use a lavatory, he will be able to go anywhere without depending on you or whoever is looking after him to carry a potty everywhere he goes.

The first step in the switch-over is to give that familiar pot a permanent home right next to the toilet so that the child gets used to going there every single time he pees. When he is calm about that, and no longer expects to find the potty in the living room, buy a child-size lavatory seat that clips over the big one and find (or buy) a stool (or sturdy box) that is the right height for climbing on and off the lavatory alone and resting his feet on while he sits there. If you buy a purpose-made step, he will be able to move it himself so he can also stand on it to reach the washbasin. Encourage your child to use this new set-up, but don't remove the pot until it is voluntarily abandoned. Once he begins to go to the bathroom on his own – which he may first do when he has a friend in to play and the two of them go together – make sure that he always finds his small seat in place. Adults who take it off to use the toilet themselves need to put it back on again when they have finished.

Once your child is happy to use the lavatory at home, you can encourage interest in lavatories all over the place. Show him the bathrooms at friends' houses; take him to the cloakrooms in shops or at the swimming pool. He should even make the acquaintance of less elegant toilet facilities in public places, so that he is not surprised and distressed when faced with a dirty, smelly toilet on a train or in a wayside garage. Unless he has met a lack of privacy and hygiene before, the toilets at some schools may be sadly off-putting.

Most three- and four-year-olds will prefer a parent to go with them to any strange lavatory and should always have an adult carer with them in a public toilet. Although small children of both sexes can go with mothers or other female caregivers to women's facilities, and little boys can accompany fathers or other males to the men's,

Help your child to get used to using different toilets in different environments.

fathers who are out and about with little girls may still find themselves in a difficult situation. Unisex public facilities are sometimes available, especially in continental Europe. Family restaurant chains and shopping malls increasingly provide family facilities and "parent and child" rather than "mother and child" rooms. If all else fails, there is sometimes a toilet intended for the use of both women and men with special needs and therefore sited in a gender-free area.

Urinating positions Most little boys urinate sitting down when they first start using a potty but by now it's a good idea to help them begin to copy fathers, older brothers and friends and pee standing up. Groups of four-year-olds at pre-school, full of their maleness, may actually tease a boy classmate who urinates sitting down. If you point out that urinating standing up means that the child need not take down his pants, the ease and speed will probably appeal to him. Do keep him in elastic-waisted trousers or shorts until peer-group fashion makes him yearn for zip flies. Elastic is both easier and safer. Once he does stand to urinate, start teaching him to lift the lavatory seat beforehand, if he can reach. If he does have older males to copy he will probably be quick to grasp the idea of aiming. If not, you may need to draw his attention to it; a piece of floating toilet paper for target practice sometimes helps. Do make sure the surrounding floor is easy to clean, though. Elegant fitted carpeting might need protecting with a machine-washable mat. His aim will often be inaccurate.

If a little girl sees a boy standing to urinate, she will probably try too. When that experiment proves wet and frustrating she may compromise by sitting backwards astride the lavatory to pee. Don't fuss. She will soon realize that standing doesn't work for her and that sitting normally suits her body best. Accepting this is part of accepting that she is female and that female bodies are not the same as male ones.

Urinating out of doors However reliable a child may be, his waiting time at this stage will still not be very long. Every child needs to learn how to urinate outdoors if family picnics or long drives are not to be ruined for everybody. Boys don't usually find this difficult. They can copy Daddy and urinate against a tree or even beside the car in a lay-by if necessary. Girls are at an unfair disadvantage that was neatly expressed by a three-year-old who after an outing with a boy cousin demanded: "Why can't I at least have one of those useful things to take on picnics?"

Very small girls may find al fresco peeing easier if they are "held out" with a parent supporting them in a squatting position. Slightly older girls who don't want to be held may like to take their knickers right off. They often find it difficult to hold pulled-down clothing out of the way. Scout out a good site for them: all ages will be thoroughly put off if they find themselves amid nettles or ants.

Bowel rhythms Many children do not need to move their bowels every day but will do so quite regularly every two, or even three days. Others go equally regularly twice, or even three times a day. The child's pattern is individual and, ideally, it should not be your concern.

If your child seems to like to go after breakfast, this makes good physiological sense, as eating after the long fast of the night often sets up a reflex bowel movement. Later on it may make social sense, too. Many children do not like using school lavatories for anything but a quick wee so they are better off if they open their bowels at home. But if this is not your child's natural pattern, do not try to impose it. Don't even set aside a ritualized 10 minutes for the child to "try". Children should go when they feel the need, just as they urinate when they need to.

Managing bowel movements independently At home, children feel more secure and independent when they can manage completely alone in the toilet. At this stage most still prefer a parent to wipe their bottoms after a bowel movement. It is really important for little girls to be wiped, and taught to wipe themselves, from the front backwards, never the other way around. Wiping forwards brings traces of the faeces into contact with the vaginal area and the urethra and can lead to urinary infections. The sooner

Your child may prefer privacy in the bathroom even if she still needs you close and ready to help.

children learn to manage even the wiping business alone, the better. Your child may be perfectly happy with a new childminder, but very anxious not to have to accept such deeply personal service from someone he does not yet know well or love at all. At school, there may not even be anyone to help in this way so the child who cannot cope for himself may be sadly caught out. Don't try to hurry it, though. Most three-year-olds are actually incapable of wiping themselves for the simple reason that their arms are not long enough relative to their bodies.

Even when children do reckon to take complete charge of themselves in the lavatory, inefficient wiping often leads to slightly stained pants. Many find it especially difficult to do a thorough job at school, where they may be short of time or privacy, and forced to use toilet paper that is much harsher and less absorbent than they are accustomed to.

Once a child has taken charge of his bowel movements, major accidents are unusual, though not as rare as many people think (see p.460). The most usual cause is a bout of diarrhoea which not only makes passage of the motion uncontrollably urgent, but alters the full-rectum signals to which the child has only just become accustomed. It is kinder to keep a young child at home while he has diarrhoea, even if he is not otherwise unwell. Being put back into nappies is undignified while the hard-to-conceal disgust of a teacher who has to clean him up is shaming.

Wetting accidents Many three- and four-year-olds wet themselves frequently. Even five- and six-year-olds have enough accidents to make a supply of spare clothes standard equipment in infant schools. Once a child has achieved basic mastery, wet pants are much more embarrassing for him than they are for you. They are horribly uncomfortable too. He certainly would not wet himself on purpose, so do be sorry for him.

Like most adults, children urinate most frequently when they are nervous or excited so don't be surprised if your child chooses all the worst times for accidents, such as birthday parties or weekends away. Many also ignore full-bladder signals if they are deeply involved in play. A tactful reminder may save a flood. Very occasionally a child under emotional stress will hold urine for so long that the bladder becomes overfull and he is unable to empty it. This sometimes happens, for example, if an unready child is left with strangers and is determined not to use the lavatory without his mother. The answer is water. The sound of a fast-running tap may release the flow. If it does not, put the child into a warm bath. It is easy to urinate there.

NIGHT-TIME DRYNESS

Many children need nappies at night well past their third birthdays. Don't leave them off too soon because that is the quickest way to turn your child into a "bedwetter". If your child still urinates every couple of hours during the day and always wakes with a wet nappy in the morning, you can be quite sure that if you put him to bed without that nappy he will wake with a wet bed. He is simply not ready to stay dry and since the urination that takes place while he is asleep is not within his control, there is nothing either of you can do to change that. You cannot teach his bladder to concentrate and hold all the urine until morning, or teach him to wake up to the signals from his full bladder. Only greater maturity will enable him to do either or both.

Moving towards staying dry at night Don't even think about leaving off those nappies until he sometimes wakes up dry after a whole night's sleep, sometimes goes for three or four hours without urinating in the daytime, and occasionally wakes in the early morning because he needs to urinate. Even when you see some or all of these signs of growing up, don't insist on leaving nappies off if he prefers to wear them. If you make him anxious about night-time urination, you will make wet beds and eventual problems more likely. When you and he together do decide to abandon nappies, do encase the mattress in a proper plastic protective cover. Small plastic sheets get horribly wrinkled and uncomfortable and they usually manage not to cover part of the flood area. Show the child the covered mattress and explain that because it is there it does not matter at all if he should wee in his sleep.

If you have just bought new pyjamas and/or bedding, casually emphasize their washability, and don't describe them as making a "lovely bed for a grown-up, dry boy". If he gets the idea that wetting his bed will spoil these nice new things, he will be anxious before the event and heartbroken after it.

Helping your child to stay dry Many young children stay dry all night with no problems and very few accidents, but a large minority are not reliably dry before their fifth birthdays, and even after that, occasional wet beds are ordinary. If mastering night-time urination is a struggle for your child, you may need to remind yourself of the difference between trying to keep the child's bed dry and helping him to keep himself dry. "Lifting" a child to urinate late at night and early in the morning may sometimes help avoid wet sheets, but it does nothing for the child's mastery. On the contrary. If he wakes when you lift him, he will be aware that you, not he, are taking responsibility for his night-time urination. If he does not wake, but urinates, almost asleep, while you hold him out, you are actually encouraging the very thing you are trying to avoid: peeing in his sleep. It is probably best not to lift a very young child. If a five- or six-year old, who is striving to keep himself dry, actually asks for you to help in this way, make sure you wake him up enough that he can register and respond to full-bladder signals for himself.

Your child should drink whenever she is thirsty even at bedtime.

Never restrict evening drinks. It is worth cutting back on fizzy drinks (even fizzy water) because they reach the bladder extra quickly, and on drinks containing caffeine which may actually stimulate the child to pass water rather than hold it. As long as he sticks to water, milk or juice, though, the child should drink as much as he likes whenever he wants. Although it may seem logical that a child who has less to drink is less likely to wet the bed – and some health personnel still suggest depriving children of fluids for up to four hours before they go to sleep – some research suggests that this actually makes bed-wetting worse. As fluids are cut back the bladder adjusts so that it feels as full now it is holding less as it did when it was holding more. Over a long period, then, restricting

How can we stop our little boy soiling?

Our four-year-old son was difficult to toilet train because he would use a potty to wee but not to poo. For a year he went in his pants or on the floor. Then that stopped and we thought the battle was won. However, now he seems to have chronic diarrhoea. His pants are always slightly dirty and although children at nursery school don't always seem to notice, we dread to think what will happen when he starts full-day school. We've tried anti-diarrhoea medicines and sending him to the toilet every two hours, but neither seems to help. It's too embarrassing to consult our health visitor, so what else can we do?

Problems with bowel mastery are far more common than most involved families realize. The conspiracy of silence that makes it difficult for you to consult local health professionals helps nobody, least of all children at school who suffer for their smell.

The difficulty arises because toddlers feel possessive about the stools that come out of their bodies while adults find stools disgusting. Instant disposal down the toilet can hurt a child's feelings so if he is looking for a battleground to fight the power adults have over him he may choose the potty and discover that faeces give him power over them. He can pass them in unconscious but active resistance, or he can withhold them in equally unconscious passive resistance. And adults care.

If a child goes almost anywhere except in the pot or lavatory and almost any time except when someone is trying to persuade him, as your son did, there has usually been too much persuasion. Maybe you lost sight of the need to help the child take charge of himself. If the pressure can be taken right off at that stage (and that's a big "if") such a child can often move forward again. If not he may move from active to passive resistance to "training", as your son seems to have done.

In order not to pass his motions in a potty or lavatory, the child has to withhold them until he gets up. Over time he may so enjoy the sensation of withholding, and get so good

at it, that he can stop putting his faeces in the "wrong" place and put them nowhere, keeping them inside his body and under his control.

If that is indeed what has happened with your son, what seems to you like chronic diarrhoea is probably chronic constipation. If a child ignores the need to go, holding on for days at a time, faeces collect in the lower bowel, harden as the body recycles their fluid, and gradually expand the rectum past the point at which he gets "need to open" signals. A child in this situation could not pass a normal movement if he wanted to. Since he goes on eating, digesting food, and producing waste, though, liquid faeces go on forming, dammed up above the obstruction, and eventually leaking past it. That's the likely physiological explanation for the constant soiling you describe.

Soiling is not deliberate. The power battle is fought on an unconscious level. Being angry with the child is unfair and useless (though feeling it, sometimes, is probably inevitable). At this point, though, just stopping that inappropriate anti-diarrhoea medicine and taking pressure off your son to use the lavatory is unlikely to be enough. *Please* seek advice from your doctor or from the paediatrician to whom she may refer you. To resolve this impasse your child may need stool softening medications and certainly needs a careful explanation of what has happened to him, and why. Above all he needs an authority figure outside the family, to assure him that it is not his fault.

Months of daily battles about his bowel movements must have left your child's self-esteem in tatters. However oblivious he may appear, he must be painfully aware of his own odour, his "difference" from other children and their (and especially your) reactions. If he takes a "don't care" attitude to his dirty pants and other children's taunts, it may well be because he feels dirty, smelly and different and therefore isn't surprised when others share his sadly poor opinion of himself.

evening drinks may actually reduce a child's bladder capacity.

Waking because he needs to pee is a sign that control is coming. Make sure he has a pot in his room and enough light to keep the monsters that live under the bed in their places. He may still need company, though. Getting out of bed alone frightens many small children. If he is not allowed to call you, he may not get out until too late. Whatever you do, though, he is bound to have some wet and some dry beds. Don't comment on either. Congratulation for dry beds and silence on wet ones is almost as bad as scolding him for wetting. If you tell him he is "good" when he is dry, he himself will feel that he is "naughty" – or at least "not good" – when he is wet. Avoid praise and blame altogether by explaining honestly that people's bladders grow up along with the rest of them and that eventually his will be able to hold all the urine all night.

Coping with wet beds Night-time accidents are very common until around five and not unusual at seven – especially in boys. Don't be in a hurry to decide that your child has a problem. Although many parents find it difficult not to worry about wet beds when a child is four or five, it's best to keep calm if you can, and keep the child calm while he matures. If calm escapes you, though, seek help from your doctor or clinic.

Sometimes children will themselves become worried about bed-wetting – usually following tactless comments by overnight guests or hostesses. They may find it difficult to accept your assurances about soon growing out of it, and put more faith in the identical message given with more authority by a doctor. If you brief your doctor privately, explaining that it is your child who is concerned, not you, he can concentrate on reassurance, and the promise of further help being available if it is needed later. If your child can be kept unconcerned – which means you controlling your natural irritation and protecting him from being shamed by visitors – he will probably become dry spontaneously by the time he is seven. If he does not, that is quite early enough to seek help from an enuresis clinic.

If bedwetting suddenly starts again when your child has been dry for months, he may be reacting to stress in his daily life. A new baby in the family may give the child an unconscious wish to be a baby again even though his conscious wish is to be grown-up enough to stay dry. A separation from you, or your separation from his other parent, a stay in hospital, the loss of a beloved grandparent or any other major upheaval can shake a child's confidence. Anything that shakes his confidence may make him temporarily unable to manage his most recent and most grown-up accomplishments. You may see other signs of regression alongside the renewed bedwetting: a resurgence of former sleeping difficulties, for example, or demands for a dummy or even for a bottle. If the reason for your child's stress is obvious, you may be able to relieve him somewhat just by talking about it and babying him a little. If you can see that the child is tense and anxious but you cannot quite see why, a trusted caregiver or teacher may be able to help you work out what may be bothering him and how he can be helped to cope. Either way don't expect an instant miracle cure for those wet beds. Relaxation and night-time mastery will both come gradually.

SLEEPING

While almost all toddlers tend to fuss about going to bed, three- and four-year-olds tend to divide fairly evenly into children who now make no fuss about it at all and children who make even more than they did when they were younger. If your child is one of the first group you're lucky. Go on doing whatever it is that you have been doing up to now and hope that it lasts. If your child is one of the others, though, it may be useful to you to take an honest look at the whole business of bedtime.

A lot of children in this age group spend a great deal more time in bed than they spend asleep. They are put to bed because their parents want peace in the evening rather than because they need to go to sleep. If you can admit to yourself that the whole bedtime business is at least as much for your sake as your child's, you will see that natural justice and self-interest both require you to make bed, and going there, as pleasant as possible for the child.

Beds and bedrooms Making beds and bedrooms places children actually enjoy to be is a
as private places great deal easier for this age group than for younger children. Toddlers tend to be anti-bed because going to bed (or to sleep) means going away from parents. Separation within the home is less of an issue for most pre-school children, indeed many are developing a sense of territory and the beginnings of a need for privacy, and enjoy a space they can call their own. Whether you have a whole bedroom available or only a sleeping corner, try to make it over to your child as her very own, consulting her about redecorating or rearranging it, and making it clear to the rest of the family that this place now belongs to her. Older brothers and sisters should not be allowed to barge in without permission and it should be left to the child to show it to visitors if, and only if, she wishes.

Remember that the child will spend at least half her time in this special place (even if she is asleep for a good deal of it) so it should be kept just as bright and clean and pretty as the more public parts of the house. Don't expect your child to keep her own room tidy yet, however much she loves it. Unless an adult does it for her, the room will soon become so littered that it is totally unappealing.

The child's bed should be the centrepiece and this is probably the sensible moment to promote her from a cot to a "big bed". It need not be full size, of course, though an ordinary adult single bed (with a removable safety rail tucked under the mattress to ease the transition from sleeping in a cot) will cost less than a junior bed and last longer. Do think carefully before you buy her a novelty bed, though. At three, she may love sleeping in a swan boat, but what will she feel about it when she is seven and crazy about ponies or soccer? If two children share a room, do avoid double decker bunk beds if you can. One or other child will always feel that the other one has the best layer; it is difficult to feel private when two of you sleep on top of one another, and nursing a child in a top bunk is impossible so every time your child is ill she will have to be moved. If one of the children only lives with you part-time – perhaps because she

Making your child's bed a place she likes to be ensures relaxation for you as well as rest for her.

comes to stay with Daddy at weekends – consider the kind of bed that has a twin stacked underneath it that you pull out and up when it's needed. Otherwise two separate beds are your best option, even if they make the room crowded.

Make the bed itself as attractive as you can. Don't decide that it is not worth buying pretty bedding and smart pyjamas while the child still wets the bed: the pretty ones wash just as well as shabby old ones. If you are buying new bedding, that's an easy and inexpensive way to introduce a favourite story character or theme. Now that your child is past the age when it's risky for her to get too warm while she's asleep, you may want to replace blankets with a washable quilt. Duvets suit a small child's instinct to snuggle, make a big bed seem more nest-like and make bed-making easy too. Do make sure that the bed is properly made every time the child gets out of it, whether in the morning or after a nap. She will not want to return to a mixed-up muddle of bedding any more than you would.

A careful arrangement of possessions around the bed will complete a sort of "mini-home" for your child, making it a place she will (hopefully) go to happily each evening and in which she will be happy to spend time awake each morning. Tastes vary, but these are some of the things which make their sleeping quarters attractive to many children:

■ A light, safely screwed to the wall and within the child's reach. It can have a 15-watt bulb for leaving on all night or a dimmer switch she can work for herself.

■ Pictures on the wall or on a magnetic board or pinboard used with sticky fixers so she can safely rearrange it herself. Mobiles over the bed and hung in the airflow from the window.

■ A bedside table or shelf stocked with her own books. Picture books meant for young children are fine; strip-cartoon annuals meant for older children are also excellent because a non-reader can follow the picture-stories.

■ Special bed-toys which usually fall into two groups: soft toys for friendship and comfort, and puzzles and fitting toys which she may attend to better in bed than she does during the day.

■ A musical box or children's cassette player. The source of friendly noise will probably be switched on the moment the child is left for the night and the moment she wakes in the morning.

■ A means of communicating with you. This may just mean an open door or it may, in a large house, mean a baby alarm or intercom.

Using beds and bedrooms Once you've made your child a place where she likes to relax and play as well as sleep, do protect its pleasant atmosphere. You will ruin it if you ever use it as a punishment-place, for example, so don't send your child to her bedroom for time-out or to bed for naughtiness. Don't even suggest the possibility indirectly by saying, "You must be over-tired or you wouldn't be so silly. I think you'd better go to bed early." Try instead to make nice things happen in her room. If a letter or postcard comes for her while she's at nursery, put it on her bed for her to find when she comes home. If you have bought her a new sweater, spread it there ready for her to try on. Keep magazine pictures for her to put on her wall or draw her a message sometimes and put it there for her to see at bedtime. If she asks to play with something of yours which she is not normally allowed – like your special chess set or pack of cards – tell her she can borrow it to play with in bed.

If you are going to put all this thought into making bed a nice place to be, you obviously want to make getting there enjoyable too. Make sure that the child has plenty of notice when bedtime is coming up. A definite evening routine and ritual usually works best, but, whatever your family's pattern or lack of one, don't expect the child to break off in the middle of a game or television programme and come instantly to bed.

Tell or read the final bedtime story with the child actually in her bed. If the story takes place downstairs, it is just one more nice thing which has to be left at bedtime. Read upstairs it is something nice to look forward to in bed.

Leave time for confidences, jokes or just chat. The more your child feels that her bed is a place where she can talk to you, tell you or ask you things, the less she will feel that going to bed is an exclusion from adult companionship.

If you want the day to end in friendship, nothing works better than bedtime stories.

When you leave the child in bed give (and keep) a definite promise of your return. You might say something like, "I'm going down to have my supper now. I'll pop up and see if you're asleep when I've finished." The child knows that if she does not go quickly to sleep you will be back before long. As a result she is likely to be fast asleep before the allotted time is over.

Once your child is in bed, getting out again should be out of the question or, better still, never considered. But if she is to take it for granted that once she is in bed she stays there, you will have to be prepared to wait on her a bit. If she may not get out of bed to tell you something interesting, how can she get her own drink of water?

Once it is dark, most children in this age group much prefer not to have to get out of bed alone, braving the bears under the bed and the monsters in the corner, so knowing that someone will always come if they call is an important part of feeling safe alone in their rooms. If your child is recently out of night-time nappies, be alert to the possibility of her being worried in case she wets herself or needs to go to the bathroom in the night. Try a night light, a potty beside the bed with permission to call for company if she needs to use it, a plastic sheet on the bed and a relaxed attitude to "accidents".

SLEEPING PROBLEMS

However attractive you can make going to bed, there are some night-time problems which are so common during this age period that you will be exceptionally fortunate if your child never presents you with any of them.

"Nasty thoughts" This is a nursery term for a kind of half-asleep nightmare which many children experience when they are drowsing off. The child herself will not be sure whether she was awake or asleep. After quite a long period of silence from her room (so that you probably thought she was fast asleep) the child either starts to cry or calls you and says that she cannot go to sleep.

It sometimes helps to ask the child what is bothering her. She may be able to tell you what monster is besetting her and make herself feel better by talking about it. But your reassurances need to be very simple and definite. If the trouble is "nasty men getting in..." remind her that nobody who does not belong in her family could possibly get in; the doors are locked and need a key to open them, the windows are too high even for a ladder to reach...

Unlike nightmares (see opposite), "nasty thoughts" often arise directly out of stories the child has heard, or seen on television. It is as if her mind replays the story to her and then, as her controls relax towards sleep, her powerful imagination takes over and embroiders it. Controlling her viewing and selecting her bedtime stories, so that she goes to bed with her head full of pleasant everyday matters rather than mysteries and miseries, may help. Some children who are prone to "nasty thoughts" and have come to dread them, actually ask for help in censoring their end-of-day images, rejecting certain stories that they love at other times of day, and refusing to look at particular illustrations.

Half-heard, half-understood snippets of real life can cause "nasty thoughts" too. A telephone conversation about Aunt May's operation; a half-heard quarrel between parents or the sound of her mother in tears can all impinge on a child so that as sleep approaches she is flooded with anxiety. It may help to talk and explain but it will not help to lie. If she did overhear a quarrel or tears, it is much better to acknowledge it calmly and tell her a suitable version of what it was about. She will accept that quarrels and upsets need not be frightening and do not mean that you don't love each other any more, if you remind her that she too sometimes has quarrels with her friends, or her brothers and sisters, and that grown-ups, too, can cry.

Nightmares Sleep alternates between cycles of lighter "paradoxical" sleep and deeper "orthodox" sleep. There are always dreams going on in the "paradoxical" phases even though it is only the frightening or disturbing dreams – the ones we call nightmares – that are usually noted or remembered. Dreams are part of inner life. If they seem to relate to external events in your child's life – to stories and so forth – it is only because those real happenings are serving as a language for fantasy. You will not prevent nightmares by banning a scary television programme; their material comes from inside the child and can only be affected by general measures which reduce her overall level of anxiety.

Almost every child sometimes has nightmares; from time to time your child may have a patch during which she has them almost every night. Unless she shows signs of stress when she is awake as well, don't worry about them. Just get to her quickly when she starts to cry. The sight, sound or touch of you will soothe her instantly back to peaceful sleep. It is only if she has time to come fully awake and be terrified by the sound of her own fear, or if the babysitter who comes to comfort her is a stranger, that the nightmare is likely to become a memorable event, which may make her afraid of going to sleep.

Night terrors Night terrors are quite different from nightmares and, fortunately, much rarer. They happen during "orthodox" rather than "paradoxical" sleep and they arise not from fantasy but from a breakthrough of primitive emotion – fear or panic. Most children never have night terrors; very few have them more than once in a while. They are sometimes precipitated by traumatic events such as surgical operations, forcible separation from parents or road accidents.

When you rush, heart thudding to the surge of your own adrenaline, to answer the scream that heralds a night terror, you will often find your child sitting up, eyes open, "looking" at some non-existent "thing" in the room. She seems not just afraid but terrified. If there is anger mixed in with the fear it will be hating anger. If there is grief it will be desolation. Although she looks awake, the child is not really conscious. Instead of being instantly comforted by your arrival (as she would be in a nightmare) she will either fail to notice you, ignore your attempts at comfort, or actually involve you in her terror. She may make you into one of the enemy with horrified screams of "go'way, go'way", or make you into a companion victim, crying "look, oh look..." Sometimes she will actually scream for you piteously: "Mummy, Mummy, I want my Mummy" even as you hug and pat her and try to make her conscious of your presence.

Such extreme fear is infectious and there is something eerie, too, about a child who seems awake but is not in touch with reality. You will probably feel uneasy and have to fight a tendency to gaze with the child into the corner she has peopled with horrors. Put the lights on. This will steady your nerves and may alter the room enough to begin to dispel whatever images the child is seeing. Even if the light has no effect on her now, it will reassure her if she comes to full wakefulness before the incident is over.

Don't argue with the child. She is not awake so she is not open to reasonable statements about monsters being made-up or there being no huge wolves in the room. Just burble soothingly along "it's all right darling" lines. If she is conscious of your voice at all, it will only be the tone she hears. Don't take any notice if the child says hurtful things. She is not conscious, so she is not responsible for anything she says. If she shouts about hating and killing you, ignore it. She doesn't mean you, she means whatever you stand for in her night terror.

Don't do anything in particular to awaken a child who stays in bed. The terror will probably recede, letting her drift straight back into normal sleep without ever knowing what has happened. It may take you some time to calm down, but she will be quite unharmed. If she gets physically involved in the terror so that she gets out of bed, runs away or begins to throw herself about or knock things over, you will have to intervene. See whether you can pick her up without increasing her panic. If she will allow you, carry and rock her so that she wakes to warmth and comfort rather than to the shock of pain when she runs into a doorpost. If she fights you, though, don't capture her by force. It's better to follow her, putting on lights as you go, and to pick her up as soon as she begins to calm down or wake up.

If your child does wake from a night terror, especially if she has ended up in a different room, she will probably be very surprised. Don't let relief at having her "normal" again make you at all dramatic. Just tell her she had a bad dream and ask if she would like a drink or to go to the lavatory. She may now be so wide awake that you have to put her to bed all over again as if it were the beginning of her night. If she remembers her strange awakening next day, dismiss it matter-of-factly: "You had a nasty dream..."

Nobody knows exactly why some children have night terrors and others do not, or even exactly where a nightmare ends and a night terror begins. Children who do have them seem to be most suscept-ible when a high fever is already making them delirious; when they are given a sedative medicine for any reason, or when they have had a severe physical and emotional shock such as being involved in a car smash. Night terrors need to be handled by calm and experienced adults – and even they don't find them pleasant to see or easy to manage. Don't leave your child with a teenage babysitter, let alone a stranger, if previous experience or present circumstances give you any reason to suppose that she might have one tonight.

Sleep talking A great many children mutter in their sleep. Some speak clearly enough for you to hear words. Sometimes a child will even laugh, or talk in a tone of voice that suggests teasing. It sounds eerie, but it is unimportant unless the child is obviously having a nightmare or starting a night terror.

Night-talking children who are calm don't need waking and they don't need listening to either. It is better not to tell them funny stories next day of the peculiar things they said, as most children find the idea of talking when they were not conscious rather scary. A talking child may wake – and frighten – a brother or sister who shares the room. If so, you may have to make other sleeping arrangements because once children start to talk in their sleep, they usually go on doing it from time to time right through childhood.

Waking in the night

Occasionally a child will wake, after several hours of sleep, for no reason that either you or she can see. She has not dreamed – as far as she knows – she is not afraid and does not need anything. She is simply wide awake and so amazed at finding herself the only conscious being in a silent house that she has to call you to make sure that the world has not emptied around her.

A reassuring visit and permission to look at a book until she is sleepy again will be all she needs, but if it happens often you may be able to explain to her that most people like to stay asleep all night and that it is a pity to wake them unless she really needs something. Her room can be arranged like the early waker's room (see below) and she can be encouraged to look after herself.

But at three or four or five a child may not be able to bear the solitude. She may have to see that there are other people left in her world. If so, being put to sleep with a brother or sister (even a tiny baby one) may work wonders. She is asked not to wake the brother or sister so she stays very quiet, but she can see his or her sleeping, breathing form and she knows she is not alone.

If no brother or sister is available, there are other forms of "company" that may work. Various families have successfully used each of the following: a bowl of goldfish; a hibernating tortoise; a clock with a friendly face that moves with each tick; a special lampshade (designed for a low-wattage night-light) with stars or pictures which flick on and off, and a photograph of the whole family.

If your child wakes in the night, she'll probably need a reassuring visit to resettle her.

Early waking

If your child is fond of her special place and her bed with all its things around it, early waking need not be a problem now. She cannot stay asleep just to please you – so it is no good being irritated with her for waking up – but she can play quietly without disturbing you. Soon after her third birthday she will probably be able to understand that she must not wake you, except for a special reason, until she hears your alarm clock or the radio or hears you moving about.

Of course she may wake you by mistake because you hear her talking to brothers or sisters, dolls or teddy bears. That is different. She cannot be expected to stay totally silent. You will just have to put your heads under the pillows and revel in your last half-hour. If she insists on calling for you, it may be because she wakes wet, urgently needing the lavatory, hungry or thirsty.

If she calls because she is wet, it is not fair either to ignore or to scold her. You want her to find it more comfortable to be dry than wet, and once she begins to move around in play she will get very cold in wet pyjamas and sheets. You will have to go to her but you need not go through the palaver of changing her bed until later. Hand her dry pyjamas to struggle into while you put an old draw-sheet or towel over the wet patch on the sheets.

If hunger and/or thirst is the problem, try leaving a drink in her old sippy-cup and a couple of rusks or biscuits by her bed. Helping herself is good entertainment as well as meeting the need.

Sometimes the world outside home can seem too much to manage.

CRYING
AND COPING

Moving on into early childhood usually means leaving behind some of the acute emotional stresses that are typical of toddlers. Your child has not changed his personality, of course. If he has always been tense, he will probably still tend that way. If he was a really balky two-year-old, turning three will not have made him entirely sweet and biddable. But overall his ability to cope with everyday stresses will have improved. You may see it clearly in his reactions to separation. A few months ago his passionate dependence on you left him bedevilled by separation anxiety. Now, the passion is as strong as ever, but the anxiety is not. He can hold himself calm through minor separations.

Words help him to cope. When you leave the room saying, "I'm just going down to the clothes line" he can understand you; see the clothes line and you moving towards it, in his mind. The beginnings of a sense of time help too. If his caregiver reminds him that you will fetch him after lunch, he cannot count the hours that must pass but he knows that they will. In the meantime, experience of other adults makes him feel more secure. He knows by now that even a world that is temporarily without you has other nice, useful people in it. A teacher can read books and sort out squabbles, a grandparent can mend a hurt knee or a broken toy, a babysitter can bring a drink of water, and an older child can hold hands on the way to the swings.

The child's own growing competence is reassuring too. He knows that he can manage a good many things for himself so he is no longer dependent on an adult for anything he might need at any moment of the day. If there are children available to him, he does not even want adults all the time. When he is involved with playmates he accepts that you are only a background figure.

But perhaps it is time and repeated experiences which give him most help in coping. Over and over again you have left him (for a minute, an hour or a day); over and over again you have come safely back to him. He has lived as your child for long enough for your trustworthiness to have built trust in him. As long as he feels as sure of your comings as your goings, and can take your affection for granted whether you are present or not, he can afford to take some of his concentrated attention off you and focus it instead on the outside world.

MEETING NEW SOCIAL CHALLENGES

It is important that your child should begin to feel safe in venturing away from home and excited rather than anxious about small flights out from under your protection. In two or three years he will enter the formal education system. Wherever he has been cared for up to then, even if he has long been accustomed to a day centre "classroom", and being attached to caregivers there, real school and a teacher whose prime purpose is his education rather than his care, will demand new levels of confident autonomy.

Getting on with other children Relationships with other children in his own age group are going to become more and more important to your child from now right through adolescence. Although babies usually find children of all ages fascinating, toddlers enjoy playing alongside each other, and a few develop real and lasting friendships, this third year typically marks the beginning of intimate individual relationships between children. Now is the time for truly co-operative play, in which shared ideas structure the game and pooled skills make it playable. If your child is used to being around a few children he knows well – with a childminder, for example – he may slip from observer to participant playmate without his carer noticing or you even knowing. The social skills he learns in that setting will then transfer, at least to some useful extent, to playgrounds, birthday parties and holiday beaches, and eventually to pre-school and school. But if your child has had very little experience of other children, there may now be problems whenever he encounters any because he wants to play the games but does not know how to join the children. Whether he does it in a nursery, a playgroup or in regular private play-dates, it is time for him to learn the vital lessons of taking turns, of sharing, of giving way. He will only do so happily if those hard lessons seem worth his while because he discovers that many games are more fun with a group and two can often succeed at a self-imposed task where one fails.

Watching older children's play helps your child see how to join in.

Trouble with peers   The lessons really are hard. Gentle, co-operative, social behaviour is a tremendous effort for most small children and those who are making the effort successfully tend to be hard on a child who cannot yet manage. If a group has just discovered how to make a sand village without trampling each other's contributions, it will be quick to turn on the big-footed newcomer who does not know the rules. So don't expect other small children to "be nice" to yours (even if he is even smaller than they are). And if there is trouble, don't waste energy on being hurt and angry with them for "picking on him".

Some children take out on others all the stresses they are feeling at home. If your three- or four-year-old bites, hits, kicks, attacks younger children, pockets other people's toys and generally makes it impossible for anyone to want to play with him, think carefully about other parts of his life. Is he hitting other children because he longs to hit your new baby and dare not? Or because now that home contains that baby, being in child care makes him feel pushed out? Does he steal other children's toys because he doesn't feel he has enough of his own, or because he feels that their toys mean they are loved, while he is not sure that he is? Does he disrupt other children's games and try to bully them because he wants to get back at you for being too bossy over him?

Some children get other children's stresses taken out on them. Bullying does happen, even at this early stage in children's lives, and aggressive children tend to pick on quiet, unassertive people who already have low self-esteem. Sometimes bullying takes a discriminatory form, focusing on unassertive children who are seen as conspicuously "different", in appearance or behaviour, or children who are part of a minority that the wider community rejects. It is crucial that discriminatory behaviour – such as teasing, name-calling or exclusion based on any aspect of a child's identity, including gender – should be taken as seriously as physical aggression. If your child should encounter or display cold shoulders and nasty names, don't let it be glossed over on the grounds that "they are too little to know what they're doing". They are too little to understand, but they are not too little to *learn* to understand. A group's ability to accommodate difference is a crucial part of its ethos and may prevent bias becoming deeply rooted in children's belief systems.

If children are neither to bully nor be bullied, they need to learn assertiveness, learn to express their own needs and feelings and defend their own rights, while respecting the rights and feelings of others. The child who runs away, howling, when another child snatches her toy, rewards his aggressive behaviour without doing anything to make herself feel safer from it. Just being rescued by an adult ("Give that back Jacko...") ends the incident but does nothing to help with the next. Both children need the victim to stop *being* a victim and hang on, saying, "I'm not finished with it yet" (or maybe, "Give that back!") herself, with an adult available to back her up if Jacko will not. Sometimes parents, in the name of peace, weigh in on the wrong side. Jacko might be told to "ask nicely" and if he then mutters "please..." the original owner of the toy is persuaded to "let him have a turn". But if she was still using the toy, another child asking for it, no matter how politely, puts her under no obligation to give it up but only to respond politely in her turn. Children need to know that they have a right to say "no" or "not till I've finished".

If your child should encounter trouble with others that is more than passing, and makes him unhappy, do talk to the teacher as calmly and undefensively as you can. If he's only just joined a group, though, the chances are that the problems are simply due to him being a newcomer to a group where the children are used to each other and he is not used to the adults. If group play is almost new to a child who has been carefully protected at home, he may find the rough-and-tumble of even the gentlest version of group life amazing. If you have always arranged for your three-year-old to win at "Snap", have the biggest strawberries and think himself stronger than his father, he is not likely to take kindly to playing with other children who expect justice and reality. "But I *want* to go first," announced one such new arrival, truly stunned that anyone else should claim the privilege. A little later she commanded another child, "Fall down. Go on, do what I say." When the other child stayed stalwartly on his feet, she pushed him over and was clearly amazed when he jumped up and said, "No pushing!" and the teacher came and reproved her.

Learning to socialize

Early childhood socializing is a skill all children have to learn, though some find it easier than others. While of course your child should not be left in a social situation where he is victimized, either by other children or by a teacher or caregiver, most difficulties in his relationships with other children just mean that he isn't very skilful yet. If you watch how he behaves with other children you will probably be able to see what it is that he does or does not do that puts them off, and teach him how to manage better. He can learn acceptable group behaviour just as easily as he can learn table manners or new words.

With adult help, children learn that "one at a time" means everyone stays safe and gets a turn.

The basic principles of "do as you would be done by" are easy to teach and interesting to learn because they start from your child and his feelings and only then move on to other children's. If you can help him to understand that every child would like to take first turn down the slide and only one can; that each would like the biggest cake he is waiting for (maybe expecting) and only one can have it; that nobody enjoys being "out" in a game any more than he does, he will at least see *how* to "play nicely", even if he cannot manage to play that way all the time. It may seem obvious to you that it is wrong to kick other people but it is not obvious to your child at this age.

It will be more difficult for your child to "play nicely" and refrain from kicking other children, literally or metaphorically, if he is encouraged to be highly competitive. Every winner leaves one or more losers, after all. The more desirable it is to win, the more shattering it is to lose. However much you may be in favour of competitive activities such as sports for older children, children first need every opportunity to realize that other people's feelings in general are usually similar to their own and always equally deserving of respect. For example, if he complains of a little boy who keeps running to the grown-ups, suggest that the child may be a bit shy and not very used to other children yet. Remind him of a time (maybe as little as two days ago) when he himself felt a bit like that and came to sit on your lap. If he screws up someone's picture and gets clobbered for it, kiss the bump but then point out that everyone likes to keep or scrumple their own pictures.

Helping your child to make friends Children in this age group should not be expected to play in company without supervision. Their social controls are not strong enough. Tempers are still precarious and new forethought can be lost in the heat of the moment. If one child lays another's scalp open with a bat, both will suffer although only one bleeds. It is adults' absolute duty to keep each and every child reasonably safe from his own and other children's aggression.

Safety is not the only criterion, though, and good play is far more likely if the adult's supervision is subtle and if she is sensitive to the line between facilitation and interference. There may be some houses your child is eager to visit if one of the parents will be in charge but not if it's the au pair who sits over the children like a policeman watching a demonstration. When your child is going to leave the arrangements you have made for his care and spend time sharing the arrangements made for another child, you (and he) are entitled to know what they are. So don't be shy to ask, or offended when you get asked the same questions.

Subtle supervision usually means finding adult occupation within the children's vicinity so that you can busy yourself but be prepared to step in before things get out of hand. If five children aged 18 months to four are armed with plastic swords and battle is hotting up, it is no use exhorting them to "be careful", even if you scoop the toddler out of harm's way as you call. Four children with weapons is at least three children too many. Take the swords away and suggest something else.

Sometimes safety demands supervision that is so up-front it is positively bossy. If children are playing on something which could be dangerous – such as a slide – you cannot rely on them to take turns and not push. After all it only takes one child one second to cause an accident. Go and take charge: "You can only use this if you do it properly; it's one at a time up the ladder, and one at a time down the slide. Now, who's first?"

Whether your child is playing with a group of others or with just one, things will not always go smoothly between them. Even "best friends" are not reliable playmates when they are only three. When things go wrong, concentrate on getting them going right again. It does not matter who began the fight. It matters only that fighting has spoiled play for everyone, so it must stop. Subtle supervision now turns into distraction with a new activity or a snack.

Even if your child spends all day at a child care centre and/or has three siblings or a twin, an easy relationship with children who live nearby is important. They are the ones who will be available at weekends, after all. If you stay put in your present home, some of them may even be around all through his childhood.

It isn't always easy for neighbouring children to find each other, though. Few modern, urban environments are considered safe enough for children to play out, even if there is traffic-free space for them to play in. In fact one of the principal stresses in young families' lives is that the real and perceived dangers of the outside world impose virtual house-arrest on children which only a chauffeuring and escort service by already over-stretched parents can relieve. If there are other small children living close by whom your child does not know because they seldom appear except in a family group, a well-timed birthday party or a few invitations to coffee issued to child and mother when you meet in the street, may help you both. He finds playmates and you, hopefully, find neighbours with whom to share car-pools and play-dates.

COPING WITH TYPICAL FEARS

Every individual child (and adult come to that) has special fears and worries of his own. However, there are some anxieties that are so widespread among children at this particular age and stage that your child is very likely to suffer from at least some of them.

Worry about disasters Your child is riding on a crest of imagination in everything he does. This makes him liable to all kinds of "supposing..." fears. Where a toddler does not worry about getting lost until he sees a likelihood of being so, a young child looks at his small self in the big park and wonders what it would be like to be lost. He may worry about more improbable possibilities, too, like the house catching fire, both his parents dying or the dog going berserk. You cannot tell him these things could not happen, of course, but you can stress their unlikeliness with concrete reassurances about smoke alarms and everybody's excellent health. If he persists with "what if...?" make sure you have a simple and reassuring answer to his real concern, which is with what would happen to *him*: "Granny (or whoever he knows best as a substitute parent) would take care of you."

Worry about injury

Awareness of self, as a whole separate person inside a body which belongs to him, may make your child very anxious about getting hurt. Sex differences come into this temporarily exaggerated fear of even minor injury. Both boys and girls are now aware of their own gender and the presence or absence of a penis. His penis is infinitely precious to a little boy, but he also tends to be afraid of losing it which is what, despite explanations, he believes must have happened to girls. A little girl tends to feel that she lacks a penis; an almost invisible vagina seems no alternative. Despite explanations she often worries that her body has been damaged by having its penis removed. So for both sexes, injury seems to start up terrible images of being broken, damaged forever, losing part of their precious selves.

Blood is often the focus of terror. Three- to five-year-olds get through more plasters than any other age group, not because they hurt themselves more often but because they cannot get on with their lives until that dreaded bead of blood is safely hidden. But pain is a focus too. A routine injection, which would have evoked nothing but a brief cry a year ago, may be dreaded, hated and remembered with horror. It may take all your tactful skill to get a splinter out of that finger.

The child with a minor bump or scrape needs reassurance at least as much as first aid.

Worry about breakages

Fear of injury to themselves spreads, in many children, to a shivery horror of injury to anything else. Your child may be disproportionately upset if he breaks a mug. If he comes across a headless doll, he may react as you would react to a dead rat. A few children cannot even enjoy jigsaw puzzles because they so dislike the incomplete and "broken" pictures.

Worry about adults' words

Although your child's language helps him to tell of his fears, his understanding of language may also cause some. He overhears fragments of adult conversation and understands the words without their context and without allowing for adult dramatizations and shorthand. If he hears you reply to a conventional, "How are you?" with, "More dead than alive", he may not take it as the wry joke which you intended. He may panic. The same applies to half-heard and partially understood fragments of TV programmes or videos. Pathetic child-victims of real or fictional horror confirm his anxious feelings that the world is a dangerous place.

Worry about strange places

The security your child gets from being with you comes partly from your shared and familiar context. He feels most confident of your ready availability when you are in familiar places doing familiar things, and even being both emotionally and physically with him may not protect him from anxiety when everything else is strange. Don't be surprised if he weeps and whines to go home from an eagerly anticipated holiday. The beach-bronzed four-year-old who announced, "I don't like it here 'cause Mummy don't do cooking," spoke for many. Don't be upset if a house move is even worse than you had expected. The intended improvement in family life may well make it worthwhile in the end, but that will not prevent the beginning from being horrible.

You can keep your child's personal disorientation to a minimum if you keep his most treasured objects with him. Don't pack his toys

When it's time to move home, let your child take personal charge of his most precious things.

and clothes and books in advance and don't let a moving firm do it. Let him "help" you pack the day before (so he knows where everything is and can keep an eye on it) and transport that lot, with him, in your car or in your hand-baggage. When you get to the strange new place concentrate on building a replica-nest – including a corner that feels like a place to play – and try to save enough time and energy to put yourself into the context he expects by cooking an ordinary supper and making him clean his teeth. In a holiday hotel, keep up as much of his home routine as will allow you to feel you are having a break. In a new house remember that you have to rebuild your context for him and that you will probably do it fastest if you actually encourage him to follow you about while you find your own way. Don't expect him to assume that you will come if he calls in the night, just as you have always done. He hasn't got your bedroom and likely whereabouts mapped in his mind; if he cannot see you, he does not know where you are. Don't try to make him sleep alone if he is homesick that first night. You don't want his new room marked with misery. If he ever sleeps with you, this is a good time to let him. Even if he has not slept with you since he was a baby it may lower the stress for both of you to invite him, "just this once, while we all get used to it..."

Helping your child cope

You can best help your child with his fears and anxieties by letting him lead the way towards independence whenever you can. But you can also help him by keeping a firm and even control over him and his life, making it clear that you do not expect him to take the responsibility for his own safety; that is still your job. If he asks permission to do something – such as sleep overnight at a friend's house – and you can see that he is not happy about it, say "no" quite firmly. He will be enormously relieved to find that you don't feel he ought to be ready for the new experience.

When he is afraid, give him reassurance in full measure. Do not ever tease him or let anyone else mock his fears. If you do, he may learn to hide them, or to mask them under a layer of cockiness, but they will still bother him inside.

The fearfulness of early childhood will diminish with time and with your child's experience of being able to cope, comfortably, with whatever happens to him. Gradually he will discover that grazed skin always heals, that falling off a tricycle does not break him into pieces, that you never lose him, forget him or go off without telling him, that baddies do not break into the house at night and that he stays quite safe and in control of whatever is asked of him. It follows that experiences of not being safe or in your or his own control are liable to delay him in reaching that happy state of confidence in himself. There is nothing whatsoever to be said for trying to toughen him up.

Don't put your child in for a race towards independence. There is no particular virtue (and there may be some risk) in having a two-year-old who will go anywhere and do anything with anyone. A shy, clingy three- or four-year-old does not reflect on you as an over-protective parent, and the kind of five-year-old who adapts slowly to new situations and people ultimately adapts as well as anyone and better than many.

A clingy child is nothing to be ashamed of; in fact an "independent" four-year-old is an idiotic idea.

COPING WITH FAMILY TROUBLES

If your family meets real disaster – death, divorce – don't try too hard to batten down misery and rage for your children's sake. When you are under such extreme stress that you feel quite unlike yourself, quite crazy, you cannot be as your child expects you to be and it may not help him to pretend that you are. If he is old enough to understand words at all, it will usually be less terrifying for him if you share at least the fact of your unhappiness. And if he must cope with you seeming strange and distant from him, he will do that better from home-base where everything else is familiar. If you cannot stand to be alone in the family home, it will probably be better to have friends or relations move in with you than to flee to them with the children.

After a death or divorce you may not want – and may not be able – to go on living where the child has always lived. But try to give him time to come to terms with the loss of a family member before you face him with the loss of his family base. If everything changes at once he will be totally bewildered.

Becoming a lone-parent family

Losing a father is a blow that can only be equalled or surpassed by losing a mother or both parents. Although there is little parallel between the loss of bereavement and that of separation or divorce, there is a parallel for a young child. He reacts to the parent's immediate absence and to the fragmentation of the family rather than to the loss of the parent's existence which is inconceivable to him. There is therefore much to be learned about helping very young children who are bereaved from research concerning marital breakdown.

A family outing is no fun for a child if he's the only reason the family is still intact.

Marriage-glue is not a good role for children who are at least as

potent a source of marital conflict as togetherness. Staying together "for the children's sake" is seldom possible or beneficial unless it is a way of buying time for a sick relationship to recover. On the other hand, once you decide to separate don't expect children – of any age – to approve or even understand your decision. All the available evidence suggests that divorce makes children extremely unhappy even if their relationship with the parent who leaves – usually, though not always or inevitably, the father – has been very distant.

Helping your child believe it

Don't expect a young child to believe in the separation. Having nerved yourself to tell him, and evoked tears in reaction to the extreme tension he senses in you, it is easy to feel that you have "done it". But by the next day he may appear so unmoved that you find him unfeeling and by the following week, when he suddenly asks, "Where's Daddy?" you're liable to scream at him. He can't believe his father has really gone because he doesn't want it to be so. Certainly at three and often at five, he still half-believes in his own magical power to alter the world by wishing. You will have to keep on telling him the unwelcome news.

Recognizing your child's feelings of guilt

Do believe in the inevitability of childish guilt. Once a child does believe his father has left he is likely to assume that he was the cause. Young children are the centre of their own lives and it takes years for them to realize that they are not the whole centre of their parents'. Many three-year-olds do not even believe that mothers exist, eat supper, watch television, take baths, after they are asleep. So a child will instantly assume that any fragmentation of his family is the result of something concerning him. He will probably focus his guilt on something he has heard his parents arguing about: his noise, his tantrums, his "cheek". There may also be a subtler sub-text to childish guilt. Small children are sexually aware people who, in the normal course of early development, dream of partnership with their opposite-sex parent and of replacing the parent of the same sex. The little boy who has wished his father out of the way so he could have his mother all to himself believes, when his father leaves, that his wishes made it happen. The little girl who wanted her father to focus on her clearly sees that her love-object has gone because he could not love a child so wicked as to want to supplant her mother.

Although some people find it hard to think about small children in relation to sexual feelings, it's important not to dismiss these ideas as far-fetched. It is guilt of this kind that fuels the anxiety which bedevils children in newly fragmented families. If their wickedness has driven out one parent, can they count on the other to stay with them? If the parent who has stayed really knew what they felt, would she still love them or would she hate them? And do such bad children really deserve to be loved and cared for, anyway? Expect your child to be extra clingy and to keep the closest possible eye on you, and don't be surprised if his conviction that he is unlovable leads him to behave as if you and he do not love each other, inviting the abandonment he feels inevitable. It will be months before the child relaxes enough to stop watching you. Only when he does stop watching you, and even willingly leaves you for an afternoon or a day, will he have begun to believe that you will not desert him.

Helping your child stay close to both parents

Don't encourage your child to "forget all about it". Fathers, as well as mothers, are psychologically essential even when they cannot be physically present. A separated child needs to talk of his father; try not to shy away from his pain as you may find that your less helpful friends do from yours.

More than half of the children of divorced parents lose touch with their fathers within a few months. In most families this is not because the fathers cannot be bothered to visit but because one or both parents decide that visits are too emotionally upsetting for the child. Don't let your child lose touch. However difficult it may be to make regular and frequent visits work – especially with a very young child – it is worth it for your child's happiness for the rest of his life. Children need to have it proved to them that the end of father-mother love is not the end of father-child or mother-child love, and that fragmentation of the family does not break their relationships. This may require enormous efforts from both parents but for the child who is stressed by incomprehensible adult behaviour it is a priority.

A young child cannot maintain a relationship with someone based solely on a monthly trip to the zoo. He needs to see his father at least once a week and they need a base so that they can talk and play and cuddle, not just wander through the rain eating too many sweets. A two- or three-year-old may not even want to leave home with his father, especially while he does not feel safe with his mother out of sight. If visits in the home really cannot be tolerated, the home of one of the child's friends may offer a haven. As soon as the father has a "home" of his own – whether or not it has a lover in it – the child should become familiar with it, because until then he will worry about his father. Banishment from the family home seems to him a horrendous exile. You may find it difficult to respond sympathetically to questions like, "But who will cook Daddy's supper?", but these are real concerns to the child. Only when he can see, and therefore believe, that both of you are "all right" as well as available, will he be able to be wholly happy again.

Parents and children who don't live together still need to be together – often.

BODIES, MINDS
AND FEELINGS

If toddlers' lives are dominated by the struggle to get their bodies under reasonable control, early childhood is dominated by the use that can be made of them. At this stage in their lives, children are their bodies, for good or ill. The knee that gets bruised, the lips that manage a first whistle or the legs that need splints, do not only belong to the child, they *are* the child.

Because young children feel at one with their bodies they do not separate physical activities from thinking activities and feeling activities, as adults tend to do. Doing helps them think; thinking makes them do. Doing helps them to understand what they feel and to stand the strength of their feelings; so feeling also makes them do. This is why attempts to modify a child's physical behaviour (to make her use her right hand for activities in which her left naturally dominates, for example) often lead to considerable confusion and emotional upset. In the absence of pressure from outside, though, young children with physical disabilities, serious illnesses or injuries are often calmer than similarly afflicted older people, and more courageous about prescribed exercises and physiotherapy. They have a developmental drive to physical improvement and no prior expectations about how easy or difficult it should be.

Physical abilities and limits Since young children feel that their bodies are "themselves", bodily strength and efficiency are very important to both sexes. They set themselves challenges and strive to meet them, continually testing their own limits. Your child knows she can walk, but needs to see how far; she knows she can run, but needs to find out whether she can run as fast as her big sister or faster than her friends. She knows she can climb, but she has to find out whether that particular tree will defeat her. While she measures herself against these self-imposed standards, she learns vital lessons about managing her physical self. She learns where the main strength of her body lies. She finds, for example, that a bed which she cannot move when she pushes from the wrist, shifts a little when she pushes from the shoulder. And if she lies on the floor and pushes the bed with her feet, legs bent at the knee are not strong enough but her straight legs, powered by her hips, move it freely.

She learns how to nurse her body along so as to get the most out of it. If she carries something heavy in one hand, the muscles tire; when she changes hands, the fresh muscles work better. When she changes back again, the first set of muscles is rested and ready for more. She discovers her most vulnerable spots too. She learns to guard her head with her arms when she falls and to let her knees take the brunt of life rather than falling flat on her belly. Painfully she – and especially her brother – discovers that private parts need respectful clearance when climbing over furniture or climbing frame bars.

Gradually she discovers more about what she can and cannot do with this body. It is solid enough to stop a rolling ball if her feet are together but if they are apart the ball will roll through. Her hands can

It's important to your child to challenge his own strength and find out what he can do.

make a cup efficient enough to carry wet sand but inefficient when the sand is dry and hopeless for water. Gravity often catches her unawares, sending her tumbling downhill (and down the stairs) but holding her back as she goes upwards. She experiments continually with balance or, as she probably sees it, "how not to fall down". She can walk along a bench with both arms outstretched but if one hand comes inwards to put a thumb in her mouth she will wobble. She can lean just so far over a fence to reach something but when she leans farther she is off-balance and cannot get back. By the time she is three she can stand on one foot but only while she concentrates; doing anything else at the same time is impossible.

The child's body and feelings Young children have to involve their bodies as well as their minds in order to understand the world and its experiences. Watching TV, the four-year-old boos the baddies, cheers the hero and gallops round the room with the horses. She neither can nor should sit quietly. If she may not engage her body as well as her mind, she will switch off her brain, if not the TV set. Her own emotions affect her in the same way. She must vent her anger in shouts and stamps, howl out her misery as she throws herself dramatically on the floor, or hop and squeak to let out just enough joy to stop herself exploding.

Unfortunately this kind of emotional display shocks and embarrasses many adults. Over many years they have learned to control themselves, use words instead of actions and keep their feelings to themselves. Now, as parents, they try to impose a similar separation between body and feeling on children who are at the stage where neither can work well without the other. It is impossible to impose complete physical restraint of this kind on a child of three or four, but even trying to do so can totally spoil things for her. If she may not roar with laughter and drum her heels when the clowns enter the circus ring, she will stop finding them funny. It can make feelings harder to bear, too. If a sudden disappointment leaves her crying bitterly and you say, "Oh don't cry", she may feel that it is her actual tears that distress you rather than her disappointed feelings. You will do more to help her recognize what it is that she feels and to learn to cope with it, if instead of trying to squash her physical displays of feeling, you accept and even encourage them. Instead of telling that disappointed child not to cry, you could say, "It has made you sad, hasn't it? Come and sit with me for a bit until you don't feel like crying any more. Then when you feel better we'll do something else..." You show the child that you understand that disappointment hurts; that tears are a perfectly acceptable response; that you will support her through the hurt and its tears and that you are confident that when the tears end, the hurt will have become manageable. On happier occasions you can even play pretend-feelings with her. She is a natural actor and will throw herself eagerly into a game of, "Be a very tired old woman; be a very angry man; be a child who's lost her puppy..." She will deliberately tense and distort her face and body, striving for the feeling-image your words have conjured up. As she does so she is learning to understand the feelings through her body; making them familiar; making them safe.

This total intermingling of body and emotion makes small

children especially vulnerable to adult abuse of either. Almost every parent recoils from the idea of sexual abuse – whether incestuous or otherwise – but there are less horrendous and less obvious kinds of abuse which may nevertheless be damaging. Being physically punished, forced or imprisoned, for example, cuts into the core of the child's new sense of self. She cannot yet say (as some prisoners of conscience have said), "Do what you like with my body; you cannot touch my mind." Whatever is done to the body is done to the mind as well. Of course any child will sometimes have to be restrained or forced, fleetingly, to prevent her from harming herself or others. But there is a difference no child will miss between action taken to prevent her from doing something, and action taken to make her pay for something she has done.

Just as physical punishment hurts a child's feelings as well as her body, so emotional neglect damages the whole child even if she is outwardly well cared-for. And being forced to make gestures of physical affection can be almost as bad as being physically punished or ignored. The child who is made to kiss Aunt Mary whom she dislikes is being asked to betray herself through her body; to use it to express an emotion she does not truly feel. Even a parent whom the child does love can demand too many kisses and hugs. The little girl who loves to sit on Daddy's knee wants to (and should) do so when she feels like it. If he grabs her and snatches kisses as she passes on other business she feels that he is using her body for his own pleasure rather than responding to love when it is offered to him. Don't demand or force physical affection. If you truly yearn for a cuddle, ask. If it is refused, accept it with good grace. For some two- and three-year-olds the power to withhold hugs is an important part of autonomy as well as a very funny tease.

It's your child's right to decide whether to give or withhold hugs and kisses.

Your child's body and the feelings it evokes are her very own and what is done to them should be up to her. A child has a right to masturbate and almost certainly will, whether you are aware of it or not. You may gently persuade her to keep this pleasure to private times, as a matter of good manners, but if you scold or shame her for the activity itself you are interfering between body and child. But if children have a right to masturbate because their bodies and their feelings are their own, the same reasoning gives them the right not to be sexually stimulated by adults or asked to stimulate them. A child who is brought up, from the very beginning, to have this dual sense of her body's worth and its privacy will have a basic protection within herself against uncomfortable approaches in the years to come.

Your body and your feelings

Early childhood is so tuned in to bodies and to physical behaviours that children read the body language of adults with uncanny skill. Whereas a toddler needs to see your face to know whether you are happy or sad, a three-year-old will often read your headache in your drooping back.

Your child will seldom be wrong about what you are feeling but she will often be wrong about what you want her to know you are feeling. Try as you may to conceal a quarrel, an illness or a work problem from her, she will know that you are miserable. Your bright, forced smile will not fool her but it may confuse her. She knows you are sad, yet you pretend to be happy. You make her doubt the evidence of her own senses. She will be better reassured by a simplified version of the truth than by attempts at total concealment of it. "Mummy is sad because her Daddy is ill" is a far less worrying thought for a small child than: "Something's wrong with Mummy..." or even, "Mummy's sad. I must have done something wrong..." The child who detects sadness in your body will use her own to try and comfort you. The best comfort she knows is the comfort she herself wants when she is miserable: a big hug. Tied up in your own problems you may feel quite unable to use a hug just now. If you reject her efforts too often, though, she may stop making them. Try to accept what she offers with a good grace. Giving your stubbed toe over to be "kissed better" is part of parenthood.

BODILY SAFETY

The physical developments of this age period demand physical adventures, and physical adventures mean a chance of physical accidents. One of the aspects of caring for young children that many parents find most conflictful is that while it is their job to keep their children safe, it is also their job to keep caretaking to a minimum. If you continually fuss at your child to "get down from there" or "be careful", you get between her and her body. You prevent her from finding out what she can and cannot do and by preventing her from learning, you may even provoke exactly the kind of accident you are working so hard to avoid.

Sometimes it is helpful to remind yourself that there is no way you could certainly prevent all possibility of accidents. Even if you followed your child around and held on to her all day, the pair of you could still fall into the nettles or under a car. Try to accept the fact that a few bumps and grazes are all in the day's work for young children. Concern yourself with preventing serious probabilities but don't drive yourself mad thinking about the thousand and one trivial possibilities, or one in a million tragic chances:

■ Trust a child who is playing alone. She will almost certainly stay within her own limits. She will not climb four rungs of the climbing frame until she can manage three. Let her set her own pace. Remember that muscles improve with use up to the point when they begin to tire; balance improves with practice; and nerves steady with experience of success.

■ Watch out when other children tease. The taunt of "baby" will drive the most sensible child to heights of idiotic daring. She needs you to remind her and the children with whom she plays of the line between bravery and folly.

■ Be wary of leaving your child in the charge of older children. She will long to emulate their exploits and they will find it easier to take her with them to the lake than to find her a safe occupation nearer home and stay with her.

■ Be careful of machines. Until she is much clearer about the workings of her own body you cannot expect her to have much idea of the workings of machines which often have quite different properties. Pedal-cars will amaze her by being more difficult to stop

If she thinks she can do it, she probably can.

Keeping children safe in busy streets requires non-stop adult vigilance.

from high than from low speed. She will not remember to keep her fingers out of tricycle spokes or her toes out from under wheel-barrow wheels. Tools like lawn mowers and hedge clippers will be especially dangerous to her because she will not easily understand, let alone allow for, the relationship between switching a switch and distant blades whirling round.

■ Above all, watch out for traffic. However sensible she seems about "road drill", she is nowhere near to being capable of applying it because she cannot accurately assess the speed or intentions of a moving vehicle. Furthermore, however obedient she seems (and means) to be to your instructions to stay on the pavement, they will be pushed straight out of her head by any distraction such as the sight of a friend on the far side of the street.

Safety from strangers When you begin to think about how you can teach your child to keep herself safe from strangers, don't dwell exclusively on the ultimate horrors of abduction, rape and murder. These disasters do happen but they are extremely rare, far rarer than other kinds of sexual abuse, and there is much less that you can do to protect your child against them. Think about daily safety rather than headline tragedy.

The conventional teaching is "never talk to strangers" but when you think about that message from a child's point of view, you'll see that it is neither easy to apply nor likely to contribute to her safety. Which strangers? You want your child to speak politely to the nurse or the shopkeeper she has never met before, and you want her to be able to ask for her fare from a bus driver or for help from a policeman, so the rule can't apply to all strangers. Furthermore, just talking will not put a child at risk. It is what may follow the talking – like holding hands or getting in cars – that matters. Furthermore, when a child is at risk, it is rather unlikely to be from a total stranger. One of the nastiest but most important facts we all have to face is that much more sexual abuse takes place within children's homes – at the hands of parents, older siblings, other relations or "friends" – than outside them. And when a child is abused outside the home, the abusers are far more likely to be family acquaintances or neighbours than complete strangers.

A more useful kind of teaching avoids the whole concept of "strangers" and who they are, avoids the idea that talking is risky and makes it unnecessary to induce fear and suspicion in a trusting and sociable small mind. All you have to teach your three- or four-year-old is that she must never go anywhere with anybody (even somebody she knows well; even a relation) without first coming to tell the adult who is looking after her.

The message is particularly easy for this age group to understand because it fits with their stage of development and therefore makes perfect sense to them. Small children always want to know where parents or carers are – even if they have only left the room to go to the lavatory – so it seems entirely reasonable to them that you should feel the same way.

The lesson is easy to remember because the child practises it every day rather than only in unusual and dramatic circumstances. If you are sitting on a bench while she plays on the swings with her friend, she is to come and tell you before she moves into the sandpit. If you know she is with the neighbours next door, she must come and tell you before the next-door Daddy takes everyone for ice cream. If she is waiting for you inside the childminder's front gate, she must run in and tell her before she comes home with you.

If your child will never deviate from her stated activities or planned path without checking in with somebody, nobody will ever be able to lure her into a car, take her to see a puppy or bribe her away with the promise of sweets. She does not have to judge whether she should go or not; judgments are left to the people who are best qualified to make them: caring adults who will say yes or no when she comes to tell what she proposes. And she will never face confusion about who is safe and who is a "stranger" ("I thought it was all right 'cause it was Daddy's friend...") because she has to come and tell, whoever it is.

Later on, well before there is any chance of your child being left, even for half an hour, without adult supervision, you will probably want to introduce her to the idea that not all adults are trustworthy, and to ways of staying safe when she is out and about with other children. But for the next two or three years it will be enough for her to know that the "rule" established between you is absolute; that other family members and close friends all agree that it's right for children to "come and tell before you go" and therefore anyone who tries to persuade her not to bother must be distrusted and disregarded.

Staying safe in strange places A lot of small children who can keep themselves reasonably safe at home come to grief when they are away on a trip or a holiday, or in the first weeks in a new home. A new environment offers new hazards. The child has never met them before and therefore cannot anticipate or even necessarily recognize them. Adults have to do both for her. If she has always lived in a flat, stairs that many children her age would manage without trouble may be risky for her. At the seaside, local children will know all about tides and collapsing sand tunnels but your child has never learned. She will see no significance in a dwindling beach, the increasing pull of a current around her legs or the tell-tale trickles of sand from a tunnel that is about to cave in.

When you take your child on holiday you will probably long to let her run free, but if her freedom is to be unsupervised you need to choose your place very carefully indeed. Even that innocent country cottage may have a bull in the next field, deadly nightshade in the hedge, a well in the garden or a delightful haystack with a pitchfork for her to jump on. When you move to a new home, all the adults may be so busy that your child gets less supervision than usual just when she needs more. Amid the myriad DIY jobs queuing for attention, try to make basic child-proofing a priority.

Whether the move is temporary or permanent the important thing is to put yourself in your child's shoes. Think about the new environment and all the things in it she has never met before. Try to foresee how they will strike her. Make a tour of inspection when you arrive. Visualize your child running around and try to spot the traps lying in wait for her. What she needs while she finds her way around is an undemanding but willing escort, ready to go with her over the rocks or down to the pool, into the ocean or over to the farm, down to the shops or into the park. If you are all on holiday, that's probably your role. If you are trying to get settled into new jobs as well as a new home, it may be a temporary extension of your usual child care.

Accident-prone children Almost all young children (and most of the rest of us, too) are more liable to accidents when tired or unwell. At this stage in her life your child's everyday life involves maximum effort from body and mind. As she tires, it gets harder to make those efforts so she becomes increasingly liable to failure and frustration. If she has been trying to ride a two-wheeler all afternoon, her performance will probably get worse as supper-time approaches and she will be infuriated. "I can, I can do it" she roars, setting off yet again. Left to fail and try again, she will get rasher and less competent as she gets crosser. If you mind her coming to grief, you have to find a tactful way to make her stop until she is rested.

Some children seem unusually accident-prone all the time. The accident and emergency department of the local hospital may come to know them by name, so often do they appear for a couple of stitches, a plaster cast or a night's observation after falling on their heads.

A few of these children may be being distracted by worries or anxieties or made careless of their own safety and bad at managing their bodies by long-term unhappiness. If you suspect that your child's liability to accidents is due to unhappiness and tension, you will need to offer extra protection by treating her as if she were somewhat younger than she is, while you try to discover and sort out the trouble.

Children vary in how well co-ordinated they are, especially in early childhood when some may have been walking for almost twice as long as others. If your child has less physical control than many others, she may come to grief during ordinary play. Try to offer practical help with the reasonable things she wants to do, rather than forbidding her to do them. Show her safe ways to climb a ladder, for instance, so that she is less likely to fall when she uses the slide or climbing frame. Teach her to wait until she has got her balance before trying to walk along a wall and to sit down when she feels herself wobbling. Make a game of setting her little obstacle courses on her bike to improve her steering.

If your child still seems clumsy at four or five, and especially if she herself is bothered by it because other children tease, she might benefit from more formal teaching directed towards muscular control. You might want to enrol her in "music and movement", dancing, gymnastic or even judo classes.

A few children seem neither unhappy nor clumsy but unreasonably fearless. They do not only climb foolishly high into trees, but also jump out again and break their legs. Speed does not frighten them so they win all the bike races at the expense of bits of skin. They are keen to try any sport from horse riding to surfing, but are sure they can do it and not at all keen on being taught how.

A child like this will learn her own lesson in time, but you want her to do it as cheaply as possible. Never congratulate her on her outrageous performances even when relief that she has come through safely makes you want to cheer. Instead of clapping her Tarzan leap, point out that her success was pure luck and that trying was stupid. If you can make her feel that you really care about her safety, she may be able to care about it too and see her rashness as babyish and silly.

Anger and physical aggression Children have the right to use their bodies to express their feelings but they do not have the right to use them to hurt anyone. Almost all parents, even the most tolerant, rightly draw the line at being hit or kicked because their child is angry.

A lot of adults believe that a child who deliberately hurts should be hurt back (see p.375). The idea is that if she really doesn't understand that hitting hurts, showing her what a good smack feels like should stop her doing it. If it doesn't stop her, and she goes on hitting, knowing she's hurting, then she deserves painful punishment this time, which will act as a deterrent in the future.

As Martin Luther King pointed out, the law of "an eye for an eye" leaves everybody blind. Although tit-for-tat arguments are so simple they sound as if they must be reasonable, they are totally illogical from a child's point of view. If your child hits you and you smack her back, the punishment doesn't show her that her own action was wrong; on the contrary, because you, an adult who can do no wrong, have done the same thing, she is more likely to see what she did as acceptable. How can she take you seriously when you punctuate the message, "I will not have you hitting people" with a good slap?

If children are to learn to use words instead of blows, they need to be with adults who really listen.

The force of the don't hit message is much stronger if nobody in your house ever hits or deliberately hurts anyone. When your child hits out at you, you take her hands and say, "No hitting. I know you're angry but we don't hit people. Hitting hurts and that's horrid..." You are bigger and stronger than your child. That means that you never have to put up with being attacked by her, or use hurtful means to stop her because if it's absolutely necessary, you can simply hold her until she calms down.

When your child is aggressive, it's important to make it clear that it's not her anger you disapprove of but only her violent way of showing it. You are not telling her not to be angry, or even not to show she's angry; you're telling her to do something constructive with that anger: to be assertive rather than aggressive (see p.473).

Physical gender differences

An only child takes the shape of her or his own body for granted and tends to assume that all other children are made in the same way. For a while, Mummy and Daddy are usually also taken for granted as just themselves. The child sees no connection between their big hairy bodies and her own smooth little one and therefore no greater similarity with one gender than the other.

First questions usually come up when the child notices a child of the opposite sex naked. "What's that?" she asks. All she wants is its name – penis – and perhaps the matching name for what she has – vagina. If you take it calmly and concentrate on giving accurate information that exactly answers the specific question you have been asked, there is no reason why the topic should get loaded with embarrassment. You do not have to "get the whole business over" by telling all. It is much better to let your child realize which bits of information she does not understand and ask, in her own time, for the missing links. She may be six or seven before she asks that crunch question: "How does the Daddy put the seed in the Mummy's va-what do you call it?" By then you will have had years of practice at giving brief specific answers and will be comfortable with, "By putting his penis into it." If you let a deadly serious "special" atmosphere build up every time your child asks a question that touches on sex, you may land yourself with pure farce. One child rushed into the kitchen saying, "Quick, Mummy, tell me where I came from. Sarah's waiting to know." Taking a deep breath, her mother launched into her long-prepared lecture, watched with amazement by her daughter who at last interrupted: "Mummy, I only said where did I come from? Was it Colchester like Sarah?"

Some parents make a point of letting their young children see them naked so that they get the chance to see the difference between adult women and men. Others make an equal point of keeping themselves covered. Where sex and young children are concerned it is probably best not to make a point of anything. It really does not matter whether or not your child sees you naked as long as the atmosphere surrounding nudity is relaxed and casual, not seductive. So don't be deliberately old-fashioned or self-consciously modern.

Deliberate displays which are intended to show children that they are made just like their parents of the same sex often misfire badly. To a child's eye there is no similarity between a small, smooth hairless girl and a fully developed woman or between a little boy with a tiny penis and almost invisible scrotum and a fully mature man. Looking at a same-sex parent, the child may see not similarity but worrying difference that suggests she or he is inadequate. Looking at an opposite-sex parent may make the child feel anxious at the thought of making a baby with someone like that. Your three- or four-year-old may give clues to worries in this area, like talking in a tone that's both excited and anxious about marrying Daddy "when I'm big". She can probably use two kinds of reassurance. Firstly, although she thinks she wants to marry her father, and may even play with fantasies of replacing you, those fantasies are scary because the reality is that you are her Mummy not her rival, and she cannot do without you. Remind her that Daddy is married to you and that she will have her own husband, from her own age group, one day. Secondly, it is comforting to point out that children are all of a piece and all the parts of their bodies grow at just the right rate to keep up with the rest. The child is just the size and shape she is meant to be now and as she grows her body will change so that it is still just the right size and shape when she is grown up.

Try not to volunteer sexual information your child has not asked for, though. She cannot use it until she needs it. In particular, avoid encouraging your child to think about herself actually having sex. Information about sex differences now and making babies in the future is important and appropriate, but sexual intercourse is just one more of the many peculiar things people get up to when they are adult. That is why sexy, teasing, innuendoes and jokes about "boyfriends" and "girlfriends" are much better avoided.

TALKING

Sometimes a young friend just won't speak when he's spoken to.

In the year or two before they start school, children are tremendously busy finding out how things work, finding out what they themselves can do, and putting themselves, imaginatively, into other people's places. Language makes it easier to think, and thinking begs for language. Language and thought are so intimately entangled that young children who use language well are more likely than others to make the most of their intellectual potential.

Using language well in early childhood does not just mean more of the same from toddlerhood. As a toddler, your child learned words mostly as labels for, and comments on, interesting things that he could actually see (like that bus) or had seen often and hoped soon to see again (like Daddy, due home from work). Your child will learn more word-labels, of course, hundreds and hundreds of them. But he will also increasingly use language for its uniquely human purpose which is not to talk about what is seen and known but about what is not. You'll hear your child talk about things that aren't there – but can be recalled or imagined or planned. And about abstract ideas and emotions that will never be "there" but can be passed as word-pictures from one person to another. Hopefully, you'll hear him using language for pure pleasure, too, his own and other people's, joking, making rhymes, telling stories.

ENRICHING YOUR CHILD'S LANGUAGE

The more you talk to your child the better, but while everyone knows that quantity is important, the importance of quality is often underestimated. Adult talk is only really useful to a young child if what the adult says affirms what the child says and gives him positive messages about himself. Even lots and lots and lots of talk will not help your child with his language (or with anything else) if it's mostly scolding and criticism.

Useful talk with an adult must also be genuine, two-way conversation, not just talk. If you let your child burble at you while you think about something else, keeping the flow going with "uh-huh" and "really?" the talk is not true communication. He will realize that you are not really listening to him and either stop talking or become very frustrated. He may even feel inadequate in the face of your obvious boredom. Monologues from adults are not very useful either. If there are no pauses for the child's contributions, or nobody listens and reacts to them, adult talk is no more than pleasant background noise like a radio left on when nobody is listening. The child will soon realize that you are not really talking to him; that you do not care whether he listens, hears or understands you.

Affirmative two-way talk with an attentive adult can supply your child with names, labels and descriptions for things or ideas at exactly the moments when he needs them. That's the best kind of help his language could have because whether he already has a large vocabulary or still uses only a few words, he needs more and more.

Suppose that he is struggling to move a fresh bag of sand towards his sandpit. He obviously needs physical help, but you can give him language-learning help at the same time by labelling his problem for him. If you just say, "Let me help you", he learns nothing new. If you say, "Let me help you to carry that bag of sand, it is too heavy for you", you offer him several new language ideas. It may not previously have occurred to him that sand in a bag is called a "bag of sand". He may now be able to connect that form of words with similar ones that are familiar, such as "cup of tea" or "drink of juice". Furthermore, the child probably had not realized that he was unable to move the bag himself because it was "too heavy". You have just taught him the label for an idea (weight) which he could sense but could not express.

You can do the same with all kinds of other ideas. You reach something for him because you are "taller"; you take some ketchup off his plate because he has taken "too much"; you dropped a dish because it was "very hot" and you rejected one of his sweaters because it had got "too small".

You can help him with words about colour, shape and number in the same way. If a friend offers him her bag of sweets to choose from and he selects a pink one, you could say, "You're going to have that one are you?" – friendly chat, but not actually helpful. If you say, "You're going to have the pink one are you?" you supply him with the word for a colour he obviously likes the look of but probably did not know was called "pink". Two sweets give you the chance to elaborate with, "Two sweets! One sweet for this hand and one sweet for that hand. Two sweets for two hands."

His imaginary games give you scope for providing words, too. Equipped with a tiny pair of gloves and a huge umbrella, he announces, "Darryl Daddy." He is obviously playing a Daddy-going-out game in his head, but does he know the names of the places his father goes to? Ask, "Is Daddy going to the office or is he going for a walk?" and you supply him with name-labels for two of the places Daddy might go. You have helped him to elaborate his thinking and enlarged the possibilities of his play.

You can carry on with this kind of elaboration almost whenever your child speaks to you, and although it looks stilted written out on the page, there is nothing difficult or phoney about it. Indeed if you are really listening to what the child is saying, what he is trying to communicate, you may find yourself doing it automatically. It is the opposite of the "uh-huh" approach to children's talk. He says, "Look! Big dog!" It is clearly an exclamation; he has obviously seen something notable about the dog. You try to see what it is and to offer him an elaboration both of the thoughts and of the words that will express them: "Yes, it is a big dog isn't it? And just look how fast he is running..."

Help your child talk to different people Most toddlers find it so difficult to communicate with strangers that someone familiar has to translate both sides of any conversation. In early childhood, though, your child will begin to understand what new people say directly to him, and will often be able to make them understand him, too, if they are trying and he is not burying a shy face in your shoulder. Help him to get the most out of every

conversation that comes his way. The more confident he feels of understanding and being understood, the better he will manage social situations with peers and adults now, and as he moves into school.

Suppose that you visit the doctor because the child has had earache, for example. Your aim is to enable the child to conduct the conversation for himself, so try not to speak for him but to help him do it. The doctor will (hopefully) address the child directly, but she may not really expect to get sensible answers from anyone but you. Don't join her in an adult conspiracy of talking over the child's head about his pain. Instead, help him to listen (if necessary, tell him what the doctor just said: "Dr Jones asked if your ear is still hurting...") to realize that he has understood what was said and to answer. If the doctor doesn't understand what he says, encourage him to say it again. Your message to your child is, "what you say is good enough". If he believes you he will enjoy having you help him say more and more. When his father comes home and asks, "What have you been doing today?", he probably means the question to be rhetorical and without your help the child will not answer because the question is incomprehensibly general. But you can help him: "Are you going to tell Daddy about the squirrel we saw in the park?" Launched into telling, the child's account will be jerky and incomplete, but you can smooth it out and keep it unrolling for him with that same elaborating technique:

"Squirrel comed. Frightened... I say 'OOOH'."

"Yes, you did say 'Ooh' didn't you? And then what happened? The squirrel ran back into the... ?"

"TREE!" supplies the child delightedly.

Sometimes people, even you, will not understand something your child says, even if he will repeat it. Don't risk a guess because if you guess wrong, he may be wildly confused ("Why did she give me a biscuit when I told her someone was at the door?"). Be honest. Admit that you haven't understood what he means and say you're sorry. It's not that you owe him an apology but that you want him to believe that you regret missing what he was trying to say. Your underlying message this time is, "What you say is interesting."

Learning to use pronouns With this kind of conversation going on, the child adds the nouns which label things, the adjectives which describe those things and the verbs which tell what they do, at a rapid rate. But he probably still finds words like "me", "you", and "him" extremely confusing because their meaning depends on who is talking and your elaborations therefore don't help. I am writing this book for you to read. But if you tell someone else about it, you will say, "I am reading this book that she wrote." I am still me and you are still you. But I have become "she" and you have become "I"!

Because this is so confusing, children usually go on using proper names (their own and other things), thus avoiding pronouns altogether: "Johnny will get Teddy" rather than, "I will get him." Trying to correct this will get you both into a monstrous mess. You say, "Say, 'I'll get Teddy', darling." The child will look at you in amazement and reiterate his first statement: "Johnny will get Teddy." What he means is that it isn't you who will get the bear, but he. Yet you said "I". Oh dear.

This kind of muddle makes things so much worse that it's better not to try to make him use pronouns until he does so spontaneously. That probably will not be long. If all the adults who look after him take trouble, now, to use pronouns correctly themselves, saying, "Shall I help you?" rather than, "Shall Mummy help Shaun?", he will gradually sort it out for himself.

Asking "what's that?" By the time he is three, or thereabouts, your child knows that he needs more words and asks for them by continually demanding, "What's that?" He is asking to be told, or reminded of the name, so don't confuse the issue by launching into elaborate answers to the different question, "What's that for?" If it is the washing machine he is pointing to, it's better to say, "That's the washing machine" than to embark on, "That's my special machine for washing clothes."

Don't hold back on big, difficult words though. Many young children love them. If you can say Diplodocus, so can he. As for Pterodactyl, it's the spelling that's tricky, not the sounds.

Soon you will be into "why?" Several hundred "why?" questions per day, including a lot of the "Why can't I?" type, quite a lot of the "Why has Daddy gone out?" variety and a few of the unanswerable genre of "Why is it hot/Sunday/morning?", can be very wearing or intensely exciting (or a bit of each). Do remember that the child is asking because he needs to know. He is adding to his store of knowledge and understanding

Your child will be amazed to find that the answers to some of his questions are in a book.

and he is doing it in the most efficient possible way – by using words. "Whys" are a clear sign of growing up. As a toddler he would either have tried to find out by doing or he would not have thought of the question in the first place.

Some "whys" are unanswerable either because the child, without realizing it of course, is tapping the edges of human knowledge, or because he is tapping the edges of yours!

"Why does it thunder/rain/blow?"

"Why is Daddy a man/big/brown?"

"Why is that lady on my TV?"

"Why do lights switch on?"

"Why won't the sun switch on?"

Try not to fall back on "because that's the way it is". If the question is answerable, answer it briefly. But don't muster everything you know about the workings of television and launch into a lecture. His question is casual; the phenomenon of the TV showing that particular picture has just caught his attention. "Because she is the lady this programme is about" is probably all he needs. If the question is answerable, but not by you, don't be afraid to say so. There is nothing but good in telling the child: "That's an interesting question but I don't know myself, let's ask Mummy/let's look in a book…" Three is not too young for a very first encyclopedia. It's not for your child to read. It's to make sure that you have a supply of pictorial information on almost any subject he is likely to enquire about. "More 'bout lizards" he demands. Without a book you may have no more 'bout lizards to offer.

Some "whys" do land you in a sort of "Alice in Wonderland" world, though:

"Why am I Rick?"

"Because when you were a new baby we decided we liked that name, so that's what we called you."

"Why?"

"Because it seemed like a nice name for a super boy."

"Why?"

The "whys" may simply be a device to keep your attention and keep the conversation going, or the child may have long ago stopped meaning literally "why?" and be meaning "tell me more". You can break it up by saying, "Shall I tell you more about when you were a new baby?"

Often, he asks "why?" but is unanswerable because "why?" is not the right question. He is using the word wrongly so it is meaningless: "Why are bulls?" Try not to dismiss him out of hand but to think what he is likely to mean. Is it, "What are bulls? What are bulls for? Are bulls dangerous? Are you frightened of bulls and should I be?" A general, "I'm not quite certain what you want to know, but let's talk about bulls and see. Do you know what a bull is? It's a man cow", may help him get started on the conversation he is really seeking.

Using words as part of self-control

After years of having their behaviour controlled and managed by adults, children begin to take over for themselves (see p.498). You will probably notice this new self-discipline first in what he says to himself as he plays. He uses to his toys or imaginary companions the

Why does my daughter talk to herself so much?

My four-year-old has always been a chatty child. I used to lie in bed in the morning and listen to her "talking" to herself in her crib. Later on she used to "read" to herself and talk to her toys in pretend games. In the last few months, though, I've noticed her talking to herself in a different way – sort of telling herself what to do. I was touched when I heard her trying to put on her shoes and saying, "The left, Ellie, find the right one," just like me. But it's happening so much now that I'm getting worried, especially as she's shortly going into a nursery class that prides itself on teaching children to concentrate through silent working. Why does Ellie still talk to herself so much? Is it a sign of slow development or lack of concentration, maybe even hyperactivity? Or is it harmless?

Children's private speech is better than harmless: it's positively helpful.

Until a generation ago, under the influence of Piaget, children's monologues were called "egocentric" and considered a sign of immaturity. It was thought that children talked to themselves because they found it impossible to imagine another person's perspective so as to join the give and take of real conversation. Private speech was expected to fade away as children became capable of social interaction.

Since the late 1970s, though, influenced by the appearance in English of much earlier work by the Russian psychologist Vygotsky, research has shown that all children use private speech (though some use it more, and for longer, than others); that it arises directly out of important social interactions and that it is crucial to early self-directed learning.

Vygotsky pointed out that for any child at any point in time there is a range of tasks and skills she's already mastered, a range that is completely beyond her and, in between, a range (known as the "zone of proximal development") that a child could master with the help of an adult. When a parent or teacher helps a child tackle such a challenging task, she first offers verbal directions about what has to be understood or done, and then suggests strategies for doing it. The child's private speech incorporates those dialogues so that when she attempts that same task on her own, she can give herself directions, suggestions and reminders. When a child is tackling a task such as putting on shoes alone for the first time, a parent may hear complete replays of familiar scenes starting, "Can't go out without your shoes Ellie... let's find your shoes." As a child becomes more confident that she can manage the job in hand, private speech contracts from whole sentences to prompt words about what is still difficult or challenging. Like many children, Ellie's main difficulty with shoes is getting the correct one on each foot, so right and left are the words she still says to herself. Eventually, children begin to be able to think words without saying them out loud. If they are beginning to read fluently they will begin to be able to do so silently. Likewise private speech becomes quiet, incomprehensible muttering and then internal speech which is not vocalized at all. It never loses all usefulness, though. Older children, even adults, faced with challenging activities, or with written material that seems incomprehensible, all tend to prompt themselves, rehearse strategies, or strive for understanding by means of private speech.

Ellie's private speech is something positive and the only associated worry may possibly be her proposed school. There are still some older teachers, who regard children's talking aloud to themselves as socially unacceptable or even disordered behaviour. Do check on the real meaning of the "silent working" this school advocates. Forbidding five-year-olds to talk to each other is controversial; forbidding them to talk at all, even to themselves as they count on their fingers, or work at a drawing, would be damaging to their development.

same kinds of controlling phrase he hears at home or at nursery: "Careful now!", "Up you come", "Leave that alone..." He is a hard taskmaster. You may overhear much fiercer tones than you are conscious of using yourself or happy for his other caregivers to use.

Later on the child begins to talk to himself in the same way, but at first his warnings come after the event. He kicks his ball into the flower bed and scolds himself, "Not in the flowers, Harry." A little while later he warns himself in advance. Poised to kick that ball, he says, "No Harry, not in the flowers" and just as if someone else had spoken, he turns and kicks it the other way.

This is an excellent sign that he really is taking the instructions and rules that come from outside into himself and making them his own. But if you often hear him fiercely instructing himself, but disobeying his own instructions, saying, "Mustn't hurt the dog, John" as he yanks its tail, be alert. You, or someone else who cares for him, may be issuing streams of instructions without making the reasons clear or making sure one is obeyed before the next is given. It may be a good moment to think, or talk, about how the child can best be helped with the important business of learning how to behave (see p.523).

Using words to control other people
Young children are on the receiving end of so much controlling talk that it is almost inevitable that they should try out this use of language for themselves. Four-year-olds, in particular, often do sound very bossy. "Stop it at once", your child may yell at the surprised baby; "Come here immejitly", he commands the unheeding dog. He is trying to find someone below him in the status hierarchy so that he can be boss as well as being bossed. He is also trying to see whether his words have as much power over other people's behaviour as yours have over him. So do try to be tolerant of this sometimes tiresome phase. He does not mean to be unpleasant. If his bossiness really upsets you, teach him to soften his commands and exhortations with "please" and "thank you", and look to the way adults speak to him. He may exaggerate the strict or hectoring tones he reproduces, but he will not invent them out of sweet reason.

Using words to boost self-esteem
Boasting is another trait that is typical of four-year-olds and not to be taken too seriously. Two children together will often have a boasting session that is almost a verbal tennis match – and recognized by both to be a game:

"My house is bigger than yours."
"My house is bigger."
"My house is as big as a palace."
"My house is as big as a park."
"My house is as big as, as, as everything!"

Although listening adults may be sensitive to the reality of one or the other child really having a smaller house, father, or income than the other, this kind of boasting is recognized by both children as verbal play. The reverse – an exchange of insults – is a different matter. One or the other of the children may get his feelings hurt and anyway it's rude. Tell them so and stop it.

If your child boasts a lot, and begins to irritate other children by doing so, you may wonder whether he needs to make himself sound very grand and big and rich because he really feels rather humble and small and poor. Lots of visible, tangible love (yes, hugs and kisses) and more congratulation and praise than criticism and reproof, may be the right prescription.

Using words to ask for approval

Your child mostly wants to be good and sometimes seems too good to be true.

Four-year-olds often sound goody-goody as well as bossy. "Nat's a good boy," he says, smugly. Don't sit on him, saying, "Well, I don't know about that." You will hurt his feelings and confuse him. It is a good sign for his future behaviour that he wants you to think him "good". And it is also a good sign of language development that he wants to use words to talk about the idea.

Sometimes this kind of talk suggests that a child wants assurance that you love him even when you do not love what he does. He is still very literal about language, so these distinctions are important to him. If he and his sister have been racketing around until you feel that the noise will drive you crazy, try to avoid saying, "Do go out into the garden you two, you're driving me round the bend." Separate them (whom you love) from their noise (which you do not) and say, "Do go out into the garden you two if you are going on with that game. The noise is driving me round the bend."

TALKING ABOUT ABSTRACT IDEAS

The more confident a child is that words will work for him, that he can express anything he thinks, and understand the expressed thoughts of others, the sooner he will begin to use them to exchange ideas. Not every child asks about God at four or five or tries to tell you how a piece of music makes him feel at five or six. It may be years yet before you share this kind of conversation with your child, and it certainly doesn't matter if it is. But it does matter if he tries it and finds himself laughed at, quoted around the family ("the things they come out with") or blocked by your obvious embarrassment. That matters because such reactions are likely to shut him up. And however much you may sometimes wish that he would shut up for a minute, talking and listening and thinking, and talking some more, are essential parts of his education in its widest sense.

Sharing thoughts and feelings with someone of such limited experience and understanding isn't always easy, especially if you are not a person who often has emotional conversations even with adults. It's easy to squash small children without meaning to as this mother almost did: "It was the winter she was four. I found her gazing out of the window, tears pouring down her face. I asked her what on earth was the matter, thinking she didn't want to go to bed or something. But what she said was, 'Oh Mummy, I don't know how to think about the moon.' It was so unexpected that I nearly laughed and said, 'Don't be silly.' I'm glad I didn't though. She wasn't being silly, far from it. We talked about things being too big or too far to understand and about why moonlight was the kind of beautiful that was sad... I don't know how to think about the moon either. But the point was that she wanted to share."

Apart from the classic conversation about the "facts of life", (see p.491) potentially difficult talk usually comes into one of the three following groups, each of which has its own useful techniques.

Talking about the way the world works When your child asks you about complicated questions of fact, you don't have to pretend to know everything. Part of your tremendous grown-up skill is that you know how to find out things you don't already know. And part of your unique value to your child is that you're interested enough to try. So if he notices flocks of birds in early winter and, not satisfied with being told that they are going to fly to a warmer country, asks where they are going, find out together from a book or from a friend who knows more about birds than you do. Often your child will ask about things you do understand but cannot think how to explain to him (infant school teachers are taught how to teach, after all). "Why don't aeroplanes fall out of the sky?", "Why do plants go yellow when we keep them on the table instead of the window-sill?" and "Why is this tooth wobbly?" are the kinds of question that may leave you groping. You need reference books which are written for young children. Finding them in the library, and perhaps enlisting the help of the children's librarian, can be fun and good practice for later on when your child will be doing projects for school.

Talking about beliefs Questions about beliefs can be even more difficult. You are being asked to explain your attitudes and you cannot look those up in a book. On the other hand you are being given the chance to pass on to your child some of what makes you the person you are and that's a precious part of being his parent. These questions come up in many different ways. Whether or not your household practises any kind of religious observance, your child will eventually notice that other families behave similarly or differently. Friends may go to different kinds of "church" on different days of the week. His best friend may never be able to sleep over with him on Fridays. An older friend may even tell him, "We don't have God, silly, we have Allah."

If you have a clear belief, share it, but try to make clear to your child that it is a belief rather than a set of facts. That will allow you to acknowledge respectfully the different beliefs held by different people. It may also help protect you both from the difficulties of religious discussion with someone whose thinking is still too concrete and based in what can be observed, experienced and proved, for easy understanding of faith. If you are not careful you may find that your child is accepting as literal truth terrifying images of hellfire and picture-postcard images of heaven presided over by a grandfatherly gentleman in blue robes sitting on a cloud.

If you have no religious belief yourself, by all means share that fact with your child, but try to help him avoid offending his grandmother with Sunday lunch stoppers like, "God's just silly. My Daddy said."

Talking about death Questions about taboo subjects are usually the most difficult of all. A couple of generations ago the most general taboo was the "facts of life"; now, it's the facts of death. Western culture is peculiarly bad at acknowledging the simple fact that death is the inevitable and universal end of life. Many people live all their lives in unspoken, semi-conscious terror of events they know must take place: their own deaths and the deaths of people they love. Terror makes us bad at talking, so terror and taboo can pass from generation to generation unless parents begin to break that cycle.

Don't shy away from talking about death.

You cannot alter the facts of death for your child. And you cannot protect him from thinking about death because he will notice it – in plants, insects, fledglings and squashed animals on our roads, if nowhere else – and he will wonder. You may be able to protect yourself from his questions, by letting him sense, the first time he asks, that death is unmentionable. But wondering, alone, will make him more liable to anxiety and deprive him of any intellectual context within which to face the first death – whether of a pet or a person – which matters directly to him.

The starting point is the most difficult. Once you have acknowledged that all living things die, your child will certainly ask – if he feels he can – "Will I die?" or "Will you die?" If you can cope with this you will be able to let him go on asking, at his own pace, so that he gets more information as and when he has a use for it. Remember, when you face these first questions, that a small child cannot anticipate or empathize with grief. He does not really know what "die" means – that is the question he is trying to explore – so although the word vibrates with pain for you it does not do so for him. You have to give him the factual answer but you can offer other facts to help guard his emotional distance. He will be fascinated to know about the different time-scales on which creatures live – from the lifespan of hours for that butterfly through the brief gestation and life of tiny mammals (like his pet mice) to the longevity of people or elephants. In that factual context you can honestly tell him that parents usually live not only through all the aeons of childhood that lie ahead of him, but also on into the time when children are parents themselves.

Natural death is linked with ageing. Even a small child observes objects, animals and people wearing out and hears adults using phrases like "past her best" of everything from cars to dogs to neighbours. So if you are asked, "Will Grandpa die soon?" try to avoid a shock-horror reaction which will make nonsense of everything you have said so far. You can be both reassuring and truthful if you say something like, "Most people live to be 70 and some live to be 100 so we don't have to worry about that..."

Childish (and not so childish) anxieties about death usually focus around the manner of dying and on what happens afterwards. Insofar as a young child has any concept of death at all it is usually violent death off the TV screen. He needs to know that natural death is usually a peaceful drifting into oblivion, a giving up of life rather than a killing. He may see a butterfly come to a permanent stop on a flower. He may find one of the goldfish just floating on the water, or go to feed his guinea pig and find it, still apparently asleep, in its nest. That may be dreadfully sad for him but he can be helped to realize that it was in no way dreadful for the guinea pig. Whatever you wish to teach him about a possible afterlife, it is vitally important that he understand that physical death, of insects, animals or people, is always final; that the dead never come alive again or have any awareness or feeling. Ghost stories are stories and funeral trappings are for the living not for the dead.

If it is important that children be helped to accept the inevitability of natural death as an end to life, it is even more important that they do not take for granted the casual slaughter in TV drama and the reported carnage on our roads and in the world's battle-zones. If your child can ask you about death, you can talk to him, in ways he will understand, about reverence for life and the importance of people looking after themselves, other people and creatures. And if this kind of talk sometimes lands you with questions you find awkward, like, "Why is it all right to squash wasps?", maybe finding answers will clarify your own thinking!

LANGUAGE PROBLEMS – GREAT AND SMALL

The most common reason for delayed language development is still deafness but the young child's language may suffer not only from today's hearing loss but from the middle-ear infections he had earlier on. Babies' hearing should be regularly checked but any child who is not talking at all by the age of two should have it checked again, by the doctor or clinic, as part of a developmental assessment. You may be referred to a special speech clinic. If nobody finds anything amiss (and they probably will not) they will suggest that you give him another six months and then bring him back if he is still not talking. Two-and-a-half is probably a reasonable time to seek advice for anything that looks as if it might be a language problem, but do be aware that a lot of slow-starters in speech seem to make some kind of breakthrough at around three.

Slower than average speech development If your child uses some words and clearly understands a lot more, you almost certainly have nothing to worry about. There is almost as much variation in young children's language progress as in toddlers' word-learning. If your three-year-old is acquiring speech more slowly than many of his friends, it may be for one of the following reasons (or for no reason other than his personal developmental timetable):

■ He is giving his concentration and energy to acquiring some other skill. He cannot do everything at once. He may talk more when walking is perfected.

■ He is a twin or has a brother or sister very close to him in age. The problem is not "private language" but the scarcity of individual attention from adults.

■ He is a boy and not a girl. Boys' developmental programming is slightly different, so the folly of comparing siblings is even greater if you're comparing across the sexes.

■ He has several older brothers and sisters. Older children may interpret so fast and skilfully that he has little need or time to speak for himself. Their talk may be so continuous that he has little chance for face-to-face talk with you.

■ He is in group care with too low a ratio of adults to children. He may lack face-to-face talk with a familiar caregiver and/or be unhappy.

■ He may be cared for by a nanny or au pair who doesn't speak his language well. Both may find gestures easier than words. He needs a fluent adult model.

■ His family may be bilingual. Learning two languages at once will take him longer than learning one.

Specific Language Impairment Some children – possibly as many as one in 1000 – do have real, if ill-understood, problems with language. They need to be recognized early so that speech therapists can give the best possible help.

Specific Language Impairment (SLI) – which you may also hear referred to as "childhood aphasia" – is a phrase used to describe slow or unusual language development that is not due to impaired hearing, a neurological problem, childhood autism or low intelligence. In other words it describes a normal child who does not achieve normal language milestones. SLI presents itself in many different forms. Some children are markedly slow in understanding and producing words; others acquire words but have great difficulty with grammar; some learn words and sentences at something close to an ordinary rate, but have very particular difficulties with remembering the names of things, or learning the rules of conversation.

Stuttering and stammering Young children's ideas are bigger than their vocabularies. They often find it difficult to express their thoughts smoothly, especially when having to search for the right word holds up the flow of what they want to say. When they are excited or upset, they want to pour something out but the words keep hiccuping. Jerky uneven speech happens to almost every young child sometimes (and to most of the rest of us, come to that) but only rarely does it turn into a stutter which happens all the time and lasts more than a few weeks.

Many children who showed disfluencies in their speech earlier on are fluent by the time they go to school, especially if they have not been made self-conscious about their talking. This is why many paediatricians encourage parents of very young stutterers to wait until they are at least five or six before seeking the professional help that will inevitably bring self-consciousness with it. However, stuttering experts increasingly recommend parents to consult speech professionals within a few weeks of a child starting to stutter.

If you are trying to decide whether a three- or four-year-old's recent stutter is a real problem, you may like to consider the following points before you seek the speech therapy that will certainly make him aware of it: does he deliberately try to control the muscles of his face, lips and tongue so that he grimaces whenever he stumbles? If so he is already conscious of some difficulty with speaking. Does he speak fluently to himself when he is alone? If so his stuttering when he speaks to other people is almost certainly due to anxiety caused by too much pressure.

Reducing stress in every area of his life and providing extra, warm, fun companionship for a while may produce an easy flow of talk again. If not, ask your doctor to refer the child to a speech therapist so that he gets help before lack of confidence in this new skill of communication saps his confidence in all his other skills as well. Whether you plan to consult a speech therapist immediately or not, how you react to your child's stutter is important. Try to stay calm yourselves (even if one of you stuttered as a child so that you are sensitized to the possibility) so that you can remain accepting of the way your child talks, and interested in what he says. The crucial thing is to make it clear that you enjoy his talking. If he feels it is not good enough for you he will become self-conscious.

Try to listen to what the child is saying rather than to how it is said. Don't hurry him or look away in ostentatious impatience while he stumbles through a sentence. Don't finish sentences for him and don't tell him to speak more slowly. Any of those (very natural) reactions to a stutter will not only embarrass and stress your child but will actually make him stutter more. Speech is conscious but the processes which produce speech sounds are not. If you make him think about how he produces a word you will make him stumble over it, just as you become breathless the moment you try to count your breathing rate or control the rise and fall of your chest. And do try to make verbal communication easy for him. If he always has to shout down his sister and repeat everything six times to make you listen, repetition and a word-jam become more likely.

Baby talk Some children go on with baby talk for a long time. It is as if they refuse to accept adult expressions in certain areas and insist on going on using the "words" they started out with. "Biccit-a-baby" demands the four-year-old who is perfectly capable of saying, "I want a biscuit."

Usually such a child has discovered that grown-ups think his baby talk is "sweet". Maybe when he uses it, your face softens. Perhaps you use it back to him. Perhaps he has overheard conversations in which you have proudly maintained to uncomprehending visitors that you "understand every word he says". Suddenly you realize that most people cannot understand him and that will make trouble when he goes to pre-school or to big school. Or you look at him one day in his new jeans and sweatshirt and realize that his talk is not appropriate to his age. It would obviously be very hurtful to the child if you suddenly turned against talk which up to then you have seemed to encourage, so don't do anything dramatic. Vow never to imitate or melt to baby talk any more; translate everything he says in it into proper English, so that you put his version alongside yours and congratulate him when he uses grown-up words and syntax – the more elaborate, the better. Over a few months the baby talk will vanish.

Some other kinds of baby talk are positively useful though. When the child does not know the word for something he wants to mention, he will often coin a highly descriptive word. That cereal which is advertised as going, "snap, crackle, pop" was christened "snapples" by a small child long before the advertisers had the same idea. Words of this kind show that the child is actually thinking about words and making them work for him. They often get adopted into family speech, and why not? They make a bridge between the child's language and the language of adults, and their use by other people shows him that he can produce good, meaningful words of his own. It is easy to tell him the "proper" name for it while letting everyone have some pleasure out of his.

The chatterbox Most three- and four-year-olds talk all the time. With perhaps 500 words in his vocabulary, the child may utter 20,000 words in a single day. That is an incredible number of repetitions. Some parents and carers get extremely bored with it.

Your child must talk, though, because he has to practise making the actual sounds. He has to try out different inflections for his words and he has to try them in different combinations.

He will practise using every word he can think of that will go with one particular one. He may say, "Daddy gone" as his father leaves for work. Then, he starts casting around the room for other words he can use with "gone": "Breakfast gone", "Water gone", "Dog gone". When he has run out of things he can see that have gone he produces more "gone" things out of his mind: "Tree gone, Jack gone, bed gone, house gone, me gone..." It is nonsense, of course, in that what he says is not true, but it is sense all the same because he is making sense of the use of the word.

Join in and make a game of it. He does not really think the tree has gone; after all, he is looking at it while he says it. He is playing with words, so you play with them too. Look straight at him and say, "Trousers gone?" or put yourself half behind the curtain and say, "Mummy gone?" He will probably roar with laughter and embroider the game even further.

Nonsense and naughty nonsense

Words are powerful things. Being able to use them makes the young child feel much more able to control the world. If he can find some words which have a particularly powerful effect on other people, he is liable to use them over and over again. "Pee-pee" he shouts. If he gets a nice strong reaction, he will add in "wee-wee" and "piss, piss, piss" for good measure. The trouble is that the more outrageous the exclamations and expletives he comes out with, the more likely it is that one of you will howl with laughter and the other with outrage.

If you ignore him, it will probably not get out of hand. If you scold, you will get into very deep water. What are you scolding for? A word? Can a word be naughty? No, obviously not. If you start trying to explain that this particular word is naughty except when used in its "proper" context, you will really confuse him. If this kind of thing bothers you, the best way to cope is to substitute your own equally absurd but less "naughty" nonsense for the child's. "Squashed tomatoes to you" is the kind of response that never fails.

All young children love nonsense rhymes and nonsense words. "Niddle, naddle, noddle, nee" they chant, enjoying the rhythm and the sounds and practising both difficult consonants and new emphases. If this chant drives you crazy, suggest a new one: "Double, double, toil and trouble," for example. A child who enjoys nonsense rhymes is ready to be introduced to the sounds and rhythms of poetry too, even if he cannot understand all the words. You could read him some of "Hiawatha" with its regular beat and lovely sounds. It will all help him to listen and think and enjoy words.

Insults and angry talk

We try to teach toddlers and young children to use words instead of blows. The trouble is that having taught these lessons parents often don't much like the angry words either. The child gets into trouble for going for you as if he would like to kill you, but he also gets into trouble for standing stock still shouting, "I hate you..." A child who says this kind of thing is usually frightened. His own powerful fury frightens him and he is still very unsure just how great his power is. He does not know that it would be virtually impossible for him really to damage you. He longs for you to keep control of him while he is out of control of himself. If you let yourself get angry because of his words and shout back at him, you add to his alarm. You have no real reason for anger. He is using great self-control in shouting rather than kicking. So try to stay calm and be the grown-up he so badly needs. Assure him that you know he does not truly hate you so you are not upset, but that you realize he feels very angry just at the moment and you are sorry for him.

As for lesser insults, these can usually be turned into a joke if you can remember that it is a little child who is calling you a "silly old cow". You really don't need to react as you would if an adult insulted you. "If I'm a silly old cow, you're a cross little calf" will often bring the whole episode to a giggly close.

It's better not to take a straightforwardly disciplinary line with any of these issues because it is important not to give your child the idea that words are ever bad in themselves. You want him to use words, to like words, to enjoy his own and other people's words. You don't want him to be afraid of them or see them as weapons. So try to apply that old adage "sticks and stones may break your bones but words will never hurt you", and help anyone else who cares for, and might be offended by, your child to remember it too. It is not entirely true, of course, but it is useful with this age group.

Angry talk can look aggressive but suggests that a child is exercising tremendous self-control.

Broadening your child's horizons is one parental duty that can also be a pleasure.

PLAYING
AND THINKING

The stages your child's playing and thinking will pass through during early childhood are not as easy to see as those of the toddler years. Then, as an explorer discovering her small world and as a scientist experimenting with its properties and behaviour, she learned a vast number of separate facts and facets and began to develop the ability to think about them. Now, it is her rapidly expanding ability to think, to imagine, to create and to "play in her head" which dominates her play learning. It is rather as if her toddler years had been spent gathering together the separate tiny pieces which go into a kaleidoscope, and these years see her able, at last, to put those pieces into her kaleidoscopic mind and shake them around to form new and different patterns at will.

It is not only your child's thinking which is maturing, of course. Her body, and especially her manual dexterity, is growing up too. Increasingly she will be able to do the things she can now think of. When she works out how to make the glove puppet dance or the friction vehicle go, there's a good chance she will actually be able to do it; if she thinks of a colour she can apply it to paper; and she can not only imagine herself as Mummy or the postman, the teacher or Mr Jones, she can also manage the "props" which help the game along.

EXPANDING YOUR CHILD'S WORLD

Your child's play-needs have not completely changed. She still needs suitable playspace, undemanding company, willing partnership and varied equipment, just as she did when she was a toddler. But what might have been ideal then will not be enough now. The familiarity of her immediate world risks becoming boring; she needs more scope. With home and all its well-known, well-loved people and things as a secure background, resting place and launching pad, she needs new experiences, new people, new objects, to feed that imagination.

What you need deliberately do to provide them depends on who else is available to your child and where and how you live. If you live in a rare close-knit village or suburban community you may not have to do very much because your child's world expands gradually as all the children grow up alongside each other. But if her daily life is rural (even idyllic), she'll need urban experience and if, like most children, yours lives in a city, without a close community or environment which she can safely explore and make her own, you are likely to have to work at expanding her lifestyle, balancing the new opportunities and challenges you offer or arrange from home against any she is being offered in a nursery or pre-school group. What is needed from home if home is your child's whole world will be very different from what is needed from home if it is the backcloth to group experience. And the specifics that she needs from you depend on the specifics that might be lacking from others. Is she in a big group at day care so that when she's at home she needs peace, even solitude? Does she get physical exercise and adventure in the daytime and need talk and books at night, or all the sit down play she can cope with at nursery so that home needs to be a place where she can run herself breathless and leap for the moon?

Gradually broadening your child's horizons demands a new level of communication between you. By listening to her and thinking about her questions (see p.493), you can keep abreast of her thought processes. By talking to her you can feed in information and ideas and involve her directly in the things you do and see together. When you are alert to the way she is likely to be thinking, and awake to her comments, you can make even the most casual encounters fascinating. An ambulance zips past. "Why," she asks you, "does it make that noise?" You can use her question to bring alive the whole drama of hurrying sick people to hospital. You could talk to her about ambulances taking priority over other traffic, and show her (on the road for real or in the playroom with toys) what that means. If it's clear that her interest in the whole topic is still smouldering, you could blow on it by taking her, then or another day, to visit your nearest hospital and see the ambulances at base and the uniformed nurses and other personnel.

You can involve her in routine things too. The supermarket has long been a favourite place but now she can look for specific items for you, fetch things which are within reach, push the trolley instead of riding in it, and even choose which particular kind of fruit juice you should buy.

Wherever you go, use her burgeoning facility with words to help her think about the people you see. The postman, to a toddler, is a person with an interesting van, a cap and a lot of letters. To your four-year-old he or she can also be somebody who has to get up very early in the morning, carry heavy bags, read people's scribbly writing and cope with their barking dogs. The adults who are part of your child's life and taken for granted, can become "real" to her, too. Help her think about you as people. Which of the things she sees you do every day do you enjoy? What are you looking forward to? How do you spend your time at that mysterious place called "work"? With her interest and her imagination well-fed by new things to see and feel and understand, you will notice her play change. And if you watch and listen, unobtrusively, as she plays, you will see new areas where she is ready to use help and ideas.

Dramatic play The three-, four- or five-year-old is usually being somebody else. She tries out every activity she notices among adults, not simply copying what they do (as a toddler might) but trying to put herself into their places and be them. When she is a builder, it is not just sand and bricks she is thinking about but sweat and language too. She may love dressing. up, but she does not need elaborate costumes. She changes character in her head, "props" are more useful than clothes. A detective needs a magnifying glass, a shopkeeper a till and a knight a sword.

Sometimes she will use dramatic play to re-live incidents which were emotionally important to her. With practice you can see these coming. A night in the hospital, for example, is bound to mean a spate of hospital games, and merits a doctor set or nurse's outfit. You

The birth of their baby sister is endlessly replayed on the doll that came with her.

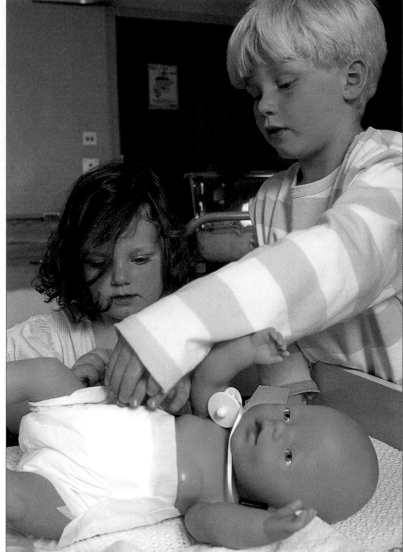

will hear her assuring her teddy that, "This is only my listening thing; keep still, it won't hurt – much."

Don't insist on taking part in dramatic play. There is only room for one author and that is the child. If she plays hospitals, she does not want you to be doctor while she plays patient. This is her script and she is the doctor. Her patient will be a junior and shadowy figure, a doll or soft toy or even an imaginary someone from out of her head. If you have a role at all, it may be required as dresser, or as provider of "pink medicine". Otherwise keep discreetly away. This is her private world which she is making for herself out of the raw material of the real world you show her.

Arts and crafts   Making and creating things with their hands is vitally important to young children. As a toddler, your child wanted to discover how things like scissors and felt-tip pens worked. Now she gradually discovers how to make them work for her. The first few times your child deliberately snips a piece of paper, don't ask her what she has made. The obvious answer is a piece of paper with snips in it, but by asking for an identification you suggest to her that the obvious isn't good enough: it "ought" to be something else. After a few days or weeks of snipping practice, she may look at her most recent piece of snipped paper and decide that it is "lace". She will have taken yet another step in creativity when she decides in advance that she is going to snip paper into lace. In the same way her collage and drawing and painting begins as an exploration of the materials. She wants to "do sticking", or to paint in order to make a painting, not in order to make a painting of a house. The medium is the message so be wary of educational groups that sit three-year-olds down to make Easter baskets or proudly show you their story illustrations.

Colours are important in all media. As she learns their names and relationships, finding that pink is somehow linked with red, your child will explore them deliberately. She may paint 57 rainbows in a week. Give her the materials and stand back. If she asks for comments, stick to what you can see on the paper. "I like those colours" is safe (she wouldn't have used them if she didn't like them too) but, "Is that Daddy?" is not. The question will either make her think you ineffably stupid (why should it be Daddy since representational painting has not entered her mind?) or make her feel inadequate: "Ought it to be Daddy?"

Young children's drawing goes through definite learning stages without anyone teaching them. At three, she finds vertical lines and circles much easier than horizontal lines. Her drawings are therefore either up and down scribble or round and round scribble. Soon the day comes when she sees something in the scribble that reminds her of a person. If she has made a circular drawing, she will add some lines for limbs and perhaps some dots for eyes. Then she will announce her first representational drawing: "A man".

By the time she is four, she may actually set out to draw a person,

Once children draw recognizable people, they soon have enough pencil control to begin to write.

rather than scribbling first and labelling afterwards. Her man will have a big roundish head, with eyes and perhaps a nose and mouth too. Straight out of the head will poke legs. The man has no separate body yet and probably no arms either. During her fifth year drawings of people get more and more lifelike. By the time your child is five her picture of you may have a separate head and body; legs with feet, arms with hands, and even clothes indicated by buttons or a waistband.

Messy play

Play with water, clay, mud, dough or sand often spans dramatic and creative play. It can be either one or both together. To some extent your child can expand these activities for herself using only her own imagination. She may spend all afternoon in the sandpit but now she is not just experimenting with the sand, she is mixing "cement" and using it to fill every crack in the paving stones. However she needs adult help if she is to apply the lessons she has learned about natural materials and learn more. She need not give much thought to what she knows about volume when she is pouring water as part of water play: an overflow is just part of the game. She needs to discover that her mug will overflow in just the same way if she does not stop pouring milk in time.

It's messy and it's play but it's also real experimental science.

Don't assume that she knows when to stop. Here is your three-year-old's beaker of juice, her other identical beaker – empty – and one of your much taller, thinner glasses. Pour the juice from one beaker to another and the child will have no doubt that she still has the same amount. She may even volunteer that it is the very same juice. Her juice. But pour that very same juice into the taller, thinner container while she watches, and she will have no doubt that there is more. She can see that there is more. Even pouring the juice backwards and forwards between the two containers with her own hands will not shift her from the evidence of her eyes. The "principle of conservation" that is dividing her reality from yours is still the other side of years of growing up and experimenting in play with all kinds of materials. Help her to use all her play-skills in ways which are obviously useful as well as "just" fun. She has messed around with dough, now it is time for real scraps of pastry. She has mixed sand and water, now it can be cupcakes and endless questions about why they "blow up" in the oven.

Building, fitting and counting play

This is the kind of play that adults most easily see as "educational" and for which a high proportion of toys are bought. But it is also a kind of play in which many young children lose interest once they have come to terms with the basic engineering toys of toddlerhood. Where there is a cupboard full of barely used toys, most of them will be construction sets, jigsaw puzzles and fitting toys. Think carefully before allocating money and space to more of these.

Your child need not use "educational" toys to educate herself. She will carry out all the intellectual activities which these toys are supposed to encourage with materials that also lend themselves to more imaginative and multiple uses. She probably already owns a good many, such as various kinds of building bricks.

Expanding this kind of play may mean helping your child to master and enjoy more and more complicated building projects.

On the other hand it may mean helping her to use her existing knowledge and skills in rewarding contexts, rather than to acquire new ones. Counting on an abacus is a game. But counting out spoons for supper or tins of cat food at the supermarket has an obvious point. She need not use a construction set to construct. She can build with her bricks; make clean pillowcases into a neat stack in the linen cupboard or put together a castle out of cardboard boxes. Careful, exact fitting is something she still finds difficult so if a mere toy is involved she may not bother. But fitting the cutlery into its compartmented drawer, or learning how to open the front door with your key, is worth much more effort.

The more you can help her to use grown-up implements, and eventually actual tools, the better. A sense of privilege because she is sharing your special things will add to your child's pleasure in using them. She will probably take as much care as she is currently capable of and that will be good for her concentration as well as her manual dexterity. Furthermore, learning safe ways to use things that might be dangerous makes it less likely that she will have careless accidents later on. Even at three, your child can use a hand whisk to beat eggs for her omelette; learn to handle a table-knife and round-ended scissors and make a start with lightweight gardening tools.

Games

Games with turns and rules (and grown-ups) can expand this kind of play in yet another direction. It takes real manual dexterity to throw dice and move little pieces around a board without the whole thing ending on the floor. Even the simplest such board games require at least the basics of counting and sequencing, and willingness to abide by its rules. Younger children in families – and more particularly youngest children in large families – usually become adept at board games rather earlier than others. It is partly because having siblings guarantees more games-playing experience and partly because games-playing experience with siblings brings them face-to-face with the brutal realities of losing. First children who play mainly with adults tend to be protected both from current pain and future skill with bent rules and extra turns. There's not much point in playing board games with a child if you don't keep the rules, but there's no point at all if she isn't ready to learn what they are and understand their point. If you are not sure whether your child has reached this point or not, try her with an old favourite such as "snakes and ladders". If she can accept that counters go down snakes and up ladders because that's the game, she is probably ready to play. But if her reaction to being told that her counter has to go down the snake it's landed on is "why should I?" she probably is not.

Each game has its own rules but they all teach social rules about taking turns and keeping tempers.

Physical play

Young children still involve their bodies in everything they do (or feel or think) so physical activity is almost non-stop – as it was in toddlerhood – and a principal purpose of physical play is to keep it safe and make it fun. Your child is going to keep trying out her physical limits, so it's better for everyone that she should feel challenged by a climbing frame or trampoline rather than by the bannisters or your settee. Children whose physical activities are somewhat limited for hours at a time, (as in a day spent in a classroom) or who are forced to keep actually still for as much as half

Physical skills learned now may stay with your child forever...

...so let her have a try at any new activity that comes her way and takes her fancy.

an hour at a time (as at a carol concert or a church service) really do experience free muscular movement as relief. If you can't stand the thought of a typhoon and its friend tearing through your home, take them to the park on the way.

Provided your child does get plenty of physical freedom, though, there's scope for helping her to expand and elaborate even this kind of play. Help her to see that some of the physical skills that are so important to her and her peers overlap the real and serious world of adults. If she can climb a ladder, she can go up the step-ladder to fetch what you need from that high shelf. If she can run fast, she can be the one to get to the telephone before it stops ringing. If she can jump, she can ford the stream by those stepping stones instead of being carried over, and she can add her small proud strength to yours in mastery of that shopping bag.

Physical skills acquired before a child is about seven years old are seldom completely lost, and learning to channel and control some of her physical energy some of the time can be exciting. Your three- or four-year-old can certainly learn to swim, for example – the earlier the better. She can master a two-wheeler with patient help and she can learn basic playground games – like hop-scotch, skipping and a range of ball games – which will help her feel at home when she goes to "big school". And if there are more specialized physical skills she will need later on, you can probably give her a start towards them now: given the chance she can learn to ski or skate or ride a horse...

Don't hurry your child towards team sports, though. In some communities these are part of every child's life once she goes to school, and there may even be "mini-leagues" practising at weekends. Your child may well be capable of grasping the rudiments of some team games by the time she is five, but ball control, "good sportsmanship" and physical courage, are all so difficult for small children that she will almost certainly be better off learning and practising in penalty-free play with a parent, sibling or friend at home, than in a more challenging atmosphere. Furthermore it will be years yet before she can make good use of sporting competition. When young children compete physically it is, and should be, with themselves and their own best performance, not against each other.

Music

Every human being has a sense of rhythm; all life, after all, is based on it, from the seasons to our heartbeats. But while every child with normal hearing can also perceive the different sounds that make up music, it has only recently been discovered that teaching can help her learn to interpret them; to hear them as music and reproduce them as such with her voice. The music of completely foreign cultures tends not to sing to us because we have not learned to hear it. The more music your child hears the more it will mean to her. The older child who cannot carry a tune or sing in key is probably not a child with an inbuilt defect, but a child who was not taught.

You can vastly increase the chances of your child being musical, although you can do nothing to engender (though a great deal to support) that still-mysterious thing called "musical talent". Listening to any and all kinds of music with you, and singing anything from nursery rhymes and children's action songs to opera, reggae or folk songs is part of it, but only part. Your child can also use more structured musical experience. A tuneful xylophone, bought from a music shop rather than from a toy shop, is a good tool; so is a piano, though an electronic keyboard makes more exciting sounds more easily, and evens out a small child's faltering finger pressure. With tools such as these, and with and without your help, your child will make and listen to sounds which get higher and lower, louder and softer, are the same as or different from each other. She will discover for herself that two notes an octave apart are the same-only-different, while two notes seven tones apart are simply different. Given similar opportunity and encouragement your three- or four-year-old may find sounds as interesting as colours or shapes.

It's good for your child to know that books aren't just for children.

Books

Almost every toddler enjoys looking at picture books as well as hearing (edited and brief) stories read aloud. But these years of early childhood are the ideal time to expand your child's acquaintance with, and affection for, every kind of book and all that they contain. She needs your direct help more where books are concerned than in almost any other area of play because the pleasures of particular books are not obvious when she sees other children reading them, nor are books advertised on TV to the extent that toys are. Your child does not know what books there are or what they say. She cannot imagine the joy they can give her. She cannot "invent" them out of her own head.

Young children need at least three kinds of book for their pleasure and as a foundation of their formal education. The order is important. At this stage in children's lives educational value is entirely dependent on pleasure.

Picture books are still important. By "reading" pictures your child prepares herself for reading words later on. Both are symbols after all, the words are just a further abstraction from the pictures. Look at them with her. Help her to milk each illustration of its last detail. How many birds are in that tree? What is the little boy in the background doing? Try to find her books with big, detailed illustrations rather than the sterile, conventional "A is for Antelope" type (how many children have ever seen an antelope anyway?).

Highly illustrated story books begin to come into their own now. If you choose good ones, your child will be able to follow the story you are reading in words on the picture pages, or at least stop you in mid-sentence to study the highlights of the plot. You have read about the children getting ready for a party. Now on this page she can study the party itself, discover what the children wore and had for tea...

Adult books matter too. She needs to get the idea that books are valuable to the adult world – as well as to children and, later, adults in the children's world of school. If you read for pleasure anyway, this will happen automatically. If you do not, try sometimes to look up the answer to one of her questions in a book, or to find her a picture of something that interests her. Help her to see books as a source of information (yours and therefore hers), as useful as well as fun.

Television, video, CD-Rom and computer games

Young children, like their elders, spend more and more time in screen-centred activities. Television can be a problem (see p.520) but it can also be a blessing. The child who will not yet sit still for a book on natural history may watch a wildlife programme and emerge with

What toys make good gifts in the year before school?

Our four-year-old daughter accumulated a lot of toys while she was a toddler and many of them are still in use. She doesn't seem ready for much more grown-up toys, like a dolls' house, for instance, but it seems dreary to go on giving her more of the same. Are we failing to think of toys, or categories of toy, that are particularly appropriate for this age?

Finding excitingly grown-up-seeming playthings that four- and five-year-olds will really enjoy is often tricky. This is an age-stage when many children's ideas outstrip their manual dexterity so that things they want to do are too difficult to be fun and things that are easy to do are soon boring. Dolls' houses are a good example: the nursery types won't leave enough to your daughter's imagination, but you are quite right in thinking that a real dolls' house will be more fun in another year or two. Right now her attempts to arrange minute furniture will founder because everything falls down.

More of the same is not necessarily dreary. A child who has accumulated numbers of cars or stuffed animals or dolls may truly want nothing so much as another.

Collections of things that she already has (or has had) some of can make excellent presents because you can gear them exactly to your own child's tastes, interests and current games. This category of toy is considerably more trouble for the giver than a straightforward purchase, but it's also likely to be cheaper and better value for money.

You could put together a post office set, using real stationery. Collect trading stamps for stamps; bank and building society slips for official-looking forms. An ink pad and stamp set and perhaps a money-box safe make good centrepieces and a collection of sticky labels and tapes are irresistible to most children.

A little extra stock turns a post office into a general store. You can use replica-foods bought from a toy shop but home-assembled mini-pots and jars of real rice and sugar, pasta and flour, and miniatures of jam and honey, sugar and salt, ketchup and mayonnaise, are more fun. There's scope for your child to make model fruits and vegetables out of playdough, too. Add a set of scales, a till and some play money, and pack the whole lot in a sturdy box that doubles as the counter.

If your child longs to make things but can never do so to her own satisfaction, you could put together some kits that are easier, and closer to her current interests, than commercial ones. A kit for dolls' house furniture, for example, means cutting out basic shapes in balsa wood, drilling holes ready for legs etc and presenting them with dowelling strips, glue, sandpaper and scraps of material for cushions. A dolls' clothes kit requires basic dresses and trousers, made with plenty of elastic and Velcro so they fit a range of dolls, presented with a collection of pretty buttons, fringes and braids, ribbons and lace. The child can finish them as elaborately as she pleases or use them just as they are. Similar levels of preparation and presentation make it possible for a young child to make many other things such as simple soft toys, and dressing-up props like masks and crowns and hats.

Finally, if your child is a paper-and-pencil person, do remember the sheer joy of having everything for drawing and painting and cutting and sticking and collage new at the same time. If you find one or two items she hasn't had before – like gold and silver pens, coloured sticky stars, black card and tracing paper – buy the glorious new felt-tip pens she was due for anyway and put it all together in a box or a home-made portfolio; it may well be the gift she uses most and remembers longest.

mental pictures of otherwise inconceivable wonders. The child who loves to be read to but cannot yet pay attention to radio, may be able to hear good children's fiction read by the best narrators of the day. The city child can find out where the milk in those bottles came from; the country child can see teeming cities and their sights; every child can discover that there are other people and lifestyles in a world far bigger and more complex than she could otherwise know.

The medium's principal problem for very young children, as for toddlers, is that it goes too fast and will not repeat. In fiction, at least, children's videos provide the answer. Your child may watch her favourite so often that she knows it by heart. Unlike you, the VCR never says, "Not that one again; can't I read something different?"

The potential benefits of CD-Rom technology and of television and computer games for very young children are still a matter for speculation. In theory, a CD-Rom could provide your child with the kinds of information you probably build into your conversations with her, at her level and pace, repeated as often as she pleased and with better pictures than you can provide even when you're in the mood to get out the children's encyclopedia. She could obtain the noises different animals make, for instance, or the names of their babies, by pressing animal-shaped icons, and get much, much more later on when she'd learned to recognize and press a further icon.

Most games are too fast-moving and complicated for three- to five-year-olds, although the performance of some younger sisters and brothers for whom an ability to play computer games is the only passport to sibling companionship, is staggering. There is more and more "educational" software available, though, some of it excellent. You don't have to believe that your child's education depends on your PC to accept that early familiarity and ease with a keyboard is likely to be useful to her.

Every child will need to take computer skills for granted as part of daily life.

PROBLEMS WITH PLAY

A child's play-world is her very own. As far as possible what your child does within that world should be her business alone, provided she does not hurt or harm anybody or anything. Inevitably, though, a child's play is influenced from outside and has some influence on her surroundings, so some troublesome issues arise.

Guns, war and violence Pretend-war and blood-curdling deeds are part of the universal currency for play in all cultures and for both sexes, especially for boys. However much energy you put into promoting non-violence, it probably won't stop a little boy using a block for a gun or turning a harmless game of "tag" into World War III. Human history, and therefore all cultures, with their fairy tales and folk-heroes, are full of blood and battle. Even if your child heard no stories except from the Bible, he would find plenty of war games to play from it.

"Real" (ie. replica) guns are different though. Research evidence strongly supports commonsense observation in suggesting that guns and weapons stimulate children to play more aggressively than they do when they provide weaponry themselves out of crooked fingers or Stickle Bricks and imagination. The mere presence of guns in a children's play environment increases both the amount and the violence of aggressive play. The suggested explanation is that whereas a gun is only one of many things that can be made out of fingers or blocks, guns have only one purpose so every time a child so much as sees a gun, he goes into bang-bang mode.

If you are thinking of banning weapons from your child's toy cupboard, do also review the place of other aggressive toys such as super-heroes. Groups of children who spend a structured play period with a layout of combat figures play more aggressively than children who spend the same period with farm animals or toy vehicles. Furthermore, during a subsequent period of free play, the children who have played with the combat toys continue to be markedly more aggressive than the others. A session listening to stories with aggressive themes – even folk stories if, like "The Three Billy Goats Gruff", they model extremes of macho behaviour – has similar effects, especially if children are encouraged to play the stories out. The same is true of older children who play violent computer games in which players score more highly by killing more people, more horribly.

Aggressive play and violent play-themes may be universal, but it is clear that arming, peopling and modelling such play enormously increases its extent and intensity. So if you want to keep your child's play as non-violent as possible, it is probably best to accept games that come out of his imagination calmly, realizing that at this stage, "Zap-Bang you're dead" means no more and no less than "I'm it", but to make this one kind of play that you do not expand or facilitate. Do remember, though, that nothing you do or avoid doing around your children's toys and games will influence their orientation towards violence as much as what you do and avoid doing in your own behaviour. All violence breeds violence, but real violence in the family, whether a child experiences or merely sees it, breeds more than play (see p.375).

Gender

Help your child to explore the whole world, not just the "male" or "female" half.

Children are human first, male or female second. If you can see gender as additional to being a person, it may help you to ensure that gender is not a limiting factor in your child's life. Try not to differentiate between "boys' toys" and "girls' toys" but to offer whatever playthings or play ideas you think your child will enjoy at a particular moment. It is not as easy as it sounds. Almost all parents will happily take a daughter out to the shops dressed up as a king, but many quail at the thought of taking a son out dressed as a queen... Some fathers who are delighted to push babies in buggies will still not be seen with a little boy pushing a doll's pram. Sometimes these adult scruples are, or masquerade as, sensitivity on the child's behalf: other people will laugh; children will tease. But your child's eventual sexual orientation will not be skewed by role-play in childhood and that needs to be acknowledged. If you try to make a boy stick to the "right" gender, however good your reasons, you deprive him of exploring the potential of half the world, and if you are happy to let a girl swap over but not a boy, you inevitably contribute to basic gender inequalities that still bedevil us all.

Those gender inequalities are still so pervasive, especially in media and advertising, that you cannot hope to protect your child from them. Children between the ages of two and five are looking out for what it means to be male or female, and are eager to identify with models of their own sex. Male models for boys are heroes whose power comes from their superior physical strength and aggression – and desirable toys and possessions reflect that preoccupation. Female role models for girls are often beautiful victims, rescued by those powerful males. If they are powerful themselves it is usually by magic, always wrapped in beauty. Little girls play at being beautiful.

Deliberate anti-sexism is important, but don't expect it to produce gender-free play – or a gender-blind child. You can make children share playspace but you cannot make boys and girls play together when they would rather play separately. Likewise, you cannot force a little girl to abandon dolls and model ponies for trains and model cars by banning one and buying the other, nor should you try. The best you can hope to do is to keep the whole world open so that she gets every chance to explore the possibilities of play with vehicles as well as animals, and play with boys as well as girls. Perhaps she (and her brother) will put them together, via model horse-trailers or doll families who have cars as well as houses, but even if she never does, it's important that she always knows she could.

Your influence doesn't stop with toys and play, either. Just as children's orientation towards violence depends on the reality of what they see and experience in the family, so does their orientation towards gender. If you want your children to grow up believing that the only areas of human experience closed to them by their sex relate to particular reproductive functions, make sure that's true of the gender role models they see all around them, and talked about where it is not.

Television and video

It is easy to make a moral case against television in children's lives. Its combination of sight and sound, movement and colour makes it an attractive and easy medium, requiring less concentration than reading or listening to the radio, and none of the active physical participation or manipulation demanded by play with real people or with objects. The more children enjoy TV the more inclined their parents are to see it as a seductive time-waster, using up hours children could spend better with books or music, or in active play today and homework tomorrow. The usually unasked question, though, is "What would your child be doing if she were not watching TV?" If the honest answer is, "Squabbling with her sister", or "Mooching about waiting for me to come home from work", it's difficult to see how viewing is wasting her time, or to avoid seeing that it's saving your sanity. Most parents find the peace which TV and video cassettes can offer at least occasionally irresistible. And if "using the screen as a baby-sitter" isn't exactly parenting to be proud of, it's surely better than letting stress and irritation build to a point where you keep putting your child down or yelling at her.

Television can take an overwhelming and negative part in young children's lives. But it can also play a positive part. The very qualities which make it seductive also make it a superb medium for education in its very widest sense. What matters, of course, is the balance between viewing and other activities, and the nature and quality of what your child watches. There's clear evidence that watching programmes with a "pro-social" (gentle, co-operative, good-citizen) ethic influences children in desirable directions just as readily as the reverse. There are not many such programmes, though, to balance children's exposure to TV violence, which clearly has a variety of negative effects. Not all children are affected in the same way or to the same degree, of course. Boys and girls are offered differing models by TV and so are children from ethnic majority and minority groups. It matters that there are still too few black characters on television and that too many of them are either violent or victims. It may matter even more that children who use wheelchairs, or children who depend on aids to sight or hearing, are offered no models at all so that for them, watching TV is like looking in a mirror and seeing nobody. Most negative effects can be softened, if not prevented, by viewing with an adult who helps the child recognize the absurdity of stereotypes and differentiate clearly between reality, fiction and fantasy (including cartoon). However, there's no doubt that all the main classes of ill-effect that researchers have identified – increased aggression; indifference towards real-life violence; fear of being a victim and a growing appetite for increasingly violent viewing – are best avoided by controlling what young children watch.

Many children begin to adopt favourite TV programmes around their third birthdays, are offered children's videos at around the same time and quickly build up viewing habits. If you offer only the few short programmes you truly approve of, and that you or another adult will often share with her, your child will accept limited, highly selective viewing. If it has never occurred to her that the television set is a source of constantly dripping, easy entertainment, she will not bully you for more and more, at least until she is old enough to read the programme guides and play out soap operas with other children in the school playground. And by then, hopefully, her life will be too full of people and activity for television to take a disproportionate part.

Unfortunately, though, highly selective and often companionable viewing is getting increasingly difficult to manage as more channels, including non-stop cartoons and inaptly named "children's" channels, become available to more people, and many adults have less time. If you switch on the set for your child (or let her switch it on herself) to get yourselves half an hour's peace from her conversation, let other caregivers use it to "entertain" her while they save their energies, or have the TV burble half-watched nonsense as a background to life and a mechanical alternative to company, she will see (or half-see) a lot, much of it violent. Many young children turn to the television whenever they finish with one activity and have not yet thought of another. Some seldom concentrate fully on play because new bursts of sound or movement from the TV set keep distracting them. Trapped by those half-understood images and attractive jingles, sucking her thumb and drifting, the child finds it more and more difficult to pay attention to anything else, to hear what you say, to break away and get on with life.

If you know that highly selective and companionable television viewing is an ideal that's unachievable in your household, your child may be better off watching (and re-watching) carefully selected videos on her own, than unselected TV programmes. She may still spend so much time viewing that her overall play activities are unbalanced, but at least what she is viewing can be harmless or better. You may need to discipline yourselves, re-educate older children and be persuasive with child care people, though. It only takes one daytime soap addict or channel-surfer to start your child towards the background TV habit.

PARENTS, TAKE NOTE

Strangulation

A child who has any kind of string around her neck with a breaking strain that approaches her body weight, is an accident waiting to happen. Supervise closely if your child is dressing up in your jewellery. If you encourage or allow her to wear a "necklace" (whether it's a religious symbol on a gold chain or beads she has threaded herself) make sure it fits so snugly that it could not catch in the car window if she operated the electrical closure by mistake, or over her tricycle handlebars as she fell off. For double safety, make that chain or thread as weak as you can. A piece of natural cotton won't strangle her; a bootlace just might.

Automatic curtain pulls and ties and the pull cords of window blinds are desperately dangerous: hung at a level that invites a child to swing; looped, ready for a head, and very strong. If you cannot banish them, at least shorten them so they are out of reach. And teach small children not to put pieces of string, neckties, dog leads or belts around their own or each other's necks with the same urgency that you teach them to be wary of plastic bags.

You can't expect a small child to be wary of her own playthings, though, so that's up to you. Could she put her head through that rope ladder (and then slip)? If she got tangled in her soft-toy hammock or a mobile, would it easily break?

And can you see to it that the real leather reins on that glorious rocking horse are attached as insecurely to the bridle as your child will be to the saddle, so that if she falls off with them round her they will come off too?

LEARNING
HOW TO BEHAVE

Children are very hard for adults to live with. In fact the real reason everyone is so interested in early childhood discipline is not that young children are so bad but that the grown-up world finds them so tiresome. Children are noisy, messy, untidy, forgetful, careless, time-consuming, demanding and ever-present. Unlike even the longest-staying visitor they don't ever go away. They can't be shelved for a few weeks when you are extra busy, like a demanding hobby; can't even be ignored, like pets, while you have a Sunday lie-in because they have an unfailing ability to make you feel guilty. The guilt-trips that come with children are worse than the upturned cereal bowls, bitten friends or walls drawn on with lipstick. Loving children (as almost every parent does) magnifies the pain of them as well as the pleasure. Loving them may even make it difficult for you to admit that they are sometimes a pain.

It is important to be able to admit that, at least to yourself, and preferably to your partner or at least one fellow parent. We all have days when we can hear our own nagging voices going on and on saying, "No", "Stop it" and "Don't do that", and when we can hear the glum silences buzzing between outbursts. We all have moments when children are removed from objects, or objects from children, with more than necessary force; when we treat our children in ways we remember from our own childhoods and swore to avoid, and when we hate those children for making us be so hateful. It helps to know that those things happen to all parents and to be aware that it isn't children's specific crimes that cause them, but general irritation with their childishness. It helps your children because if they cannot be childish at two or four, when can they be? It helps you by preventing you from deciding that your children are especially disobedient, ill-disciplined and spoiled, and therefore blaming yourself for being a bad parent – which is the biggest guilt-trip of all. And it reminds everyone who ever has any contact with your children not to stick onto them the problem-labels that so easily become self-fulfilling prophecies. Tell a child that you think he is naughty and nasty and he will live up to your view and probably come to share it himself and make sure that his teachers do too. But hang onto the truth, which is that he is very young and family life is difficult, and you aren't perfect and shouldn't expect yourself to be, and things will change for the better. You can count on that because the one thing that's certain is that your child is going to grow older.

Getting the timing right   The socialization that preoccupies parents and toddlers, and transforms them from babies to (very) young children, is focused on their mastery of their own impulses and bodies and therefore their management of themselves within the familiar confines of home or day care, and in relation to loved family members and caregivers. When children have achieved enough of that autonomy to be ready to move from toddlerhood into childhood they are ready to move out of the confines of that small circle. From now on your child will need more and more from the wider world in which his home is set and therefore it is now that he must begin to behave in ways which will make him acceptable to people outside his family. Every society has countless expectations for different people's behaviour under different circumstances, and nobody will expect a three-year-old to meet all of them all the time. Nevertheless these years of early childhood are the ideal period for coming to terms with what will be expected in the future, as well as practising the behaviours that are a social priority right now.

Small children will learn almost anything adults try to teach because they want to know everything. They particularly want to know how to behave because they very much want to be like you and to please you. Try not to let the heavy word "discipline" with all its related spectres such as "disobedience" and "dishonesty" bedevil a process which should be always interesting and often agreeable, both for you and your child.

If you like your child as well as loving him, and you are pleased with yourselves for having done a good job as parents so far, you may be able to get right through his childhood without ever thinking about his "discipline" at all. If you can, do. An absence of rules and rows in your household does not mean that you are being lax. Your child has moods and so do you. He makes mistakes just as you do and he sometimes does what he wants instead of what he ought, just as everybody does. If you are just getting on with life together, treating each other as human beings, that may be all there is to it. If so, do not bother with this chapter. It is meant for the millions of parents who need more structured assurance that their children will not "get out of hand", or who feel that they already have problems with discipline.

Discipline and self-discipline According to dictionary definitions, the word "discipline" means "teaching rules and forms of behaviour by continual repetition and drill..." and a disciplined person is "one whose obedience is unquestioning..." That isn't what most modern parents mean by discipline. You could insist on instant obedience and formal good manners; ensure that your child behaved as you told him and feared your displeasure. But none of that would help to keep him good or safe or honest when you were not there to tell him what to do. You are not going to be with him forever. Good parents work themselves out of the job – slowly.

Although every parent has moments when he wishes his children took "instant obedience" for granted, so that just saying "sit down and keep quiet" produced stationary, silent children, the only kind of discipline that is really worthwhile is the self-discipline that will one day keep him doing what he should and behaving as he ought when there is nobody to tell him what to do or to notice if he does wrong. Apart from the immediate necessity of keeping him safe, telling a child what he must and must not do is only a means to that end. Your endless exhortations and instructions are only raw materials; they get their value added once he takes them inside himself and makes them his own instructions to himself: part of his conscience.

Learning even the rudiments of self-discipline takes much longer than the years of early childhood. Some children don't acquire enough in time to keep themselves steady through adolescent upheavals. Some individuals' self-control remains rudimentary so that even as adults they can never entirely trust their own value-judgments or impulse-control. When your child was a baby you had to be him, acting for him in all the ways he could not act for himself and thinking for him when he could not think for himself. When he became a toddler you had to be with him, keeping final control over his safety, security and social acceptability, yet letting him begin to manage himself. Now that he is a young child he is ready to begin to learn how to keep himself safe, secure and socially acceptable. In the next couple of years you will show him how to behave in thousands of different situations and circumstances and help him see that all those different, often individually unimportant bits of behaviour are linked by a few basic and vitally important principles, such as honesty or kindness. As his understanding grows, you will withdraw your control, bit by bit, trusting him to apply the principles for himself because doing so is no longer a matter of obeying you but of being true to himself.

Showing your child how to behave

"Show" is a key word because your child will model his behaviour on your example far more than he'll adapt it to what you say. In fact if there's a credibility gap between what you say and what you do, he'll do what you do no matter what you say, so beware of old-fashioned disciplinary techniques like "biting back" children who bite. "How to" is also an important concept because children find it much easier to understand and remember positive instructions than negative ones: what they should do than what they shouldn't, and much prefer action to inaction. Try to say, "Like this" rather than, "Not like that" and to say, "Yes" and, "Go for it" at least as often as you say, "No" and, "Stop that."

With a new baby, showing a child how to be helps him to be caring as well as careful.

Although different parents want their children to behave in different ways, there are some useful rules-of-thumb that seem to cover all value-systems:

■ "Do as you would be done by." Your child will not give you (much) more politeness, consideration and co-operation than you give him – and he's likely to produce the same language (good and bad) and many of the same attitudes. There can be few double standards here. If you are always too busy to help with his puzzle and you scream at him when he accidentally trips over your feet, he will not take helping you get supper for granted or quickly forgive you when the comb pulls his hair.

■ Make sure that good behaviour gets rewarded and bad behaviour does not. It sounds obvious, but it is not. If your child ever gets sweets at the supermarket check-out, is he more likely to get them to keep him quiet because he's whining and embarrassing you, or as a reward to thank him because he's been co-operative and helpful?

■ Remember that adult attention acts as a reward and that young children would often rather have cross attention than none at all. Try not to take a "let sleeping dogs lie" approach to family life. If you ignore your child whenever he is quietly occupied and pay attention to him only when you must, you keep rewarding him for being a pain and punishing him for being a pleasure.

■ Be sure that as well as being positive, you are clear. Even positive instructions don't work very well if they are vague. "Behave yourself" sounds like a positive instruction, but it is meaningless to a child of this age. What you really mean is "don't do anything I don't like" which is an impossible command because he does not know what you don't like!

■ Apart from emergencies, when reasons must wait until later, always tell your child why he should (or shouldn't) behave in particular ways. You don't have to get into elaborate explanations for every little request, let alone into argument, but if you insist that "because I say so" is all the reason he needs, he will not be able to fit this particular instruction into the general pattern of "how to behave" that he is building up in his mind. "Put that shovel back" you say crossly. Why? Because it is dangerous? Dirty? Breakable? Because you want to be sure of being able to find it next time? If you tell him that it belongs to the builders who don't like other people moving their things, he can apply that thought to other occasions. But if you say, "Just do as you're told", you teach him nothing.

■ Try to keep "don't" for actual rules. Telling your child not to do things really only works when you want to rule a specific action out once and for all. If you only want to forbid a piece of behaviour now, at this moment and under these particular circumstances, you will do better to turn it around and phrase it positively. Think of that familiar, "Don't interrupt while I'm talking." It's really not surprising that small children ignore it because there are many times when adults actually want them to interrupt – to say the potatoes are boiling over, the baby is crying or they need to go to the lavatory. You will probably get a better reaction to, "Please wait a minute until we have finished talking." Specific "don'ts" become rules. As long as you keep them to a minimum the child will probably accept them easily,

Showing your child how to do difficult things safely will protect her better than telling her not to.

especially if you explain your reasons. Tell your child, "Don't ever climb in that tree, it's not safe." And provided your partner backs you up and doesn't let him risk it "just for once", that particular tree will be recognized as forbidden. "Don't cross any roads without a grown-up" is another useful rule that a three- or four-year-old will easily accept just as long as you don't send him across to the corner shop for a newspaper because the road concerned is only a small one.

Rules can play a useful part in keeping a small child safe (though when his safety is at stake, his self-discipline can't be relied upon to keep him obeying without supervision) but they don't really play much part in teaching him how to behave because they are too rigid and inflexible to be very useful in ordinary life. Try to keep rules to definite, here-and-now issues and avoid making them about issues of principle that will matter all his life.

You obviously cannot show your child how to behave if you your-selves are not sure how people should behave, so being consistent in your principles is important. Other kinds of consistency don't always matter, though. Your child is not a circus animal, being taught to respond to a specific signal with a particular trick. He is a human being, and human beings aren't consistent. He has to learn to respond to a vast range of signals as best he can and that involves realizing that circumstances alter cases. Although encouraging a two-year-old to draw on a whiteboard on his bedroom wall *would* make him more likely to draw on the living room walls, by the age of four, and provided people take the time to explain and discuss things with him, he'll understand where it is and is not acceptable to draw. What's more, sweets ad lib at Christmas will not make him expect them when the holiday is over, and permission to jump on Granny's bed won't make him forget that your bed is forbidden.

Trusting and being trustworthy

Being trusted transforms the fun of domestic play into real job satisfaction.

Trust your child to mean well even when he doesn't do well. If he feels that there's always an adult standing over him, ready to correct or instruct him, he probably will not bother to think very much about what he ought or ought not to do. Within the limits of his age and stage, pass as much responsibility for his own behaviour as you can over to him, and make him feel trusted to handle it.

If he is to go to a friend's house, for example, don't smother him with anxious instructions such as, "Remember to say thank you for having me" and, "Don't forget to wipe your feet." If you are willing to let him go at all, you must let him take charge of himself. Your exhortations will not help him to behave nicely, they will merely make him feel uneasy about going.

When you are wrong – and especially when you find you have been unfair – do admit it. Don't let false adult dignity prevent you from showing him the right way to behave. He is modelling himself to some extent on you so it is important to apologise to him when you make a mistake, just as you want him to apologise to you. Suppose you accuse him of breaking a glass and refuse to believe his denial. You later discover that your partner broke it. By all the standards you are trying to teach your child, you owe him a sincere apology. You were wrong and you were unjust. If you ask him to forgive you, he will respect you more, not less.

Problems of Behaviour

If you are truly thinking about "discipline" as a matter of showing your child how to behave, you will find that most "behaviour problems" are problems of maturity rather than morality and that most of the problematic issues of discipline can be easily resolved. Some degree of "attention-seeking" behaviour, for example, is a normal way for a very young child to respond to rationed attention from busy adults. If the ration of pleasant attention can be increased, he won't have to clamour to make you scold him.

Disobedience Instant and unquestioning obedience probably kept life peaceful for Victorian parents with large families, but it cannot produce children who think for themselves and can therefore be trusted to look after themselves from an early age. The difference was sharply illustrated when three small girls were abducted in a car from outside their school. A fourth child ran home and raised the alarm so rapidly that the car was chased and stopped and the children were home again within the hour. One distraught father asked: "Why did you go with the man in the car? We've always told you not to go with strangers." Huge-eyed and reproachful, his daughter replied, "But he said, 'Your father says you're to come with me at once. He sent me to fetch you.' So I did. You always say, 'you must do what I tell you.' You always say it." The child who raised the alarm was questioned by police: "What made you run home instead of getting in the car with your friends?" "My Daddy and Mummy are always saying, 'think!'" she answered. "So I thought that if Daddy really wanted us he'd have come; and the man only said one Daddy and we've got three Daddies, all of us have I mean. And then I thought I'd like to ask my Mummy. So I ran."

Getting rid of "obedience" and "disobedience" and thinking instead about getting your child's co-operation, defuses a lot of issues. Sometimes he will not do what you want because he wants to do something different. He will not go to bed because he wants to finish his game. It is not his disobedience that is causing trouble, it is a simple conflict of interests. A compromise like "five more minutes" is far more likely to work than yelling, "Do as I say this moment." Sometimes he will not do what you want because he has not understood what you do want. Told to stay at the table until lunch is finished he may get down when his plate is empty. He did not realize you meant that he was to stay put until everyone had finished. He has not failed to obey, he has failed to understand. Occasionally he will not do what you want because he is out to annoy you. He feels bolshy. You tell him not to touch your new book and he goes straight to it. This, and out of all these examples only this, is true disobedience. It is a deliberate attempt to provoke you and how well the attempt succeeds probably depends on what damage has been done. If the shiny dustjacket is torn, you will be furious with him. That's reality. He would be cross if you had spoiled something of his; he has provoked a universal human reaction. But it is the damage that merits wrath, not the "disobedience". If no real harm has been done you can defuse the whole situation by refusing to rise to his bait: "Fancy going off and doing the one thing I asked you not to. You must be in a silly mood." Where is the argument he was looking forward to?

Lying Small children live in a world that's difficult for them to manage and in which they often stand accused of doing damage of one kind or another. Denying wrongdoing is therefore their most usual kind of lie and the kind that most often gets them into trouble. Your child breaks his sister's doll by mistake. Faced with it he denies the whole incident. You are probably angrier with him for the lie than you are about the breakage.

If you feel strongly that your child should own up when he has done something wrong, do make it easy. "This doll is broken. I wonder what happened?" is much more likely to enable him to say "I broke it, I'm sorry" than, "You've broken this doll, haven't you, you naughty, careless boy." But if your child does admit to something, of his own accord or because you force it out of him, do make sure that you don't overwhelm him with anger and punishments. You cannot have it both ways. If you want him to tell you when he has done something wrong, you cannot also be furious with him. If you are furious, he would be foolish to tell you next time, wouldn't he?

Tall stories get some children into trouble too. In early childhood, a lot of children still confuse reality and fantasy, and what they wish had happened with what really did. After all, they can happily accept stories about the Easter Bunny while keeping a quite unmagic rabbit of their own; they see no conflict between the two.

If you are going to read your child stories and help him to enjoy the mythology of childhood in his culture, such as Santa Claus, it is unreasonable to jump on him for lying when he comes in from a walk with an elaborate story of his own. Of course he didn't really meet a spacelady. He probably doesn't even think he did. But just as it's sad if older children force a four-year-old to pick holes in the fantasy of Father Christmas ("We haven't even got a chimney, silly"), so it's a pity if his own fantasies are beyond the pale. Enjoy the story. Being not true does not make it a lie in any moral sense.

Parents sometimes worry because their children seem to have no regard for the truth at all. They may overhear them mentioning Mummy's new dress when she hasn't got one, or announcing that they were sick last night when they weren't, or just telling a friend that they are going out for tea when they aren't. There are lots of reasons for casually inaccurate talk and an important one is that the child hears it from adults. Adults tell endless untruths out of tact, kindness, a desire to avoid hurting other people's feelings or to save their own time. Children hear them. Your child hears you agreeing with Mrs Smith that the weather is much too hot when you have just told him how much you like the heat; hears you on the telephone excusing yourself from something because you have invisible visitors. Unless the reasons for these "white" lies are explained to him, he cannot be expected to see why he must never exaggerate or falsify when you can.

If your child tells so many stories and adds so much embroidery to his accounts of daily life that you really cannot be sure what is true and what is not, it may be time to make it clear to him why truth matters. Don't fall back on it being "naughty" to tell lies. Instead, try him with the story of "The boy who cried wolf". It is a good story. He will enjoy it. Having told it you can discuss it with him. Point out that you, and all the people who help take care of him, really need to be able to distinguish between what is true and what is not, so as to be sure of knowing when something important has happened to him or when he is really feeling ill or scared. Phrase the whole conversation so that he feels you care about him telling the truth because you care about him and want to be sure you look after him properly: a matter of accurate communication rather than "being good".

Stealing

Property rights are complicated. Teach your child exactly what he may and may not keep.

Many young children, especially those with no older brothers and sisters to keep asserting "that's mine!", are as vague about property rights as they are about truth. Within the family there will be lots of things that belong to everybody; some that belong to particular people but can be freely borrowed and a few that are "private possessions" for the use of the owner only. Outside the family there are complications too. It is all right to keep the little ball you found in the bushes in the park but it is not all right to keep a purse. It is all right to bring your painting home from nursery school but not a piece of playdough. People are allowed to take leaflets from shops (though not the whole boxful) but not packets of soup (not even one). There's no purpose in making a moral issue out of a young child's collecting of things that catch his fancy until he's able to understand all this. You cannot afford to take it entirely casually, though, because, even at the age of three or four, other people may call it stealing and make a major song and dance about it.

You might find it useful to separate the issue of principle from the complexities of daily behaviour. Discuss the first and have some rules to guide the second, such as: don't bring anything away from somebody else's house without asking; always ask a grown-up if you may keep anything you find; don't pick anything up in a shop unless a grown-up says it's all right. Try not to be especially moralistic about money. If your child takes some from your purse, stop and ask yourself what you would have said if it had been a lipstick he took, and then say the same about the money. To young children both are the same. Treasure. They know money is precious, of course, because they hear you talking about it and see you exchanging it for nice things. But to children, money is like those tokens you put in slot machines; they have no concept of real money.

The child who behaves like a magpie, collecting in a bottom drawer money he never tries to use and other people's possessions he does not even really want, may be in emotional trouble. He may be trying to take in a symbolic way something that he does not feel he is being given. It is probably love or approval that he feels short of. Instead of being furious and upset and making him feel disgraced, could you try to offer what he needs? If you cannot, and if the stealing goes on, you would probably be sensible to ask for professional help before your child reaches school age. It is very much easier for a child to acquire a label such as "thief" than to get rid of it.

Arguing and bargaining

All children prevaricate when they are asked to do something they don't want to do. It can be maddening to talk to a child who pretends not to hear you, or says, "okay" but doesn't do anything. It's even more irritating when a child actually argues with every suggestion, request or instruction. Life just isn't long enough to spend five minutes persuading a four-year-old that he needs shoes to go out and another five getting him to the front door... But it's worth thinking about how maddening it must also be for a young child to be so low in the family pecking order that he can be interrupted whatever he is doing and given orders by almost any adult who happens to be around. A bit of mutual give and take, based on doing as you would be done by, will help much more than yelling. It also helps to be aware that many young children find transitions from one activity to another difficult. They need plenty of warning that a meal, an outing, or bedtime is coming up, and plenty of time to make the move.

Some children, especially rather intelligent ones, are quick to catch on to the idea that if you want them to do something they don't want to do, they have bargaining power. Rather than go silently upstairs to change into a clean shirt, your son may say, "If I get clean for you, will you get out my bike for me?" Unfortunately, parents often feel that this, even more than argument, is in some way "cheeky". They have the right to tell their children what to do and they certainly don't want to concede them any right to do the same. "Do as your mother tells you and don't argue!" roars father. We are really back with instant obedience.

Bargaining can be a very useful form of human exchange as every adult society throughout history has discovered. But you will obviously get bored with it if your child tries to exact a return for every single thing you remind him to do, especially if it's his responsibility, not yours, so why should you pay? Confine bargains to exceptional requests or ones that are unusually tiresome for the child, and then offer one yourself, sometimes, rather than always waiting for him to propose them.

PROBLEMS OF HANDLING

There's an irony about small children's behaviour: the more worried you are about it and the harder you try to change it, the worse it's liable to get.

That's because children are easiest to live with when adults take a positive approach to their behaviour, assuming that they mean well; noticing when they do well; making sure they understand what is wanted of them under different circumstances, and rewarding good behaviour so as to motivate more of the same. Parents who decide that their children are especially badly behaved, or are told so by relatives and carers, risk slipping into a negative way of handling them that's the opposite of all that. Negative discipline focuses on bad behaviour; expects it; watches for it, punishes it, so as to motivate change, but gets more – and more and *more* of the same.

Punishment The idea of formal punishment sits better with "discipline" than with "learning how to behave". Older people, who know how they should behave but do not always want to do so, may sometimes be kept from transgression by its cost – detention for talking in class or getting the car towed for illegal parking. Such considerations don't always work for us, though, and don't ever work for young children because they aren't yet able to weigh future penalties against present impulses. The only sanction that works at all reliably with children under four, or even five, is other people's disapproval. Whatever punishment you may announce when you get cross, it is your crossness that punishes. If that statement makes you laugh because your child is currently putting on a don't-careish front, see through it by considering how differently he would react to a formal punishment ("No ice cream for dinner") if you announced it in different ways. Tell him, "No ice cream for dinner" in cheerful, matter-of-fact tones and he is unlikely to turn a hair. (Does he usually have ice cream for dinner? Does he especially want ice cream for dinner? What is he going to get for dinner?) But tell him angrily, "That's it. Just for that you'll get no ice cream for dinner" and he will probably cry or rage. He may or may not have expected or even wanted ice cream, but he certainly did not want you to be cross with him.

You probably made the angry statement about the ice cream in the (righteous) heat of the moment and it had the desired effect of making your feelings clear. But so would any other statement of those feelings, like "You're being so silly that I'm simply not enjoying this walk, so we're going home." The trouble with the "no ice cream"

You punish because you're cross, but it's your crossness that really punishes.

version is that by the time it is dinner-time the whole row will probably be long over and forgotten. In order to stick to your formal guns you have to drag the whole episode up again and, in effect, punish the child a second time. How awkward if he has been especially charming and helpful ever since...

Your disapproval, or anger, is your most effective sanction. If it leads you to immediate and spontaneous "punishment" so that the child can clearly see that his behaviour has directly caused it, the punishment may strengthen your point. You will not go on standing in the queue for ice cream while he behaves so badly, so he doesn't get the ice cream right now. He has done himself out of it rather than being "punished" for his behaviour. You cannot let him go on pulling packets out of the supermarket stacks so you pick him up and put him in the trolley seat. He has abused his liberty and thus sacrificed it. Are those actions "punishments"? If they were cold and calculated they would be, and as cold, calculated punishments, they probably wouldn't work. As heated reactions to immediate situations, though, they are the direct results of the child's own ill-advised actions. And that's the one and only kind of punishment that may work.

The most common heat-of-the-moment punishments – smacks and spankings, yells and insults – are not direct results of a child's actions and don't work, although they may seem to have done so at the time. If your child is doing something really irritating (like fiddling with the TV or the dog or the baby) and you've tried telling him not to, moving him away, distracting him, and he just goes straight back and does it again, yelling at him or smacking him will stop him (and maybe relieve your feelings), and that makes it seem to have worked better than any of those other techniques. But hurting his feelings and his hand stopped him fiddling because being hurt made him cry. It didn't teach him not to fiddle and won't stop him doing it again.

It sounds obvious that smacking a child every time he does something wrong will teach him not to. But not to what? Being "naughty" in early childhood is a complicated business. It can mean doing something dangerous to himself (like running into the road), or dangerous to someone else (like tipping over the baby's pushchair) or doing any number of things that (predictably or just today) irritate, embarrass or disappoint adults. Being smacked may tell a child that he's done wrong; even tell him what he's done wrong this time, but it cannot tell him what would have been right and it certainly won't make him try harder to please you. Smacking children can't teach them how to behave and the proof is that once a child starts to be punished that way, he'll get smacked all through childhood. In fact it's because physical punishments are so ineffective that they tend to escalate. Most of your child's wrongdoing is caused by impulse and forgetfulness. Today you spend all afternoon telling him not to run over the flower bed. You yell at him to come off but because he's excited with all the running, he laughs. Finally you smack him and he cries and comes indoors. Tomorrow, cheerful and outside again, he does the same thing. In the name of consistency you have to smack him again – harder. Once you're into that particular vicious circle, this year's smack can easily become next year's spanking.

Research shows that children who are physically punished are far more likely to remember the smack than what it was for, because they are often too angry to listen to explanations or crying too hard to hear them. Asked why they were smacked, four- and five-year-olds usually say "you were cross". So don't rely on physical punishments to teach your child good behaviour. You cannot get the co-operation you need merely through using your superior physical strength.

Be careful how you use your superior emotional strength, too. Punishments which are designed to make children feel silly or undignified are just as ineffective and emotionally dangerous as the physical kind. If you take away a child's shoes because he ran away, or force him to wear a baby's bib because he spills food down his clothes, you make him feel helpless, worthless and quite incapable of learning the growing-up lessons you are trying to teach. If untidy eating is making a real laundry problem he needs neat eating made easier. Does he need a booster cushion on that chair now he's out of his highchair? Is he allowed to use his fingers as well as a spoon?

If you are truly trying to show your child how to behave (rather than pay him back for misbehaviour) you will usually do better without formal punishments, especially in these early years, because they will make him less, rather than more, inclined to listen to what you say and try to please you. The effective alternative to punishing children who do wrong so that they feel bad, is rewarding children who do right so that they feel good. Your child will learn something from the explosions that occur when you all get cumulatively across each other, a great deal from your displeasure when he gets things wrong, but most of all from being praised and congratulated when he behaves as you wish.

Rewards, prizes and bribes Just as the principal element of any punishment is adult disapproval, so the principal element of any reward is adult approval. A reward tells your child, "I love you/approve of you/appreciate you/like being with you." Tangible things like sweets or treats can convey those messages but so can smiles and praise and hugs. A child's rewards, like his punishments, are often the direct result of his own behaviour which has put you in a good mood: "We got through the checkout so quickly because of you unloading for me while I packed, that we've got time to go and have a coffee..."

Sometimes, though, material bribes or, if you think they sound less immoral, prizes, can be very useful. Small children have a clear and simple sense of justice and are clear-sighted about other people's goodwill. If you have to make your child do something he very much dislikes, offering a prize may have the dual effect of making it seem worth his while to co-operate and making him realize that you are on his side. Suppose, for example, that it is a hot afternoon and he is enjoying himself in his paddling pool. You have to pick up something for work tomorrow and you cannot leave him behind because there is nobody else in the house. What is wrong with a simple bribe honestly proposed? "I know you'd rather we stayed at home but we've got to do this errand. What about coming home by the shop and seeing if your new story-tape is in? Would that help?" It is a bribe but it is also a perfectly reasonable bargain.

An actual prize sometimes makes all the difference to a child who has to put up with something genuinely unpleasant like stitches in his head. It doesn't much matter what the object is (as long as it isn't something he was expecting to be given anyway) what matters is having something nice dangling just the other side of the nasty few minutes. Don't make this kind of prize conditional on good behaviour though. A prize "if you don't make any fuss", may put your child under terrible strain. He may need to make a fuss. And he certainly needs to feel that you will support him however he behaves.

Spoiling Everybody knows that spoiled children are a misery to themselves and to everyone else, and most people assume that they reflect badly on their parents' good sense. But few people stop to consider what it is that makes them consider a child "spoiled" or what it is that the parents have done wrong. As a result, "spoiled" is a sort of spectre haunting parents who live in dread of hearing the word used either of their child or of their child-handling. Some describe a child as "spoiled" when they really mean only that they love and indulge him. Some even withhold treats and presents from normally appreciative, not especially unmannerly children because "we don't want him getting spoiled..."

That's a sad misunderstanding. Spoiling isn't about indulgence and fun, it's about bullying and blackmail. You can't spoil your child with too much talk, play and laughter; too many smiles and hugs, or even too many presents, provided you give them because you want to. Your child will not get spoiled because you buy sweets in the supermarket or 15 birthday gifts. But he may get spoiled if he learns that he can blackmail you into reversing a "no sweets" decision by throwing a tantrum in public, or get anything he wants out of you if he goes on and on and on... The most "spoiled" child you know may not get much more – may even get less – than most children, but he gets whatever comes his way by bullying it out of his parents against their better judgment. Spoiling is the result of the family balance of power getting out of line.

Limits, and adults Children need adults who have the courage of their convictions and
who stick to them the courage to set limits or draw boundaries for them, within which they know they can stay safe – and good. Limits are not just something adults impose on children. We all have to observe the limits that mark out our space from other people's – sometimes literally as well as figuratively. Children need additional limits, laid down by parents and carers, to keep them safe while they learn to keep themselves safe; to control them while they develop self-control, and to make sure they don't lose their own space or trespass on other people's while they learn the lessons of socialized living like "do as you would be done by".

Limits are only limits if children cannot break them. And they only give children safe freedom of action if they know they cannot. Parents who say their children will not stay within limits are usually confusing obedience – which does rely on co-operation from the child – with limits (or boundaries) which do not. If you set a limit, make sure the child *cannot* overstep it. If the boundary of the front garden is the limit of his playspace, for example, don't wait for him to open the front gate and then scold and punish him. Put a loop of wire around that latch from the beginning.

If you're not prepared to do whatever it takes to make a limit stick, it's better not to set it in the first place. Parents sometimes say they cannot make a limit stick when they really mean that the necessary action is too much effort. Millions of "extra" hours of television must be watched each week by children whose parents mean to limit their viewing to a particular programme or time, but cannot face the fuss that would result from pulling out the plug. If you aren't sure it's going to be worth your while to enforce a boundary, don't set it – even if your mother-in-law says you should. It's far better for your child's behaviour (and your temper) if he is allowed to watch two hours of TV than if he is allowed to watch one and watches another that was forbidden.

Some children do have phases when they seem intent on doing so much that's beyond the pale that parents' ability to keep track and keep calm is seriously tested. If making sure that your child, or one particular child, stays within your limits is especially demanding, set as few as you possibly can. Make sure that each one concerns an issue you really care about so that you are motivated to do everything you have to do to make it stick and *ignore the rest*.

Moving towards power-sharing

As young children come to see themselves as individuals among other individuals they become concerned about the extent to which they can manage those others as well as themselves. So this is an age-stage when power-games are common. Your child may test the limits of his influence, and seek to increase it, just as he tests and exercises his muscles.

It is right that your child should discover that he has some influence over people and practise exercising it – he cannot grow up if he is kept totally powerless and dependent. However it is important not to let him override your power by bullying, or wearing you down with endless whining. He needs to learn acceptable ways of asserting his own power, or influencing things his way.

Try to react more positively to reason and charm than to tears and tantrums. Although his self-control is still very limited, you want your child to begin to realize that you are far more likely to be persuaded than frightened into saying "yes" to a request.

Encourage your child to join in decision-making processes that affect him. It's very important that he should have his say even when he cannot have his way. As he gets older he will discover what is permitted to other children of his age, hear about television programmes he has never seen and generally seek new privileges. Because these are new issues you will not have ready-made answers. Don't feel pressured into responding off the top of your head. Discuss them with your partner and your child, and with other carers or members of the family if that seems appropriate. Whether the matter goes for or against him, your child will know that the adults in his world are agreed and he has had his chance to speak too.

It's good for your child to learn that "asking nicely" often works.

Show your child that you try to balance his rights against yours just as you balance the rights of his sister against his, or your partner's against your own. You all live together and the downside of loving companionship is that you all have to leave each other space, and sometimes shift over a bit to give somebody a temporary extra share. Your child will not always do as you wish. You do not always have to do as he wishes. The clashes have to be sorted out between you. If you want to read and he wants a walk, there's a problem. Discuss it honestly. If you simply can't stand the idea of a walk, say so. It's better to refuse him than to go every inch with dragging footsteps, feeling a martyr and making it impossible for him to enjoy it. But if you feel he's entitled to his walk, as you are to your reading, compromise on a half-hour each and feel entitled to insist that he, too, fulfils his half of what amounts to a bargain.

Help your child to understand other people's feelings. The more interested you can make him in how you and other people feel and in how similar others feelings are to his own, the more sensitive to them he will be able to be. Understanding the feelings of others is the root of unselfishness and therefore the opposite of being spoiled. When an opportunity comes up, grab it. Talk to him about what the little girl next door felt when the big ones stole her bike. If he says calmly that she can buy another, point out that parents often want to buy things for their children but cannot always afford to. When you are making family plans, let him in on the difficulties of arranging treats and holidays so that all the different people involved get what they enjoy. You can even help him see that while it would be unfair to him if you served the cabbage he hates every night of the week, it is equally unfair to his father if you never serve what happens to be his favourite vegetable...

At this stage in his life your child longs for conversation with adults and for information of all kinds. As long as you don't do this kind of teaching as a set of lectures, each cued off by some misdemeanour of his own, he will enjoy it enormously. You are doing him the honour of discussing feelings with him as well as things. You are helping him in the age-appropriate task of putting himself into other people's shoes. And you are calling his attention to a whole area of experience he might not yet have noticed for himself. The more you can do this, the sooner and the more clearly will he come to understand that he is one very important and much-loved person in a world of equally important other people.

EARLY YEARS EDUCATION

This chapter is not called *pre-school* education because the years between three-ish and five-ish are much more than a waiting time before school or a time of preparation for school. In fact although people refer to "under-fives" as if they were a recognizable group, notably different from fives and sixes, it isn't a meaningful phase in any developmental sense. As children move out of toddlerhood they enter a period, properly called "early childhood", which lasts until the five-to-seven shift takes them into "middle childhood". Seven years is a far more meaningful age-maker than five, and under-eights *are* fairly distinct from junior school children.

Early childhood has a developmental agenda of its own that has little to do with school, and is similar in societies where "starting school" happens much later or not at all. Early childhood education is just as important to children's overall education and long-term success as primary, or secondary, or further education, but it is more

Early years education is full of amazement...

different from all of them than they are different from each other. Early years education is as much concerned with feelings and emotions and ways of expressing and managing them, as with cognitive processes. And more concerned with social skills than with academic skills. While skills like reading and writing that are learned unusually early can certainly place a child ahead of most of her peers when they first enter the compulsory school system, they alone will not keep her ahead. Research has shown that the lasting value of "pre-school education" is not that it gives children a head start in school but a head start in life.

When the term "pre-school education" was freshly coined, the interval between the end of toddlerhood and the start of academic schooling was longer, in most countries, than it is today and beginning to be recognized as a developmental period in its own right which needed to be facilitated with richly varied and largely social play. It was the difficulty of providing for play in small families and urban homes that inspired the first pre-school playgroups two generations ago, and play was serious business in British infant schools and American kindergartens, until seven-year-olds moved on into middle childhood and primary school or first grade.

...at mysteries like these vanishing dinosaurs.

Early education is different for the current generation though. All over the world parents are aware that they are bringing children up in a highly competitive world of global markets, and that those children's futures depend on education. They want children to have more of it than they had themselves, and earlier in their lives, and although that's being provided in different ways in different places, more and sooner is certainly the general trend. Many Western European countries regard three years of early childhood education prior to starting school at six or seven, as every child's right, and integrate it with whatever day care the family needs. Best practice, in northern Italy, for example, offers care, education and a number of other services such as after-school activities for older children, in integrated children's centres.

In the UK, and in North America, however, a welcome backdating of the age at which it is considered important to provide children with stimulating "educational" play, from three- and four-year-olds to babies and toddlers, is parallelled by a less welcome tendency to backdate the start of academic learning. Laws still say that American and British children must start school (or its approved equivalent) soon after their sixth and fifth birthdays respectively, but whatever the locally compulsory starting age, more and more children are being sent to school – rather than nursery school – as early as their fourth birthdays, and sometimes into programmes originally designed for children two years (which is half of their lifetimes) older.

The early years education scene is further complicated by the fact that the same competitive world pressures that make parents anxious for more and more education for younger and younger children also compel them to demand more and more day care. Care and education should go together whether a child is five months or five years old; in fact care cannot be of high quality unless it is educational, and education cannot be good without being caring. Discussions of "educare" usually assume that it will come from paying extra attention to educational activities in a child care centre or to adding care during parental working hours to a playgroup or nursery school. But how much should be added, and what should it be? Knowing that parents are susceptible, some child care businesses compete for their custom by offering more and more academic-sounding curricula even for babies. Biology and physics for one-year-olds sounds – and is – absurd, but how can parents be *sure* that it does not mean anything more than opportunities to plant seeds in a garden and play with a water wheel? The more some establishments claim to offer, the more parents are liable to feel that children who are getting less cannot be getting enough.

"Educare" need not come from an institution at all, of course. Your child may already be receiving all the educational input she needs while being cared for by her parents, a childminder or relation, a nanny or a share in one, or some combination of some of those. If you can see that your three-year-old is curious, energetic and busy, you know that her daily life is full of varied, interesting experiences and you're drawn into her enthusiasm for books and toys and friends of all ages, you may see no reason to change anything – yet.

But the early years education picture, and your assessment of your own child's needs, are further complicated by issues that are nothing to do with her personal or intellectual development but to do with the kind of society she lives in. It's fine for a young child to be home-and-individual-based provided there's plenty of stimulation and companionship available to her. But if she lives as a three-plus in a community where most of her age-mates are in child care all day, or in pre-school education facilities, such as nursery schools, at least half the day, playgrounds may be empty except at weekends; facilities designed for under-eights may be non-existent and even the children's library may not open until 3pm. Your child may be solitary now and come to see her lifestyle as odd in the near future.

On the other hand, some communities still have so many young children at home, that there are well-supported local swimming classes or "tumble tots", sometimes soft rooms and, best of all, drop-in playgroups. Such facilities offer your child and her adult companion more than (rather expensive) opportunities to make friends, and do something different on a wet winter day, they also show that there are plenty of children around to be met, for free, in the park.

But even if there are plenty of children around, you yourself don't need to put your child in a child care centre and you don't feel that she needs, or is ready for any kind of educational group, don't let the whole matter slip from your mind so that her life goes on indefinitely in its present mould. One day it will be time for her to go to big school. When that day comes she will have to go, whether she wants to or not, and in many communities she will have to go all day, every weekday and manage without you almost from the beginning. No programme of outings with you or a carer is enough to prepare her for being a regular member of a class of other children and managing with only a small share in an adult's attention. When you started school – or certainly when your father did – a first day in the class-room was often also a child's first day away from home and mother and in a group of children. But that's rare, nowadays, and because it's rare teachers and helpers aren't ready for it; other children aren't in the same bewilderment and it's too many "firsts" for any small person to cope with comfortably. However idyllic her present lifestyle, by the time she is rising four she really will benefit from some more formal early years education and group experience.

Your child's early years education

It's easy to confuse what you want from early years education with what you will later want from a school. Even if you are looking for a more directly educational group for a child who is in a child care centre or a regular playgroup but "does nothing but play", don't be tempted by the other extreme with rows of tiny desks. Young children learn by playing and therefore optimal learning means being encouraged to play: to choose what to do, when and for how long; to touch, manipulate and experiment as well as look and listen; to move about and involve body and feelings as well as mind and, always, to talk. Attempts to teach three- and four-year-olds directly, making them sit still and keep quiet while they are shown and told things, or making them memorize what has not yet been made meaningful by action, are misguided, even if they work in the sense of producing children who know the names of all the letters in the

Your child will need to play at learning before she learns to play.

alphabet at four. Indeed attempts to teach them by *making* them do anything are ill-judged. If you want your child to learn as much as she is able, you have to keep her wanting to. Young children know no difference between play and learning, but they often make clear distinctions between play and lessons. It's fine for your child to know the difference, but sad if she decides lessons are boring and play is more fun.

Teaching a child who is still in early childhood something she does not especially want to know, or getting her to do or make something that looks good to adults although the criteria by which they judge it mean nothing to the child, is at best a meaningless waste of everybody's time and at worst a turn-off from being taught. If your three-year-old bangs the piano with concentrated enjoyment, the chances are that she is playing more in her head than on the keyboard; that she is being somebody – Daddy, or the entertainer from a recent TV show – and that the sound she is making is irrelevant to the role play. Nevertheless, she may be delighted if her father shows her how to pick out a familiar tune, and delight him with her performance and pleasure in it. But what happens if that delighted Daddy now arranges piano lessons for her and explains that if she practises 10 minutes each day she will be able "to play better and better"? Nothing whatsoever. The child's interest in piano-playing vanishes and if lessons or practice are imposed on her she will resist. Playing the piano "better" was not on her agenda. She wanted to play at playing the way she could play now, not work at playing so as to play differently in an inconceivable future.

Play does not always mean undirected "free play", though. The hallmark of a good early years teacher is his ability to understand a young child's agenda as revealed by her play, and use his own knowledge and experience to help her move forward educationally within it. Many adults – parents, caregivers, relations – can facilitate children's play, as earlier chapters have shown, but a trained early years teacher's skills are special. Above all he will be uniquely skilled at recognizing where a child has got to in any particular respect. He sees what she can do now and is already trying to do; sees what she might be able to do beyond that, and provides sensitive, well-timed, well-paced help and support to bridge the gap (known as the zone of "proximal development") between the two.

Finding the early years education that's right for you

Groups providing early years education are as variable as schools, within and between countries so if you are fortunate enough to have a choice of affordable groups available, you will need local advice.

Early years education programmes are affected by their setting and hours. You may not be in a position to choose solely according to which seems educationally best, because the logistics imposed by where your child attends, and when, will very much affect your daily life. If you need full-day child care, that may have to be the first consideration, although the educational programme within a child care centre may have a different emphasis or impact from the pro-gramme of a nursery school or nursery class.

If, on the other hand, you are happy for your child to attend half-time, that may increase your chances of a place in a popular establishment. In many communities your chances go up even more if you volunteer your child for afternoon sessions rather than the mornings most families prefer. Understandably, few nursery schools or classes will allow your child to attend for flexible hours (a stable group and an ongoing curriculum is important to the children, after all) but some do offer two or three full days per week as an alternative to five halves, and this might fit better with your work or child care arrangements, or save some travelling time.

Important though it is, try not to let part-time education add too many complications to life. If your child is already in day care, perhaps with a childminder, their accustomed two mornings a week at playgroup may be too much when five afternoons in a nursery class are added. Two or three changes of caregiver in a day, and not even the same ones on all five days of the week, can be very stressful for her to live through and for you to keep track of.

Early years education establishments that are not part of schools or child care centres, but stand on their own are usually known as nursery schools, though the term "pre-school" is also used. These tend to be relatively small and intimate and especially strongly influenced by the senior teachers. If you put your child's name down for a well-recommended nursery school a year or more ahead of time, changes in staffing during the intervening period just may have changed everything you most liked about it. Before you take up the offered place, check it out again as if you'd only just heard of it.

When you're looking for a group be wary of tying yourself to particular requirements, such as links with a particular religion. A nursery school that is just what you want from that one specific point of view may not be at all what you want from most others. Likewise, don't be much influenced by a group's stated philosophy. For example, "Montessori", in the modern world, can mean a programme in which your child's activities are rigidly controlled by the materials offered (even permitted) to her. However it may mean a programme whose only noticeable Montessori features are those outstanding materials freely offered alongside many others, or an unusually high level of staff training.

Teacher training is crucial to high quality early years education. Do look into exactly what qualifications the staff hold. Remember that child care or play worker qualifications, though highly desirable for day care workers, are not at all the same as early years teaching qualifications. An educational establishment should not only have a trained teacher in overall charge but should be staffed by teachers also. High quality education for your child usually depends on being taught by someone who is trained to teach her.

Parent involvement, with shared values and close co-operation between home and school, is important too. Even groups that do not rely on parent volunteers should be eager to get to know them.

Choosing a group for your child However popular and over-subscribed a nursery school, or the pre-school education facility of a child care centre may be, don't feel you have to accept it at face value. Even if its reputation is well-deserved it may not be the right place for your child. Make an appointment to visit (without your child in the first place) during its open hours.

Meet the person in charge, by all means, but if the children are divided into several groups or classrooms, make sure you also meet the person who will be directly responsible for teaching, comforting and disciplining your child. Do you like her? Does she seem to like small children, speaking sympathetically of them and not being too ready to joke with you at their expense or to dismiss them as "all the same at that age"? Does she ask you anything about your child that suggests she is trying to get a picture of a person rather than a type?

Ask to be allowed to watch the group in action. Do the children seem happy and busy? Do they talk freely to each other, to themselves and to the adults? Are boys and girls encouraged to engage in all activities and to play together or at least respect each other's play? Does there seem to be some planning and choice of activities so that a child who does not want to join in a song can play, rather than sit in a corner as if in disgrace? Is there adequate tactful supervision during "free play", or are these periods a chaos of fights, tumbles and tears? Are policies on matters such as hitting and hitting back, standing up for yourself and seeking help from an adult, so clear that you can see what they are from watching the children work within them?

Consider the accommodation. A dreary building is not a sensible reason to turn down a school or class that is otherwise good: people and programmes matter more than buildings. But if the dreariness isn't even relieved by bright paint and curtains, and children's artwork, you may wonder whether the staff have really shown dedication and enthusiasm by doing the best that can be done with the unpromising material they had to start off with. And you may suspect that parents are not taking much interest. Equally some facilities matter so much that their absence really would be a strike against a group. Clean, warm, friendly toilets, for example; safe, interesting outdoor playspace and a few comfortable hidey-holes where a person can escape the group and rest for a few minutes.

Think about the size of the establishment and, far more important, the size of the groups within it. A small nursery school will not feel small to your child if all the 30 children in it spend their days as a

It takes a skilled teacher to plan group activities that involve and enrapture every single child.

single group. Most three- and four-year-olds are more comfortable in groups of not more than 10 to 15 children. If the classes are kept small, both large and small establishments have some advantages. A large one may give you better access to specialist services such as music teachers or speech therapists, and give your child a wide range of other children to make friends with (possibly including much younger and older ones) and the possibility of "promotion" with age. A small setting may give you more and closer interaction with your child's teacher and quicker, more direct action if problems arise, by a head teacher who really knows all the children. From your child's point of view, small may mean safe and cosy; large may mean exciting and challenging, and whatever she feels now, she may feel differently as she settles in and grows up.

Preparing your child for pre-school

The ease with which your child joins a pre-school education group depends as much on where she is coming from as on where she is going to. While of course the impact is greatest on the child who has never before been in a group without her own carer, even a child who has been in a day care centre for as long as she can remember and is being moved in search of educational enrichment, may not take the change in her stride. She already knows a lot about group life and she is accustomed to being away from home and home people, but changes of place and routine are always stressful, and while this change does not involve new separation from you or from home, it does involve separation from friends and familiar – possibly beloved – carers.

If you are pregnant, arrange for her to start at the group well before the birth, or not until several months after it. Becoming a big sister is as much change as any child ought to have to cope with.

The timing matters most if this will be her first experience of group life, or even of being cared for anywhere but at home. If you launch her into a classroom just when the new baby comes into her home, she is bound to feel banished and rejected. If you try and launch her immediately afterwards, you will not have the time or energy to support her properly through her first weeks.

If she is currently in all-day child care, though, and that's going to be replaced by the nursery school plus time at home with you during a long maternity leave, do try to take at least a couple of weeks off before the birth and get her started then. Some extra time on her own with you will give her an excellent start into being a sibling, and neither of the alternatives – going to child care all day when you are at home with the baby, or staying at home all day when she's accustomed to being with her own age group – will be ideal.

Staying and going

Most small children reckon to be able to cope with almost anything as long as a parent or loved caregiver is there. As long as the school or class encourages adults to stay with children until they are ready to be left, the first days should be easy, especially if your child is starting at the same time as several others who know each other.

Be honest with the child about your movements and make sure that her father, or anyone else who takes her in these early days, agrees to be honest too. If you mean to stay all morning, every morning, until she is happy to be left, tell her so and mean it. Don't suddenly decide to slip away after all in the middle of the session because she seems so happy. Later on, if you mean to stay for half an hour, tell her that too and say, "Goodbye" when you are leaving. She cannot concentrate on group activities if she is continually looking over her shoulder to see if you have vanished.

Although it's very important that you take your child and that you stay, it's also important that you stay in the right spirit. Don't treat this educational group as something for joint parent and child participation, like a toddler group or music class. You are only there temporarily to support your child while she gets to know the people – adults and children – who are permanent members of the class. If you play with your child, get things out for her and take her to the toilet, you will be a barrier between her and the other adults as well as between her and the other children. She may need you to stand between her and them on the very first day, but after that you have to help her behave as if you were not there, ready for the day when you will not be. Try, over the first few sessions, to become more and more invisible. If she keeps coming to show you things, try saying, "It's lovely, why don't you show it to Adela?" If she tells you she needs to go to the toilet, say "I'm sure Adela will take you, just as she does the others." Above all, try not to interfere between your child and the other children. The teachers will protect her if she needs protecting, or control her if they think that she is being too rough or aggressive.

When you and the teacher decide that she is ready for you to leave her for the first time, tell her, in a confident and congratulatory way. Remind her, by name, of all the people she knows now, and all the things she likes doing. Point out to her that only new children have their own adults with them and that she is not new any more.

Take the child to the group yourself, leave her with the adult she knows best and say that you will be there, on that same spot, to take her back again at going home time. She needs to feel quite sure of passing seamlessly from your care to the teacher's. Nothing is more likely to make her anxious than the possibility of being left

If your child is new to group life, the home corner is often the best place to start.

Be on time (or early) to collect your child. Being late really matters.

Trouble?

There's a lot the teacher can do to help a new child who's bravely struggling to cope.

somewhere between the two of you and in the care of neither.

Go back early on the first two or three days. She does not, of course, know the actual time, but it's an excellent idea to ensure that you arrive before the last activity of the session ends and therefore before she even has time to start looking for you.

Make being on time to collect her a real priority for at least her first few weeks. A child left waiting after the others have gone home feels abandoned. The understandable irritation of the adult left in charge (who may not even be the child's own teacher) gets through to her and makes her feel rejected, however kindly she conceals it. For some children, being collected late is enough to make them decide that it is not safe to be left in the first place.

Leaving a child who doesn't want you to leave her is a hateful way to start the day, her day and yours. It's hateful when it's nursery school and it's hateful when it's real school too. Whether she is three or five, though, if parting tears are the only sign that your child is unhappy, try not to take them too seriously. Many children who are genuinely enjoying and benefiting from school life find the parting moment hard, and many parents do too. A good teacher will tell you honestly whether or not your child cheers up and joins in as soon as you have left. If, despite her assurances, you still don't feel comfortable about leaving her, find a way to see her without her seeing you – over the garden wall or through the door crack. Her teacher can probably show you the vantage point used by the hundreds of parents who have gone through this before you. If your child is drearily watching the door and sucking her thumb, you need to look again (later if you can; next day if you can't stay now) in case you picked a bad moment. If you see a similar sad sight, tell the teacher, give her a day or two to observe the child and talk to other teachers and then ask for a conference to consider what is going wrong and how it can be put right.

Probably, though, your very first check will show you your child happily doing whatever the others are doing. If it is only "goodbye" which is causing trouble, tell her you're sorry it makes her sad, but don't let her think that her tears upset you or she may deduce that letting you go really is dangerous. Instead, talk to her about how difficult partings can be, and enlist her help in thinking of ways to make this kind easier for her. Something from home to take to school might reassure her, acting as a symbolic bridge between the two, rather as a cuddly can bridge the space between a baby who's been settled for the night and her mother who's gone to cook dinner. If the teacher prefers children not to bring toys from home in case they get lost, appropriated or quarrelled over, she can have a tissue out of your handbag to keep in her pocket, or an apple out of the home fruit bowl to eat at snack-time.

Provided she likes her teacher (and there's probably not much future in her membership of that class if she doesn't) ask your child's permission to tell her about the goodbye troubles and seek her help. A positive greeting, a hand to hold and her full attention for one minute will help the child make the transition from you to her. And if the teacher will entrust her with a regular job, such as mixing the paint, her immediate busy importance may solve the whole problem.

Surely our hyperactive five-year-old should be on medication?

Our five-year-old son was diagnosed ADHD almost a year ago in the United States after being banned from two day care centres and a nursery school. He was eventually admitted to pre-kindergarten on condition he took Ritalin, and he did well. Now we are in the UK where we shall live for three years and, to my horror, the doctor refuses to prescribe for Caleb and the school won't support us in pressuring him. They say he has some behaviour problems but nothing they can't cope with. Can these professionals do this? Don't they realize that they're condemning Caleb to being constantly in trouble and the rest of his family to trying to live with and love a child who's unmanageable?

Attention Deficit Hyperactivity Disorder is diagnosed, and treated with stimulant drugs such as Ritalin, far more frequently in North America than in Europe. But while the US figure of 5% of all children is high by any European standard, there is wide variation even within individual countries such as the UK. When professionals differ, children and parents tend to get caught in the middle but the answer to your question, "Can professionals do this?" has to be that they can (and indeed must) do what they themselves believe to be their professional best.

Some psychologists and doctors are reluctant to diagnose as a "disorder" a combination of characteristics – hyperactivity, distractibility and impulsivity – that all children display to *some* extent under some circumstances. They are very aware that a child may disrupt his class at school because the work is boring, his parents are separating, his way of learning is out of kilter with his teacher's way of teaching, he's depressed, allergic to the additives in his favourite fizzy drink or being bullied. That doesn't mean that they don't "believe in" ADHD or have

any concern for the very real suffering of parents with hyperactive children. But it does mean that they want to explore social, emotional and environmental reasons for a child's behaviour and difficulties before assuming that the brain's filtering system is at fault and prescribing accordingly.

Few doctors or psychologists are wholly opposed to medication for ADHD – Ritalin has many success stories to its credit – but many are concerned about the ethics of using psychoactive drugs to control behaviour, especially as the more widespread and easily available drug treatments become, the less likely it is that other forms of help and support, social, psychological and educational, will be made available to parents and children. They therefore prefer to consider drugs as a last resort rather than an easy option. Teachers, hard-pressed though they are, often feel the same way, priding themselves on being able to catch and contain the interest and energy of almost any child, especially a child under seven, sufficiently to teach him or her. Suspension of such young children from school or day care is a very new and very unwelcome phenomenon.

While your anxiety over being refused Ritalin for your son is entirely understandable, it is possible that this move to a new country and a different set of professional attitudes will prove it ill-founded. After all, Caleb is *not* constantly in trouble in this school. Maybe it suits him better than the last one; maybe its difference enables him to be different. He is not unmanageable at home either – yet. Perhaps he will not be. Perhaps being deprived of the drug will prove to be an opportunity for you to discover that he can manage and be managed without it now. If the school is willing, isn't it worth a try?

If none of that is enough, perhaps you can find another parent and child to travel with so that the two children can go in together. Or perhaps she might find it easier to part from her father, having left you at home where (in her view!) you belong. Or maybe part of the problem is that her day has too many transitions from one adult to another. It might seem more comfortably predictable if it started, as well as finished, at her childminder's house, and she took her to school as well as fetching her at lunch-time.

STARTING "BIG SCHOOL"

The beginning of "big school" is the beginning of a new life for your child, whether she starts at four, five or six, and from nursery school or child care or the school's own nursery class. School will dominate everything she does for the next 12 or more years and the imperatives of her attendance and the school's hours, half-term breaks and holidays will probably dominate yours. A good start may affect her attitude to school (and therefore your Sunday nights and Monday mornings) for years to come and there is quite a lot you can do to ensure it. You need to start early, though. You can equip your child with school clothes and a school bag the day before she starts, but confidence and competence take longer. To build them you may need to work closely with her childminder, or anyone who cares for her when you are not there, and with her pre-school group.

You may need to do some advance work with the school as well. If your child has any special needs and will be going to a mainstream school, she will – and should – be aware of the particular challenges she will meet and any special arrangements that are being made for her. If she is a twin and there are decisions to be made about whether or not both children should be in the same class or the same within-class group, they should have a part in any discussions (see p.550).

Help your child to acquire the kinds and levels of independence you know she'll need. A sense of being able to cope with all that's expected is a vital part of self-confidence for all of us at any time. Your small child cannot know what will be expected of her at school so it is up to you to know for her and ensure that when she gets there it all seems manageable. You know, for example, that she will be expected to manage her own clothes when she goes to the toilet. Of course there will be an adult who can be asked for help but, unlike day care, or even playgroup, there will not be an adult routinely offering it. Having to ask for help will make your child feel very incompetent compared with her new classmates, so make it easy for her with elastic-waisted trousers or skirts rather than zips or dungarees.

If asking for help will make your child feel helpless, struggling to manage without help may make her feel late, lost and panicky. Go for shoes with Velcro instead of knot-prone laces; make sure that dressing and undressing herself is a daily routine she takes for granted, and check that the new items she's so proud of – such as her lunch box and school bag – are easily opened. It's worth finding her opportunities to practise any school-techniques which will be new to her, too, such as drinking from a drinking fountain or finding the coat-hook with her name on it. A child who copes confidently with

Help your child have confidence in her competence and pride in her new role.

these everyday matters saves the teacher time and trouble but she saves herself something even more important: anxiety.

Going to school means meeting many adults. The more easily your child can speak up, the more she'll find herself understood, so in the months before school begins look for ways to help her practise and make sure that other adults do so too. You could make a point of

---

PARENTS ASK

Should twins be together or apart at school?

Our twin boys will be starting school soon. They have naturally always been very close – in fact they've seldom been apart – so we were surprised when during a family visit to the school the head teacher raised the possibility that they might go into two different classes. I'd hate them to lose their togetherness and would have dismissed the idea without further discussion only she asked the boys directly, and one of them said two different classes would be fun. When we asked him, later, why he'd said that, he said he'd "like to be just me a bit". But his brother says he won't go to school at all unless they can sit next to each other. I wish the teacher had talked to us about it privately because I don't think the twins are old enough to make decisions like that for themselves. Anyway, can it be right to separate twins so young?

If parents of twins have anything particular to worry about it isn't that the children may lose their togetherness but that they may fail to achieve separateness. While of course it's a pity that your two feel differently about being in the same class when they start school, it's a good thing that even one of them feels ready for more independence from the twin relationship. It would surely be very wrong to refuse him the opportunity to be "just me" because his brother is still dependent on being "we".

Although it took you aback, the teacher did your family a service by raising this issue with the people most personally concerned – the children themselves. Their input helped you to understand dynamics in the twin relationship of which you hadn't previously been aware. Now you know that their closeness shouldn't be taken for granted; that

security for one can smother the other, you can concentrate on meeting the different needs of what are, after all, two different children. The twin who feels he is never "just me" needs to be able to be that at home as well as at school, and when he's with his brother as well as when he's not. If you have been dressing them alike, assuming that they want the same food and the same amount of sleep, taking it for granted that they will share friends, baths, TV programmes and stories, this is an excellent time to stop. Try to play down the fact that they are twins (nobody, especially them, is going to forget that anyway) and play up the fact that they are brothers who can agree to differ about anything and everything without threatening the fact that they love each other.

If you can do that successfully you will also meet the needs of your other son whose security is in being half of a pair but whose future lies in being a whole individual. If he can learn not to feel uncomfortable when his brother opts to wear a different outfit from himself, he'll be on the way to being able to choose his own outfit without reference to his brother. If he can accept that his brother's friendships with other children offer no threat to what they share, he'll be on the way to making separate friendships of his own. And if he can do all that by the time they start school, he may take being in a separate class from his twin in his stride. If he finds it difficult to settle into school, though, do try not to blame that separation. Many children find the beginning of school stressful. For most of them there's no question of a twin's hand to hold. Your child can be helped to settle just the way others are. And when he is settled it will be as one individual class member among many, not as one of a pair of twins.

For many children, crowds and noise are the worst aspects of school.

having her greet visitors to the house and perhaps show them her room or her guinea pig. Shopping is good practice, whether it is for her own snacks or your wholemeal loaf, and she can have a go at speaking for herself to the doctor, the bus driver and the librarian. The practice she needs is not only in overcoming her shyness and making the effort to face strangers, but also in practicalities. Help her find out how loudly she needs to speak in order to be understood and make sure that if she still uses baby-slang for people, body parts or functions, she knows the generally understood words as well. Teach her to repeat herself (rather than bury her head in the nearest skirt) if she is not understood the first time. Remind her to listen to the adult's answer and "de-code" it, even though the voice or the accent is unfamiliar.

Even after three years in a day care centre or one or two in a nursery class or school, a lot of small children still dislike crowds, especially noisy ones. And 25 (or more) strange children in a class-room can certainly seem like a noisy crowd when you are used to 15 friends. But when a new school child is really fighting for self-control it is often the even larger and noisier groups at assembly, at lunch or in the playground, which finally defeat her. Try to build some crowded fun occasions into your child's life, and persist with them for practice even if, for her, "crowded fun" is a contradiction in terms. If your child can learn to take the swimming pool and its café on a Saturday morning in her stride, and join in the noise at a puppet show, a circus or a pantomime, she'll be less inclined to panic the first time she sits down to eat in the school lunch room.

A school child in the family

The five-to-seven shift into middle childhood is a watershed in learning and in cognitive and cultural growth that is recognized in every culture, and has been since Aristotle. As she crosses it your child will become increasingly aware of the wider community that surrounds her family, and become a person who can learn, and wants to learn its history, knowledge and skills. Children are supremely social animals, so she will also learn, and come to share, the values of the people around her, children as well as adults. There is no chance at all of her failing to learn right from wrong, but she just might learn from the wrong people. Moving into middle childhood will not wipe out your child's desire to please and be like you and other beloved adults; you will not lose your enormous influence. But her powerful new desire to be popular with peers and conform to their tastes and behaviour may give it some competition. If you want to influence the child you have made towards being the kind of person you want her to be, these first school years give you the best opportunities you will ever have.

Not all parents take those opportunities though. Some seem unaware of their own enormous importance in the five-to-seven shift and seem to regard the run up to it, and indeed middle childhood itself, as an "easy phase" in children's lives; a rest pause for parents between the exhausting business of caring for babies and very small children and the stressful upheavals of safeguarding adolescents. It's as if once children are safely into school, parents feel able to relax because school takes the strain and children's lives revolve around it.

Schools are an educational tool, and a very useful one; the best we have to help children who have reached that five-to-seven shift along the road towards a good education. Academics – or any kind of formal education – involve the acquisition of a wider range of knowledge and skills than any child could learn for herself by observation and hands-on investigation in play. Furthermore much of the knowledge must be developed, and many of the skills perfected, by more repetition and practice than most children will always enjoy. Even the best teachers cannot ensure that every child enjoys every lesson she must learn in school, or would always choose to spend the allotted amount of her time at home on homework. But teachers' particular skills, exercised within groups of peers, and supported by the institutional structure of school settings, make it as easy as it can be for children to devote time and effort to acquiring skills such as legible handwriting or fluent times-tables, that are not pleasurable play now, but will be crucial to their happiness later on.

But while schools are vital as main sources of academic learning and scaffolders of children's intellectual growth, they are not, cannot, and should not be the focal point for every aspect of their lives. Schools are institutions; as such they cannot stand in for family or for community in children's lives, nor do their best for children in isolation from their homes. Schools and homes, teachers and parents share the culture that soaks into children. If there is violence on the streets taking children into school will not keep them safe because violence will squeeze in with them. If homes have fashion and sports and porno magazines and no books, even the most dedicated teacher of English will not get many children reading the literature they might passionately enjoy. And no teacher could ever have enough time to talk with children to compensate them for homes full of half-heard talk from a TV that's always on, or empty of talk because parents are absent or too busy. A school cannot succeed where home fails. It is more likely that home will succeed where school fails. But if a good school and a good home work together, teachers' chances of succeeding in their roles with children will be increased by working alongside parents who are succeeding in theirs and then nobody will fail, least of all the children.

So don't let yourselves feel that once your child has made the school world into her world you will have lost her, or can leave her to it because you will never again know and control every detail of her days. You won't have lost her; you will have launched her on the next stage of the journey towards the grown-up world you'll share.

Your child has a long way to go, though, before she'll feel at home in this new world that does not have you in it. As she gets started she needs to feel that you go with her into school and that you confidently swap yourself for her teacher. At first you may do it literally: taking her all the way into the classroom and swapping her hand from yours to hers. Then you may do it symbolically: taking her as far as the cloakroom where she sheds the coat that brought her from home, and then waving her down the corridor that separates you from her teacher. And even after that you will need to do it in spirit and in talk, so that home and school still make a whole for your child and she knows for sure that she can safely leave you because she will never lose you.

INDEX

As your child grows up he needs to leave you but know he won't lose you.